Red Hat Linux:
The Complete Reference

Richard Petersen

Osborne/**McGraw-Hill**

Berkeley   New York   St. Louis   San Francisco
Auckland   Bogotá   Hamburg   London   Madrid
Mexico City   Milan   Montreal   New Delhi   Panama City
Paris   São Paulo   Singapore   Sydney
Tokyo   Toronto

Osborne/**McGraw-Hill**
2600 Tenth Street
Berkeley, California 94710
U.S.A.

For information on translations or book distributors outside the U.S.A., or to arrange
bulk purchase discounts for sales promotions, premiums, or fundraisers, please contact
Osborne/McGraw-Hill at the above address.

Red Hat Linux: The Complete Reference

234567890 DOC DOC 019876543210

Book P/N 0-07-212535-7   and   CD P/N 0-07-212536-5
parts of
ISBN 0-07-212537-3

Publisher
  Brandon A. Nordin

**Associate Publisher and
Editor-in-Chief**
  Scott Rogers

Acquisitions Editor
  Jane Brownlow

Project Editor
  Mark Karmendy

Acquisitions Coordinator
  Tara Davis

Technical Editor
  Steve Shah

Copy Editor
  Marcia Baker

Proofreader
  Carol Burbo

Indexer
  Jack Lewis

Computer Designers
  Jani Beckwith
  Lucie Erickson
  Roberta Steele

Illustrators
  Robert Hansen
  Michael Mueller
  Beth Young

This book was composed with Corel VENTURA™ Publisher.

About the Author ...

Richard Petersen holds a master's degree in
Library and Information Studies. He currently
teaches Unix and C/C++ courses at the
University of California, Berkeley.

To my sisters-in-law,
Marylou and Valerie

Contents at a Glance

Part III Internet

Part IV Servers

Part V Administration

Part VI Network Administration

Part VII   Applications

Contents

Part I

Introduction

Part II

Environments

Part III

Internet

Part VI

Network Administration

Part VII

Applications

Acknowledgments

I would like to thank all those at Osborne/McGraw-Hill who made this book a reality, particularly Jane Brownlow, acquisitions editor, for her continued encouragement and analysis as well as management of such a complex project; Eric Richardson and Steve Shah, the technical editors, whose analysis and suggestions proved very insightful and helpful; Tara Davis, aquisitions coordinator, who provided needed resources and helpful advice; Marcia Baker, copy editor, for her excellent job editing as well as her insightful comments; and project editor Mark Karmendy, who incorporated the large number of features found in this book as well as coordinated the intricate task of generating the final version. Thanks also to Scott Rogers, who initiated the project.

Special thanks to Linus Torvalds, the creator of Linux, and to those who continue to develop Linux as an open, professional, and effective operating system accessible to anyone. Thanks also to the academic community whose special dedication has developed Unix as a flexible and versatile operating system. I would also like to thank professors and students at the University of California, Berkeley, for the experience and support in developing new and different ways of understanding operating system technologies.

I would also like to thank my parents, George and Cecelia, and my brothers, George, Robert, and Mark, for their support and encouragement with such a difficult project. Also Valerie and Marylou and my nieces and nephews, Aleina, Larisa, Justin, Christopher, and Dylan, for their support and deadline reminders.

Introduction

The Red Hat Linux operating system has become one of the major Linux distributions, bringing to the PC all the power and flexibility of a Unix workstation as well as a complete set of Internet applications and a fully functional desktop interface. This book is designed not only to be a complete reference on Red Hat Linux, but also to provide clear and detailed explanations of Linux features. No prior knowledge of Unix is assumed; Linux is an operating system anyone can use.

This book identifies six major Linux topics: Environments, the Internet, Servers, Administration, Network Administration, and Applications. Gnome and the K Desktop Environment (KDE) are two new desktop Graphical User Interfaces (GUIs) for Linux, noted for their power, flexibility, and ease-of-use. These are complete desktop environments that are more flexible than either Windows or the Mac OS. They support standard desktop features such as menus, taskbars, and drag-and-drop operations. But they also provide virtual desktops, panel applets and menus, and Internet capable file managers. Gnome has become the standard graphical user interface for Red Hat Linux systems, though Red Hat also provides full support for KDE, including it in its standard distribution. You can install both, run applications from one on the other, and easily switch between them. Both Gnome and KDE were designed with software development in mind, providing a firm foundation that has encouraged the development of a massive number of new applications for these interfaces. They have become integrated components of Linux, with applications and tools for every kind of task and operation. Instead of treating Gnome and KDE as separate entities, Gnome and KDE tools and applications are presented throughout the book. For example, Gnome and KDE mail clients are discussed in the chapter on Internet mailers, along with other mail clients. Gnome and KDE FTP clients, editors, graphics tools, and administration tools, among others, are also handled in those respective chapters.

Red Hat Linux is also a fully functional Unix operating system. It has all the standard features of a powerful Unix system, including a complete set of Unix shells such as BASH, TCSH, and the Z-shell. Those familiar with the Unix interface can use any of these shells with the same Unix commands, filters, and configuration features.

For the Internet, Linux has become a platform for very powerful Internet applications. You not only use the Internet but, with Linux, also become a part of it, creating your own Web, FTP, and Gopher sites. Other users can access your Linux systems, several at the same time, using different services. You can also use very powerful Gnome, KDE, and Unix clients for mail and news. Linux systems are not limited to the Internet. You can use it on any local intranet, setting up an FTP or Web site for your network. The Red Hat Linux system provided on the CD-ROM with this book comes equipped with a variety of fully functional FTP and Web servers already installed and ready to use. All you need to do is add the files you want onto your site.

Red Hat Linux has the same level of administration features that you find on standard Unix systems as well as several user-friendly GUI configuration tools that make any administration task a simple matter of choosing items on a menu or clicking a check box. It has the same multiuser and multitasking capabilities. You can set up accounts for different users and each can access your system at the same time. Each user can have several programs running concurrently. With Linux you can control access, set up network connections, and install new devices. Red Hat Linux includes very powerful and easy-to-use window-based configuration utilities like Linuxconf, Setup, and the Control Panel, which you can use to perform system administration tasks, such as installing printers, adding users, and establishing new network connections.

A wide array of applications operates on Linux. Many personal versions of commercial applications are available for Linux free of charge, such as WordPerfect, StarOffice, and Sybase database. You can download them directly from the Internet. Numerous Gnome and KDE applications are continually released through their respective Web sites. The GNU public licensed software offers professional-level applications, such as programming development tools, editors, and word processors, as well as numerous specialized applications, such as those for graphics and sound. A massive amount of software is available at online Linux sites where you can download applications and then easily install them onto your system.

Since this book is really five books in one—an Internet book, a Gnome and KDE book, a Server book, an Applications book, and an Administration book—how you choose to use it depends upon how you want to use your Linux system. Almost all Linux operations can be carried out using either the Gnome or KDE interface. You need to use the Unix command line interface very little, if at all. You can focus on the Gnome and KDE chapters and their corresponding tools and applications in the different chapters throughout the book. If you want to delve deeper into the Unix aspects of Linux, you can check out the Shell chapters and the corresponding shell-based applications in other chapters. If you want to use Linux only for its Internet services, then concentrate on the Internet clients and servers, most of which are already installed for you. If you want to use Linux as a multiuser system servicing many users or integrate it into a local network, you can use the detailed system, file, and network administration information provided in the administration chapters. None of these tasks are in any way exclusive. If you are working in a business environment, you will probably make use of all three aspects. Single users may concentrate more on the desktops and the Internet features, whereas administrators may make more use of the Unix features.

The book is designed to help you start using Linux quickly. After a streamlined installation procedure for Red Hat (taking about 30 minutes or less), basic Gnome and KDE interface operations and system configuration tasks are discussed. Here you learn the essentials of using both Gnome and KDE. System configuration tasks like mounting CD-ROMs and adding new user accounts are presented with the easiest methods, without much of the complex detail described in the administration chapters that is unnecessary for basic operations.

In Part II, you are introduced to the different kinds of user environments available for Linux, starting with KDE and Gnome. Different features, such as applets, the Panel, and configuration tools, are described in detail. With either of these interfaces, you can run all your applications using icons, menus, and windows. At any time, you can open up a terminal window through which you can enter standard Linux commands on a command line. Linux makes a distinction between a desktop and window managers; a window manager controls basic window operations like window appearance, movement, and elements. You have a variety of very powerful Linux window managers to choose from, such as AfterStep, WindowMaker, and Enlightenment. You can also choose to use just the standard Unix command line interface to run any of the standard Unix commands. The remaining chapters in this section discuss the BASH shell and its various file, directory, and filter commands.

Part III discusses the many Internet applications you can use on your Linux system. Red Hat Linux automatically installs mail, news, FTP, and Web browser applications, as well as FTP and Web servers. Both KDE and Gnome come with a full set of mail, news, FTP clients, and Web browsers. These are described in detail along with Netscape Communicator, now an integrated part of all Linux systems. Your CD-ROM offers other mail clients, newsreaders, and Internet tools that you can easily install from your desktop. In addition, the book describes Internet clients like IglooFTP and Balsa that you can download from Internet sites and install on your system.

Part IV discusses Internet servers, including FTP, Web, Gopher, and DNS servers. Internet servers have become integrated components of most Linux systems. Both the standard wu-ftpd FTP server and the newer ProFTPD server with its directive format are presented. ProFTPD covers features such as guest and virtual FTP sites. The Apache Web server chapter covers standard configuration directives like those for automatic indexing as well as and the newer virtual host directives. Apache GUI configuration tools, such as comanche, are also presented. The different Gopher servers like GN are discussed with their respective configurations. Configuration files and features for the Domain Name System and its BIND server are examined along with features such as virtual domains and IP aliases. With Linux you can easily set up your own Domain Name server for a home or small local network. The sendmail mail sever, INN news server, Squid proxy server, and the ht:/DIG and WAIS search servers are also examined.

Part V discusses file system, system, and X Window system administration. These chapters emphasize the use of GUI system management configuration tools, Linuxconf, the Control Panel, and Setup. Although Linuxconf is now the official Red Hat Linux configuration tool, many of the older Red Hat configuration tools available in the Control Panel and the Setup menu are still effective and, in some ways, easier to use. You can use them to set up your network, add users, and configure devices such as printers. Linuxconf also lets you configure your Internet servers. There are also detailed descriptions of the configuration files used in administration tasks and how to make entries in them.

Different file system tasks are covered such as mounting file systems, selecting device names, accessing DOS files. System administration tasks like managing users and groups, installing devices, and monitoring your system presentations include both the GUI tools you can use for these tasks and the underlying configuration files and commands. Using, updating, and configuring the Linux kernel with its modules are addressed along with procedures for installing new kernels. X Window system topics cover the XFree86 servers, window manager configuration, X Window system startup methods like the display manger, and X Window system configuration commands. The discussion of XFree86 servers includes a detailed explanation of the /etc/XF86Config configuration file used to configure your card.

Part VI covers network administration, dealing with topics such as configuring remote file system access and setting up firewalls. Most network administration tasks can be performed using configuration tools such as Linuxconf and Red Hat's netcfg utility. These are discussed in detail first. Next, the various network file system interfaces like NFS for Unix, Samba for Windows file systems, and Netatalk for AppleTalk networks are presented. Then, the different aspects of network administration are addressed, such as network connections and routes, Domain Name services, Hostname designations, IP virtual hosts, and IP masquerading. Network security topics include firewalls and encryption using ipchains to protect your system and the Secure Shell (SSL) to provide secure remote transmissions.

Part VII reviews applications available for Linux, beginning with Office suites, such as StarOffice and KOffice. The different database management systems available are then discussed along with the Web site locations where you can download them. Software installation has been simplified with the Red Hat Package Management System (RPMS). There are several GUI tools like the KDE kpackage and Gnome gnomeRPM that you can use to easily install and uninstall software, much as you would with the Windows install wizard. A variety of different text editors are also available, including several Gnome and KDE editors, as well as the Vim (enhanced VI), gvim (graphical Vi), and GNU Emacs editors.

Finally, you'll find an "About the CD" page at the back of the book, which covers what is available on the CD-ROM included with this book.

The Complete Reference

Linux

Part I

Introduction

Chapter 1

Introduction to Red Hat Linux

3

Linux is an operating system for PC computers and workstations that now features a fully functional *graphical user interface (GUI)*, just like Windows and the Mac (though more stable). Linux was developed in the early 1990s by Linus Torvald, along with other programmers around the world. As an operating system, Linux performs many of the same functions as UNIX, Mac, Windows, and Windows NT. However, Linux is distinguished by its power and flexibility. Most PC operating systems, such as Windows, began their development within the confines of small, restricted personal computers, which have only recently become more versatile machines. Such operating systems are constantly being upgraded to keep up with the ever-changing capabilities of PC hardware. Linux, on the other hand, was developed in a different context. Linux is a PC version of the UNIX operating system that has been used for decades on mainframes and minicomputers, and is currently the system of choice for workstations. Linux brings the speed, efficiency, and flexibility of UNIX to your PC, taking advantage of all the capabilities that personal computers can now provide. Along with its UNIX capabilities come powerful networking features, including support for Internet, intranet, Windows, and AppleTalk networking. As a standard, Linux is distributed with fast, efficient, and stable Internet servers, such as the Web, FTP, and Gopher servers, along with domain name, proxy, news, mail, and indexing servers. In other words, Linux has everything you need to set up, support, and maintain a fully functional network.

Now, with both Gnome and K Desktop, Linux also provides GUI interfaces with that same level of flexibility and power. Unlike Windows and the Mac, you can choose the interface you want, and then customize it further, adding panels, applets, virtual desktops, and menus, all with full drag-and-drop capabilities and Internet-aware tools. On your desktop, a file manager window can access any Internet site, enabling you to display Web pages and download files with a few simple mouse operations. To print a file, simply drag it to a Printer icon.

Linux does all this at a great price. Linux is free, including the network servers and GUI desktops. Unlike the official UNIX operating system, Linux is distributed freely under a GNU General Public License as specified by the Free Software Foundation, making it available to anyone who wants to use it. Linux is copyrighted and it is not public domain. However, a GNU public license has much the same effect as being in the public domain. The GNU public license is designed to ensure Linux remains free and, at the same time, standardized. Only one official Linux exists. GNU stands for Gnu's Not UNIX and is a project initiated and managed by the Free Software Foundation to provide free software to users, programmers, and developers. The list of software available under the GNU Public License is extensive, including environments, programming languages, Internet tools, and text editors. People sometimes have the mistaken impression that Linux is somehow less than a professional operating system because it is free. Linux is, in fact, a PC and workstation version of UNIX. Many consider it far more stable and much more powerful than Windows. This power and stability have made Linux an operating system of choice as a network server.

To appreciate Linux completely, you need to understand the special context in which the UNIX operating system was developed. UNIX, unlike most other operating systems, was developed in a research and academic environment. In universities and research laboratories, UNIX is the system of choice. Its development paralleled the entire computer and communications revolution over the past several decades. Computer professionals often developed new computer technologies on UNIX, such as those developed for the Internet. Although a sophisticated system, UNIX was designed from the beginning to be flexible. The UNIX system itself can be easily modified to create different versions. In fact, many different vendors maintain different official versions of UNIX. IBM, Sun, and Hewlett-Packard all sell and maintain their own versions of UNIX. People involved in research programs often create their own versions of UNIX, tailored to their own special needs. This inherent flexibility in the UNIX design in no way detracts from its quality. In fact, this flexibility attests to the ruggedness of UNIX, allowing it to adapt to practically any environment. This is the context in which Linux was developed. Linux is, in this sense, one other version of UNIX—a version for the PC. The development of Linux by computer professionals working in a research-like environment reflects the way UNIX versions have usually been developed. Linux is publicly licensed and free, and reflects the deep roots UNIX has in academic institutions, with their sense of public service and support. Linux is a top-rate operating system accessible to everyone, free of charge.

As a way of introducing Linux, this chapter discusses Linux as an operating system, the history of Linux and UNIX, the overall design of Linux, and Linux distributions. This chapter also discusses online resources for documentation, software, and newgroups, plus Web sites with the latest news and articles on Linux. Web and FTP site listings are placed in tables at the end of this chapter for easy reference. Here you can find sites for different distributions, Linux publications, software repositories, and Linux development, as well as for office suites and commercial databases.

Red Hat Linux

Red Hat Linux is currently the most popular Linux distribution. Red Hat originated the RPM package system used on several distributions that automatically installs and removes software packages. Red Hat is also providing much of the software development for the Gnome desktop, and it is a strong supporter of KDE. Its distribution includes both Gnome and KDE. Red Hat maintains software alliances with major companies like Oracle, IBM, and Sun. The Red Hat distribution of Linux is available online at numerous FTP sites. It maintains its own FTP site at **ftp.redhat.com** where you can download the entire current release of Red Hat Linux, as well as updates and third-party software. Red Hat was designed from its inception to work on numerous hardware platforms. Currently, Red Hat supports Sparc, Intel, Alpha, PPC, ARM, m68k, and SGI platforms. See **www.redhat.com** for more information, including extensive documentation such as Red Hat manuals, FAQs, and links to other Linux sites.

If you purchase Red Hat Linux from Red Hat, you are entitled to online support services. Although Linux is free, Red Hat as a company specializes in support services, providing customers with its expertise in developing solutions to problems that may arise or using Linux to perform any of several possible tasks, such as e-commerce or database operations.

Red Hat maintains an extensive library of Linux documentation that is freely accessible online. On its Web page, you can link to its support page, which lists the complete set of Red Hat manuals, all in Web page format for easy viewing with any Web browser. These include the Reference Guide, the Getting Started Guide, and the Installation Guide. Tip, HOWTO, and FAQ documents are also provided. Of particular note is the Hardware Compatibility Lists. This documentation lists all the hardware compatible with Red Hat Linux. For PC users, this includes most hardware, with few exceptions. All the Red Hat documentation is freely available under the GNU Public License.

Operating Systems and Linux

An *operating system* is a program that manages computer hardware and software for the user. Operating systems were originally designed to perform repetitive hardware tasks. These tasks centered around managing files, running programs, and receiving commands from the user. You interact with an operating system through a user interface. This user interface allows the operating system to receive and interpret instructions sent by the user. You only need to send an instruction to the operating system to perform a task, such as reading a file or printing a document. An operating system's user interface can be as simple as entering commands on a line or as complex as selecting menus and icons on a desktop.

An operating system also manages software applications. To perform different tasks, such as editing documents or performing calculations, you need specific software applications. An *editor* is an example of a software application, which enables you to edit a document, making changes and adding new text. The editor itself is a program consisting of instructions to be executed by the computer. To use the program, it must first be loaded into computer memory, and then its instructions are executed. The operating system controls the loading and execution of all programs, including any software applications. When you want to use an editor, simply instruct the operating system to load the editor application and execute it.

File management, program management, and user interaction are traditional features common to all operating systems. Linux, like all versions of UNIX, adds two more features. Linux is a multiuser and multitasking system. As a multitasking system, you can ask the system to perform several tasks at the same time. While one task is being done, you can work on another. For example, you can edit a file while another file is being printed. You do not have to wait for the other file to finish printing before you edit. As a multiuser system, several users can log in to the system at the same time, each interacting with the system through his own terminal.

Operating systems were originally designed to support hardware efficiency. When computers were first developed, their capabilities were limited and the operating system had to make the most of them. In this respect, operating systems were designed with the hardware in mind, not the user. Operating systems tended to be rigid and inflexible, forcing the user to conform to the demands of hardware efficiency.

Linux, on the other hand, is designed to be flexible, reflecting its UNIX roots. As a version of UNIX, Linux shares the same flexibility designed for UNIX, a flexibility stemming from UNIX's research origins. The UNIX operating system was developed by Ken Thompson at AT&T Bell Laboratories in the late 1960s and early 1970s. The UNIX system incorporated many new developments in operating system design. Originally, UNIX was designed as an operating system for researchers. One major goal was to create a system that could support the researchers' changing demands. To do this, Thompson had to design a system that could deal with many different kinds of tasks. Flexibility became more important than hardware efficiency. Like UNIX, Linux has the advantage of being able to deal with the variety of tasks any user may face.

This flexibility allows Linux to be an operating system that is accessible to the user. The user is not confined to limited and rigid interactions with the operating system. Instead, the operating system is thought of as providing a set of highly effective tools that the user can use. This user-oriented philosophy means you can configure and program the system to meet your specific needs. With Linux, the operating system becomes an operating environment.

History of Linux and UNIX

As a version of UNIX, the history of Linux naturally begins with UNIX. The story begins in the late 1960s when a concerted effort to develop new operating system techniques occurred. In 1968, a consortium of researchers from General Electric, AT&T Bell Laboratories, and the Massachusetts Institute of Technology carried out a special operating system research project called *MULTICS* (*MULTiplexed Information Computing System*). MULTICS incorporated many new concepts in multitasking, file management, and user interaction. In 1969, Ken Thompson, Dennis Ritchie, and the researchers at AT&T Bell Laboratories developed the UNIX operating system, incorporating many of the features of the MULTICS research project. They tailored the system for the needs of a research environment, designing it to run on minicomputers. From its inception, UNIX was an affordable and efficient multiuser and multitasking operating system.

The UNIX system became popular at Bell Labs as more and more researchers started using the system. In 1973, Dennis Ritchie collaborated with Ken Thompson to rewrite the programming code for the UNIX system in the C programming language. Dennis Ritchie, a fellow researcher at Bell Labs, developed the C programming language as a flexible tool for program development. One of the advantages of C is it can directly access the hardware architecture of a computer with a generalized set of programming commands. Up until this time, an operating system had to be specially rewritten in a hardware-specific assembly language for each type of computer. The C programming language allowed Dennis Ritchie and Ken Thompson to write only one version of the UNIX operating system, which could then be compiled by C compilers on different computers. In effect, the UNIX operating system became transportable, able to run on a variety of different computers with little or no reprogramming.

UNIX gradually grew from one person's tailored design to a standard software product distributed by many different vendors, such as Novell and IBM. Initially, UNIX was treated as a research product. The first versions of UNIX were distributed free to the computer science departments of many noted universities. Throughout the 1970s, Bell Labs began issuing official versions of UNIX and licensing the systems to different users. One of these users was the Computer Science department of the University of California, Berkeley. Berkeley added many new features to the system that later became standard. In 1975, Berkeley released its own version of UNIX, known by its distribution arm, *Berkeley Software Distribution* (*BSD*). This BSD version of UNIX became a major contender to the AT&T Bell Labs version. Other independently developed versions of UNIX sprouted up. In 1980, Microsoft developed a PC version of UNIX called *Xenix*. AT&T developed several research versions of UNIX and, in 1983, it released the first commercial version, called System 3. This was later followed by System V, which became a supported commercial software product. You can find more information on UNIX in *UNIX: The Complete Reference*, written by the UNIX experts at AT&T labs, Kenneth Rosen, Doug Host, James Farber, and Richard Rosinski.

At the same time, the BSD version of UNIX was developing through several releases. In the late 1970s, BSD UNIX became the basis of a research project by the *Department of Defense's Advanced Research Projects Agency* (*DARPA*). As a result, in 1983, Berkeley released a powerful version of UNIX called BSD release 4.2. This release included sophisticated file management, as well as networking features based on TCP/IP network protocols—the same protocols now used for the Internet. BSD release 4.2 was widely distributed and adopted by many vendors, such as Sun Microsystems.

The proliferation of different versions of UNIX led to a need for a UNIX standard. Software developers had no way of knowing on what versions of UNIX their programs would actually run. In the mid-1980s, two competing standards emerged, one based on the AT&T version of UNIX and the other based on the BSD version. In bookstores today, you can find many different books on UNIX for one or the other version. Some specify System V UNIX, while others focus on BSD UNIX.

AT&T moved UNIX to a new organization, called UNIX System Laboratories, which could focus on developing a standard system, integrating the different major versions of UNIX. In 1991, UNIX System Laboratories developed System V release 4, which incorporated almost all the features found in System V release 3, BSD release 4.3, SunOS, and Xenix. In response to System V release 4, several other companies, such as IBM and Hewlett-Packard, established the *Open Software Foundation* (*OSF*) to create their own standard version of UNIX. Two commercial standard versions of UNIX existed then—the OSF version and System V release 4. In 1993, AT&T sold off its interest in UNIX to Novell. UNIX Systems Laboratories became part of Novell's UNIX

Systems Group. Novell issued its own versions of UNIX based on System V release 4, called UNIXWare, designed to interact with Novell's NetWare system. UNIX Systems Laboratories is currently owned by the Santa Cruz Operation. With Solaris, Sun has introduced System V release 4 onto its Sun systems. Two competing GUIs for UNIX, called Motif and Open-Look, have been merged into a new desktop standard called the *Common Desktop Environment (CDE)*.

Throughout much of its development, UNIX remained a large and demanding operating system requiring a workstation or minicomputer to be effective. Several versions of UNIX were designed primarily for the workstation environment. SunOS was developed for Sun workstations and AIX was designed for IBM workstations. As personal computers became more powerful, however, efforts were made to develop a PC version of UNIX. Xenix and System V/386 are commercial versions of UNIX designed for IBM-compatible PCs. AUX is a UNIX version that runs on the Macintosh. A testament to UNIX's inherent portability is that it can be found on almost any type of computer: workstations, minicomputers, and even supercomputers. This inherent portability made possible an effective PC version of UNIX.

Linux was originally designed specifically for Intel-based personal computers. Linux started out as a personal project of a computer science student named Linus Torvald at the University of Helsinki. At that time, students were making use of a program called *Minix,* which highlighted different UNIX features. Minix was created by Professor Andrew Tannebaum and widely distributed over the Internet to students around the world. Linus's intention was to create an effective PC version of UNIX for Minix users. He called it Linux, and in 1991, Linus released version 0.11. Linux was widely distributed over the Internet and, in the following years, other programmers refined and added to it, incorporating most of the applications and features now found in standard UNIX systems. All the major window managers have been ported to Linux. Linux has all the Internet utilities, such as FTP, telnet, and SLIP. It also has a full set of program development utilities, such as C++ compilers and debuggers. Given all its features, the Linux operating system remains small, stable, and fast. In its simplest format, Linux can run effectively on only 4MB of memory.

Although Linux has developed in the free and open environment of the Internet, it adheres to official UNIX standards. Because of the proliferation of UNIX versions in the previous decades, the *Institute of Electrical and Electronics Engineers (IEEE)* developed an independent UNIX standard for the *American National Standards Institute (ANSI)*. This new ANSI-standard UNIX is called the *Portable Operating System Interface for Computer Environments (POSIX)*. The standard defines how a UNIX-like system needs to operate, specifying details such as system calls and interfaces. POSIX defines a universal standard to which all UNIX versions must adhere. Most popular versions of UNIX are now POSIX-compliant. Linux was developed from the beginning according to the POSIX standard. Linux also adheres to the *Linux filesystem standard (FSSTND)*, which specifies the location of files and directories in the Linux file structure. See **www.pathname.com/fhs** for more details.

Linux Overview

Like UNIX, Linux can be generally divided into three major components: the kernel, the shell, the file structure. The *kernel* is the core program that runs programs and manages hardware devices, such as disks and printers. The *environment* provides an interface for the user. It receives commands from the user and sends those commands to the kernel for execution. The *file structure* organizes the way files are stored on a storage device, such as a disk. Files are organized into directories. Each directory may contain any number of subdirectories, each holding files. Together, the kernel, the environment, and the file structure form the basic operating system structure. With these three, you can run programs, manage files, and interact with the system.

An environment provides an interface between the kernel and the user. It can be described as an interpreter. An environment interprets commands entered by the user and sends them to the kernel. Linux provides several kinds of environments: desktops, window managers, and command line shells. Each user on a Linux system has her own user interface. Users can tailor their environments to their own special needs, whether they be shells, window managers, or desktops. In this sense, for the user, the operating system functions more as an operating environment, which the user can control.

The shell interface is simple and usually consists of a prompt at which you type a command, and then press ENTER. In a sense, you are typing the command on a line; this line is often referred to as the *command line*. You will find the commands entered on the command line can become quite complex. Over the years, several different kinds of shells have been developed and, currently, three major shells exist: Bourne, Korn, and C-shell. The *Bourne shell* was developed at Bell Labs for System V. The *C-shell* was developed for the BSD version of UNIX. The *Korn shell* is a further enhancement of the Bourne shell. Current versions of UNIX, including Linux, incorporate all three shells, enabling you to choose the one you prefer. However, Linux uses enhanced or public domain versions of these shells: the Bourne Again shell, the TC-shell, and the Public Domain Korn shell. When you start your Linux system, you are placed in the *Bourne Again shell*, an updated version of the Bourne shell. From there, you can switch to other shells as you choose.

As an alternative to a command line interface, Linux provides both desktops and window managers. These use a GUI based on the X Windows system developed for UNIX by the Open Group consortium (**www.opengroup.org**). A *window manager* is a reduced version of a desktop, supporting only window operation, but it still enables you to run any application. A desktop provides a complete GUI, much like Windows and the Mac. You have windows, icons, and menus, all managed through mouse controls. Currently, two desktops are freely available and both are included with most distributions of Linux: Gnome and KDE.

In Linux, files are organized into directories, much as they are in Windows. The entire Linux file system is one large interconnected set of directories, each containing files. Some directories are standard directories reserved for system use. You can create your own directories for your own files, as well as easily move files from one directory to another. You can even move entire directories, and share directories and files with other users on your system. With Linux, you can also set permissions on directories and files, allowing others to access them or restricting access to you alone. The directories of each user are, in fact, ultimately connected to the directories of other users. Directories are organized into a hierarchical tree structure, beginning with an initial root directory. All other directories are ultimately derived from this first root directory.

Desktops

With the *K Desktop Environment* (*KDE*) and the *GNU Network Object Model Environment* (*Gnome*), Linux now has a completely integrated GUI interface. You can perform all your Linux operations entirely from either interface. Previously, Linux did support window managers that provided some GUI functionality, but they were usually restricted to window operations. KDE and Gnome are fully operational desktops supporting drag-and-drop operations, enabling you to drag icons to your desktop and to set up your own menus on an Applications panel. Both rely on an underlying X Windows system, which means as long as they are both installed on your system, applications from one can run on the other desktop. You can run KDE programs like the KDE mailer or the newsreader, on the Gnome desktop. Gnome applications like the Gftp FTP client can run on the KDE desktop. You can even switch file managers, running the KDE file manager on Gnome. You lose some desktop functionality, such as drag-and-drop operations, but the application runs fine.

Both desktops can run any X Windows system program, as well as any cursor-based program like Emacs and Vi, which were designed to work in a shell environment. At the same time, a great many applications are written just for those desktops and included with your distributions. The K Desktop has a complete set of Internet tools, along with editors and graphic, multimedia, and system applications. Gnome has slightly fewer applications, but a great many are currently in the works. Check their Web sites at **www.gnome.org** and **www.kde.org** for new applications. As new versions are released, they include new software.

Linux Software

Linux was developed as a cooperative effort over the Internet, so no company or institution controls Linux. Software developed for Linux reflects this background. Development often takes place when Linux users decide to work on a project together. When completed, the software is posted at an Internet site, and any Linux user can then access the site and download the software. The potential for Linux-based software is explosive. Linux software development has always operated in an Internet environment and it is global in scope, enlisting programmers from around the world. The only thing you need to start a Linux-based software project is a Web site.

Most Linux software is copyrighted under a GNU public license provided by the Free Software Foundation, and is often referred to as GNU software (see **www.gnu.org**). GNU software is distributed free, provided it is freely distributed to others. GNU software has proven both reliable and effective. Many of the popular Linux utilities, such as C compilers, shells, and editors, are all GNU software applications. Installed with your Linux distribution are the GNU C++ and Lisp compilers, Vi and Emacs editors, BASH and TCSH shells, as well as TeX and Ghostscript document formatters. Many other GNU software applications are available at different Internet sites and these are listed in Table 1-7. Chapter 3 and Chapter 32 describe in detail the process of downloading software applications from Internet sites and installing them on your system.

Under the terms of the GNU General Public License, the original author retains the copyright, although anyone can modify the software and redistribute it, provided the source code is included. Also, no restriction exists on selling the software or giving it away free. One distributor could charge for the software, while another one could provide it free of charge.

Lately, major software companies are also developing Linux versions of their most popular applications. Netscape provides a Linux version of its popular Web browser, which is now included as standard on most Linux distributions. A Linux version of Sun's *Java Development Kit* (*JDK*) is also available through **ftp.blackdown.org**. Corel has developed a Linux version of WordPerfect, while Oracle provides a Linux version of its Oracle database. (At present, no plans seem in the works for Microsoft applications.)

Until recently however, many of these lacked a true desktop interface, but this has changed dramatically with the introduction of KDE and Gnome. These desktops are not merely interfaces: they both provide extensive, flexible, and powerful development libraries that software developers can use to create almost any kind of application, which they are.

One of the most important features of Linux, as well as all UNIX systems, is its set of Internet clients and servers. The Internet was designed and developed on UNIX systems, and Internet clients and servers, such as those for FTP and the Web, were first implemented on BSD versions of UNIX. DARPANET, the precursor to the Internet, was set up to link UNIX systems at different universities across the nation. Linux contains a full set of Internet clients and servers including mail, news, FTP, and Web, as well as proxy clients and servers.

Software packages are distributed either in compressed archives or in RPM packages, and these RPM packages are those archived using the Red Hat Package Manager. Compressed archives have an extension such as **.tar.gz** or **.tar.Z**, whereas RPM packages have an **.rpm** extension. For Red Hat, downloading the RPM package versions of software from their FTP sites is best. Whenever possible, you should try to download software from a distribution's FTP site, but you could also download the source version and compile it directly on your system. This has become a simple process, almost as simple as installing the compiled versions (see Chapter 4).

Distributions, such as Red Hat, also have a large number of mirror sites from which you can download their software packages. Red Hat mirror sites are listed at

www.redhat.com/mirrors.html. Most Linux Internet sites that provide extensive software archives have mirror sites, such as **www.kernel.org,** that hold the new Linux kernels. If you have trouble connecting to a main FTP site, try one of its mirrors.

Online Information Sources

Extensive online resources are available on almost any Linux topic. The tables at the end of the chapter list sites where you can obtain software, display documentation, and read articles on the latest developments. Many Linux Web sites provide news, articles, and information about Linux. Several are based on popular Linux magazines, such as **www.linuxjournal.com** and **www.linuxgazzette.com**. Others operate as Web portals for Linux such as **www.linux.com, www.linuxworld.org**, and **www.linux.org**. Some specialize in particular topics, such as **kernelnotes.org** for news on the Linux kernel and **www.linuxgames.org** for the latest games ported for Linux. You can find their Web site addresses listed in Table 1-4.

Distribution FTP and Web sites, such as **www.redhat.com** and **ftp.redhat.com,** provide extensive Linux documentation and software. The **www.gnome.org** site holds software and documentation for the Gnome desktop, while **www.kde.org** holds software and documentation for the KDE desktop. The tables in this chapter list many of the available sites. You can find other sites through resource pages that hold links to other Web sites—for example, the Linux Web site on the World Wide Web at **www.linuxdoc.org/links.html**.

Documentation

Linux documentation has also been developed over the Internet. Much of the documentation currently available for Linux can be downloaded from Internet FTP sites. A special Linux project called the *Linux Documentation Project* (*LDP*), headed by Matt Welsh, is currently developing a complete set of Linux manuals. The documentation, at its current level, is available at the LDP home site at **www.linuxdoc.org**.

An extensive number of mirrors are maintained for the Linux Documentation Project. You can link to any of them through a variety of sources, such as the LDP home site **www.linux.org** and **www.linuxjournal.org**. The documentation includes a user's guide, an introduction, and administration guides. These are available in text, PostScript, or Web page format. Table 1-3 lists these guides. You can also find briefer explanations, in what are referred to as HOW-TO documents. HOW-TO documents are available for different subjects, such as installation, printing, and e-mail. The documents are available at Linux FTP sites, usually in the directory **/pub/Linux/doc/HOW-TO**.

You can find a listing of different Linux information sites in the file **META-FAQ** located at Linux FTP sites, usually in the directory **/pub/Linux/doc**. On the same site and directory, you can also download the *Linux Software Map* (*LSM*). This is a listing of most of the software currently available for Linux. Also, many software companies have Web sites that provide information about their Linux applications. Several of these are listed in Tables 1-7 and 1-8.

In addition to FTP sites, Linux Usenet newsgroups are also available. Through your Internet connection, you can access Linux newsgroups to read the comments of other Linux users and to post messages of your own. Several Linux newsgroups exist, each beginning with **comp.os.linux**. One of particular interest to the beginner is **comp.os.linux.help**, where you can post questions. Table 1-6 lists the different Linux newsgroups available on Usenet.

Most of the standard Linux software and documentation currently available is already included on your Red Hat CD-ROM. HOW-TO documents are all accessible in HTML format, so you can view them easily with your Web browser. In the future, though, you may need to access Linux Internet sites directly for current information and software.

Linux Distributions

Although there is only one standard version of Linux, there are actually several different releases that exist. Different companies and groups have packaged Linux and Linux software in slightly different ways. Each company or group then releases the Linux package, usually on a CD-ROM. Later releases may include updated versions of programs or new software. Some of the more popular releases are Red Hat, OpenLinux, SuSE, and Debian. Several distributions, such as Caldera and Red Hat, also offer their systems bundled with commercial software. The Linux kernel is, of course, centrally distributed through **www.kernel.org**. All distributions use this same kernel, although it may be configured differently.

Linux Resources

The following tables list various Linux resources available on the Internet. Many of these sites have links to other popular sites. Table 1-1 lists the Web site for several of the more popular Linux distributions. Listed here also are Linux kernel sites where the newest releases of the official Linux kernel are provided. These sites have corresponding FTP sites where you can download updates and new releases, as well as third-party software packaged for these distributions (see Table 1-2). For those not listed check their Web sites for FTP locations. Linux documentation provided by the LDP are listed in Table 1-3, along with their Internet sites. Currently, many Linux Web sites provide news, information, and articles on Linux developments, as well as documentation, software links, and other resources. These are listed in Table 1-4. Desktop and window manager sites are listed in Table 1-5. The Gnome and KDE sites are particularly helpful for documentation, news, and software you can download for those desktops. Table 1-6 lists some of the Usenet Linux newsgroups you can check out, particularly for posting questions. The following tables list different sites for Linux software. Repositories and archives for Linux software are listed in Table 1-7, along with several specialized sites, such as those for commercial and game software. Table 1-8 lists sites for office suites and databases. Most of these sites provide free personal versions of their software for Linux, which you can download from them directly and install on your Linux system. Sites for Internet server software available for Linux are listed in Table 1-9. Most of these are already included on the Red Hat CD-ROM included with this book, however, you can obtain news, documentation, and recent releases directly from the server's Web sites. Table 1-10 lists different sites of interest for Linux programming, including Perl, Tcl/Tk, and Linux kernel sites.

When downloading software packages, always check to see if versions are packaged for your particular distribution. For example, Red Hat will use RPM packages. Many sites provide packages for the different popular distributions, such as Red Hat, Caldera, and Debian. For others, first check the distribution FTP sites for a particular package. For example, a Red Hat package version for ProFTPD is located at the **ftp.redhat.com** FTP site. **rpmfind.net** and **www.linuxapps.com** are also good places for locating RPM packages for particular distributions.

URL	Internet Site
www.redhat.com	Red Hat Linux
www.calderasystems.com	OpenLinux (Caldera)
www.suse.com	SuSE Linux
www.debian.org	Debian Linux
www.infomagic.com	Infomagic
www.linuxppc.com	LinuxPPC (Mac PowerPC version)
www.turbolinux.com	Turbo Linux (Pacific Hi-Tech)
www.slackware.com	Slackware Linux Project
www.kernel.org	The Linux Kernel
www.kernelnotes.org	Linux Kernel release information

Table 1-1. *Linux Distributions and Kernel Sites*

URL	Internet Site
ftp.redhat.com	Red Hat Linux and Updates
ftp.redhat.com/contrib	Software packaged for Red Hat Linux
ftp.calderasystem.com	OpenLinux (Caldera)
ftp.suse.com	SuSE Linux
ftp.debian.org	Debian Linux
ftp.linuxppc.com	LinuxPPC (Mac PowerPC version)
ftp.turbolinux.com	Turbo Linux (Pacific Hi-Tech)

Table 1-2.   *Linux Distribution FTP Sites*

Sites	Description
www.linuxdoc.org	LDP Web site
ftp.linuxdoc.org	LDP FTP site

Guides	Document Format
Linux Installation and Getting Started Guide	DVI, Postscript, LaTeX, PDF, and HTML
Linux User's Guide	DVI, Postscript, HTML, LaTeX, and PDF
Linux System Administrator's Guide	Postscript, PDF, LaTeX, and HTML
Linux System Administration Made Easy	Postscript, PDF, LaTeX, and HTML
Linux Network Administrator's Guide	DVI, Postscript, PDF, and HTML
The Linux Kernel Module Programming Guide	DVI, Postscript, PDF, LaTeX, and HTML

Table 1-3.   *Linux Documentation Project*

Guides	Document Format
Get Acquainted with Linux Security and Optimization System	PDF
Linux Administrator's Security Guide	HTML
Linux Programmer's Guide	DVI, Postscript, PDF, LaTeX, and HTML
The Linux Kernel	HTML, LaTeX, DVI, and Postscript
Linux Kernel Hacker's Guide	DVI, PostScript, and HTML
Linux HOWTOs	HTML, PostScript, SGML, and DVI
Linux FAQs	HTML, PostScript, and DVI
Linux Man Pages	Man page format

Table 1-3. *Linux Documentation Project* (continued)

URL	Internet Site
www.linuxdoc.org	Web site for Linux Documentation Project
www.lwn.net	Linux Weekly News
www.linux.com	Linux.com
www.linuxtoday.com	Linux Today
www.linuxpower.org	Linux Power
www.linuxfocus.org	Linux Focus
www.linuxworld.org	Linux World
www.linuxmall.com	Linux Mall
www.linuxjournal.com	Linux Journal
www.linuxgazette.com	Linux Gazette

Table 1-4. *Linux Information and News Sites*

URL	Internet Site
www.linux.org	Linux Online
www.li.org	Linux International Web site
www.uk.linux.org	Linux European Web site
www.kernelnotes.org	Latest news on the Linux kernel
slashdot.org	Linux forum
webwatcher.org	Linux Web site watcher

Table 1-4. *Linux Information and News Sites* (continued)

URL	Internet Site
www.gnome.org	Gnome Web site
www.kde.org	K Desktop Environment Web site
www.x11.org	X Windows system Web site, with links
www.fvwm.org	FVWM window manager
www.windowmaker.org	WindowMaker window manager
www.enlightenment.org	Enlightenment window manager
www.afterstep.org	AfterStep window manager
www.blackbox.org	Blackbox window manager
www.lesstif.org	Hungry Programmers OSF/Motif
www.themes.org	Desktop and Window manager themes, including KDE and Gnome
www.xfree86.org	XFree86, GNU version of the X Windows system provided for Linux
www.themes.org	Themes for window mangers and desktops
www.eazel.com	Eazel Mac-like Gnome interface

Table 1-5. *Linux Desktops and Window Managers*

Newsgroup	Title
comp.os.linux.announce	Announcements of Linux developments
comp.os.linux.development.apps	For programmers developing Linux applications
comp.os.linux.development.system	For programmers working on the Linux operating system
comp.os.linux.hardware	Linux hardware specifications
comp.os.linux.admin	System administration questions
comp.os.linux.misc	Special questions and issues
comp.os.linux.setup	Installation problems
comp.os.linux.answers	Answers to command problems
comp.os.linux.help	Questions and answers for particular problems
comp.os.linux.networking	Linux network questions and issues

Table 1-6.   *Usenet Newsgroups*

URL	Internet Site
www.linuxapps.com	Linux Software Repository
www.uk.linux.org/Commercial.html	Linux Commercial Vendors Index
linuxwww.db.erau.edu/	Linux archive
http://www.happypenguin.org/	Linux Game Tome
www.linuxgames.org	Linux games
www.linuxquake.com	Quake
http://www.xnet.com/~blatura/linapps. shtml	Linux applications and utilities page

Table 1-7.   *Linux Software Archives, Repositories, and Links*

URL	Internet Site
freshmeat.net	New Linux software
www.linuxlinks.com	Linux links
filewatcher.org	Linux FTP site watcher
www.linuxdoc.org/links.html	Linux links
rpmfind.net	RPM package repository
www.gnu.org	GNU archive
www.opensound.com	Open sound system drivers
www.blackdown.org	Web site for Linux Java
www.fokus.gmd.de/linux	Woven goods for Linux
metalab.unc.edu	Mirror site for Linux software and distributions

Table 1-7.   *Linux Software Archives, Repositories, and Links* (continued)

URL	Databases
www.oracle.com	Oracle database
www.sybase.com	Sybase database
www.software.ibm.com/data/db2/linux	IBM database
www.informix.com/linux	Informix database
www.cai.com/products/ingres.htm	Ingress II
www.softwareag.com	Adabas D database
www.mysql.com	MySQL database
www.ispras.ru/~kml/gss	The GNU SQL database
www.postgresql.org	The PostgreSQL database

Table 1-8.   *Database and Office Software*

URL	Databases
www.fship.com/free.html	Flagship (Interface for xBase database files)
koffice.kde.org	Katabase (KOffice desktop database)
gaby.netpedia.net	Gaby (Gnome desktop personal database)
	Office Software
koffice.kde.org	KOffice
linux.corel.com	WordPerfect
www.sun.com	Star Office (Sun Microsystems product)
www.gnome.org/gw.html	Gnome Workshop Project
www.helixcode.com	Helix Code, Office Applications for Gnome
www.redhat.com	Applixware (commercial)

Table 1-8. *Database and Office Software* (continued)

URL	Servers
www.apache.org	Apache Web server
www.proftpd.org	ProFTPD FTP server
www.isc.org	Internet Software Consortium: BIND, INN, and DHCPD
www.sendmail.org	Sendmail mail server
www.squid.org	Squid proxy server
www.samba.org	Samba SMB (Windows network) server
boombox.micro.umn.edu/pub/gopher	Gopher server
www.eudora.com/free/qpop.html	Qpopper pop3 mail server

Table 1-9. *Network Servers*

URL	Internet Sites
www.linuxprogramming.org	Linux programming resources
www.scriptics.com	Tk/Tcl Products
java.sun.com	Sun Java Web site
www.perl.com	Perl Web site with Perl software
www.blackdown.org	Sun's Java Development Kit for Linux
developer.gnome.org	Gnome developers Web site
www.openprojects.nu	Open Projects Network
developer.kde.org	Developer's library for KDE

Table 1-10.   *Linux Programming*

Chapter 2

Installing Red Hat Linux

23

This chapter describes the installation procedure for the Red Hat software. The installation includes the Linux operating system, a great many Linux applications, and a complete set of Internet servers. Different Linux distributions usually have their own installation programs. The Red Hat installation program is designed to be efficient and brief, while installing as many features as possible. Certain features, such as Web server support, would ordinarily require specialized and often complex configuration operations. Red Hat automatically installs and configures many of these features.

Red Hat provides a detailed installation manual both on the CD-ROM provided with this book and at its Web site. The manual consists of Web pages you can view using any browser. They include detailed figures and step-by-step descriptions. Checking this manual before you install is advisable. This chapter presents all the steps in the installation process, but is not as detailed as the Red Hat manual. On the CD-ROM, the Red Hat Installation manual is located at:

```
doc/install-guide/index.htm
```

On the Red Hat Web site at **www.redhat.com**, click Support and choose the Installation Guides, Manuals, & FAQs entry. This presents a menu on which the first entry is the Red Hat Linux 6.0 Installation Guide.

Installing Linux involves several steps. First, you need to determine whether your computer meets the basic hardware requirements. These days, most Intel-based PC computers do. If you want to have your Linux system share a hard drive with another operating system, you may need to repartition your hard disk. Several different options exist for partitioning your hard drive, depending on whether it already contains data you need to preserve.

Red Hat supports several methods for installing Linux. You can install from a Local source such as a CD-ROM or a hard disk, or from a network or Internet source. For a network and Internet source, Red Hat supports NFS, FTP, and HTTP installations. With FTP, you can install from an FTP site. With HTTP, you can install from a Web site. NFS enables you to install over a local network. For a Local source, you can install from a CD-ROM or a hard disk. In addition, you can start the installation process by booting from your CD-ROM, from a DOS system, or from boot disks that can then use the CD-ROM or hard disk repository. Red Hat documentation covers each of these methods in detail. This chapter deals with the installation using the CD-ROM provided by this book and a boot disk created from a boot image on the CD-ROM. This is the most common approach.

Once the installation program begins, you simply follow the instructions, screen by screen. Most of the time, you only need to make simple selections or provide yes and no answers. The installation program progresses through several phases. First, you create Linux partitions on your hard drive, and then you install the software packages. After that, you can configure your network connection, and then your X Window System for graphical user interface support. Both X Windows and network configurations can be performed independently at a later time.

Once your system is installed, you are ready to start it and log in. You will be logging in to a simple command line interface. From the command line, you can then invoke X Windows, which provides you with a full graphical user interface.

You have the option of installing just the operating system, the system with a standard set of applications, or all the software available on the CD-ROM. If you choose a standard installation, you can add the uninstalled software packages later. Chapter 3 and Chapter 24 describe how you can use the GnomeRPM utility or the Red Hat Package Manager to install, or even uninstall, the software packages.

Hardware, Software, Information Requirements

Before installing Linux, you must be sure your computer meets certain minimum hardware requirements. You also need to have certain specific information ready concerning your monitor, video card, mouse, and CD-ROM drive. All the requirements are presented in detail in the following sections. Be sure to read them carefully before you begin installation. During the installation program, you need to provide responses based on the configuration of your computer.

Hardware Requirements

Listed here are the minimum hardware requirements for installing a Linux system:

- A 32-bit Intel-based personal computer. An Intel or compatible 80386, 80486, or Pentium microprocessor is required.
- A 3 1/2 inch floppy disk drive
- At least 32MB RAM, though 64MB are recommended
- At least 1GB free hard disk space; 1 to 2GB are recommended. You need at least 1.2GB to load and make use of all the software packages on your CD-ROM. The Standard installation of basic software packages takes 500MB, plus 32 to 64MB for swap space. If you have less than 500MB, you can elect to perform a minimum install, installing only the Linux kernel without most of the applications. You could later install the applications you want, one at a time.
- A 3 1/2-inch, DOS-formatted, high-density (HD) floppy-disk drive, to be used to create an install disk.
- A CD-ROM drive
- Two empty DOS-formatted, 3 1/2-inch, high-density (HD) floppy disks

If you plan to use the X Windows graphical user interface, you will also need:

- A video graphics card
- A mouse or other pointing device

Software Requirements

Only a few software requirements exist. If you intend to install using the floppy disks, you need an operating system from which you can create the disks. The DOS operating system is required to enable you to prepare your installation disks. Using a DOS system, you can access the CD-ROM and issue DOS-like commands to create your installation disks. Any type of DOS will do. You can even use the same commands on OS/2. However, you do not need DOS to run Linux. Linux is a separate operating system in its own right.

If you want to have Linux share your hard disk with another operating system, Windows, for example, you need certain utilities to prepare the hard disk for sharing. For Windows, you need either the **defrag** and **fips** utilities or disk management software like Partition Magic 4.0. The **fips** utility is provided on your CD-ROM. This utility essentially frees space by reducing the size of your current extended or primary partition. **Defrag** and **fdisk** are standard DOS utilities, usually located in your **dos** directory. **Defrag** is used with **fips** to defragment your hard disk before **fips** partitions it. This collects all files currently on the partition into one area, leaving all the free space grouped in one large chunk. If you are installing on a new empty hard drive and you want to use part of it for Windows, you can use **fdisk** to set up your Windows partitions. All these tasks can also be carried out using Partition Magic 4.0, a commercial product that now supports Linux partitions.

Information Requirements

Part of adapting a powerful operating system like Linux to the PC entails making the most efficient use of the computer hardware at hand. To do so, Linux requires specific information about the computer components with which it is dealing. For example, special Linux configuration files are tailored to work with special makes and models of video cards and monitors. Before installing Linux, you need to have such information on hand. The information is usually available in the manual that came with your hardware peripherals or computer.

CD-ROM, Hard Disk, and Mouse Information

For some older SCSI CD-ROM drives, you need the manufacturer's name and model.

Decide how much of your hard drive (in megabytes) you want to dedicate to your Linux system. If you are sharing with Windows, decide how much you want for Windows and how much for Linux.

Decide how much space you want for your swap partition. Your *swap partition* must be between 16MB and 64MB, with 32MB appropriate for most systems, and is used by Linux as an extension of your computer's RAM.

Find the make and model of the mouse you are using. Linux supports both serial and bus mice. Most mice are supported, including Microsoft, Logitech, and Mouse Systems.

Know what time zone you are in and to what time zone your hardware clock is set. This can be either Greenwich Mean Time (GMT) or your local time zone.

Know which serial port your mouse is using: COM1, COM2, or none, if you use the PS/2 mouse port.

Video and Monitor Information

Although most monitors and video cards are automatically configured during installation, you still need to provide the manufacturer's make and model. Find out the manufacturer for your monitor and its model, such as Iiyama VisionMaster 450 or NEC E500. Do the same for your video card, for example, Matrox Millennium G200 or ATI XPERT@Play 98 (you can find a complete list of supported cards at www.xfree86.org). For some of the most recent monitors and video cards, and some older, uncommon ones, you may need to provide certain hardware specifications. Having this information on hand, if possible, is advisable, just in case. At the end of the installation process, you are presented with lists of video cards and monitors from which to choose your own. These lists are extensive. In case your card or monitor is not on the list, however, you need to provide certain hardware information about them. If the configuration should fail, you can always do it later using an X Window System configuration utility such as Xconfigurator and XF86Setup. Of particular importance is the monitor information, including the vertical and horizontal refresh rates.

VIDEO CARD INFORMATION

- What is the make and model of your video card?
- What chipset does your video card use?
- How much memory is on your video card?

MONITOR INFORMATION

- What is the manufacturer and model of your monitor? Linux supports an extensive list of monitors, covering almost all current ones. You only have to select yours from the list. If, however, your monitor is not on this list, you need to provide the following information. Be sure this information is correct. Should you enter a horizontal or vertical refresh rate that is too high, you can seriously damage your monitor. You can choose a generic profile or you can enter information for a custom profile. To do that, you need the following information:
  - The horizontal refresh rate in Hz
  - The vertical refresh rate in Hz

Network Configuration Information

Except for deciding your hostname, you do not have to configure your network during installation. You can put configuration off until a later time and use network configuration utilities like Linuxconf or netcfg to perform network configuration. If the information is readily available, however, the installation procedure will automatically configure your network, placing needed entries in the appropriate configuration files. If you are on a network, you must obtain most of this information from your network administrator. If you are setting up a network yourself, you have to determine each piece of information. If you are using a dial-up Internet service provider, you configure your network access using a PPP dial-up utility, such as kppp or Linuxconf after you have installed the system. The installation program will prompt you to enter in these values:

- Decide on a name for your computer (this is called a *hostname*). Your computer will be identified by this name on the Internet. Do not use "localhost"; that name is reserved for special use by your system.

- Your domain name.

- The Internet Protocol (IP) address assigned to your machine. Every host on the Internet is assigned an IP address. This address is a set of four numbers, separated by periods, which uniquely identifies a single location on the Internet, allowing information from other locations to reach that computer.

- Your network IP address. This address is usually the same as the IP address, but with an added 0.

- The netmask. This is usually 255.255.255.0 for class C IP addresses. If, however, you are part of a large network, check with your network administrator.

- The broadcast address for your network. Usually, your broadcast address is the same as your IP address with the number 255 added at the end.

- If you have a gateway, you need the gateway (router) IP address for your network.

- The IP address of any name servers your network uses.

- NIS domain and IP address if your network uses an NIS server.

Upgrade Information for Currently Installed Linux Systems

If you already have installed a previous version of Red Hat Linux (kernel 2.0 and above), you may have personalized your system with different settings that you would like to keep. If you choose the Upgrade option rather than Install during the installation process, these settings will be kept. All your previous configuration files are saved in files with a .rpmsave extension. However, upgrade only works for Red Hat kernel 2.0 and above (Red Hat 5.0 and up).

For earlier Red Hat versions or other installed Linux distributions, you must save your settings first. You may want to back up these settings anyway as a precaution. These settings are held in configuration files that you can save to a floppy disk and then use on your new system, in effect, retaining your original configuration (if you use `mcopy` be sure to use the `-t` option). You may want to preserve directories and files of data, such as Web pages used for a Web site. You may also want to save copies of software packages you have downloaded. For these and for large directories, using the following **tar** operation is best.

```
tar cvMf /dev/fd0   directory-or-package
```

Make copies of the following configuration files and any other files you want to restore. You only need to copy the files you want to restore.

Files	Description
/etc/XF86Config	X Windows configuration file
/etc/lilo.conf	Boot manager configuration file
/etc/hosts	IP addresses of connected systems
/etc/resolv.conf	Domain name server addresses
/etc/fstab	File systems mounted on your system
/etc/passwd	Names and passwords of all users on your system
/home/user	Any home directories of users with their files on your system, where *user* is the username. (For a large number of files use **tar cfM/dev/fd0/home/user**)
.netscape	Each home directory has its own .netscape subdirectory with Netscape configuration files such as your bookmark entries
Web site pages and FTP files	You may want to save any pages used for a Web site or files on an FTP site you are running. On CND versions these are located at /home/httpd/ and /home/ftpd.

Once you have installed your system, you can mount the floppy disk and copy the saved files from the floppy to your system, overwriting those initially set up. If you use the **/etc/XF86Config** file from your previous system, you needn't run XF86Setup to set up X Windows. The **/etc/XF86Config** file includes all the X Windows setup information.

If you want to restore the **/etc/lilo.conf** file from your previous system, you must also install it, using the following command.

```
# lilo /etc/lilo.conf
```

To restore archives that you saved on multiple disks using the **tar** operation, place the first disk in the floppy drive and use the following command.

```
tar xvMf  /dev/fd0
```

Opening Disk Space for Linux Partitions

If you are using an entire hard drive for your Linux system or if you are upgrading a currently installed Linux system and you want to use the same partitions, you can skip this section and go on to installing Linux. If, however, your Linux system is going to share a hard drive with your Windows or DOS system, you have the option of a partitionless installation or creating separate partitions for Windows and Linux. Partitionless installation is a new feature of Red Hat 6.2. You can just use a Windows partition for your Linux system, provided it is large enough. You do not have to create a partition for Linux. If, instead, you want to manually create separate Linux and Windows partitions, you need to organize your hard drive so part of it is used for DOS and the remaining part is free for Linux installation. How you go about this process depends on the current state of your hard disk. If you have a new hard disk and you are going to install both Windows and Linux on it, you need to be sure to install Windows on only part of the hard drive, leaving the rest free for Linux. This means specifying a size smaller than the entire hard disk for your Windows partition that you set up during the Windows install procedure. You could also use **fdisk** to create partitions manually for Windows that will take up only a part of the hard disk. If you want to install Linux on a hard disk that already has Windows installed on the entire hard disk, however, you need to resize your primary or extended partition, leaving part of the disk free for Linux. The objective in each situation is to free space for Linux. When you install Linux, you will then partition and format that free space for use by Linux. Red Hat 6.2 supports partitionless installation. With partitionless installation, you will be able to access Linux using only the Linux boot disk that you create at the end of the installation. Furthermore, Linux systems using paritionless installation will run significantly slower.

A hard disk is organized into partitions. The partitions are further formatted to the specifications of a given operating system. When you installed Windows, you first needed to create a primary partition for it on your hard disk. If you have only one disk on your hard drive, then you only have a primary partition. To add more partitions, you create an extended partition and then, within that, logical partitions. For example, if you have C, D, and E disks on your hard drive, your C disk is your primary partition and the D and E disks are logical partitions set up within your extended partition. You then used the DOS **format** operation to format each partition into a Windows disk, each identified by a letter. For example, you may have divided your disk into two partitions, one formatted as the C disk and the other as the D disk. Alternatively, you may have divided your hard disk into just one partition and formatted it as the C disk. To share your hard drive with Linux, you need to free some space by either reducing the size of or deleting some of those partitions.

First, decide how much space you need for your Linux system. You probably need a minimum of 1GB, though more is recommended. As stated earlier, the basic set of Linux software packages takes up 500MB, whereas the entire set of software packages, including all their source code files, takes 1.2GB. In addition, you need space for a Linux swap partition used to implement virtual memory. This takes between 16 and 32MB.

Once you determine the space you need for your Linux system, you can then set about freeing that space on your hard drive. To see what options are best for you, you should first determine what your partitions are and their sizes. You can do this with the **fdisk** utility. To start this utility, type **fdisk** at the DOS prompt, and press ENTER.

```
C:\> fdisk
```

This brings up the menu of fdisk options. Choose Option 4 to display a list of all your current partitions and the size of each. Press ESC to leave the **fdisk** utility. You can use the DOS **defrag** and Linux **fips** utilities to reduce the size of the partitions, creating free space from unused space on your hard drive. You should still make a backup of your important data for safety's sake. First, check if you already have enough unused space on your hard drive that can be used for Linux. If you do not, you must delete some files. When Windows creates and saves files, it places them in different sectors on your hard disk. Your files are spread out across your hard disk with a lot of empty space in between. This has the effect of fragmenting the remaining unused space into smaller sections, separated by files. The **defrag** utility performs a defragmentation process that moves all the files into adjoining space on the hard disk, thereby leaving all the unused space as one large continuous segment. Once you have defragmented your disk, you can use the **fips** utility to create free space using part or all of the unused space. **fips** is a version of **fdisk** designed to detect continuous unused space and remove it from its current Windows partition, opening unpartitioned free space that can then be used by Linux. All your Windows partitions and drives remain intact with all their data and programs. They are just smaller.

To run the **defrag** utility, enter the command **defrag**. This is a DOS command usually found in the **dos** or **windows** directory. You can also run it from Windows.

```
C:\> windows\defrag
```

Defrag displays a screen with colored blocks representing the different sectors on your hard disk. It carries out an optimization of your hard disk, moving all your used sectors, your data and programs, together on the hard disk. This may take a few minutes. When it is complete, you will see the used sectors arranged together on the screen. You can then exit the **defrag** utility.

Now you are ready to run the **fips** utility to free space. **fips** is located on your RedHat Linux CD-ROM, also in the directory named **dosutils**. Change to your CD-ROM drive and run the **fips** utility. In the following example, the CD-ROM drive is drive E.

```
C:\> e:
E:\> \dosutils\fips
```

fips displays a screen showing the amount of free space. Use your arrow keys to make the space smaller if you do not need all your free space for Linux. You should leave some free space for your Windows programs. Then press ENTER to free the space.

Creating the Red Hat Boot Disks

You can install Red Hat using an install disk whose image is located on the Red Hat CD-ROM. You create the install disk using the MS-DOS program **rawrite** and a install disk image. The install disk has to be created on a computer that runs DOS. Install disk images exist for local installation (**boot.img**), installing from an network source like a Web site (**netimage.img**) and installing with PCMCIA support (**pcmcia.img**). Begin by first starting your computer and entering DOS. Then perform the following steps.

Insert the Red Hat CD-ROM into your CD-ROM drive. At your DOS prompt, change to your CD-ROM drive, using whatever the letter for that drive may be. For example, if your CD-ROM drive is the E drive, just type **e:** and press ENTER. Once you have changed to the CD-ROM drive, you then need to change to the **\images** directory. The Install disk images are there, **boot.img**, **pcmia.img**, and **netboot.img**. The **rawrite** command is in the **dosutils** directory, **\dosutils\rawrite**.

To create the install disk, insert a blank floppy disk into your floppy drive. Now start the **rawrite** command. The **rawrite** command will actually write the disk image to your floppy disk. The **rawrite** command first prompts you for the name of the disk image file you want to copy. Enter the full name of the install image file (in this example **boot.img**). It then asks you to enter the letter of the floppy drive where you put your floppy disk. On many systems this is the A drive.

```
E:\> cd images
E:\col\launch\floppy > e:\dosutils\rawrite
Enter source file name: boot.img
Enter destination drive (A or B) and press ENTER: a
```

Press ENTER to confirm that you have a blank floppy disk in the drive. **rawrite** will then copy the image file to your floppy disk, creating your install disk. When it finishes, remove your disk from the floppy drive. This is the disk that the installation procedure (described later) refers to as the Install diskette. If you need to create a network boot disk, use **netimage.img** instead. For PCMCIA support use **pcmcia.img**.

Installing Linux

Installing Linux involves several processes, beginning with creating Linux partitions, and then loading the Linux software, configuring your X Windows interface, installing the Linux Loader (LILO) that will boot your system, and creating new user accounts. The installation program is a screen-based program that takes you through all these processes, step-by-step, as one continuous procedure. You can use either your mouse or the keyboard to make selections. When you finish with a screen, click the Next button at the bottom to move to the next screen. If you need to move back to the previous screen, click the Back button. You can also use the TAB, the arrow keys, SPACEBAR, and ENTER to make selections. You have little to do, other than make selections and choose options. Some screens provide a list of options from which you make a selection. In a few cases, you are asked for information you should already have if you followed the steps earlier in this chapter. You are now ready to begin installation. The steps for each part of the procedure are delineated in the following sections. This should not take more than an hour.

Starting the Installation Program

If you followed the instructions in the first part of the chapter, you have freed space on your hard drive, and created your install and module disks. Now you are ready to create your Linux partitions. To do this, you need to boot your computer using the install disk you made earlier. When you start your computer, the installation program will begin and, during the installation, you can create your Linux partitions.

You can start the installation using one of several methods. If your computer can boot from the CD-ROM, you can start the installation directly from the CD-ROM. Just place the Red Hat CD-ROM in the CD-ROM drive before you start your computer. If you have a DOS system installed on your hard drive, you can start up DOS and then use the **autoboot.bat** command in the **dosutils** directory to start the installation, as shown here. You have to execute this command from a DOS system, not the Windows DOS window. Only DOS can be running for this command to work.

```
e:\dosutils\autoboot.bat
```

If neither of these options is feasible for you, you can use the install floppy disk (see the previous section on creating a boot disk). This is perhaps the most fail-safe method of installing Linux. Insert the Linux install disk into your floppy drive and reboot your computer. Performing a cold boot is best: turn off the computer completely and then turn it on again with the install disk in the floppy drive.

The installation program will start, presenting you with an Introduction screen. After a moment, the following prompt will appear at the bottom of your screen:

```
boot:
```

Press ENTER. (If necessary, you can enter boot parameters as described in the Red Hat manual.) Configuration information will fill your screen as the installation program attempts to detect your hardware components automatically.

Your system then detects the type of CD-ROM you have. If it cannot do so, your system will ask you to select yours from a list. If you have an IDE CD-ROM and the system fails to detect it, this may be because it is not connected on the default HDC device interface. You must restart the installation, providing the CD-ROM device name at the boot prompt.

```
Boot: linux hdX=cdrom
```

Replace the *X* with one of the following letters, depending on the interface the unit is connected to, and whether it is configured as master or a slave: a—First IDE controller master, b—First IDE controller slave, c—Second IDE controller master, d—Second IDE controller slave.

As an alternative to the CD-ROM installation, you can copy the entire CD-ROM to a Window partition (one large enough), and then install using that partition instead of the CD-ROM. You need to know the device name of the partition and the directory to which you should copy the CD-ROM files. When asked to choose the installation method, you can select hard disk. You then have to specify the partition name and the directory.

Red Hat Installation

The first screen asks you to select the language you want to use. Click the language you want and then click the Next button. On the following screen, you will configure your keyboard. The screen displays lists for selecting your keyboard model, layout, and options. A generic model works in most cases.

On the next screen, you configure your mouse (see Figure 2-1). The screen lists the different mouse brands along with specific models. Click a + symbol to expand a model list. Select your mouse. You can also check a button at the bottom of the screen to have a two-button mouse emulate a three-button mouse. A generic PS/2 or serial mouse will work if your model is not listed. If you select a serial mouse, you also must select the port and device to which it is connected.

Now that the keyboard and mouse are configured, you can begin the installation process. The next screen displays a Welcome to Red Hat message. Click the Next button to continue.

On the following screen labeled Install Path, you select whether you want to install a new system or upgrade a previous one. On the panel labeled Install Type, click the button for either Install or Upgrade. You use the Upgrade option to upgrade a version of Red Hat (2.0 or higher) that is already on your system. All your current configuration files are preserved in files with a .rpmsave extension. You can use them to restore your system configuration. With new software versions, configuration files sometimes change format, so be sure to check for any changes.

Should you select the Install option, you can then specify a different class of installation. You can select a Gnome or KDE workstation, a server installation, or a custom installation. Most first-time users will want to use a custom installation. The other classes of installation also perform automatic formatting of your partitions, erasing all current data on them. Use them only if you are sure of what you are doing. Gnome and KDE workstation installations automatically erase any and all Linux partitions on your computer and use them to install Red Hat Linux. Be very careful

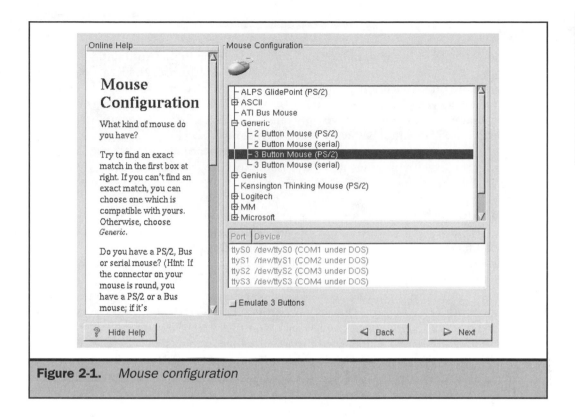

Figure 2-1.   *Mouse configuration*

with the Server installation. The Server installation will erase all partitions on your computer hard drives, including Windows and OS/2 partitions. The Server installation is intended for computers that will operate as dedicated servers, performing only network server tasks. Should you be using Windows on the same computer as you want to use Linux, do NOT select the Server option.

The Gnome and KDE workstation installations will install all the needed applications for a Linux workstation with either the Gnome or KDE desktops as your default desktop. Server installation will install server programs to enable your Linux system to operation as a network server. The custom installation enables you to choose what software packages you want installed on your system.

If you chose the Workstation or Server options, then an Automatic Partitioning screen is displayed with two options, Manually partition and Remove data. If you choose Manually partition, then you can control and select the partitions you want set up and formatted. If you choose Remove data, then the Workstation will erase any current Linux partition on your system, whereas the Server install will erase all your partitions (including Windows). Should you want to back out to select a custom installation, you can just click the Back button.

Partitions

If you choose a Custom installation or the Manual partition in the Automatic Partitioning screen, the Partitions screen is displayed (see Figure 2-2). Here, you can manually create Linux partitions or select the one where you want to install Red Hat. The top pane lists your Partitions and the lower pane lists the hard drives on your computer (many computers will have only one hard drive). Selecting a hard drive will list its partitions. The button below the Partitions pane enables you to create, edit, and delete partitions. The Partitions screen is actually an interface for the Red Hat Disk Druid program, used in previous Red Hat installation programs. By default, Red Hat will use Disk Druid to create partions; however, you can choose to use Linux `fdisk` instead.

If you are using partitionless installation and you have already installed Windows, a DOS/FAT Windows partition will be displayed. Simply click the edit button and enter the mount point for the root, /, and the size of Linux usage. If, instead, you are creating separate partitions, you are advised to set up at least two Linux partitions, a swap partition and a root partition. The *root partition* is where the Linux system and application files are installed. If you have a large hard drive, one over 8.4 gigs, you should set up another partition to be used to boot your Linux system. This "boot" partition will hold the Linux kernel and other files needed to start up Linux. Application and other files will be installed on the root partition. If you are sharing a large hard drive with other systems like Windows, be sure to install the Linux boot partition within the first 8.4 gigs of the hard drive. Boot loaders

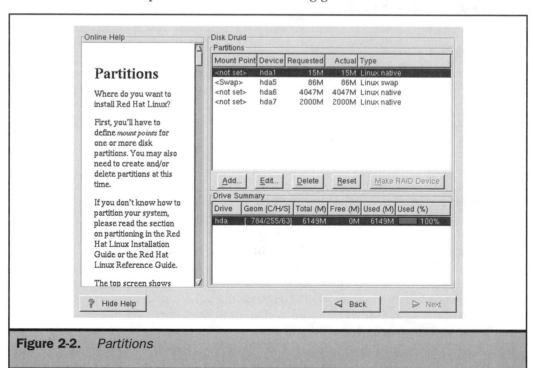

Figure 2-2. *Partitions*

like LILO can only boot systems that are located within the first 8.4 gigs. The root and swap partitions, however, can be located anywhere on the hard drive, even past the first 8.4 gigs.

Except for the swap partition, when setting up a Linux partition you must specify a mount point. A *mount point* is a directory where the files on that partition are connected to the overall Linux file structure for your system. The mount point for your root partition is the root directory represented by a single slash, /. The mount point for your boot partition is the path **/boot**.

When creating a new partition, you must specify its size. Be sure enough space is available for it on your hard drive. If not, you will receive a Unallocated Requested Partition message. You can free space by deleting unwanted partitions already set up or edit the new partition's entry and change its requested size. Check the entry for your hard drive in the Drive summaries pane to find out how much free space is available on your hard drive.

To create the new partition, click the Add button to display a dialog box where you can enter the mount point, size (in megabytes), the partition type, and the hard disk on which you want to create the partition. For the size, you can select a "Grow to fill disk" option to have the partition automatically expand to the size of the remaining free space on the disk. You can have this option selected for more than one partition. In that case, the partition size will be taken as a required minimum and the remaining free space will be shared equally among the partitions. For partition type, select Linux native for standard Linux partitions and select the Linux swap type for your swap partition. You can even use Disk Druid to create DOS partitions. To make any changes later, you can Edit a partition by selecting it and clicking the Edit button.

If you want to change the size of a partition that has been already created, you first must delete it and then create a new one. Remember, deleting a partition erases all data on it. To delete a partition, select it and click the Delete button.

Once you create your partitions, you can format them. The next screen is the Choose Partitions to Format screen, which lists the Linux partitions on your system. Click the ones you want to format. You should format all new Linux partitions and any old ones you may have that you no longer need. However, if you already have a Linux system and have installed Red Hat on it, then you will most likely have several Linux partitions already. Some of these may be used for just the system software, such as a boot and root partitions. These should be formatted. Other may have extensive user files such as a /home partition that normally holds user home directories and all the files they have created. You should *not* format such partitions.

LILO

Once your partitions are prepared, you install LInux LOader (LILO). You use LILO to start Red Hat Linux from your hard drive. You can also use it to start any other operating system you may have installed on your computer, such as Windows. You have two choices on where to install LILO: the Master Boot Record (MBR) or the root partition. The recommended place is the MBR.

The LILO Configuration screen lists various LILO options (see Figure 2-3). Here you can select where to install LILO (MBR or root partition), a label for the Linux system (usually linux), whether it is to be the default system (if you have more than one operating system), and specify any kernel parameters your system may require for Linux. At the top of the screen are options for creating a boot disk and NOT to install LILO. The boot disk option is automatically selected for you. You can use the boot disk to start your Linux system should there ever be a problem starting from your hard drive (for example, if you reinstall Windows on your hard drive, LILO is removed and you will need to use the boot disk to start Linux so you can reinstall LILO).

The bottom of the screen displays a list of bootable partitions. Selecting one enables you to enter specific information for the partition in the top pane, such as the label you want to give to this partition and any kernel parameters required. The root or boot linux partition is usually given a label named "linux" and a Window partition could be given a label like "win".

Network Configuration

The Network Configuration screen displays tabbed panes in the top-half for the different network devices on your computer (see Figure 2-4). Click the tab for the device you want to configure. For computers already connected to a network with an Ethernet card, the tab is usually labeled eth0. Such a tab displays a pane with boxes for

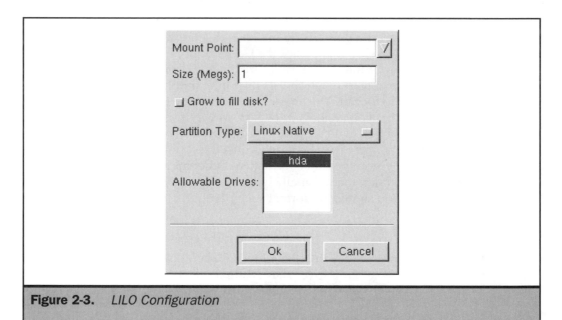

Figure 2-3.   *LILO Configuration*

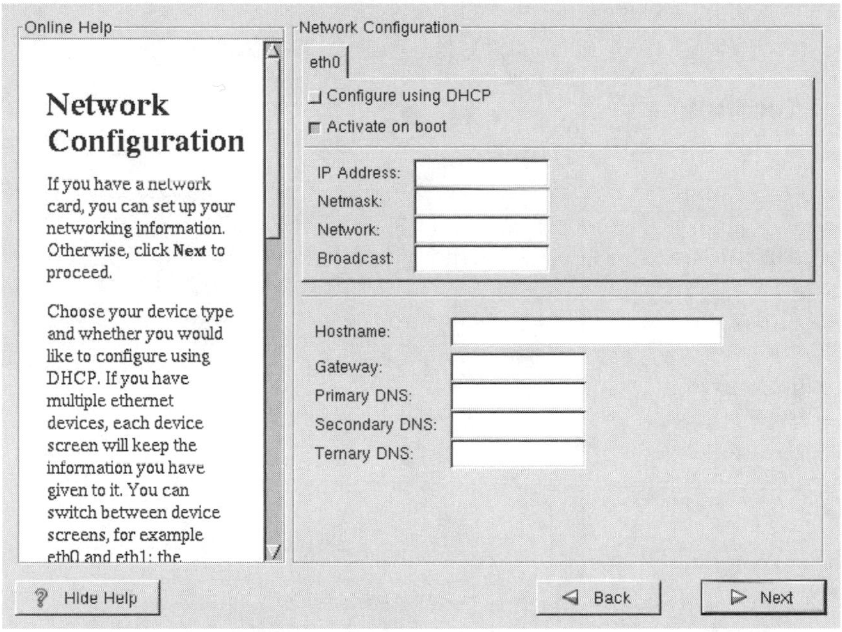

Figure 2-4.   *Network Configuration*

entering the various IP addresses for the network accessible through this device. These include the device's IP address (usually your computer's IP address), the network's address, and the broadcast address, along with the netmask. You could have a computer with several Ethernet devices, each connected to a different (or the same) network. If your network supports DHCP, then you can click the DHCP button instead of manually entering in these addresses. DHCP automatically provides your computer with the needed IP addresses. You can also choose to have the device activated when your system boots or not.

The bottom pane holds boxes for entering the IP addresses for your network's Domain Name Servers (DNS) and Gateway computer, as well as the host name you want to give to your system. In the Hostname box, enter the fully qualified domain name for your computer.

On the Time Zone Configuration screen, you have the option of setting the time using a map to specify your location or by using Universal Coordinated Time (UTC) entries.

On the Account Configuration screen, shown in Figure 2-5, you can set the root password for the root account on our system. This is the account used for system administration operations, such as installing software and managing users. On this same screen, you can also add ordinary user accounts. In the boxes for the Account

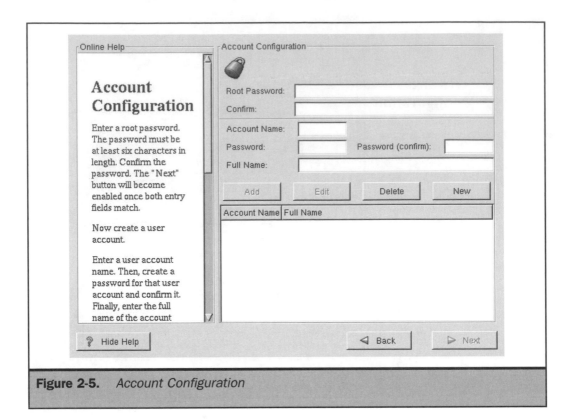

Figure 2-5.   *Account Configuration*

name, password, and Full name, enter the username, the password for that account, and the user's full name. Then click the Add button to create the account. You will see it displayed in the following list. To add another user, first click the New button, enter the new user's information, and then click the Add button. You can add as many users as you wish. You can also add users at any time after you install your system.

On the Authentication Configuration screen, you can add further levels of security for passwords. MD5 allows for long passwords up to 256 characters and shadow passwords will save password information in a secure file on your system. Also, if your network supports the Network Information Service (NIS), you can enable the service and enter its domain name and server address.

For Custom installations, you are presented with a Package Group Selection screen. Here you can choose to install whole sets of packages for different categories. For example, you can install all the packages you would need for the Gnome desktop or the X Window System. To install all packages, select the Everything entry at the end of the list.

If you want to select individual software packages, click the Select individual packages check box. This will display a new screen with two panes, the left showing an expandable tree of software categories and the right displaying icons for the individual software packages. To select a package for installation, double-click it. You can also single click, and then click the "Select package for installation" check box below. Whenever you single click any icon, a description of the package is displayed on the bottom pane. Many software package require that other software packages also be installed. Should you not have these already selected for installation, then an Unresolved dependencies screen is displayed showing the packages you need to install. You can then select them for installation.

X Window System Configuration

The X Configuration screen then configures the X Window System. This enables GUI interfaces, such as Gnome and KDE. X configuration uses the Xconfigurator utility to detect your Video card and monitor automatically. The detected card and monitor are listed under "Autoprobe results." If Xconfigurator fails to detect your card or monitor, it will provide a list of video cards and monitors from which you can select yours. You need to know the brand and model number for your card and monitor. If your video card does not appear on the list, XFree86 may not support it. If you have technical knowledge about your card, however, you may choose Unlisted Card and attempt to configure it by matching your card's video chipset with one of the available X servers. If the video card you select has a video clock chip, Xconfigurator will presents a list of clock chips. The recommended choice is No Clockchip Setting because, in most cases, XFree86 can automatically detect the proper clock chip.

Once you select your video card, the installation program installs the appropriate XFree86 server and Xconfigurator presents a list of monitors. If your monitor appears on the list, select it and press ENTER. If your monitor is not on the list, select Custom. This displays a screen where you enter the horizontal sync range and vertical sync range of your monitor (these values are generally available in the documentation that accompanies your monitor or from your monitor's vendor or manufacturer). Be careful to enter the correct horizontal and vertical frequencies. If you enter values that are too high, you could overclock your monitor and possibly damage or destroy it. Do not select a monitor "similar" to your monitor unless you are certain the monitor you are selecting does not exceed the capabilities of your monitor.

You can specify your card's resolution and color depth by clicking the Customize X Configuration check box. A screen appears where you can enter the resolution and the color depth you want.

You can choose to use a graphical login instead of the command line login. Click the graphical login check box. If you choose this option, when you start, the Gnome Desktop Manager (GDM) will start and display a login screen where you can enter the username and password. A Sessions menu in the Options menu enables you to choose whether to start KDE, Gnome, or the Another Level window manager. The default is Gnome. When you log in, Gnome automatically starts up. When you log out of Gnome, the GDM login window is redisplayed. Select Shutdown from the Options menu to shut down Linux.

If you do not choose this option, then you will start up with the command line interface. Enter the username at the login prompt and the password at the password prompt to log in. Use **startx** to start Gnome and **switchdesk** to switch to KDE or Another Level. The **logout** command logs out, and CTRL-ALT-DEL will shut down Linux.

When you finish, Xconfigurator will generate an X Window System configuration file called **/etc/X11/XF86Config**. This is the file the X Window System uses to start up.

If you are having difficulty, you can always click the Skip X Configuration check box to skip the X Window System configuration and perform it later, after you have installed your system.

The Installing Packages screen is then displayed, which shows each package as it is installed and the progress of the installation. When the installation finishes, the Next button will become active. You can then move on to the Boot Disk Creation screen. Here, you can create a boot disk using a standard floppy disk (or you can elect to skip it). Once your Boot disk is created, installation is finished. Click the Exit button on the final screen. Your system will reboot, displaying a LILO boot prompt. If you set up Linux as your default operating system, just press return or do nothing. Linux will then start up. If Linux is not your default, then enter the label you gave it when configuring LILO (usually "linux").

When your system restarts, the login prompt or the GDM login screen will appear, depending upon whether you chose to have the X Window System start up automatically. You can then log into your Linux system using a login name and a password for any users you have set up. If you log in as the root user, you can perform administrative operations, such as installing new software or creating more users. To log in as the root user, enter **root** at the login prompt and the root user password at the password prompt.

If you are upgrading from a previously installed Red Hat Linux system and used the upgrade options, you can restore your previous configuration files, which are currently saved on your new system with the .rpmsave extension to their filenames. If you are upgrading from another Linux system and have manually saved configuration files, you can restore them now. Mount the floppy disk on which you saved these files and copy the configuration files to your new system. You can also restore any **tar** archived files and packages with the **tar xvMf /dev/fd0** command.

When you finish, log out of your account using the command **logout**. You then need to shut down the entire system. From the GDM login window, select Shutdown from the Options menu. From the command line interface, hold down the CTRL and ALT keys and press DEL (CTRL-ALT-DEL). Remember, you must always use CTRL-ALT-DEL to shut down the system. Never turn it off as you do with DOS.

Should your Linux system fail to boot at any time, you can use the boot disk you created to perform an emergency boot. You can also use the install disk and, at the boot prompt, enter: **boot rw root=** with the device name of the root Linux partition. For example, if your root Linux partition is **/dev/hda4**, then you would enter **boot rw root=/dev/hda4** as shown here:

```
boot> boot rw root=/dev/hda4
```

Chapter 3

Interface Basics and System Configuration

To start using Linux, you must know how to access your Linux system and, once you are on the system, how to execute commands and run applications. Accessing Linux involves more than just turning on your computer. Once Linux is running, you have to log in to the system using a predetermined login name and password. Once on the system, you can start executing commands and running applications. You can then interact with your Linux system using either a command line interface or a *graphical user interface* (*GUI*). The Linux systems use desktops to provide a fully functional GUI with which you can use windows, menus, and icons to interact with your system.

Obtaining information quickly about Linux commands and utilities while logged in to the system is easy. Linux has several online utilities that provide information and help. You can access an online manual that describes each command or obtain help that provides more detailed explanations of different Linux features. A complete set of manuals provided by the Linux Documentation Project is on your system and available for you to browse through or print.

To make effective use of your Linux system, you must know how to configure certain features. Administrative operations such as adding users, specifying network settings, accessing CD-ROM drives, and installing software can now be performed with user-friendly system tools.

This chapter discusses how to access your Linux system, including logging in and out of user accounts, as well as starting the system and shutting it down. Linux commands and utilities are also covered, along with basic operations of the Gnome and KDE desktops. The chapter ends with an explanation of basic system administration operations, such as creating new user accounts and installing software packages.

User Accounts

You never directly access a Linux system. Instead, Linux sets up an interface through which you can interact. A Linux system can actually set up and operate several user interfaces at once, accommodating several users simultaneously. In fact, you can have many users working off the same computer running a Linux system. Each particular user appears to be the only one working on the system, as if Linux can set up several virtual computers and each user can then work on her own virtual computer. Such virtual computers are actually individually managed interfaces whereby each user interacts with the Linux system.

These user interfaces are frequently referred to as *accounts.* UNIX, which Linux is based on, was first used on large minicomputers and mainframes that could accommodate hundreds of users at the same time. Using one of many terminals connected to the computer, users could log in to the UNIX system using their login names and passwords. All of this activity was managed by system administrators. To gain access to the system, you needed to have a user interface set up for you. This was commonly known as "opening an account." A system administrator created the account on the UNIX system, assigning a login name and password for it. You then used your account to log in and use the system.

Each account is identified by a login name with access protected by a password. Of course, you can access any account if you know its login name and password. On your Linux system, you can create several accounts, logging into different ones as you choose. Other people can access your Linux system, making use of login names and passwords you provide for them. In effect, they have their own accounts on your system. Recall that in the previous chapter on installing Linux, you created a login name and password for yourself. These are what you use to access Linux regularly. When you created the login name and password, you were actually creating a new user account for yourself.

You can, in fact, create other new user accounts using special system administration tools. These tools become available to you when you log in as the root user. The *root user* is a special user account reserved for system administration tasks, such as creating users and installing new software. Basic system administration operations are discussed briefly in this chapter, but they are discussed in detail in Chapters 20 through 31. For now, you only need your regular login name and password.

Accessing Your Linux System

To access and use your Linux system, you must carefully follow required startup and shutdown procedures. You do not simply turn off and turn on your computer. If you have installed the Linux Loader, LILO, when you turn on or reset your computer, LILO first decides what operating system to load and run. You see the following prompt: enter **linux** to start up the Linux operating system:

```
LILO: linux
```

If, instead, you wait a moment or press the ENTER key, LILO loads the default operating system. (Recall that earlier you designated a default operating system.) If you want to run Windows instead, LILO gives you a moment at the prompt to type in the name you gave for Windows, such as **dos** or **win**.

You can think of your Linux operating system as operating on two different levels, one running on top of the other. The first level is when you start your Linux system, and the system loads and runs. It has control of your computer and all its peripherals. You still are not unable to interact with it, however. After Linux starts, it displays a login prompt, waiting for a user to come along and log in to the system to start using it. To gain access to Linux, you have to log in first.

You can think of logging in and using Linux as the next level. Now you can issue commands instructing Linux to perform tasks. You can use utilities and programs, such as editors or compilers, or even games. Depending on a choice you made during installation, however, you may either be interacting with the system using a simple command line interface or using the desktop directly. There are both command line login prompts and Graphical login windows. In the case of Red Hat, if you choose to use a graphical interface at the end of the installation, you are presented with a graphical login window at which you enter your login and password. If you choose not to use the graphical interface, you are presented with a simple command line prompt to enter your login name.

On the command line interface, you are presented with a simple prompt, such as a $ or # symbol. You type in a command and press ENTER to have the system perform actions. You can start up the GUI desktop from the command line interface, if you want. In Linux, the command **startx** starts the X Window System along with a GUI, which then enables you to interact with the system using windows, menus, and icons. On Red Hat, the **startx** command starts the Gnome desktop by default, though you can configure it to start up other window managers, such as WindowMaker.

Shutting down from a command line interface involves several steps. If you are using the GUI started from the command line interface, you first need to exit the GUI, returning to the command line interface. Then you log out of your account and return to the system's login prompt. Logging out does *not* shut down the system: it is still running and has control of your machine. You then need to tell the system to shut itself down by issuing a shutdown command: Hold down the CTRL and ALT keys, and then press the DEL key (CTRL-ALT-DEL). The system shuts itself down and reboots. This involve a series of important actions, such as unmounting file systems and shutting down any servers (never simply turn off the computer). When rebooting starts, only then can you turn off your computer. Or, you can log in as the root user and issue a shutdown command. The **-h** option simply shuts down the system, whereas the **-r** option shuts down the system, and then reboots it. In the next example, the system is shut down after five minutes. To shut down the system immediately, you can use **+0** or the word **now** (see Chapter 27 for more details).

```
# shutdown -h +5
```

With the graphical login, your X Window System starts up immediately and displays a login window with boxes for a user login name and a password. When you enter your login name and password, and then click the OK or GO button, your default GUI starts up. On Red Hat, this is Gnome. On Red Hat, you can easily change this to KDE or another window manager. When you quit your GUI, you are also logging out of your account. The login window is then redisplayed. To shut down, you simply select the Shutdown entry in the Options menu or click Shutdown.

Graphical logins are handled by the *Gnome Display Manager* (*GDM*). The GDM manages the login interface along with authenticating a user password and login name, and then starting up a selected desktop. If problems ever occur using the X Window System display of the GUI interface, you can force a shutdown of the X Window System and the GUI with the CTRL-ALT-BACKSPACE keys. Also, from the GDM, you can shift to the command line interface with the CTRL-ALT-F1 keys, and then shift back to the X Window System with the CTRL-ALT-F7 keys.

Gnome Display Manager: GDM

When the GDM starts up, it shows this login window with a box for login:

Three menus are at the top of the window labeled Session, Language, and System. To log in, enter your login name in the Login box and press ENTER. Then you are prompted to enter your password. Do so, and press ENTER. By default, the Gnome desktop is started up. When you log out from the desktop, you return to the GDM login window. To shut down your Linux system, click the System menu to display the entries Reboot or Halt. Select Halt to shut down your system.

From the Session menu, you can select the desktop or window manager you want to start up. Here are the default entries for Red Hat's Session menu:

You can select KDE to start up the K Desktop instead of Gnome, among others. The Language menu lists a variety of different languages Red Hat Linux supports. Choose one to change the language interface.

Command Line Interface

For the command line interface, you are initially given a login prompt. The system is now running and waiting for a user to log in and use it. You can enter your user name and password to use the system. The login prompt is preceded by the hostname you gave your system. In this example, the hostname is **turtle**. When you finish using Linux, you first log out. Linux then displays exactly the same login prompt, waiting for you or another user to log in again. This is the equivalent of the login window provided by the GDM.

```
Red hat Linux release 6.2 (Piglet)
Kernel 2.2.5-15 on i686

turtle login:
```

If you want to turn off your computer, you must first shut down Linux. If you don't shut down Linux, you could require Linux to perform a lengthy systems check when it starts up again. You shut down your system by holding down both the CTRL and ALT keys, and then pressing the DEL key, CTRL-ALT-DEL. You then see several messages as Linux shuts itself down. Linux then reboots your computer. During the reboot process, you can turn off your computer. The following steps include all the startup and shutdown procedures for the command line interface.

1. Boot your computer.

2. At the LILO prompt, type **linux** and press ENTER. (Or, press ENTER if Linux is your default.)

3. After a few messages, the login prompt appears, and then you can log in to the system and use it.

4. When you finish using Linux, you can log out. The login prompt then reappears.

5. At the login prompt, you can also shut down the system with CTRL-ALT-DEL. The system first shuts down and then restarts, at which time you can turn off your computer.

Once you log in, you can enter and execute commands. After you finish, you need to log out of the system before you shut it down. (If you don't want to shut down the system, you needn't do so.) You are then presented with a login prompt: you can then log in using a different user name or log in as the root user.

Logging in to your Linux account involves two steps: entering your user name, and then your password. You already know what the login prompt looks like. Type in the login name for your user account. If you make a mistake, you can erase characters with the BACKSPACE key. In the next example, the user enters the user name richlp and is then prompted to enter the password.

```
Red hat Linux release 6.2 (Piglet)
Kernel 2.2.5-15 on i686

turtle login: richlp
Password:
```

When you type in your password, it does not appear on the screen. This is to protect your password from being seen by others. If you enter either the login or password incorrectly, the system will respond with the error message "Login incorrect" and will ask for your login name again, starting the login process over. You can then reenter your login name and password.

Once you enter your user name and password correctly, you are logged in to the system. Your command line prompt is displayed, waiting for you to enter a command. Notice the command line prompt is a dollar sign (**$**), not a sharp sign (**#**). The **$** is the prompt for regular users, whereas the **#** is the prompt solely for the root user. In this version of Linux, your prompt is preceded by the hostname and the directory you are in. Both are bounded by a set of brackets.

```
[turtle /home/richlp]$
```

To end your session, issue the **logout** command. This returns you to the login prompt, and Linux waits for another user to log in.

```
$ logout
```

Once logged into the system, you have the option of starting an X Window System GUI, such as Gnome or KDE, and using it to interact with your Linux system. You start the X GUI by entering **startx** on the command line (open a terminal window to enter it). On Red Hat, you can use the **switchdesk** command, while in your desktop, to switch between Gnome, KDE, or the FVWM window manager. You make your selection, and then quit the desktop to return to the command line interface. When you start up the GUI again, the desktop you selected is used.

Gnome Desktop

The Gnome desktop display, shown in Figure 3-1, displays a panel at the bottom of the screen, as well as any icons for folders and Web pages initially set up by your distribution. For Red Hat, you see several Web page icons and a folder for your home directory. The panel at the bottom of the screen contains icons for starting applications, such as Netscape (the Netscape logo) and the Help system (the question mark logo). You can start applications using the main menu, which you display by clicking the Gnome icon (the image of a bare foot print), located on the left side of the panel.

When you click the folder for your home directory on your desktop or select the File Manager entry on the main menu, a file manager window opens showing your home directory. You can display files in your home directory and use the up arrow button to move to the parent directory. Back and Forward buttons move through previously displayed directories. In the location window you can enter the pathname for a directory to move directly to it. The file manager is also Internet-aware. You can use it to access remote FTP directories and to display or download their files (though it cannot display Web pages).

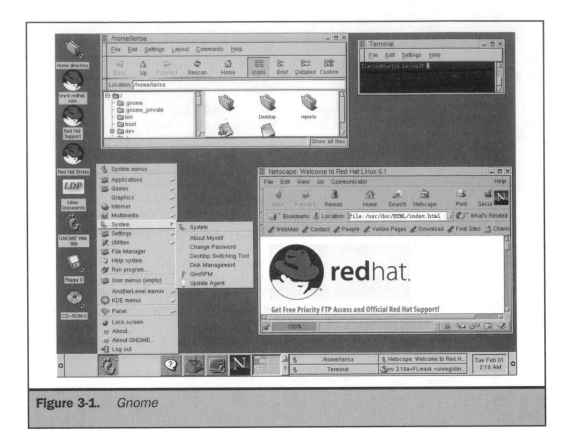

Figure 3-1. *Gnome*

To move a window, click-and-drag its title bar or right-click its other borders. Each window supports Maximize, Minimize, and Close buttons, as well as a stick pin. Double-clicking the title bar reduces the window to only its title bar; you can redisplay the window with another double-click. The desktop supports full drag-and-drop capabilities. You can drag folders, icons, and applications to the desktop or other file manager window open to other folders. The move operation is the default drag operation. CTRL-click to copy files and middle-click to create links. In most cases, you would use links for desktop icons.

The panel also contains a pager for desktop areas, which appears as four squares. Clicking a square moves you to that area. You can think of the desktop work area as being four times larger than your monitor screen, and you can use the pager to display different parts. You can configure your Gnome interface, setting features such as the background by using the Gnome Control panel. Click the image of a toolbox on the panel. To execute a command using the command line interface, open a Terminal window and click the image of a monitor on the panel. In that window, at the $ prompt, type in your command.

To quit the Gnome desktop, select the logout entry at the bottom of the main menu. If you entered from a login window, you are then logged out of your account and returned to the login window. If you started Gnome from the command line, you are returned to the command line prompt, still logged into your account.

The K Desktop

Although Gnome is the default desktop for Red Hat, you can easily switch to the KDE desktop. Red Hat installs the complete KDE desktop as part of its distribution. If you are performing a graphical login using the Gnome Desktop Manager, you can use the Session menu to select KDE as the desktop you want to run. If you are logging in to Linux using the command line interface, and then starting the desktop with the `startx` command, you can start the Gnome desktop, and then use the Desktop Switcher located in the System directory to select KDE. When you quit Gnome and restart with the `startx` command, KDE is used as your desktop instead of Gnome. On KDE, you can then use the Desktop Switcher located in the Red Hat System menu to switch back to Gnome:

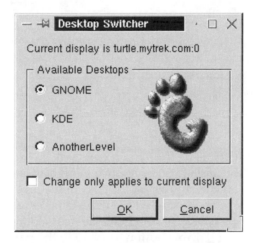

The KDE desktop display, shown in Figure 3-2, initially displays a panel at the bottom of the screen, as well as any icons for folders and Web pages initially set up by your distribution. In the upper-left corner, you can see folder icons labeled Autostart, Trash, and Templates. When a user starts KDE for the first time, the KDE Setup Wizard is run, displaying a series of four windows, advising you to set up icons for KDE Web pages, as well as CD-ROM and printer icons. Initially, the KDE wizard enables you to choose a theme, such as a Windows, KDE standard, or Mac theme. You can change this later if you want. The next windows ask if you want to add icons for your CD-ROM and printer, and links to certain Web sites, such as the KDE Web site.

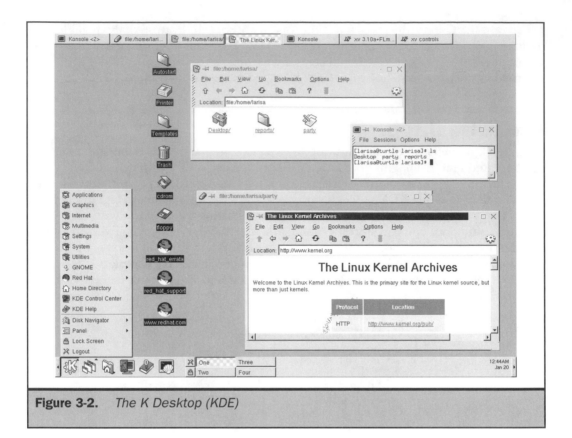

Figure 3-2. *The K Desktop (KDE)*

You can start applications using the main menu, which you display by clicking the button in the panel with the large *K* on a cogwheel. This button is located on the left side of the panel. When you click the folder for your home directory on your panel (the icon of a folder with a house on it) or select the File Manager entry on the main menu, a file manager window opens, showing your home directory. You can display files in your home directory and use the up arrow button to move to the parent directory. Back and Forward buttons move through previously displayed directories. In the location window, you can enter the pathname for a directory to move directly to it. The file manager is also Internet-aware and a fully functional Web browser. You can use it to access remote Web and FTP sites, displaying Web pages or downloading files from an FTP site.

To move a window, click-and-drag its title bar or click-and-drag its other borders. Each window supports Maximize, Minimize, and Close buttons, as well as a stick pin. Double-clicking the title bar reduces the window to only its title bar, which can redisplay with another double-click. The desktop supports full drag-and-drop capabilities. You can drag folders, icons, and applications to the desktop or to another file manager window open to other folders. Clicking the cogwheel in the right corner of a file manager window opens a duplicate window.

Selection of an icon in a file manager window is different than in other GUIs. To select an item, CTRL-click, instead of making a single left-click. The single left-click is the same as a double-click on other GUIs, executing the item or opening it with its associated application. So, if you single-click on a folder icon, you open the folder (as opposed simply to selecting it). If you single-click a file, you start up the application using that file. To select items, be sure to CTRL-click them. To unselect a selected item, be sure to CTRL-click again. When you click-and-drag a file to the desktop or another file manager window, a pop-up menu appears, which then enables you to choose whether you want to move, copy, or create a link for the item.

The panel also contains a pager for virtual desktops. This appears as four squares. Clicking a square moves you to that desktop. You can think of the virtual desktops as separate desktops, and you can use the pager to move to the different ones. To execute a command using the command line interface, open a Console window. Click the image of a monitor on the panel. In that window, at the $ prompt, type in your command. You can modify your KDE interface at any time using the KDE Control Center. Click the image of a monitor with a circuit board on the panel or select the KDE Control Center from the main menu.

To quit the KDE desktop, select the logout entry at the bottom of the main menu. If you entered from a login window, you are logged out of your account and returned to the login window. If you started KDE from the command line, you are returned to the command line prompt, still logged in to your account.

Command Line Interface

When using the command line interface, you are given a simple prompt at which you type in your command. Even with a GUI, you sometimes need to execute commands on a command line. Linux commands make extensive use of options and arguments. Be careful to place your arguments and options in their correct order on the command line. The format for a Linux command is the command name followed by options, and then by arguments, as shown here:

```
$ command-name   options   arguments
```

An *option* is a one-letter code preceded by a dash, which modifies the type of action the command takes. Options and arguments may or may not be optional, depending on the command. For example, the **ls** command can take an option, **-s.** The **ls** command displays a listing of files in your directory, and the **-s** option adds the size of each file in blocks. You enter the command and its option on the command line as:

```
$ ls -s
```

An *argument* is data the command may need to execute its task. In many cases, this is a filename. An argument is entered as a word on the command line after any options. For example, to display the contents of a file, you can use the **more** command with the file's name as its argument. The **more** command used with the filename mydata would be entered on the command line as:

```
$ man mydata
```

The command line is actually a buffer of text you can edit. Before you press ENTER, you can perform editing commands on the existing text. The editing capabilities provide a way to correct mistakes you may make when typing in a command and its options. The BACKSPACE and DEL keys enable you to erase the character you just typed in. With this character-erasing capability, you can BACKSPACE over the entire line if you want, erasing what you entered. CTRL-U erases the whole line and enables you to start over again at the prompt.

You can also use UP ARROW to redisplay your previously executed command. You can then reexecute that command, or you can edit it and execute the modified command. This is helpful when you have to repeat certain operations over and over, such as editing the same file. This is also helpful when you've already executed a command you entered incorrectly.

Help

A great deal of help is already installed on your system, as well as accessible from online sources. Both the Gnome and KDE desktops feature Help systems that use a browser-like interface to display help files. To start KDE Help, click the book icon in the panel. Here, you can select from the KDE manual, the Linux man pages, or the GNU info pages. KDE help features browser capabilities, including bookmarks and history lists for documents you view.

To start the Gnome Help browser, click the icon with the question mark (?) in the panel. You can then choose from the Gnome user guide, man pages, and info pages (see Figure 3-3). The Gnome Help browser also features bookmarks and history lists.

Both Gnome and KDE, along with other applications, such as Linuxconf, also provide context-sensitive help. Each KDE and Gnome application features detailed manuals that are displayed using their respective Help browsers. Also, applications like Linuxconf feature detailed context-sensitive help. Most panels on Linuxconf have help buttons that display detailed explanations for the operations on that panel.

In addition, extensive help is provided online. The Red Hat desktop displays Web page icons for support pages, including online manuals and tutorials.

On your system, the **/usr/doc** directory contains documentation files installed by each application. Within this directory, you can also find a **HOWTO** directory that lists

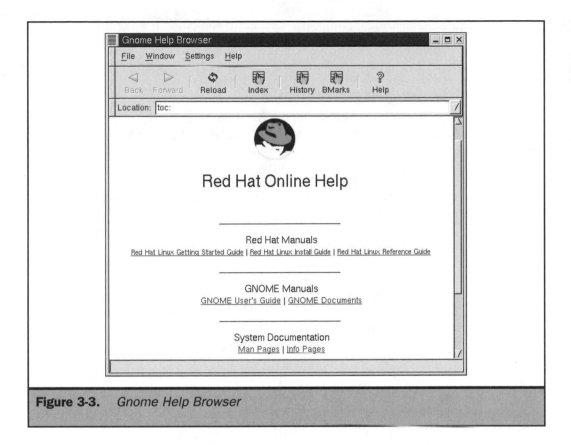

Figure 3-3.   *Gnome Help Browser*

all the Linux HOWTO documents. The **HTML** directory holds these same documents in Web page form. You can view them with your Web browser.

You can also access the online manual for Linux commands from the command line interface using the **man** command. Enter **man** with the command on which you want information.

```
$ man ls
```

Pressing either the SPACEBAR or the F key advances you to the next page. Pressing the B key moves you back a page. When you finish, press the Q key to quit the **man** utility and to return to the command line. You activate a search by pressing either the slash (/) or question mark (**?**). The **/** searches forward and the **?** searches backward. When you press the **/**, a line opens at the bottom of your screen, and you then enter a word to search for. Press ENTER to activate the search. You can repeat the same search by pressing the N key. You needn't reenter the pattern. Other utilities, such as **Xman** and **Tkman** provide a GUI front end for the man pages. You can also use either the Gnome or KDE Help systems to display man pages.

Online Documentation

When you start up your browser, a default Web page lists links for documentation both on your own system and at the Red Hat Web site. To use the Red Hat Web site, you first must be connected to the Internet. However, your CD-ROM and your system contain extensive documentation showing you how to use the desktop and take you through a detailed explanation of Linux applications, including the Vi editor and shell operations. The links to this documentation are listed here. Other documentation provides detailed tutorials on different Linux topics.

The **/usr/doc** directory contains the online documentation for many Linux applications, including subdirectories with the names of installed Linux applications that contain documentation, such as README files. You can access the complete set of HOW-TO text files in the **/usr/doc/HOWTO** directory. The HOW-TO series contains detailed documentation on all Linux topics from hardware installation to network configuration. In addition, **/usr/doc/HOWTO/HTML** holds documentation in the form of Web pages you display with a Web browser. You can use the following URL on a Web browser, such as Netscape, to view the documents.

```
file:/usr/doc/HOWTO/HTML
```

Online documentation for GNU applications, such as the gcc compiler and the Emacs editor, also exists. You can access this documentation by entering the command **info.** This brings up a special screen listing different GNU applications. The info interface has its own set of commands. You can learn more about it by entering **info info**. Typing **m** opens a line at the bottom of the screen where you can enter the first few letters of the application. Pressing ENTER brings up the info file on that application. You can also display **info** documents using either the Gnome or KDE help browsers.

Red Hat Configuration

The official Red Hat configuration tool is Linuxconf. Red Hat also provides a collection of older configuration tools accessible through an Icon bar called the *Control panel*. These are discussed in detail in Chapter 21. Red Hat, however, recommends you use Linuxconf, which supports three interfaces: an X Window System interface, a cursor-based interface, and a Web interface. You use the cursor-based interface from a Linux command line, and you needn't be running a GUI. The interface presents a full-screen display on which you can use arrow keys, the TAB key, the SPACEBAR, and the ENTER key to make selections. With the Web-based interface, you use your Web browser to make selections (though this is meant for use on local networks). Use the URL for your system with a :90 attached, as in **turtle.mytrek.com:90**.

Linuxconf provides an extensive set of configuration options, enabling you to configure features, such as user accounts and file systems, as well as your Internet servers, dial-up connections, and LILO. You can access the main Linuxconf interface with its entire set of configuration options or use specialized commands that display entries for a particular task, such as configuring user's accounts or entering your network settings. The specialized commands include **userconf** for user accounts, **fsconf** for file systems, and **netconf** for networks. In all cases, you need to log in as the root user. Configuration tools are only accessible by the root user.

Users: userconf

To add users on Red Hat, use the **userconf** command. If you are using Gnome or KDE, open a terminal window and enter the command **userconf** and then press ENTER. You see a window displayed showing buttons for users and groups, as shown in Figure 3-4. Clicking User accounts displays a window listing all the users on your system. Click Add here to add a new user. This opens another window where you can

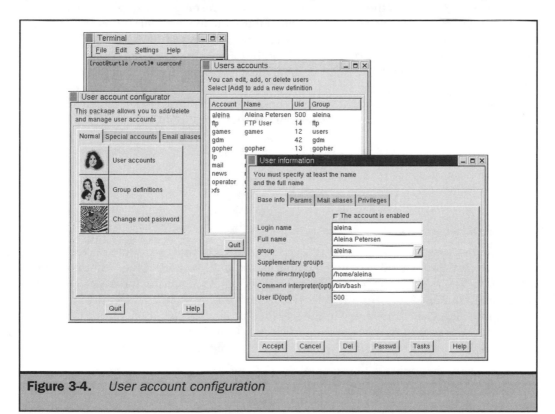

Figure 3-4.   *User account configuration*

enter the user login, home directory, and login shell, though you can use defaults for the login shell. You can use the other panels in this window to add mail aliases or set privileges, such as allowing the user to mount a CD-ROM. When you finish, another window opens that prompts you to specify a password for the user.

To change any settings for a user, double-click its entry in the User Accounts window. This displays the User Information for this user. Click Passwd to change the password, if you want.

File Systems

Files and directories contained on different hardware devices such as floppy disks, CD-ROMs, and hard disk partitions are called *file systems*. The Linux partition you used to install your Linux system on is called the *root partition*. The root partition contains the main file system with a directory tree, starting from the root and spreading out to different system and user subdirectories. To access files on another file system, say, a CD-ROM disc, you need to attach that file system to your main system. Attaching a file system is called *mounting the file system*. You first set up an empty directory to which you want to mount the file system. On Red Hat, the **/mnt/cdrom** directory is already reserved for mounting CD-ROMs and the **/mnt/floppy** directory is reserved for floppy disks.

Although you can mount a CD-ROM using Linuxconf, the Red Hat Gnome interface also provides a simple method for mounting and unmounting a CD-ROM. Simply insert the CD-ROM into your CD-ROM drive and, on the Gnome desktop, you'll see an icon labeled CD-ROM appear. A CD-ROM is automatically mounted. A Gnome file manager window automatically appears, which shows the contents of the CD-ROM. You can also mount and unmount the CD-ROM using a pop-up menu on the CD-ROM icon. Right-click it to display a pop-up menu with options to mount, unmount, or eject the CD-ROM:

You can access the CD-ROM you placed in your CD drive by double-clicking the CD-ROM icon. Your CD-ROM drive remains locked until you select the Unmount entry that is now displayed on the pop-up menu. If you do not see an icon for your CD-ROM, you must first make it user-mountable. Use **fsconf** or Linuxconf to select the local drive and double-click the cdrom entry in the Local volume window. Then, on the Options panel select the user mountable option. Click Act/Changes to register the change. Then right-click the desktop and select Rescan Devices from the pop-up menu.

To mount a file system, you first start up Linuxconf with the **fsconf** command. This displays a Filesystem Configurator window with a button for the local drive. Click this button to display the local volume window. This lists the entries for all the file systems currently accessible on your system. To mount your CD-ROM, double-click the **/mnt/cdrom** entry to open a Volume specification window, and then click the Mount button. Now you can access the contents of the CD-ROM at the **/mnt/cdrom** directory on your system. The CD-ROM remains locked until you click Unmount.

You can also use the Local volume window to add new entries for mounting any Windows partitions that may be on your system's hard drives. Figure 3-5 shows the entries for a Windows partition (type **vfat**) to be mounted at the **/dos** directory. If you have another CD-ROM drive on your system, you can add another entry for it (use the iso9660 type).

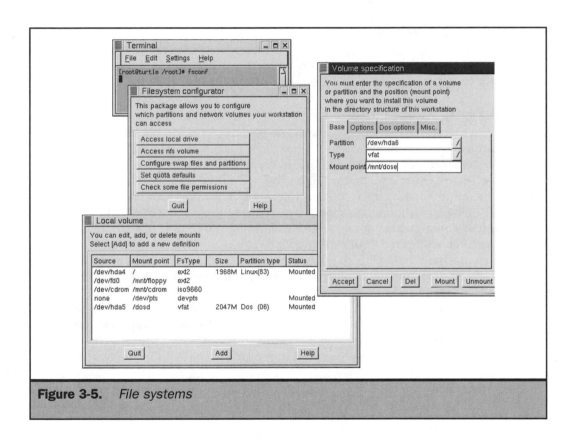

Figure 3-5. *File systems*

Network

Network configuration differs depending on whether you are connected to a *local area network* (*LAN*) with an Ethernet card or you use a dial-up ISP connection. You had the opportunity to enter your LAN network settings during the installation process. You can configure either connection by accessing Linuxconf with the **netconf** command. This displays the Network Configurator window that lists buttons for different network settings. (As an alternative to Linuxconf, you can use **netcfg** in the Control panel or **kppp,** as described in Chapter 28). For PPP connections, you can use RP3, the Red Hat PPP Dialer, as well as **netconf**, **kppp**, or **netcfg**. The Red Hat PPP Dialer utility provides an easy-to-use interface with panels for login information, modem configuration, and dial-up connections.

LAN

To configure a LAN connection, click the Basic Host Information button to display the host configuration window. In the first Adapter panel, you can enter the IP address, network device, and the kernel module to use (the drivers for your Ethernet card). Then, in the Network configurator window, click the Name Server Specification button to display the Resolver Configuration window, where you can enter the IP addresses for the Domain Name servers on your network (see Figure 3-6).

The Red Hat PPP Dialer

If you have a dialup connection to a *Internet service provider* (*ISP*), you need to configure a PPP interface. Almost all ISPs currently use PPP connections. You can easily set up a PPP connection using the Red Hat PPP Dialer (rp3). Select Dialup Configuration Tool entry in the Internet submenu on the Gnome desktop. If you do not have any Internet connections set up already, the Add New Internet Connection dialog box starts up (to add a new connection, you can click the New button on the Red Hat Dialup Configuration Tool window, opened from its entry on the Gnome Internet menu). If you have not yet configured your modem, the Dialer attempts automatically to detect your modem and to provide information, such as the speed and serial device it uses. You see a screen displaying this information, along with the sound level, which you can adjust (see Figure 3-7).

Next, you are asked to enter the name you want to use to identify this connection on your system, the account name (see Figure 3-8). You also enter the phone number used to dial your ISP.

You then enter the user name for your ISP account, along with its password (see Figure 3-9).

When you finish, the final screen appears listing the account name, user name, and phone number, as shown in Figure 3-10.

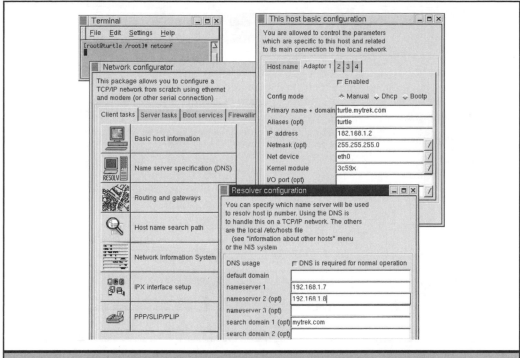

Figure 3-6. *An example of netconf for LAN network settings*

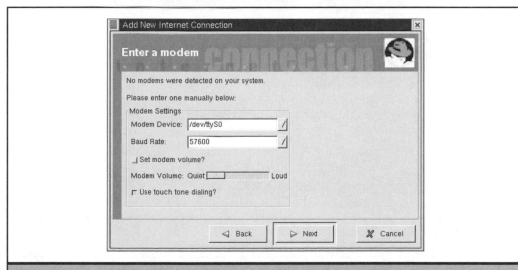

Figure 3-7. *Red Hat PPP Dialer modem configuration*

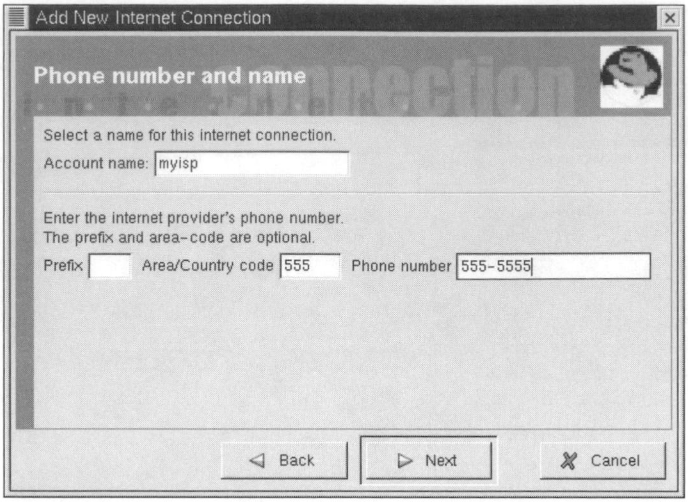

Figure 3-8.   *Red Hat PPP Dialer name and phone number*

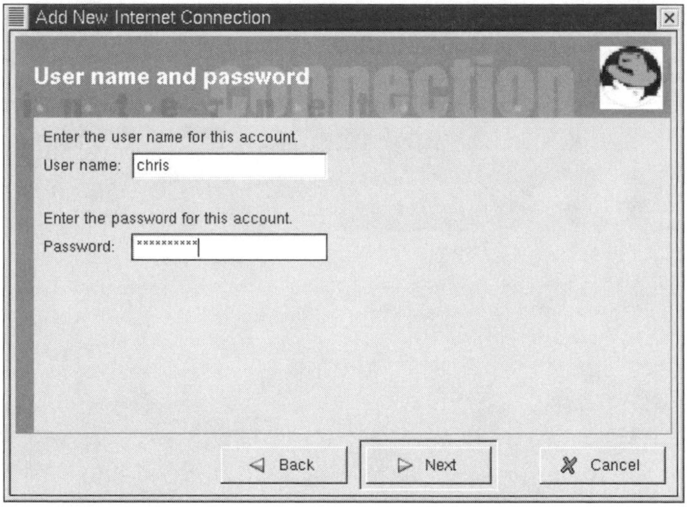

Figure 3-9.   *Red Hat PPP Dialer user name and password*

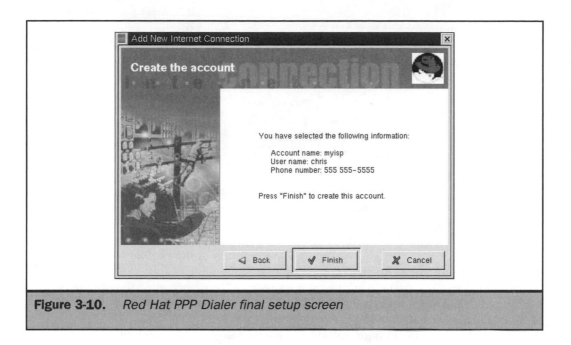

Figure 3-10. *Red Hat PPP Dialer final setup screen*

Each time you want to connect, select the Red Hat PPP Dialer entry from the Gnome Internet menu. This displays a Choose window listing all your network connections, including any you created with the Red Hat PPP Dialer:

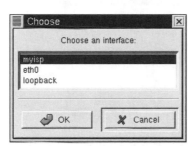

Double-click the account name you set up for your PPP connection. In this illustration, the account name used for the PPP connection is **myisp**, which also shows an Ethernet connection (eth0) and the localhost connection.

You are then prompted as to whether you want to start up the connection. Click the Yes button. A window appears that monitors the connection, showing a graph indicating the current activity on it:

You can minimize the monitor, docking it to the Gnome panel. Right-clicking the monitor icon displays a menu with entries for starting, stopping, and configuring the connections, along with the connection Properties. The Properties dialog box enables you to set such features as calculating the time and the cost of a connected session. The monitor is actually part of the Red Hat Network Monitor Tool. You can select this tool independently on the Gnome Internet menu and display monitors for all your network connections.

You can also place the network monitor for your PPP connection on the Gnome panel. Here it is displayed in a smaller size as a Gnome applet. To start your PPP connection, you only need to double-click the PPP network monitor. Right-clicking the monitor image displays a menu with options for starting and configuring your connection. To add a monitor to the Gnome panel, use the Panel menu on the Gnome Main menu. In the Panel menu, select Add Applet, and then the Network submenu, and, from there, select the RH PPP Dialer entry. This displays a list of all the network connections on your system:

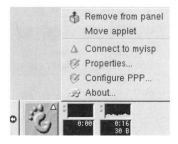

Select the one you want placed on the panel. The monitor bears the name you have given to the PPP connection. In this illustration, the PPP network monitor has the name myisp. You can place any of your network monitors on the Gnome panel. This illustration shows a monitor for both the Ethernet and PPP connections.

To change your setting or to add a new connection, use the Red Hat PPP Dialer Configuration Tool. On the Gnome Internet menu, select the Dialer Configuration Tool entry to start up the configuration tool. It then displays a window with two tabbed panels: one listing your accounts and the other for your modem configuration. Buttons on the right side of the Accounts panel enable you to add new connections or to edit current ones:

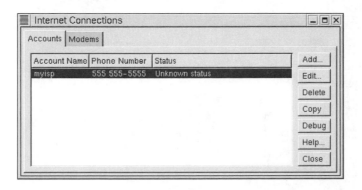

The Edit button opens a window with panels for modifying connection and modem information, as shown next. On the Account Info panel, you can change your login name (user name), password, and phone number for your ISP. On the Advanced panel, you can enter information such as the IP address of your ISP's domain name servers.

The Red Hat PPP Dialer uses **wvdial** utility to perform the connection operations. You can find the configuration information for your connections in the **/etc/wvdial.conf** file. You can, if you choose, edit this file directly to configure your PPP connections.

Linuxconf PPP Configuration

To use **netconf** to configure PPP connections, click the PPP/SLIP/PLIP button on the Network Configurator window. A window then opens that asks you to choose the type of interface you want. Select PPP. Then a small window opens displaying a ppp0 entry. Double-click it to display the PPP interface window with panels for setting your modem connections, the phone number to dial, and the Expect and Send entries for your login name and password (see Figure 3-11). To activate a connection, click Connect. You can also use dialup managers like **kppp**, **xisp**, and **gnomeppp** to setup and manager your PPP connections.

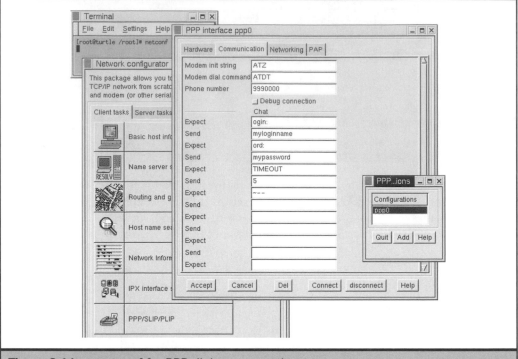

Figure 3-11. *netconf for PPP dial-up connections*

Printer Configuration

As part of the installation procedure for Red Hat Linux, you configured a printer connected to your computer. To change configurations or to add a new printer later, you can use the Red Hat Linux Print Manager, also known as *printtool*. You can access printtool through the Control panel on the Gnome System menu or from the Another Level menu and the Administration submenu. The Red Hat Print Manager enables you to select the appropriate driver for your printer, as well as to set print options such as paper size and print resolutions. You can use the Red Hat Print Manager to access a printer connected directly to your local computer or to a printer on a remote system on your network (see Chapter 25).

When you start up the Red Hat Print Manager, you are presented with a window that lists your installed printers (see Figure 3-12). To add a new printer, click the Add button. To edit an installed printer, double-click its entry. For a new printer, you are first asked to specify whether the printer is local or remotely connected through a UNIX, Windows (SMB), or NetWare network. Then a window opens with entries for the printer device, spool directory, and input filter (see Figure 3-12). Default settings are entered for each.

The name can be any name you choose to give your printer. The device is the port to which the printer is connected. For the first three parallel ports, these are **lp0**, **lp1**, **lp2**; for serial ports, these are **ttyS0**, **ttyS1**, and **ttyS2**, and so on. The input filter entry is your print driver. Click the filter button to open a Configure Printer window where you can select your printer and configure the print settings (see Figure 3-13). The Printer Type panel on this window lists an extensive number of printers. Choose the one for the printer you are adding. The Driver Description pane in the upper-right corner displays a short description of the selected printer driver. Use the Resolution, Paper Size, and Color Depth panels to configure these features. You can also choose the margins, number of copies, and print speed. You can use the Configure Printer window on an installed printer to change these features later, if you want.

Configuration Using Red Hat Setup

Red Hat also provides a setup utility with which you can configure different devices and system settings, such as your keyboard, mouse, and time zone. The Setup utility is useful if you have changed any of your devices—say, installed a new mouse, keyboard, or sound card—and is designed to be run from the command line interface. Several of its components, such as **kbdconfig** and **mouseconfig**, only work from that interface. You start the utility with the command **setup**, which you enter at a shell command line. Setup provides a full-screen, cursor-based interface where you can use arrow, TAB, and ENTER keys to make your selections. Initially, Setup displays a menu, shown

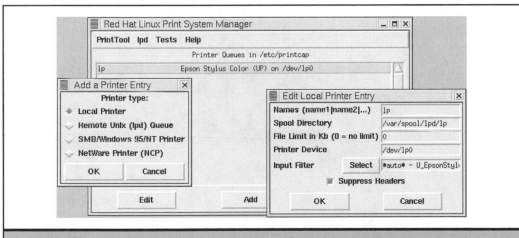

Figure 3-12. *Red Hat Print Manager printer dialog box*

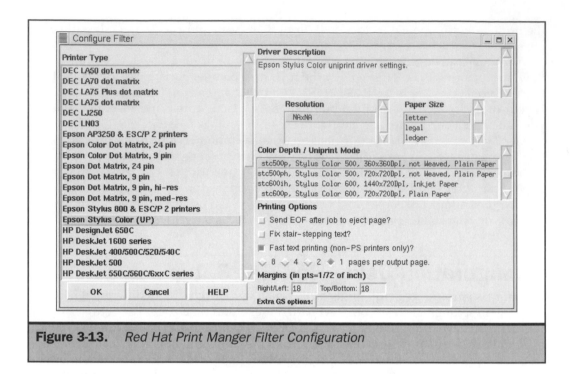

Figure 3-13. *Red Hat Print Manger Filter Configuration*

next, of configuration tools from which you can choose. Use the arrow keys to select one, and then press the TAB key to move to the Run Tool and Quit buttons.

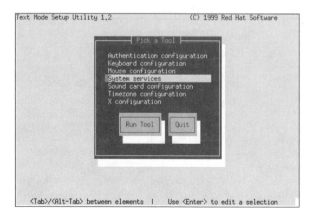

Setup is actually an interface for running several configuration tools (see Table 3-1). You can call any of these tools separately using their commands. For example, the **kbdconfig** command starts the keyboard configuration utility that enables you to select the type of keyboard, while the **mouseconfig** command enables you to select the type of mouse.

Tools	Description
setup	Red Hat setup interface listing configuration tools for system and device setting
authconfig	Authentication options, such as enabling NIS, shadow passwords, and MD5 passwords
kbdconfig	Selects the keyboard type
mouseconfig	Selects the mouse type
ntsysv	Selects servers and daemons to start up at boot time
sndconfig	Detects and configures your sound card
timeconfig	Selects the time zone
Xconfigurator	Configures your X Window System for your video card and monitor

Table 3-1. *Setup Tools*

kbdconfig

With **kbdconfig**, you can select the type of keyboard you are using. A cursor-based dialog box appears with a list of different keyboard types, which should be run from the command-line interface, not a desktop.

mouseconfig

With **mouseconfig**, you can select the type of mouse you are using. A cursor-based dialog box appears with a list of different mouse device types:

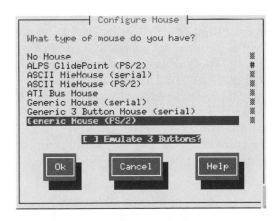

Your system is automatically probed for the type of the mouse connected to your system and the cursor is positioned at that entry. If you have a two-button mouse, you can select the three-button emulation option to let a simultaneous click on both the left and right mouse buttons emulate a third mouse button. This should be run from the command line interface, not from a desktop.

ntsysv

ntsysv is a simple utility for specifying which servers and services should be automatically started at boot time (see Chapter 15). The dialog box lists the possible servers and services from which to choose. Move to the entry you want and use the spacebar to toggle it on or off. An entry with an asterisk next to it is selected and is started automatically the next time you boot your system.

sndconfig

The **sndconfig** utility enables you to select and configure your sound card. Initially, the **sndconfig** utility tries to detect your sound card automatically. If the automatic detection fails, a dialog box appears with a listing of different sound cards. Select the one on your system. Another dialog box appears where you need to enter the setting for your sound card. **sndconfig** then tries to play sample sound and MIDI files to test the card. As an alternative to **sndconfig**, you can obtain, load, and configure sound drivers yourself (see Chapter 25). This should be run from the command-line interface, not from a desktop.

Xconfigurator

One important utility is the X Window System configuration provided by Xconfigurator. If you have trouble with your X Window System configuration, you can use this utility to configure it again. Xconfigurator is also helpful for updating X-Windows if you change your video card. Simply run Xconfigurator again and select the card. You can run Xconfigurator by entering the **Xconfigurator** command on the command line, or by selecting the X configuration entry in the Setup utility's menu.

Xconfigurator first probes your system in an attempt to determine what type of video card you have. Failing that, Xconfigurator presents a list of video cards. Select your video card from the list and press ENTER. If your video card does not appear on the list, XFree86 may not support it. If you have technical knowledge about your card, however, you may choose Unlisted Card and attempt to configure it by matching your card's video chipset with one of the available X servers.

Once you select your video card, the installation program installs the appropriate XFree86 server, and Xconfigurator presents a list of monitors, as shown here:

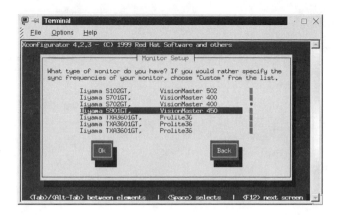

If your monitor appears on the list, select it and press ENTER. If it is not on the list, select Custom. This displays a screen where you enter the horizontal sync range and vertical sync range of your monitor (these values are generally available in the documentation that accompanies your monitor or from your monitor's vendor or manufacturer). Be careful to enter the correct horizontal and vertical frequencies. If you enter values that are too high, you may overclock your monitor, and damage or destroy it. Do not select a monitor similar to your monitor unless you are certain the monitor you are selecting does not exceed the capabilities of your monitor.

The next screen prompts you for the amount of video memory installed on your video card. If you are not sure, please consult the documentation accompanying your video card. Choosing more memory than is available does not damage your video card, but the XFree86 server may not start correctly if you do.

If the video card you selected has a video clock chip, Xconfigurator presents a list of clock chips. The recommended choice is No Clockchip Setting because, in most cases, XFree86 can automatically detect the proper clock chip.

In the next screen, Xconfigurator prompts you to select the video modes you want to use. These are screen resolutions you may want to use. You can select one or more by moving to it and pressing the SPACEBAR. Xconfigurator then starts the X Window System and displays a dialog box asking if you can see it.

Xconfigurator then generates an X Window System configuration file called **/etc/X11/XF86Config**. This is the file the X Window System uses to start up.

Command Line Configuration

When logged in as the root user, you can also perform certain configuration operations from the command line. You can manually access system configuration files, editing them and making entries yourself. For example, the domain name server entries are kept in the **/etc/resolv.conf** file. You can edit this file and type in the addresses.

You can use the **useradd** command to add user accounts and the **userdel** command to remove them. One common operation performed from the command line is to change a password. Any user can change his own password with the **passwd** command. The command prompts you for your current password. After entering your current password and pressing ENTER, you are then prompted for your new password. After entering the new password, you are asked to reenter it. This is to make sure you actually entered the password you intended to enter. Because password characters are not displayed when you type them, it is easy to make a mistake and to press a wrong key.

```
$ passwd
Old password:
New password:
Retype new password:
$
```

File Systems

You can easily mount and unmount file systems with the **mount** and **umount** commands. To mount your CD-ROM, you only have to enter the command **mount** and the directory **/mnt/cdrom**. You can then access the contents of the CD-ROM at the **/mnt/cdrom** directory.

```
$ mount /mnt/cdrom
```

When you finish, unmount the CD-ROM with the **umount** command.

```
$ umount /mnt/cdrom
```

You can also manually mount and unmount floppy disks and hard disk partitions. See Chapter 26 for a detailed discussion.

Network

To configure a LAN connection, you make entries in network configuration files in the **/etc** directory (see Chapter 28). If, for some reason, you have been unable to set up your X Window System, you may have to set up such a connection. For dialup PPP connections you can use either the wvdial dialer or pppd.wvdial is the same dialer used for the Red Hat PPP Dialer. wvdial is an intelligent dialer, which not only dials up an ISP service, but also perform login operations, supplying your user name and password. wvdial first loads its configuration from the **/etc/wvdial.conf** file. In here, you can place modem and account information, including modem speed and serial device, as well as ISP phone number, user name, and password. The **wvdial.conf** file is organized into sections, beginning with a section label enclosed in brackets. A section holds variables for different parameters that are assigned values, such as username = chris. The default section holds default values inherited by other sections, so you needn't repeat them. Table 3-2 lists the wvdial variables.

Variable	Description
Inherits	Explicitly inherits from the specified section. By default, sections inherit from the [Dialer Defaults] section
Modem	The device wvdial should use as your modem. The default is /dev/modem
Baud	The speed at which wvdial communicates with your modem. The default is 57600 baud
Init1 ... Init9	Specifies the initialization strings to be used by your modem. wvdial can use up to 9. The default is "ATZ" for Init1
Phone	The phone number you want wvdial to dial
Area Code	Specifies the area code, if any
Dial Prefix	Specifies any needed dialing prefix, for example, 70 to disable call waiting or 9 for an outside line
Dial Command	Specifies the dial operation. The default is "ATDT"
Login	Specifies the user name you use at your ISP
Login Prompt	If your ISP has an unusual login prompt, you can specify it here
Password	Specifies the password you use at your ISP
Password Prompt	If your ISP has an unusual password prompt, you can specify it here
PPPD PATH	If pppd is installed on your Linux system somewhere other than /usr/sbin/pppd, you need to specify its location with this option
Force Address	Specifies a static IP address to use (for ISPs that provide static IP addresses to users)

Table 3-2. *wvdial Variables*

Variable	Description
Remote Name	For PAP or CHAP authentication, you may have to change this to your ISP's authentication name. The default value is *
Carrier Check	Setting this option to No disables the carrier check by your modem. Used for a modem that reports its carrier line is always down
Stupid Mode	In Stupid Mode, wvduak does not attempt to interpret any prompts from the terminal server and starts pppd after the modem connects
New PPPD	Enable this option for use with pppd version 2.3.0 or newer. Instructs pppd to look for a required file /etc/ppp/peers/wvdial
Default Reply	Specifies the default response for prompts that wvdial does not recognize. The default is **ppp**
Auto Reconnect	If enabled, wvdial attempts to reestablish a connection automatically if you are randomly disconnected by the other side. This option is **on** by default

Table 3-2. *wvdial Variables* (continued)

The following example shows the **/etc/wvdial.conf** file generated by the example used in Figure 3-10.

/etc/wvdial.conf

```
[Modem0]
Modem = /dev/ttyS0
Baud = 57600
Init1 = ATZ
SetVolume = 0
Dial Command = ATDT

[Dialer Defaults]
Modem = /dev/ttyS0
Baud = 57600
Init1 = ATZ
SetVolume = 0
Dial Command = ATDT

[Dialer myisp]
```

```
Username = chris
Password = mypassword
Modem = /dev/ttyS0
Phone = 555-5555
Area Code = 555
Baud = 57600
Stupid mode = 0
```

To start wvdial, enter the command **wvdial,** which then reads the connection configuration information from the **/etc/wvdial.conf** file. **wvdial** then dials the ISP and initiates the PPP connection, providing your user name and password when requested.

```
$ wvdial
```

You can set up connection configurations for any number of connections in the **/etc/wvdial.conf** file. To select one, enter its label as an argument to the **wvdial** command, as shown here:

```
$ wvdial myisp
```

As an alternative to using **wvdial**, you can use the **pppd** command directly. The **connect** option instructs to make a connection. The **pppd** command takes as its argument a Linux command that will actually make the connection—usually the **chat** command. You enter **pppd**, followed by the **connect** option and the **chat** command with its expect-reply pairs. The entire chat operation is encased in single quotes. In the next example, the user invokes **pppd** with the chat operation. The modem is connected to port 2, **/dev/ttyS0**, and the speed is 57600 baud. Notice the single quotes around the entire chat operation with its expect-reply pairs.

```
# pppd connect  'chat -v "" ATDT5556666 ogin: mylogin  word: mypass'  /dev/ttyS0    57600
```

Modem Setup

If you have a modem connected to your PC, it is connected to one of four communications ports. The PC names for these ports are COM1, COM2, COM3, and COM4. These ports can also be used for other serial devices, such as a serial mouse (though not for PS/2 mice). Usually, a serial mouse is connected to COM1 and a modem is connected to COM2, though, in many cases, your modem may be connected to COM4. Find out which ports your modem and mouse are connected to because you must know this to access your modem. On the PC, COM1 and COM3 share the same access point to your computer; the same is true of COM2 and COM4. For this reason, if you have a serial mouse connected to COM1, you should not have your modem on COM3. You could find your mouse cutting out whenever you use your modem. If your mouse is on COM1, then your modem should either be on COM2 or COM4.

In Linux, you use the serial communication ports for your modem. Serial ports begin with the name **/dev/ttyS,** with an attached number from 0 to 3. (Notice the numbering begins from 0, not 1.) The first port, COM1, is **/dev/ttyS0,** and **/dev/ttyS1** is the second port. The third and fourth ports are **/dev/ttyS2** and **/dev/ttyS3**. In many Linux communication programs, you need to know the port for your modem, which is either **/dev/ttyS1** for COM2 or **/dev/ttyS3** for COM4.

Some communication programs try to access the modem port using only the name **/dev/modem**. This is meant to be an alias, another name, for whatever your modem port actually is. If your system has not already set up this alias, you can easily create this alias using the `ln -s` command or the `modemtool` utility. `modemtool` has a GUI interface and is run on an X Window System desktop, such as Gnome or KDE. It displays four entries, one for each serial port. Click the one that applies to your system (see Chapter 22).

You can also create an alias on the command line using the `ln` command. The following example creates an alias called **modem** for the COM2 port, **/dev/ttyS1**. If your modem port is **/dev/ttyS3,** use that instead. (You must be logged in as a root user to execute this command.) The following example sets up the **/dev/modem** alias for the second serial port, **/dev/ ttyS1**.

```
# ln -s /dev/Stty1  /dev/modem
```

Your **/dev/mouse** alias should already be set up for the port it uses. For a serial mouse, this is usually the COM1 port, **/dev/ ttyS0**. If the alias is not set up or if you need to change it, you can use the `ln -s` command. The following example sets up the **/dev/mouse** alias for the first serial port, **/dev/ ttyS0**.

```
# ln -s /dev/ttyS0  /dev/mouse
```

Installing Software Packages

Now that you know how to start Linux and access the root user, you can install any other software packages you may want. Installing software is an administrative function performed by the root user. Unless you chose to install all your packages during your installation, only some of the many applications and utilities available for users on Linux were installed on your system. Red Hat uses the *Red Hat Package Manager* (*RPM*) to organize Linux software into packages you can automatically install or remove. An RPM software package operates like its own installation program for a software application. A Linux software application often consists of several files that must be installed in different directories. The program itself is most likely placed in a directory called **/usr/bin**, online manual files go in another directory, and library files, in yet another directory. In addition, the installation may require modification of certain configuration files on your system. The RPM software packages on your Red Hat CD-ROM performs all these tasks for you. Also, if you later decide you don't want a specific application, you can uninstall packages to remove all the files and configuration information from your system (see Chapter 32 or more details).

The RPM packages on your CD-ROMs only represent a small portion of the software packages available for Linux. You can download additional software in the form of RPM packages from distribution contrib sites, such as **contrib.redhat.com** for Red Hat packages. In addition, these packages are organized into **lib5** and **lib6** directories. **lib5** refers to the packages using the older libraries, whereas **lib6** refers to those using the new GNU 2.*x* libraries. For Red Hat 6.0, you should use the **lib6** versions, though **lib5** versions also work. An extensive repository for RPM packages is located at http://rpmfind.net/. Packages here are indexed according to distribution, group, and name. This includes packages for every distribution, including previous versions of those distributions. You can also locate many of the newest Linux applications from **freshmeat.net**. Here, you can link to the original development sites for these applications and download documentation and the recent versions.

To install packages on Red Hat, you use the `GnomeRPM` utility or the Gnome file manager. Select the GnomeRPM entry in the Gnome main menu under Systems. With GnomeRPM, you can locate packages on your file system. For your Red Hat CD-ROM, first be sure to mount the CD-ROM, and then use GnomeRPM to access the **/mnt/cdrom/RedHat/RPMS** directory, where you will find your packages listed. Choose the packages you want to install. GnomeRPM lists packages already installed. You can select them to view their details and file list.

Instead of GnomeRPM, you can use the Gnome file manager to install RPM packages. This is actually easier to do for individual packages. Use the file manager window to access the directory with your package. Then right-click the package name or icon. In the pop-up menu, you can select the Install option to install the package. You can use this same method for FTP sites. The Gnome file manager is Internet-aware. You can enter a URL for an FTP site in its location box to access the site. When you locate the package, right-click it and select Install or Update. The file is downloaded, and then automatically installed on your system.

Updating Red Hat

New versions of distributions are often released every 6 to 12 months. In the meantime, new updates are continually being prepared for particular software packages. These are posted as updates you can download from a distribution's FTP site and install on your system. These include new versions of applications, servers, and even the kernel. Downloading and installing updates is a fairly straightforward process, made even easier with the Gnome and KDE desktops.

In the period between major releases, Red Hat posts RPM package updates for software installed from your CD-ROM in its **update** directory at its FTP site at **ftp.redhat.com**. Such updates may range from single software packages to whole components, for instance, all the core, applications, and development packages issued when a new release of Gnome, KDE, or XFree86 are made available.

With version 6.1, Red Hat now provides an Update Agent that automatically locates, downloads, and installs any updates for your Red Hat System:

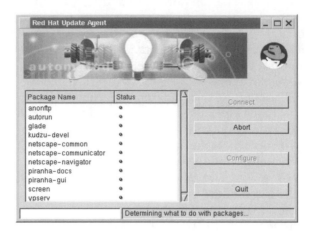

To use Update Agent, however, you first must register your copy of Red Hat at the Red Hat Web site at **www.redhat.com**. You are then provided with a user name and password with which you can configure Update Agent to access Red Hat's special secure server at **priority.redhat.com.** To start Update Agent, select its entry in the System menu in the Gnome main menu. On starting Update Agent, you are asked for your root user password as an added precaution.

The first time you use Update Agent, you will have to configure it, providing information about your system. Click on the Configure button to display the Configuration dialog box with three tabbed panels. One exists for user, retrieval, and exceptions. The User panel holds your registration information and your e-mail address. The Retrieval panel is where you enter in the server you want to use (for example priority.redhat.com) as well as download instructions and the download directory you want to use. The Exception panel holds the names of any packages you do not want to automatically update.

To use Update Agent, click the Connect button. Update Agent connects to the FTP server, opens your Web browser (such as Netscape), and displays a Web page listing the possible updates it found. You can select individual packages by clicking the check boxes next to them, and then click the Request Selected packages button. To select all packages, click the Request ALL packages button. Once you select your packages, you can click the Request Packages button. The browser then closes and the Update Agent begins downloading the selected packages. The packages are listed with a Status icon. The packages are first downloaded, during which time the Status icon is a button, and then they are installed, which is indicated by a red arrow. When finished, the status icon becomes a check mark.

Updating Red Hat with Gnome

Or, you can upgrade manually by first downloading all the packages and installing them yourself. For example, to install new releases of the K Desktop, you can download distribution versions of their packages from the KDE FTP site at **ftp.kde.org** or from distribution FTP sites. You can use an FTP client, such as **ncftp**, to download them all at once, including any subdirectories (see Chapter 12). Then change to that directory and use the **rpm -Uvh** command to install the packages.

RPM update packages are kept in the Red Hat update site at **ftp.redhat.com** and its mirror sites. You can access the site, locate the updates for your distribution version, and then download them to your system. Then you can install them using an RPM utility, such as GnomeRPM, or the **rpm** command using the update option, **-U.** Perhaps the easiest way to do this is to use the Gnome file manager to download the files first (see Figure 3-14). First, open a file manager window, enter the URL for the Red Hat update site in its location box, and then access the update site. For Red Hat 6.1, the updates are in the **6.1** directory. Within that directory, move to the **current** directory, where you can see a list of all the updates. Download any new updates or all of them if this is the first update for your version. To download, open another file manager window and create a new directory to hold your update. Now open that directory. Then select-and-drag the update files from the file manager window for the update site to that new directory. You may not need all the files. In the case of kernel updates, you only need the kernel file for your processor: i386, i586 (Pentium), or i686 (Pentium II). As files are downloaded, a dialog box displays the filename and the percentage downloaded.

Once the update is downloaded, you can open a Terminal window and change to that new directory. You open a Terminal window by clicking the Monitor icon in the panel. Then use the **cd** command to change to that directory. If the directory name is **redup**, you would enter

```
# cd redup
```

Then issue the following **rpm** update command. The **nodeps** option uses two dashes. If you simply want to start by installing certain packages, you can refine your installation, as shown in the previous example for XFree86.

```
$ rpm -Uvh --nodeps *rpm
```

Or, you can open the GnomeRPM utility, and then open the dialog box for installing packages. From the file manager window displaying the packages, you can drag-and-drop the files to the GnomeRPM install dialog box. You may receive error messages noting dependency requirements. You usually can safely ignore these messages. If you also receive install conflicts, you may be trying to install two versions of the same package. In that case, you must install one or the other.

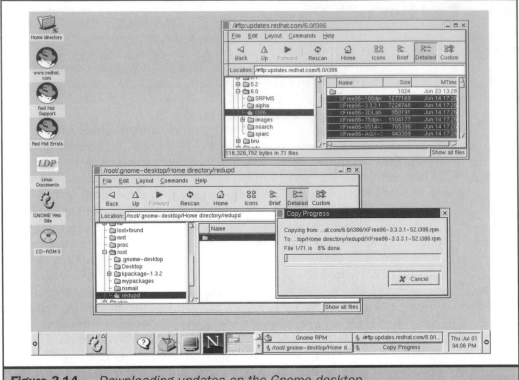

Figure 3-14. *Downloading updates on the Gnome desktop*

Updating Red Hat with KDE

To update with KDE, you can perform much the same kind of operation. Use the KDE file manager window to access the Red Hat update directory. Then open another file manager window to a new directory where you want to store your update files. Select all the files, and then drag-and-drop them to that new file manager window. A dialog box appears as each file is downloaded, showing the percentage of the download. Once the download is complete, you individually install packages with **kpackage** or use the **rpm** command. If many files exist, you may want to use the **rpm** command. Open a Terminal window by clicking the Monitor icon in the panel. Then use the **cd** command to change to that directory. If the directory name is **redup**, enter

```
# cd redup
```

Then use the **rpm** command with the **–Uvh** options and ***rpm** to select all the RPM packages at once. You can refine the install using more refined filename matching.

```
# rpm -Uvh --nodeps  *rpm
```

Command Line Installation

If you do not have access to the desktop or you prefer to work from the command line interface, you can use the **rpm** command to manage and install software packages. The command name stands for the Red Hat Package Manager. This is the command that actually performs installation, removal, and verification of software packages. In fact, both LISA and glint use the **rpm** command to install and remove packages. Each software package is actually an RPM package, consisting of an archive of software files and information about how to install those files. Each archive resides as a single file with a name that ends with **.rpm**, indicating it is a software package that can be installed by the Red Hat Package Manager.

You can use the **rpm** command either to install or uninstall a package. The **rpm** command uses a set of options to determine what action to take. Table 3-3 lists the set of **rpm** options. The **-i** option installs the specified software package, and the **-U** option updates a package. With an **-e** option, rpm uninstalls the package. A *q* placed before an *i* (**-qi**) queries the system to see if a software package is already installed and displays information about the software (**-qpi** queries an uninstalled package file). The **-h** option provides a complete list of **rpm** options. A helpful option is the **—nodeps** option, which installs without performing dependency checks. The syntax for the **rpm** command is as follows (*rpm-package-name* is the name of the software package you want to install):

rpm *options rpm-package-name*

The software package name is usually quite lengthy, including information about version and release date in its name. All end with **.rpm**. In the next example, the user installs the Linuxconf package using the **rpm** command. Notice the full filename is entered. To list the full name, you can use the **ls** command with the first few characters and an asterisk, **ls linuxconf***. You can also use the * to match the remainder of the name, as in **linuxconf-1.16*.rpm**. In most cases, you are installing packages with the **-U** option, update. Even if the package is not already installed, **-U** still installs it.

```
$ rpm   -Uvh linuxconf-1.16r-1-1.i386.rpm
```

When RPM performs an installation, it first checks for any dependent packages. These are other software packages with programs the application you are installing needs to use. If other dependent packages must be installed first, RPM cancels the installation and lists those packages. You can install those packages, and then repeat the installation of the application. In a few situations, such as a major distribution update where packages may be installed out of order, installing without dependency checks is all right. For this, you use the **—nodeps** option. This assumes all the needed packages are being installed, though.

To determine if a package is already installed, use the **-qi** option with rpm. The **-q** stands for query. To obtain a list of all the files the package has installed, as well as the directories it installed to, use the **-ql** option.

To query package files, add the **p** option. The **-qpi** option displays information about a package and **-qpl** lists the files in it. The following example lists all the files in the Linuxconf package.

```
$ rpm -qpl linuxconf-1.16r-1-1.i386.rpm
```

To remove a software package from your system, first use **rpm -qi** to make sure it is actually installed, and then, use the **-e** option to uninstall it. As with the **-qi** option, you needn't use the full name of the installed file. You only need the name of the application. In the next example, the user removes the xtetris game from the system:

```
$ rpm  -e  xtetris
```

An important update you may need to perform is to update the Xfree86 packages. If you install a new video card or a monitor, and the current Xfree86 package does not support it, chances are the new one should. Simply download those packages from the distribution update sites and install them with the RPM update operation, as shown here.

```
$ rpm -Uvh  --nodeps  XFree86*rpm
```

-U	Update package
-i	Install package
-e	Remove package
-qi	Display information for an installed package
-ql	Display file list for installed package
-qpi	Display information from an RPM package file (used for uninstalled packages)
-qpl	Display file list from an RPM package file (used for uninstalled packages)

Table 3-3. *RPM Options*

The Complete Reference

Linux

Part II

Environments

Chapter 4

Gnome

The *GNU Network Object Model Environment*, also known as *Gnome,* is a powerful and easy-to-use environment consisting primarily of a panel, a desktop, and a set of GUI tools with which program interfaces can be constructed. Gnome is designed to provide a flexible platform for the development of powerful applications. Currently, Gnome is strongly supported by Red Hat and is its primary GUI interface. When you install Red Hat, the default interface used is Gnome. Gnome is completely free under the GNU Public License with no restrictions. You can obtain the source directly from the Gnome Web site at **www.gnome.org**.

The core components of the Gnome desktop consist of a panel for starting programs and desktop functionality. Other components normally found in a desktop, such as a file manager, Web browser, and window manager are provided by Gnome-compliant applications. Gnome provides libraries of Gnome GUI tools that developers can use to create Gnome applications. Programs that use buttons, menus, and windows that adhere to a Gnome standard can be said to be Gnome-compliant. For a file manager, the Gnome desktop uses a new Gnome version of Midnight Commander. Window managers must be Gnome-compliant. The Gnome desktop does not have its own window manager as KDE does. The Gnome desktop uses any Gnome-compliant window manager. Currently, the Enlightenment window manager is the one commonly used for the Gnome desktop.

Integrated into Gnome is support for component model interfaces, allowing software components to interconnect, regardless of the computer language in which they are implemented or the kind of machine on which they are running. The standard used in Gnome for such interfaces is the *Common Object Request Broker Architecture* (*CORBA*), developed by the Object Model Group for use on UNIX systems. Gnome uses the ORBit implementation of CORBA. With such a framework, Gnome applications and clients can directly communicate with each other, enabling you to use components of one application in another.

You can find out more about Gnome at its Web site at **www.gnome.org**. This site not only provides a detailed software map of current Gnome projects with links to their development sites, it also maintains extensive mailing lists for Gnome projects to which you can subscribe. The Web site provides online documentation, such as the Gnome User's Guide and FAQs. If you want to develop Gnome programs, check the Gnome developer's Web site at **developer.gnome.org.** The site provides tutorials, programming guides, and development tools. The Gnome Web site also includes detailed online documentation for the GTK+ library, Gnome widgets, and the Gnome desktop.

For Gnome program development check **developer.gnome.org.** Here you can find the complete API reference manual online, as well as extensive support tools such as a tutorial and *Interactive Development Environments (IDE).*

GTK+

GTK+ is the widget set used for Gnome applications. Its look and feel was originally derived from Motif. The widget set is designed from the ground up for power and flexibility. For example, buttons can have labels, images, or any combination thereof. Objects can be dynamically queried and modified at run time. It also includes a theme engine that enables users to change the look and feel of applications using these widgets. At the same time, the GTK+ widget set remains small and efficient.

The GTK+ widget set is entirely free under the *Library General Public License* (*LGPL*). The LGPL enables developers to use the widget set with proprietary, as well as free, software. The widget set also features an extensive set of programming language bindings, including C++, Perl, Python, Pascal, Objective C, Guile, and Ada. Internalization is fully supported, permitting GTK+-based applications to be used with other character sets, such as those in Asian languages. The drag-and-drop functionality supports both Xdnd and Motif protocols, allowing drag-and-drop operations with other widget sets that support these protocols, such as Qt and Motif.

The Gnome Interface

The Gnome interface consists of the panel and a desktop, as shown in Figure 4-1. The panel appears as a long bar across the bottom of the screen. It holds menus, programs, and applets. An *applet* is a small program designed to be run within the panel. On the panel is

Figure 4-1.   *Gnome*

a button with a large barefoot imprint on it. This is the Gnome applications menu, the main menu. The menu operates like the Start menu in Windows, listing entries for applications you can run on your desktop. You can display panels horizontally or vertically, and have them automatically hide, to show you a full screen.

The remainder of the screen is the desktop. Here, you can place directories, files, or programs. You can create them on the desktop directly or drag them from a file manager window. A click-and-drag operation with the middle mouse button enables you to create links on the desktop to installed programs. Initially, the desktop only holds an icon for your home directory. Clicking it opens a file manager window to that directory.

From a user's point of view, you can think of the Gnome interface as having four components: the desktop, the panel, the main menu, and the file manager. In its standard default configuration, the Gnome desktop displays a folder icon for your home directory in the upper-left corner. Some distributions may include other icons, such as links to the Gnome Web site or to the Linux Documentation site. Initially, a file manager window opens on the desktop displaying your home directory. The panel has several default icons: The main menu (bare foot), the Terminal program (monitor), the Gnome Help System (question mark), the Gnome Control Center (toolbox), the Gnome pager (squares), and a clock. Red Hat also includes the Netscape Web browser.

To start a program, you can select its entry in the main menu, click its application launcher button in the panel (if there is one), double-click its icon in either the desktop or the file manager window, drag a data file to its icon, or select the Run Program entry in the main menu. This opens a small window where you can type in the program name.

To quit Gnome, you select the Logout entry in the main menu. You can also add a Logout button to the panel you could use instead. To add the Logout button, right-click the panel and select the Add Logout Button entry. A Logout button then appears in the panel. When you log out, the Logout dialog box is displayed. You have three options. The first option, Logout, quits Gnome, returning you to your command line shell still logged in to your Linux account. The second option, Halt, not only quits Gnome, but also shuts down your entire system. The third option, the Reboot entry, shuts down and reboots your system. The Logout entry is selected by default. Halt and Reboot are only available to the root user. If normal users execute them, they are prompted to enter the root user password to shut down. You can also elect to retain your desktop by clicking the Save current setup check box. This reopens any programs or directories still open when you logged out. Gnome-compliant window managers also quit when you log out of Gnome. You then must separately quit a window manager that is not Gnome-compliant after logging out of Gnome.

The Gnome Help system, shown in Figure 4-2, provides a browser-like interface for displaying the Gnome users manual, man pages, and info documents. It features a toolbar that enables you to move through the list of previously viewed documents. You can even bookmark specific items. A Web page interface enables you to use links to connect to different documents. You can easily move the manual, or the list of man pages and info documents. You can place entries in the location box to access specific documents directly. Special URL-like protocols are supported for the different types

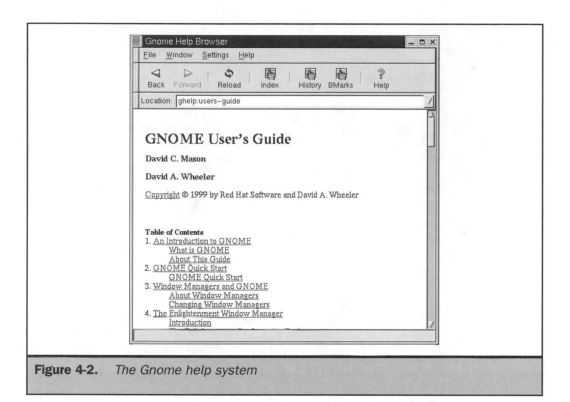

Figure 4-2.   *The Gnome help system*

of documents: ghelp: for Gnome help, man: for man pages, and info: for the info documents.

The Gnome Desktop

The Gnome desktop provides you with all the capabilities of GUI-based operating systems (see Figure 4-3). You can drag files, applications, and directories to the desktop, and then back to Gnome-compliant applications. If the desktop stops functioning, you can restart it by starting the Gnome file manager. The desktop is actually a backend process in the Gnome file manager. But you needn't have the file manager open to use the desktop.

Although the Gnome desktop supports drag-and-drop operations, these work only for applications that are Gnome- or Motif-compliant. You can drag any items from a Gnome-compliant application to your desktop, and vice versa. Any icon for an item that you drag from a file manager window to the desktop also appears on the desktop. However, the default drag-and-drop operation is a move operation. If you select a file in your file manager window and drag it to the desktop, you are actually moving the file from its current directory to the .gnome-desktop directory, which is located in your

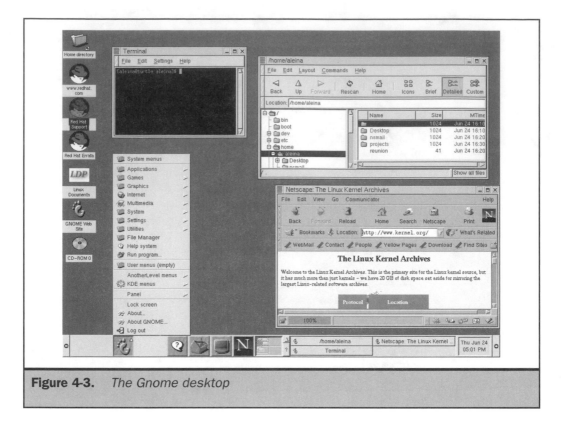

Figure 4-3.   *The Gnome desktop*

home directory and holds all items on the desktop (notice this is a dot file). In the case of dragging directory folders to the desktop, the entire directory and its subdirectories would be copied to the .gnome-desktop directory.

In most cases, you only want to create on the desktop another way to access a file without moving it from its original directory. You can do this by creating a link or a program launcher, instead of moving the file. To create a link, drag the file while holding down the middle mouse button. When you release the mouse button, a pop-up menu appears with entries for copy, move, or link. Select the link entry. A copy of the icon then appears with a small arrow in the right corner indicating it is a link. You can then click this link to start the program, open the file, or open the directory, depending on what kind of file you linked to. To create a program launcher, right-click anywhere on the desktop and choose the Create Launcher applet entry. This opens a dialog box where you can enter the program name, select an icon for it, and set its permissions.

You can then use that icon to access the item directly. This is often used for starting common programs. For example, you can middle-click-and-drag the Netscape icon to the desktop and select Link from the pop-up menu to create a link icon for Netscape. Double-clicking the icon starts Netscape. You can do the same with files. In this case, their respective program is started. If the item is a directory, then the file manager starts up, opened to that directory. If you want to have an application placed on your desktop that is not Gnome-compliant, you can manually place a link in your home directory's .gnome-desktop directory.

As an alternative to the desktop, you can drag any program, file, or directory to the panel; a launcher applet is then automatically created for it on the panel. The item is not moved or copied. You can also right-click anywhere on the empty desktop to display a menu, some of whose entries will start applications. The entries for this menu are listed in Table 4-1. You will notice entries for a new directory. Remember, this entry creates a new directory on your desktop, specifically in the your .gnome-desktop directory.

The desktop also displays icons for any drives you have access to ,such as a CD-ROM or floppy drive, provided they are user mountable. You can easily do this with Linuxconf. Select the Access Local Drive entry, and then select the drive and the Options panel for that drive. On this panel, select the User Mountable option. If you do not have Linuxconf, you must make the appropriate entry in the **fstab** file, adding "user" to the options field for that device.

Menu Item	Description
New | Terminal	Launches a new Gnome Terminal window that navigates to the ~/.gnome-desktop directory
New | Directory	Creates a new directory on your desktop
New | Launcher	Places a new application launcher on the desktop. Uses the Application Launcher dialog box to have you specify the application and its properties
New | [application]	Some Gnome applications place entries in the New menu that enable you to start new sessions easily for those applications
Arrange Icons	Arranges your desktop icons
Create New Window	Launches a new Gnome File Manager window showing your Home directory
Rescan Mountable Devices	Rescans the mountable devices on your machine and displays an icon for any new devices
Rescan Desktop	Rescans the files in your ~/.gnome-desktop directory

Table 4-1. *The Gnome Desktop Menu*

You can mount file systems on these devices by right-clicking their icons and choosing the Mount Device entry. For example, to mount a floppy disk, right-click the floppy disk icon and select the Mount Device entry. You can then access the disk in the floppy disk drive either by double-clicking it or right-clicking and selecting the Open entry. A file manager window opens to display the contents of the CD-ROM disk. To unmount a floppy disk, right-click the CD-ROM icon and select the Unmount Device entry. You can then safely remove the floppy disk. Be sure you don't remove a mounted floppy disk until you have first unmounted it, selecting the Unmount Device entry in the pop-up menu. A CD-ROM is automatically mounted when you put it in the CD-ROM drive. A file manager window will open showing its contents. To remove the CD-ROM first, right-click and select unmount and then select eject. Devices need to be set to user mount for them to show on the desktop (see Chapter 24).

Usually a window manager extends a desktop into several areas that appear as different screens. Gnome's drag-and-drop operation works on desktop areas provided by a Gnome-compliant window manager. Gnome does not directly manage desktop areas, though you can use the Gnome pager to move to them. You use the window manager configuration tool to configure them. In addition, most window managers also support virtual desktops. Instead of being extensions of the same desktop area, virtual desktops are separate entities. Gnome does not support its drag-and-drop capabilities on virtual desktops. It is aware of only a single desktop with multiple areas. An *area* is an extension of a desktop, making it larger than the screen, whereas virtual desktops are entirely separate entities. KDE implements virtual desktops, whereas Gnome supports desktop operations only on desktop areas. The Gnome pager, however, does support virtual desktops, creating icons for each in the panel, along with task buttons for any applications open on them. You can use the Gnome pager to move to different virtual desktops and their areas.

Window Managers

Gnome works with any window manager. However, desktop functionality, such as drag-and-drop capabilities and the Gnome pager, only work with window managers that are Gnome-compliant. Currently, only the Enlightenment window manager is completely Gnome-compliant, though others, such as FVWM, IceWin, and Window Maker, are partially compliant and soon will be fully so. Check a window manager's documentation to see it is Gnome-compliant.

Enlightenment employs much the same window operations as used on other window managers. You can resize a window by clicking any of its sides or corners and dragging. You can move the window with a click-and-drag operation on its title bar. You can also right-click and drag any border to move the window, as well as ALT-click anywhere on the window. The upper-right corner lists the Maximize, Minimize, and Close buttons. If the Gnome pager is running in your panel, then Minimize creates a button for the window in the panel that you can click to restore it. If the Gnome pager is not present, then the window will iconify, minimizing to an icon on the desktop. You can click the upper-left corner of a window to display a window menu with entries for window operations. These include a desktop entry to move the window to another desktop area and the Stick option, which displays the window no matter to what desktop area you move.

You can also access the Enlightenment desktop menu. To display the menu, middle-click anywhere on the desktop (hold both mouse buttons down at the same time for a two-button mouse). A pop-up menu then appears with submenus for Gnome, user, and other applications, as well as the Desktop, Themes, and Enlightenment configuration. You can use this menu to start any application, if you want. With the desktop menus you move to different desktop areas and virtual desktops. The Themes menu enables you to choose different Enlightenment themes (these are separate from KDE themes). Enlightenment also has extensive configuration options discussed in a later section.

If you have several window managers installed on your system, then you can change from one to the other using the Window Manager capplet in the Gnome Control Center. *capplet* is the term used for a *control applet*, a module used to configure your desktop. Select the Control Center entry in the main menu to start the Control Center. In the Control Center window, select Window Manager, listed under Desktop in the tree on the left. A panel is displayed listing your window managers. Initially, only Enlightenment is listed. To add others to the list, click the Add button on the right side of the panel. This opens a window that prompts you to enter an identifying name for the window manager, the command that starts the window manager, and any configuration tool it may use. If the window manager is Gnome-compliant, you can click the button Window Manager Is Session Managed. Once you finish making your entries and click OK, the new window manager appears in the list on the Control Center panel. Select it and click Try to run that window manager. If you want to run the window manager's configuration tool, click the Run Configuration Tool button.

The Gnome File Manager

Gnome uses *GNU Midnight Commander* (*GMC*, shown in Figure 4-4) for its file manager. This is the Midnight Commander file manager with a Gnome front end. The GMC window consists of a menu bar, a toolbar, a location box, and two panes. The left pane displays a directory tree from which you can directly select directories. The right pane is the Directory view, which displays the files and subdirectories for the currently selected directory. The directory tree maps all the directories on your system, starting from the root directory. You can expand or shrink any directory by clicking the + or – symbol before its name. Select a directory by clicking the directory name. The contents of that directory are then displayed in the right-hand pane, the Directory view.

The Directory view has several viewing options. You can view a directory's contents as icons, a brief list, a detailed list, or a custom view. You select the different

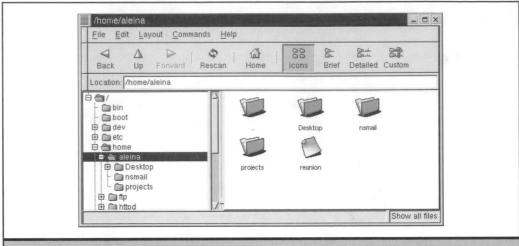

Figure 4-4.   *Gnome file manager*

options from the Layout menu or by clicking their respective buttons in the toolbar. The brief list simply provides the name, whereas the detailed list provides the name, permissions, size, date, owner, and group. For a custom view, you can select the informational fields you want displayed for your files. In all the list views, buttons are displayed for each field across the top of the Directory View pane. You can use these buttons to sort the lists according to that field. For example, to sort the files by date, click the Date button; to sort by size, click the Size button. You can also select a field from the Sort By entry in the Layout menu.

The GMC file manager operates similarly to a Web browser. It maintains a list of previously viewed directories; you can move back and forth through that list using the toolbar buttons. The left-arrow button moves you to the previously displayed directory, and the right-arrow button moves you to the next displayed directory. The up-arrow button moves you to the parent directory, and the Home button moves you to your home directory. To use a path name to go directly to a given directory, you can type the path name in the Location box and press ENTER. GMC is also Internet-aware. You can use the location box to access an FTP site and display the directories on that remote site, and then drag-and-drop files to another file manager window to download them to your system. Be sure to include the FTP protocol specification, **ftp://**.

To open a subdirectory, you can double-click its icon, or single-click the icon and select Open from the File menu. If you want to open a separate GMC window for that directory, click the middle mouse button on the directory's icon (for two-button mice, click the right and left buttons at the same time).

As a Gnome-compliant file manager, Midnight Commander supports GUI drag-and-drop operations for copying and moving files. To move a file or directory, click-and-drag from one directory to another, as you would on Windows or Mac interfaces. The move operation is the default drag-and-drop operation in Gnome. To copy a file, hold the CTRL key down while you click the item and drag it.

If you click-and-drag a file with the middle mouse button, when you reach the destination and lift up on the mouse button, a pop-up menu appears listing several options: Copy, Move, Link, or Cancel drag. This is a convenient way to create a link to a file, such as an application. Just click-and-drag with the middle mouse button, and then choose Link from the pop-up menu.

You can also perform file operations on a file by right-clicking its icon and selecting the action you want from the pop-up menu that appears (see Table 4-2). For example, to delete an item, right-click it and select the Delete entry from the pop-up menu. To move a file, select the Move entry. This displays a dialog box where you can change the path name of the file you want to rename. A Browse button enables you to use a directory tree to select a new directory location. The Advanced Options panel in this dialog box enables you to select a Preserve Symlinks option. With this option, any symbolic links to this file are changed to point to the new location. To copy a file, you can select Copy from the pop-up menu and use the dialog box to select the new location for the copy and a new name if you want. The destination directory displayed in the Move, Copy, or Links menu is that of the currently active file manager window. To move a file from one directory to another, open a file manager window to that new directory, click it, and then, in your source window, right-click directly on the file icon for the file you are moving. The location box in the Move window shows the path name for the directory whose file manager window you just selected. The same process works for Copy and Link operations. For example, to create a link in the **presents** directory to the **party** file in the **birthday** directory, you open a file manager window for both the **birthday** and **presents** directory, click the **presents** directory, and then right-click the **party** file in the **birthday** directory and select the link entry. You see the location box in the Link window showing the path name for the **birthday** directory. Add in the name you want to give to the link file.

You can use this same procedure to rename a file. Right-click and select the Move entry from the pop-up menu. In the dialog box, enter a new name for the file. You can also rename a file either by entering a new name in its Properties dialog box or by slowly clicking the name displayed under the icon. Use a right-click and select Properties from the pop-up menu to display the Properties dialog box.

File operations can be performed on a selected group of files and directories. You can select a group of items in several ways. You can click the first item and then hold down the Shift key while clicking the last item. You can also click-and-drag the mouse across items you want to select. To select separated items, hold the CTRL key down as you click the individual icons. If you want to select all the items in the directory, choose the Select All entry in the Edit menu. You can also select files based on pattern matches on the file names. Choose the Select Files entry in the Edit menu. You can then enter a pattern using Linux file matching wildcard symbols such as * (See Chapter 6). For example, the pattern *.c would select all C source code files. You can then click-and-drag a set of items at once. This enables you to copy, move, or even delete several files at once. To move files

Menu Item	Description
Open	Open the file with its associated application
Open With	Select an application with which to open this file
View	View the file with a basic text viewer
Edit	Use an editor to edit the file
Copy	Copy the file to the clipboard so it can be pasted elsewhere
Delete	Delete the file
Move	Display the Move dialog box with which you can move the file
Properties	Display the Properties dialog box for this file. There are three panels: Statistics, Options, and Permissions.

Table 4-2. *The File Pop-Up Menu*

between directories, open two file manager windows to the respective directories. Then click-and-drag the items from one window to the other.

You can start any application in the file manager by double-clicking either the application itself or a data file used for that application. If a file does not have an associated application, you can right-click the file and select the Open With entry. A dialog box is then displayed where you can choose the application with which you want to open this file. Drag-and-drop operations are also supported for applications. You can drag a data file to its associated application icon (say, one on the desktop); the application then starts up using that data file.

With the Properties dialog box, you can view detailed information on a file and set options and permissions. A Properties box has three panels: Statistics, Options, and Permissions. The *Statistics panel* shows detailed information such as size, date, and ownership. The *Options panel* enables you to set the open, view, and edit operations for this file. You can choose the application to open it with, which one to use to view it, and which one to use to edit it. The *Permissions panel* shows the read, write, and execute permissions for user, group, and other, as set for this file. You can change any of the permissions here, provided the file belongs to you.

You can set preferences for your GMC file manager in the Preferences dialog box. Access this dialog box by selecting the Preferences item in the Edit menu. The Preferences dialog box has five panels: File Display, Confirmation, Custom View, Caching, and VFS. On the File Display panel, you can select such features as hiding or showing hidden (dot) files. The Confirmation panel is where confirmation checks are specified for deleting and overwriting files. The Virtual File System (VFS) panel enables you to set options for accessing remote file systems, such as FTP sites. You can specify an anonymous FTP password, a timeout period, and whether you have to use an FTP proxy server. The Caching panel enables you to specify caching options for directory and FTP information. GMC keeps a copy of displayed directories for a given amount of time per session, which allows fast reload of previously displayed directories. You use the Custom View panel to select the fields you want displayed in your custom view of a directory listing. These are such fields as date, time, and permissions. You have two panes: one listing possible fields (Possible Columns) and the other listing the fields you have chosen (Displayed Columns). Use the Add button to add a field to your list; use the Remove button to remove one. You can drag entries up or down in the Displayed Columns pane to reorder them.

The Gnome Panel

The *panel* is the center of the Gnome interface, as shown next. Through it you can start your applications, run applets, and access desktop areas. You can think of the Gnome panel as a type of tool you can use on your desktop. You can have several Gnome panels displayed on your desktop, each with applets and menus you have placed in them. In this respect, Gnome is flexible, enabling you to configure your panels any way you want. You can customize a panel to fit your own needs, holding applets and menus of your own selection. You may add new panels, add applications to the panel, and add various applets.

You can hide the panel at any time by clicking either of the Hide buttons located on each end of the panel. The Hide buttons are thin buttons showing a small arrow. This is the direction in which the panel will hide. To redisplay the panel, move your mouse off the screen in that direction at the bottom of the screen. If you want the panel to automatically hide when you are not using it, select the Autohide option in the panel configuration window. Moving the mouse to the bottom of the screen redisplays the panel. You can also move the panel to another edge of the screen by clicking-and-dragging it with your middle mouse button (both buttons simultaneously for two-button mice).

To add a new panel, select the Add New Panel entry in the Panel menu located in the main menu. You can choose from edge or corner panels. An *edge panel* is displayed across one of the edges of the screen. Your original panel is an edge panel. *A corner panel* is a smaller panel that does not extend across the entire screen. It only extends as far as it must to contain whatever applets and menu button you place in it. It is anchored on one corner of the screen. If you click the Hide button on the corner, you hide the panel. But, if you click the other Hide button, it merely moves the panel to the other corner. Clicking it again hides the panel. You can change a panel's type at any time by right-clicking the panel and selecting the alternate configuration. A right-click at an edge panel displays a "Convert to edge panel" entry you can use to change the edge panel to a corner panel.

Adding Applications and Applets

Adding applications to a panel is easy. For an application already in the main menu, you only need to go to its entry and right-click it. Then select the Add This Launcher To Panel entry. An application launcher for that application is then automatically added to the panel. Suppose you use gEdit frequently and want to add its icon to the panel, instead of having to go through the main menu all the time. Right-click the gEdit menu entry and select the Add This Launcher To Panel option. The gEdit icon now appears in your panel.

To add an application icon not in the Mail menu, first right-click the panel to display the pop-up menu and select the Add New Launcher entry. This opens the Create Launcher Applet window for entering properties for the applications launcher. You are prompted for the application name, the command that invokes it, and its type. To select an icon for your launcher, click the Icon button. This opens the icon picker window, listing icons from which you can choose.

You can also group applications under a Drawer icon. Clicking the Drawer icon displays a list of the different application icons you can then select. To add a drawer to your panel, right-click the panel and select the Add Drawer entry. If you want to add a whole menu of applications on the main menu to your panel, right-click the menu item and select the Add This As Drawer To Panel entry. The entire menu appears as a drawer on your panel, holding icons instead of menu entries, as shown next. For example, suppose you want to place the Internet applications menu on your panel. Right-click the Internet item and select Add This As Drawer To Panel. A drawer appears on your panel labeled Internet and clicking it displays a pop-up list of icons for all the Internet applications.

A menu differs from a drawer in that a *drawer* holds application icons instead of menu entries. You can add menus to your panel, much as you add drawers. To add a submenu in the main menu to your panel, right-click the menu title and select the Add This As Menu To Panel entry. The menu title appears in the panel; you can click it to display the menu entries.

You can also add directory folders to a panel. Click-and-drag the folder icon from the file manager window to your panel. Whenever you click this folder button, a file manager window opens, displaying that directory. You already have a folder button for your home directory. You can add directory folders to any drawer on your panel.

Main Menu

You open the main menu by clicking its button on the panel. The Main Menu button is a stylized picture of a bare foot. It is initially located on the left side of your panel, the lower left-hand corner of your screen. You only need to single-click the Main Menu button. You needn't keep holding your mouse button down. The menu pops up much like the Start menu in Windows.

You can configure menus using the Menu Properties dialog box. To change the properties for a menu on the panel, including the main menu, right-click its icon in the panel and select the Properties entry. This displays the Menu Properties dialog box, which has two sections: Menu Type and Main Menu. In the Main Menu section, you can set properties for that main menu. Several possible submenus can be displayed on the main menu, either directly or in other submenus. You can choose from the System, User, Red Hat, KDE, and Debian menus. Red Hat and Debian menus are those used for specific Red Hat or Debian programs installed by those distributions that are not specifically Gnome applications. KDE is used for KDE applications, if the KDE desktop is also installed on your system.

You can customize the main menu, adding your own entries, with the Menu editor. The main menu is divided into two sections: the Systems menu and the User menu. The *Systems menu,* which can be changed only by the system administrator—the root user—contains the default Gnome applications installed with Gnome. The *User menu* can be changed by individual users, adding entries for applications a user frequently runs. To start the Menu editor, select the Menu Editor entry in the Setting submenu located in the main menu. The Menu editor is divided into two panes, the left being a tree view of the main menu. You can expand or shrink any of the submenus. The right pane holds configuration information for a selected entry. There are two panels: basic and advanced. The basic panel displays the name, command, and application type, as well as the icon. You can click the icon to change it. You can also change the name, command, or type fields.

To add a new application, click the New Item button on the toolbar. The new item is placed in the currently selected menu. Enter the name, command, and type information, and then select an icon. Then click the Save button to add the entry to the menu. You can move the menu item in the menu by clicking the up or down arrow button in the toolbar, or by dragging it with the mouse. If you are a user, remember you can only add entries to the User menu, not to the Systems menu.

An easier way to add an application is to use the drag-and-drop method. Locate the application you want to add with the file manager, and then drag-and-drop its icon to the appropriate menu in the Menu editor. The entry is made automatically, using configuration information provided for that application by the file manager.

Panel Configuration

You use the Global Panel Configuration dialog box to configure properties for all Gnome panels. Either right-click the panel and select Global Properties, or select Global Properties in the Panel submenu in the main menu to display this dialog window. The Global Panel Configuration dialog box has six tabbed panels: Animation, Launcher Icon, Drawer Icon, Menu Icon, Logout Icon, and Miscellaneous. With the animation panel, you can enable panel animations, setting various options for them. The various Icon panels enable you to select the images you want to use to denote active or inactive elements, among other features, such as border and depth. On the miscellaneous panel, you set certain options, such as allowing pop-up menus on the desktop, prompting before logout, or keeping panels below windows.

To configure individual panels, you use the Panel Properties dialog box. To display this dialog box, you right-click the particular panel and select the This Panel Properties entry in the pop-up menu, or select This Panel Properties in the main menu's Panel menu. For individual panels, you can set features for edge panel configuration and the background. The Panel Properties dialog box includes a tabbed panel for each. On the Edge panel, you can choose options for positioning an edge panel and for minimizing it, including the autohide feature. The Hide Buttons feature enables you to hide the panel yourself.

On the Background panel, you can change the background image used for the panel. You can select an image, have it scaled to fit the panel, and select a background color. For an image, you can also drag-and-drop an image file from the file manager to the panel, and that image then becomes the background image for the panel.

Gnome Applets

As previously stated, applets are small programs that perform tasks within the panel. To add an applet, right-click the panel and select Add New Applet from the pop-up menu. This, in turn, displays other pop-up menus listing categories of applets with further listings of available applets. Select the one you want. For example, to add the clock to your panel, select Clock from the Utility menu. To remove an applet, right-click it and select Remove from panel.

Gnome features a number of helpful applets, such as a CPU monitor and a mail checker. Some applets monitor your system, such as the Battery Monitor, which checks the battery in laptops, CPU/MEM Usage, which shows a graph indicating your current CPU and memory use, as well as separate applets for CPU and memory load: CPULoad and MemLoad. The Mixer applet displays a small scrollbar for adjusting sound levels. The CD player displays a small CD interface for playing music CDs.

For Network tasks, there are MailCheck, PPP dialer, and Web Control applets. MailCheck checks for received mail. To configure MailCheck, right-click it and select the Properties entry. You can set the frequency of checks, as well as specify a more sophisticated mail checker to run, such as **fetchmail**. The PPP dialer sets up a PPP connection to an ISP. This requires you have a PPP dialer program, such as **gnomeppp** already configured. Web Control enables you to start your Web browser with a specified URL.

Several helpful utility applets provide added functionality to your desktop. The Clock applet can display time in a 12- or 24-hour format. Right-click the Clock applet and select the Properties entry to change its setup. You use the Printer applet to print your files. To print a file, drag its icon to the Printer applet. To configure the Printer applet, right-click it and select Properties. Here you can specify the printer name and the printer command to use, helpful if you have more than one printer.

The Drive Mount applet enables you to mount a drive using a single click. You can create a Drive Mount applet for each device you have, such as a floppy drive and a CD-ROM. To mount a file system, all you have to do is click the appropriate Drive Mount icon in the panel. The applet originally displays a small image of a floppy drive. By default, the applet mounts the floppy drive. You can change its configuration to mount a CD-ROM, a hard drive, or a Zip drive, by first right-clicking an applet and selecting the Properties entry. This displays a Drive Mount Settings dialog box. Here you can select the icon the applet should display and its mount point, the directory on your file system to which it will be attached. For a CD-ROM, this is usually **/mnt/cdrom**. You have four icons to choose from: Floppy, CDROM, Zip Disk, and Hard Drive. Select the one you want. Now, you can click the icon in the panel to mount the device. Normally, only the root user can mount floppy disks or CD-ROMS. If you want to allow users to mount floppies or a CD-ROM disk, you have to set the appropriate permissions on these devices. You can easily use Linuxconf to do this (see File Administration Chapter 24).

Gnome Pager

The *Gnome pager*, shown next, appears in the panel and shows a pager for your desktop areas, as well as buttons for each window open on the desktop. A window may be part of an application such as Netscape or the file manager displaying a directory. The Gnome pager is a panel applet that works only in the panel. If it is not already active, you can activate the Gnome pager by right-clicking the panel and selecting Add New Applet from the pop-up menu. This, in turn, displays other pop-up menus listing categories of applets and their listings of available applets. Select the Utility category and, in that menu, select Gnome Pager.

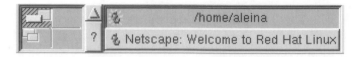

The Gnome pager is divided into two areas: the Pager view and the Task List view. The *Pager view* shows all your areas as small adjoining rectangles. Applications show up as small outlines in these rectangles. If you click the small arrow to the right of the Desktop view, the areas are displayed with a listing of the applications on them. The *Task list* view arranges applications in a series of buttons, one for each open application (window). Clicking an application button moves you to that window.

To configure the pager, right-click it and select Properties to display the Gnome Pager Setting dialog box. You can also click the small icon with the question mark. Here you can set the width of the task list, and the number of rows and columns. You can also control how the pager is displayed, suppressing either the Pager view or the Task List view, including icons in the Task List view, or using small pages for the desktop areas. Remember, the window manager you are using may also have a pager you can use. Check your window manager documentation on how to activate it.

Quicklaunch

You can use the Quicklaunch applet in the panel to start programs. The *Quicklaunch applet* holds a collection of small icons for application launchers. Click them to launch your application. The Quicklaunch applet can use only launchers that are already set up either on the main menu or on your desktop. To add a launcher to Quicklaunch, drag-and-drop the launcher to the Quicklaunch applet in the panel. A small icon is then created for it in the Quicklaunch applet. For main menu items, click an item and drag it to the Quicklaunch applet. Right-click a particular application's icon and select Properties to configure that launcher.

Gnome Configuration: Control Center

With the Gnome Control Center, shown in Figure 4-5, you can configure different parts of your system using tools called *capplets.* Think of capplets as modules or plug-ins that can be added to the Control Center to enable you to configure various applications. Capplets exist for the core set of Gnome applications, as well as for other applications for which developers may have written capplets. You can either start the Control Center directly or start up a particular capplet that starts the Control Center open to that capplet. To start the Control Center directly, select the Control Center entry in the System menu located in the main menu or on its applet in the panel (icon of a toolbox). The Control Center menu also lists the capplets currently available on your system. To start using a capplet, select the particular application capplet you want from the Control Center menu.

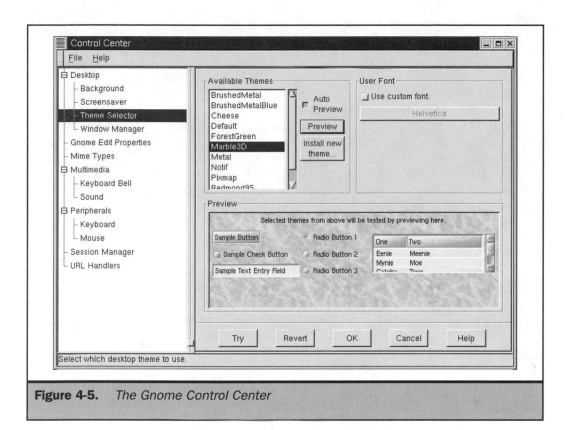

Figure 4-5.   *The Gnome Control Center*

The Control Center window is divided into two panes. The left one is a tree view of the capplets available on your system, which are arranged into categories you can expand or shrink. The left pane displays the panel for configuring that particular application. Click the entry in the view tree for the application you want to configure, and its configuration panel then appears to the left.

Your Gnome system provides several desktop capplets you can use to configure your desktop: Background, Screensaver, Theme Selector, and Window Manager. You use the Background capplet to select a background color or image, the Screensaver to select the screensaver images and wait time, the Theme selector to choose a theme, and the Window Manager to choose the window manager you want to use.

Gnome Edit Properties enables you to choose an editor as your default editor for Gnome, the editor the Gnome file manager uses to open text files. Gnome MIME Types enables you to specify *Multipurpose Internet Mail Extensions* (*MIME*) type entries for your system, associating given MIME types with certain applications. Notice basic MIME type entries are already present. You can edit an entry and change its associated application.

Also listed are Multimedia and Peripheral capplets. For the sound configuration, you can select sound files to play for events in different Gnome applications. For your keyboard, you can set the repeat sensitivity and click sound. You can configure mouse buttons for your right or left hand, and adjust the mouse motion. With the Session Manager capplet, you can configure certain Gnome session features, specifying non-Gnome programs to start up and whether you want a logout prompt.

Several User Interface capplets enable you to configure different interface components, such as menus, toolbars, and status bars. There are capplets for setting these features for applications, dialog boxes, and the *Multiple Document Interface* (*MDI*). You can specify whether toolbars and menus can be detached, whether they have relief borders, and whether they include icons. For dialog boxes, you can set features such as the arrangement of buttons or the position of the dialog box on the screen when it appears. The default MDI used for Gnome is notebook. The notebook interface consists of tabbed panels used in many applications, such as the Control Center. You can choose two other interfaces: toplevel and modal. You can also adjust the way the notebook interface displays its tabs.

Gnome sets up several configuration files and directories in your home directory. The **.gnome** directory holds configuration files for different desktop components, such as **gmc** for the file manager, panel for the panels, and **gmenu** for the main menu. **.gtkrc** holds configuration directives for the GTK+ widgets. The .gnome-desktop holds all the items you placed on your desktop.

Gnome Directories and Files

Most distributions install Gnome binaries in the **/usr/bin** directory on your system. Gnome libraries are located in the /usr/lib directory. Gnome also has its own include directories with header files for use in compiling and developing Gnome applications, **/usr/include/libgnome** and **/usr/include/libgnomeui** (see Table 4-3). The directories located in **/usr/share/gnome** contain files used to configure your Gnome environment.

Gnome sets up several hidden directories for each user in their home directory that begin with ".gnome" and include a preceding period in the name. **.gnome** holds files used to configure a user's Gnome desktop and applications. Configuration files for the panel, Control Center, GnomeRPM, MIME types, and sessions, among others, are located here. The files **Gnome**, **GnomeHelp**, **Background**, and **Terminal** all hold Gnome configuration commands for how to display and use these components. For example, **Gnome** holds general display features for the desktop, while **GnomeHelp** specifies the history and bookmark files for the help system. Configuration files for particular Gnome applications are kept in the subdirectory **apps**. On Red Hat, the **redhat-apps** directory holds **.desktop** files containing Gnome instructions on how to handle different Red Hat utilities, such as **netcfg**. .gnome-desktop holds any files, folders, or links the user has dragged to the desktop. **.gnome-help-browser** holds the Bookmark and History files for the Gnome Help System. These are the bookmarks and

ENVIRONMENTS

System Gnome Directories	Contents
/usr/bin	Gnome programs
/usr/lib	Gnome libraries
/usr/include/libgnome	Header files for use in compiling and developing Gnome applications
/usr/include/libgnomeui	Header files for use in compiling and developing Gnome user interface components
/usr/share/gnome/apps	Files used by Gnome applications
/usr/share/gnome/help	Files used by Gnome Help System
/usr/doc/gnome*	Documentation for various Gnome packages, including libraries
/etc/X11/gdm/gnomerc	Gnome configuration file invoked with the Gnome Display Manager (GDM)
User Gnome Directories	**Contents**
.gnome	Holds configuration files for the user's Gnome desktop and Gnome applications. Includes configuration files for the panel, Control Center, background, GnomeRPM, MIME types, and sessions
.gnome-desktop	Directory where files, directories, and links you place on the desktop will reside
.gnome-help-browser	Contains Gnome Help System configuration files, including History and Bookmarks set up by the user
.gnome_private	The user private Gnome directory
.gtkrc	GTK+ configuration file
.mc	Configuration files for the Midnight Commander File Manager

Table 4-3.   *Gnome Configuration Directories*

the list of previous documents the user consulted with the Gnome Help browser. **.gtckrc** is the user configuration file for the GTK+ libraries, which contains current desktop configuration directives for resources such as keybindings, colors, and window styles.

Enlightenment

Currently, Gnome is distributed with the Enlightenment window manager. *Enlightenment* is fully Gnome-compliant and also has its own display features and functionality. You can configure Enlightenment from within Gnome, by first selecting it in the Control Center's Window Manager panel, and then selecting Run Configuration Tool For Enlightenment. This runs the e-conf Enlightenment configuration program, displaying the Enlightenment Configuration window shown in Figure 4-6.

The Enlightenment Configuration window displays a list of configuration topics on the left and the panel for the selected topic on the right. Basic options set window displays, enabling you to select resize and move methods. With the Desktops option, you can create virtual desktops and specify the number of desktop areas for each one. On the panel are two configuration tools. The left one, labeled Size Of Virtual Screen, is used to determine the number of desktop areas. The right one, labeled Separate Desktops, is used to specify the number of virtual desktops. Recall, however, that the Gnome desktop is only supported on the first virtual desktop, not on any others. This means drag-and-drop operations do not work on the other virtual desktops. They do, however, work on any of the desktop areas on that first virtual desktop. The Gnome pager supports all the virtual desktop, displaying rectangles for each in the panel. Other topics cover features such as

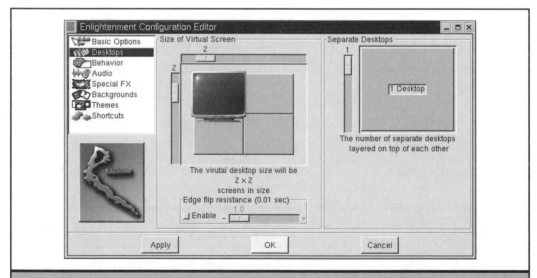

Figure 4-6. *Enlightenment configuration*

sounds, special effects, window focus, keyboard shortcuts, and backgrounds. You can set different backgrounds for each virtual desktop.

The Themes panel enables you to use an Enlightenment theme, from which there are many to choose. Enlightenment is known for its magnificent themes. See **e.themes.org** for themes you can download. To make a theme available, place it in your home directory's **.enlightenment/themes** directory. Make sure that file has an **.etheme** extension. Enlightenment maintains its own configuration directory, called **.enlightenment,** in your home directory. It contains subdirectories for themes, backgrounds, and windows.

Gnome Themes

You can display your Gnome desktop using different themes that change the appearance of desktop objects such as windows, buttons, and scrollbars. Gnome functionality is not affected in any way. You can choose from a variety of themes. Many are posted on the Internet at **gtk.themes.org**. Technically, these are referred to as *GTK themes*, which allow the GTK widget set to change their look and feel.

To select a theme, use the Gnome Control Center and select Themes in the Desktop listing. You can select a theme from the Available Themes list on the Configuration panel. The Auto Preview button enables you to see an example of the theme. To use the theme, click Try. To install a theme you have downloaded from the Internet, click the Install New Theme button and locate the theme file. The theme is then installed on your system, and an entry for it appears in the Available Themes list.

Updating Gnome

Currently, new versions of Gnome are being released frequently, sometimes every few months. Gnome releases are designed to enable users to upgrade their older versions easily. Be sure to obtain the release for your particular distributions (though you can install from the source code if you want). Packages tailored for various distributions can be downloaded through the Gnome Web site at **www.gnome.org** or directly from the Gnome FTP site at **ftp.gnome.org** and its mirror sites. RPM packages for Red Hat can also be obtained from the updates directory for the current distributions located on the Red Hat FTP site at **ftp.redhat.com**. You can use the Red Hat update agent to update any Gnome updates located on the Red Hat FTP site automatically.

Or, you can manually download the update files and install them yourself. First, log in as the root user and then create a directory to hold the Gnome files. Then connect to an FTP site. You can use a Web browser, such as Netscape, but using an FTP client, such as **ftp**, IglooFTP, or even the Gnome file manager, is preferable. Download the files for the new version to your new directory. For Red Hat these are a series of RPM package files. To download using the Gnome file manager, enter the FTP URL in a file manager window's Location box to access the site. Move to the directory holding the Gnome files.

Then select the files and drag-and-drop them to another file manager window that is open to the local directory in which you want them placed. The files are downloaded for you. To download using FTP, be sure to turn off prompts with the **prompt** command and use **mget *** to download all the files at once. Once they are downloaded, you can use the **rpm** command with the **–Uvh** option to install them or the GnomeRPM utility. Be sure to read any installation instructions first. These can be found in README or INSTALL files. You may have to install some packages before others.

To install a particular Gnome RPM package manually, use the **rpm** command with the **–Uvh** options or an RPM package utility like GnomeRPM (see Chapter 4 and Chapter 30). This example installs the games package.

```
rpm -Uvh gnome-games-1.0.51-3.i386.rpm
```

Many of the most recent updates are provided in the form of source files that you can download and compile. These are usually packages in compressed archives with **.tar.gz** extensions. At **ftp.gnome.org,** these are currently located in **pub/Gnome/sources**. Check the Gnome Web site for announcements. For example, a new version of the Gnome core programs could be:

```
ftp.gnome.org/pub/GNOME/sources/gnome-core/gnome-core-1.0.54-2.tar.gz
```

Once you download the archive, use the **tar** command with the **xvzf** options to decompress and extract it. In the directory generated, use the **./configure**, **make**, and **make install** commands to configure, create, and install the programs.

```
tar xvzf gnome-core-1.0.54-2.tar.gz
```

The Complete Reference

Linux

Chapter 5

The K Desktop Environment: KDE

The *K Desktop Environment* (*KDE*) is a network transparent desktop that includes the standard desktop features, such as a window manager and a file manager, as well as an extensive set of applications that cover most Linux tasks. Like Gnome, KDE is fully supported by Red Hat and is included as a fully functional alternate desktop with Red Hat Linux distributions. A standard installation of Red Hat installs KDE and you can easily select it as your working desktop.

KDE is an Internet-aware system that includes a full set of integrated network/Internet applications, including a mailer, a newsreader, and a Web browser. The file manager doubles as a Web and FTP client, enabling you to access Internet sites directly from your desktop. KDE aims to provide a level of desktop functionality and ease of use found in MAC/OS and Windows systems, combined with the power and flexibility of the UNIX operating system. Although the UNIX system has long been prevalent in scientific and server applications, it has not been used extensively by ordinary users because of its somewhat difficult interface. KDE aims to make UNIX and Linux systems as easy to use for the ordinary user as Windows and MAC/OS systems, and then some. KDE bears an interface that will be familiar to users of Window 98 and Windows 2000.

The KDE desktop is developed and distributed by the KDE project. This a large open group of hundreds of programmers around the world. KDE is entirely free and open software provided under a GNU public license, and is available free of charge along with its source code. KDE development is managed by a core group: The KDE Core Team. Anyone can apply, though membership is based on merit. KDE applications are developed using the Compound Document Framework called KOM/OpenParts. To allow applications to share objects such as images, spreadsheets, and documents, a desktop like KDE uses a technology for managing distributed objects called the *Common Object Request Broker Architecture* (*CORBA*). KDE has added to CORBA an additional object management capability called the *K Object Manager* (*KOM*). KOM provides functionality not found in the CORBA standard. KOM/OpenParts enables developers to develop KDE applications quickly. You can think of KOM as being similar to IBM/Apple's SOM/OpenDoc or Microsoft's DCOM/OLE/ActiveX.

Numerous applications written specifically for KDE are easily accessible from the desktop. These include editors, photo and paint image applications, spreadsheets, and office applications. Such applications usually have the letter *k* as part of their name—for example, **kedit** or **kpaint**. Provided with the KDE desktop are a variety of tools. These include calculators, console windows, notepads, and even software package managers. On a system administration level, KDE provides several tools for configuring your system. With **kuser**, you can manage user accounts, adding new ones or removing old ones. **kppp** enables you to connect easily to remote networks with *Point-to-Point Protocol* (*PPP*) using a modem. Practically all of your Linux tasks can be performed from the KDE desktop. KDE applications also feature a built-in Help application. Choosing the Contents entry in the Help menu starts the KDE Help viewer. The Help viewer provides a Web page–like interface with links for navigating through the Help documents. The Red Hat configuration of KDE includes a menu listing traditional Red Hat GUI-capable applications. Here, you find GUI-based Internet clients, editors, system tools, and even games. Red Hat also has a menu for Gnome applications. You can run any Gnome application on KDE (provided Gnome is already installed). On Red Hat, to switch from the KDE desktop to Gnome, you can use the Desktop Switcher located in the Red Hat menu under System.

KDE version 2.0 and on includes an office application suite called *KOffice*, based on KDE's KOM/OpenParts technology. KOffice includes a presentation application, a spreadsheet, an illustrator, and a word processor, among other components (see Chapter 29 for more details). In addition, an *Interactive Development Environment* (*IDE*), called *Kdevelop,* is also available to help programmer's create KDE-based software.

KDE was initiated by Matthias Ettrich in October 1996, and it has an extensive list of sponsors, including SuSE, Caldera, Red Hat, O'Reilly, DLD, Delix, Live, Linux Verband, and others. KDE is designed to run on any UNIX implementation, including Linux, Solaris, HP-UX, and FreeBSD. The official KDE Web site is **www.kde.org**, which provides news updates, download links, and documentation. KDE software packages can be downloaded from the KDE FTP site at **ftp.kde.org** and its mirror sites. Several KDE mailing lists are available for users and developers, announcements, administration, and other topics. See the KDE Web site to subscribe.

Qt and Harmony

KDE uses as its library of GUI tools the Qt library, developed and supported by Troll Tech (**www.troll.no**). *Qt* is considered one of the best GUI libraries available for UNIX/Linux systems. Using Qt has the advantage of relying on a commercially developed and supported GUI library. Also, using the Qt libraries drastically reduced the development time for KDE. Troll Tech provides the Qt libraries as open source software that is freely distributable. Certain restrictions exist however: Qt-based (KDE) applications must be free and open sourced, with no modifications made to the Qt libraries. If you develop an application with the Qt libraries and want to sell it, then you have to buy a license from Troll Tech. In other words, the Qt library is free for free applications, but not for commercial ones.

The Harmony Project is currently developing a free alternative to the Qt libraries. Harmony will include all Qt functionality, as well as added features, such as mutlithreading and theming. It will be entirely compatible with any KDE applications developed using Qt libraries. Harmony will be provided under the *GNU library public license* (*LGPL*). See **www.harmony.org** for more information.

KDE Desktop

One of KDE's aims is to provide users with a consistent integrated desktop, where all applications use GUI interfaces (see Figure 5-1). To this end, KDE provides its own window manager (kwm), file manager (kfm), program manager, and desktop panel.

You can run any other X Window system compliant application, such as Netscape in KDE, as well as any Gnome application. In turn, you can also run any KDE application, including the kfm file manager, with any other Linux window manager like Blackbox, Afterstep, and even Enlightenment. You can even run KDE applications in Gnome.

When you first start KDE, the initial file manager window is displayed on your screen showing your current working directory. At the bottom of the screen is the KDE panel. Located on the panel are icons for menus and programs, as well as buttons for different desktop screens. The icon for the Applications Starter shows a large *K* on a cog wheel with a small arrow at the top indicating it is a menu. Click this icon to display the menu listing all the applications you can run. The Applications Starter operates somewhat like the Start menu in Windows. The standard KDE applications installed with the KDE can be accessed through this menu. You can find entries for different categories such as Internet,

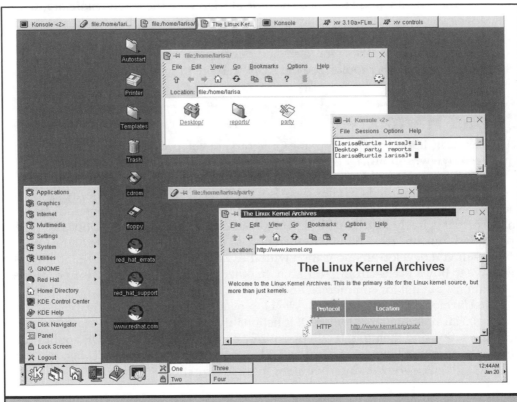

Figure 5-1.   *The KDE desktop*

Systems, Multimedia, and Utilities. These submenus list KDE applications you can use. For example, to start the KDE mailer, select the Mail Client entry in the Internet submenu. At the top of the screen is a taskbar showing buttons for different programs you are running or windows you have open. This is essentially a docking mechanism that enables you to change to a window or application just by clicking its button. To quit KDE, you can select the Logout entry in the Applications Starter menu. You can also right-click anywhere on the desktop and select the Logout entry from the pop-up menu. If you leave any KDE or X11 applications or windows open when you quit, they are automatically restored when you start up again.

Three icons are initially displayed in the upper-right corner of the desktop. The Trash icon operates like the Recycle Bin in Windows or the trash can on the Mac. Drag items to it to hold them for deletion. The AutoStart folder holds programs you want automatically started whenever KDE starts. The Templates folder holds templates for easily creating documents. You can place default document files here, such as default files for Web links, makefiles, or editor files. The panel initially shows small icons for the Applications Starter, window list, your **home** directory, a terminal window, and buttons for virtual desktops, among others. The Window List icon looks like several grouped windows. It displays a list of all open windows and the desktop they are on. The Home Directory icon shows a folder with a house. Click it to open a file manager window showing your **home** directory. The Help Viewer icon is an image of a book. The Terminal Window icon is a picture of a two computer monitors. Click this to open a terminal window where you can enter Linux shell commands.

The desktop supports drag-and-drop operations. For example, to print a document, drag it to the Printer icon. You can place any directories on the desktop by simply dragging them from a file manager window to the desktop. You can also create new ones on the desktop by right-clicking anywhere on the desktop and selecting New and then Directory from the pop-up menu. All items that appear on the desktop are located in the **Desktop** directory in your **home** directory. There you can find the **Trash**, **Templates**, and **AutoStart** directories, along with any others you place on the desktop. To configure your desktop, either click the Desktop icon located on the right of your panel, or right-click the desktop and select the Display Properties entry. This displays a window with several tabbed panels for different desktop settings, such as the background or style.

kdelink Files

On the KDE desktop, special files called *kdelink* files are used to manage a variety of tasks, including device management, Internet connections, program management, and document types. You create a kdelink file by right-clicking the desktop and then selecting New. From this menu, you choose the type of kdelink file you want to create. Application is for launching applications. The File System Devices option creates a kdelink file that can mount devices on your system such as CD-ROMs and floppy disks. The MIME Types option is for kdelink files used to define new MIME types and their associated applications. The Internet Address entry enables you to define a simple kdelink file you can use to access a Web or FTP site. The application, device, and MIME type functions are covered in later sections.

You can create a kdelink file that holds an Internet URL address and then use that kdelink file to access that site directly. You can place the kdelink file on your desktop or put it in your panel, where it is easily accessible. You can configure the file to display any icon you choose. In effect, you can have an icon on your desktop you can click to immediately access a Web site. When you click the URL kdelink file, the file manager starts up and accesses that address, displaying the Web page. For FTP sites, it performs an anonymous login and displays the **remote** directory.

To create a URL kdelink file, right-click the desktop and select the New menu. You then have three possible kinds of URL kdelink files from which to choose. They are all URL kdelink files, but they have different defaults, depending on what use you want. There are entries for an FTP, a Web, and a generic Internet address: FTP URL, World Wide Web URL, and *Internet kAddresss* (*URL*). For a Web URL, select World Wide Web URL. A window appears that displays a box with the name **WWWUrl.kdelink** (for FTP, this is **FTPUrl.kdelink**, and for the Internet address it is **URL.kdelink**—see the following illustration). Replace the prefix, in this case **WWWUrl**, with a name of your own choosing. Be sure to keep the **.kdelink** extension (this is important). For example, to create a kdelink file for the KDE themes Web site, you would enter something like **kdethemes.kdelink**. A kdelink dialog box for URL access is then displayed. This dialog box has three tabbed panels: General, Permissions, and URL. On the General panel is the name of your kdelink file. Go to the URL panel. There, you see a box labeled URL with a default Web URL already in it. Replace it with the URL you want. For example, for KDE themes the URL would be **http://kde.themes.org**. Be sure to include the protocol, such as **http://** or **ftp://**. An Icon button on this panel shows the icon that will be displayed for this kdelink file on your desktop. The default is a Web World icon. You can change it if you want by clicking the Icon button to open a window that lists icons you can choose from. Click OK when you are finished. The kdelink file then appears on your desktop with that icon. Click it to access the Web site. An alternative and easier way to create a URL kdelink file is simply to drag a URL from a Web page displayed on the file manager to your desktop. A kdelink file is automatically generated with that URL. To change the default icon used, you can right-click the file and choose Properties to display the kdelink dialog box. Click the Icon button to choose a new icon.

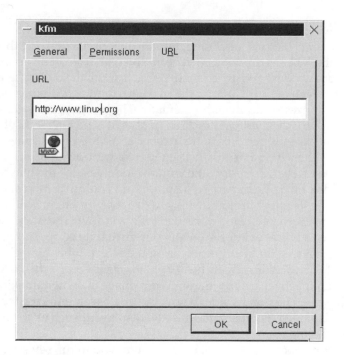

KDE Windows

A KDE window has the same functionality you find in other window managers and desktops. You can resize the window by clicking-and-dragging any of its corners or sides. A side extends the window in that dimension, whereas a corner extends both height and width at the same time. Notice the corners are slightly enhanced. The top of the window has a title bar showing the name of the window. This is the program name in the case of applications and the current directory name for the file manager windows. The active window has the title bar highlighted. Here is an example of a KDE window:

To move the window, click this title bar and drag it where you want. In the right side of the title bar are small buttons for closing, minimizing, or maximizing the window. The button with the X closes the window. The button with a small box maximizes the window, letting the window take up the entire screen. Click the button again to restore the window to its previous size. Clicking the Maximize button with the middle or right mouse button maximizes vertically or horizontally. The button showing a simple period minimizes it. On KDE, when you minimize a window, it is no longer displayed on the desktop, but its button entry remains in the taskbar at the top of the screen. Click that button to redisplay the window. You can also reduce a window to its title bar by double-clicking the title bar. To restore the window, double-click the title bar again.

On the left side of the title bar are two buttons: a Window button and a Stick Pin button. Clicking the Window button displays a drop-down menu with entries for window operations, such as closing or resizing the window. The Stick Pin button next to it is used to have a window appear on all your virtual desktops, no matter to which one you change. In effect, the window sticks on the screen when you change to another virtual desktop. When active, only its head appears, as if you pushed a stick pin into the desktop. When inactive, a side view stick-pin image is shown, making the window appear as if it has been laid on its side. Below the title bar, menus for the particular application are displayed. Toolbars may also be displayed, such as the navigation toolbar used for the file manager.

As a multitasking operating system, Linux enables you to run several applications at the same time. This means you can have several applications open and running on your desktop, each with its own window. You can switch between them by moving from one window to another. When an application is open, a button for it is placed in the taskbar at the top of the desktop. You can switch to that application at any time by clicking its Taskbar button. From the keyboard, you can use the ALT-TAB key combination to display a list of current applications. Holding down the ALT key and sequentially pressing TAB moves you through the list. You can hide an application at any time by clicking its window's Minimize button. The Taskbar button entry for it remains. Click this to restore the application. Table 5-1 shows the KDE keyboard shortcuts.

Virtual Desktops

KDE, as with most Linux window managers, supports virtual desktops. In effect, this extends the desktop area on which you can work. You could have Netscape running on one desktop and be using a text editor in another. KDE can support up to eight virtual desktops, though the default is four. The KDE panel holds a button for each virtual desktop. The buttons are displayed with the names One, Two, Three, and Four:

Keys	Effect
ALT-ESC or CTRL-ESC	Current Session–manager with Logout button
ALT-TAB and ALT-SHIFT-TAB	Traverse the windows of the current desktop
CTRL-TAB and CTRL-SHIFT-TAB	Traverse the virtual desktops
ALT-F2	Open small command-line window
ALT-F3	Window operation menu
ALT-F4	Close window
CTRL-F[1..8]	Switch to a particular virtual desktop
CTRL-ALT-ESC	Force shutdown of X-windows.

Table 5-1.   *KDE Keyboard Shortcuts*

ENVIRONMENTS

As you shall see, you can change these names to whatever you want. To move from one desktop to another, click its button. Clicking Three displays the third desktop, and clicking One moves you back to the first desktop.

Normally, when you open an application on a particular desktop, it appears only in that desktop. When you move to another desktop, the application disappears from your screen. Moving back again shows the application. For example, if you open kmail on the third desktop, and then move to the second desktop, kmail disappears from your screen. Moving back to the third desktop causes kmail to appear again. Selecting the Taskbar button for an application also switches you to the desktop on which the application is open. For example, clicking the kmail Taskbar button switches to the third desktop. You can also use the Window list menu in the panel to display a listing of all open windows in each desktop. Selecting a window entry moves to that desktop. If you want an application to appear on all desktops, no matter which one you move to, click its window's Pin button in the upper-left corner.

If you want to move a window to a different desktop, first open the window's menu by clicking the Window button in the upper-left corner. Then, select the To desktop entry, which lists the available desktops. Choose the one you want. You can also right-click the window's title bar to display the window's menu.

Most window managers use a pager to enable you to switch from one desktop to another. KDE also has a pager, though it is not initially displayed. To display the pager, select Desktop Pager from the System menu in the Applications Starter menu. A four-squared rectangle is displayed, one for each desktop. Click a rectangle to move to that desktop.

You can also configure KDE so if you move the mouse over the edge of a desktop screen, it automatically moves to the adjoining desktop. You need to imagine the desktops arranged in a four-square configuration, with two top desktops next to each other and two desktops below them. You enable this feature by selecting the Active Desktop Borders entry in the Desktop panel in the KDE Control Center.

To change the number of virtual desktops, you use the KPanel configuration window. From the Applications Starter menu, select Panel and then Configure. On the Kpanel configuration window, select the Desktop panel. You then see entries for the current desktops. The visible bar controls the number of desktops. Slide this to the right to add more and to the left to reduce the number. The width bar controls the width of the desktop buttons on the panel. You can change any of the desktop names by clicking a name and entering a new one.

You can also configure desktop features, such as color background, for each virtual desktop. In the Applications Starter menu, select Settings and then Desktop. From this menu, you can choose various features to change. Selecting Background displays a Display Settings window. A list of virtual desktops is then shown. Select the one whose background you want to change, and then you can choose from colors and wallpaper. You can select wallpaper from a preselected list or choose your own.

KDE Panel and Applications Starter

The KDE panel is located at the bottom of the screen:

Through it, you can access most KDE functions. The panel includes icons for menus, directory windows, specific programs, and virtual desktops. At the left end of the panel is an icon with a large *K* on a cog wheel. This is the icon for the KDE Application Starter. Click this icon to display the menu of applications you run. From the KDE menu, you can access numerous submenus for different kinds of applications. You can also open the Application Starter with the ALT-F1 key.

To add an application to the panel, select the Add application entry in the panel submenu located in the Applications Starter. This menu displays all installed KDE applications. To add a button for an application to the panel, click the application entry. You can also drag applications from a File Manager window to the panel directly and have them automatically placed in the panel. The panel only displays kdelink files. When you drag-and-drop a file to the panel, a kdelink file for it is automatically generated.

To configure the panel position and behavior, right-click the panel and select the configure entry. This displays a panel configuration dialog box with several tabbed panels. The Positions panel enables you to specify the edges of the screen where you want your panel and taskbar displayed. You can also enlarge or reduce it in size. On the Options panel, you can set auto-hide options for the panel and taskbar. The

Desktops panel is used for configuring your virtual desktops, enabling you to add more desktops and rename the current ones.

You can add or remove menu items in your Applications Starter menu using the Edit Menus program. Right-click its *K* icon and select Configure. This launches the Edit Menus window, displaying the Applications Starter menu to the right and a menu button to the left, labeled Empty. To add a new item, drag this button to the Launcher menu. You can even place it in a submenu. To enter a label and an application for it to start, you right-click the button. This displays a dialog box with fields for the application program, menu item name, and the MIME types to be associated with the program. You can also specify if you want the program opened in a terminal window. For example, to create a menu entry for the notorious Vi editor, drag the Empty button to the Launcher menu. Right-click it and enter **vi** as the command and **The Vi Editor** as the name. Click the check box for Open in terminal window because Vi is a shell-based program. Before you quit, be sure to select Save from the File menu. You then see an entry for the Vi editor in the Applications Starter menu. You can also delete entries using Edit Menus. On Red Hat systems, when you first start Edit Menus, another menu item is under the empty item labeled Red Hat Menus. These are menus already set up for all your applications that were installed by Red Hat. You can place all these menus on the Applications Starter by dragging this button to the Starter menu. You then see an entry for Red Hat menus that expands to numerous submenus.

KDE Themes

For your desktop, you can select a variety of different themes. A *theme* changes the look and feel of your desktop, affecting the appearance of GUI elements, such as scrollbars, buttons, and icons. For example, you use the Mac OS theme to make your K desktop look like a Macintosh. Themes for the K desktop can be downloaded from the **kde.themes.org** Web site. Information and links for themes for different window managers can be found at **www.themes.org**. You can use the KthemeMgr program to install and change your themes.

The KDE Help System

The KDE Help viewer provides a browser-like interface for accessing and displaying both KDE Help files and Linux man and info files. You can start the Help system either by selecting its entry in the Applications Starter menu or by right-clicking the desktop and selecting the Help entry (see Figure 5-2). You can use a URL format to access man and info pages, info: and man:. For example, man:cp displays the man page for the **cp** command. A navigation toolbar enables you to move through previously viewed documents. KDE Help documents use an HTML format with links you can click to access other documents. Initially, the KDE Help system displays a list of contents with links for access in the KDE applications index for application documentation, the system man pages, and **system info** directory where you can access info documents for

TeX, emacs, and gcc, among others. The **Back** and **Forward** commands move you through the list of previously viewed documents. **Prev**, **Next**, **Up**, and **Top** are commands used for man and info documents. These are arranged in a tree through which you can move up and down. The KDE Help system provides an effective search tool for searching for patterns in Help documents, including man and info pages. Select the Search entry to display a page where you can enter your pattern. You can also click the small icon in the toolbar of a page with a spyglass.

Applications

You can start an application in KDE in several ways. If an entry for it is in the Applications Starter menu, you can select that entry to start the application. Some applications also have buttons on the KDE panel you can click to start them. The panel already holds several of the commonly used programs, such as the kmail and kcalendar. You can also use the file manager to locate a file using that application or the application program itself. Clicking its icon starts the application. Or, you can open a shell window and enter the name of the application at the shell prompt and press ENTER to start an application. You can also use the ALT-F2 keys to open a small window consisting of a box to enter a single command. You can use the up and down arrow keys to display previous commands, and the right and left arrow keys or the backspace keys to edit any of them. Press ENTER to execute a command.

Figure 5-2. *KDE Help System*

You can also access applications directly from your desktop. To access an application from the desktop, either create a kdelink or a standard link file that can link to the original application program. With a kdelink file, you can choose your own icon and specify a tooltip comment. You can also use a kdelink file to start a shell-based application running in its own terminal window. A standard link, on the other hand, is a simple reference to the original program file. Using a link starts the program up directly with no arguments. To create a standard link file, locate the application on your file system, usually in the **/usr/bin** or **/usr/sbin** directory. Then, click-and-drag the application icon to your desktop. In the pop-up menu, select Link. The link has the same icon as the original application. Whenever you click that icon, you can select Start from the pop-up menu to start the application.

To create a kdelink file, you right-click anywhere on the empty desktop, select New from the pop-up menu, and then choose Application. Enter the name for the program and a kdelink file with that name appears on the desktop. A kfm dialog box then opens with four panels: General, Permissions, Execute, and Application. The General panel displays the name of the link with the extension **.kdelink**. To specify the application the kdelink file runs, go to the Execute panel and either enter the application's program name in the Execute box or click Browse to select it. KDE applications are often located in the **/usr/bin** directory and begin with *k*. To select an icon image for the kdelink file, click the Cog icon. The Select icon window is displayed, listing icons from which you can choose. To run a shell-based program such as Vi or Pine, click the Run in terminal check box and specify any terminal options. Certain KDE programs can minimize to a small icon while they are running, and can be displayed in the panel. This is referred to as *Swallowing on the panel*. Enter the name of the program in that Execute box.

On the Permissions panel, be sure to set execute permissions so the program can be run. In the Application panel, you can specify the type of documents to be associated with this application. The bottom of the panel shows two lists. The left list is for MIME types you want associated with this program, and the right list is the listing of available MIME types from which to choose. To add a MIME type, select an entry in the right list and click the Left Arrow button. Use the Right Arrow button to remove a MIME type. On the panel, you also specify the comment, the file manager program name, and the name in your language. The comment is the Help note that appears when you pass your mouse over the icon. For the file manager program name, enter the name followed by a semicolon. This is the name used for the link, if you use the file manager to display it. kdelinks needn't reside on the desktop. You can place them in any directory and access them through the file manager. You can later make changes to a kdelink file by right-clicking its icon and selecting Properties from the pop-up menu. This again displays the kfm dialog box for this file. You can change its icon and even the application it runs. You can download other icons from **icons.themes.org**.

You can have KDE automatically display selected directories or start certain applications whenever it starts up. To do so, place links for these windows and applications in the **AutoStart** directory. You see the AutoStart folder displayed on your desktop. To place a link for a directory in the AutoStart folder, first locate the Directory icon using the file manager. Then, click-and-drag the icon to the AutoStart folder. From the pop-up menu that appears, select Link (do not select Copy or Move). Whenever you start KDE, that directory is displayed in a file manager window. You can do the same for applications and files. Locate the application with the file manager and click-and-drag it to the AutoStart folder, selecting Link. For a file, do the same. Whenever KDE starts, those applications automatically start. For files, the application associated with it starts using that file. For example, to start kmail automatically, click-and-drag its icon to the AutoStart folder, selecting Link.

Mounting CD-ROMs and Floppy Disks from the Desktop

With KDE, you can create icons on your desktop that you can use to easily access a CD-ROM or floppy disk. The icons are *kdelink files,* which are special files that can perform a variety of tasks, including accessing devices such as CD-ROMs. Once you set up a kdelink file for your CD-ROM, to access a CD-ROM disk, place the CD-ROM disk in your CD-ROM drive and click the CD-ROM icon. The file manager window then opens, displaying the contents of the CD-ROM's top-level directory. You can also right-click the icon to display a pop-up menu with an entry to mount the disk. When the CD-ROM holds a mounted CD disk, the CD-ROM icon displays a small red rectangle on its image. Unlike Windows systems, the CD-ROM disk remains locked in the CD-ROM drive until you unlock it. To unmount the CD, right-click the CD-ROM's icon and select Unmount from the pop-up menu. You can then open the CD-ROM drive and remove the CD.

To access a floppy disk, you can perform a similar operation using the Floppy Disk icon. Place the floppy disk in the disk drive and click the Floppy Disk icon. This displays a file manager window with the contents of the floppy disk. Or, you can right-click the ion to display a pop-up menu with an entry to mount the disk. Once mounted, you can access it, copying files to and from the disk. Be careful not to remove the disk unless you first unmount it. To unmount the disk, right-click its icon and select Unmount from the icon's pop-up menu. You can perform one added operation with the floppy disk. If you put in a blank disk, you can format it. You can choose from several file system formats, including MS-DOS. To format a standard Linux file system, select the ext2 entry.

A kdelink you use for your CD-ROM is a special kind of kdelink file designed for file system devices. To create one, first right-click anywhere on the desktop, select New, and then File System Device. A window appears prompting you for a filename for the kdelink file. It shows a default name **device.kdelink**. Replace **device** with the name you want, and be sure to keep the **.kdelink** extension. For example, for a CD-ROM, you could have **cdrom.kdelink**. The kdelink icon then appears on your desktop with a question mark, indicating the device is not yet configured. Right-click this icon and select the Properties entry. In the Properties window, change to the Device panel and, in the box labeled Device, enter the full pathname for the device (see Figure 5-3). Devices are located in the **/dev** directory. A device name for an IDE CD-ROM is usually **/dev/hdc**. For the mount point, enter the directory where you want the device mounted. For a CD-ROM, this is usually **/mnt/cdrom**. See the chapter on file administration, Chapter 26, for a discussion on devices and file systems. You can then select images for Unmounted and Mounted icons. To select the Mounted icon, click the Mounted icon to display a list of icons from which to choose. Do the same for the Unmounted icon. The kdelink file does not perform the necessary system administration operations that enable access to the CD-ROM by ordinary users. Normally, only the systems administrator (root user) can mount or unmount CD-ROMS and floppy disks. You also must make sure an entry is in the /etc/fstab file for the CD-ROM or floppy drive. If not, you have to add one. Such operations are fairly easy to perform using the file system management tools provided by Linuxconf and fsconf. Check Chapter 3 and Chapter 24 for the procedures to use.

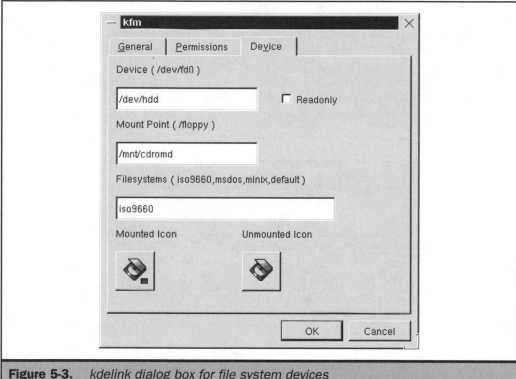

Figure 5-3.   *kdelink dialog box for file system devices*

KDE File Manager and Internet Client: kfm

The *KDE file manager* is a multifunctional utility with which you can manage files, start programs, browse the Web, and download files from remote sites (see Figure 5-4). Traditionally, the term "file manager" was used to refer to managing files on a local hard disk. The KDE file manager extends its functionality well beyond this traditional function because it is Internet capable, seamlessly displaying remote file systems as if they were your own, as well as viewing Web pages with browser capabilities.

A KDE file manager window consists of a menu bar, a navigation toolbar, a location field, a status bar, and a pane of file and directory icons for the current working directory. When you first display the file manager window, it displays the file and subdirectory icons for your **home** directory. The files listed in a directory can be viewed in several different ways. You can view files and directories as icons, small icons, or in a detailed listing. The detailed listing provides permissions, owner, group, and size information. Permissions are the permissions controlling access to this file (see Chapter 8). Configuration files are not usually displayed. These are files beginning with a period and are often referred to as *dot files*. To have the file manager display these files, select Show Dot Files from the View menu.

To search for files, select the Find entry in the File menu. This opens a dialog box with which you can search for filenames using wildcard matching symbols, such as *****. Click the small image of a looking glass in the toolbar to run the search and on the stoplight to stop it (see Figure 5-5). The search results are displayed in a pane in the lower half of the search window. You can click a file and have it open with its appropriate application. Text files are displayed by the kwrite text editor and images are displayed by kview. Applications

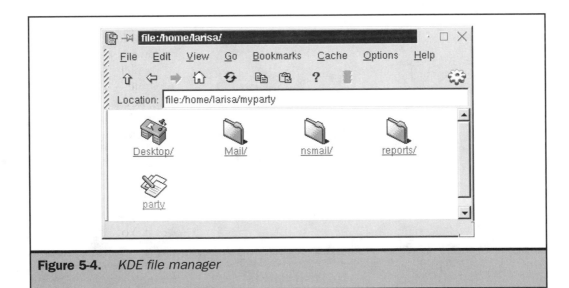

Figure 5-4.   *KDE file manager*

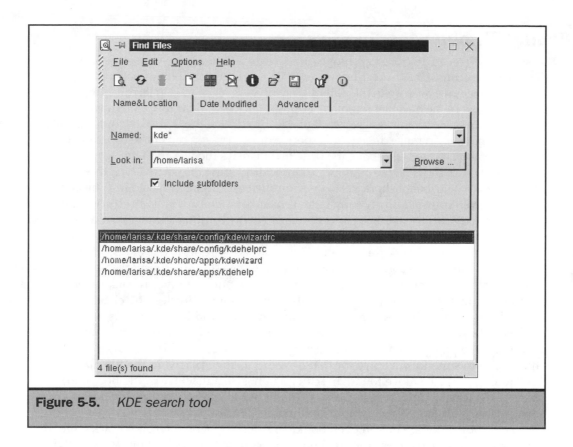

Figure 5-5.   *KDE search tool*

are run. The search program also enables you to save your search results for later reference. You can even select files from the search and add them to an archive.

You can open a file either by clicking it or by selecting it, and then choosing the Open entry in the File menu. A single-click opens the file, not a double-click. If you want to select the file or directory, you need to hold down the CTRL key while you click it. A selection is performed with a CTRL-click. If the file is a program, that program starts up. If it is a data file, such as a text file, then the associated application is run using that data file. For example, if you click a text file, the kwrite application starts displaying that file. If KFM cannot determine the application to use, it opens a dialog box prompting you to enter the application name. You can click the Browse button on this box to use a directory tree to locate the application program you want.

The file manager can also extract tar archives and install RPM packages. An *archive* is a file ending in **.tar.gz**, **.tar**, or **.tgz**. Clicking the archive lists the files in it. You can extract a particular file simply by dragging it out the window. Clicking a text file displays it with kwrite, while clicking an image file displays it with kview. Selecting an RPM package opens it with the kpackage utility, which you can then use to install the package.

Moving Through the File System

A single-click on a Directory icon moves to that directory and displays its file and Subdirectory icons. Unlike other interfaces, KDE does not use double-clicking to open a directory. To move back up to the parent directory, you click the Up Arrow button located on the left end of the navigation toolbar. A single-click on a Directory icon moves you down the directory tree, one directory at a time. By clicking the Up Arrow button, you move up the tree. To move directly to a specific directory, you can enter its pathname in the location box located just above the pane that displays the File and Directory icons. Figure 5-4 shows the KDE file manager window displaying the current directory. You can also use several keyboard shortcuts to perform such operations, as listed in Table 5-2.

Like a Web browser, the file manager remembers the previous directories it has displayed. You can use the Back and Forward Arrow buttons to move through this list of prior directories. For example, a user could use the Location field to move to the **~/birthday** directory, and use it again to move to the **~/reports** directory. Clicking the Back Arrow button displays the ~/**birthday** directory (the ~ represents the user's home directory). Then, clicking the Forward Arrow button moves it back to the **~/reports** directory. You can move directly to your **home** directory by clicking the Home button. This has the same effect as the **cd** command in the shell. If you know you want to access particular directories again, you can bookmark them, much as you do a Web page. Just open the directory and select the Add Bookmarks entry in the Bookmarks menu. An entry for that directory is then placed in the file manager's Bookmark menu. To move to the directory again, select its entry in the Bookmark menu. This is helpful for directories you might use frequently or for directories you must access with lengthy or complex pathnames. Bookmarks also apply to individual files and applications. You can even bookmark desktop icons. To bookmark a file, first select a file, and then choose the Add Bookmarks entry in the Bookmark menu. Later, selecting that bookmark opens that file. You can do the same thing with applications, where selecting the application's bookmark starts the application. Each bookmark is a file placed in your **.kde/share/apps/kfm/bookmarks** directory. You can go to this directory and change the names of any of the files and they then appear as changed on your Bookmark menu. These files are kdelink files. To change their names, right-click the file and select Properties from the pop-up menu. In the dialog box displayed, you see the filename is the full pathname with a **.kdelink** extension on a panel tabbed General. You can replace the pathname with one of your own choosing, but keep the **.kdelink** extension—for example, **myreport.kdelink**. This bookmark would then appear as **myreport**. The pathname used to access the file is actually on the URL panel.

To help you navigate from one directory to another, you can use the Location field or the directory tree. In the Location field, you can enter the pathname of a directory, if you know it, and press ENTER. The file manager then displays that directory. The directory tree provides a tree listing all directories on your system and in your **home** directory. You can activate the directory tree by selecting Show Tree entry in the View

KEYS	Description
ALT-LEFT ARROW	Back in History
ALT-RIGHT ARROW	Forward in History
ALT-UP ARROW	One directory up
ENTER	Open a file/directory
ESC	Open a pop-up menu for the current file
LEFT/RIGHT/UP/DOWN ARROWS	Move among the icons
SPACEBAR	Select/unselect file
PAGE UP	Scroll up fast
PAGE DOWN	Scroll down fast
RIGHT ARROW	Scroll right (on Web pages)
LEFT ARROW	Scroll left (on Web pages)
UP ARROW	Scroll up (on Web pages)
DOWN ARROW	Scroll down (on Web pages)
CTRL-C	Copy selected file to Clipboard
CTRL-V	Paste files from Clipboard to current directory
CTRL-S	Select files by pattern
CTRL-T	Open a terminal in the current directory
CTRL-L	Open new location
CTRL-F	Find files
CTRL-W	Close window

Table 5-2.   *KDE File Manager Keyboard Shortcuts*

menu. The directory tree has three main entries: **Root**, **My Home**, and **Desktop**. The **Root** entry displays the directories starting from the system root directory, the **My Home** entry displays directories starting from your **home** directory, and the **Desktop** entry displays the files and links on your desktop. Click a side triangle to expand a directory entry, and click a down triangle of an expanded directory entry to hide it.

ENVIRONMENTS

Internet Access

The KDE file manager doubles as a Web browser and an FTP client. It includes a box for entering either a pathname for a local file, or an URL for a Web page on the Internet or your intranet. A navigation toolbar can be used to display previous Web pages or previous directories. When accessing a Web page, the page is displayed as on any Web browser. With the navigation toolbar, you can move back and forth through the list of previously displayed pages in that session. This feature is particularly convenient for displaying local Web pages, such as documentation in HTML format. Most Linux distributions provide extensive documentation in the form of Web pages you can easily access and display using a KDE file manager window. Red Hat Web page documentation is located at **/usr/doc/HTML**. Figure 5-6 shows the KDE file manager window, operating as a Web browser, displaying a Web page.

The KDE file manager also operates as an FTP client. When you access an FTP site, you navigate the remote directories as you would your own. The operations to download a file are the same as copying a file on your local system. Just select the file's

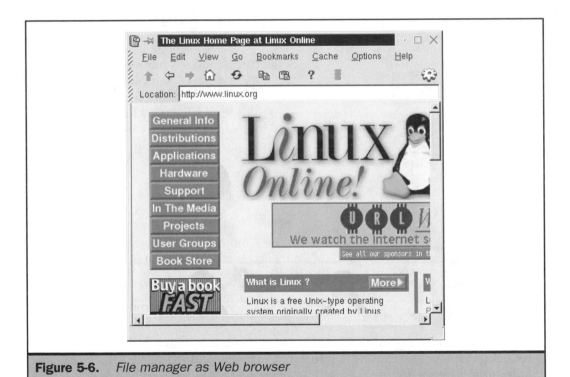

Figure 5-6.   *File manager as Web browser*

icon or entry in the file manager window and drag it to a window showing the local directory to which you want it downloaded. Then, select the Copy entry from the pop-up menu that appears.

By default, KDE attempts an anonymous login. If you want to perform a nonanonymous login as a particular user, add the username with an @ symbol before the FTP address. You are then prompted for the user password. For example, the following entry logs in to the **ftp.mygames.com** server as the chris user:

```
ftp://chris@ftp.mygames.com
```

Copy, Move, Delete, and Archive Operations

To perform an operation on a file or directory, you first have to select it. In KDE, to select a file or directory, you hold the CTRL key down, while clicking the file's icon or listing. To select more than one file, continually hold the CTRL key down while you click the files you want. Or, you can use the keyboard arrow keys to move from one file icon to another, and then use the spacebar to select the file you want.

To copy and move files, you can use the standard drag-and-drop method with your mouse. To copy a file, you locate it by using the file manager. Open another file manager window to the directory to which you want the file copied. Then, click-and-drag the File icon to that window (be sure to keep holding down the mouse button). A pop-up menu appears with selections for Move, Copy, or Link. Choose Copy. To move a file to another directory, follow the same procedure, but select Move from the pop-up menu. To copy or move a directory, use the same procedure as for files. All the directory's files and subdirectories are also copied or moved.

You can also move or copy files using the **Copy** and **Paste** commands. First, use a CTRL-click to select a file or directory (hold the CTRL key down while clicking the File icon). Either select the Copy entry from the Edit menu or click the Copy button in the navigation bar. Change to the directory to which you want to copy the selected file. Then, either select Paste from the Edit menu or click the Paste button. Follow the same procedure for moving files, using the Move entry from the Edit menu or the Move button in the navigation toolbar. Most of the basic file manager operations can be selected from a pop-up menu displayed whenever you right-click a file or directory. Here, you can find entries for copying, moving, and deleting the file, as well as navigating to a different directory.

Distinguishing between a copy of a file or directory and a link is important. A *copy* creates a duplicate, whereas a *link* is just another name for the same item. Links are used extensively as ways of providing different access points to the same document. If you want to access a file using an icon on your desktop, creating a link on the desktop, rather than a copy, is best. With a copy, you have two different documents, whereas, with a link, you are accessing and changing the same document. To create a link on your desktop, click-and-drag the File icon from the directory window to the desktop and select Link from the pop-up menu. Clicking the link brings up the original document. Deleting the link only removes the link, not the original document. You can create links for directories or applications using the same procedure. You can also place links in a directory: click-and-drag the files to which you want to link in to that directory and select Link from the pop-up menu.

You delete a file by removing it immediately or placing it in a Trash folder to delete later. To delete a file, select it and then choose the Delete entry in the Edit menu. You can also right-click the icon and select Delete. To place a file in the Trash folder, click-and-drag it to the Trash icon on your desktop or select Move to Trash from the Edit menu. You can later open the Trash folder and delete the files. To delete all the files in the Trash folder, right-click the Trash icon and select Empty Trash Bin from the pop-up menu. To restore any files in the Trash bin, open the Trash bin and drag them out of the Trash folder.

Each file and directory has properties associated with it that include permissions, the filename, and its directory. To display the properties window for a given file, right-click the file's icon and select the Properties entry. On the General panel, you see the name of the file displayed. To change the file's name, replace the name there with a new one. Permissions are set on the Permissions panel. Here, you can set read, write, and execute permissions for user, group, or other access to the file. See Chapter 8 for a discussion of permissions. The group entry enables you to change the group for a file.

.directory

KDE automatically searches for and reads an existing **.directory** file located in a directory. A **.directory** file holds KDE configuration information used to determine how the directory is displayed. You can create such a file in a directory and place a setting in it to set display features, such as the icon to use to display the directory folder.

KDE Configuration: KDE Control Center

With the KDE Control Center, you can configure your desktop and system, changing the way it is displayed and the features it supports (see Figure 5-7). You can open the Control Center directly to a selected component by selecting its entry in the Applications Starter Settings menu. The Settings menu displays a submenu listing the configuration categories. Select a category, and then select the component you want. For example, to configure your screen saver, select the screen saver config entry in the Desktop menu located in the Settings menu. The Control Center can be directly started by either clicking the Control Center icon in the panel or selecting Control Center from the Applications Starter menu.

The Control Center window is divided into two panes. The left pane shows a tree view of all the components you can configure and the right pane displays the dialog windows for a selected component. On the left pane, components are arranged into categories whose titles you can expand or shrink. The Applications heading holds entries for configuring the KDE file manager's Web browser features, as well as its file

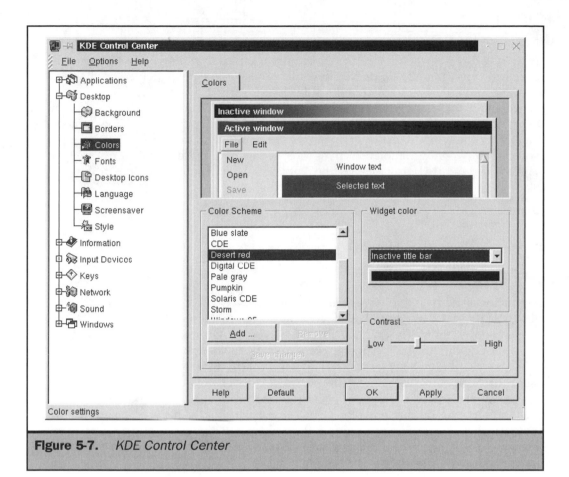

Figure 5-7.   *KDE Control Center*

management operations. Under Desktop, you can set different features for displaying and controlling your desktop. For example, the Background entry enables you to select a different background color or image for each one of your virtual desktops. Other desktop entries enable you to configure components such as the screen saver, the language used, and the window style. Some entries enable you to configure your mouse, key mappings, network connections, sound events, and window components. You can change key bindings for any of the window operations or standard operations, such as cut-and-paste. You can also change any of the specialize key mappings, such as the ALT-TAB key, that moves through your open applications, CTRL-TAB that moves through your virtual desktops, or ALT-F2 that display a dialog box for executing commands. Configuration components are actually modules. In future releases, more modules will be included as more applications and tools are added to the K desktop. See the Help viewer for a current listing of K desktop configuration modules.

ENVIRONMENTS

.kde/share/config

Your **.kde** directory holds files and directories used to maintain your KDE desktop. The **.desktops** directory holds KDE link files whose icons are displayed on the desktop. Configuration files are located in the **.kde/share/config** directory. Here, you can find the general KDE configuration file **kfmrc,** as well as configuration files for different KDE components. **krootwmrc** holds configuration commands for your root window, **kwmrc** for the window manager, **ksoundrc** for sound, and **kcmpanelrc** for your panel. You can place configuration directives directly in any of these files—for example, to have the left mouse button display the Applications Starter menu on the desktop, place the following lines in your **krootwmrc** file:

```
[MouseButtons]
 Left=Menu
```

MIME Types

As you install new kinds of programs, they may use files of a certain type. In that case, you must register the type with KDE, so it can be associated with a given application or group of applications. For example, the MIME type for **.Gif** images is **image/gif**, which is associated with image-viewing programs. You use a kdelink file to create a new MIME type for KDE. Right-click the desktop and select MIME from the New menu. Type the name for the kdelink file, keeping the **.kdelink** extension, and click OK. The Properties dialog box then appears with three panels: General, Permissions, and Bindings. Click the Bindings tab, and then enter the possible extensions for the file type, using an * to match the prefix. For example, ***.gif; *.GIF** would match any file ending with **.gif**. Type a comment and then the MIME type, such as **image/gif**. Select a default application and an icon to use for files of that type.

KDE Directories and Files

On Red Hat systems, KDE is installed in the standard system directories, such as /usr/bin, /usr/lib, and /usr/share, whereas on other distributions, KDE is installed in the **/opt/kde** directory. KDE core programs, along with KDE applications, are held in the **/usr/bin** directory. KDE libraries are located in the **/usr/lib** directory.

The directories located in **/usr/share** contain files used to configure your KDE environment. **/usr/share/applnk** maps its files to the Applications Launcher menu. Its directories and subdirectories appear as menu items and submenus on the main menu. Their contents consist of kdelink files, one for each menu entry. The **/usr/share/apps** file contains files and directories set up by KDE applications. **/usr/share/mimelnk** holds MIME type definitions. **/usr/share/config** contains the configuration files for particular KDE applications. For example, **kfmrc** holds configuration entries for displaying and using the kfm file manager. These are the system-wide defaults that can be overridden by a user's own configurations in their own **.kde/share/config** directory. **/opt/share/icons** holds the default icons used on your KDE desktop and by KDE applications. The **/usr/share** directory also holds files for other configuration elements such as wallpaper, toolbars, and languages.

The **.kde** directory holds a user's own KDE configuration for the desktop and its applications. The **.kde/share** directory holds user versions of the **/usr/kde/share** directories, specifying user configurations for menus, icons, MIME types, sounds, and applications. **.kde/share/config** holds configuration files with users' own configuration specifications for their use of KDE applications. For example, **desktop4rc** holds display configurations the user set up for the fourth virtual desktop. **.kde/share/icons** holds the icons for a user's particular themes, and **.kde/share/sounds** holds sound files. **.kde/share/applnk** holds the kdelink files for the menu entries in the Personal section of the Applications Launcher menu added by the user. In a user's **home** directory, the **.kderc** file contains current desktop configuration directives for resources such as key bindings, colors, and window styles.

Each user has a **Desktop** directory that holds KDE link files for all icons and folders on the user's desktop (see Table 5-3). These include the AutoStart, Trash, and Template folders. The AutoStart folder holds links to applications that are automatically started

System KDE Directories	Description
/usr/bin	KDE programs
/usr/lib	KDE libraries
/usr/man	KDE **man** directory
/usr/include	Header files for use in compiling and developing KDE applications
/usr/share/config	KDE desktop and application configuration files
/usr/share/applnk	kdelink files used to build the main menu
/usr/share/apps	Files used by KDE applications
/usr/share/icons	Icons used in KDE desktop and applications
/usr/share/sounds	Sounds used in KDE desktop and applications
/usr/share/doc	KDE Help system
/usr/doc/kde	KDE documentation
KDEDIR	System variable that holds KDE directory for other distributions, **KDEDIR=/opt/kde**

Table 5-3.   *KDE Installation Directories*

User KDE Directories	Description
.kde/share/config	User KDE desktop and application configuration files for user-specified features
.kde/share/applnk	kdelink files used to build the user's personal menu entries on the KDE main menu
.kde/share/apps	Directories and files used by KDE applications.
.kde/share/icons	Icons used in the user's KDE desktop and applications, such as the ones for the user-specified theme
.kde/share/sounds	Sounds used in KDE desktop and applications
.kderc	User configurations directives for desktop resources
Desktop	Holds kdelink files for icons and folders displayed on the user's KDE desktop
Desktop/Templates	Template kdelink files
Desktop/Trash	Trash folder for files marked for deletion
Desktop/AutoStart	Applications automatically started up with KDE.

Table 5-3.   *KDE Installation Directories* (continued)

up whenever KDE starts. The Trash folder holds files you want to delete, and the Templates folder holds default kdelink files you can use as a basis for creating particular kdelink files.

System Configuration Using KDE

KDE provides some system administration tools, though for most tasks, using Linuxconf is preferable. You can easily run Linuxconf or any of the Red Hat system tools on your KDE desktop. You can access the KDE system administration tools through the root desktop. Log in as the root user and start KDE. You then find system tools in both the System and the Utilities menu in the Applications Starter menu. **kuser** provides a KDE interface for managing users on your system. You can add or remove users, or set permissions for current ones. The K desktop provides two utilities for viewing and managing your processes: the KDE Task Manager (KTop) and the KDE Process Manager (**kpm**). The SysV Init Editor is a version of the System V Init Manager (see Chapter 16). You can use the SysV Init Editor to start and stop servers and to determine at what run level they will start. See the chapter on system administration, Chapter 27, for a more detailed discussion on administration tasks. With **kppp**, you can connect to the Internet using a modem. Use **kppp** to connect to *an Internet service provider (ISP)* that supports the PPP protocols. **kppp** is discussed in more detail in the chapter on network administration, Chapter 28. **kpackage** enables you to manage the RPM packages you have installed. You can use it to install new packages, see the ones that are installed, and easily display information about the package. With **kpackage**, you can list the files in a particular package and display the release information. You can even display text files, such as Readme and configuration files. This is an easy way to find out exactly where an application's program and configuration files are installed on your system.

Updating KDE

Currently, new versions of KDE are being released frequently, sometimes every few months. KDE releases are designed to enable users to upgrade their older versions easily. Be sure to obtain the release for your particular distributions (though you can install from the source code if you want). Packages tailored for various distributions can be downloaded through the KDE Web site at **www.kde.org** or directly from the KDE FTP site at **ftp.kde.org** and its mirror sites. RPM packages for Red Hat can be obtained from its FTP site in the **updates** directory for the current Red Hat distribution, **ftp.redhat.com**.

First, log in as the root user, and then create a directory to hold the KDE files. Then connect to an FTP site. You can use a Web browser such as Netscape, but using an FTP client such as FTP, IglooFTP, or even the KDE file manager is preferable. Download the files for the new version to your new directory. For Red Hat, these are a series of RPM package files. To download using FTP, be sure to turn off prompts with the **prompt** command and use **mget *** to download all the files at once. With GUI FTP clients like IglooFTP, you may be able to select the entire directory at once to download. With the KDE file manager, select the files and drag them to a window open to the local directory and select Copy from the pop-up menu.

Current KDE releases from the KDE FTP site feature an install script called **install-kde**. For distributions that use RPM packages, you first install the kde-installer package. This installs the install script. Then execute the following command. The various KDE packages are then installed in proper order, replacing or upgrading older versions. For RPM packages obtained from Red Hat, you can simply install the KDE packages along with any other RPM updated packages, or use the Red Hat update agent to install any KDE updates automatically on the Red Hat FTP site.

```
rpm -Uvh kde-installer-1.1.2-*rh*.i386.rpm
install-kde-1.1.2
```

To install a particular KDE RPM package manually, you use the **rpm** command with the **-Uvh** options. This example installs the kdenetwork package:

```
Rpm -Uvh  kdenetwork-1.1.2.2.i386.rpm
```

The
Complete
Reference

Chapter 6

The X Window System
and Window Managers

Instead of the command line interface, you can use an *X Window System* (*X*) GUI to interact with your Linux system. With such an interface, you can use icons, windows, and menus to issue commands and run applications. Unlike PC-based GUIs, such as Windows or the Mac OS, Linux and UNIX systems divide the GUI into three separate components: The X Window System, window managers, and program/file managers. The X Window System, also known as *X* and *X11*, is an underlying standardized graphic utility that provides basic graphic operations, such as opening windows or displaying images. A window manager handles windowing operations, such as resizing and moving windows. Window managers vary in the way windows are displayed, using different borders and window menus. All, however, use the same underlying X graphic utility. A file manager handles file operations using icons and menus, and a program manager runs programs, often enabling you to select commonly used programs from a taskbar. Unlike window managers, file and program managers can differ greatly in their capabilities. In most cases, different file and program managers can run on the same window manager.

All Linux and UNIX systems use the same standard underlying X graphics utility. This means, in most cases, that an X Window System–based program can run on any of the window managers and desktops. X Window System–based software is often found at Linux or UNIX FTP sites in directories labeled **X11**. You can download these packages and run them on any window manager running on your Linux system. Some may already be in the form of Linux binaries you can download, install, and run directly. Netscape is an example. Others are in the form of source code that can easily be configured, compiled, and installed on your system with a few simple commands. Some applications, such as Motif applications, may require special libraries.

With a window manager, you can think of a window as taking the place of a command line. Operations you perform through the window are interpreted and sent to the Linux system for execution. Window managers operate off the underlying X Window System, which actually provides the basic window operations that enable you to open, move, and close windows, as well as to display menus and select icons. FVWM2 and AfterStep manage these operations, each in its own way, providing their own unique interfaces. The advantage of such a design is that you can have different window managers that can operate on the same Linux system. In this sense, Linux is not tied to one type of *graphical user interface* (*GUI*). On the same Linux system, one user may be using FVWM, another may be using the Xview window manager, and still another may be using, the Enlightenment window manager, all at the same time. You can find out detailed information about different window managers available for Linux from the X11 Web site at **www.X11.org**. The site provides reviews, screenshots, and links to home sites, as well as a comparison table listing the features available for the different window managers. Linux window mangers are listed in Table 6-1 along with the Web sites where you can access them.

Window Manager	Command	Description	Internet Sites
AfterStep	**afterstep**	Based on the NeXTSTEP interface	**www.afterstep.org ftp.afterstep.org afterstep.themes.org**
amiwn	**amiwn**	An Amiga window manager interface	**www.lysator.liu.se/ ~marcus/amiwn.html**
Blackbox	**blackbox**	Simple and fast window manager	**blackbox.wiw.org blackbox.themes.org**
Enlightenment	**enlightenment**	Window manager supporting themes	**www.enlightenment.org e.themes.org**
eXode		Enhanced X Open Desktop	**http://www.simplicity .net/exode/**
FVWM2	**fvwm2**	The Free Virtual Window Manager (v. 1.24)	**www.fvwm.org fvwm.themes.org**
FVWM95	**fvwm95**	Windows 95 interface	**ftp://mitac11.uia.ac.be /html-test/fvwm95.html**
Gnome	**gnome-session**	GNU Network Object Model-Environment	**www.gnome.org ftp.gnome.org gnome.themes.org**
IceWM	**icewm**	Ice window manager	**www.kiss.uni-lj.si /~k4fr0235/icewm/**

Table 6-1.   *Window Managers*

Window Manager	Command	Description	Internet Sites
The K desktop	**startkde**	The K Desktop Environment	**www.kde.org ftp.kde.org kde.themes.org**
LessTif	**mwm**	A clone of Motif	**www.lesstif.org**
Macintosh-like Virtual Window Manager	**mlvwm**	A clone of the Macintosh interface	**http://www2u.biglobe.ne .jp/~y-miyata/mlvwm.html**
Motif	**mwm**	Motif window manager	
Q Virtual Window Manager	**qvwm**	Windows 95 interface	**qvwm.kuntrynet.com**
Scheme-Configurable Window Manager	**scwn**	Highly configurable, based on FVWM2	**huis-clos.mit.edu/scwm**
TWM	**twm**	Tom's window manager	
WindowMaker	**wmaker**	Originally based on NeXTSTEP	**www.windowmaker.org ftp.windowmaker.org wm.themes.org**
Xview	**olwm olvwm**	The Xview window manager (OpenLook)	**metalab.unc.edu/pub /Linux/libs/X/xview**

Table 6-1.   *Window Managers* (continued)

Window, File, and Program Managers

With a window manager, you can use your mouse to perform windowing operations, such as opening, closing, resizing, and moving windows. Several window managers are available for Linux (see Table 6-1). Some of the more popular ones are

Enlightenment (enlightenment), Window Maker (wmaker), AfterStep (afterstep), and the Free Virtual Window Manager 2.0 (FVWM2). Window Maker and AfterStep are originally based on the NeXTSTEP interface used for the NeXT operating system. Enlightenment is the default window manager for Gnome. Red Hat provides its own configuration of FVWM2 called Another Level. Red Hat distributions currently include Enlightenment, Window Maker, AfterStep, and Another Level (FVWM2). Enlightenment is used as the default window manager for Gnome and Another Level for a standard X Window system environment.

Window managers operate through the underlying X graphics utility. The X Window System actually provides the basic operations that enable you to open, move, and close windows, as well as display menus and select icons. Window managers manage these operations each in their own way, providing different interfaces from which to choose. All window managers, no matter how different they may appear, use X Window System tools. In this sense, Linux is not tied to one type of graphical user interface. On the same Linux system, one user may be using the FVWM2 window manager, another may be using Enlightenment, and yet another, Window Maker.

Window managers originally provided only basic window-management operations such as the opening, closing, and resizing of windows. Their features have been enhanced in the more sophisticated window managers, such as Window Maker and Enlightenment, to include support for virtual desktops, docking panels, and themes that enable users to change the look and feel of their desktop. However, to work with files and customize applications, you need to use file and program managers. With a file manager, you can copy, move, or erase files within different directory windows. With a program manager, you can execute commands and run programs using taskbars and program icons. A desktop program combines the capabilities of window, file, and program managers, providing a desktop metaphor with icons and menus to run programs and access files. Gnome and the K Desktop are two such desktop programs. See Table 6-1 for a listing of window managers and desktops along with their Web sites where you can obtain more information.

Several window managers have been enhanced to include many of the features of a desktop. The window managers included on many Linux distributions have program management capabilities in addition to window handling. FVWM2 and Afterstep have a taskbar and a workplace menu you can use to access all your X programs. With either the menu or the taskbar, you can run any X program directly from FVWM2. Window Maker provides a NeXTSTEP interface that features a docking panel for your applications with drag-and-drop support. You can drag files to the application icon to start it with that file.

Using only a window manager, you can run any X program. Window managers have their own workspace menu and taskbar. You can also run any X program from an Xterm terminal window. You can type the name of an X application there. When you press ENTER, the X application starts up with its own window. Invoking an X application as a background process is best accomplished by adding an ampersand after the command. A separate window opens for the X application in which you can work. Selecting one window manager over another does not, in any way, preclude you from running any X applications. All X applications run on any window manager. Even Gnome and KDE applications run on any window manager, provided you have installed Gnome and KDE.

Window Managers

Instead of the command line interface, you can use an X window manager and file manager, which enable you to interact with your Linux system using windows, buttons, and menus. Window managers provide basic window management operations such as opening, closing, and resizing windows, and file managers enable you to manage and run programs using icons and menus. The X Window System supports a variety of window managers. Several of these are listed in Table 6-1, along with Web sites from which you can download them.

Windows and Icons

You run applications, display information, or list files in windows. A window is made up of several basic components. The outer border contains resize controls. Various buttons enable you to control the size of a window or to close the window. Inside the outer border are the main components of the window: The title bar, which displays the name of the window; the menu, through which you can issue commands; and the window pane, which displays the contents of a window. You can change a window's size and shape using buttons and resize areas. The resize areas are the corner borders of the window. Click and hold a resize area and move the mouse to make the window larger or smaller in both height and width. You can make the window fill the whole screen using a maximize operation. Most windows managers include a small button in the upper-right corner, which you can click to maximize the window. To reduce the window to its original size, click the Maximize button again. If you want to reduce the window to an icon, click the Minimize button. (it's the small square with a dot in the center next to the Maximize button). Once you reduce the window to an icon, you can reopen it later by double-clicking that icon.

You can move any window around the desktop by selecting either its title bar or its border (not a corner). Move your mouse pointer to the window's title bar; and then click and hold it while you move your mouse pointer. You can see the window move. When you reach the position you want, release the mouse button. Clicking the title bar moves the window to the front of any overlapping windows. The same process holds true for borders. Move the mouse pointer to the edge of the window until you see the pointer transform into a small straight line. Then click and hold that edge, and then move the mouse pointer. You can then see the entire window move.

Applications designed as X programs have their own menus, buttons, and even icons within their windows. You execute commands in such X applications using menus and icons. If you are running an application, such as an editor, the contents of the window are data on which the menus operate. If you are using the file manager, the contents are icons representing files and directories. The desktop file manager is discussed in the next chapter on directories and files. Some windows, such as terminal windows, do not have menus.

You can have several windows open at the same time. Only one of those windows will be active, however. The active windows have dark borders, and the inactive windows have light borders. On some window managers, just moving your mouse pointer to a particular window makes it the active window, rendering all others inactive. On others, you need to click its title bar. Most window managers enable the user to configure the method for making the window active. In FVWM2, overlapping windows sometimes cause confusion. Making a window active does not automatically bring it to the front. An active window could still be partially hidden by other overlapping windows. To bring a window to the front, you need to click that window's title bar. Clicking anywhere else on the window only makes it the active window; it does not bring the window to the front (though this is configurable). Icons represent either applications you can run or data files for those applications. They appear on your desktop window and within file manager windows, with the name of the file or application below them. To run an application, double-click its icon.

Themes

Many window managers such as Enlightenment, Window Maker, AfterStep, and FVWM2 support themes. Themes change the look and feel for widgets on your desktop, providing different background images, animation, and sound events. With themes, users with the same window manager may have desktops that appear radically different. The underlying functionality of the window manager does not change. You can easily download themes from Web sites and install them on your window manager. New ones are constantly being added. Information and links to window manager theme sites can be found at **http://themes.org**.

Workspace Menu

Most window managers provide a menu through which you can start applications, perform window configurations, and exit the window manager. This menu operates similarly to the Start window on Microsoft Windows. Window managers give it different names: Enlightenment calls it the applications menu, Window Maker refers to it as the root-window menu, and FVWM2 calls it the workplace menu. In this chapter, it is referred to as the *workspace menu*. This menu is usually a pop-up menu you can display by clicking anywhere on the desktop. The mouse button you use differs with window managers. Enlightenment uses a middle-click, whereas Window Maker uses a right-click, and FVWM2 uses a left-click. Many of the entries on this workspace menu lead to submenus, which, in turn, may have their own submenus. For example, applications bring up a submenu listing categories for all your X programs. Selecting the graphics item brings up a list of all the X graphic programs on your system. If you choose Xpaint, the Xpaint program start up. On some window managers, you find entries for window configuration and themes. Here are items and submenus for configuring your window manager. For example, both AfterStep and Enlightenment have menus for changing your theme.

Desktop Areas and Virtual Desktops

Initially, you may find desktop areas disconcerting—they provide a kind of built-in enlargement feature. You discover the area displayed on your screen may be only part of the desktop. Moving your mouse pointer to the edge of your screen moves the screen over the hidden portions of the desktop. You also notice a small square located on your desktop or in your window manager's icon bar, taskbar, or panel. This is called the *pager,* and you use it to view different areas of your virtual desktop. The pager displays a rectangle for every active virtual desktop. Some window managers, such as FVWM2, display only two, others such as AfterStep have four, and others, such as FVWM, start out with only one.

Each desktop rectangle is divided into smaller squares called *desktop areas.* You can think of each desktop area as a separate extension of your desktop. It's as if you have a large desk, only part of which is shown onscreen. The active part of the desk is a highlighted square, usually in white. This is the area of the desktop currently displayed by your screen. A desktop can have as many as 25 squares, though the default is usually 4. You can click one of the squares in the rectangle to move to that part of your desk. You could place different windows in different parts of your desk, and then move to that part when you want to use them. In this way, everything you want on your desktop needn't be displayed on your screen at once, cluttering it. If you are working on the desktop and everything suddenly disappears, it may be you accidentally clicked one of the other squares. Certain items are always displayed on your screen, no matter what part of the virtual desktop you display. These are called *sticky* items. The pager is one, along with taskbars or panels. For example, the taskbars and iconbar's pager always show up on your screen, no matter what part of the virtual desktop you are viewing. Windows by default are not sticky, though you can make them sticky.

Most window managers also support virtual desktops. A *virtual desktop* includes all the desktop areas, along with the items displayed on them, such as icons, menus, and windows. Window managers such as Enlightenment, AfterStep, and FVWM2 enable you to use several virtual desktops. Unlike desktop areas that just extend a desktop, virtual desktops are separate entities. Most pagers display the different virtual desktops as separate rectangles, each subdivided into its respective desktop areas. To move to a virtual desktop, you click its rectangle. In some window managers, such as Window Maker, you select the desktop from a list. Window managers provide entries on their main menus for selecting virtual desktops and even moving windows from one desktop to another. Use a window manager's configuration program or configuration files to specify the number of virtual desktops you want.

Panels, Buttonbars, Taskbars, and Window Lists

A panel displays buttons for frequently used X Window System commands. Popular panels include Wharf and Zharf for AfterStep and FVWM2, the Clip on Window Maker, and GoodStuff for FVWM. Each icon on the panel displays an image and the name of a program. Click the button to start that program. For example, to open an Xterm window, click the icon labeled Xterm. Each window manager has different ways to add applications to the panel. Adding an entry in Window Maker is as simple as dragging an application's icon to the docking panel. In most cases, you can edit the panel entries in the window manager configuration files. For example, the entries beginning with the keyword `*GoodStuff` configure the GoodStuff panel in FVWM2 configuration files. In addition, some window managers support button bars with small icons for applications. A taskbar shows tasks that are running, and it can hold menu buttons for displaying menus. The FVWM2 taskbar features a Start menu for applications and lists buttons for current tasks. Windows can be minimized to the taskbar, much like docking in Windows 95. Open windows are also listed in the taskbar. Most window managers also provide a window list. Window lists are handy if you have work spread across different desktop areas and virtual desktops. Selecting a window entry in the window list moves you directly to that window and its virtual desktop/area.

The Terminal Window: Xterm

From within a Linux window manager, you can open a special window called a *terminal* window, which provides you with a standard command line interface. You can then enter commands on a command line with options and arguments at the prompt displayed in this window. You can use any of several programs to create a terminal window, the most commonly used program is called *Xterm. Rxvt* is an alternative terminal window program that is a stripped-down version of Xterm, lacking some configuration and emulation features, but smaller and faster. Most window manager workspace menus and panels have entries for starting a terminal window with either Xterm or Rxvt. An entry may be labeled with one of those names or an icon of a monitor.

Once opened, the window displays a shell prompt, usually the $, where you can enter Linux commands, just as you would on the command line. You see any results of your commands displayed within the terminal window, followed by a shell prompt indicating the beginning of the command line. An Xterm window supports several text-handling features. To the left of the window is a scroll bar you can use to scroll back to view previously displayed text. As text moves off the top of the screen, you can scroll back to see it. This is particularly helpful if you are displaying directories with a large number of files that do not fit on one screen. Xterm also enables you to copy text and paste it to the command line. You use the left mouse button to copy text and the second mouse button to paste it. You can copy any of the text previously displayed, such as previous commands or output from those commands. To copy text, click and hold down the left mouse button, while dragging it across the text you want to copy, letting up when you reach the end. Also, double-clicking selects a word, and a triple-click selects a line. If you want to extend the selected text, use the third mouse button. Once you select text, click the second mouse button. This automatically pastes the text to the end of the command line. Repeating clicks repeats the paste. The copy-and-paste operation is particularly helpful for constructing a complex command from previous ones. You can also copy and paste across different terminal windows.

The terminal window has the special capability of being able to run any X program from its command line. The terminal window operates within the X Window System environment. To run any X program, open an Xterm window and enter the command, terminating it by pressing ENTER. The X program then starts up in its own window. For example, to run Netscape, you could open a terminal window and type the command **netscape**. A new window then opens up running Netscape. You can open as many terminal windows as you want, and then start an X program from each. However, closing a terminal window also closes the program started from it.

Notice the terminal window in which you entered the X command appears to suspend itself. No following prompt appears after you press ENTER to run the program. This is because the terminal window is currently busy running the X program you just executed. You can free the terminal window to execute other commands while that program is running by invoking the program with an ampersand (&). Technically, this places it in the background as far as the terminal window is concerned (see Chapter 8). But you are free to move to that X program's window and run it there. The following example would run Netscape, freeing the terminal window to run other commands. Notice the prompt:

```
$ netscape  &
```

When you finish using the terminal window, close it by typing the command **exit** on the command line. Each terminal window is its own shell, and **exit** is the command to end a shell. (Shells are discussed in detail in Chapter 8.) Figure 6-1 shows the terminal window. The user has entered several commands, and the output is displayed in the window. As you reach the bottom of the window, the text displayed scrolls up, line by line, just as a normal terminal screen would. You can, of course, use the window controls to make the terminal window larger or smaller. You can even minimize it to an icon and later reopen it.

An Xterm window has four menus: The main menu, a VT options menu, a VT font menu, and a Tektronix window options menu. To bring up the main menu, hold down the CTRL key and click the left mouse button. For the VT options menu, hold down the CTRL key and click the second (right or middle) mouse button. To bring up the font menu, use the CTRL key and the third mouse button. You can then set the font and size of characters displayed. The terms *second mouse button* and *third mouse button* can be

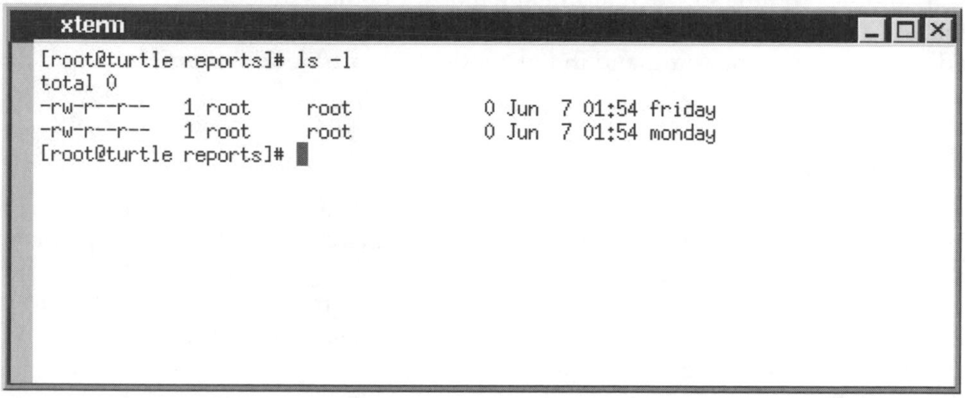

```
xterm                                                    _ □ ✕
[root@turtle reports]# ls -l
total 0
-rw-r--r--    1 root     root          0 Jun  7 01:54 friday
-rw-r--r--    1 root     root          0 Jun  7 01:54 monday
[root@turtle reports]# █
```

Figure 6-1.   *The terminal window*

confusing. On a two-button mouse, the second button is the right button, and the third button is the left and right buttons held down at the same time. On a three-button mouse, the second button is the middle button, and the third button is the rightmost button.

X Window System Multitasking

One of the most useful features of your Linux X Window System interface is its capability to open several operations at the same time, each with its own window. Notice in the command line interface you can only work on one task at a time (an exception is discussed in Chapter 8 dealing with what are called background processes). You issue a command and, after it executes, you can execute another. In the X Window System, you can have several different applications running at once. Moving your mouse pointer from one window to another effectively moves you from one application to another. This feature of the X Window System illustrates one of the most useful capabilities of Linux: *Concurrency*, the capability to have several processes operating at the same time. In your X Window System interface, you can have several applications running at the same time, each with its own window.

This feature can be easily illustrated using terminal windows. You can have several terminal windows open at the same time, each with its own command line. From the window manager's Main menu you can open terminal windows. Each terminal window has its own command line, and moving your mouse pointer from one window to another moves you from one command line to another. You can type a command in the active window and execute it. You can then move to another terminal window and type in another command. Each terminal window operates independently of the other. If you issue a command that takes a while to execute, and then you move to another window, you notice the command in the window you just left is still executing.

File Managers

A *file manager* uses directory windows that enable you to use menus, icons, and windows to manage files and directories. A *directory* is displayed as a window, with files displayed as icons. Directories are usually represented by icons that look like folders. You open a directory and examine the files in it, just as you would open a folder and examine its contents. A directory window has menus for performing standard file and directory operations, such as opening or deleting a file. Most file managers can also display files as lists providing details like the sizes and dates. Desktop file managers, such as gmc in Gnome and kfm in KDE, support drag-and-drop operations where you can copy or move files with a click-and-drag operation from one file manager window to another. You can also use gmc and kfm without their desktop interface, running on any window manager, though Gnome and KDE still must be installed on your system. Xfm is another popular file manager that provides basic directory and file operations.

Desktops

A *desktop* is an integrated program and file manager, providing you with menus and icons with which you can manage your files, run programs, and configure your system. Two desktops currently included in most Linux distributions are the *K Desktop Environment* (*KDE*) and the Gnome. They provide easy access to Internet tools, as well as the many Linux programs written for them or for the X Window System. You can take full advantage of all desktop features, such as toolbars, configuration utilities, file management windows, and automatic history lists. KDE includes its own window manager with its desktop, though you can use any window manager. Gnome uses a separate window manager, but it should be Gnome-compliant like Enlightenment. Red Hat provides both KDE and Gnome. To switch between the two, you use the desktop switching tool, *switchdesk.* The interfaces vary, but both include certain basic features: Desktop drag-and-drop operations are supported; a panel holds an application's starter menu, small utility programs, and icons for starting programs. The desktops also include an Internet-aware file manager that can access FTP sites and, in the case of KDE, operate as a Web browser. For each directory, you can open a window that shows all the files in that directory, displayed as icons. You can then run applications by double-clicking their icons (for KDE, you single-click), or you can move the icons out of the file manager window and onto the desktop for easier access. By selecting different windows, menus, and icons on your screen using a mouse, you can run the application associated with the icon, opening a new window for it.

Starting Window Managers

As noted in Chapter 4, either the X Window System is started automatically using a display manager with a login window, or from the command line by entering the `startx` command. Your X Window System server will then load, followed immediately by the window manager. You exit the window manager by choosing an exit or quit entry in the desktop workspace menu. The display manager and some window managers, like FVWM2 and WindowMaker, give you the option of starting other window managers. If you get into trouble and the window manager hangs, you can forcibly exit the X Window System with the keys CTRL-ALT-BACKSPACE.

The window manager you start is the default one set up by your Linux distribution when you installed your system. Many distributions now use as their default either Gnome or KDE. For Gnome and the K Desktop different window managers are used: kwm for the K Desktop and Enlightenment for Gnome. You can run Gnome or KDE applications on most window managers. To have Gnome use a particular window manager, you need to select it using the Gnome Control Center. You can use a window manager in place of kwm for KDE. Check the window manager's Web site for current information on Gnome and KDE compatibility. Currently, Enlightenment is fully Gnome-compliant, and AfterStep and Window Maker are nearly so.

To use a different window manager, first install it. RPM packages install with a default configuration for the window manager. If you are installing from source code you compiled, follow the included installation instructions. You can then configure Gnome or KDE to use that window manager, provided it is compliant with them. Or, you can configure your system to start a particular window manager without either desktop. To do this, place an entry for your window manager in an X Window System startup file. Different startup files exist for the display manager and the **startx** command. The startup file for the display manager is called **/etc/X11/xdm/Xsession** and the one for the **startx** command is called **/etc/X11/xinit/xinitrc**. For **startx**, users can also setup their own **.xinitrc** file in their home directories in place of the system's **xinitrc** file. Modifying these files can be a complex process. The procedure is described in detail in Chapter 28.

Window managers provide default configuration files and include utilities for changing your configuration. Red Hat features a customized configuration of FVWM2 called *AnotherLevel,* carried out using M4 macros. You can also use the **wmconfig** program to generate workspace menu entries for different window managers. Currently, AfterStep and FVWM2 are supported. Both AfterStep and Window Maker use the GNUstep configuration standard, placing configuration files in a directory named GNUstep in a user's home directory. The common X Window System and window manager configuration files are listed in Table 6-1 for your Linux system and user home directories.

Window Managers for Linux

Several of the more popular Linux window managers are the *Free Virtual Window Manager 2.0 (FVWM2)*, Enlightenment (enlightenment), Window Maker (wmaker), Blackbox

(blackbox), ICEWin, Xview (olwm), twm, LessTif (mwm), AfterStep (afterstep), and Motif (mwm). All except Motif are free. Most are easily configurable and provide theme support. Enlightenment is currently the default window manager for Gnome. AfterStep and Window Maker are based on the NeXTSTEP interface. Xview is the Linux version of the Sun System's OpenLook interface. FVWM2 is the replacement for the original FVWM window manager, which was, until recently, the standard window manager used by most Linux distributions. LessTif is a free Motif clone that provides a Motif interface and runs many Motif applications. twm is an older window manager that provides basic windowing capabilities. AfterStep, Window Maker, FVWM2, twm, and Enlightenment are included with most major distributions, including Red Hat. The other window managers you can download from their Web sites, Linux sites, or the Red Hat contrib site, **contrib.redhat.com**. You can download and install recent versions of any window manager as they become available. These window managers are GNU public-licensed software—they are yours free of cost.

Enlightenment

Enlightenment aims to provide a highly configurable graphical shell for a user's work environment. It is still undergoing development, though releases are stable. Enlightenment is currently the default window manager distributed with Gnome. You can download new releases from the Enlightenment Web site at **www.enlightenment.org**, which also includes documentation. RPM packages for Red Hat are available on the Red Hat FTP site. Enlightenment has the same window operations as used on other window managers. You can resize a window by clicking-and-dragging any of its sides or corners. You can move the window with a click-and-drag operation on its title bar. You can also right-click and drag any border to move the window. The upper-right corner lists the Maximize, Minimize, and Close buttons. The Minimize button minimizes to an icon on the desktop. You can click the upper-left corner of a window to display a window menu with entries for window operations. These include a Desktop entry to move the window to another desktop area and the Stick option, which displays the window no matter to what desktop area you move.

To access the Enlightenment workspace menu, middle-click anywhere on the desktop (hold both mouse buttons down at the same time for a two-button mouse). Entries exist for applications, as well as the desktop, themes, and Enlightenment configuration. With the desktop menus, you move to different desktop areas and virtual desktops. The themes menu enables you to choose different Enlightenment themes. Enlightenment also has extensive configuration options, discussed in a later section.

To configure Enlightenment, use its GUI configuration tool. The Enlightenment Configuration window, shown in Figure 6-2, displays a list of configuration topics on the left and the panel for the selected topic on the right. Basic options set window displays, enabling you to select resize and move methods. With the Desktops option, you can create virtual desktops and specify the number of desktop areas for each one. Other topics cover features such as sounds, special effects, window focus, keyboard

shortcuts, and backgrounds. You can set different backgrounds for each virtual
desktop. The Themes panel enables you to use an Enlightenment theme, of which there
are many from which to choose. Enlightenment is known for its impressive themes. See
e.themes.org for themes you can download. To make a theme available, place it in your
home directory's **.enlightenment/themes** directory. Make sure that file has a **.etheme**
extension. Enlightenment maintains its own configuration directory in your home
directory called **.enlightenment**. It contains subdirectories for themes, backgrounds,
and windows.

AfterStep

Originally based on the NeXTSTEP interface used on the NeXT operating system,
AfterStep has evolved into a window manager in its own right. *AfterStep* includes the
advantages of the NeXTSTEP interface, while adding features of its own. AfterStep

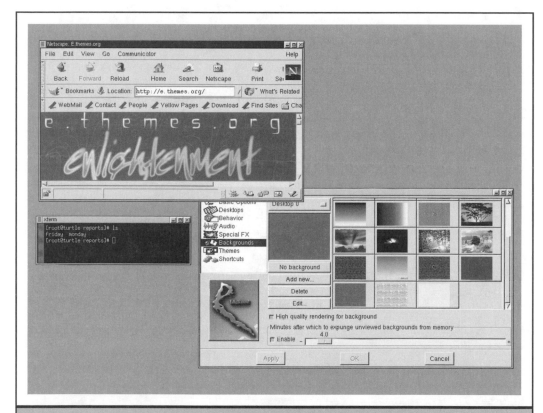

Figure 6-2.   *The Enlightenment window manager*

began as a continuation of the BowMan window manager, which, in turn, was based on FVWM. It is available free under the GNU Public License. You can download AfterStep from the AfterStep Web site (**www.afterstep.org**) or obtain the RPM version from the Red Hat FTP site.

Windows, menus, and icons are intentionally similar to NeXTSTEP (see Figure 6-3). Clicking anywhere on the desktop displays the workspace menu. Clicking-and-dragging a menu title tears it off from the menu and lets it stick to the desktop. To start applications, you can also access features from an icon bar called *Wharf,* which is initially displayed on the left side, though it can be placed on any edge. Double-click an application's icon to start it. Wharf can contain folders, which, themselves, expand to rows of application icons. A Windows list also maintains a list of all open windows. The pager initially displays pages for four virtual desktops, each with four desktop areas. These appear above Wharf. Click a desktop or a desktop area to move to it.

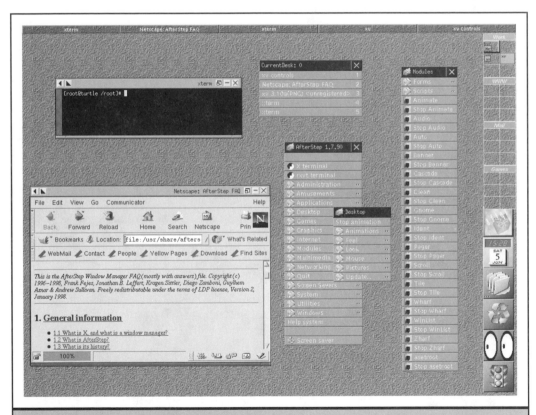

Figure 6-3.   *The AfterStep window manager*

AfterStep includes an extensive set of modules and support themes. You can download themes from the **as.themes.org** Web site. The AfterStep Web site contains documentation, themes, and current releases. It also maintains links to sites that provide added material, such as the AfterStep configuration guide, applets, and themes. AfterStep is *Inter-Client Communications Conventions Manual* (*ICCCM*), Gnome, and KDE-compliant. To start AfterStep, use the command **afterstep** where your X-Windows configuration files start your window manager (usually **.xinitrc** or **.Xclients**). The AfterStep configuration files are located in the directory **GNUstep/Library/AfterStep** in a user's home directory. Configuration follows the GNUstep/Library standard. Separate configuration files are used for different components, such as Wharf, Pager, and other modules and applications. A standard configuration is included with the installation, and you can download others from AfterStep sites. Most AfterStep material, including the current release, can be downloaded from the AfterStep FTP site at **ftp.afterstep.org**.

Window Maker

Window Maker is designed to emulate NeXTSTEP closely and it includes additional support for GNUstep applications. GNUstep is an attempt to develop a GNU version of NeXT's OpenStep API. Window Maker plans to be Gnome and KDE-compliant (see the Web site for current status). The Window Maker Web site at **www.windowmaker.org** provides online documentation, links, screenshots, and new releases. You can download the newest version directly from **ftp.windowmaker.org**.

A right-click displays the root-window menu (workspace). A middle-click displays a window list of currently opened windows (see Figure 6-4). You can make frequently used menus "stick" to the desktop by dragging the title bar of the menu. This makes a Close button appear in the menu title bar. If you want to close the menu, click that button. Docked icons are listed in a icons bar. Initially, this is shrunk to the GNUstep logo. Click-and-drag the logo to display the dock. To start an application, double-click its icon. Whenever you start an application, a small icon for it, known as an *appicon*, is placed on the desktop. To add that application to the dock, drag this icon to it. The dock icons support drag-and-drop operations. Drag a file to an application's icon to start the application with that file. Window Maker supports multiple desktops, which it calls *workspaces*. You use the Workspaces menu to create new workspaces and to change to current ones. On a workspace-dependent dock called the *Clip*, you can have different clips of programs for each workspace.

You resize windows using a resize bar at the bottom of a window. You can move a window by dragging the title bar. To the left of the title bar is a miniaturizing window that reduces the window to a miniature window with its own title bar. To restore the window, double-click its miniature. To maximize the window, hold the CTRL key down while you double-click the title bar. Do the same to restore it.

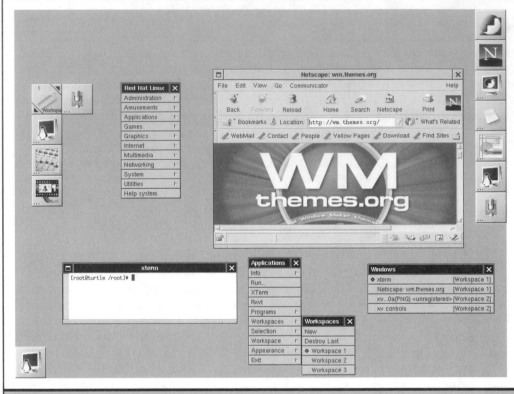

Figure 6-4.   *The Window Maker window manager*

Window Maker also supports themes. You can download Window Maker themes from **wm.themes.org**. To install a theme, extract its archive in your **GNUstep/Library/WindowMaker/Themes** directory. Then, from the root-window menu, select Themes and choose the theme from the list. Window Maker also features an extensive number of dock applications specifically designed to run within the dock (like Gnome applets in the panel). For example. you can run a miniature network interface monitor, a POP3 mail checker, or, of course, a CD player.

Window Maker is configured using a GUI configuration utility, WPrefs. A Wmakerconf utility also automatically generates the configuration files. Configuration files are kept in your **GNUstep/WindowMaker** directory, while attributes for different applications are kept in the **GNUstep/Defaults** directory. For example, the entries for the application's menu are kept in the **GNUstep/Defaults/WMRootMenu** file.

Blackbox

The *Blackbox* window manager is designed to be simple and fast. It provides multiple workspaces and small menus. Its source code can be compiled using only a C++ compiler and the X11 development libraries. The Blackbox uses no special graphic libraries. It is nearly compliant with the ICCCM. Although it has an interface similar to Window Maker, the Blackbox is an entirely original program written in C++, sharing no common code with any other window manager. Blackbox was written by Brad Hughes, who currently maintains it. Blackbox provides support for KDE and Motif, but not for Gnome. Blackbox also supports themes. You can download Blackbox themes from **blackbox.themes.org**, and you can find out more about Blackbox from its Web site, **blackbox.wiw.org**. Blackbox comes with a standard configuration, though you can set up your own in a **.blackboxrc** configuration file.

Scwm

The *Scheme-Configurable Window Manager* (*Scwm*) provides powerful customization capabilities using a configuration language based on Guile Scheme. Originally based on FVWM2, it has developed its own capabilities while maintaining compatibility with FVWM2, including support for FVWM2 modules. With Guile Scheme, Scwm is fully programmable. Configurations can be made and implemented while running the window manager, without having to restart it. You can find out more about Scwm at **http://huis-clos.mit.edu/scwm**.

IceWM

The *IceWM* window manager supports many of the same features as FVWM, including themes. You can obtain recent releases, screenshots, and themes from the IceWM Web page currently at **http://www.kiss.uni-lj.si/~k4fr0235/icewm/**. IceWM features a taskbar where open windows and running applications are docked. A sequence of labeled buttons represents different desktops. Click one to move to that desktop. To the left is a Linux button you can click to display the Workspace menu. Next to the Linux button is a Window List button to display your open windows. Windows have Minimize, Maximize, and Close buttons in the upper-right corner. Resize borders are on every corner of a window. Clicking anywhere on the desktop displays the workspace menu. Configuration can be performed using the IcePref configuration tool.

FVWM2 and Another Level

FVWM2 supports features such as the taskbar, workplace menu, modules, and themes. *Modules* are small programs that can be loaded and run dynamically. FVWM2 replaces FVWM, which is no longer under development. You can obtain newer versions of

FVWM2 as they come out, from the FVWM2 Web page, currently located at **www.fvwm.org**. RPM packages of the new FVWM2 versions are also available at the Red Hat FTP sites. You can download FVWM2 themes from **fvwm.themes.org**.

FVWM2 is usually the default window manager for most distributions, used when you have not specified a window manager (Gnome or KDE specify their own window managers). FVWM2 extends the capabilities of FVWM to provide better configuration files, allows customization of individual windows, and provides better module support. There are modules for a taskbar that adds Windows 95–like docking and Start menu capabilities. FVWM2 supports virtual desktops and desktop areas. FVWM2 also supports the Wharf icon bar. A pager display enables you to move from one desktop to another. Clicking anywhere on the desktop displays a workplace menu, as shown in Figure 6-5. To quit FVWM2, select the Quit entry from this menu.

When the FVWM window manager starts up, it executes its own configuration file, performing tasks such as displaying buttons on the FVWM taskbar, setting up entries in the workplace menu, and determining what programs to start up initially, if any. The

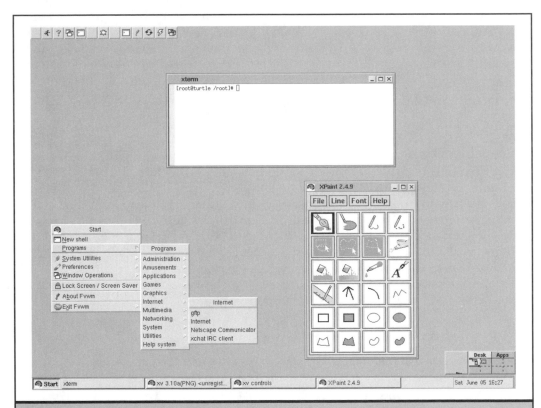

Figure 6-5.   *The FVWM2 window manager with Red Hat AnotherLevel*

default configuration file is **/etc/X11/fvwm2/system.fvwm2rc**. The configuration file for the older FVWM window manager is **/etc/X11/fvwm/system.fvwmrc**. You can modify any of these files to configure your FVWM window manager as you want. For example, if you want to set the number of virtual desktops, you can modify the DeskTopNum entry in this file. Changes to this file are global for all users. Individual users can create their own **.fvwm2rc** files in their home directories and edit entries to customize their window managers. To start, users can copy the **system.fvwm2rc** file to their home directories as their **.fvwm2rc** file to use as a basis for their own configurations. The following entry determines the number of desktop areas to support in a virtual desktop. It is measured by the number of squares on the length and width, so 3 × 3 would be nine desktop areas.

```
DeskTopSize 2x2
```

Red Hat uses the AnotherLevel configuration for FVWM2 to create a custom FVWM2 desktop with Red Hat icons and menus. AnotherLevel uses a set of M4 macro files located in the **/etc/X11/AnotherLevel** directory. Different configuration features are organized into separate files, such as **fvwm2rc.keys.m4** for key bindings and **fvwm2rc.modules.m4** for modules used. The **fvwm2rc.defines.m4** file holds definitions for many configuration values, including the number of virtual desktops and the number of areas set up for them. Values are defined using macros:

```
# NUM_DESKTOPS is number of desktops
# -- each desktop is DESKTOP_SIZE panes
define(`NUM_DESKTOPS',2)

# DESKTOP_SIZE is a geometry specifying horizontal
# desktop x vertical desktops
# So 3x3 gives 9 panes per desktop
define(`DESKTOP_SIZE',2x2)
```

To create your own customized AnotherLevel, copy the **fvwm2rc.defstyles.m4** and **fvwm2rc.defines.m4** files to your home directory as **.fvwm2rc.defstyles.m4** and **.fvwm2rc.defines.m4**. Workspace menus are defined using **wmconfig**. The **wmconfig** application configuration is located in **/etc/X11/wmconfig**. You can copy this directory to your home directory as **.wmconfig,** and then change the entries in those files as you want, adding, changing, or removing application entries.

Xview: olwm and olvwm

Xview is the implementation of Sun System's OpenLook interface. Those familiar with OpenLook should find the Linux version runs in much the same way. You can download Xview from metalab.unc.edu FTP site. The Xview archive files are located in the **/pub/Linux/libs/X/xview** directory, currently **xview-3.2p1.4. bin.tar.gz**. This Xview package includes both the olwm and olvwm window managers, as well as several utilities, such as a clock and a text editor. The olvwm version of Xview supports a virtual desktop.

The Xview package contains a set of shared libraries that provide OpenLook menus, buttons, and other widgets. These are used in many Linux applications. Although applications that use these Xview widgets needn't use the Xview window manager, they do use the Xview libraries. So, you can run applications such as the textedit Xview editor in the FVWM window manager. The buttons and menus textedit uses are Xview widgets, though it can operate in an FVWM window. Such an Xview package is not the full Xview window manager. It is a subset of libraries with a few popular applications.

To install the full Xview window manager, first download its tar archive from **metalab.unc.edu.** If your distribution previously installed the Xview package, you need to remove the **/usr/openwin** directory. Then unpack the Xview package you downloaded with the **tar xvf** command. This creates a subdirectory named **usr** in your current directory. In this **usr** directory is a subdirectory named **openwin**, which you move into the **/usr** directory (notice the forward slash).

```
# mv usr/openwin  /usr
```

Then run the **ldconfig** command on the **/usr/openwin/lib** directory. This sets up the Xview libraries.

```
# ldconfig /usr/openwin/lib
```

Make sure a **/usr/openwin/lib** entry is in the **/etc/ld.so.config** file. Because the Xview archive is not an RPM package, you have to perform the installation tasks yourself, such as moving files to the right directory and running **ldconfig**. Other window managers can be obtained in RPM format that automatically installs and configures their files for you. You then place an entry for start olvwm in either the **.xinitrc** or **.xsessions** file.

When you first bring up the olvwm window manager, you are presented with a blank screen and a pager with six squares displayed in the upper-left corner. Double-click any square to move to that screen. To bring up the Xview workspace menu, click anywhere on the screen with the right mouse button. The workspace menu is a *pinnable* menu. You see a picture of a push-pin at the top. If you click it, the workplace menu remains displayed at that place on the screen. Click the pin again to remove the workplace menu. The X11 Progs entry in the workspace menu automatically lists installed X11 programs, and the Xview Progs entry lists all Xview programs (those installed in **/usr/openwin/bin**).

Window components are slightly different from other window managers, though they serve much the same function. Menus are displayed with the right mouse button. On the workspace menu, you bring up submenus by right-clicking the small triangle to the right of a menu item. To move windows and pinned menus, you click-and-drag with the left mouse button on the edge of the window.

Xview components are installed in the **/usr/openwin** directory. Here you find subdirectories, such as **/usr/openwin/bin,** which hold Xview programs, and **/usr/openwin/lib,** which hold Xview libraries. When the X Window System starts up, it must have a shell variable called OPENWINHOME set to the Xview directory, **/usr/openwin**. Such assignments should also be placed in the respective X startup files like **.xinitrc** or **.xessions**.

The **/usr/openwin/lib** directory contains the menu files used to display the Xview workspace menu and its submenus. You can add entries to these menus if you want. An entry consists of the label to be displayed, followed by the action to take. For example, to add an entry to the workspace menu for Netscape, place the following entry in the **openwin-menu** file. The Xview man pages have a detailed explanation of Xview menus and the kind of entries you can make.

```
"Netscape"      exec /usr/bin/netscape.
```

LessTif: mwm

LessTif is a Motif clone designed to run any Motif program. It describes itself as the Hungry Programmers' version of OSF/Motif. LessTif is currently source-compatible with OSF/Motif® 1.2; that is, the same source code compiles with either LessTif or Motif. LessTif is provided free under the GNU *Library General Public License* (*LGPL*). You can download it from the LessTif Web site at **www.lesstif.org**. You can also download RPM versions from the Redhat contrib site, **contrib.redhat.com**. The Web site also provides documentation and a listing of applications that currently work under LessTif. You invoke LessTif with the command **mwm**. It uses a global configuration file **/etc/X11/mwm/system.mwmrc** and a user configuration file **.mwmrc**. Currently, LessTif does not run all Motif programs. The project is still under development, but it provides the same window management look and feel as that of Motif. Plans are to provide compatibility first with Motif 1.2, and then with version 2.0.

Motif

Motif is proprietary software you must purchase from a vendor for about $150. Motif and Xview were the two major competing window interfaces provided for UNIX, representing two different window standards. These two standards have recently been integrated into a new GUI standard for UNIX called the *Common Desktop Environment* (*CDE*).

The Common Desktop Environment (CDE)

The *Common Desktop Environment* (*CDE*) provides a common set of desktop interface standards proposed by Hewlett-Packard, Novell, IBM, and Sun in 1995. It was designed to merge OpenLook and Motif into one standard interface that could be used on all versions of UNIX. Commercial versions of CDE, such as TriTeal CDE, are available for Linux (**www.triteal.com**). The CDE desktop provides an interface somewhat similar to Gnome and KDE. Along with window and desktop support, it provides a panel for launching applications. Most CDE desktops include a set of CDE applications, such as a file manager, a mail client, and a text editor. Like other desktops and window managers, CDE supports virtual desktops. Help is context-sensitive, enabling you to display information about a component by clicking a help entry in its pop-up menu.

DOS and Windows Emulators: VMware, DOSemu, and Wine

Emulators are available for Linux that enable you to run DOS and Windows programs. These are projects still in development and their success is only partial, to date. As emulators, they run programs slower than DOS or Windows would.

An extremely efficient Windows platform for Linux is *VMware*. Using VMware's virtual platform technology, you can run any Windows application directly on your Linux system. For more information, check the VMware Web site at **www.vmware.com.**

The DOS emulator is *DOSemu*. It includes sample configuration files called **config.dist** located in the **examples** directory. This contains a long list of configuration options. All are commented out with a preceding **#** symbol. You need to copy this file to **dosemu.conf**. Edit the **dosemu.conf** file, removing the **#** from the entries that apply to your system. Explanations are given for each section in the file. To create a bootable floppy DOS disk, use **mcopy** to copy the **command.com**, **sys.com**, **emufs.sys**, **ems.sy.cdrom.sys**, and **exitemu.com** files to that disk. To run the DOS emulator, enter **dos** on the command line. To exit the emulator, entering `exitemu.dos -?` gives you a list of **dos** command options.

The *Wine* emulator is designed to run Windows 3.1 and 32-bit programs. It is still in development, with new versions continually being released. At this point, the Wine emulator is considered experimental. You can download a version from the Web site at **www.winehq.com**. The Windows FAQ provides detailed information.

Chapter 7

Shell Operations

The *shell* is a command interpreter that provides a line-oriented interactive interface between the user and the operating system. You enter commands on a command line, they are interpreted by the shell, and then sent as instructions to the operating system. This interpretive capability of the shell provides for many sophisticated features. For example, the shell has a set of wildcard characters that can generate filenames. The shell can redirect input and output, as well as run operations in the background, freeing you to perform other tasks.

Several different types of shells have been developed for Linux: the *Bourne Again shell* (*BASH*), the *Public Domain Korn shell* (*PDKSH*), the *TCSH shell*, and the *Z-shell*. All shells are available for your use, although the BASH shell is the default. You only need one type of shell to do your work. Red Hat Linux includes all the major shells, although it installs and uses the BASH shell as the default. If you use the Red Hat Linux command-line shell, you will be using the BASH shell, unless you specify another. This chapter discusses the BASH shell that shares many of the same features as other shells.

The Command Line

The Linux command line interface consists of a single line into which you enter commands with any of their options and arguments. Red Hat Linux installs with the BASH shell. The BASH shell has a dollar sign prompt, but Linux has several other types of shells, each with its own prompt. A shell *prompt*, such as the one shown here, marks the beginning of the command line:

$

The prompt designates the beginning of the command line. You are now ready to enter a command and its arguments at the prompt. In the next example, the user enters the **date** command, which displays the date. The user types the command on the first line, and then presses ENTER to execute the command.

```
$ date
Sun July 8 10:30:21 PST 2000
```

The *command line interface* is the primary interface for the shell, which interprets the commands you enter and sends them to the system. The shell follows a special syntax for interpreting the command line. The first word entered on a command line must be the name of a command. The next words are options and arguments for the command. Each word on the command line must be separated from the others by one or more spaces or tabs.

```
$ Command     Options     Arguments
```

An *option* is a one-letter code preceded by a dash that modifies the type of action the command takes. One example of a command that has options is the **ls** command. The **ls** *command*, with no options, displays a list of all the files in your current directory. It merely lists the name of each file with no other information.

With a **-1** option, the **ls** command modifies its task by displaying a line of information about each file, listing such data as its size, and the date and time it was last modified. In the next example, the user enters the **ls** command followed by a **-1** option. The dash before the **-1** option is required. Linux uses it to distinguish an option from an argument.

```
$ ls -1
```

Another option, **-a**, lists all the files in your directory, including what are known as hidden files. *Hidden files* are often configuration files and they always have names beginning with a period. For this reason, hidden files are often referred to as *dot files*. In most cases, you can also combine options. You do so by preceding the options with an initial dash, and then listing the options you want. The options **-al**, for example, list information about all the files in your directory, including any hidden files. Another option for the **ls** command is **-F**. With this option, the **ls** command displays directory names with a preceding slash, so you can easily identify them.

```
$ ls -al
```

Most commands are designed to take arguments. An *argument* is a word you type in on the command line after any options. Many file management commands take filenames as their arguments. For example, if you only wanted the information displayed for a particular file, you could add that file's name after the **-1** option:

```
$ ls -1 mydata
```

The shell you will start working in is the BASH shell, your default shell. This shell has special command-line editing capabilities that you may find helpful as you learn Linux. You can easily modify commands you have entered before executing them, moving anywhere on the command line and inserting or deleting characters. This is particularly helpful for complex commands. You can use the CTRL-F or RIGHT ARROW key to move forward a character, or the CTRL-B or LEFT ARROW key to move back a character. CTRL-D or DEL deletes the character the cursor is on, and CTRL-H or BACKSPACE deletes the character before the cursor. To add text, you use the arrow keys to move the cursor to where you want to insert text and type in the new characters. At any time, you can press ENTER to execute the command. For example, if you make a spelling mistake when entering a command, rather than reentering the entire command, you can use the editing operations to correct the mistake.

You can also use the UP ARROW key to redisplay your previously executed command. You can then reexecute that command or edit it and execute the modified command. You'll find this capability helpful when you have to repeat certain operations over and over, such as editing the same file. This capability is also helpful when you've already executed a command you had entered incorrectly. In this case, you would be presented with an error message and a new, empty command line. By pressing the UP ARROW key, you can redisplay your previous command, make corrections to it, and then execute it again. This way, you would not have to enter the whole command again.

The BASH shell keeps a list, called a *history list*, of your previously entered commands. You can display each command, in turn, on your command line by pressing the UP ARROW key. The DOWN ARROW key moves you down the list. You can modify and execute any of these previous commands when you display them on your command line. This history feature is discussed in more detail in Chapter 15.

Some commands can be complex and take some time to execute. When you mistakenly execute the wrong command, you can interrupt and stop such commands with the interrupt keys—CTRL-C or DEL.

You can enter a command on several lines by typing a backslash just before you press ENTER. The backslash "escapes" the ENTER key, effectively continuing the same command line to the next line. In the next example, the **cp** command is entered on three lines. The first two lines end in a backslash, effectively making all three lines one command line.

```
$ cp -i \
mydata \
newdata
```

Wildcards and Filename Arguments: *, ?, [ ]

Filenames are the most common arguments used in a command. Often you may know only part of the filename, or you may want to reference several filenames that have the same extension or begin with the same characters. The shell provides a set of special characters called *wildcards* that search out, match, and generate a list of filenames. The *wildcard characters* are the asterisk, the question mark, and brackets (*, ?, [ ]). Given a partial filename, the shell uses these matching operators to search for files and generate a list of filenames found. The shell replaces the partial filename argument with the list of matched filenames. This list of filenames can then become the arguments for commands such as **ls**, which can operate on many files. Table 7-1 lists the shell's wildcard characters.

Common Shell Symbols	Execution
ENTER	Execute a command line
;	Separate commands on the same command line
`command`	Execute a command
\	Quote the following character. Used to quote special characters
|	Pipe the standard output of one command as input for another command
&	Execute a command in the background
!	History command

Wildcard Symbols	Execution
*	Match on any set of characters in filenames
?	Match on any single character in filenames
[]	Match on a class of possible characters in filenames

Redirection Symbols	Execution
>	Redirect the standard output to a file or device, creating the file if it does not exist and overwriting the file if it does exist
>!	The exclamation point forces the overwriting of a file if it already exits. This overrides the noclobber option
<	Redirect the standard input from a file or device to a program
>>	Redirect the standard output to a file or device, appending the output to the end of the file

Standard Error Redirection Symbols	Execution
2>	Redirect the standard error to a file or device
2>>	Redirect and append the standard error to a file or device
2>&1	Redirect the standard error to the standard output
>&	Redirect the standard error to a file or device
|&	Pipe the standard error as input to another command

Table 7-1.   *Shell Symbols*

ENVIRONMENTS

The *asterisk, *,* references files beginning or ending with a specific set of characters. You place the asterisk before or after a set of characters that form a pattern to be searched for in filenames. If the asterisk is placed before the pattern, filenames that end in that pattern are searched for. If the asterisk is placed after the pattern, filenames that begin with that pattern are searched for. Any matching filename is copied into a list of filenames generated by this operation. In the next example, all filenames beginning with the pattern "doc" are searched for and a list generated. Then all filenames ending with the pattern "day" are searched for and a list is generated.

```
$ ls
doc1 doc2 document docs mydoc monday tuesday
$ ls doc*
doc1 doc2 document docs
$ ls *day
monday tuesday
$
```

Filenames often include an extension specified with a period and followed by a single character. The extension has no special status and is only part of the characters making up the filename. Using the asterisk makes it easy to select files with a given extension. In the next example, the asterisk is used to list only those files with a **.c** extension. The asterisk placed before the **.c** constitutes the argument for **ls**.

```
$ ls *.c
calc.c main.c
```

You can use ***** with the **rm** command to erase several files at once. The asterisk first selects a list of files with a given extension, or beginning or ending with a given set of characters, and then it presents this list of files to the **rm** command to be erased. In the next example, the **rm** command erases all files beginning with the pattern "doc":

```
$ rm doc*
```

The asterisk by itself matches all files. If you use a single asterisk as the argument for an **rm** command, all your files will be erased. In the next example, the **ls *** command lists all files, and the **rm *** command erases all files.

```
$ ls *
doc1 doc2 document docs mydoc myletter yourletter
$ rm *
```

```
$ ls
$
```

Use the ***** wildcard character carefully and sparingly with the **rm** command. The combination can be dangerous. A misplaced ***** in an **rm** command without the **-i** option could easily erase all your files. The first command in the next example erases only those files with a **.c** extension. The second command, however, erases all files. Notice the space between the asterisk and the period in the second command. A space in a command line functions as a *delimiter*, separating arguments. The asterisk is considered one argument, and the **.c**, another argument. The asterisk by itself matches all files and, when used as an argument with the **rm** command, instructs **rm** to erase all your files.

```
$ rm *.c
$ rm * .c
```

The *question mark, ?*, matches only a single incomplete character in filenames. Suppose you want to match the files **doc1** and **docA**, but not **document**. Whereas the asterisk will match filenames of any length, the question mark limits the match to just one extra character. The next example matches files that begin with the word "doc" followed by a single differing letter.

```
$ ls
doc1 docA document
$ ls doc?
doc1 docA
```

Whereas the ***** and **?** wildcard characters specify incomplete portions of a filename, the *brackets, [ ]*, enable you to specify a set of valid characters to search for. Any character placed within the brackets will be matched in the filename. Suppose you want to list files beginning with "doc", but only ending in *1* or *A*. You are not interested in filenames ending in *2* or *B*, or any other character. Here is how it's done:

```
$ ls
doc1 doc2 doc3 docA docB docD document
$ ls doc[1A]
doc1 docA
```

You can also specify a set of characters as a range, rather than listing them one by one. A dash placed between the upper and lower bounds of a set of characters selects all characters within that range. The range is usually determined by the character set in use. In an ASCII character set, the range "a–g" will select all lowercase alphabetic characters from *a* through *g,* inclusive. In the next example, files beginning with the pattern "doc" and ending in characters *1* through *3* are selected. Then those ending in characters *B* through *E* are matched.

```
$ ls doc[1-3]
doc1 doc2 doc3
$ ls doc[B-E]
docB docD
```

You can combine the brackets with other wildcard characters to form flexible matching operators. Suppose you only want to list filenames ending in either a **.c** or **.o** extension, but no other extension. You can use a combination of the asterisk and brackets: *** [co]**. The asterisk matches all filenames, and the brackets match only filenames with extension **.c** or **.o**.

```
$ ls *.[co]
main.c   main.o   calc.c
```

At times, a wildcard character is actually part of a filename. In these cases, you need to quote the character by preceding it with a backslash to reference the file. In the next example, the user needs to reference a file that ends with the **?** character, **answers?**. The **?** is, however, a wildcard character and would match any filename beginning with "answers" that has one or more characters. In this case, the user quotes the **?** with a preceding backslash to reference the filename.

```
$ ls answers\?
answers?
```

Standard Input/Output and Redirection

When UNIX was designed, a decision was made to distinguish between the physical implementation and the logical organization of a file. Physically, UNIX files are accessed in randomly arranged blocks. Logically, all files are organized as a continuous stream of bytes. Linux, as a version of UNIX, has this same organization. Aside from special system calls, the user never references the physical structure of a file. To the user, all files have the same organization—a byte stream. Any file can be easily copied or appended to another because all files are organized in the same way. In this sense, only one standard type of file exists in Linux, the *byte-stream file.* Linux makes no implementational distinction between a character file and a record file, or a text file and a binary file.

This logical file organization extends to input and output operations. The data in input and output operations is organized like a file. Data input at the keyboard is placed in a data stream arranged as a continuous set of bytes. Data output from a command or program is also placed in a data stream and arranged as a continuous set of bytes. This input data stream is referred to in Linux as the *standard input*, while the output data stream is called the *standard output*.

Because the standard input and standard output have the same organization as that of a file, they can easily interact with files. Linux has a redirection capability that lets you easily move data in and out of files. You can redirect the standard output so that, instead of displaying the output on a screen, you can save it in a file. You can also redirect the standard input away from the keyboard to a file, so that input is read from a file instead of from your keyboard.

When a Linux command is executed that produces output, this output is placed in the standard output data stream. The default destination for the standard output data stream is a device, in this case, the screen. *Devices*, such as the keyboard and screen, are treated as files. They receive and send out streams of bytes with the same organization as that of a byte-stream file. The screen is a device that displays a continuous stream of bytes. By default, the standard output will send its data to the screen device, which will then display the data.

For example, the `ls` command generates a list of all filenames and outputs this list to the standard output. Next, this stream of bytes in the standard output is directed to the screen device. The list of filenames is then printed on the screen. The `cat` command also sends output to the standard output. The contents of a file are copied to the standard output whose default destination is the screen. The contents of the file are then displayed on the screen.

Redirecting the Standard Output: > and >>

Suppose that instead of displaying a list of files on the screen, you would like to save this list in a file. In other words, you would like to direct the standard output to a file rather than the screen. To do this, you place the *output redirection operator*, **>** (greater-than sign), and the name of a file on the command line after the Linux command. Table 7-2 lists the different ways you can use the redirection operators. In the next example, the output of the `cat` command is redirected from the screen device to a file.

```
$ cat myletter > newletter
```

The redirection operation creates the new destination file. If the file already exists, it will be overwritten with the data in the standard output. You can set the `noclobber` feature to prevent overwriting an existing file with the redirection operation. In this case, the redirection operation on an existing file will fail. You can overcome the `noclobber` feature by placing an exclamation point after the redirection operator. The

Command	Execution
ENTER	Execute a command line
;	Separate commands on the same command line
command\ *opts args*	Enter backslash before carriage return to continue entering a command on the next line
\`*command*\`	Execute a command
BACKSPACE CTRL-H	Erase the previous character
CTRL-U	Erase the command line and start over
CTRL-C	Interrupt and stop a command execution

Special Characters for Filename Generation	Execution
*	Match on any set of characters
?	Match on any single characters
[]	Match on a class of possible characters
\	Quote the following character. Used to quote special characters

Redirection	Execution
command > *filename*	Redirect the standard output to a file or device, creating the file if it does not exist and overwriting the file if it does exist
command < *filename*	Redirect the standard input from a file or device to a program
command >> *filename*	Redirect the standard output to a file or device, appending the output to the end of the file
command >! *filename*	In the C-shell and the Korn shell, the exclamation point forces the overwriting of a file if it already exits. This overrides the noclobber option
command 2> *filename*	Redirect the standard error to a file or device in the Bourne shell

Table 7-2. *The Shell Operations*

Redirection	Execution
command **2>>** *filename*	Redirect and append the standard error to a file or device in the Bourne shell
command **2>&1**	Redirect the standard error to the standard output in the Bourne shell
command **>&** *filename*	Redirect the standard error to a file or device in the C-shell

Pipes	Execution
command **|** *command*	Pipe the standard output of one command as input for another command
command **|&** *command*	Pipe the standard error as input to another command in the C-shell

Background Jobs	Execution
&	Execute a command in the background
fg *%jobnum*	Bring a command in the background to the foreground or resume an interrupted program
bg	Place a command in the foreground into the background
CTRL-Z	Interrupt and stop the currently running program. The program remains stopped and waiting in the background for you resume it
notify *%jobnum*	Notify you when a job ends
kill *%jobnum* **kill** *processnum*	Cancel and end a job running in the background
jobs	List all background jobs. The **jobs** command is not available in the Bourne shell, unless it is using the jsh shell
ps	List all currently running processes including background jobs
at *time date*	Execute commands at a specified time and date. The time can be entered with hours and minutes and qualified as A.M. or P.M.

Table 7-2.   *The Shell Operations* (continued)

ENVIRONMENTS

next example sets the **noclobber** feature for the BASH shell and then forces the overwriting of the **oldletter** file if it already exists.

```
$ set -o noclobber
$ cat myletter >! oldletter
```

Although the redirection operator and the filename are placed after the command, the redirection operation is not executed after the command. In fact, it is executed before the command. The redirection operation creates the file and sets up the redirection before it receives any data from the standard output. If the file already exists, it will be destroyed and replaced by a file of the same name. In effect, the command generating the output is executed only after the redirected file has been created.

In the next example, the output of the **ls** command is redirected from the screen device to a file. First the **ls** command lists files and, in the next command, **ls** redirects its file list to the **listf** file. Then the **cat** command displays the list of files saved in **listf**. Notice the list of files in **listf** includes the **listf** filename. The list of filenames generated by the **ls** command include the name of the file created by the redirection operation—in this case, **listf**. The **listf** file is first created by the redirection operation, and then the **ls** command lists it along with other files. This file list output by **ls** is then redirected to the **listf** file, instead of being printed on the screen.

```
$ ls
mydata intro preface
$ ls > listf
$ cat listf
mydata intro listf preface
```

Errors occur when you try to use the same filename for both an input file for the command and the redirected destination file. In this case, because the redirection operation is executed first, the input file, because it exists, is destroyed and replaced by a file of the same name. When the command is executed, it finds an input file that is empty.

In the **cat** command shown next, the file **myletter** is the name for both the destination file for redirected output and the input file for the **cat** operation. As shown in the next example, the redirection operation is executed first, destroying the **myletter** file and replacing it with a new and empty **myletter** file. Then the **cat** operation is executed and attempts to read all the data in the **myletter** file. However, nothing new is now in the **myletter** file.

```
$ cat myletter > myletter
```

You can also append the standard output to an existing file using the **>>** redirection operator. Instead of overwriting the file, the data in the standard output is added at the end of the file. In the next example, the **myletter** and **oldletter** files are appended to the **alletters** file. The **alletters** file will then contain the contents of both **myletter** and **oldletter**.

```
$ cat myletter >> alletters
$ cat oldletter >> alletters
```

The Standard Input

Many Linux commands can receive data from the standard input. The standard input itself receives data from a device or a file. The default device for the standard input is the keyboard. Characters typed into the keyboard are placed in the standard input, which is then directed to the Linux command. The **cat** command without a filename argument reads data from standard input. When you type in data on the keyboard, each character will be placed in the standard input and directed to the **cat** command. The **cat** command then sends the character to the standard output—the screen device—which displays the character on the screen.

If you combine the **cat** command with redirection, you have an easy way of saving what you have typed to a file. As shown in the next example, the output of the **cat** operation is redirected to the **mydat** file. The **mydat** file will now contain all the data typed in at the keyboard. The **cat** command, in this case, still has no file arguments. It will receive its data from the standard input, the keyboard device. The redirection operator redirects the output of the **cat** command to the file **mydat**. The **cat** command has no direct contact with any files; it is simply receiving input from the standard input and sending output to the standard output.

```
$ cat > mydat
This is a new line
for the cat
command
^D
$
```

Just as with the standard output, you can also redirect the standard input. The standard input may be received from a file rather than the keyboard. The operator for redirecting the standard input is the less-than sign, **<**. In the next example, the standard input is redirected to receive input from the **myletter** file, rather than the keyboard device. The contents of **myletter** are read into the standard input by the redirection operation. Then the **cat** command reads the standard input and displays the contents of **myletter**.

ENVIRONMENTS

```
$ cat < myletter
hello Christopher
How are you today
$
```

You can combine the redirection operations for both standard input and standard output. In the next example, the `cat` command has no filename arguments. Without filename arguments, the `cat` command receives input from the standard input and sends output to the standard output. However, the standard input has been redirected to receive its data from a file, while the standard output has been redirected to place its data in a file.

```
$ cat < myletter > newletter
```

Pipes: |

You may find yourself in situations in which you need to send data from one command to another. In other words, you may want to send the standard output of a command to another command, not to a destination file. Suppose you want to send a list of your filenames to the printer to be printed. You need two commands to do this: the `ls` command to generate a list of filenames and the `lpr` command to send the list to the printer. In effect, you need to take the output of the `ls` command and use it as input for the `lpr` command. You can think of the data as flowing from one command to another. To form such a connection in Linux, you use what is called a *pipe*. The *pipe operator*, |, (vertical bar character) placed between two commands forms a connection between them. The standard output of one command becomes the standard input for the other. The pipe operation receives output from the command placed before the pipe and sends this data as input to the command placed after the pipe. As shown in the next example, you can connect the `ls` command and the `lpr` command with a pipe. The list of filenames output by the `ls` command is piped into the `lpr` command.

```
$ ls | lpr
```

You can combine the pipe operation with other shell features, such as wildcard characters, to perform specialized operations. The next example prints only files with a .c extension. The `ls` command is used with the asterisk and ".c" to generate a list of filenames with the .c extension. Then this list is piped to the `lpr` command.

```
$ ls *.c | lpr
```

In the previous example, a list of filenames was used as input, but what is important to note is pipes operate on the standard output of a command, whatever that might be. The contents of whole files or even several files can be piped from one command to another. In the next example, the **cat** command reads and outputs the contents of the **mydata** file, which are then piped to the **lpr** command.

```
$ cat mydata | lpr
```

Linux has many commands that generate modified output. For example, the **sort** command takes the contents of a file and generates a version with each line sorted in alphabetic order. The **sort** command works best with files that are lists of items. Commands such as **sort** that output a modified version of its input are referred to as *filters*. Filters are often used with pipes and are discussed in detail in Chapter 14. In the next example, a sorted version of **mylist** is generated and piped into the **more** command for display on the screen. Note, the original file, **mylist**, has not been changed and is not itself sorted. Only the output of **sort** in the standard output is sorted.

```
$ sort mylist | more
```

You can, of course, combine several commands, connecting each pair with a pipe. The output of one command can be piped into another command, which, in turn, can pipe its output into still another command. Suppose you have a file with a list of items you want to print both numbered and in alphabetical order. To print the numbered and sorted list, you can first generate a sorted version with the **sort** command and then pipe that output to the **cat** command. The **cat** command with the **-n** option then takes as its input the sorted list and generates as its output a numbered, sorted list. The numbered, sorted list can then be piped to the **lpr** command for printing. The next example shows the command.

```
$ sort mylist | cat -n | lpr
```

The standard input piped into a command can be more carefully controlled with the standard input argument, **-**. When you use the dash as an argument for a command, it represents the standard input. Suppose you want to print a file with the name of its directory at the top. The **pwd** command outputs a directory name, and the **cat** command outputs the contents of a file. In this case, the **cat** command needs to take as its input both the file and the standard input piped in from the **pwd** command. The **cat** command will have two arguments: the standard input as represented by the dash and the filename of the file to be printed.

In the next example, the **pwd** command generates the directory name and pipes it into the **cat** command. For the **cat** command, this piped-in standard input now contains the directory name. As represented by the dash, the standard input is the first argument to the **cat** command. The **cat** command copies the directory name and the contents of the **mylist** file to the standard output, which is then piped to the **lpr** command for printing. If you want to print the directory name at the end of the file instead, simply make the dash the last argument and the filename the first argument, as in **cat mylist -** .

```
$ pwd | cat - mylist | lpr
```

Redirecting and Piping the Standard Error: >&, 2>

When you execute commands, an error could possibly occur. You may give the wrong number of arguments or some kind of system error could take place. When an error occurs, the system issues an error message. Usually such error messages are displayed on the screen, along with the standard output. Linux distinguishes between standard output and error messages, however. Error messages are placed in yet another standard byte stream called the *standard error*. In the next example, the **cat** command is given as its argument the name of a file that does not exist, **myintro**. In this case, the **cat** command simply issues an error:

```
$ cat myintro
cat : myintro not found
$
```

Because error messages are in a separate data stream from the standard output, error messages still appear on the screen for you to see even if you have redirected the standard output to a file. In the next example, the standard output of the **cat** command is redirected to the file **mydata**. However, the standard error, containing the error messages, is still directed to the screen.

```
$ cat myintro > mydata
cat : myintro not found
$
```

You can redirect the standard error as you can the standard output. This means you can save your error messages in a file for future reference. This is helpful if you need a record of the error messages. Like the standard output, the standard error has the screen device for its default destination, but you can redirect the standard error to any file or device you choose using special redirection operators. In this case, the error messages will not be displayed on the screen.

Redirection of the standard error relies on a special feature of shell redirection. You can reference all the standard byte streams in redirection operations with numbers. The numbers 0, 1, and 2 reference the standard input, standard output, and standard error, respectively. By default, an output redirection, >, operates on the standard output, 1. You can modify the output redirection to operate on the standard error, however, by preceding the output redirection operator with the number 2. In the next example, the **cat** command again will generate an error. The error message is redirected to the standard byte stream represented by number 2, the standard error.

```
$ cat nodata 2> myerrors
$ cat myerrors
cat : nodata not found
$
```

You can also append the standard error to a file by using the number 2 and the redirection append operator, >>. In the next example, the user appends the standard error to the **myerrors** file, which then functions as a log of errors.

```
$ cat nodata 2>> myerrors
```

Shell Variables

You define variables within a shell, and such variables are known—logically enough—as *shell variables*. Many different shells exist. Some utilities, such as the *mailx utility*, have their own shells with their own shell variables. You can also create your own shell using what are called *shell scripts*. You have a user shell that becomes active as soon as you log in. This is often referred to as the *login shell*. Special system variables are defined within this login shell. Shell variables exist as long as your shell is active, that is, until you exit the shell. For example, logging out will exit the login shell. When you log in again, any variables you may need in your login shell must be defined once again.

Definition and Evaluation of Variables: =, $, set, unset

You define a variable in a shell when you first use the variable's name. A variable's name may be any set of alphabetic characters, including the underscore. The name may also include a number, but the number cannot be the first character in the name. A name may not have any other type of character, such as an exclamation point, an ampersand, or even a space. Such symbols are reserved by the shell for its own use. Also, a name may not include more than one word. The shell uses spaces on the command line to distinguish different components of a command such as options, arguments, and the name of the command.

You assign a value to a variable with the assignment operator, =. You type in the variable name, the assignment operator, and then the value assigned. Do not place any spaces around the assignment operator. The assignment operation **poet** = Virgil, for example, will fail. (The C-shell has a slightly different type of assignment operation that is described in the section on C-shell variables later in this chapter.) You can assign any set of characters to a variable. In the next example, the variable **poet** is assigned the string **Virgil**.

```
$ poet=Virgil
```

Once you have assigned a value to a variable, you can then use the variable name to reference the value. Often you use the values of variables as arguments for a command. You can reference the value of a variable using the variable name preceded by the **$** operator. The dollar sign is a special operator that uses the variable name to reference a variable's value, in effect, evaluating the variable. Evaluation retrieves a variable's value, usually a set of characters. This set of characters then replaces the variable name on the command line. Wherever a **$** is placed before the variable name, the variable name is replaced with the value of the variable. In the next example, the shell variable **poet** is evaluated and its contents, **Virgil**, are then used as the argument for an **echo** command. The **echo** command simply echoes or prints a set of characters to the screen.

```
$ echo $poet
Virgil
```

You must be careful to distinguish between the evaluation of a variable and its name alone. If you leave out the **$** operator before the variable name, all you have is the variable name itself. In the next example, the **$** operator is absent from the variable name. In this case, the **echo** command has as its argument the word "poet", and so prints out "poet".

```
$ echo poet
poet
```

The contents of a variable are often used as command arguments. A common command argument is a directory pathname. It can be tedious to retype a directory path that is being used over and over again. If you assign the directory pathname to a variable, you can simply use the evaluated variable in its place. The directory path you assign to the variable is retrieved when the variable is evaluated with the **$** operator. The next example assigns a directory pathname to a variable and then uses the evaluated variable in a copy command. The evaluation of **ldir** (which is **$ldir**) results in the pathname **/home/chris/letters**. The copy command evaluates to **cp myletter /home/chris/letters**.

```
$ ldir=/home/chris/letters
$ cp myletter $ldir
```

You can obtain a list of all the defined variables with the **set** command. The next example uses the **set** command to display a list of all defined variables and their values.

```
$ set
poet   Virgil
ldir   /home/chris/letters/old
$
```

If you decide you do not want a certain variable, you can remove it with the **unset** command. The **unset** command undefines a variable. The next example undefines the variable **poet**. Then the user executes the **set** command to list all defined variables. Notice that **poet** is missing.

```
$ unset poet
$ set
ldir   /home/chris/letters/old
$
```

Shell Scripts: User-Defined Commands

You can place shell commands within a file and then have the shell read and execute the commands in the file. In this sense, the file functions as a shell program, executing shell commands as if they were statements in a program. A file that contains shell commands is called a *shell script*.

You enter shell commands into a script file using a standard text editor such as the Vi editor. The **sh** or **.** command used with the script's filename will read the script file and execute the commands. In the next example, the text file called **lsc** contains an **ls** command that displays only files with the extension **.c**.

lsc
```
ls *.c
```

```
$ sh lsc
main.c calc.c
$ . lsc
main.c calc.c
```

You can dispense with the **sh** and **.** commands by setting the executable permission of a script file. When the script file is first created by your text editor, it is only given read and write permission. The **chmod** command with the **+x** option will give the script file executable permission. (Permissions are discussed in Chapter 7.) Once it is executable, entering the name of the script file at the shell prompt and pressing ENTER will execute the script file and the shell commands in it. In effect, the script's filename becomes a new shell command. In this way, you can use shell scripts to design and create your own Linux commands. You only need to set the permission once. In the next example, the **lsc** file's executable permission for the owner is set to on. Then the **lsc** shell script is directly executed like any Linux command.

```
$ chmod u+x lsc
$ lsc
main.c calc.c
```

Just as any Linux command can take arguments, so also can a shell script. Arguments on the command line are referenced sequentially starting with **1**. An argument is referenced using the **$** operator and the number of its position. The first argument is referenced with **$1**, the second, with **$2**, and so on. In the next example, the **lsext** script prints out files with a specified extension. The first argument is the extension. The script is then executed with the argument **c** (of course, the executable permission must have been set).

lsext
```
ls *.$1
```

```
$ lsext c
main.c calc.c
```

In the next example, the commands to print out a file with line numbers have been placed in an executable file called **lpnum**, which takes a filename as its argument. The command to print out the line numbers is executed in the background.

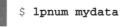

lpnum
```
pr -t -n $1 | lp &
```

```
$ lpnum mydata
```

You may need to reference more than one argument at a time. The number of arguments used may vary. In **lpnum,** you may want to print out three files at one time and five files at some other time. The **$** operator with the asterisk, **$***, references all the arguments on the command line. Using **$*** enables you to create scripts that take a varying number of arguments. In the next example, **lpnum** is rewritten using **$*** so it can take a different number of arguments each time you use it.

lpnum
```
pr -t -n $* | lp &
```

```
$ lpnum mydata preface
```

Jobs: Background, Kills, and Interruptions

In Linux, you not only have control over a command's input and output, but also over its execution. You can run a job in the background while you execute other commands. You can also cancel commands before they have finished executing. You can even interrupt a command, starting it again later from where you left off. Background operations are particularly useful for long jobs. Instead of waiting at the terminal until a command has finished execution, you can place it in the background. You can then continue executing other Linux commands. You can, for example, edit a file while other files are printing.

Canceling a background command can often save you a lot of unnecessary expense. If, say, you execute a command to print all your files and then realize you have some large files you do not want to print, you can reference that execution of the print command and cancel it. Interrupting commands is rarely used and sometimes, it is unintentionally executed. You can, if you want, interrupt an editing session to send mail and then return to your editing session, continuing from where you left off. The background commands, as well as commands to cancel and interrupt jobs, are listed in Table 7-2.

In Linux, a command is considered a *process*—a task to be performed. A Linux system can execute several processes at the same time, just as Linux can handle several users at the same time. Commands to examine and control processes exist, though they are often reserved for system administration operations. Processes actually include not only the commands a user executes, but also all the tasks the system must perform to keep Linux running.

The commands that users execute are often called *jobs* to distinguish them from system processes. When the user executes a command, it becomes a job to be performed by the system. The shell provides a set of job control operations that enable the user to control the execution of these jobs. You can place a job in the background, cancel a job, or interrupt one.

You execute a command in the background by placing an ampersand on the command line at the end of the command. When you do so, a user job number and a system process number are displayed. The user job number, placed in brackets, is the number by which the user references the job. The system process number is the number by which the system identifies the job. In the next example, the command to print the file **mydata** is placed in the background.

ENVIRONMENTS

```
$ lpr mydata &
[1]  534
$
```

You can place more than one command in the background. Each is classified as a job and given a name and a job number. The command **jobs** lists the jobs being run in the background. Each entry in the list consists of the job number in brackets, whether it is stopped or running, and the name of the job. The **+** sign indicates the job currently being processed, and the **-** sign indicates the next job to be executed. In the next example, two commands have been placed in the background. The **jobs** command then lists those jobs, showing which one is currently being executed.

```
$ lpr intro &
[1]  547
$ cat *.c > myprogs &
[2]  548
$ jobs
[1]  +  Running  lpr intro
[2]  -  Running  cat *.c > myprogs
$
```

If you wish, you can place several commands at once in the background by entering the commands on the command line, separated by an ampersand, **&**. In this case, the **&** both separates commands on the command line and executes them in the background. In the next example, the first command, to **sort** and redirect all files with a **.l** extension, is placed in the background. On the same command line, the second command, to print all files with a **.c** extension, is also placed in the background. Notice the two commands each end with **&**. The **jobs** command then lists the **sort** and **lpr** commands as separate operations.

```
$ sort *.l > ldocs & lpr *.c &
[1]  534

[2]  567
$ jobs
[1]  +  Running  sort *.l > ldocs
[2]  -  Running  lpr
$
```

After you execute any command in Linux, the system tells you what background jobs, if you have any running, have been completed so far. The system does not interrupt any operation, such as editing, to notify you about a completed job. If you want to be notified immediately when a certain job ends, no matter what you are doing on the system, you can use the **notify** command to instruct the system to tell you. The **notify** command takes a job number as its argument. When that job is finished, the system interrupts what you are doing to notify you the job has ended. The next example tells the system to notify the user when job 2 has finished.

```
$ notify %2
```

You can bring a job out of the background with the foreground command, **fg**. If only one job is in the background, the **fg** command alone will bring it to the foreground. If more than one job is in the background, you must use the job's number with the command. You place the job number after the **fg** command, preceded with a percent sign. A **bg** command also places a job in the background. This command is usually used for interrupted jobs. In the next example, the second job is brought back into the foreground. You may not immediately receive a prompt again because the second command is now in the foreground and executing. When the command is finished executing, the prompt appears, and you can execute another command.

```
$ fg %2
cat *.c > myprogs
$
```

If you want to stop a job running in the background, you can force it to end with the **kill** command. The *kill command* takes as its argument either the user job number or the system process number. The user job number must be preceded by a percent sign, **%**. You can find out the job number from the **jobs** command. In the next example, the **jobs** command lists the background jobs; then job 2 is canceled.

```
$ jobs
[1]   +   Running   lpr intro
[2]   -   Running   cat *.c > myprogs
$ kill %2
$
```

You can also cancel a job using the system process number, which you can obtain with the **ps** command. The **ps** command displays a great deal more information than the **jobs** command does. It is discussed in detail in Chapter 20 on systems administration. The next example lists the processes a user is running. The *PID* is the *system process number*, also known as the *process ID*. TTY is the terminal identifier. The time is how long the process has taken so far. COMMAND is the name of the process.

ENVIRONMENTS

```
$ ps
PID      TTY       TIME      COMMAND
523      tty24     0:05      sh
567      tty24     0:01      lpr
570      tty24     0:00      ps
```

You can then reference the system process number in a **kill** command. Use the process number without any preceding percent sign. The next example kills process 567.

```
$ kill 567
```

You can interrupt a job and stop it with the CTRL-Z command. This places the job to the side until it is restarted. The job is not ended; it merely remains suspended until you want to continue. When you're ready, you can continue with the job in either the foreground or the background using the **fg** or **bg** command. The **fg** command restarts an interrupted job in the foreground. The **bg** command places the interrupted job in the background.

At times, you may need to place a currently running job in the foreground into the background. However, you cannot move a currently running job directly into the background. You first need to interrupt it with CTRL-Z, and then place it in the background with the **bg** command. In the next example, the current command to list and redirect **.c** files is first interrupted with a CTRL-Z. Then that job is placed in the background.

```
$ cat *.c > myprogs
^Z
$ bg
```

Filters and Regular Expressions

Filters are commands that read data, perform operations on that data, and then send the results to the standard output. Filters generate different kinds of output, depending on their task. Some filters only generate information about the input, other filters output selected parts of the input, and still other filters output an entire version of the input, but in a modified way. Some filters are limited to one of these, while others have options that specify one or the other. You can think of a filter as operating on a stream of data; receiving data and generating modified output. As data is passed through the filter, it is analyzed, screened, or modified.

The data stream input to a filter consists of a sequence of bytes that can be received from files, devices, or the output of other commands or filters. The filter operates on the data stream, but it does not modify the source of the data. If a filter receives input from a file, the file itself is not modified. Only its data is read and fed into the filter.

The output of a filter is usually sent to the standard output. It can then be redirected to another file or device, or piped as input to another utility or filter. All the features of redirection and pipes apply to filters. Often data is read by one filter and its modified output piped into another filter. Data could easily undergo several modifications as it is passed from one filter to another. However, it is always important to realize the original source of the data is never changed.

Many utilities and filters use patterns to locate and select specific text in your file. Sometimes, you may need to use patterns in a more flexible and powerful way, searching for several different variations on a given pattern. You can include a set of special characters in your pattern to enable a flexible search. A pattern that contains such special characters is called a *regular expression*. Regular expressions can be used in most filters and utilities that employ pattern searches such as Ed, **sed**, **awk**, **grep**, and **egrep**. Although many of the special characters used for regular expressions are similar to the shell wildcard characters, they are used in a different way. Shell wildcard characters operate on filenames. Regular expressions search text.

In Linux, as in UNIX, text files are organized into a series of lines. For this reason, many editors and filters are designed to operate on a text file line by line. The first UNIX editor, *Ed*, is a line editor whose commands reference and operate on a text file one line at a time. Other editing utilities and filters operate on text much the same way as the Ed line editor. In fact, the Ed editor and other editing filters use the same set of core line editing commands. The editing filters such as **sed** and **diff** use those same line-editing commands to edit filter input. An edit filter receives lines of text as its input and performs line-editing operations on them, outputting a modified version of the text. Three major edit filters exist: **tr**, which translates characters; **diff**, which outputs editing information about two files; and **sed**, which performs line-editing operations on the input. Table 7-3 lists the different editing filters.

Using Redirection and Pipes with Filters

Filters send their output to the standard output and so, by default, display their output on the screen. The simplest filters merely output the contents of files. You have already seen the **cat** commands. What you may not have realized is that **cat** is a filter. It receives lines of data and outputs a version of that data. The **cat** filter receives input and copies it out to the standard output, which, by default, is displayed on the screen.

You can save the output of a filter in a file or send it to a printer. To do so, you need to use redirection or pipes. To save the output of a filter to a file, you redirect it to a file using the redirection operation, **>**. To send output to the printer, you pipe the output to the **lpr** utility, which then prints it. In the next command, the **cat** command pipes its output to the **lpr** command, which then prints it.

```
$ cat complist | lpr
```

Command	Execution
sed *editing-command file-list*	Outputs an edited form of its input. **sed** takes as an argument an editing command and a file list. The editing command is executed on input read from files in the file list. **sed** then outputs an edited version of the files. The editing commands are line-editing commands similar to those used for the Ed line editor.
n	With this option, **sed** does not output lines automatically. This option is usually used with the **p** command to output only selected lines.
f *filename*	With this option, **sed** reads editing commands *filename*
Line Commands	(You need to quote any new line characters if you are entering more than one line)
a	Appends text after a line
I	Inserts text before a line
c	Changes text
d	Deletes lines
p	Prints lines
w	Writes lines to a file
r	Reads lines from a file
q	Quits the **sed** editor before all lines are processed
n	Skips processing to next line
s /*pattern*/*replacement*/	Substitutes matched pattern with replacement text
g s/*pat*/*rep*/**g**	Global substitution on a line
p s/*pat*/*rep*/**p**	Outputs the modified line
w s/*pat*/*rep*/**w** *fname*	Writes the modified line to a file
/*pattern*/	A line can be located and referenced by a pattern
diff *filename filename*	Compares two files and outputs the lines that are different as well as the editing changes needed to make the first file the same as the second file

Table 7-3. *Edit Filters*

Command	Execution
f1-linenum **a** *f2-line1, f2-line2*	Appends lines from file2 to after *f1-linenum* in file1
f1-line1, f1-line2 **d** *f1-linenum*	Deletes the lines in file1
f1-line1, f1-line2 **c** *f2-line1, f2-line2*	Replaces lines in file1 with lines in file2
b	Ignores any trailing or duplicate blank
c	Outputs a context for differing lines. Three lines above and below are displayed.
e	Outputs a list of Ed editing commands that, when executed, change the first file into an exact copy of the second file
tr *first-character-list* *second-character-list*	Outputs a version of the input in which characters in the first character list that occur in the input are replaced in the output by corresponding characters in the second character list

Table 7-3.   *Edit Filters* (continued)

ENVIRONMENTS

Other commands for displaying files, such as **more**, may seem to operate like a filter, but they are not filters. You need to distinguish between filters and device-oriented utilities, such as **lpr** and **more**. Filters send their output to the standard output. A device-oriented utility such as **lpr**, though it receives input from the standard input, sends its output to a device. In the case of **lpr**, the device is a printer; for **more**, the device is the terminal. Such device-oriented utilities may receive their input from a filter, but they can only output to their device.

All filters accept input from the standard input. In fact, the output of one filter can be piped as the input for another filter. Many filters also accept input directly from files, however. Such filters can take filenames as their arguments and read data directly from those files. The **cat** and **sort** filters operate in this way. They can receive input from the standard input or use filename arguments to read data directly from files.

One of the more powerful features of **cat** is it can combine the contents of several files into one output stream. This output can then be piped into a utility or even another filter, allowing the utility or filter to operate on the combined contents of files as one data stream. For example, if you want to view the contents of several files at once, screen by screen, you must first combine them with the **cat** filter and then pipe the combined data into the **more** filter. The **more** command is, then, receiving its input from the standard input. In the following set of examples, the **cat** filter copies the contents of **preface** and **intro** into a combined output. In the first example, this output is piped into the **more** command. The **more** filter then enables you to view the combined text, screen by screen. In the second, the output is piped to the printer using the **lpr** command and, in the third, the output is redirected to a file called **frontdata**.

```
$ cat preface intro | more
$ cat preface intro | lpr
$ cat preface intro > frontdata
```

Types of Filter Output: wc, spell, and sort

The output of a filter may be a modified copy of the input, selected parts of the input, or simply some information about the input. Some filters are limited to one of these, while others have options that specify one or the other. The **wc**, **spell**, and **sort** filters illustrate all three kinds of output. The **wc** filter merely prints counts of the number of lines, words, and characters in a file. The **spell** filter selects misspelled words and outputs only those words. The **sort** command outputs a complete version of the input, but in sorted order. These three filters are listed in Table 7-4 with their more commonly used options.

The *wc filter* takes as its input a data stream, which is usually data read from a file. It then counts the number of lines, words, and characters (including the newline character, found at the end of a line) in the file and simply outputs these counts. In the next example, the **wc** command is used to find the number of lines, words, and characters in the **preface** file.

```
$ wc preface
6       27      142     preface
```

The *spell filter* checks the spelling of words in its input and outputs only the misspelled.

```
$ spell foodlistsp
soop
vegetebels
```

Using redirection, you can save those words in a file. With a pipe, you can print them. In the next example, the user saves the misspelled words to a file called **misspell**.

```
$ spell foodlistsp > misspell
```

Command	Execution
`cat` *filenames*	Displays a file. It can take filenames for its arguments. It outputs the contents of those files directly to the standard output, which, by default, is the screen.
`tee` *filename*	Copies the standard input to a file while sending it on to the standard output. It is usually used with another filter and enables you to save output to a file while sending the output on to another filter or utility.
`head` *filename*	Displays the first few lines of a file. The default is ten lines, but you can specify the number of lines
`tail` *filename*	Displays the last lines in a file. The default is ten lines, but you can specify the number of lines `$ tail` *filenames*.
`wc` *filename*	Counts the number of lines, words, and characters in a file and outputs only that number
`c`	Counts the number of characters in a file
`l`	Counts the number of lines in a file
`w`	Counts the number of words in a file
`spell` *filename*	Checks the spelling of each word in a file and outputs only the misspelled words
`sort` *filename*	Outputs a sorted version of a file
`cmp` *filename filename*	Compares two files, character by character, checking for differences. Stops at the first difference it finds and outputs the character position and line number
`comm` *filename filename*	Compares two files, line by line, and outputs both files according to lines that are similar and different for each
`grep` *pattern filenames*	Searches files for a pattern and lists any matched lines
`I`	Ignores uppercase and lowercase differences

Table 7-4.   *Filters*

Command	Execution
c	Only outputs a number—the count of the lines with the pattern
l	Displays the names of the files that contain the matching pattern
n	Outputs the line number along with the text of those lines with the matching pattern
v	Outputs all those lines that do not contain the matching pattern
fgrep *patterns file-list*	Searches files in the file list for several patterns at the same time. Executes much faster than either **grep** or **egrep**; however, **fgrep** cannot interpret special characters and cannot search for regular expressions.
egrep *pattern file-list*	Searches files in the file list for the occurrence of a pattern. Like **fgrep**, it can read patterns from a file. Like **grep**, it can use regular expressions, interpreting special characters. However, unlike **grep**, it can also interpret extended special characters such as **?**, **|**, and **+**.
pr	Outputs a paginated version of the input, adding headers, page numbers, and any other specified format
cpio *generated-filenames* | **cpio -o** > *archive-file* **cpio -i** *filenames* < *archive-file*	Copies files to an archive and extracts files from an archive. Has two modes of operation: one using the **-o** option to copy files to an archive and the other using the **-i** option to extract files from an archive. When copying files to an archive, you need first to generate the list of filenames using a command such as **ls** or **find**.

Table 7-4.   *Filters* (continued)

You can pipe the output of one filter into another filter, in effect, applying the capabilities of several filters to your data. For example, suppose you only want to know how many words are misspelled. You could pipe the output of the **spell** filter into the **wc** filter, which would count the number of misspelled words. In the next example, the words in the **foodlistsp** file are spell-checked, and the list of misspelled words is piped to the **wc** filter. The **wc** filter, with its **-w** option, then counts those words and outputs the count.

```
$ spell preface | wc -w
2
```

The *sort* *filter* outputs a sorted version of a file. **sort** is a useful utility with many different sorting options. These options are primarily designed to operate on files arranged in a database format. In fact, **sort** can be thought of as a powerful data manipulation tool, arranging records in a database-like file. This chapter examines how **sort** can be used to alphabetize a simple list of words. The **sort** filter sorts, character by character, on a line. If the first character in two lines is the same, then **sort** will sort on the next character in each line. You can, of course, save the sorted version in a file or send it to the printer. In the next example, the user saves the sorted output in a file called **slist**.

```
$ sort foodlist > slist
```

Searching Files: grep and fgrep

The *grep* and *fgrep* *filters* search the contents of files for a pattern. They then inform you of what file the pattern was found in and print the lines in which it occurred in each file. Preceding each line is the name of the file in which the line is located. **grep** can search for only one pattern, whereas **fgrep** can search for more than one pattern at a time. The **grep** and **fgrep** filters, along with their options, are described in Table 7-4.

The **grep** filter takes two types of arguments. The first argument is the pattern to be searched for; the second argument is a list of filenames, which are the files to be searched. You enter the filenames on the command line after the pattern. You can also use special characters, such as the asterisk, to generate a file list.

```
$ grep pattern filenames-list
```

In the next example, the **grep** command searches the lines in the **preface** file for the pattern "stream".

```
$ grep stream preface
 consists of a stream of
```

If you want to include more than one word in the pattern search, you enclose the words within single quotation marks. This is to quote the spaces between the words in the pattern. Otherwise, the shell would interpret the space as a delimiter or argument on the command line, and **grep** would try to interpret words in the pattern as part of the file list. In the next example, **grep** searches for the pattern "text file".

```
$ grep 'text file' preface
A text file in Unix
text files, changing or
```

If you use more than one file in the file list, **grep** will output the name of the file before the matching line. In the next example, two files, **preface** and **intro**, are searched for the pattern "data". Before each occurrence, the filename is output.

```
$ grep data preface intro
 preface: data in the file.
 intro: new data
```

As mentioned earlier, you can also use shell wildcard characters to generate a list of files to be searched. In the next example, the asterisk wildcard character is used to generate a list of all files in your directory. This is a simple way of searching all of a directory's files for a pattern.

```
$ grep data *
```

The special characters are often useful for searching a selected set of files. For example, if you want to search all your C program source code files for a particular pattern, you can specify the set of source code files with a ***.c**. Suppose you have an unintended infinite loop in your program and you need to locate all instances of iterations. The next example searches only those files with a **.c** extension for the pattern "while" and displays the lines of code that perform iterations.

```
$ grep while *.c
```

Regular Expressions

Regular expressions enable you to match possible variations on a pattern, as well as patterns located at different points in the text. You can search for patterns in your text that have different ending or beginning letters, or you can match text at the beginning or end of a line. The regular expression special characters are the circumflex, dollar sign, asterisk, period, and brackets: **^, $, *, ., []**., as shown in the following table.

Character	Match	Operation
^	Start of a line	References the beginning of a line
$	End of a line	References the end of a line
.	Any character	Matches on any one possible character in a pattern
*	Repeated characters	Matches on repeated characters in a pattern
[]	Classes	Matches on classes of characters (a set of characters) in the pattern

The circumflex and dollar sign match on the beginning and end of a line. The asterisk matches repeated characters, the period matches single characters, and the brackets match on classes of characters. Regular expressions are used extensively in many Linux filters and applications to perform searches and matching operations. The Vi and Emacs editors and the **sed**, **diff**, **grep,** and **gawk** filters all use regular expressions.

To match on patterns at the beginning of a line, you enter the ^ followed immediately by a pattern. The ^ special character makes the beginning of the line an actual part of the pattern to be searched. In the next example, ^**consists** matches on the line beginning with the pattern "consists".

```
^consists
consists of a stream of
```

The next example uses the $ special character to match patterns at the end of a line.

```
such$
 be used to create such
```

The *period* is a special character that matches any one character. Any character will match a period in your pattern. The pattern **b.d** will find a pattern consisting of three letters. The first letter will be *b*, the third letter will be *d*, and the second letter can be any character. It will match on "bid", "bad", "bed", "b+d", or "b d", for example. Notice the space is a valid character (so is a tab).

For the period special character to have much effect, you should provide it with a context—a beginning and ending pattern. The pattern **b.d** provides a context consisting of the preceding *b* and the following *d*. If you specified **b.** without a *d*, then any pattern beginning with *b* and having at least one more character would match. The pattern would match on "bid", "bath", "bedroom", and "bump", as well as "submit", "habit", and "harbor".

The asterisk special character, *****, matches on zero or more consecutive instances of a character. The character matched is the one placed before the asterisk in the pattern. You can think of the asterisk as an operator that takes the preceding character as its operand. The asterisk will search for any repeated instances of this character. Here is the syntax of the asterisk special character:

```
c*    matches on zero or more repeated occurrences of whatever
      the character c is:
c cc ccc cccc  and so on.
```

The asterisk comes in handy when you need to replace several consecutive instances of the same character. The next example matches on a pattern beginning with *b* and followed by consecutive instances of the character *o*. This regular expression will match on "boooo", "bo", "boo", and "b".

```
bo*
    book
    born
    booom
    zoom     no match
```

The **.*** pattern used by itself will match on any character in the line; in fact, it selects the entire line. If you have a context for **.***, you can match different segments of the line. A pattern placed before the **.*** special characters will match the remainder of the line from the occurrence of the pattern. A pattern placed after the **.*** will match the beginning of the line up until the pattern. The **.*** placed between patterns will match any intervening text between those patterns on the line. In the next example, the pattern **.*and** matches everything in the line from the beginning up to and including the letters "and". Then the pattern **and.*** matches everything in the line from and including the letters "and" to the end of the line. Finally, the pattern **/o.*F/** matches all the text between and including the letters *o* and *F*.

```
.*and     Hello to you and to them Farewell

and.*     Hello to you and to them Farewell

o.*F      Hello to you and to them Farewell
```

Because the * special character matches zero or more instances of the character, you can provide a context with zero intervening characters. For example, the pattern I.*t matches on "It" as well as "Intelligent".

Suppose instead of matching on a specific character or allowing a match on any character, you need to match only on a selected set of characters. For example, you might want to match on words ending with an *A* or *H*, as in "seriesA" and "seriesH", but not "seriesB" or "seriesK". If you used a period, you would match on all instances. Instead, you need to specify that *A* and *H* are the only possible matches. You can do so with the brackets special characters.

You use the brackets special characters to match on a set of possible characters. The characters in the set are placed within brackets and listed next to each other. Their order of listing does not matter. You can think of this set of possible characters as defining a class of characters, and characters that fall into this class are matched. You may notice the brackets operate much like the shell brackets. In the next example, the user searches for a pattern beginning with "doc" and ending with either the letters *a*, *g*, or *N*. It will match on "doca", "docg", or "docN", but not on "docP".

```
doc[agN]
     List of documents
     doca docb
     docg docN docP
```

The brackets special characters are particularly useful for matching on various suffixes or prefixes for a pattern. For example, suppose you need to match on filenames that begin with the pattern "week" and have several different suffixes, as in **week1**, **week2**, and so on. To match on just those files with suffixes 2, 4, and 5, you enclose those characters within brackets. In the next example, notice the pattern **week[245]** matches on **week2** and **week4**, but not on **week1**.

```
week[245]
     week2 weather
     reports on week4
     week1 reports          no match
```

The brackets special characters are also useful for matching on a pattern that begins in either uppercase or lowercase. Linux distinguishes between uppercase and lowercase characters. The pattern "computer" is different from the pattern "Computer"; "computer" would not match on the version beginning with an uppercase *C*. To match on both patterns, you need to use the brackets special characters to specify both *c* and *C* as possible first characters in the pattern. Place the uppercase and lowercase versions of the same character within brackets at the beginning of the pattern. For example, the pattern `[Cc]omputer` searches for the pattern "computer" beginning with either an uppercase *C* or a lowercase *c*.

You can specify a range of characters within the brackets with the dash. Characters are ranged according to the character set being used. In the ASCII character set, lowercase letters are grouped together. Specifying a range with `[a-z]` selects all the lowercase letters. In the first example, shown next, any lowercase letter will match the pattern. More than one range can be specified by separating the ranges with a comma. The ranges `[A-Za-z]` select all alphabetic letters, both uppercase and lowercase.

```
doc[a-z]        doca docg docN docP
doc[A-Za-z]     doca docg docN docP
```

Although shell file matching characters enable you to match on filenames, regular expressions enable you to match on data within files. Using **grep** with regular expressions, you can locate files and the lines in them that match a specified pattern. You can use special characters in a **grep** pattern, making the pattern a regular expression. **grep** regular expressions use the `*`, `.`, and `[]` special characters, as well as the `^` and `$` special characters.

Suppose you want to use the long form output of **ls** to display just your directories. One way to do this is to generate a list of all directories in the long form and pipe this list to **grep**, which can then pick out the directory entries. You can do this by using the `^` special character to specify the beginning of a line. Remember, in the long-form output of **ls**, the first character indicates the file type. A **d** represents a directory, an **l** represents a symbolic link, and an **a** represents a regular file. Using the pattern `^d`, **grep** will match only on those lines beginning with a *d*.

```
$ ls -l | grep '^d'
drwxr-x---  2  chris 512 Feb 10 04:30   reports
drwxr-x---  2  chris 512 Jan 6  01:20   letters
```

If you only want to list those files that have symbolic links, you can use the pattern `^l`:

```
$ ls -l | grep '^l'
lrw-rw-r-- 1  chris  group 4    Feb 14   10:30  lunch
```

Be sure to distinguish between the shell wildcard character and special characters used in the pattern. When you include special characters in your **grep** pattern, you need to quote the pattern. Notice regular-expression special characters and shell wildcard characters use the same symbols: the asterisk, period, and brackets. If you do not, then any special characters in the pattern will be interpreted by the shell as shell wildcard characters. Without quotes, an asterisk would be used to generate filenames. rather than being evaluated by **grep** to search for repeated characters. Quoting the pattern guarantees that **grep** will evaluate the special characters as part of a regular expression. In the next example, the asterisk special character is used in the pattern as a regular expression and in the filename list as a shell wildcard character to generate filenames. In this case, all files in the current directory will be searched for patterns with zero or more *s*'s after "report".

```
$ grep 'reports*' *
mydata: The report was sitting on his desk.
weather: The weather reports were totally accurate.
```

The brackets match on either a set of characters, a range of characters, or a nonmatch of those characters. For example, the pattern **doc[abc]** matches on the patterns "doca", "docb", and "docc", but not on "docd". The same pattern can be specified with a range: **doc[a-c]**. However, the pattern **doc[^ab]** will match on any pattern beginning with "doc", but not ending in *a* or *b*. Thus, "docc" will be retrieved, but not "doca" or "docb". In the next example, the user finds all lines that reference "doca", "docb", or "docc".

```
$ grep 'doc[abc]' myletter
File letter doca and docb.
We need to redo docc.
```

Certain Linux utilities, such as **egrep** and **awk**, can make use of an extended set of special characters in their patterns. These special characters are |, ( ) , +, and ?, and are listed here:

Character	Execution
pattern	*pattern*	Logical OR for searching for alternative patterns
(*pattern*)	Parentheses for grouping patterns
char+	Searches for one or more repetitions of the previous character
char?	Searches for zero or one instance of the previous character

The + and ? are variations on the * special character, whereas | and ( ) provide new capabilities. Patterns that can use such special characters are referred to as full regular expressions. The Ed and Ex standard line editors do not have these extended special characters. Only **egrep**, which is discussed here, and **awk** have extended special characters.

The + sign matches one or more instances of a character. For example, **t+** matches at least one or more *t*'s, just as **tt*** does. **t+** matches on "sitting" or "biting", but not "ziing". The **?** matches zero or one instance of a character. For example, **t?** matches on one *t* or no *t*'s, but not "tt". The expression **it?i** matches on "ziing" and "biting", but not "sitting". In the next examples, repeated *n* characters followed by an *e* are searched for. With the + special character, the regular expression **an+e** matches on one or more instances of *n* preceded by *a* and followed by *e*. The "ane" is matched in "anew", and "anne" is matched on "canned".

The **|** and **( )** special characters operate on pattern segments, rather than just characters. The **|** is a logical OR special character that specifies alternative search patterns within a single regular expression. Although part of the same regular expression, the patterns are searched for as separate patterns. The search pattern **create|stream** searches for either the pattern "create" or "stream".

```
create|stream
 consists of a stream of
 be used to create such
```

The **egrep** command combines the capabilities of **grep** and **fgrep**. Like **fgrep**, it can search for several patterns at the same time. Like **grep**, it can evaluate special characters in its patterns and search for regular expressions. Unlike **grep**, however, it can evaluate extended special characters, such as the logical OR operator, **|**. In this respect, **egrep** is the most powerful of the three search filters.

To search for several patterns at once, you can either enter them on the command line separated by a newline character as **fgrep** does, or you can use the logical OR special character in a pattern to specify alternative patterns to be searched for in a file. The patterns are actually part of the same regular expression, but they are searched for as separate patterns. The pattern **create|stream egrep** will search for either the pattern "create" or the pattern "stream".

```
$ egrep 'create|stream' preface
consists of a stream of
 be used to create such
```

Chapter 8

The Linux File Structure

In Linux, all files are organized into directories that, in turn, are hierarchically connected to each other in one overall file structure. A file is referenced not just according to its name, but also according to its place in this file structure. You can create as many new directories as you want, adding more directories to the file structure. The Linux file commands can perform sophisticated operations, such as moving or copying whole directories along with their subdirectories. You can use file operations such as **find**, **cp**, **mv**, and **ln** to locate files and copy, move, or link them from one directory to another. Desktop file managers, such as kfm and midnight commander used on the KDE and Gnome desktops, perform the same operations using icons, windows, and menus.

Together, these features make up the Linux file structure. This chapter first examines different types of files, as well as file classes. Then, the chapter examines the overall Linux file structure and how directories and files can be referenced using pathnames and the working directory. The last part of the chapter discusses the different file operations such as copying, moving, and linking files, as well as file permissions.

Linux Files

You can name a file using any alphabetic characters, underscores, and numbers. You can also include periods and commas. A number cannot begin a filename, however, and except in certain special cases, you should never begin a filename with a period. Other characters, such as slashes, question marks, or asterisks, are reserved for use as special characters by the system and cannot be part of a filename. Filenames can be as long as 256 characters.

You can include an extension as part of a filename. A period is used to distinguish the filename proper from the extension. Extensions can be useful for categorizing your files. You are probably familiar with certain standard extensions that have been adopted by convention. For example, C source code files always have an extension of **.c**. Files that contain compiled object code have a **.o** extension. You can, of course, make up your own file extensions. The following examples are all valid Linux filenames:

```
preface
chapter2
New_Revisions
calc.c
intro.bk1
```

Special initialization files are also used to hold shell configuration commands. These are the hidden, or dot files, referred to in Chapter 5 that begin with a period. Dot files have predetermined names. Recall that when you use **ls** to display your filenames, the dot files will not be displayed. To include the dot files, you need to use **ls** with the **-a** option. Dot files are discussed in more detail in the chapter on shell configuration, Chapter 9.

As shown in Figure 8-1, the `ls -l` command displays detailed information about a file. First the permissions are displayed, followed by the number of links, the owner of the file, the name of the group the user belongs to, the file size in bytes, the date and time the file was last modified, and the name of the file. Permissions indicate who can access the file: The user, members of a group, or all other user. Permissions are discussed in detail in Chapter 9. The group name indicates the group being given group permission. In Figure 8-1, the file type for **mydata** is that of an ordinary file. Only one link exists, indicating the file has no other names and no other links. The owner's name is **chris**, the same as the login name, and the group name is **weather**. Other users probably also belong to the weather group. The size of the file is 207 bytes and it was last modified on February 20, at 11:55 A.M. The name of the file is **mydata**.

If you want to display this detailed information for all the files in a directory, simply use the `ls -l` command without an argument.

```
$ ls -l
-rw-r--r--  1  chris weather 207  Feb 20  11:55  mydata
-rw-rw-r--  1  chris weather 568  Feb 14  10:30  today
-rw-rw-r--  1  chris weather 308  Feb 17  12:40  monday
```

All files in Linux have one physical format—a byte stream. A *byte stream* is just a sequence of bytes. This allows Linux to apply the file concept to every data component in the system. Directories are classified as files, as are devices. Treating everything as a file allows Linux to organize and exchange data more easily. The data in a file can be sent directly to a device such as a screen because a device interfaces with the system using the same byte-stream file format as regular files.

This same file format is used to implement other operating system components. The interface to a device, such as the screen or keyboard, is designated as a file. Other

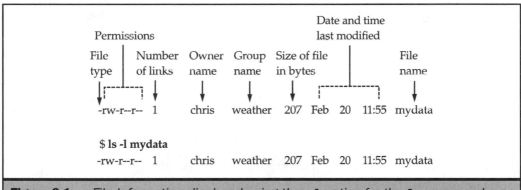

Figure 8-1.   *File Information displayed using the* `-l` *option for the* `ls` *command*

components, such as directories, are themselves byte-stream files, but they have a special internal organization. A directory file contains information about a directory, organized in a special directory format. Because these different components are treated as files, they can be said to constitute different *file types*. A character device is one file type. A directory is another file type. The number of these file types may vary according to your specific implementation of Linux. Four common types of files exist, however: ordinary files, directory files, character device files, and block device files. Although you may rarely reference a file's type, it can be useful when searching for directories or devices. Later in the chapter, you see how to use the file type in a search criterion with the **find** command to search specifically for directory or device names.

Although all ordinary files have a byte-stream format, they may be used in different ways. The most significant difference is between binary and text files. Compiled programs are examples of binary files. However, even text files can be classified according to their different uses. You can have files that contain C programming source code or shell commands, or even a file that is empty. The file could be an executable program or a directory file. The Linux file command helps you determine for what a file is used. It examines the first few lines of a file and tries to determine a classification for it. The **file** command looks for special keywords or special numbers in those first few lines, but it is not always accurate. In the next example, the **file** command examines the contents of two files and determines a classification for them:

```
$ file monday reports
monday:      text
reports:       directory
```

If you need to examine the entire file byte-by-byte, you can do so with the **od** command. The **od** command performs a dump of a file. By default, it prints every byte in its octal representation. However, you can also specify a character, decimal, or hexadecimal representation. The **od** command is helpful when you need to detect any special character in your file, or if you want to display a binary file. If you perform a character dump, then certain nonprinting characters will be represented in a character notation. For example, the carriage return is represented by a \n. Both the **file** and **od** commands, with their options, are listed in Table 8-1.

The File Structure

Linux organizes files into a hierarchically connected set of directories. Each directory may contain either files or other directories. In this respect, directories perform two important functions. A *directory* holds files, much like files held in a file drawer, and a directory connects to other directories, much like a branch in a tree is connected to other branches. With respect to files, directories appear to operate like file drawers, with each drawer holding several files. To access files, you open a file drawer. Unlike

Commands	Execution
`file`	Examines the first few lines of a file to determine a classification
`-f` *filename*	Reads the list of filenames to be examined from a file
`od`	Prints the contents of a file byte-by-byte in either octal, character, decimal, or hexadecimal; octal is the default
`-c`	Outputs character form of byte values; nonprinting characters have a corresponding character representation
`-d`	Outputs decimal form of byte values
`-x`	Outputs hexadecimal form of byte values
`-o`	Outputs octal form of byte values

Table 8-1.   *The `file` and `od` Commands*

ENVIRONMENTS

file drawers, however, directories can contain not only files, but other directories, as well. In this way, a directory can connect to another directory.

Because of the similarities to a tree, such a structure is often referred to as a *tree structure*. This structure could more accurately be thought of as an upside-down bush rather than a tree, however, because no trunk exists. The tree is represented upside down, with the root at the top. Extending down from the root are the branches. Each branch grows out of only one branch, but it can have many lower branches. In this respect, it can be said to have a *parent-child structure*. In the same way, each directory is itself a subdirectory of one other directory. Each directory may contain many subdirectories, but is itself the child of only one parent directory.

The Linux file structure branches into several directories beginning with a root directory, */*. Within the root directory several system directories contain files and programs that are features of the Linux system. The root directory also contains a directory called **home** that may contain the home directories of all the users in the system. Each user's home directory, in turn, contains the directories the user has made for his use. Each of these could also contain directories. Such nested directories would branch out from the user's home directory, as shown in Figure 8-2.

Home Directories

When you log in to the system, you are placed within your home directory. The name given to this directory by the system is the same as your login name. Any files you create when you first log in are organized within your home directory. Within your home directory, however, you can create more directories. You can then change to

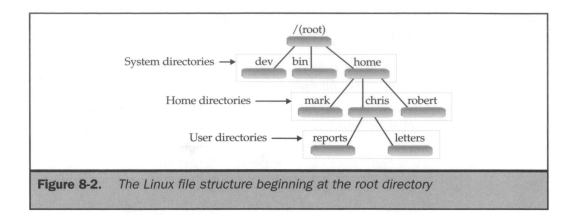

Figure 8-2. *The Linux file structure beginning at the root directory*

these directories and store files in them. The same is true for other users on the system. Each user has her own home directory, identified by the appropriate login name. Users, in turn, can create their own directories.

You can access a directory either through its name or by making it the default directory. Each directory is given a name when it is created. You can use this name in file operations to access files in that directory. You can also make the directory your default directory. If you do not use any directory names in a file operation, then the default directory will be accessed. The default directory is referred to as the *working directory*. In this sense, the working directory is the one from which you are currently working.

When you log in, the working directory is your home directory, usually having the same name as your login name. You can change the working directory by using the **cd** command to designate another directory as the working directory. As the working directory is changed, you can move from one directory to another. Another way to think of a directory is as a corridor. In such a corridor, there are doors with names on them. Some doors lead to rooms; others lead to other corridors. The doors that open to rooms are like files in a directory. The doors that lead to other corridors are like other directories. Moving from one corridor to the next corridor is like changing the working directory. Moving through several corridors is like moving through several directories.

Pathnames

The name you give to a directory or file when you create it is not its full name. The full name of a directory is its *pathname*. The hierarchically nested relationship among directories forms paths, and these paths can be used to identify and reference any directory or file unambiguously. In Figure 8-3, a path exists from the root directory, **/**, through the **home** directory to the **robert** directory. Another path exists from the root directory through the **home** and **chris** directories to the **reports** directory. Although parts of each path may at first be shared, at some point they differ. Both the directories **robert** and **reports** share the two directories, **root** and **home**. Then they differ. In the

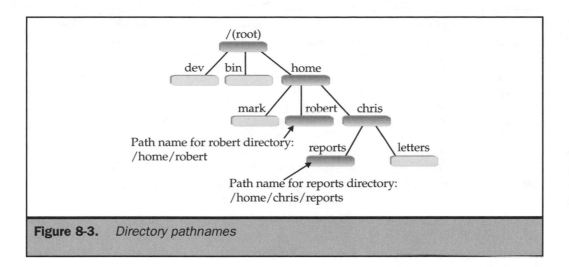

Figure 8-3. *Directory pathnames*

home directory, **robert** ends with **robert**, but the directory **chris** then leads to **reports**. In this way, each directory in the file structure can be said to have its own unique path. The actual name by which the system identifies a directory always begins with the root directory and consists of all directories nested above that directory.

In Linux, you write a pathname by listing each directory in the path separated by a forward slash. A slash preceding the first directory in the path represents the root. The pathname for the **robert** directory is **/home/robert**. The pathname for the **reports** directory is **/home/chris/reports**. Pathnames also apply to files. When you create a file within a directory, you give the file a name. The actual name by which the system identifies the file, however, is the filename combined with the path of directories from the root to the file's directory. In Figure 8-4, the path for the **weather** file consists of the

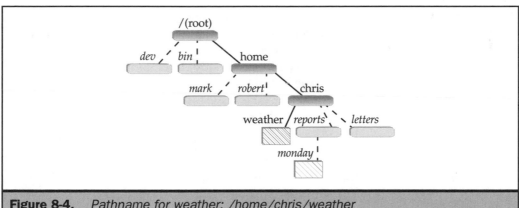

Figure 8-4. *Pathname for weather: /home/chris/weather*

root, **home**, and **chris** directories and the filename **weather**. The pathname for **weather** is **/home/chris /weather** (the root directory is represented by the first slash).

Pathnames may be absolute or relative. An *absolute pathname* is the complete pathname of a file or directory beginning with the root directory. A *relative pathname* begins from your working directory; it is the path of a file relative to your working directory. Using the directory structure described in Figure 8-4, if **chris** is your working directory, the relative pathname for the file **monday** is **/reports/monday**. The absolute pathname for **monday** is **/home/chris/reports/monday**.

The absolute pathname from the root to your home directory could be especially complex and, at times, even subject to change by the system administrator. To make it easier to reference, you can use a special character, the tilde ~, which represents the absolute pathname of your home directory. In the next example, from the **thankyou** directory, the user references the **weather** file in the home directory by placing a tilde and slash before **weather**:

```
$ pwd
/home/chris/letters/thankyou
$ cat ~/weather
raining and warm
$
```

You must specify the rest of the path from your home directory. In the next example, the user references the **monday** file in the **reports** directory. The tilde represents the path to the user's home directory, **/home/chris**, and then the rest of the path to the **monday** file is specified.

$ cat ~/reports/monday

System Directories

The root directory that begins the Linux file structure contains several system directories. The system directories contain files and programs used to run and maintain the system. Many contain other subdirectories with programs for executing specific features of Linux. For example, the directory **/user/bin** contains the various Linux commands that users execute, such as cp and mv. The directory **/bin** holds interfaces with different system devices, such as the printer or the terminal. Table 8-2 lists the basic system directories, and Figure 8-5 shows how they are organized in the tree structure.

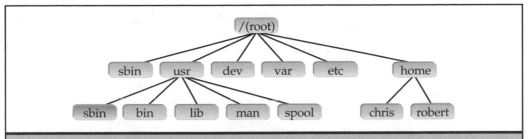

Figure 8-5. *System directories in Linux*

Directory	Function
/	Begins the file system structure, called the *root*
/home	Contains users' **home** directories
/bin	Holds all the standard commands and utility programs
/usr	Holds those files and commands used by the system; this directory breaks down into several subdirectories
/usr/bin	Holds user-oriented commands and utility programs
/usr/sbin	Holds system administration commands
/usr/lib	Holds libraries for programming languages
/usr/doc	Holds Linux documentation
/usr/man	Holds the online manual **man** files
/usr/spool	Holds spooled files, such as those generated for printing jobs and network transfers
/sbin	Holds system administration commands for booting the system
/var	Holds files that vary, such as mailbox files
/dev	Holds file interfaces for devices such as the terminals and printers
/etc	Holds system configuration files and any other system files

Table 8-2. *Standard System Directories in Linux*

Listing, Displaying, and Printing Files: ls, cat, more, and lpr

One of the primary functions of an operating system is the management of files. You may need to perform certain basic output operations on your files, such as displaying them on your screen or printing them. The Linux system provides a set of commands that perform basic file-management operations, such as listing, displaying, and printing files, as well as copying, renaming, and erasing files. These commands are usually made up of abbreviated versions of words. For example, the **ls** command is a shortened form of "list" and lists the files in your directory. The **lpr** command is an abbreviated form of "line print" and will print a file. The **cat** and **more** commands display the contents of a file on the screen. Table 8-3 lists these commands with their different options. When you log in to your Linux system, you may want a list of the files in your home directory. The **ls** command, which outputs a list of your file and directory names, is useful for this. The **ls** command has many possible options for displaying filenames according to specific features. These are discussed in more detail at the end of the chapter.

Displaying Files: cat and more

You may also need to look at the contents of a file. The **cat** and **more** commands display the contents of a file on the screen. **cat** stands for *concatenate.* **cat** is a complex and versatile command, as described in Chapter 7. Here it is used in a limited way, displaying the text of a file on the screen:

```
$ cat mydata
computers
```

The **cat** command outputs the entire text of a file to the screen at once. This presents a problem when the file is large because its text quickly speeds past on the screen. The **more** command is designed to overcome this limitation by displaying one screen of text at a time. You can then move forward or backward in the text at your leisure. You invoke the **more** command by entering the command name followed by the name of the file you want to view.

```
$ more mydata
```

When **more** invokes a file, the first screen of text is displayed. To continue to the next screen, you press the **f** key or the SPACEBAR. To move back in the text, you press the **b** key. You can quit at any time by pressing the **q** key.

Printing Files: lpr, lpq, and lprm

With the printer commands like lpr and lprm you can perform printing operations like printing files or canceling print jobs (see Table 8-3). When you need to print files, use the **lpr** command to send files to the printer connected to your system. In the next example, the user prints the **mydata** file:

```
$ lpr mydata
```

Command or Option	Execution
ls	This command lists file and directory names: **$ ls**
cat	This filter can be used to display a file. It can take filenames for its arguments. It outputs the contents of those files directly to the standard output, which, by default, is directed to the screen: **$ cat** *filenames*
more	This utility displays a file screen-by-screen. It can take filenames for its arguments. It outputs the contents of those files to the screen, one screen at a time: **$ more** *filenames*
+num	Begins displaying the file at page *num*
*num***f**	Skips forward *num* number of screens
*num***b**	Skips backward *num* number of screens
d	Displays half a screen
h	Lists all **more** commands
q	Quits more utility
lpr	Sends a file to the line printer to be printed; a list of files may be used as arguments
-P *printer-name*	Selects a specific printer
lpq	Lists the print queue for printing jobs
lprm	Removes a printing job from the printing queue

Table 8-3.   *Listing, Displaying, and Printing Files*

If you want to print several files at once, you can specify more than one file on the command line after the **lpr** command. In the next example, the user prints out both the **mydata** and **preface** files:

```
$ lpr mydata preface
```

Printing jobs are placed in a queue and printed one, at a time, in the background. You can continue with other work as your files print. You can see the position of a particular printing job at any given time with the **lpq** command. **lpq** gives the owner of the printing job (the login name of the user who sent the job), the print job ID, the size in bytes, and the temporary file in which it is currently held. In this example, the owner is chris and the print ID is 00015:

```
$ lpq
Owner     ID       Chars      Filename
chris     00015    360        /usr/lpd/cfa00015
```

If you need to cancel an unwanted printing job, you can do so with the **lprm** command. lprm takes as its argument either the ID number of the printing job or the owner's name. lprm then removes the print job from the print queue. For this task, lpq is helpful, for it provides you with the ID number and owner of the printing job you need to use with **lprm**. In the next example, the print job 15 is canceled:

```
$ lprm  00015
```

You can have several printers connected to your Linux system. One of these will be designated the default printer, and **lpr** prints to this printer, unless another printer is specified. With **lpr**, you can specify the particular printer on which you want your file printed. Each printer on your system will have its own name. You can specify which printer to use with the **-P** option followed by that printer's name. In the next example, the file **mydata** is printed on the evans1 printer:

```
$ lpr -Pevans1 mydata
```

Managing Directories: mkdir, rmdir, ls, cd, and pwd

You can create and remove your own directories, as well as change your working directory, with the **mkdir**, **rmdir**, and **cd** commands. Each of these commands can take as its argument the pathname for a directory. The **pwd** command displays the absolute pathname of your working directory. In addition to these commands, the special characters represented by a single dot, a double dot, and a tilde can be used to reference the working directory, the parent of the working directory, and the home directory, respectively. Taken together, these commands enable you to manage your directories. You can create nested directories, move from one directory to another, and use pathnames to reference any of your directories. Those commands commonly used to manage directories are listed in Table 8-4.

Command	Execution
`mkdir`	Creates a directory: `$ mkdir` reports
`rmdir`	Erases a directory: `$ rmdir` letters
`ls -F`	Lists directory name with a preceding slash: `$ ls -F` today /reports /letters
`ls -R`	Lists working directory as well as all subdirectories
`cd` *directory name*	Changes to the specified directory, making it the working directory. `cd` without a directory name changes back to the home directory: `$ cd` reports `$ cd`
`pwd`	Displays the pathname of the working directory: `$ pwd` /home/chris/reports
directory name/filename	A slash is used in pathnames to separate each directory name. In the case of pathnames for files, a slash separates the preceding directory names from the filename: `$ cd` /home/chris/reports `$ cat` /home/chris/reports/mydata
`..`	References the parent directory. You can use it as an argument or as part of a pathname: `$ cd ..` `$ mv ..`/larisa oldletters

Table 8-4.   *Directory Commands*

Command	Execution
.	References the working directory. You can use it as an argument or as part of a pathname: $ **ls** . $ **mv** ../aleina .
~/*pathname*	The tilde is a special character that represents the pathname for the **home** directory. It is useful when you need to use an absolute pathname for a file or directory: $ **cp** monday ~/today $ **mv** tuesday ~/weather

Table 8-4.   *Directory Commands* (continued)

You create and remove directories with the **mkdir** and **rmdir** commands. In either case, you can also use pathnames for the directories. In the next example, the user creates the directory **reports**. Then, the user creates the directory **letters** using a pathname.

```
$ mkdir reports
$ mkdir /home/chris/letters
```

You can remove a directory with the **rmdir** command followed by the directory name. In the next example, the user removes the directory **reports** with the **rmdir** command. Then, the directory **letters** is removed using its pathname.

```
$ rmdir reports
$ rmdir /home/chris/letters
```

You have seen how to use the **ls** command to list the files and directories within your working directory. To distinguish between file and directory names, however, you need to use the **ls** command with the **-F** option. A slash is then placed after each directory name in the list.

```
$ ls
weather reports letters
$ ls -F
weather reports/ letters/
```

The **ls** command also takes as an argument any directory name or directory pathname. This enables you to list the files in any directory without first having to change to that directory. In the next example, the **ls** command takes as its argument the name of a directory, **reports**. Then the **ls** command is executed again, only this time the absolute pathname of **reports** is used.

```
$ ls reports
monday tuesday
$ ls /home/chris/reports
monday tuesday
$
```

Within each directory, you can create still other directories; in effect, nesting directories. Using the **cd** command, you can change from one directory to another. No indicator tells you what directory you are currently in, however. To find out what directory you have changed to, use the **pwd** command to display the name of your current working directory. The **pwd** command displays more than just the name of the directory—it displays the full pathname, as shown in the next example. The pathname displayed here consists of the **home** directory, **dylan**, and the directory it is a part of, **home**. Each directory name is separated by a slash. The root directory is represented by a beginning slash.

```
$ pwd
/home/dylan
```

As you already know, you can change directories with the **cd** command. Changing to a directory makes that directory the working directory, which is your default directory. File commands, such as **ls** and **cp**, unless specifically told otherwise, operate on files in your working directory.

When you log in to the system, your working directory is your home directory. When a user account is created, the system also creates a home directory for that user. When you log in, you are always placed in your home directory. The **cd** command enables you to make another directory the working directory. In a sense, you can move from your home directory into another directory. This other directory then becomes the default directory for any commands and any new files created. For example, the **ls** command now lists files in this new working directory.

The **cd** command takes as its argument the name of the directory to which you want to change. The name of the directory can be the name of a subdirectory in your working directory or the full pathname of any directory on the system. If you want to change back to your home directory, you only need to enter the **cd** command by itself, without a filename argument.

```
$ pwd
/home/dylan
$ cd props
$ pwd
/home/dylan/props
$ cd /home/chris/letters
$ pwd
/home/chris/letters
$
```

You can use a double dot symbol, **..**, to represent a directory's parent. This literally represents the pathname of the parent directory. You can use the double dot symbol with the **cd** command to move back up to the parent directory, making the parent directory the current directory. In the next example, the user moves to the **props** directory and then changes back to the home directory:

```
$ cd props
$ pwd
/home/dylan/props
$ cd ..

$ pwd
/home/dylan
```

A directory always has a parent (except, of course, for the root). For example, in the last listing, the parent for **thankyou** is the **letters** directory. When a directory is created, two entries are made: one represented with a dot, **.**, and the other represented by a double dot, **..** . The dot represents the pathnames of the directory, and the double dot represents the pathname of its parent directory. The double dot, used as an argument in a command, references a parent directory. The single dot references the directory itself. In the next example, the user changes to the **letters** directory. The **ls** command is used with the **.** argument to list the files in the **letters** directory. Then, the **ls** command is used with the **..** argument to list the files in the parent directory of **letters**, the **chris** directory.

```
$ cd letters
$ ls .
thankyou
$ ls ..
weather letters
$
```

You can use the single dot to reference your working directory, instead of using its pathname. For example, to copy a file to the working directory retaining the same name, the dot can be used in place of the working directory's pathname. In this sense, the dot is another name for the working directory. In the next example, the user copies the **weather** file from the **chris** directory to the **reports** directory. The **reports** directory is the working directory and can be represented with the single dot.

```
$ cd reports
$ cp /home/chris/weather   .
```

The **..** symbol is often used to reference files in the parent directory. In the next example, the **cat** command displays the **weather** file in the parent directory. The pathname for the file is the **..** symbol followed by a slash and the filename.

```
$ cat ../weather
raining and warm
```

You can use the **cd** command with the **..** symbol to step back through successive parent directories of the directory tree from a lower directory. In the next example, the user is placed in the **thankyou** directory. Then, the user steps back up to the **chris** directory by continually using the command **cd ..** .

File and Directory Operations: find, cp, mv, rm, and ln

As you create more and more files, you may want to back them up, change their names, erase some of them, or even give them added names. Linux provides you with several file commands that enable you to search for files, copy files, rename files, or remove files (see Table 8-6). If you have a large number of files, you can also search them to locate a specific one. The commands are shortened forms of full words, consisting of only two characters. The **cp** command stands for "copy" and copies a file, mv stands for "move" and renames or moves a file, rm stands for "remove" and erases a file, and ln stands for "link" and adds another name for a file. One exception to this rule is the **find** command, which performs searches of your filenames to find a file.

Searching Directories: find

Once you have a large number of files in many different directories, you may need to search them to locate a specific file, or files, of a certain type. The **find** command enables you to perform such a search. The **find** command takes as its arguments directory names followed by several possible options that specify the type of search and the criteria for the search. find then searches within the directories listed and their subdirectories for files that meet these criteria. The **find** command can search for a file based on its name, type, owner, and even the time of the last update.

```
$ find directory-list -option  criteria
```

The **-name** option has as its criteria a pattern and instructs find to search for the filename that matches that pattern. To search for a file by name, you use the **find** command with the directory name followed by the **-name** option and the name of the file.

```
$ find directory-list -name filename
```

The **find** command also has options that merely perform actions, such as outputting the results of a search. If you want find to display the filenames it has found, you simply include the **-print** option on the command line along with any other options. The **-print** option instructs find to output to the standard output the names of all the files it locates. In the next example, the user searches for all the files in the **reports** directory with the name **monday**. Once located, the file, with its relative pathname, is printed.

```
$ find reports -name monday -print
reports/monday
```

The **find** command prints out the filenames using the directory name specified in the directory list. If you specify an absolute pathname, the absolute path of the found directories will be output. If you specify a relative pathname, only the relative pathname is output. In the previous example, the user specified a relative pathname, **reports**, in the directory list. Located filenames were output beginning with this relative pathname. In the next example, the user specifies an absolute pathname in the directory list. Located filenames are then output using this absolute pathname.

```
$ find /home/chris -name monday -print
/home/chris/reports/monday
```

If you want to search your working directory, you can use the dot in the directory pathname to represent your working directory. The double dot would represent the parent directory. The next example searches all files and subdirectories in the working directory, using the dot to represent the working directory. If you are located in your **home** directory, this is a convenient way to search through all your own directories. Notice the located filenames are output beginning with a dot.

```
$ find . -name weather -print
./weather
```

You can use shell wildcard characters as part of the pattern criteria for searching files. The special character must be quoted, however, to avoid evaluation by the shell. In the next example, all files with the **.c** extension in the **programs** directory are searched for:

```
$ find programs -name '*.c' -print
```

You can also use the **find** command to locate other directories. In Linux, a directory is officially classified as a special type of file. Although all files have a byte-stream format, some files, such as directories, are used in special ways. In this sense, a file can be said to have a file type. The **find** command has an option called **-type** that searches for a file of a given type. The **-type** option takes a one-character modifier that represents the file type. The modifier that represents a directory is a **d**. In the next example, both the directory name and the directory file type are used to search for the directory called **thankyou**:

```
$ find /home/chris -name thankyou -type d -print
/home/chris/letters/thankyou
$
```

File types are not so much different types of files, as they are the file format applied to other components of the operating system, such as devices. In this sense, a device is treated as a type of file, and you can use find to search for devices and directories, as well as ordinary files. Table 8-5 lists the different types available for the **find** command's **-type** option.

Moving and Copying Files

To make a copy of a file, you simply give cp two filenames as its arguments. The first filename is the name of the file to be copied—the one that already exists. This is often referred to as the *source file*. The second filename is the name you want for the copy. This will be a new file containing a copy of all the data in the source file. This second argument is often referred to as the *destination file*. The syntax for the **cp** command follows:

```
$ cp source-file destination-file
```

In the next example, the user copies a file called **proposal** to a new file called **oldprop**:

```
$ cp proposal oldprop
```

Command or Option	Execution
`find`	Searches directories for files based on search criteria. This command has several options that specify the type of criteria and actions to be take.
`-name` *pattern*	Searches for files with the *pattern* in the name
`-group` *name*	Searches for files belonging to this group *name*
`-size` *numc*	Searches for files with the size *num* in blocks. If `c` is added after *num*, then the size in bytes (characters) is searched for
`-mtime` *num*	Searches for files last modified *num* days ago
`-newer` *pattern*	Searches for files modified after the one matched by *pattern*
`-print`	Outputs the result of the search to the standard output. The result is usually a list of filenames, including their full pathnames
`-type` *filetype*	Searches for files with the specified file type
`b`	Block device file
`c`	Character device file
`d`	Directory file
`f`	Ordinary (regular) file
`p`	Named pipes (fifo)
`l`	Symbolic links

Table 8-5. The `find` Command

When the user lists the files in that directory, the new copy will be among them.

```
$ ls
proposal  oldprop
```

You could unintentionally destroy another file with the **cp** command. The **cp** command generates a copy by first creating a file and then copying data into it. If another file has the same name as the destination file, then that file is destroyed and a new file with that name is created. In a sense, the original file is overwritten with the new copy. In the next example, the **proposal** file is overwritten by the **newprop** file. The **proposal** file already exists.

```
$ cp newprop  proposal
```

Most Linux distributions configure your system to detect this overwrite condition. If not, you can use the **cp** command with the **-i** option to detect it. With this option, cp first checks to see if the file already exists. If it does, you are then asked if you want to overwrite the existing file. If you enter **y**, the existing file is destroyed and a new one created as the copy. If you enter anything else, this is taken as a negative answer and the **cp** command is interrupted, preserving the original file.

```
$ cp -i  newprop  proposal
Overwrite proposal?  n
$
```

To copy a file from your working directory to another directory, you only need to use that directory name as the second argument in the **cp** command. The name of the new copy will be the same as the original, but the copy will be placed in a different directory. Files in different directories can have the same names. Because files in different directories are registered as different files.

```
$ cp filenames directory-name
```

The **cp** command can take a list of several filenames for its arguments, so you can copy more than one file at a time to a directory. Simply specify the filenames on the command line, entering the directory name as the last argument. All the files are then copied to the specified directory. In the next example, the user copies both the files **preface** and **doc1** to the **props** directory. Notice **props** is the last argument.

```
$ cp preface doc1 props
```

You can use any of the wildcard characters to generate a list of filenames to use with **cp** or **mv**. For example, suppose you need to copy all your C source code files to a given directory. Instead of listing each one individually on the command line, you could use a * character with the **.c** extension to match on and generate a list of C source code files (all files with a **.c** extension). In the next example, the user copies all source code files in the current directory to the **sourcebks** directory:

```
$ cp *.c sourcebks
```

ENVIRONMENTS

If you want to copy all the files in a given directory to another directory, you could use ***.*** to match on and generate a list of all those files in a **cp** command. In the next example, the user copies all the files in the **props** directory to the **oldprop** directory. Notice the use of a **props** pathname preceding the ***.*** special characters. In this context, **props** is a pathname that will be appended before each file in the list that ***.*** generates.

```
$ cp props/*.* oldprop
```

You can, of course, use any of the other special characters, such as **.**, **?**, or **[]**. In the next example, the user copies both source code and object code files (**.c** and **.o**) to the **projbk** directory:

```
$ cp *.[oc] projbk
```

When you copy a file, you may want to give the copy a different name than the original. To do so, place the new filename after the directory name, separated by a slash.

```
$ cp filename directory-name/new-filename
```

In the next example, the file **newprop** is copied to the directory **props** and the copy is given the name **version1**. The user then changes to the **props** directory and lists the files. Only one file exists, which is called **version1**.

```
$ cp newprop props/version1
$ cd props
$ ls
version1
```

You can use the **mv** command either to change the name of a file or to move a file from one directory to another. When using mv to rename a file, you simply use the new filename as the second argument. The first argument is the current name of the file you are renaming.

```
$ mv original-filename   new-filename
```

In the next example, the **proposal** file is renamed with the name **version1**:

```
$ mv proposal version1
```

As with cp, it is easy for mv to erase a file accidentally. When renaming a file, you might accidentally choose a filename already used by another file. In this case, that other file will be erased. The **mv** command also has a **-i** option that checks first to see if a file by that name already exists. If it does, then you are asked first if you want to overwrite it. In the next example, a file already exists with the name **version1**. The overwrite condition is detected and you are asked whether you want to overwrite that file.

```
$ ls
proposal version1
$ mv -i  version1  proposal
Overwrite proposal?  n
$
```

You can move a file from one directory to another by using the directory name as the second argument in the **mv** command. In this case, you can think of the **mv** command as simply moving a file from one directory to another, rather than renaming the file. After you move the file, it will have the same name as it had in its original directory, unless you specify otherwise.

```
$ mv filename directory-name
```

If you want to rename a file when you move it, you can specify the new name of the file after the directory name. The directory name and the new filename are separated by a forward slash. In the next example, the file **newprop** is moved to the directory **props** and renamed as **version1**:

```
$ mv newprops props/version1
$ cd props
$ ls
version1
```

You can also use any of the special characters described in Chapter 5 to generate a list of filenames to use with **mv**. In the next example, the user moves all source code files in the current directory to the **newproj** directory:

```
$ mv *.c newproj
```

If you want to move all the files in a given directory to another directory, you can use ***.*** to match on and generate a list of all those files. In the next example, the user moves all the files in the **reports** directory to the **repbks** directory:

```
$ mv reports/*.*  repbks
```

Moving and Copying Directories

You can also copy or move whole directories at once. Both **cp** and **mv** can take as their first argument a directory name, enabling you to copy or move subdirectories from one directory into another. The first argument is the name of the directory to be moved or copied, while the second argument is the name of the directory within which it is to be placed. The same pathname structure used for files applies to moving or copying directories.

You can just as easily copy subdirectories from one directory to another. To copy a directory, the **cp** command requires you to use the **-r** option. The **-r** option stands for "recursive." It directs the **cp** command to copy a directory, as well as any subdirectories it may contain. In other words, the entire directory subtree, from that directory on, will be copied. In the next example, the **thankyou** directory is copied to the **oldletters** directory. Now two **thankyou** subdirectories exist, one in **letters** and one in **oldletters**.

```
$ cp -r letters/thankyou oldletters
$ ls -F letters
/thankyou
$ ls -F oldletters
/thankyou
```

Erasing a File: the rm Command

As you use Linux, you will find the number of files you use increases rapidly. Generating files in Linux is easy. Applications such as editors, and commands such as **cp**, easily create files (see Table 8-6). Eventually, many of these files may become outdated and useless. You can then remove them with the **rm** command. In the next example, the user erases the file **oldprop**:

```
$ rm oldprop
```

The **rm** command can take any number of arguments, enabling you to list several filenames and erase them all at the same time. You just list them on the command line after you type rm.

```
$ rm proposal version1 version2
```

Be careful when using the **rm** command because it is irrevocable. Once a file is removed, it cannot be restored. Suppose, for example, you enter the **rm** command by accident while meaning to enter some other command, such as cp or mv. By the time you press ENTER and realize your mistake, it is too late. The files are gone. To protect against this kind of situation, you can use the **rm** command's **-i** option to confirm you want to erase a file. With the **-i** option, you are prompted separately for each file and asked whether to remove it. If you enter **y**, the file will be removed. If you enter anything else, the file is not removed. In the next example, the **rm** command is instructed to erase the files **proposal** and **oldprop**. The **rm** command then asks for confirmation for each file. The user decides to remove **oldprop,** but not **proposal**.

```
$ rm -i proposal oldprop
Remove proposal? n
Remove oldprop? y
$
```

Command	Execution
cp *filename filename*	Copies a file. cp takes two arguments: the original file and the name of the new copy. You can use pathnames for the files to copy across directories: $ **cp** today reports/monday
cp -r *dirname dirname*	Copies a subdirectory from one directory to another. The copied directory includes all its own subdirectories: $ **cp -r** letters/thankyou oldletters
mv *filename filename*	Moves (renames) a file. mv takes two arguments: the first is the file to be moved. The second argument can be the new filename or the pathname of a directory. If it is the name of a directory, then the file is literally moved to that directory, changing the file's pathname: $ **mv** today /home/chris/reports
mv *dirname dirname*	Moves directories. In this case, the first and last arguments are directories: $ **mv** letters/thankyou oldletters
ln *filename filename*	Creates added names for files referred to as links. A link can be created in one directory that references a file in another directory: $ **ln** today reports/monday
rm *filenames*	Removes (erases) a file. Can take any number of filenames as its arguments. Literally removes links to a file. If a file has more than one link, you need to remove all of them to erase a file: $ **rm** today weather weekend

Table 8-6. *File Operations*

Links: the ln Command

You can give a file more than one name using the **ln** command. You might want to reference a file using different filenames to access it from different directories. The added names are often referred to as *links*.

The **ln** command takes two arguments: the name of the original file and the new, added filename. The **ls** operation lists both filenames, but only one physical file will exist.

```
$ ln original-file-name added-file-name
```

In the next example, the **today** file is given the additional name **weather**. It is just another name for the **today** file.

```
$ ls
today
$ ln today weather
$ ls
today weather
```

You can give the same file several names by using the **ln** command on the same file many times. In the next example, the file **today** is given both the name **weather** and **weekend**:

```
$ ln today weather
$ ln today weekend
$ ls
today weather weekend
```

You can use the **ls** command with the **-l** option to find if a file has several links. **ls** with **-l** lists several pieces of information, such as permissions, the number of links a file has, its size, and the date it was last modified. In this line of information, the first number, which precedes the user's login name, specifies the number of links a file has. The number before the date is the size of the file. The date is the last time a file was modified. In the next example, the user lists the full information for both **today** and **weather**. Notice the number of links in both files is two. Furthermore, the size and date are the same. This suggests both files are actually different names for the same file.

```
$ ls -l today weather
-rw-rw-r-- 2  chris  group 563  Feb  14   10:30  today
-rw-rw-r-- 2  chris  group 563  Feb  14   10:30  weather
```

This still does not tell you specifically what filenames are linked. You can be somewhat sure if two files have exactly the same number of links, sizes, and modification dates, as in the case of the files **today** and **weather**. To be certain, however, you can use the **ls** command with the **-i** option. With the **-i** option, the **ls** command lists the filename and its inode number. An *inode* number is a unique number used by the system to identify a specific file. If two filenames have the same inode number, they reference exactly the same file. They are two names for the same file. In the next example, the user lists **today**, **weather**, and **larisa**. Notice that **today** and **weather** have the same inode number.

```
$ ls -i today weather larisa
1234 today     1234 weather    3976 larisa
```

The added names, or links, created with ln are often used to reference the same file from different directories. A file in one directory can be linked to and accessed from another directory. Suppose you need to reference a file in the home directory from within another directory. You can set up a link from that directory to the file in the home directory. This link is actually another name for the file. Because the link is in another directory, it can have the same name as the original file.

To link a file in the home directory to another directory, use the name of that directory as the second argument in the **ln** command.

```
$ ln filename directory-name
```

In the next example, the file **today** in the **chris** directory is linked to the **reports** directory. The **ls** command lists the **today** file in both the **chris** directory and the **reports** directory. In fact, only one copy of the **today** file exists, the original file in the home directory.

```
$ ln today reports
$ ls
today reports
$ ls reports
today
$
```

Just as with the **cp** and **mv** commands, you can give another name to the link. Simply place the new name after the directory name, separated by a slash. In the next example, the file **today** is linked to the **reports** directory with the name **wednesday**. Only one actual file still exists, the original file called **today** in the **chris** directory. However, **today** is now linked to the directory **reports** with the name **wednesday**.

In this sense, **today** has been given another name. In the **reports** directory, the **today** file goes by the name **wednesday**.

```
$ ln today reports/wednesday
$ ls
today reports
$ ls reports
wednesday
$
```

You can easily link a file in any directory to a file in another directory by referencing the files with their pathnames. In the next example, the file **monday** in the **reports** directory is linked to the directory, **chris**. Notice the second argument is an absolute pathname.

```
$ ln monday /home/chris
```

To erase a file, you need to remove all its links. The name of a file is actually considered a link to that file. Hence the command **rm** that removes the link to the file. If you have several links to the file and remove only one of them, the others stay in place and you can reference the file through them. The same is true even if you remove the original link—the original name of the file. Any added links will work just as well. In the next example, the **today** file is removed with the **rm** command. However, a link to that same file exists, called **weather**. The file can then be referenced under the name **weather**.

```
$ ln today weather
$ rm today
$ cat weather
The storm broke today
and the sun came out.
$
```

Symbolic Links and Hard Links

Linux supports what are known as symbolic links. Links, as they have been described so far, are called *hard links*. Although hard links will suffice for most of your needs, they suffer from one major limitation. A hard link may fail when you try to link to a file on some other user's directory. This is because the Linux file structure can be physically segmented into what are called file systems. A *file system* can be made up of any physical memory device or devices, from a floppy disk to a bank of hard disks. Although the files and directories in all file systems are attached to the same overall directory tree, each file system physically manages its own files and directories. This means a file in one file system cannot be linked by a hard link to a file in another file system. If you try to link to a file on another user's directory that is located on another file system, your hard link will fail.

To overcome this restriction, you use symbolic links. A *symbolic link* holds the pathname of the file to which it is linking. It is not a direct hard link but, rather, information on how to locate a specific file. Instead of registering another name for the same file as a hard link does, a symbolic link can be thought of as another symbol that represents the file's pathname. A symbolic link is another way of writing the file's pathname.

You create a symbolic link using the **ln** command with the **-s** option. In the next example, the user creates a link called **lunch** to the file **/home/george/veglist**:

```
$ ln -s lunch /home/george/veglist
```

If you list the full information about a symbolic link and its file, you will find the information displayed is different. In the next example, the user lists the full information for both **lunch** and **/home/george/veglist** using the **ls** command with the **-l** option. The first character in the line specifies the file type. Symbolic links have their own file type represented by a l. The file type for **lunch** is l, indicating it is a symbolic link, not an ordinary file. The number after the term "group" is the size of the file. Notice the sizes differ. The size of the **lunch** file is only 4 bytes. This is because **lunch** is only a symbolic link—a file that holds the pathname of another file—and a pathname takes up only a few bytes. It is not a direct hard link to the **veglist** file.

```
$ ls lunch /home/george/veglist
lrw-rw-r-- 1  chris   group 4    Feb  14   10:30  lunch
-rw-rw-r-- 1  george  group 793  Feb  14   10:30  veglist
```

To erase a file, you need to remove only its hard links. If any symbolic links are left over, they will be unable to access the file. In this case, a symbolic link would hold the pathname of a file that no longer exists.

Unlike hard links, you can use symbolic links to create links to directories. In effect, you can create another name with which you can reference a directory. If you use a symbolic link for a directory name, however, remember the **pwd** command always displays the actual directory name, not the symbolic name. In the next example, the user links the directory **thankyou** with the symbolic link **gifts**. When the user uses **gifts** in the **cd** command, the user is actually changed to the **thankyou** directory. **pwd** displays the pathname for the **thankyou** directory.

```
$ ln -s /home/chris/letters/thankyou  gifts
$ cd gifts
$ pwd
/home/chris/letters/thankyou
$
```

If you want to display the name of the symbolic link, you can access it in the **cwd** variable. The *cwd variable* is a special system variable that holds the name of a directory's symbolic link, if one exists. Variables such as **cwd** are discussed in Chapter 15. You display the contents of **cwd** with the command **echo $cwd**.

```
$ pwd
/home/chris/letters/thankyou
$ echo $cwd
/home/chris/gifts
```

File and Directory Permissions: chmod

Each file and directory in Linux contains a set of permissions that determines who can access them and how. You set these permissions to limit access in one of three ways: You can restrict access to yourself alone, you can allow users in a predesignated group to have access, or you can permit anyone on your system to have access; and, you can control how a given file or directory is accessed. A file and directory may have read, write, and execute permission. When a file is created, it is automatically given read and write permissions for the owner, enabling you to display and modify the file. You may change these permissions to any combination you want. A file could have read-only permission, preventing any modifications. A file could also have execute permission, allowing it to be executed as a program.

Three different categories of users can have access to a file or directory: the owner, the group, or others. The owner is the user who created the file. Any file you create, you own. You can also permit your group to have access to a file. Often, users are collected into groups. For example, all the users for a given class or project could be formed into a group by the system administrator. A user can give access to a file to other members of the group. Finally, you can also open up access to a file to all other users on the system. In this case, every user on your system could have access to one of your files or directories. In this sense, every other user on the system makes up the "others" category.

Each category has its own set of read, write, and execute permissions. The first set controls the user's own access to his files—the owner access. The second set controls the access of the group to a user's files. The third set controls the access of all other users to the user's files. The three sets of read, write, and execute permissions for the three categories—owner, group, and other—make a total of nine types of permissions.

As you saw in the previous section, the **ls** command with the **-1** option displays detailed information about the file, including the permissions. In the next example, the first set of characters on the left is a list of the permissions set for the **mydata** file.

```
$ ls -l mydata
-rw-r--r--  1  chris weather 207 Feb  20  11:55    mydata
```

An empty permission is represented by a dash, **-**. The read permission is represented by *r*, write by *w*, and execute by *x*. Notice there are ten positions. The first character indicates the file type. In a general sense, a directory can be considered a type of file. If the first character is a dash, a file is being listed. If it is *d*, information about a directory is being displayed.

The next nine characters are arranged according to the different user categories. The first set of three characters is the owner's set of permissions for the file. The second set of three characters is the group's set of permissions for the file. The last set of three characters is the other users' set of permissions for the file. In Figure 8-6, the **mydata** file has the read and write permissions set for the owner category, the read permission only set for the group category, and the read permission set for the other users category. This means, although anyone in the group or any other user on the system can read the file, only the owner can modify it.

You use the **chmod** command to change different permission configurations. chmod takes two lists as its arguments: permission changes and filenames. You can specify the list of permissions in two different ways. One way uses permission symbols and is referred to as the *symbolic method*. The other uses what is known as a "binary mask" and is referred to as either the *absolute* or the *relative method*. Of the two, the symbolic method is the more intuitive and will be presented first. Table 8-7 lists options for the **chmod** command.

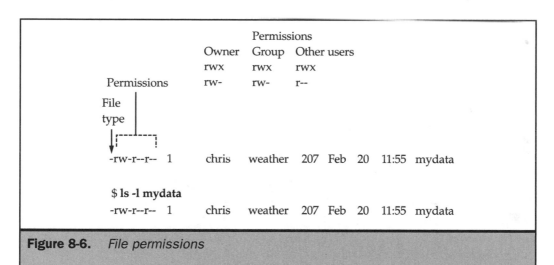

Figure 8-6.   *File permissions*

Command or Option	Execution
chmod	Changes the permission of a file or directory
Options	
+	Adds a permission
–	Removes a permission
=	Assigns entire set of permissions
r	Sets read permission for a file or directory. A file can be displayed or printed. A directory can have the list of its files displayed.
w	Sets write permission for a file or directory. A file can be edited or erased. A directory can be removed.
x	Sets execute permission for a file or directory. If the file is a shell script, it can be executed as a program. A directory can be changed to and entered.
u	Sets permissions for the user who created and owns the file or directory
g	Sets permissions for group access to a file or directory
o	Sets permissions for access to a file or directory by all other users on the system
a	Sets permissions for access by the user, group, and all other users
s	Sets User ID and Group ID permission; program owned by owner and group
t	Set sticky bit permission; program remains in memory
chgrp *groupname filenames*	Changes the group for a file or files

Table 8-7.   *File and Directory Permission Operations*

Options	
chown *user-name* *filenames*	Changes the owner of a file or files
ls -l *filename*	Lists a filename with its permissions displayed
ls -ld *directory*	Lists a directory name with its permissions displayed
ls -l	Lists all files in a directory with its permissions displayed

Table 8-7.   *File and Directory Permission Operations* (continued)

ENVIRONMENTS

Setting Permissions: Permission Symbols

As you might have guessed, the symbolic method of setting permissions uses the characters *r, w,* and *x* for read, write, and execute, respectively. Any of these permissions can be added or removed. The symbol to add a permission is the plus sign, +. The symbol to remove a permission is the minus sign, -. In the next example, the **chmod** command adds the execute permission and removes the write permission for the **mydata** file. The read permission is not changed.

```
$ chmod +x-w mydata
```

Permission symbols also specify each user category. The owner, group, and others categories are represented by the *u, g,* and *o* characters, respectively. Notice the owner category is represented by a *u* and can be thought of as the user. The symbol for a category is placed before the read, write, and execute permissions. If no category symbol is used, all categories are assumed, and the permissions specified are set for the user, group, and others. In the next example, the first **chmod** command sets the permissions for the group to read and write. The second **chmod** command sets permissions for other users to read. Notice no spaces are between the permission specifications and the category. The permissions list is simply one long phrase, with no spaces.

```
$ chmod g+rw mydata
$ chmod o+r mydata
```

A user may remove permissions as well as add them. In the next example, the read permission is set for other users, but the write and execute permissions are removed.

```
$ chmod o+r-wx mydata
```

Another permission symbol exists, **a**, which represents all the categories. The *a* symbol is the default. In the next example, both commands are equivalent. The read permission is explicitly set with the *a* symbol denoting all types of users: other, group, and user.

```
$ chmod a+r mydata
$ chmod +r mydata
```

One of the most common permission operations is setting a file's executable permission. This is often done in the case of shell program files, which are discussed in Chapters 8 and 16. The executable permission indicates a file contains executable instructions and can be directly run by the system. In the next example, the file **lsc** has its executable permission set and then executed:

```
$ chmod u+x lsc
$ lsc
main.c lib.c
$
```

In addition to the read/write/execute permissions, you can also set ownership permissions for executable programs. Normally, the user who runs a program owns it while it is running, even though the program file itself may be owned by another user. The User ID permission allows the original owner of the program to own it always, even while another user is running the program. For example, most software on the system is owned by the root user, but is run by ordinary users. Some such software may have to modify files owned by the root. In this case, the ordinary user would need to run that program with the root retaining ownership so the program could have the permissions to change those root-owned files. The Group ID permission works the same way, except for groups. Programs owned by a group retain ownership, even when run by users from another group. The program can then change the owner group's files.

To add both the User ID and Group ID permissions to a file, you use the **s** option. The following example adds the User ID permission to the **pppd** program, which is owned by the root user. When an ordinary user runs pppd, the root user retains ownership, allowing the pppd program to change root-owned files.

```
#   chmod +s /usr/sbin/pppd
```

The User ID and Group ID permissions show up as an *s* in the execute position of the owner and group segments. User ID and Group ID are essentially variations of the execute permission, *x*. Read, write, and User ID permission would be *rws* instead of just *rwx*.

```
# ls -l /usr/sbin/pppd
-rwsr-sr-x  1 root root  84604 Aug 14  1996 /usr/sbin/pppd
```

One other special permission provides efficient use of programs. The sticky bit instructs the system to keep a program in memory after it finishes execution. This is useful for small programs used frequently by many users. The sticky bit permission is *t*. The sticky bit shows up as a *t* in the execute position of the other permissions. A program with read and execute permission with the sticky bit would have its permissions displayed as *r-t*.

```
# chmod +t  /usr/X11R6/bin/xtetris
# ls -l /usr/X11R6/bin/xtetris
-rwxr-xr-t  1 root   root   27428 Nov 19  1996
/usr/X11R6/bin/xtetris
```

Absolute Permissions: Binary Masks

Instead of permission symbols, many users find it more convenient to use the absolute method. The *absolute method* changes all the permissions at once, instead of specifying one or the other. It uses a binary mask that references all the permissions in each category. The three categories, each with three permissions, conform to an octal binary format. Octal numbers have a base eight structure. When translated into a binary number, each octal digit becomes three binary digits. A binary number is a set of 1 and 0 digits. Three octal digits in a number translate into three sets of three binary digits, which is nine altogether—and the exact number of permissions for a file.

You can use the octal digits as a mask to set the different file permissions. Each octal digit applies to one of the user categories. You can think of the digits matching up with the permission categories from left to right, beginning with the owner category. The first octal digit applies to the owner category, the second to the group, and the third to the others category.

The actual octal digit you choose determines the read, write, and execute permissions for each category. At this point, you need to know how octal digits translate into their binary equivalents. The following table shows how the different octal digits, 0 to 7, translate into their three-digit binary equivalents. You can think of the octal digit first being translated into its binary form, and then each of those three binary digits being used to set the read, write, and execute permissions. Each binary digit is then matched up with a corresponding permission, again moving from left to right. If a binary digit is 0, the permission is turned off. If the binary digit is 1, the permission is turned on. The first binary digit sets the read permission on or off, the second sets the write permission, and the third sets the execute permission. For example, an octal digit 6 translates into the binary digits 110. This would set the read and write permission on, but set the execute permission off.

Octal	Binary
0	000
1	001
2	010
3	011
4	100
5	101
6	110
7	111

When dealing with a binary mask, you need to specify three digits for all three categories, as well as their permissions. This makes a binary mask less versatile than the permission symbols. To set the owner execute permission on and the write permission off for the **mydata** file, as well as retain the read permission, you need to use the octal digit 5 (101). At the same time, you need to specify the digits for group and other users access. If these categories are to retain read access, you need the octal number 4 for each (100). This gives you three octal digits, 544, which translate into the binary digits 101 100 100.

```
$ chmod 544 mydata
```

One of the most common uses of the binary mask is to set the execute permission. As you learned in Chapter 7 , you can create files that contain Linux commands, and these files are called shell scripts. To have the commands in a shell script executed, you must first indicate the file is executable—that it contains commands the system can execute. You can do this in several ways, one of which is to set the executable permission on the shell script file. Suppose you just completed a shell script file and you need to give it executable permission to run it. You also want to retain read and write permission, but deny any access by the group or other users. The octal digit 7 (111) will set all three permissions, including execute (you can also add 4-read, 2-write, and 1-execute to get 7). Using 0 for the group and other users denies them access. This gives you the digits 700, which are equivalent to the binary digits 111 000 000. In the next example, the owner permission for the **myprog** file is set to include execute permission:

```
$ chmod 700 myprog
```

If you want others to be able to execute and read the file, but not change it, you can set the read and execute permissions and turn off the write permission with the digit 5 (101). In this case, you would use the octal digits 755, having the binary equivalent of 111 101 101.

```
$ chmod 755 myprog
```

For the ownership and sticky bit permissions, you add another octal number to the beginning of the octal digits. The octal digit for User ID permission is 4 (100); for Group ID, it is 2 (010); and for the sticky bit, it is 1 (001). The following example sets the User ID permission to the **pppd** program, along with read and execute permissions for the owner, group, and others:

```
$  chmod 4555 /usr/sbin/pppd
```

The following example sets the sticky bit for the **xtetris** program:

```
$ chmod 1755  /usr/X11R6/bin/xtetris
```

The next example would set both the sticky bit and the User ID permission on the **xman** program. The permission 5755 has the binary equivalent of 101 111 101 101.

```
$ chmod 5755 /usr/X11R6/bin/xman
$ ls -l /usr/X11R6/bin/xman
-rwsr-xr-t   1 root  root   44364 Mar 26 04:28 /usr/X11R6/bin/xman
```

Directory Permissions

You can also set permissions on directories. The read permission set on a directory allows the list of files in a directory to be displayed. The execute permission enables a user to change to that directory. The write permission enables a user to create and remove her files in that directory. If you allow other users to have write permission on a directory, they can add their own files to it. When you create a directory, it is automatically given read, write, and execute permission for the owner. You may list the files in that directory, change to it, and create files in it.

Like files, directories have sets of permissions for the owner, the group, and all other users. Often, you may want to allow other users to change to and list the files in one of your directories, but not let them add their own files to it. In this case, you would set read and execute permissions on the directory, but not write permission. This would allow other users to change to the directory and list the files in it, but not to create new files or to copy any of their files into it. The next example sets read and execute permission for the group for the **thankyou** directory, but removes the write permission. Members of the group may enter the **thankyou** directory and list the files there, but they may not create new ones.

```
$ chmod g+rx-w letters/thankyou
```

Just as with files, you can also use octal digits to set a directory permission. To set the same permissions as in the previous example, you would use the octal digits 750, which have the binary equivalents of 111 101 000.

```
$ chmod 750 letters/thankyou
```

As you know, the **ls** command with the **-l** option will list all files in a directory. To list only the information about the directory itself, add a **d** modifier. In the next example, **ls -ld** displays information about the **thankyou** directory. Notice the first character in the permissions list is *d*, indicating it is a directory.

```
$ ls -ld thankyou
drwxr-x---  2  chris 512 Feb 10 04:30  thankyou
```

If you have files you want other users to have access to, you not only need to set permissions for that file, you also must make sure the permissions are set for the directory in which the file is located. Another user, to access your file, must first access the file's directory. The same applies to parents of directories. Although a directory may give permission to others to access it, if its parent directory denies access, the directory cannot be reached. In this respect, you must pay close attention to your directory tree. To provide access to a directory, all other directories above it in the directory tree must also be accessible to other users.

Changing a File's Owner or Group: chown and chgrp

Although other users may be able to access a file, only the owner can change its permissions. If, however, you want to give some other user control over one of your file's permissions, you can change the owner of the file from yourself to the other user. The **chown** command transfers control over a file to another user. This command takes as its first argument the name of the other user. Following the user name, you can list the files you are giving up. In the next example, the user gives control of the **mydata** file to Robert:

```
$ chown robert mydata
$ ls -l mydata
-rw-r--r--  1  robert weather 207  Feb  20 11:55  mydata
```

You can also, if you wish, change the group for a file, using the **chgrp** command. **chgrp** takes as its first argument the name of the new group for a file or files. Following the new group name, you list the files you want changed to that group. In the next example, the user changes the group name for **today** and **weekend** to the **forecast** group. The **ls -l** command then reflects the group change.

```
$ chgrp forecast today weekend
$ ls -l
-rw-r--r--  1  chris weather 207  Feb  20 11:55  mydata
-rw-rw-r--  1  chris forecast 568  Feb  14 10:30  today
-rw-rw-r--  1  chris forecast 308  Feb  17 12:40  weekend
```

ENVIRONMENTS

The
Complete
Reference

Chapter 9

Shell Features and Configuration

Four different major shells are commonly used on Linux systems: the Bourne Again shell (BASH), the Public Domain Korn shell (PDKSH), the TCSH shell, and the Z-shell. The BASH shell is an advanced version of the Bourne shell, which includes most of the advanced features developed for the Korn shell and the C-shell. TCSH is an enhanced version of the C-shell, originally developed for BSD versions of UNIX. PDKSH is a subset of the UNIX Korn shell, whereas the Z-shell is an enhanced version of the Korn shell. Although their UNIX counterparts differ greatly, the Linux shells share many of the same features. In UNIX, the Bourne shell lacks many capabilities found in the other UNIX shells. In Linux, however, the BASH shell incorporates all the advanced features of the Korn shell and C-shell, as well as the TCSH shell.

All four shells are available for your use, though the BASH shell is the default.

So far, all examples in this book have used the BASH shell. You log into your default shell, but you can change to another shell by entering its name. **tcsh** invokes the TCSH shell, **bash** the BASH shell, **ksh** the PDKSH shell, and **zsh** the Z-shell. You can leave a shell with the CTRL-D or **exit** command. You only need one type of shell to do your work. This chapter describes common features of the BASH shell, such as history and aliases, as well as how to configure the shell to your own needs using shell variables and initialization files. The other shells share many of the same features, and use similar variables and initialization files.

Command and File Name Completion

The BASH command line has a built-in feature that performs command and filename completion. If you enter an incomplete pattern as a command or filename argument, you can then press the TAB key to activate the command and filename completion feature, which completes the pattern. If more than one command or file has the same prefix, the shell simply beeps and waits for you to add enough characters to select a unique command or filename. In the next example, the user issues a **cat** command with an incomplete filename. Upon pressing the TAB key, the system searches for a match and, when it finds one, fills in the filename. The user can then press ENTER to execute the command.

```
$ cat pre tab
$ cat preface
```

The shell can also perform filename completion to list the partially matching files in your current directory. If you press ESC followed by a question mark, ESC-?, the shell lists all filenames matching the incomplete pattern. In the next example, the ESC-? after the incomplete filename generates a list of possible filenames. The shell then redraws the command line, and you can type in the complete name of the file you want, or type in distinguishing characters and press the TAB key to have the filename completed.

```
$ ls
document docudrama
$ cat doc escape ?
document
docudrama
$ cat docudrama
```

Command Line Editing

The BASH shell has built-in command-line editing capabilities that enable you to easily modify commands you have entered before executing them. If you make a spelling mistake when entering a command, rather than reentering the entire command, you can use the editing operations to correct the mistake before executing the command. This is most helpful for commands that use arguments with lengthy pathnames. The command-line editing operations are a subset of the Emacs editing commands (see Table 9-1). You can use CTRL-F or the RIGHT ARROW key to move forward a character, and the CTRL-B or the LEFT ARROW key to move back a character. CTRL-D or DEL deletes the character the cursor is on. To add text, you move the cursor to where you want to insert text and type in the new characters. At any time, you can press ENTER to execute the command. As described in the next section, you can also use the command-line editing operations to modify history events—previous commands you have entered.

History

In the BASH shell, the *history utility* keeps a record of the most recent commands you have executed. The commands are numbered starting at 1 and a limit exists to the number of commands remembered—the default is 500. The history utility is a kind of short-term memory, keeping track of the most recent commands you have executed. To see the set of your most recent commands, type **history** on the command line and press ENTER. A list of your most recent commands is then displayed, preceded by a number.

```
$ history
1 cp mydata today
2 vi mydata
3 mv mydata reports
4 cd reports
5 ls
```

Each of these commands is technically referred to as an "event." An *event* describes an action that has been taken—a command that has been executed. The events are

Command-Line Editing

CTRL-B or LEFT ARROW	Moves left one character (backward to the previous character)
CTRL-F or RIGHT ARROW	Moves right one character (forward to the next character)
CTRL-A	Moves to the beginning of a line
CTRL-E	Moves to the end of a line
ESC-F	Moves forward one word
ESC-B	Moves backward one word
DEL	Deletes the character the cursor is on
BACKSPACE or CTRL-H	Deletes the character before the cursor
CTRL-D	Deletes the character after the cursor
CTRL-K	Removes (kills) the remainder of a line

History Commands

CTRL-N or DOWN ARROW	Moves down to the next event in the history list	
CTRL-P or UP ARROW	Moves up to the previous event in the history list	
ESC-<	Moves to the beginning of the history event list	
ESC->	Moves to the end of the history event list	
ESC-TAB	History of event matching and completion	
fc *event-reference*	Edits an event with the standard editor and then executes it	
	options	
	−1	List recent history events; same as **history** command
	−e *editor* *event-reference*	Invokes a specified editor to edit a specific event

History Event References

!*event num*	References an event with an event number
!*characters*	References an event with beginning characters
!?*pattern*?	References an event with a pattern in the event
!−*event num*	References an event with an offset from the first event
!*num−num*	References a range of events

Table 9-1.   *Command-Line Editing, History Commands, and History Event References*

numbered according to their sequence of execution. The most recent event has the highest number. Each of these events can be identified by its number or beginning characters in the command.

The history utility enables you to reference a former event, placing it on your command line and enabling you to execute it. The easiest way to do this is to use the UP ARROW and DOWN ARROW keys to place history events on your command line, one at a time. You needn't display the list first with `history`. Pressing the UP ARROW key once places the last history event on your command line. Pressing it again places the next history event on your command. Pressing the DOWN ARRROW key places the previous event on the command line.

The BASH shell also has a history event completion operation invoked by the ESC-TAB command. Much like standard command-line completion, you enter part of the history event you want. Then you press ESC, followed by TAB. The event that matches the text you have entered is then located and used to complete your command line entry. If more than one history event matches what you have entered, you will hear a beep, and you can then enter more characters to help uniquely identify the event you want.

You can then edit the event displayed on your command line using the command-line editing operations. The LEFT ARROW and RIGHT ARROW keys move you along the command line. You can insert text wherever you stop your cursor. With BACKSPACE and DEL, you can delete characters. Once the event is displayed on your command line, you can press ENTER to execute it.

You can also reference and execute history events using the ! history command. The ! is followed by a reference that identifies the command. The reference can be either the number of the event or a beginning set of characters in the event. In the next example, the third command in the history list is referenced first by number and then by the beginning characters:

```
$ !3
mv mydata reports
$ !mv
mv mydata reports
```

You can also reference an event using an offset from the end of the list. A negative number will offset from the end of the list to that event, thereby referencing it. In the next example, the fourth command, **cd mydata**, is referenced using a negative offset, and then executed. Remember that you are offsetting from the end of the list—in this case, event 5, up toward the beginning of the list, event 1. An offset of 4 beginning from event 5 places you at event 2.

```
$ !-4
vi mydata
```

If no event reference is used, then the last event is assumed. In the next example, the command ! by itself executes the last command the user executed—in this case, **ls**:

```
$ !
ls
mydata today reports
```

History Event Editing

You can also edit any event in the history list before you execute it. In the BASH shell, you can do this two ways. You can use the command-line editor capability to reference and edit any event in the history list. You can also use a history **fc** command option to reference an event and edit it with the full Vi editor. Each approach involves two different editing capabilities. The first is limited to the commands in the command-line editor, which edits only a single line with a subset of Emacs commands. At the same time, however, it enables you to reference events easily in the history list. The second approach invokes the standard Vi editor with all its features, but only for a specified history event.

With the command-line editor, not only can you edit the current command, but you can also move to a previous event in the history list to edit and execute it. The CTRL-P command then moves you up to the prior event in the list. The CTRL-N command moves you down the list. The ESC-< command moves you to the top of the list, and the ESC-> command moves you to the bottom. You can even use a pattern to search for a given event. The slash followed by a pattern searches backward in the list, and the question mark followed by a pattern searches forward in the list. The **n** command repeats the search.

Once you locate the event you want to edit, you use the Emacs command-line editing commands to edit the line. CTRL-D deletes a character. CTRL-F or the RIGHT ARROW moves you forward a character, and CTRL-B or the LEFT ARROW moves you back a character. To add text, you position your cursor and type in the characters you want. Table 9-1 lists the different commands for referencing the history list.

If you want to edit an event using a standard editor instead, you need to reference the event using the **fc** command and a specific event reference, such as an event number. The editor used is the one specified by the shell as the default editor for the **fc** command. The next example will edit the fourth event, **cd reports**, with the standard editor and then execute the edited event:

```
$ fc 4
```

You can select more than one command at a time to be edited and executed by referencing a range of commands. You select a range of commands by indicating an identifier for the first command followed by an identifier for the last command in the range. An identifier can be the command number or the beginning characters in the command. In the next example, the range of commands 2 through 4 are edited and executed, first using event numbers and then using beginning characters in those events:

```
$ fc 2 4
$ fc vi c
```

fc uses the default editor specified in the **FCEDIT** special variable. Usually, this is the Vi editor. If you want to use the Emacs editor instead, you use the **-e** option and the term **emacs** when you invoke **fc**. The next example will edit the fourth event, **cd reports**, with the Emacs editor and then execute the edited event:

```
$ fc -e emacs 4
```

Configuring History: HISTFILE and HISTSAVE

The number of events saved by your system is kept in a special system variable called **HISTSIZE**. By default, this is usually set to 500. You can change this to another number by simply assigning a new value to **HISTSIZE**. In the next example, the user changes the number of history events saved to 10 by resetting the **HISTSIZE** variable:

```
$ HISTSIZE=10
```

The actual history events are saved in a file whose name is held in a special variable called **HISTFILE**. By default, this file is the **.bash_history** file. You can change the file in which history events are saved, however, by assigning its name to the **HISTFILE** variable. In the next example, the value of **HISTFILE** is displayed. Then a new filename is assigned to it, **newhist**. History events are then saved in the **newhist** file.

```
$ echo $HISTFILE
.bash_history
$ HISTFILE="newhist"
$ echo $HISTFILE
newhist
```

Aliases

You use the **alias** command to create another name for a command. The **alias** command operates like a macro that expands to the command it represents. The alias does not literally replace the name of the command; it simply gives another name to that command. An **alias** command begins with the keyword **alias** and the new name for the command, followed by an equal sign and the command the alias will reference. No spaces can be around the equal sign. In the next example, `list` becomes another name for the `ls` command:

```
$ alias list=ls
$ ls
mydata today
$ list
mydata today
$
```

You can also use an alias to substitute for a command and its option, but you need to enclose both the command and the option within single quotes. Any command you alias that contains spaces must be enclosed in single quotes. In the next example, the alias `lss` references the `ls` command with its `-s` option, and the alias `lsa` references the `ls` command with the `-F` option. `ls` with the `-s` option lists files and their sizes in blocks, and the `ls` with the `-F` option places a slash before directory names. Notice single quotes enclose the command and its option.

```
$ alias lss='ls -s'
$ lss
mydata 14   today  6    reports  1
$ alias lsa='ls -F'
$ lsa
mydata today /reports
$
```

You may often use an alias to include a command name with an argument. If you execute a command that has an argument with a complex combination of special characters on a regular basis, you may want to alias it. For example, suppose you often list just your source code and object code files—those files ending in either a **.c** or **.o**. You would need to use as an argument for `ls` a combination of special characters such as `*.[co]`. Instead, you could alias `ls` with the `*.[co]` argument, giving it a simple name. In the next example, the user creates an alias called **lsc** for the command `ls*.[co]`:

```
$ alias lsc='ls *.[co]'
$ lsc
main.c main.o lib.c lib.o
```

You can also use the name of a command as an alias. This can be helpful in cases where you should only use a command with a specific option. In the case of the **rm**, **cp**, and **mv** commands, the **-i** option should always be used to ensure an existing file is not overwritten. Instead of constantly being careful to use the **-i** option each time you use one of these commands, the command name can be aliased to include the option. In the next example, the **rm**, **cp**, and **mv** commands have been aliased to include the **-i** option:

```
$ alias rm='rm -i'
$ alias mv='mv -i'
$ alias cp='cp -i'
```

The **alias** command by itself provides a list of all aliases in effect and their commands. You can remove an alias by using the **unalias** command. In the next example, the user lists the current aliases and then removes the **lsa** alias:

```
$ alias
lsa=ls -F
list=ls
rm=rm -i
$ unalias lsa
```

Controlling Shell Operations

The BASH shell has several features that enable you to control the way different shell operations work. For example, setting the **noclobber** feature prevents redirection from overwriting files. You can turn these features on and off like a toggle, using the **set** command. The **set** command takes two arguments: an option specifying on or off and the name of the feature. To set a feature on, you use the **-o** option, and to set it off, you use the **+o** option. Here is the basic form:

```
$ set -o feature        turn the feature on
$ set +o feature        turn the feature off
```

Three of the most common features are described here: **ignoreeof**, **noclobber**, and **noglob**. Table 9-2 lists these different features, as well as the **set** command. Setting **ignoreeof** enables a feature that prevents you from logging out of the user shell with a CTRL-D. CTRL-D is not only used to log out of the user shell, but also to end user input entered directly into the standard input. CTRL-D is used often for the Mailx program or for utilities such as **cat**. You could easily enter an extra CTRL-D in such circumstances and accidentally log yourself out. The **ignoreeof** feature prevents such accidental logouts. In the next example, the **ignoreeof** feature is turned on using the

set command with the **-o** option. The user can now only log out by entering the **logout** command.

```
$ set -o ignoreeof
$ ctrl-d
Use exit to logout
$
```

Setting **noclobber** enables a feature that safeguards existing files from redirected output. With the **noclobber** feature, if you redirect output to a file that already exists, the file will not be overwritten with the standard output. The original file is preserved. Situations may occur in which you use, as the name for a file to hold the redirected output, a name you have already given to an existing file. The **noclobber** feature prevents you from accidentally overwriting your original file. In the next example, the user sets the **noclobber** feature on and then tries to overwrite an existing file, **myfile**, using redirection. The system returns an error message.

```
$ set -o noclobber
$ cat preface > myfile
myfile: file exists
$
```

At times, you may want to overwrite a file with redirected output. In this case, you can place an exclamation point after the redirection operator. This will override the **noclobber** feature, replacing the contents of the file with the standard output.

```
$ cat preface >! myfile
```

Setting **noglob** enables a feature that disables special characters in the user shell. The characters *****, **?**, **[]**, and **~** will no longer expand to matched filenames. This feature is helpful if you have special characters as part of the name of a file. In the next example, the user needs to reference a file that ends with the **?** character, **answers?**. First, the user turns off special characters using the **noglob** feature. Now the question mark on the command line is taken as part of the filename, not as a special character, and the user can reference the **answers?** file.

```
$ set -o noglob
$ ls answers?
answers?
```

Environment Variables and Subshells: export

When you log in to your account, Linux generates your user shell. Within this shell, you can issue commands and declare variables. You can also create and execute shell scripts. When you execute a shell script, however, the system generates a subshell. You then have two shells, the one you logged into and the one generated for the script. Within the script shell, you could execute another shell script, which would have its own shell. When a script has finished execution, its shell terminates and you return to the shell from which it was executed. In this sense, you can have many shells, each nested within the other. Variables you define within a shell are local to it. If you define a variable in a shell script, then, when the script is run, the variable is defined with that script's shell and is local to it. No other shell can reference that variable. In a sense, the variable is hidden within its shell.

You can define environment variables in all types of shells including the BASH, Z-shell, and TCSH shells. The strategy used to implement environment variables in the BASH shell, however, is different from that of the TCSH shell. In the BASH shell, environment variables are exported. That is to say, a copy of an environment variable is made in each subshell. For example, if the myfile variable is exported, a copy is automatically defined in each subshell for you. In the TCSH shell, on the other hand, an environment variable is defined only once and can be directly referenced by any subshell.

In the BASH shell, an environment variable can be thought of as a regular variable with added capabilities. To make an environment variable, you apply the `export` command to a variable you have already defined. The `export` command instructs the system to define a copy of that variable for each new shell generated. Each new shell will have its own copy of the environment variable. This process is called *exporting variables.* Thinking of exported environment variables as global variables is a mistake. A new shell can never reference a variable outside of itself. Instead, a copy of the variable with its value is generated for the new shell. You can think of exported variables as exporting their values to a shell, not to themselves. For those familiar with programming structures, exported variables can be thought of as a form of "call by value."

Configuring Your Shell with Special Shell Variables

When you log in to your account, the system generates a shell for you. This shell is referred to as either your login shell or your user shell. When you execute scripts, you are generating subshells of your user shell. You can define variables within your user shell, and you can also define environment variables that can be referenced by any subshells you generate. Linux sets up special shell variables you can use to configure your user shell. Many of these special shell variables are defined by the system when you log in, but you define others yourself. See Table 9-2 for a list of the commonly used ones.

A reserved set of keywords is used for the names of these special variables. You should not use these keywords as the names of any of your own variable names. The special shell variables are all specified in uppercase letters, making them easy to identify. Shell feature variables are in lowercase letters. For example, the keyword **HOME** is used by the system to define the **HOME** variable. **HOME** is a special environment variable that holds the pathname of the user's **home** directory. On the other hand, the keyword **noclobber**, covered earlier in the chapter, is used to set the **noclobber** feature on or off.

Common Special Variables

Many of the special variables automatically defined and assigned initial values by the system when you log in can be changed, if you wish. Some special variables exist whose values should not be changed, however. For example, the **HOME** variable holds the pathname for your **home** directory. Commands, such as **cd**, reference the pathname in the **HOME** special variable to locate your **home** directory. Some of the more common of these special variables are described in this section. Other special variables are defined by the system and given an initial value that you are free to change. To do this, you redefine them and assign a new value. For example, the **PATH** variable is defined by the system and given an initial value; it contains the pathnames of directories where commands are located. Whenever you execute a command, the shell searches for it in these directories. You can add a new directory to be searched by redefining the **PATH** variable yourself, so it will include the new directory's pathname. Still other special variables exist that the system does not define. These are usually optional features, such as the **EXINIT** variable that enables you to set options for the Vi editor. Each time you log in, you must define and assign a value to such variables. You can obtain a listing of the currently defined special variables using the **env** command. The **env** command operates like the **set** command, but it only lists special variables.

You can automatically define special variables using special shell scripts called "initialization files." An *initialization file* is a specially named shell script executed whenever you enter a certain shell. You can edit the initialization file and place in it definitions and assignments for special variables. When you enter the shell, the initialization file will execute these definitions and assignments, effectively initializing special variables with your own values. For example, the BASH shell's **.bash_profile** file is an initialization file executed every time you log in. It contains definitions and assignments of special variables. However, the **.bash_profile** file is basically only a shell script, which you can edit with any text editor such as the Vi editor; changing, if you wish, the values assigned to special variables.

In the BASH shell, all the special variables are designed to be environment variables. When you define or redefine a special variable, you also need to export it to make it an environment variable. This means any change you make to a special variable must be accompanied by an **export** command. You shall see that at the end of the login initialization file, **.bash_profile**, there is usually an **export** command for all the special variables defined in it.

The **HOME** variable contains the pathname of your **home** directory. Your **home** directory is determined by the system administrator when your account is created. The pathname for your **home** directory is automatically read into your **HOME** variable when you log in. In the next example, the **echo** command displays the contents of the **HOME** variable:

```
$ echo $HOME
/home/chris
```

The **HOME** variable is often used when you need to specify the absolute pathname of your **home** directory. In the next example, the absolute pathname of **reports** is specified using **HOME** for the **home** directory's path:

```
$ ls $HOME/reports
```

Some of the more common special variables are **SHELL**, **PATH**, **PS1**, **PS2**, and **MAIL**. The **SHELL** variable holds the pathname of the program for the type of shell you log in to. The **PATH** variable lists the different directories to be searched for a Linux command. The **PS1** and **PS2** variables hold the prompt symbols. The **MAIL** variable holds the pathname of your mailbox file. You can modify the values for any of them to customize your shell.

The **PATH** variable contains a series of directory paths separated by colons. Each time a command is executed, the paths listed in the **PATH** variable are searched one-by-one for that command. For example, the **cp** command resides on the system in the directory **/usr/bin**. This directory path is one of the directories listed in the **PATH** variable. Each time you execute the **cp** command, this path is searched and the **cp** command located. The system defines and assigns **PATH** an initial set of pathnames. In Linux, the initial pathnames are **/usr/bin** and **usr/sbin**.

The shell can execute any executable file, including programs and scripts you have created. For this reason, the **PATH** variable can also reference your working directory; so if you want to execute one of your own scripts or programs in your working directory, the shell can locate it. No spaces can be between the pathnames in the string. A colon with no pathname specified references your working directory. Usually, a single colon is placed at the end of the pathnames as an empty entry specifying your working directory. For example, the pathname **/usr/bin:/usr/sbin:** references three directories: **/usr/bin**, **/usr/sbin**, and your current working directory.

```
$ echo $PATH
/usr/bin:/usr/sbin:
```

You can add any new directory path you want to the **PATH** variable. This can be useful if you have created several of your own Linux commands using shell scripts. You could place these new shell script commands in a directory you created and then add that directory to the **PATH** list. Then, no matter what directory you are in, you can execute one of your shell scripts. The **PATH** variable will contain the directory for that script, so that directory will be searched each time you issue a command.

You add a directory to the **PATH** variable with a variable assignment. You can execute this assignment directly in your shell. In the next example, the user **chris** adds a new directory, called **mybin,** to the **PATH**. Although you could carefully type in the complete pathnames listed in **PATH** for the assignment, you can also use an evaluation of **PATH**, **$PATH**, in their place. In this example, an evaluation of **HOME** is also used to designate the user's **home** directory in the new directory's pathname. Notice the empty entry between two colons, which specifies the working directory.

```
$ PATH=$PATH:$HOME/mybin:
$ export PATH
$ echo $PATH
/usr/bin:/usr/sbin::/home/chris/mybin
```

If you add a directory to **PATH** yourself while you are logged in, the directory would be added only for the duration of your login session. When you log back in, the login initialization file, **.bash_profile**, would again initialize your **PATH** with its original set of directories. The **.bash_profile** file is described in detail a bit later in the chapter. To add a new directory to your **PATH** permanently, you need to edit your **.bash_profile** file and find the assignment for the **PATH** variable. Then, you simply insert the directory, preceded by a colon, into the set of pathnames assigned to **PATH**.

The **PS1** and **PS2** variables contain the primary and secondary prompt symbols, respectively. The primary prompt symbol for the BASH shell is a dollar sign, **$**. You can change the prompt symbol by assigning a new set of characters to the **PS1** variable. In the next example, the shell prompt is changed to the **->** symbol:

```
$ PS1="->"
-> export PS1
->
```

You can change the prompt to be any set of characters, including a string, as shown in the next example:

```
$ PS1="Please enter a command: "
Please enter a command: export PS1
Please enter a command: ls
mydata /reports
Please enter a command:
```

The **PS2** variable holds the secondary prompt symbol, which is used for commands that take several lines to complete. The default secondary prompt is >. The added command lines begin with the secondary prompt instead of the primary prompt. You can change the secondary prompt just as easily as the primary prompt, as shown here:

```
$ PS2="@"
```

Like the TCSH shell, the BASH shell provides you with a predefined set of codes you can use to configure your prompt. With them you can make the time, your user name, or your directory pathname a part of your prompt. You can even have your prompt display the history event number of the current command you are about to enter. Each code is preceded by a \ symbol. **\w** represents the current working directory, **\t** the time, and **\u** your user name. **\!** will display the next history event number. In the next example, the user adds the current working directory to the prompt:

```
$ PS1="\w $"
/home/dylan $
```

The codes must be included within a quoted string. If no quotes exist, the code characters are not evaluated and are themselves used as the prompt. **PS1=\w** sets the prompt to the characters **\w**, not the working directory. The next example incorporates both the time and the history event number with a new prompt:

```
$ PS1="\t \! ->"
```

The following table lists the codes for configuring your prompt.

Prompt codes	Description
\!	Current history number
\$	Use $ as prompt for all users except the root user, which has the # as its prompt
\d	Current date
\s	Shell currently active
\t	Time of day
\u	User name
\w	Current working directory

If **CDPATH** is undefined, then when the **cd** command is given a directory name as its argument, it searches only the current working directory for that name. If **CDPATH** is defined, however, **cd** also searches the directories listed in **CDPATH** for that directory name. If the directory name is found, **cd** changes to that directory. This is helpful if you are working on a project in which you constantly must change to directories in another part of the file system. To change to a directory that has a pathname very different from the one you are in, you would need to know the full pathname of that directory. Instead, you could simply place the pathname of that directory's parent in **CDPATH**. Then, **cd** automatically searches the parent directory, finding the name of the directory you want. Notice that you assign to **CDPATH** the pathname of the parent of the directory you want to change to, not the pathname of the directory itself.

Using the **HOME** variable to specify the home directory part of the path in any new pathname added to **CDPATH** is advisable. This is because the pathname for your home directory could possibly be changed by the system administrator during a reorganization of the file system. **HOME** will always hold the current pathname of the **home** directory. In the next example, the pathname **/home/chris/letters** is specified with **$HOME/letters**:

```
$ CDPATH=$CDPATH:$HOME/letters
$ export CDPATH
$ echo $CDPATH
:/home/chris/letters
```

Several shell special variables are used to set values used by network applications, such as Web browsers or newsreaders. **NNTPSERVER** is used to set the value of a remote news server accessible on your network. If you are using an ISP, the ISP usually provides a news server you can access with your newsreader applications. However, you first have to provide your newsreaders with the Internet address of the news server. This is the role of the **NNTPSERVER**. News servers on the Internet usually use the NNTP protocol. **NNTPSERVER** should hold the address of such a news server. For many ISPs, the news server address is a domain name that begins with **nntp**. The following example assigns the news server address **nntp.myservice.com** to the **NNTPSERVER** special variables. Newsreader applications automatically obtain the news server address from **NNTPSERVER**. Usually, this assignment is placed in the shell initialization file, **.bash_profile**, so it is automatically set each time a user logs in.

```
NNTPSERVER=nntp.myservice.com
export NNTPSERVER
```

Other special variables are used for specific applications. The **KDEDIR** variable holds the pathname for the KDE Desktop program files. If you install KDE using its source code, instead of the Red Hat RPM pakage, its default directory will be **/opt/kde**. At the time of installation, you can choose to install KDE in a different directory and then change the value of **KDEDIR** accordingly.

```
export KDEDIR=/opt/kde
```

Configuring Your Login Shell: .bash_profile

The **.bash_profile** file is the BASH shell's login initialization file, which can also be named **.profile**. It is a script file that is automatically executed whenever a user logs in. The file contains shell commands that define special environment variables used to manage your shell. They may be either redefinitions of system-defined special variables or definitions of user-defined special variables. For example, when you log in, your user shell needs to know what directories hold Linux commands. It will reference the **PATH** variable to find the pathnames for these directories. However, first, the **PATH** variable must be assigned those pathnames. In the **.bash_profile** file, an assignment operation does just this. Because it is in the **.bash_profile** file, the assignment is executed automatically when the user logs in.

Special variables also need to be exported, using the **export** command, to make them accessible to any subshells you may enter. You can export several variables in one **export** command by listing them as arguments. Usually, at the end of the **.bash_profile** file is an **export** command with a list of all the variables defined in the file. If a variable is missing from this list, you may be unable to access it. Notice the **export** command at the end of the **.profile** file in the example described next. You can also combine the assignment and **export** command in to one operation as show here for **NNTPSEVER**.

```
export NNTPSERVER=nntp.myservice.com
```

A copy of the standard **.bash_profile** file provided for you when your account is created is listed in the next example. Notice how **PATH** is assigned, as is the value of

BAS Shell Special Variables	Description
HOME	Path name for user's home directory
LOGNAME	Login name
USER	Login name
TZ	Time zone used by system
SHELL	Path name of program for type of shell you are using
PATH	List of pathnames for directories searched for executable commands
PS1	Primary shell prompt
PS2	Secondary shell prompt
IFS	Interfield delimiter symbol
MAIL	Name of mail file checked by mail utility for received messages
MAILCHECK	Interval for checking for received mail
MAILPATH	List of mail files to be check by mail for received messages
TERM	Terminal name
CDPATH	Path names for directories searched by **cd** command for subdirectories
EXINIT	Initialization commands for Ex/Vi editor
BASH Shell Features	

$ set -+o *feature*	Korn shell features are turned on and off with the **set** command; **-o** sets a feature on and **+o** turns it off:
	 $ set -o noclobber *set noclobber on*
	 $ set +o noclobber *set noclobber off*

ignoreeof	Disabled CTRL-D logout
noclobber	Does not overwrite files through redirection
noglob	Disables special characters used for filename expansion: *, ?, ~, and []

Table 9-2.   *BASH Shell Special Variables and Features*

$HOME. Both **PATH** and **HOME** are system special variables the system has already defined. **PATH** holds the pathnames of directories searched for any command you enter, and **HOME** holds the pathname of your **home** directory. The assignment **PATH=$PATH:$HOME/bin** has the effect of redefining **PATH** to include your **bin** directory within your **home** directory. So, your **bin** directory will also be searched for any commands, including ones you create yourself, such as scripts or programs. Notice **PATH** is then exported, so it can be accessed by any subshells. Should you want to have your **home** directory searched also, you can use any text editor to modify this line in your **.bash_profile** file to **PATH=$PATH:$HOME\bin:$HOME**, adding **:$HOME** at the end. In fact, you can change this entry to add as many directories as you want searched.

.bash_profile

```
# .bash_profile

# Get the aliases and functions
if [ -f ~/.bashrc ]; then
       . ~/.bashrc
fi

# User specific environment and startup programs

PATH=$PATH:$HOME/bin
BASH_ENV=$HOME/.bashrc
USERNAME=""

export USERNAME BASH_ENV PATH
```

Your Linux system also has its own profile file that it executes whenever any user logs in. This system initialization file is simply called **profile** and is found in the **/etc** directory, **/etc/profile**. This file contains special variable definitions the system needs to provide for each user. A copy of the system's **.profile** file follows. Notice how **PATH** is redefined to include the **/usr/X11R6/bin** directory. This is the directory that holds the X Windows commands you execute when using the desktop. Also, **PATH** includes the pathname for programs **/usr/local/bin**. **HISTFILE** is also redefined to include a larger number of history events. An entry has been added here for the **NNTPSERVER** variable. Normally, a news server address is a value that needs to be set for all users. Such assignments should be made in the system's **/etc/profile** file by the system administrator, rather than in each individual user's own **.bash_profile** file. The **/etc/profile** file also executes any scripts in the directory **/etc/profile.d**. This design allows for a more modular structure. Rather than make entries by editing the **/etc/profile** file, you can just add a script to **profile.d** directory. The scripts for the BASH shell have the extension **.sh**. For example, the **qt.sh** script in the **profile.d** directory checks for a definition of the **QTDIR** variable and makes one if none is in effect.

/etc/profile

```
# /etc/profile

# System wide environment and startup programs
# Functions and aliases go in /etc/bashrc

PATH="$PATH:/usr/X11R6/bin:/usr/local/:"
PS1="[\u@\h \W]\\$ "

ulimit -c 1000000
if [ `id -gn` = `id -un` -a `id -u` -gt 14 ]; then
    umask 002
else
    umask 022
fi

USER=`id -un`
LOGNAME=$USER
MAIL="/var/spool/mail/$USER"

HOSTNAME=`/bin/hostname`
HISTSIZE=1000
HISTFILESIZE=1000
NNTPSERVER=nntp.myservice.com
export PATH PS1 HOSTNAME HISTSIZE HISTFILESIZE MAIL NNTPSERVER

for i in /etc/profile.d/*.sh ; do
    if [ -x $i ]; then
      . $i
    fi
done

unset i
```

Your **.bash_profile** initialization file is a text file that can be edited by a text editor, like any other text file. You can easily add new directories to your **PATH** by editing **.bash_profile** and using editing commands to insert a new directory pathname in the list of directory pathnames assigned to the **PATH** variable. You can even add new variable definitions. If you do so, however, be sure to include the new variable's name in the **export** command's argument list. For example, if your **.bash_profile** file does not have any definition of the **EXINIT** variable, you can edit the file and add a new line that assigns a value to **EXINIT**. The definition **EXINIT='set nu ai'** will configure the Vi editor with line numbering and indentation. You then need to add **EXINIT** to the **export** command's argument list. When the **.bash_profile** file executes again, the **EXINIT** variable will be set to the command **set nu ai**. When the Vi editor is invoked, the command in the **EXINIT** variable will be executed, setting the line number and auto-indent options automatically.

In the following example, the user's **.bash_profile** has been modified to include definitions of **EXINIT** and redefinitions of **PATH**, **CDPATH**, **PS1**, and **HISTSIZE**. The **PATH** variable has $HOME: added to its value. $HOME is a variable that evaluates to the user's **home** directory and the ending colon specifies the current working directory, enabling you to execute commands that may be located in either the **home** directory or the working directory. The redefinition of **HISTSIZE** reduces the number of history events saved, from 1,000 defined in the system's **.profile** file, to 30. The redefinition of the **PS1** special variable changes the prompt to include the pathname of the current working directory. Any changes you make to special variables within your **.bash_profile** file override those made earlier by the system's **.profile** file. All these special variables are then exported with the **export** command.

.bash_profile
```
# .bash_profile
# Get the aliases and functions
if [ -f ~/.bashrc ];
  then
      . ~/.bashrc
fi
# User-specific environment and startup programs
PATH=$PATH:$HOME/bin:$HOME:
ENV=$HOME/.bashrc
USERNAME=""
CDPATH=$CDPATH:$HOME/bin:$HOME
HISTSIZE=30
EXINIT='set nu ai'
PS1="\w \$"
export USERNAME ENV PATH CDPATH HISTSIZE EXINIT PS1
```

Although **.profile** is executed each time you log in, it is not automatically reexecuted after you make changes to it. The **.profile** file is an initialization file that is *only* executed whenever you log in. If you want to take advantage of any changes you make to it without having to log out and log in again, you can reexecute .**profile** with the dot (.) command. **.profile** is a shell script and, like any shell script, can be executed with the . command.

```
$ .bash_profile
```

Configuring the BASH Shell: .bashrc

The **.bashrc** file is a configuration file executed each time you enter the BASH shell or generate any subshells. If the BASH shell is your login shell, **.bashrc** is executed along with your **.bash_login** file when you log in. If you enter the BASH shell from another shell, the **.bashrc** file is automatically executed, and the variable and alias definitions it contains will be defined. If you enter a different type of shell, then the configuration file for that shell will be executed instead. For example, if you were to enter the TCSH shell with the **tcsh** command, then the **.tcshrc** configuration file is executed instead of **.bashrc**.

The **.bashrc** shell configuration file is actually executed each time you generate a BASH shell, such as when you run a shell script. In other words, each time a subshell is created, the **.bashrc** file is executed. This has the effect of exporting any local variables or aliases you have defined in the **.bashrc** shell initialization file. The **.bashrc** file usually contains the definition of aliases and any feature variables used to turn on shell features. Aliases and feature variables are locally defined within the shell. But the **.bashrc** file defines them in every shell. For this reason, the **.bashrc** file usually holds such aliases as those defined for the **rm**, **cp**, and **mv** commands. The next example is a **.bashrc** file with many of the standard definitions:

.bashrc

```
# Source global definitions
if [ -f /etc/bashrc ];
 then
      . /etc/bashrc
fi
set  -o ignoreeof
set  -o noclobber
alias rm 'rm -i'
alias mv 'mv -i'
alias cp 'cp -i'
```

Linux systems usually contain a system **.bashrc** file executed for all users. This may contain certain global aliases and features needed by all users whenever they enter a BASH shell. This is located in the **/etc** directory, **/etc/.bashrc**. A user's own **.bashrc** file, located in the **home** directory, contains commands to execute this system **.bashrc** file. The **./etc/bashrc** command in the previous example of **.bashrc** does just that. You can add any commands or definitions of your own to your **.bashrc** file. If you have made changes to **.bashrc** and you want them to take effect during your current login session, you need to reexecute the file with either the **.** or the **source** command.

```
$ . .bashrc
```

The BASH Shell Logout File: .bash_logout

The **.bash_logout** file is also a configuration file, which is executed when the user logs out. It is designed to perform any operations you want done whenever you log out. Instead of variable definitions, the **.bash_logout** file usually contains shell commands that form a kind of shutdown procedure—actions you always want taken before you log out. One common logout command is to clear the screen and then issue a farewell message.

As with **.bash_profile**, you can add your own shell commands to **.bash_logout**. In fact, the **.bash_logout** file is not automatically set up for you when your account is first created. You need to create it yourself, using the Vi or Emacs editor. You could then add a farewell message or other operations. In the next example, the user has a **clear** and an **echo** command in the **.bash_logout** file. When the user logs out, the **clear** command clears the screen, and then the **echo** command displays the message "Good-bye for now."

.bash_logout

```
clear
echo "Good-bye for now"
```

Other Initialization and Configuration Files

Each type of shell has is its own set of initialization and configuration files. The TCSH shell used **.login**, **.tcshrc**, **.logout** files in place of **.bash_profile**, **.bashrc**, and **.bash_logout**. The Z-shell has several initialization files: **.zshenv**, **.zlogin**, **.zprofile**, **.zschrc**, and **.zlogout**. See Table 9-3 for a listing. Check the Man pages for each shell to see how they are usually configured. When you install a shell, default versions of these files are automatically placed in the **home** directories. Except for the TCSH shell, all shells use much the same syntax for variable definitions and assigning values (TCSH uses a slightly different syntax, described in its Man pages).

Configuration Directories and Files

Applications often install configuration files in a user's **home** directory that contain specific configuration information, which tailors the application to the needs of that particular user. This may take the form of a single configuration file that begins with a period, or a directory that contains several configuration files. The directory name will also begin with a period. For example, Netscape installs a directory called **.netscape** in the user's **home** directory that contains configuration files. On the other hand, the mailx application uses a single file called **.mailrc** to hold alias and feature settings set up

BASH Shell	Function
.bash_profile	Login initialization file
.bashrc	BASH shell configuration file
.bash_logout	Logout name
TCSH Shell	
.login	Login initialization file
.tcshrc	TCSH shell configuration file
.logout	Logout file
Z-shell	
.zshenv	Shell login file (first read)
.zprofile	Login initialization file
.zlogin	Shell login file
.zshrc	Z-shell shell configuration file
.zlogout	Logout file
PDKSH Shell	
.profile	Login initialization file
.kshrc	PDKSH shell configuration file

Table 9-3. *Shell Configuration Files*

by the user. Most single configuration files end in the letters **rc**. **ftp** uses a file called **.netrc**. Most newsreaders use a file called **.newsrc**. Entries in configuration files are usually set by the application, though you can usually make entries directly by editing the file. Applications have their own set of special variables to which you can define and assign values. Of particular interest is the **.wm_style** file that holds the name of the Window manager the user wants to use. You can edit and change the name there to that of another window manager to start up a new one. You can list the configuration files in your **home** directory with the **ls -a** command.

The
Complete
Reference

Linux

Part III

Internet

The Complete Reference

Chapter 10

Mail Clients

Your Linux system has electronic mail clients that enable you to send messages to other users on your system or other systems, such as those on the Internet. You can send and receive messages in a variety of ways, depending on the type of mail client you use. Although all electronic mail utilities perform the same basic tasks of receiving and sending messages, they tend to have different interfaces. Some mail clients operate on a desktop, such as KDE or Gnome. Others run on any X Windows window managers. Several popular mail clients were designed to use a screen-based interface and can run from only the command line. Other traditional mail clients were developed for just the command-line interface, which requires you to type your commands. Most mail clients described here are included in standard Linux distributions and come in a standard rpm package for easy installation. For Web-based Internet mail services, such as Hotmail, Lycos, and Yahoo!, you use a Web browser instead of a mail client to access mail accounts provided by those services.

Mail is transported to and from destinations using mail transport agents. sendmail and smail send and receive mail from destinations on the Internet or at other sites on a network. To send mail over the Internet, they use the Simple Mail Transport Protocol (SMTP). sendmail is a smaller agent that is easy to configure, whereas smail is both more complex and more powerful. Most Linux distributions, such as Red Hat and OpenLinux, automatically install and configure sendmail for you. On starting up your system, you can send and receive messages over the Internet.

Local and Internet Addresses

Each user on a Linux system has a mail address and, whenever you send mail, you are required to provide the address of the user to whom you are sending the message. For users on your local Linux system, addresses can consist of only the user's login name. When sending messages to users on other systems, however, you need to know not only the login name, but also the address of the system they are on. Internet addresses require the system address to be uniquely identified.

Most systems have Internet addresses you can use to send mail. Internet addresses use a form of addressing called *domain addressing*. A system is assigned a domain name, which when combined with the system name, gives the system a unique address. This domain name is separated from the system name by a period and may be further qualified by additional domain names. Here is the syntax for domain addresses:

```
login-name@system-name.domain-name
```

Systems that are part of a local network are often given the same domain name. The domain name for both the **garnet** and **violet** systems at U.C. Berkeley is **berkeley.edu**. To send a message to **chris** on the **garnet** system, you simply include the domain name:

```
chris@garnet.berkeley.edu.
```

In the next example, a message is sent to **chris,** located on the **garnet** system, using domain addressing:

```
$ mail chris@garnet.berkeley.edu < mydata
```

Early domain names reflect that the Internet was first developed in the United States. They qualify Internet addresses by category, such as commercial, military, or educational systems. The domain name *.com* indicates a commercial organization, whereas *.edu* is used for educational institutions. As the Internet developed into a global network, a set of international domain names was established. These domain names indicate the country in which a system is located—for example, *.fr* represents France, *.jp* represents Japan, and *.us* represents the United States.

Signature Files: .signature

You can end your e-mail message with the same standard signature information, such as your name, Internet address or addresses, or farewell phrase. Having your signature information automatically added to your messages is helpful. To do so, you need to create a signature file in your **home** directory and enter your signature information in it. A *signature file* is a standard text file you can edit using any text editor. Mail clients, such as kmail enable you to specify a file to function as your signature file. Others, such as Mail, expect the signature file to be named **.signature**.

The K Desktop Mail Client: kmail

The K Desktop mail client, *kmail*, provides a full-featured GUI interface for composing, sending, and receiving mail messages. The kmail window displays three panes for folders, headers, and messages, as shown in Figure 10-1. The upper-left pane displays your mail folders. You have an inbox folder for received mail, an outbox folder for mail you have composed, but have not sent yet, and a sent-mail folder for messages you have previously sent. You can create your own mail folders and save selected messages in them, if you wish. The top-right pane displays mail headers for the currently selected mail folder. You can use the scroll bar to the right to move through the list of headers. The headers are segmented according to fields, beginning with sender and subject. A color code is used to indicate read and unread messages. New messages are listed in red. Read messages are in green. A bullet symbol also appears at the beginning of unread message headers. To display a message, click its header. The message is then displayed in the large pane below the header list. You can also send and receive attachments, including binary files. Pictures and movies that are received are displayed using the appropriate K Desktop utility. If you right-click the message, a pop-up menu displays options for actions you may want to perform on it. You can move or copy it to another folder, or simply delete it. You can also compose a reply or forward the message.

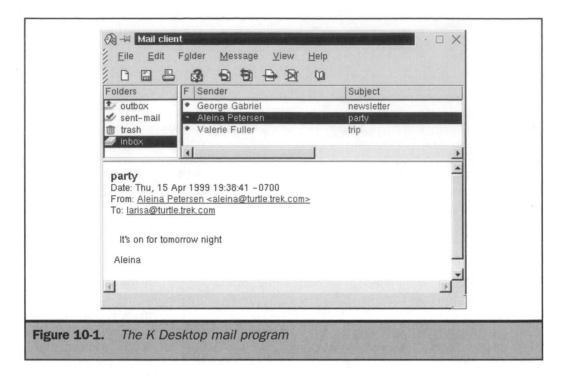

Figure 10-1. *The K Desktop mail program*

The menus in the menu bar at the top of the window contain the commands and options you can use for managing your mail. An icon bar for commonly used mail commands is displayed below the menu bar. To get new mail, click the icon showing a page with a question mark (?). To print a message, click the Printer icon. To save a message, click the Disk icon. If you hold the mouse over an icon, a short description of its function is displayed. The icon of an open book opens the kmail address book. Here, you can enter a list of e-mail addresses. Also, a right-click on a displayed message gives you the option of automatically adding its e-mail address to your address book. You can use the Help button or the Help menu to obtain more detailed descriptions of the different kmail features. The Help button opens the kmail Handbook, which provides easy reference to different operations.

You click the Blank Page icon to compose and send a new message. If you want to compose a reply, select the header of the message you want to reply to, and then click the icon showing a page with a single curved arrow. A message window opens with the To entry already filled with the sender's address, the From entry with your address, and the Subject line with the sender's subject with a preceding RE:. To forward a message, select the message's header and click the icon showing a page with two curved arrows.

When you compose a message, a new window opens with entries for the e-mail address, Carbon-copy (CC), and Subject. A button with three dots is placed next to address entries like From and CC. Clicking one of these buttons invokes your K address book, from which you can select an e-mail address. You enter the message in the body of the window. You can use any of the standard mouse-based editing capabilities to cut, copy, paste, and select text. All commands available to you for composing messages are listed in the menus in the menu bar at the top of the window. A button bar of commonly used functions is displayed just below the menu bar. To send the message, click the Envelope button. To attach a file, you can select the Attach entry in the Attach menu or click the Paper Clip button. This menu also has entries for inserting the text of files into the message or appending a signature file. Other composition features, such as the spell-checker and encryption, are also supported. The standard message window does not display all the header entries unless you select All from the View menu. You can also individually select the fields you want displayed. The Options menu enables you to mark a message as urgent or request a delivery confirmation.

To set up kmail for use with your mail accounts, you must enter account information. Select the Settings entry in the File menu. Several panels are available on the Settings window, which is then displayed. For accounts, you select the Network panel. Two sections are on this panel: one for sending mail and one for receiving mail. In the sending-mail section, enter the SMTP server you use. If you have an ISP or you are on a LAN, enter the server name for your network. The default is the sendmail utility on your own Linux system. In the receiving mail section, you can add any mail accounts you may have. You may have more than one mail account on mail servers maintained by your ISP or LAN. A configure window is displayed where you can enter login, password, and host information. The *host* is the name of the POP server this particular account uses.

Gnome Mail Clients: Balsa, Gmail, Mahogany, and so forth

Currently, several Gnome-based mail clients are under development, many of which you can currently use (see Table 10-1). These include Balsa, Mahogany, gmail, GnoMail, Eucalyptus, Glacier, Pygmy, Spruce and N-tool (both Balsa and Mahogany are discussed further). Check the Gnome Web site for more mail clients as they come out. Many are based on the gnome-mail client libraries (camel) currently under development, which provides support for standard mail operations. *Balsa* is a Gnome mail client with extensive features, though it can operate under any window manager, including KDE, as long as Gnome is installed on your system. The *Mahogany* mail client is a Gnome mail client that also has versions for other platforms. *Gmail* is meant to be a light and fast e-mail client, supporting basic mail operations, such as forwarding, replies, and mailboxes. GnoMail is yet another Gnome mail client that also uses the gnome-mailer libraries. Glacier is a GNU mail client with extensive MIME support. *Eucalyptus* is a MIME-compliant mail client that supports unlimited folders, addresses, filters, and multiple POP servers. Eucalyptus was previously implemented on the Amiga. Pygmy is a simple GNOME mail client written in the Python programming language and supports attachments and MIME messages. The

N-tool is a Gnome mail client with Japanese language support, providing standard features, including mailboxes and full MIME support. *Spruce* is a Gnome e-mail client with support for multiple accounts. *LinPopUp* is a port of WinPopUp that operates on Samba-connected networks and can send messages to users on Windows machines running WinPopUp.

Balsa provides a full-featured GUI interface for composing, sending, and receiving mail messages. The Balsa window displays three panes for folders, headers, and messages, as shown in Figure 10-2. The left-side pane displays your mail folders. You initially have three folders: an inbox folder for received mail, an outbox folder for mail you have composed, but have not sent yet, and a trash folder for messages you have deleted. You can also create your own mail folders in which you can store particular messages. To place a message in a folder you have created, click-and-drag the message header for that message to the folder.

Mail Client	Description
Balsa	Balsa is an e-mail client for GNOME that supports POP3, IMAP, local folders, and multithreading.
Eucalyptus	Eucalyptus is an advanced MIME-compliant e-mail application.
Glacier	Glacier is an e-mail client for Gnome that supports MIME parsing.
Gmail	Gmail is an experimental vfolder-based e-mail system (using mysql).
GnoMail	GnoMail is a mail user agent that uses gnome-mailer interface.
LinPopUp	LinPopUp is an X Window graphical port of Winpopup, running over Samba.
Mahogany	Mahogany is a cross-platform e-mail application.
Ntool	N-Tool is a GUI Mail tool that supports Japanese language (ISO-2022-JP).
Pygmy	Pygmy is a GNOME mail client written in the Python programming language.
Spruce	Gnome is an e-mail client with support for multiple accounts.

Table 10-1.   *Gnome Mail Clients*

The right side of the Balsa window consists of two panes. The top-right pane lists the message headers for the currently selected folder. Message headers are displayed showing the subject, sender, and date. An Envelope icon indicates an unread message and a Trash Can icon indicates a message to be deleted. Headers are segmented into fields with buttons for the fields shown at the top of the pane. You can click these buttons to sort headers by different fields, such as subject or sender. To display a message, you click it. It is then displayed in the pane below the message headers. You can click the Right and Left Arrow icons in the icon bar to move through the header list.

To display message headers for a particular folder, you first must open that folder. Double-clicking the folder's icon both opens the folder and selects it, with its headers displayed. You can also single-click the folder's icon and select Open from the Mailbox menu. This opens the folder and displays a button for it in the bar separating the folder pane from the right-side panes. You can open several folders at once. Each will have its own button in the bar. To have an open folder's message headers display, you can click its button in this middle bar. To close a folder, select it and then choose the Close entry on the Mailbox menu.

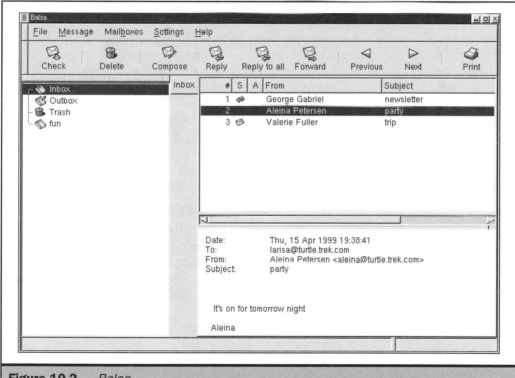

Figure 10-2. *Balsa*

You can access commands for managing your mail through the menus on the menu bar located at the top the Balsa window. An icon bar for commonly used mail commands is displayed below the menu bar. To retrieve new messages, click the Check icon or select the Get New Mail item in the File menu. To print a message, click its header and then the Printer icon. To delete a message, select its header and click the Delete icon. The icons featuring envelopes are different forms of message composition: One for new messages, one for replies, and one for forwarding messages. Balsa also supports filters for automatically performing operations on received mail. You can create a filter that matches a specified string in a header field and then automatically perform an operation on that message. For example, you could have any message from a certain person automatically deleted or messages on a certain subject automatically printed.

To compose a message, click the Compose icon or select the New item on the Message menu. A new message window opens with entries for the To, From, Subject, and Carbon copy header fields. If you select the Reply or Forward icons, the To, From, and Subject fields are already filled in with your address and the sender's address, and the sender's subject with a preceding Re: for replies and Fwd: for forwards. Fields that use addresses have a small Address Book button at the end of their fields. You can click this button to use the address book to enter an address for a field. Enter the message in the body of the window. The standard GUI editing operations are supported, enabling you to use your mouse to select, cut, copy, and move text. To send the message, click the Send icon in the icon bar or select the Send entry in the File menu. Icons also exist for operations such as selecting attachments or printing the message. Attachments added to a message are displayed in a pane just below the icon bar.

You can configure Balsa to access any number of mail accounts. Select the Preferences entry to bring up a window with panels for configuring Balsa. The Mail Servers panel shows three sections: one for remote mailbox servers, another for local mail, and the last for outgoing mail. In the remote mailbox servers section, you can add the server information for your network. Clicking the Add button opens a mailbox configurator window where you can enter your account's username and password, as well as the server name for that mailbox server. The mailbox name is any name you want to use to identify this mail service.

The Mahogany mail client window uses a format similar to Balsa. Three panes are there: A left pane for listing folders, and two other panes on the right side for headers and message text. The headers pane has buttons for sorting headers by different fields, such as subject or sender. Mail operations can be performed using the menus or the button bar at the top of the window. To compose a message, you can click the Envelope button. This opens a window with entries for From, To, and Subject header fields. Mouse-based editing operations, such as cut-and-paste are currently not supported, though you can invoke an external editor. A menu bar and icon bar at the top of the window list the different message operations you can perform, such as the spell-checker and printing.

X Window Mail Clients: Netscape and exmh

Although many of the newer mail clients are being designed for either Gnome or the K Desktop, several mail clients were developed for use on X Windows and operate under any window manager or desktop. They do not require either Gnome or the K Desktop. Netscape Messenger and exmh are two of the more popular mail clients. The Emacs mail clients are integrated into the Emacs environment, of which the Emacs editor is the primary application. They are, however, fully functional mail clients. The GNU Emacs mail client can operate either with X Windows capabilities or with a screen-based interface like Pine. The XEmacs mail client operates solely as an X Windows application.

Netscape Messenger

Netscape Communicator includes a mail client called Messenger. To use the mail client, you have to select the mail window item in Navigator's window menu or select the Messenger icon in the Communicator window. Account information, such as your mail server, username, and password must be entered in the Mail panel in the Preferences window, accessible from the Edit menu. Received messages are displayed in the Messenger window. The window is divided into two panes, the upper one listing headers of received messages and the lower one for displaying messages. To display a message, click its header. The icon bar displays icons for several common mail operations, such as sending, deleting, or forwarding messages.

To send a message, click the New Message icon. This opens a window that displays three sections. The middle section is for entering the subject line and the bottom section is for entering the text of your message. The top section switches among three alternate panes: address, attachments, and options. You can use the small buttons on the left side of the section to switch between panes. The address pane features a drop-down menu for selecting which address field you want to fill. Entries exist for the To, From, Cc, and Bcc fields. The attachments pane lists files attached to this message. Use the Attachment's icon in the icon bar to add attachments. The options pane lists several options, such as priority, encryption, and receipts. For the text section, Messenger supports a wide range of composition features, such HTML addresses, fonts, formatting, and spell-checker. It supports standard GUI editing operations including cut-and-paste, though you use the ALT key instead of the CTRL key for keyboard equivalents.

exmh

exmh is an X Windows version of the MH mail client, described later in this chapter. It displays a window with two panes (see Figure 10-3). The upper pane lists the headers for received mail and the lower pane displays a selected message. Above each pane is a button bar for various MH commands (these are the same as the commands for the MH

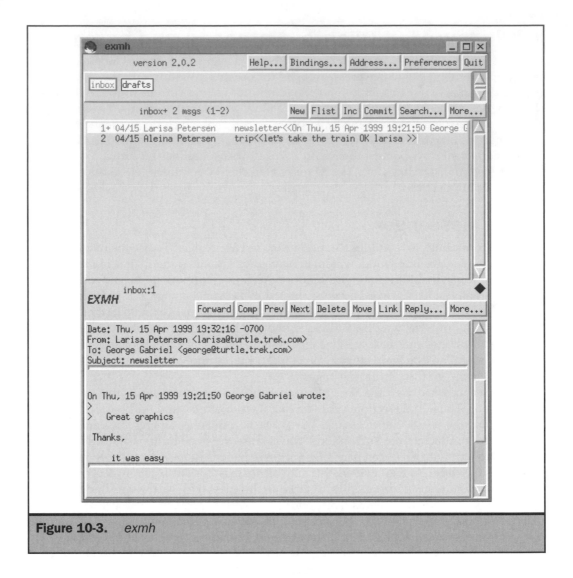

Figure 10-3. *exmh*

mail client). To check for new mail, you press the Inc button on the top pane. Headers for unread messages are colored blue and the selected header is displayed in red. You can add new mailbox folders by pressing the New button.

To read a message, click its header, which is displayed in the lower pane. Buttons for managing a message are listed across the top of that pane. Long messages are displayed screen by screen, and you can see the next screen by clicking the More button. The Next and Previous buttons move you directly to the next or previous message. Comp, Reply, and Forward all open a new message window for composing and sending a message. Comp is for new messages, and Reply and Forward include your address, the sender's, and the current message's subject.

To compose a new message, click the Comp button in the lower pane. Header fields and their titles are listed from the top. Click next to a header title and enter its value. For example, to enter a value for the To field, click after "To" and type the address you want. A line below the header separates the header from the text of the message. Click below this line and enter your message. You can change any of the header fields and the text of your message at any time. Click the Send button to send the message.

The Emacs Mail Client: GNU Emacs and XEmacs

The GNU version of Emacs includes a mail client along with other components, such as a newsreader and editor. GNU Emacs is included on Red Hat distributions. Check the Emacs Web site at **www.emacs.org** for more information. When you start up GNU Emacs, menu buttons are displayed across the top of the screen. If you are running Emacs in an X Windows environment, then you have full GUI capabilities and can select menus using your mouse. To access the Emacs mail client, select from the mail entries in the Tools menu. To compose and send messages, just select the Send Mail item in the Tools menu. This opens a screen with a prompt for To: and Subject: header entries (see Figure 10-4). You then type the message below them, using any of the Emacs editing capabilities. On the menu bar, a new menu is added labeled Mail. When you are ready to send the mail, choose the Send Mail entry in this menu. To read mail, select the Read Mail item in the Tools menu, which displays the first mail message received. Use entries in the Move menu to move to the next message or back to a previous one, and use entries in the Delete menu to remove a message. The Mail

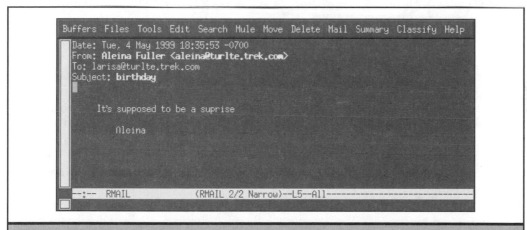

Figure 10-4.   *Emacs mail client*

menu lists entries for message operations, such as sending replies or forwarding the message. GNU Emacs is a working environment within which you can perform a variety of tasks, with each task having its own buffer. When you read mail, a buffer is opened to hold the header list, and when you read a message, another buffer will hold the contents. When you compose a message, yet another buffer holds the text you wrote. The buffers you have opened for mail, news, or editing notes or files are listed in the Buffers menu. You can use this menu to switch among them.

XEmacs is another version of Emacs designed to operate solely with a GUI interface. The Internet applications, which you can easily access from the main XEmacs button bar, includes a Web browser, a mail utility, and a newsreader. Currently, XEmacs is distributed on OpenLinux. Clicking the Mail button brings up another window that lists received messages and also enables you to compose new ones. You can compose, reply, or print messages using buttons on the side of the window. To display a message, click its header and press the SPACEBAR. You can display the headers by choosing the Display item in the Folder menu. When composing a message, you have full use of the Emacs editor with all its features, including the spell-checker and search/replace. A new window is opened that prompts you for the address and subject. When you finish editing your message, choose Send and Exit in the Mail menu located at the end of the menu bar.

Screen-Based Mail Clients

You can invoke several powerful mail clients on the command line that provide a full-screen, cursor-based interface. Menus are displayed on the screen whose entries you can select using your keyboard. Basic cursor movement is supported with arrow keys. Pine, Elm, and Mutt are all mail clients that provide a screen-based interface. Although screen-based, the mail clients are capable. Pine, in particular, has an extensive set of features and options.

Pine

Pine stands for *Program for Internet News and E mail.* It features full MIME support, enabling you to send messages, documents, and pictures easily. Pine has an extensive list of options, and it has flexible Internet connection capabilities, letting you receive both mail and Usenet news. Pine also enables you to maintain an address book where you can place frequently used e-mail addresses. You can find more information about Pine, including documentation and recent versions, from the Pine Information Center Web site at **www.washington.edu/pine**. The Pine newsgroup is **comp.mail.pine,** where you can post questions.

Pine runs from the command line using a simple cursor-based interface. Enter the **pine** command to start Pine. Pine supports full-screen cursor controls. It displays a menu whose items you can select by moving the cursor with the arrow keys to the entry of your choice and pressing ENTER. Each item is labeled with a capital letter, which you use to select it. The O command brings up a list of other Pine commands you can use.

To send a message, select the Compose Message item. This brings up a screen where you can enter your message. You are first taken through the different entries for the header, which prompts you for an e-mail address and subject. You can even attach files. Then, you type in the text of the message. A set of commands listed at the bottom of the screen specify different tasks. You can read a file with CTRL-R and cancel the message with CTRL-C. Use CTRL-X to send the message, as shown in Figure 10-5.

Pine organizes both sent and received messages into folders that you select using the Folder List entry on the main menu. The different available folders are listed from left to right. Three folders are automatically set up for you: INBOX, sent-mail, and saved-messages. The INBOX folder holds mail you have received, but have not yet read. Sent-mail is for messages you have sent to others, while saved-messages are messages you have read and want to keep. Use the LEFT and RIGHT ARROW keys to select the one you want and then press ENTER. Selecting the INBOX folder will list the messages you have received. Headers for received messages are then displayed, and you can choose a specific header to view your message. The folder you select becomes your default folder. You can return to it by selecting the Folder Index entry in the main menu.

Mutt

Mutt incorporates many of the features of both Elm and Pine. It has an easy-to-use screen-based interface similar to Elm. Like Pine, Mutt has an extensive set of features,

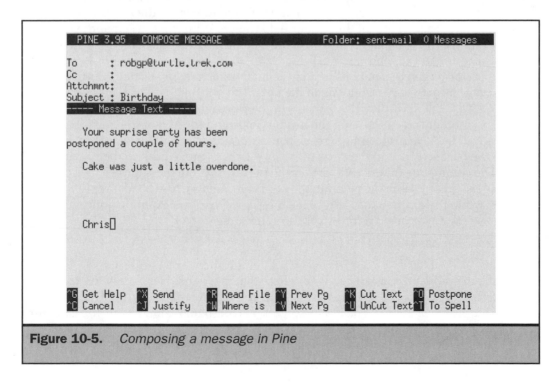

Figure 10-5.   *Composing a message in Pine*

such as MIME support. You can find more information about Mutt from the Mutt Web page at **www.mutt.org**. Here, you can download recent versions of Mutt and access online manuals and help resources. On most distributions, the Mutt manual is located in the **/usr/doc** directory under Mutt. The Mutt newsgroup is **comp.mail.mutt** where you can post queries and discuss recent Mutt developments.

Mutt screens have both an index mode and a pager mode. The *index mode* is used to display and manage message header lists, while the *pager mode* is used to display and compose messages. Mutt screens support ANSI escape sequences for color coding, displaying commands, prompts, and selected entries in different colors. You invoke Mutt with the command **mutt** entered on a Linux shell command line. Mutt displays a list of common commands across the top of the screen. Pressing the single key listed before the command executes that command. For example, pressing **q** quits Mutt, **s** saves the current message, and **r** enables you to send a reply to a message. Press the **?** key to obtain a complete listing of Mutt commands.

To compose a new message, press **m**. On the bottom line, you are then sequentially prompted to enter the address of the person to whom you are sending a message, the subject line, and a carbon copy list. Then you are placed in the standard editor, usually Vi or Emacs, and you can use the editor to enter your message. If you are using Vi, you first have to press the **a** or **i** command before you can enter text. After entering your text, you press ESC to return to the Vi command mode. When you finish entering your message, you save and exit Vi with the **ZZ** command. After editing the message, Mutt displays the header and a list of possible commands at the top of the screen. You can then edit the message or any of the header fields again. With the **a** command, you can add attachments to the message, and with the **q** command you can cancel the message. Press the **y** command to send the message

Headers for received mail are listed in the main screen upon starting Mutt. You can use the arrow keys to move from one to the next. The selected header is highlighted. Press the ENTER key to display the contents of the message, as shown in Figure 10-6. This opens another screen showing the header fields and the text of the message. Long messages are displayed screen by screen. You can use the PAGE UP or SPACEBAR keys to move to the next screen, and the PAGE DOWN or – keys to move back to the previous screen. The commands for operations you can perform on the message are listed across the top of the screen. With the **r** command, you can compose and send a reply to the message, while the **d** command deletes the message. Once you examine your message, you can use the **i** command to return to the main screen.

Elm

Elm has a screen-oriented, user-friendly interface that makes mail tasks easy to execute. Messages are displayed one screen at a time, and you can move back and forth through the message screen by screen. The Elm newsgroup is **comp.mail.elm,** where you can post queries for problems you may encounter. To send a message using Elm, you type **elm** along with the address of the person to whom you are sending the message. When you

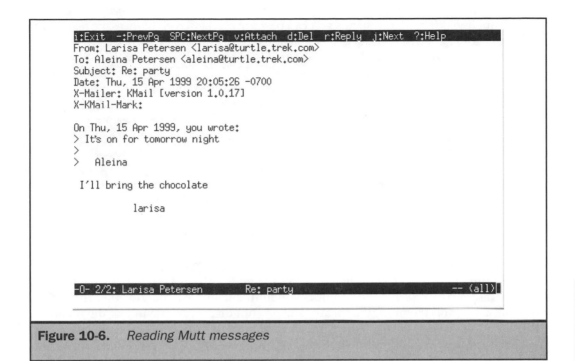

```
i:Exit  -:PrevPg  SPC:NextPg  v:Attach  d:Del  r:Reply  j:Next  ?:Help
From: Larisa Petersen <larisa@turtle.trek.com>
To: Aleina Petersen <aleina@turtle.trek.com>
Subject: Re: party
Date: Thu, 15 Apr 1999 20:05:26 -0700
X-Mailer: KMail [version 1.0.17]
X-KMail-Mark:

On Thu, 15 Apr 1999, you wrote:
> It's on for tomorrow night
>
>    Aleina

  I'll bring the chocolate

          larisa



-O- 2/2: Larisa Petersen         Re: party                    -- (all)
```

Figure 10-6.   *Reading Mutt messages*

press ENTER, Elm displays the name of the person to whom you are sending the message and then prompts you for the subject. Elm displays the actual name of the person, not the address. At the subject prompt, you enter a subject. Then Elm prompts you for a carbon copy list. You can then enter the addresses of other users whom you want to have a copy of the message, or you can simply press ENTER if you do not want any carbon copies sent. Upon pressing ENTER at this point, you are placed in the standard editor, either Vi or Emacs, and you can use the editor to enter your message. After editing the message, Elm prompts you for an action, at which time you can send it, quit without sending, edit the message again, or edit its headers, as shown here. Each option is listed with a single-letter command. The **h** option displayed in the Elm message menu is for editing the header. With this option, you can change any of the entries in your message header, and you can enter other header values, such as addresses for blind carbon copies.

```
Please choose one of the following options by parenthesized letter:
e)dit message, edit h)eaders, s)end it, or f)orget it
```

To receive mail using Elm, you enter **elm** by itself on the command line. Elm then displays a list of message headers representing messages you have received. The headers are displayed from the top of the screen. At the bottom of the screen is an information menu listing the different commands you can perform on the screen of message headers (see Figure 10-7). This list of headers is referred to in Elm as the *index*. If you have more than one screen of message headers, you can move to the next screen with the + key. You can also move back a screen with the – key. An Elm header displays the status, message number, date, name of the sender, number of lines in the message, and the subject. The message status is represented by a letter code. An **N** indicates a newly received message, and an **O** indicates an old message—one that is still unread. The current header is either preceded by an arrow, **->**, or highlighted by the background. The arrow or highlight moves as you use arrow keys to move to the next or previous message header. To display the current message, press ENTER. A new screen appears in which the message is displayed. If the message is larger than a screen, you can move through it, screen by screen, using the same commands as those in the **more** utility. Pressing the SPACEBAR moves you to the next screen, and pressing **b** moves you back a screen. You can even search for particular patterns in the message. Once you examine your message, you can use the **i** command to return to the header screen. The **i** stands for *index,* which is the term Elm uses to refer to the list of headers. You quit Elm by pressing the **q** key.

With Elm, you create any number of different mailbox files in which you can save your messages. The **c** command prompts you for the name of a mailbox file. Simply press the **c** key and the prompt appears. The prompt displays the name of the mailbox file used to hold received messages from the sender in the current message header. You can specify your own mailbox file by entering the name of the file preceded by a = sign. **=birthdays** specifies the **birthdays** mailbox file. Once you change to the other folder, the headers for all the messages in this mailbox file are displayed and you can display the messages, delete them from the file, or send replies. The folder's name is displayed at the top of the screen.

Elm maintains an **.elm** directory in your home directory with which it configures your use of Elm. Each time you invoke Elm, it generates a shell for your own use,

```
Mailbox is '/usr/spool/mail/richpete' with 3 messages
 N 1  Gabriel Matoza       Feb 11        (5)       "Budget"
 N 2  Aleina Petersen      Feb 12        (28)      "Birthday"
 N 3  Marylou Carrion      Feb 14        (16)      "Homework"




    You can use any of the following commands by pressing the first character;
    d)elete or u)ndelete mail, m)ail a message, r)eply or f)orward mail, q)uit
      To read a message, press <return>.  j = move down, k = move up, ? = help

  Command:
```

Figure 10-7.   *Elm header list*

within which you can define your own aliases and configuration variables. The **.elm** directory contains special configuration files in which you can place alias or variable definitions. You can set options either by entering assignments to the **.elmrc** file in your **.elm** directory or by using the Options menu within Elm (command **o** displays the options menu). Elm also enables you to create mail aliases. You can create aliases either by using the Alias menu within the utility or by entering aliases in the **aliases.text** file in the **.elm** directory.

Command Line Mail Clients

Several mail clients use a simple command line interface. They can be run without any other kind of support, such as X Windows, desktops, or cursor support. They are simple and easy to use, but include an extensive set of features and options. Two of the more widely used mail clients of this type are Mail and Mail Handler (MH). Mail is the mailx mail client that was developed for the UNIX system. It is considered a kind of default mail client that can be found on all UNIX and Linux systems. You can also use the Emacs mail client from the command line, as described in the previous section.

Mail

What is known now as the mail utility was originally created for BSD UNIX and called, simply, mail. Later versions of UNIX System V adopted the BSD mail utility and renamed it *mailx*. Now, it is simply referred to as *Mail*. Mail functions as a de facto default mail client on UNIX and Linux systems. All systems have the Mail mail client, whereas they may not have other mail clients.

To send a message with Mail, type **mail** along with the address of the person to whom you are sending the message. Press ENTER and you are prompted for a subject. Enter the subject of the message and press ENTER again. At this point, you are placed in input mode. Anything typed in is taken as the contents of the message. Pressing ENTER adds a new line to the text. When you finish typing your message, press CTRL-D on a line of its own to end the message and send it. You see *EOT* (*end-of-transmission*) displayed after you press CTRL-D. In the next example, the user sends a message to another user whose address is **robert**. The subject of the message is Birthday. After typing in the text of the message, the user presses CTRL-D.

```
$ mail robert
Subject: Birthday
     Your present is in the mail
really.

^D
EOT
$
```

INTERNET

The Mail utility receives input from the standard input. By default, the standard input is taken from what the user enters on the keyboard. With redirection, however, you can use the contents of a file as the message for the Mail program. In the next example, the file **mydata** is redirected as input for the Mail utility and sent to **robert**.

```
$ mail robert < mydata
```

You can send a message to several users at the same time by listing those users' addresses as arguments on the command line following the `mail` command. In the next example, the user sends the same message to both **chris** and **aleina**.

```
$ mail chris aleina
```

You may also want to save a copy of the message you are sending for yourself. You can copy a mail message to a file in your account by specifying a filename on the command line after the addresses. The filename must be a relative or full pathname, containing a slash. A pathname identifies an argument as a filename to which Mail saves a copy of the message being sent. In the next example, the user saves a copy of the message to a file called **birthnote**. A relative pathname is used, with the period denoting the current working directory: **./birthnote**.

```
$ mail robert ./birthnote
```

To receive mail, you enter only the `mail` command and press ENTER. This invokes a Mail shell with its own prompt and mail commands. A list of message headers is displayed. Header information is arranged into fields beginning with the status of the message and the message number. The status of a message is indicated by a single uppercase letter, usually **N**, for *new*, or **U**, for *unread*. A message number, used for easy reference to your messages, follows the status field. The next field is the address of the sender, followed by the date and time the message was received, and then the number of lines and characters in the message. The last field contains the subject the sender gave for the message. After the headers, the Mail shell displays its prompt, a question mark, **?**. At the Mail prompt, you enter commands that operate on the messages. The commonly used Mail commands are listed in Table 10-2. An example of Mail headers and prompts follows:

```
$ mail
Mail version 5.5-kw 5/30/95. Type ? for help.
"/var/spool/mail/chris": 3 messages 3 new
>N  1 valerie    Tue Feb 11 10:14:32 5/44   "Budget"
 N  2 aleina     Wed Feb 12 12:30:17 28/537 "Birthday"
 N  3 robert     Fri Feb 14  8:15:24 16/293 "Homework"
?
```

Status Codes	Description
N	Newly received messages
U	Previously unread messages
R	Reads messages in the current session
P	Preserved messages, read in previous session and kept in incoming mailbox
D	Deleted messages; messages marked for deletion
O	Old messages
*	Messages you saved to another mailbox file
Display Messages	**Description**
H	Redisplay the message headers
z+ z-	If header list takes up more than one screen, scrolls header list forward and backward
t *message-list*	Displays a message referenced by the message list; if no message list is used, the current message is displayed
p *message-list*	Displays a message referenced by the message list; if no message list is used, the current message is displayed
n or +	Displays next message
-	Displays previous message
top *message-list*	Displays the top few lines of a message referenced by the message list; if no message list is used, the current message is displayed
Message Lists	**Description**
message-number	References message with message number
num1-num2	References a range of messages beginning with *num1* and ending with *num2*
.	Current message
^	First message
$	Last message
*	All the messages waiting in the mailbox

Table 10-2. *Mail Commands*

INTERNET

Message Lists	Description
lpattern	All messages with pattern in the subject field
Address	All messages sent from user with address

:*c*	All messages of the type indicated by *c*; message types are as follows:
	     n newly received messages
	     o old messages previously received
	     r read messages
	     u unread messages
	     d deleted messages

Deleting and Restoring Messages	Description
d *message-list*	Deletes a message referenced by the indicated message list from your mailbox
u *message-list*	Undeletes a message referenced by the indicated message list that has been previously deleted
Q	Quits the Mail utility and saves any read messages in the **mbox** file
x	Quits the Mail utility and does *not* erase any messages you deleted; this is equivalent to executing a **u** command on all deleted messages before quitting
pre *message-list*	Preserves messages in your waiting mailbox even if you have already read them

Sending and Editing Messages	Description
R	Sends a reply to all persons who received a message
R	Sends a reply to the person who sent you a message
m *address*	Sends a message to someone while in the Mail utility
v *message-list*	Edits a message with the Vi editor

Table 10-2. *Mail Commands* (continued)

Saving Messages	Description
s *message-list filename*	Saves a message referenced by the message list in a file, including the header of the message
S *message-list*	Saves a message referenced by the message list in a file named for the sender of the message
w *message-list filename*	Saves a message referenced by the message list in a file without the header; only the text of the message is saved
`folder` *mailbox-filename*	Switches to another mailbox file
%	Represents the name of incoming mailbox file: `folder %` switches to incoming mailbox file
#	Represents name of previously accessed mailbox file: `folder #` switches to previous mailbox file
&	Represents name of mailbox file used to save your read messages automatically; usually called **mbox**: `folder &` switches to **mbox** file
General Commands	**Description**
?	Displays a list of all the Mail commands
! *command*	Executes a user shell command from within the Mail shell

Table 10-2. *Mail Commands* (continued)

Mail references messages either through a message list or through the current message marker (>). The greater-than sign (>) is placed before a message considered the current message. The current message is referenced by default when no message number is included with a Mail command. You can also reference messages using a message list consisting of several message numbers. Given the messages in the previous example, you can reference all three messages with 1-3. The ^ references the first message; for example, ^-3 specifies the range of messages from the first message to the third message. The $ references the last message. The period, ., references the current message. And the asterisk, *****, references all messages. Simply entering the number of the message by itself will display that message. The message is then output screen by screen. Press the SPACEBAR or the ENTER key to continue to the next screen.

You use the **R** and **r** commands to reply to a message you have received. The **R** command entered with a message number generates a header for sending a message and then places you into the input mode to type in the message. The **q** command quits Mail. When you quit, messages you have already read are placed in a file called **mbox** in your **home** directory. Instead of saving messages in the **mbox** file, you can use the **s** command to save a message explicitly to a file of your choice. The **s** command, however, saves a message with its header, in effect, creating another mailbox file. You can then later access a mailbox file either by invoking the Mail utility with the **-f** option and the mailbox filename or, if you are already using Mail, by executing the **folder** command that switches to a specified mailbox file. For example, the command **mail -f family_msgs** accesses the mailbox file **family_msgs**. Each message in the **family_msgs** mailbox file is then displayed in a message list.

Mail has its own initialization file, called **.mailrc**, that is executed each time Mail is invoked, either for sending or receiving messages. Within it, you can define Mail options and create Mail aliases. You can set options that add different features to mail, such as changing the prompt or saving copies of messages you send. To define an alias, you enter the keyword **alias**, followed by the alias you have chosen and then the list of addresses it represents. In the next example, the alias **myclass** is defined in the **.mailrc** file.

.mailrc
```
alias myclass chris dylan aleina justin larisa
```

In the next example, the contents of the file **homework** are sent to all the users whose addresses are aliased by **myclass**.

```
$ mail myclass < homework
```

The Mail Handler Utility: MH

The Mail Handler mail client, commonly known as MH, takes a different approach to managing mail than most other mail clients. MH consists of a set of commands you execute within your user shell, just as you would execute any other UNIX command. No special mail shell exists, as there is for Mail. One MH command sends a message, another displays your incoming messages, and still another saves a message. The MH commands and their options are listed in Table 10-3. A set of environment variables provides a context for the MH commands you execute, such as keeping track of the current messages or mail folders. Instead of working from a command line interface, you can use xmh or ezmh, which provide an X Windows interface for accessing MH messages.

Commands	Descriptions
`inc`	Places received mail in your incoming mailbox and displays message headers
`show` *num*	Displays current message or specified messages
`prev`	Displays the previous message
`next`	Displays the next message
`scan`	Redisplays message headers
`mhl`	Displays formatted listing of messages
`folders`	Lists all mail folders
`forw`	Forwards a message
`repl`	Replies to a message
`send`	Resends a message or sends a file as a message
`pick`	Selects messages by specified criteria and assigns them a sequence
`folder`	Changes to another mailbox file (folder)

Table 10-3. *MH Commands*

INTERNET

To send a message using MH, you first need to compose the message using the **comp** command, and then send the message with the **send** command. To compose a message, type in the word **comp** on the command line by itself and press RETURN. Then you are prompted for each header component, beginning with the address of the user to whom you are sending the message. After entering a subject, you are placed in an input mode for the default editor used for MH (usually the Vi editor). Next, you type the contents of the message, and then save and quit the editor as you normally would (ESC-SHIFT-**ZZ** for Vi). At the **What now?** prompt, you can send the message, edit it, save it to a file, display it again, or quit without sending the message. The **send** command sends the message. Pressing ENTER at the **What now?** prompt displays a list of commands you can enter. In the next example, the user composes a message for another user whose address is **robert**.

```
$ comp
To: robert
cc:
```

```
Subject: Birthday
------------------
Your present is in the mail
really.

What now? send
$
```

To read your mail with MH, you first need to store newly received mail into a designated MH mailbox file with the **inc** command. The **inc** command displays a list of headers for each mail message in your incoming mailbox. A MH message header consists only of the message number, the month and year, the address of the sender, and the beginning of the message text.

```
$ inc
1+  02/97  To:valerie    budget <<You are way under
2   02/97  To:aleina     birthday <<Yes, I did remember
$
```

If you want to redisplay the headers, you need to use another MH command called **scan**.

```
$ scan
1+  02/97  To:valerie    budget <<You are way under
2   02/97  To:aleina     birthday <<Yes, I did remember
$
```

You use the **show, next**, and **prev** commands to display a message. The **show** command displays the current message, the **next** command displays the message after the current one, and the **prev** command displays the message before the current one. Initially, the current message is the first of the newly received messages. If you want to display a particular message, you can use the **show** command with the number of the message. **show** 2 displays message 2. You can also reference several messages at once by listing their message numbers. The command **show 1 3** displays messages 1 and 3. You can also designate a range of messages by specifying the first message number in the range, and the last number, separated by a minus sign. **show 1-3** displays messages 1, 2, and 3.

```
$ show
$ next
```

To print a message, you first output it with **show,** and then pipe the output to a printer. You save a message to a text file in much the same way. First you output the message using the **show** command, and then redirect that output to a file.

```
$ show | lpr
$ show > myfile
```

You reply to the current message using the **repl** command. You need to know either the message number or the address and subject of the message to reply to it. You delete the current message using the **rmm** command. To delete a specific message, using the message number with **rmm**. **rmm** 2 deletes the second message. You can create your own mailbox files for MH using the **folder** command. MH mailbox files are commonly referred to as *folders*. To create a new folder, enter in the **folder** command followed by the name of your folder preceded by a + sign. The + sign identifies an argument as a folder name.

```
$ repl 2
$ rmm 2
$ folder +mybox
```

Notifications of Received Mail: From and biff

As your mail messages are received, they are automatically placed in your mailbox file, but you are not automatically notified when you receive a message. To find out if you have any messages waiting, you can either use a mail client to retrieve messages or you can use the From and biff utilities to tell you if you have any mail waiting.

The From utility tells what messages you have received and are waiting to be read. For each waiting message, it lists the senders' addresses and times each message was received. To use From, you enter the keyword **from** and press ENTER.

```
$ from
1 From valerie Sun Feb 11 10:14:32 1996
  Subject: Budget
2 From aleina Mon Feb 12 12:30:17 1996
  Subject: Birthday
3 From robert Wed Feb 14  8:15:24 1996
  Subject: Homework
$
```

biff notifies you immediately when a message is received. This is helpful when you are expecting a message and want to know as soon as it arrives. biff automatically displays the header and beginning lines of messages as they are received. To turn on biff, you enter **biff y** on the command line. To turn it off, you enter **biff n**. To find out if biff is turned on, enter **biff** alone. biff displays a message notification whenever a message arrives, no matter what you may be doing at the time. You could be in the middle of an editing session and biff will interrupt it to display the notification on your screen. You can then return to your editing session. In the next example, the user first sets biff on. Then biff notifies the user that a message has been received. The user then checks to see if biff is still on.

```
$ biff y
$
New mail for chris has arrived:
--Date: Sun Feb 11 12:30:21
From: dylan
To: chris
Subject: Food
    Chris,
        Have you tried the chocolate
...more...

$
$ biff
is y
$
```

You can temporarily block biff by using the **mesg n** command to prevent any message displays on your screen. **mesg n** not only stops any Write and Talk messages, it also stops biff and Notify messages. Later, you can unblock biff with a **mesg y** command. A **mseg n** command comes in handy if you don't want to be disturbed while working on some project.

If you are running a window manager, such as fvwm or Afterstep, you can use the xbiff utility to perform the same function. xbiff displays an icon of a mailbox, which has a flag on it, on your desktop. When mail arrives, the flag goes up. xbiff can also beep or produce some other sound, if you prefer.

The K Desktop has a biff utility called *Kbiff* that performs much in the same way. With Kbiff, you can set numerous options. Kbiff can show an empty inbox tray when there is no mail and a tray with slanted letters in it when mail arrives. If old mail is still in your mailbox, letters are displayed in a neat square. You can set these icons as any image you want. You can also specify the mail client to use and the polling interval for checking for new mail. If you have several mail accounts, you can set up a Kbiff profile for each one. Different icons can appear for each account telling you when mail arrives in one of them.

Accessing Mail on Remote POP Mail Servers

Most newer mail clients are equipped to access mail accounts on remote servers. For such mail clients, you can specify a separate mail account with its own mailbox. For example, if you are using an ISP, most likely you will use that ISP's mail server to receive mail. You will have set up a mail account with a username and password for accessing your mail. Your e-mail address is usually your username and the ISP's domain name. For example, a username of larisa for an ISP domain named **mynet.com** would have the address **larisa@mynet.com**. The username would be larisa. The address of the actual mail server could be something like **mail.mynet.com**. The user larisa would log in to the **mail.mynet.com** server using the username larisa and her password to access mail sent to the address **larisa@mynet.com**. Newer mail clients, such as kmail, Balsa, and Netscape enable you to set up a mailbox for such an account and access your ISP's mail server to check for and download received mail. You must specify what protocol a mail server uses. This is usually the *Post Office Protocol* (*POP*). This procedure is used for any remote mail server. Using a mail server address, you can access your account with your username and password.

Instead of creating separate mailboxes in different mail clients, you can arrange to have mail from different accounts sent directly to the inbox maintained by your Linux system for your Linux account. All your mail, whether from other users on your Linux system or from ISP mail servers, will appear in your local inbox. Such a feature is helpful if you are using a mail client, such as Elm or Mail, that does not have the capability to access mail on your ISP's mail server. You can implement such a feature with Fetchmail. *Fetchmail* checks for mail on remote mail servers and downloads it to your local inbox, where it appears as newly received mail.

To use Fetchmail, you have to know a remote mail server's Internet address and mail protocol. Most remote mail servers use the POP3 protocol, but others may use IMAP, ETRM, or POP2 protocols. Enter **fetchmail** on the command line with the mail server address and any needed options. The mail protocol is indicated with the **-p** option and the mail server type, usually POP3. If your e-mail username is different from your Linux login name, then you use the **-u** option and the e-mail name. Once you execute the **fetchmail** command, you are prompted for a password. The syntax for the **fetchmail** command for a POP3 mail server follows:

```
fetchmail -p POP3 -u username mail-server
```

To use Fetchmail, connect to your ISP, and then enter the **fetchmail** commands with the options and the POP server name on the command line. You will see messages telling you if mail is there and, if so, how many messages are being downloaded. You can then use a mail client to read the messages from your inbox. You can run Fetchmail in daemon mode to have it automatically check for mail. You have to include an option specifying the interval in seconds for checking mail.

INTERNET

```
fetchmail -d  1200
```

You can specify options such as the server type, username, and password in a **.fetchmailrc** file in your **home** directory. You can also have entries for other mail servers and accounts you may have. Instead of entering options directly into the **.fetchmailrc** file, you can use the `fetchmailconf` program. `fetchmailconf` provides a GUI interface for selecting Fetchmail options and entering mail account information. `fetchmailconf` runs only under X Windows and requires Python and Tk be installed (most distributions automatically install these during installation). It displays windows for adding news servers, configuring a mail server, and configuring a user account on a particular mail server. The expert version displays the same kind of windows, but with many more options. Initially, `fetchmailconf` displays a window with buttons for choosing a novice or expert version (see Figure 10-8). Choosing the novice version displays a window with an entry labeled "New Server." Type the address of your mail server in the adjoining box and press ENTER. The server address then appears in a list below. To configure that server, click the server name and then the Edit button at the bottom of the window. A new window opens with entries such as user accounts and server protocols. You can add as many user accounts as you may have on that server. You can then further configure an individual account by selecting the username and clicking the Edit button. This opens another window for user

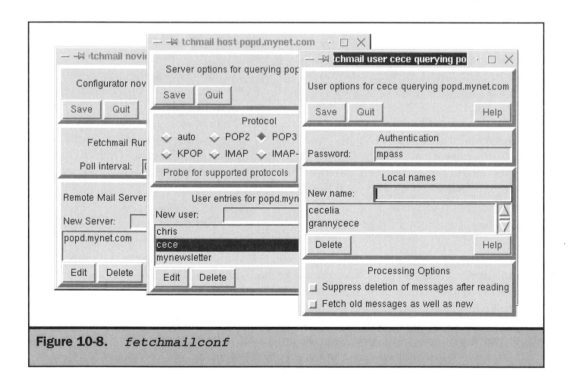

Figure 10-8.   *fetchmailconf*

account options. You can specify a password and specify any corresponding local users for which you want mail for this account downloaded.

Once configured, you can enter **fetchmail** with no arguments; it will read entries from your **.fetchmailrc** file. Accounts you have specified are checked and any new mail is placed in your inbox. If you want Fetchmail to check automatically for new mail periodically, you can activate its daemon mode. To do so, place a daemon entry in the **.fetchmailrc** file. The following entry activates the Fetchmail daemon mode, checking for mail every 1,200 seconds:

```
Set daemon  1200
```

You can also make entries directly in the **.fetchmailrc** file. An entry in the **.fetchmailrc** file for a particular mail account consists of several fields and their values: poll, protocol, username, and password. *Poll* is used to specify the mail server name, and *protocol* for the type of protocol used. Notice you can also specify your password, instead of having to enter it in each time Fetchmail accesses the mail server. The syntax for an entry follows:

```
poll SERVERNAME protocol PROTOCOL username NAME password PASSWORD
```

You can use abbreviations for certain field names if you want: *proto* for protocol, *user* for username, and *pass* for password. An example follows for a POP3 server and an account with the username chris and the password mypass:

```
poll popd.mynet.com proto pop3 user chris password mypass
```

You can specify a default entry for any of these fields and not have to repeat them for each account entry. The default must be placed before the mail server entries. The following example sets the default protocol to POP3 and the username to chris:

```
defaults protocol pop3 user chris
```

This next example would reference the chris account with the password newpass on the **popd.train.com** mail server using the POP3 protocol. The missing fields are filled in by default.

```
poll popd.train.com password newpass
```

Fetchmail enables you to download messages to a specific user on your local system. In fact, you can access several accounts on the remote system and have them downloaded to specific users on the your local system. This is useful when running

INTERNET

Fetchmail in daemon mode. Essentially, Fetchmail is transferring mail from one set of remote accounts to corresponding ones on your local system. You could even have Fetchmail download from one remote account to several local ones, sending copies of the same mail to each. This is helpful if you are using several accounts on your Linux system,or if a group of users is using an account on the remote server for group mail. Local users are specified with the keyword **is** or **to** followed by the usernames, terminating with the keyword **here**. The following examples show different ways of specifying local users. The last entry will send all mail retrieved from the mynewsletter account to the users larisa, aleina, and dylan.

```
poll popd.mynet.com proto pop3 user chris password mypass is chris here
poll popd.othernet.com proto pop3 user neil password mypass is chris here
poll popd.mynet.com proto pop3 user cece password mypass to cecelia grannycece here
poll popd.mynet.com proto pop3 user mynewsletter password mypass to larisa aleina dylan here
```

Fetchmail also supports a multidrop mailbox feature. You can have several users' mail sent to one mailbox on the mail server, and then download it from there to the inboxes for their Linux accounts.

The Complete Reference

Chapter 11

Usenet and Newsreaders

senet is an open mail system on which users post news and opinions. It operates like a system-wide mailbox that any user on your Linux system can read or send messages. Users' messages are incorporated into Usenet files, which are distributed to any system signed up to receive them. Each system that receives Usenet files is referred to as a *site.* Certain sites perform organizational and distribution operations for Usenet, receiving messages from other sites and organizing them into Usenet files, which are then broadcast to many other sites. Such sites are called *backbone sites* and they operate like publishers, receiving articles and organizing them into different groups.

To access Usenet news, you need access to a news server. A news server receives the daily Usenet newsfeeds and makes them accessible to other systems. Your network may have a system that operates as a news server. If you are using an Internet service provider (ISP), a news server is probably maintained for your use. To read Usenet articles, you use a *newsreader*—a client program that connects to a news server and accesses the articles. On the Internet and in TCP/IP networks, news servers communicate with newsreaders using the *Network News Transfer Protocol* (*NNTP*) and are often referred to as NNTP news servers. Or, you could also create your own news server on your Linux system to run a local Usenet news service or to download and maintain the full set of Usenet articles. Several Linux programs, called *News Transport Agents,* can be used to create such a server.

Usenet News

Usenet files were originally designed to function like journals. Messages contained in the files are referred to as *articles.* A user could write an article, post it in Usenet, and have it immediately distributed to other systems around the world. Someone could then read the article on Usenet, instead of waiting for a journal publication. Usenet files themselves were organized as journal publications. Because journals are designed to address specific groups, Usenet files were organized according to groups called *newsgroups.* When a user posts an article, it is assigned to a specific newsgroup. If another user wants to read that article, she looks at the articles in that newsgroup. You can think of each newsgroup as a constantly updated magazine. For example, to read articles on computer science, you would access the Usenet newsgroup on computer science. More recently, Usenet files have also been used as bulletin boards on which people carry on debates. Again, such files are classified into newsgroups, though their articles read more like conversations than journal articles. You can also create articles of your own, which you can then add to a newsgroup for others to read. Adding an article to a newsgroup is called *posting* the article.

Each newsgroup has its own name, which is often segmented to classify newsgroups. Usually, the names are divided into three segments: a general topic, a subtopic, and a specific topic. The segments are delimited by periods. For example, you may have several newsgroups dealing with the general topic *rec,* which stands for recreation. Of those, some newsgroups may deal with only the subtopic food. Again, of those, a group may only discusses a specific topic, such as recipes. In this case, the newsgroup name would be **rec.food.recipes**.

Many of the bulletin board groups are designed for discussion only, lacking any journal-like articles. A good number of these begin with either alt or talk as their general topic. For example, **talk.food.chocolate** may contain conversations about how wonderful or awful chocolate is perceived, while **alt.food.chocolate** may contain informal speculations about the importance of chocolate to the basic structure of civilization as we know it. Here are some examples of Usenet newsgroup names:

```
comp.ai.neural-nets
comp.lang.pascal
sci.physics.fusion
rec.arts.movies
rec.food.recipes
talk.politics.theory
```

Linux has newsgroups on various topics. Some are for discussion, others are sources of information about recent developments. On some, you can ask for help for specific problems. A current list of some of the popular Linux newsgroups is provided here.

Newsgroup	Topic
comp.os.linux.announce	Announcements of Linux developments
comp.os.linux.admin	System administration questions
comp.os.linux.misc	Special questions and issues
comp.os.linux.setup	Installation problems
comp.os.linux.help	Questions and answers for particular problems

You read Usenet articles with a newsreader, such as krn, Gnews Gone, elknews, trn or tin, which enables you first to select a specific newsgroup and then read the articles in it. A newsreader operates like a user interface, enabling you to browse through and select available articles for reading, saving, or printing. Most newsreaders employ a sophisticated retrieval feature called *threads* that pulls together articles on the same discussion or topic. Numerous newsreaders currently are under development for both Gnome and KDE. You can check for KDE newsreaders on the software list on the K Desktop Web site at **www.kde.org**. For Gnome newsreaders, check Internet tools on the software map on the Gnome Web site at **www.gnome.org**.

Most newsreaders can read Usenet news provided on remote news servers that use the NNTP. Many such remote news servers are available through the Internet. Desktop newsreaders, such as krn and Netscape Collabra, have you specify the Internet address for the remote newsreader in their own configuration settings. Several shell-based newsreaders, however, such as trn, tin, and Pine, obtain the newsreader's Internet address from the **NNTPSERVER** shell variable. Before you can connect to a remote news server with such newsreaders, you first have to assign the Internet address of the news server to the **NNTPSERVER** shell variable, and then export that variable. You can place the assignment and export of **NNTPSERVER** in a login initialization file, such as **.bash_profile,** so it is performed automatically whenever you log in.

```
$ NNTPSERVER=news.servdomain.com
$ export NNTPSERVER
```

News Transport Agents

Usenet news is provided over the Internet as a daily newsfeed of articles for thousands of newsgroups. This newsfeed is sent to sites that can then provide access to the news for other systems through newsreaders. These sites operate as news servers; the newsreaders used to access them are their clients. The news server software, called *News Transport Agents,* is what provides newsreaders with news, enabling you to read newsgroups and post articles. For Linux, three of the popular News Transport Agents are INN, nntp, and Cnews. Both Cnews and nntp are smaller and simpler, and useful for small networks. INN is more powerful and complex, designed with large systems in mind (see **www.isc.org** for more details).

Daily newsfeeds on Usenet are often large and consume much of a news server's resources in both time and memory. For this reason, you may not want to set up your own Linux system to receive such newsfeeds. If you are operating in a network of Linux systems, you can designate one of them as the news server and install the News Transport Agent on it to receive and manage the Usenet newsfeeds. Users on other systems on your network can then access that news server with their own newsreaders.

If your network already has a news server, you needn't install a News Transport Agent at all. You only have to use your newsreaders to remotely access that server remotely (see **NNTPSERVER** in the previous section). In the case of an ISP, such providers often operate their own news servers, which you can also remotely access using your own newsreaders, such as trn and tin. Remember, though, trn and tin must take the time to download all the articles for selected newsgroups, as well as updated information on all the newsgroups.

You can also use News Transport Agents to run local versions of news for only the users on your system or your local network. To do this, install INN or Cnews and configure them just to manage local newsgroups. Users on your system could then post articles and read local news. You could also use INN, though the other agents would be adequate for local networks.

Mailing Lists

As an alternative to newsgroups, you can subscribe to an mailing lists. Users on a mailing lists automatically receive messages and articles sent to it. Mailing lists work much like a mail alias, broadcasting messages to all users on the list. Mailing lists were designed to serve small, specialized groups of people. Instead of posting articles for anyone to see, only those who subscribe receive them. Numerous mailing lists, as well as other subjects, are available for Linux. For example, at the **www.gnome.org** site, you can subscribe to any of several mailing lists on Gnome topics, such as **gnome-themes-list@gnome.org**, which deals with Gnome desktop themes. At **www.liszt.com,** you can search for mailing lists on various topics. By convention, to subscribe to a list, you send a request to the mailing list address with a –request term added to its user name. For example, to subscribe to **gnome-themes-list@gnome.org,** you send a request to **gnome-themes-list-request@gnome.org.** At **www.linux.org,** you can link to sites that support Linux-oriented mailing lists, such as Majordomo and the Linux Mailing Lists Web site. Lists exist for such topics as the Linux kernel, administration, and different distributions.

Gnome Newsreaders

Several Gnome newsreaders are under development, including elknews, Gnews, GNONews, Gone, and Pan. Check the Internet tool section on the Gnome software map at **www.gnome.org** for current versions and updates. *Elknews* is a simple newsreader featuring threading, sorting, posting, group listing, and custom-port connections. *GNews* is a newsreader that supports multithreading with pthreads. *GNONews* newsreader plans to implement Agent-like features to Gnome. *Gone,* which stands for *Gnome's Other News Editor,* is a GNU news reader that features MIME support, drag-and-drop attachments, inline image viewing, and plug-in filter support. *Pan* is a newsreader modeled after the Windows program, Agent, featuring decoding of binaries and automatic grouping of multipart posts.

The K Desktop Newsreader: krn

krn is a newsreader for the K Desktop. To start krn, select the news entry in the K Internet submenu located on the K menu. When you first use krn, you must configure the Internet settings. A window is displayed, titled KRN-NNTP Settings. In the Servers section, enter the NNTP and SMTP server Internet addresses. Specify any of the other options you want. You can enter more than one NNTP server address and it is added to a pop-up menu on the NNTP entry box. You can then use the pop-up menu to change news servers.

The krn newsreader window displays two folders: one for subscribed newsgroups and one for all newsgroups. You can expand or contract either by clicking their Folder icon. A menu bar is at the top of the window for newsgroup and configuration operations. An icon bar just below the menus lists several common newsgroup operations. To connect to your news server, click the first icon on this list. The second icon then disconnects. The icon with several lines downloads a current, complete list of newsgroups. The Curved Arrow icon checks to see if new articles have been posted for your newsgroups. The icon of a sheet of paper with a small, blue line partway through its left side is used to subscribe or unsubscribe to a newsgroup. To subscribe to a newsgroup, you first select it from the list of All Newsgroups. Then, click the Subscribe icon on the icon bar. It automatically appears in your list of subscribed-to newsgroups.

To display articles in a newsgroup, double-click the newsgroup entry. A window opens up consisting of two panes. The top pane lists the headers for articles in the newsgroup. You can scroll through the list using the scroll bar to the right. Articles you have read appear in blue type. If you right-click an article header, a pop-up menu displays options for moving or copying it to another folder, or deleting it. Buttons appear at the top of the header pane for each of the header fields. Fields for subject, sender, and date exist. Clicking a button sorts the headers by that field. For example, clicking the date field sorts all headers by date. Another field is named *score.* This is for score rules you can set up for the newsgroup. A score rule searches for keywords in certain fields and gives a score you specified to the articles if the keywords are found.

To read an article, click its header. The text of the article appears in the pane below (see Figure 11-1). A menu bar at the top of the window holds commands for accessing articles. Two icon bars below enable you to execute commonly used commands. In the top icon bar, the arrows move through the list of articles. The icon with a looking glass opens a find window for searching articles by subject, sender, text, or other fields. The blank page posts a new article and the icon with lines in it downloads a current list of articles for the group. To the left is a box for adjusting the number of articles you want displayed.

If you want to post an article of your own to this newsgroup, click the icon of a blank paper. This opens a new window with the newsgroup name already entered. Enter your own address and then enter the text of the article. You can add other newsgroups to which you want the article posted. To attach a file, click the Attach entry in the Attach menu. To post a follow-up article, click the icon of a page with lines in it. This opens a similar window with entries for Subject, Newsgroup, and a Follow-up-to entry. Enter your message and then click the Envelope icon to send it. If, instead, you want only to send a reply to the author, then click the Envelope icon. A window opens a Kmail message window with entries already filled for the address and subject. The article is displayed in the window with preceding >> signs. You can edit and add to the message, as you want.

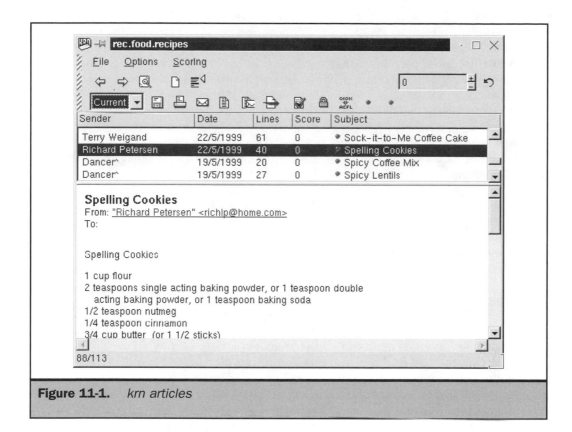

Figure 11-1.   *krn articles*

Netscape Newsreader

The Netscape newsreader is part of the Netscape Communicator package. You can configure the newsreader function by editing the Netscape Preferences for news. From the Edit menu in Netscape Navigator, select the Preferences entry. Then, select News from the list on the left. This displays a pane that includes an entry for your news server. Here, you enter the address of your news server. You can set other options here also, such as the number of articles to display at a time for a newsgroup.

To access a newsgroup, select the Newsgroups entry from the Communicator menu. This opens a Netscape Messenger window with the mailbox folders listed to the left. Below the mailbox folders is the list of news servers. Most likely, you have only one. Click this entry to expand to a list of newsgroups to which you have subscribed. Then, double-click the newsgroup name to see its articles.

When you select a newsgroup, a new window opens with two panes. The pane on top lists the headers for articles in the newsgroup. Use the scroll bar to the right to move through the list. To display the contents of the article, click it and it is displayed in the large pane in the lower-half of the window. Header information is shown first. If the article is a picture file, then the picture is automatically decoded and displayed in the pane. If the article is a video file, then the appropriate program for running video starts up and runs it. You can search for articles by subject or sender by selecting the Search Messages entry in the Edit menu. The icons in the icon bar at the top can be used to post new articles or follow-ups to the current newsgroup. A new window opens that appears much like a Netscape Mail message window.

You can subscribe to newsgroups by selecting the Subscribe entry in the File menu. This opens a window that shows a list of all available newsgroups. The list is compressed, with beginning strings that can be expanded by clicking the + signs next to them. Select the one you want and click the Join button in the upper-right corner. When you close the window, the newsgroups appears under your newsgroup server name.

Pine and slrn

Pine is designed to work with the Internet and is capable of reading Internet newsgroups. The Config entry listed on the Setup screen opens an options list in which you can place entries for your Internet mail server or news server. If you are using an ISP or LAN, you can enter the domain names for your news server or mail server. Newsgroups are treated by Pine as just another mail folder. To list a newsgroup, select the Folder List entry and use the **A** command to add the name of the newsgroup. It is then listed as another folder. When you select it, the newsgroup headers are listed instead of mail headers. You can also post news using Pine, just as you would send a message. Pine has an extensive list of options with which you can customize its operations. These options are accessed through the Config selection in the Setup screen, which is accessible from the main menu. The options you change are saved in a **.pinrc** file in your **home** directory.

slrn is a screen-based newsreader that has an interface similar to Pine's. Commands are displayed across the top of the screen and can be executed using the listed keys. Different types of screens exist for the newsgroup list, article list, and article content, each with its own set of commands. An initial screen lists your subscribed newsgroups with commands for posting, listing, and subscribing to your newsgroups. Selecting a newsgroup opens a screen that initially displays only the newsgroup's articles. Article headers are listed with different colors for the article number, author, and subject fields. Selecting an article splits the screen, showing the contents of the article in a larger portion below, and a smaller portion showing the article list. The ARROW keys as well as the PAGE UP and PAGE DOWN keys move you through the article list, whereas the SPACEBAR and **b** keys move you forward and backward through the currently displayed article text. Selecting a new article displays it in the lower section of the screen. Commands you can perform on an article are shown at the bottom of the screen. They include commands for posting follow-ups and paging operations.

Emacs News

The GNU version of Emacs also includes a newsreader along with other components, such as a mailer and editor. GNU Emacs is included on Red Hat distributions. Check the Emacs Web site at **www.emacs.org** for more information. When you start up GNU Emacs, menu buttons are displayed across the top of the screen. If you are running Emacs in an X-Windows environment, then you have full GUI capabilities and can select menus using your mouse. Be sure the NNTPSERVER variable is set to your news server address in your .bash_profile file and it is exported.

To access the Emacs newsreader, select from the Read Net News entry in the Tools menu. A listing of newsgroups is displayed. The menus across the top of the screen change, adding Misc, Groups, and Groups menu. The Groups menu holds entries for managing newsgroups, such as sorting and searching for groups, as well as subscribing to new ones or listing only subscribed or unsubscribed groups. To select a group, click it or move to it with the arrow keys, and then press the spacebar.

When you select a newsgroup, a split screen is displayed where the headers for the newsgroup articles are listed in the top screen, while the contents of the currently selected article are shown in the bottom screen. Use the Tab key or the mouse to select the screen you want. When you select the header screen, the menus change, listing Search, Misc, Post, Threads, and Article menus. These hold commands for managing the headers. For example, you can post a follow-up by selecting the article and choosing the Followup entry in the Post menu. In the Article menu, you can move to the bottom of the header list or the top, highlight selected headers, and save articles. In the Thread menu, you can move to the header for the next thread or toggle threads on or off. From the Search menu, you can search for headers using patterns and regular expressions. When you finish with a newsgroup, choose Exit from the Misc menu.

On the bottom screen, an article is displayed. When you select this screen, the menus change to Search, Misc, Post, Treatment, and Article. Here the Article menu enables you to page forward and backward through the article. The Treatment menu has entries for hiding or showing headers and signatures. From the Post menu you can post follow-ups and replies for this particular article. The Search menu now performs searches on the article text.

GNU Emacs is a working environment in which each task has its own buffer. When you read news, a buffer is opened to hold the newsgroup and article headers, and when you read an article, another buffer holds the contents. When you compose an article, yet another buffer holds the text you wrote. The buffer you opened for mail, news, or editing notes or files is listed in the Buffers menu. You can use this menu to switch among them.

XEmacs is the complete Emacs editor with a graphical user interface and Internet applications. The Internet applications, which you can easily access from the main XEmacs button bar, include a Web browser, a mail utility, and a newsreader. Clicking the News button brings up another window that displays the newsreader, listing your Usenet newsgroups. If you are using an ISP, it uses the name of the news server in the **NNTPSERVER** variable. You can then access newsgroups, displaying articles.

trn

With the trn newsreader, you can display and search articles by subject, article, or threads. To use trn to access remote news servers, be sure the NNTPSERVER variable is set in your **.bash_profile** file. The trn interface has several powerful features, such as pattern searches for groups of articles. The *t* in trn stands for *threaded*. A *thread* is any connection between articles, such as articles that share the same subject or follow-up articles to a previously posted article. trn's special interface, called a *selector,* enables you to move through a threaded set of articles. For example, if you are reading an article on a particular subject and you give an **n** command to go to the next article, you go to the next article on that subject (in the thread), not to the next sequentially posted article, as you would normally do. Instead of moving through a newsgroup's articles according to their posted order, you can move through them using different threads, examining articles according to different subjects. The same is true for an article and its follow-up articles. An article and its follow-ups are threaded, so upon reading an article, pressing the **n** command moves you to the first follow-up to that article, not to the next sequentially posted article. Using threads, you can use the **n** command to read an article with all of its follow-ups, instead of searching separately for each one.

trn operates on two levels: the newsgroup list and the article list. When you first execute trn, you select a newsgroup from a list of newsgroups. Commands move you from one newsgroup to another in the list. Once you find the one you want, you can then select articles to read in that newsgroup. When you finish reading, you can leave that newsgroup and select another in the newsgroup list. You use the trn selector to display, organize, and move through the article list, though you can also use the standard **rn** commands to manage the article list.

You enter the trn newsreader by typing the command **trn** at your Linux prompt. The **trn** command initially displays a short list of newsgroup headers. Before doing so, however, the **trn** command first checks an official list of new newsgroups with those listed in your **.newsrc** file. If any new newsgroups are not yet listed in your **.newsrc** file, then trn asks, one by one, if you want to subscribe to them. At each prompt, you can enter **y** to add the newsgroup and **n** not to add it. With **-q, trn** goes directly to displaying the newsgroup headers, skipping any new newsgroup queries.

```
$ trn -q
```

After the subscription phase, trn checks to see if any newsgroups are listed in your **.newsrc** file that have unread news in them. If so, the newsgroup headers for the first few of these are displayed. Each newsgroup header tells how many unread articles remain in a given newsgroup. trn then prompts you as to whether you want to read articles in the first newsgroup. If not, you can enter the **n** command to move to the next newsgroup. The **p** command moves you back to the previous newsgroup.

To list articles in a newsgroup, you enter **+** at the prompt. This displays the trn selector from which you can select the article you want to display. If you enter **y,** you skip the list of articles and display the first article in the newsgroup. You are then prompted to read the next article or quit and return to the newsgroup list. You can leave the newsgroup and return to the newsgroup list by entering **q** at the prompt.

trn has a variety of commands for moving through the list of newsgroups. You can move to the first or last newsgroup, the next or previous newsgroup, or the newsgroup whose name has a specific pattern. For example, a **$** places you at the end of the newsgroup list. Many commands are designed to distinguish between read and unread newsgroups. The **^** places you at the first newsgroup with unread news, whereas the number **1** places you at the first newsgroup in the list, whether or not it is read. The lowercase **n** and **p** commands place you at the next and previous unread newsgroups. To move to the next or previous newsgroup, regardless of whether it is read, use the uppercase **N** and **P** commands. The pattern searching commands give trn great versatility in locating newsgroups. To perform a pattern search for a newsgroup, at the prompt, enter a **/** followed by the pattern. The **/** performs a forward search through the list of newsgroups. The **?** performs a backward search.

As mentioned earlier, typing **+** at the trn prompt enters the selector, which enables you to use threads. The selector consists of a screen that lists each article's author, thread count, and subject. Any follow-up articles are preceded by a **>** symbol. Articles are grouped according to the threads to which they belong. The first article in each thread is preceded by an ID, consisting of a lowercase alphabetic character or a single digit, starting from *a*.

The selector has three display modes—article, subject, and thread—which correspond to how the selector displays articles. You can easily choose the mode you want by pressing the **S** command and entering **a** for article, **s** for subject, or **t** for thread. You can also switch back and forth between the different modes by pressing the **=** key. A subject is whatever a user enters into the subject field of an article's header. Articles with the same subject entry are threaded together. When using the thread mode, articles are grouped with any posted follow-ups, as well as with articles of the same subject. The follow-up articles are preceded by a **>** symbol. The article mode does not display threads. Articles are listed individually, each preceded by its own ID, in posted sequence.

When you display an article in a thread, a thread tree appears in the upper-right corner of the screen. A thread tree represents the connections between articles in a thread. Each unread article is represented by a number starting from 1, with each enclosed in brackets. Lines connect the different article numbers. The number representing the article you are currently displaying is highlighted in the thread tree. Once you read an article and move on to another, the read article's number is enclosed in parentheses and the next article's number is highlighted.

Although most newsreaders let you post news, some such as trn, do not. You can post articles directly using Pnews. *Pnews* prompts you for certain header information, places you in an editor in which you can type in your article, and then prompts you either to send, edit, save, or quit the article. Pnews operates directly from the command line, providing you with a full-screen interface, much like other screen-based applications such as Pine, mutt, and tin. To begin, enter the **Pnews** command at your Linux shell prompt. You are then prompted to enter the newsgroup for the article. To see the full list of newsgroups, enter a **?** at the newsgroups prompt. (A good idea is, in advance, to decide on what newsgroups you want.) You can obtain a listing of newsgroups at any time from the newsgroup file located in the **news** directory on your system.

You usually end an article with the same standard signature information, such as your name, Internet address or addresses, and a polite sign-off. As you write more articles, having your signature information automatically added to your articles is helpful. To do so, you need to create a file called **.signature** in your **home** directory and enter your signature information in it. Pnews then reads the contents of the **.signature** file and places them at the end of your article. You can use any standard editor to create your **.signature** file.

tin

The *tin* newsreader operates using a selector much like the one used in the trn newsreader. However, tin has a screen selector for both newsgroups and articles. When you enter tin, the selector displays the screen listing your newsgroups. You can then select the newsgroup you want and display a screen for its articles. One set of screen movement commands is used for all screens, whether for newsgroups, article lists, or article text. CTRL-D, CTRL-F, and SPACEBAR all move you forward to the next screen. CTRL-U, CTRL-B, and **b** all move you backward to the previous screen. The UP ARROW and the **k** key move you up one line on the screen, while the DOWN ARROW and **j** key move you down one line. The **q** command moves you back from one selector to another. For example, if you are in the article selector, pressing **q** moves you back to the newsgroup selector. **Q** quits the tin newsreader entirely.

tin also has a set of editing and history commands you can use to edit any commands you enter. ESC always erases a command you have entered and lets you start over. The editing commands are a subset of the Emacs commands. CTRL-D deletes a character, CTRL-F and the RIGHT ARROW key move right one character. CTRL-B and the LEFT ARROW key move back one character. To insert new text, move your cursor to the position you want and start typing. tin also keeps a history of the commands you enter. You can recall the previous commands with CTRL-P, moving back, one by one, through a list of your previously entered commands. CTRL-N moves you forward through the list. You can find a complete listing of all tin commands in the tin manual pages, which you can invoke by typing **man tin**.

When you start tin, it first displays a screen of newsgroups. The term "Group Selection" is shown at the top of the screen. To its right is "h=help." Pressing the **h** key brings up a Help menu. The newsgroups are listed with a selection number that identifies the newsgroup, followed by the number of unread articles, and then by the name of the newsgroup. To select a newsgroup, you must first move to it. You can do this in a variety of ways. If you see your newsgroup displayed on the screen, you can use your UP ARRROW and DOWN ARROW keys to move to it. CTRL-D moves you to the next screen; CTRL-U moves you back. Instead of using the arrow keys, you can move directly to a newsgroup by entering its index number. You can also locate a newsgroup by using pattern searches. You enter the / followed by a pattern. **?** performs a backward search.

Once you locate the newsgroup you want, press ENTER to display a list of its articles. A list of commonly used commands are displayed at the bottom of the screen. The **s** command subscribes to a new newsgroup and the **u** command unsubscribes.

The tin newsreader displays the subject and author of each article in the newsgroup preceded by an index number and, if unread, a +. The + sign indicates all unread articles. Working from the selector, you can choose articles you want to display. You select an article by moving the cursor to that article and pressing ENTER. Both the newsgroup and article selector screens use many of the same commands. The UP ARROW and DOWN ARROW keys move you from one article to the next. If more than one screen of articles exists, you can move back and forth through them using CTRL-U or CTRL-D. You can also move to an article by typing its index number. An example of the tin article selector screen follows:

```
rec.food.recipes (119T 124A 0K 0H R)          h=help

65    +    Fruit Salad                 Dylan Chris
66    +    Fudge Cake                  Cecelia Petersen
67    +    Chocolate News              Richard Leland
68    +    Chocolate News              Larisa@atlash
69    +    Apple Muffins               George Petersen
70    +    REQUEST: romantic dinners   Marylou Carrion
71    +    REQUEST: Dehydrated Goodies Valerie Fuller
72    +    REQUEST: Devonshire Cream   Carolyn Blacklock
73    +    Sauces                      Bonnie Matoza
74    +    Passion Fruit               Gabriel Matoza
75    +    REQUEST: blackened (red)fish Ken Blacklock
76    +    REQUEST: Cheese Toast       dylan@sf
77    +    REQUEST: Sausage Recipes    Penny Bode
78    +    Biscuit Recipe              gloria@stlake
```

INTERNET

```
79     +      >blackened (red)fish              augie@napa
80     +      Oatmeal Cookies                   John Gunther
81     +      REQUEST: Potato Salad             Margaret
82     +      REQUEST: Sesame Chicken           Frank Moitoza
83     +      >Summer desserts                  maryann@sebast


    <n>=set current to n, TAB=next unread, /=search pattern,
^K)ill/select,
  a)uthor search, c)atchup, j=line down, k=line up, K=mark read,
l)ist thread,
    |=pipe, m)ail, o=print, q)uit, r=toggle all/unread, s)ave,
t)ag, w=post
```

The commonly used commands for accessing articles are displayed at the bottom of the screen. You can search articles for a specified pattern with the **/** command. The **a** command enables you to search for articles by a specified author. The **s** command saves an article. You can post an article of your own to the newsgroup by pressing the **w** command. You are prompted for header information, and then you enter the text of your message. Once you select an article, it is displayed. If the article takes up more than one screen, you can move forward by pressing the SPACEBAR and backward by pressing the **b** key. With the **B** command, you can search the article for a specified pattern, and with the **s** command you can save it. With the **f** command, you can post a follow-up to the article, while with the **r** command, you can send a message to the author.

tin supports an extensive set of options, features, attributes, and variables. Configuration files are placed in the **.tin** directory maintained in your **home** directory. Options can be set using the tin Global Options menu or by entering them directly in the **tinrc** file in the **.tin** directory. Attributes for particular newsgroups can be set in the **.tin** attributes file. For accessing remote news servers, be sure the **NNTPSERVER** variable is set in your **.bash_profile** file.

The Complete Reference

Linux

Chapter 12

FTP Clients

The *Internet* is a network of computers around the world you can access with an Internet address and a set of Internet tools. Many computers on the Internet are configured to operate as servers, providing information to anyone who requests it. The information is contained in files you can access and copy. Each server, often referred to as a *site,* has its own Internet address by which it can be located. Linux provides a set of Internet tools you can use to access sites on the Internet, and then locate and download information from them. These tools are known as *clients.* A client application, such as an FTP or a Web client, can communicate with a corresponding server application running on a remote system. An FTP client can communicate with an FTP server program on another system. The server lets the client access certain specified resources on its system and lets an FTP client transfer certain files.

To access Internet sites, your computer must be connected to the Internet. You may be part of a network already connected to the Internet. If you have a standalone computer, such as a personal computer, you can obtain an Internet connection from an *Internet service provider (ISP).* Once you have an Internet address of your own, you can configure your Linux system to connect to the Internet and use various Internet tools to access different sites.

The primary tools for accessing Internet sites are FTP clients and Web browsers. With FTP clients, you can connect to a corresponding FTP site and download files from it. FTP clients are commonly used to download software from FTP sites that operate as software repositories. Most Linux software applications can be downloaded to your Linux system from such sites. A distribution site like **ftp.redhat.com** is an example of one such FTP site, holding an extensive set of packaged Linux applications you can download using an FTP client and then easily install on your system. In the last few years, the Web browsers have become the primary tool for accessing information on the Internet. Most of the tasks you perform on the Internet may be done easily with a Web browser. You only need to use an FTP client to download or upload files from or to a specific FTP site.

Other Internet tools are also available for your use, such as Gopher, telnet, and IRC clients. *Gopher* is a kind of hybrid of FTP and Web clients. It provides you with a series of menus listing different topics. You move from one menu to the other, narrowing your topic until you find the information you want. Often, this is in the form of a file that you download by selecting its menu entry. The *telnet* protocol enables you to log into an account directly on another system. *IRC clients* set up chat rooms through which you can communicate with other users over the Internet. Web clients are discussed in the next chapter. telnet and IRC clients are discussed in Chapter 14.

Internet Addresses

The Internet uses a set of network protocols called *TCP/IP,* which stands for *Transmission Control Protocol/Internet Protocol.* In a TCP/IP network, messages are broken into small components called *datagrams,* which are then transmitted through various interlocking routes and delivered to their destination computers. Once received, the datagrams are reassembled into the original message. Datagrams are also referred to as *packets*. Sending messages as small components has proved far more reliable and faster than sending them as one large bulky transmission. With small components, if one is lost or damaged, only that component has to be resent, whereas if any part of a large transmission is corrupted or lost, the entire message must be resent.

On a TCP/IP network such as the Internet, each computer is given a unique address called an *IP address*. The IP address is used to identify and locate a particular host—a computer connected to the network. IP addressing can be either class-based or Classless (CNDR). Class-based addressing is described here. (See Chapter 30.) An IP address consists of a set of four segments, each pair separated by a period. The segments consist of numbers that range from 0 to 255, with certain values reserved for special use. The IP address is divided into two parts: one part identifies the network and the other part identifies a particular host. The number of segments used for each is determined by the class of the network. On the Internet, networks are organized into three classes depending on their size—classes A, B, and C. A class A network uses only the first segment for the IP address and the remaining three for the host, allowing a great many computers to be connected to the same network. Most IP addresses reference smaller, class C, networks. For a class C network, the first three segments are used to identify the network and only the last segment identifies the host. The syntax looks like this:

```
net.net.net.host
```

In a class C network, the first three numbers identify the network part of the IP address. This part is divided into three network numbers, each identifying a subnet. Networks on the Internet are organized into subnets, beginning with the largest and narrowing to small subnetworks. The last number is used to identify a particular computer, referred to as a *host*. You can think of the Internet as a series of networks with subnetworks, and these subnetworks have their own subnetworks. The rightmost number identifies the host computer, and the number preceding it identifies the subnetwork of which the computer is a part. The number to the left of that identifies the network the subnetwork is part of, and so on. The Internet address 192.168.187.4 references the fourth computer connected to the network identified by the number 187. Network 187 is a subnet to a larger network identified as 168. This larger network is itself a subnet of the network identified as 192. Here's how it breaks down:

192.168.187.4	IP address
192.168.187	Network identification
4	Host identification

IP addresses are officially managed by the Internet Assigned Numbers Authority (IANA). You can obtain your own Internet address from an Internet service provider (ISP) or, if you are on a network already connected to the Internet, your network administrator can assign you one. If you are using an ISP, the ISP may temporarily assign one from a pool it has on hand, each time you connnect.

Certain numbers are reserved. The numbers 127, 0, or 255 cannot be part of an official IP address. The address 127.0.0.0 is the loopback address that enables users on your computer to communicate with each other. The number 255 is a special broadcast identifier you can use to broadcast messages to all sites on a network. Using 255 for any part of the IP address references all nodes connected at that level. For example, 192.168.255.255 broadcasts a message to all computers on network 192.18, all its subnetworks, and their hosts. The address 192.168.187.255 broadcasts to every computer on the local network. If you use 0 for the network part of the address, the host number references a computer within your local network. For example, 0.0.0.6 references the sixth computer in your local network. If you want to broadcast to all computers on your local network, you can use the number 0.0.0.255.

A special set of numbers is reserved for use on non-Internet local area networks. These are numbers that begin with the special network number 192.168., as used in these examples. If you are setting up a local area network, such as a small business or home network, you are free to use these numbers for your local machines. You can set up an intranet using network cards such as Ethernet cards and Ethernet hubs, and then configure your machines with IP addresses starting from 192.168.1.1. The host segment can go up to 255. If you have three machines on your home network, you could give them the addresses 192.168.1.1, 192.168.1.2, 192.168.1.3. You can implement "Internet" services, such as FTP, Web, and mail services on your local machines, and use any of the "Internet" tools to make use of those services. They all use the same TCP/IP protocols as used on the Internet. For example, with FTP tools you can transfer files between the machines on your network, with mail tools you can send messages from one machine to the other, and with a Web browser you can access local "Web" sites that may be installed on a machine running its own "Web" servers. If you want to have one of your machines connected to the Internet or some other network, you can set it up to be a gateway machine. By conventions, the gateway machine is usually given the address 192.168.1.1. With a method called *IP masquerading*, you can have any of the non-Internet machines use a gateway to connect to the Internet.

All hosts on the Internet are identified by their IP addresses. When you send a message to a host on the Internet, you must provide its IP address. Using a sequence of four numbers of an IP address, however, can be difficult. They are hard to remember and it's easy to make mistakes when typing them. To make identifying a computer on the Internet easier, the *Domain Name Service* (*DNS*) was implemented. The DNS establishes a domain name address for each IP address. The domain name address is a series of names separated by periods. Whenever you use a domain name address, it is automatically converted to an IP address, which is then used to identify that Internet host. The domain name address is far easier to use than its corresponding IP address.

A domain name address needs to be registered with the NIC so each computer on the Internet can have a unique name. Creating a name follows specified naming conventions, as discussed earlier, in Chapter 11. The domain name address consists of the hostname, the name you gave to your computer; a domain name, the name that identifies your network; and an extension that identifies the type of network you are on. Here is the syntax for domain addresses:

```
host-name.domain-name.extension
```

In the following example, the domain address references a computer called sunsite on a network referred to as unc. It is part of an educational institution, as indicated by the extension edu.

```
sunsite.unc.edu
```

The conversion of domain addresses to IP addresses used to be performed by each individual host. And, for a few frequently used addresses for which you know the IP address, this can still be done. So many computers are now connected to the Internet, however, domain name conversion has to be performed by special servers known as *Domain Name Servers* or simply name servers. A *name server* holds a database of domain name addresses and their IP addresses. Local networks sometimes have their own name servers. If a name server does not have the address, then it may call on other name servers to perform the conversion. A program on your computer called a *resolver* obtains the IP address from a name server and then uses it in the application where you specified the domain name address.

With the **whois** and **nslookup** commands, you can obtain information for domain name servers about different networks and hosts connected to the Internet. Enter **whois** and the domain name address of the host or network, and **whois** displays information about the host, such as the street address and phone number, as well as contact persons.

```
$ whois   domain-address
```

The **nslookup** command takes a domain address and finds its corresponding IP address.

```
$ nslookup  domain-address
```

nslookup has an interactive mode you enter by not specifying any domain name. You can then use **nslookup** to search for other kinds of information about a host. For example, the HINFO option finds out what type of operating system a host uses. The **nslookup** man page specifies a list of different options and how to use them.

Network File Transfer: FTP

You can use *File Transfer Protocol* (*FTP*) clients to transfer extremely large files directly from one site to another. FTP can handle both text and binary files. This is one of the TCP/IP protocols, and it operates on systems connected to networks that use the TCP/IP protocols, such as the Internet. FTP performs a remote login to another account on another system connected to you on a network, such as the Internet. Once logged into that other system, you can transfer files to and from it. To log in, you need to know the login name and password for the account on the remote system. For example, if you have accounts at two different sites on the Internet, you can use FTP to transfer files from one to the other. Many sites on the Internet allow public access using FTP, however. Many sites serve as depositories for large files anyone can access and download. Such sites are often referred to as *FTP sites* and, in many cases, their Internet address begins with the word "*ftp*," such as **ftp.redhat.com**. Others begin with other names, such as **metalab.unc.edu.** These public sites allow anonymous FTP login from any user. For the login name, you use the word "anonymous," and for the password you use your Internet address. You can then transfer files from that site to your own system.

You can perform FTP operations using any one of a number of FTP client programs. For Linux systems, you can choose from several FTP clients. Many now operate using GUI interfaces such as Gnome. Some, such as Netscape, have limited capabilities, whereas other such as IglooFTP and ncftp include an extensive set of enhancements. The original FTP client is just as effective, though not as easy to use. It operates using a simple command-line interface and requires no GUI or cursor support as do other clients.

Web Browser-Based FTP: Netscape

You access an FTP site and download files from it with any Web browser. A Web browser is effective for checking out an FTP site to see what files are listed there. When you access an FTP site with a Web browser, the entire list of files in a directory is listed as a Web page. You can move to a subdirectory by clicking its entry. Click the .. entry at the top of the page to move back up to the parent directory. With Netscape Navigator, you can easily browse through an FTP site to download files. To download a file, you left-click or SHIFT left-click its entry (not right-click). This opens a box for selecting your local directory and the name for the file. The default name is the same as on the remote system. Netscape Navigator has some important limitations. You cannot upload a file, and you cannot download more than one file at a time. Navigator is useful for locating individual files, though not for downloading a large set of files, as is usually required for a system update.

The K Desktop File Manager: kfm

On the K Desktop, the desktop file manager has a built-in FTP capability, as shown in Figure 12-1. The FTP operation has been seamlessly integrated into standard desktop file operations. Downloading files from an FTP site is as simple as copying files from one directory to another, but one of the directories happens to be located on a remote FTP site. On the K Desktop, you can use a file manager window to access a remote FTP site. Files in the remote directory are listed just as your local files are. To download files from an FTP site, you open a window to access that site. Open the directory you want, and then open another window for the local directory to which you want the remote files copied. In the window showing the FTP files, select the ones you want to download. Then, simply click-and-drag those files to the window for the local directory. A pop-up menu appears with choices for copy or move. Select move. The selected files are then downloaded. Another window then opens, showing the download progress and displaying the name of each file in turn, and a bar indicating the percentage downloaded so far.

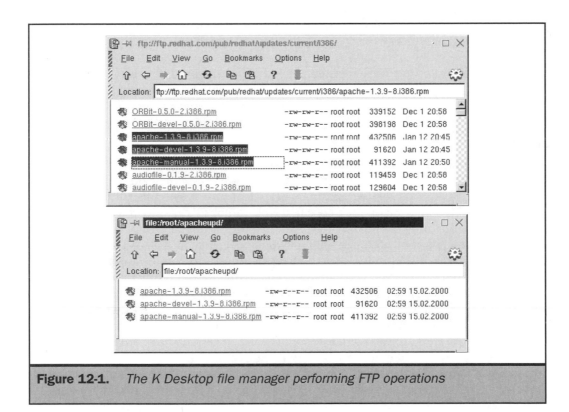

Figure 12-1. *The K Desktop file manager performing FTP operations*

INTERNET

Gnome FTP: Gnome file manager, gFTP, and IglooFTP

The easiest way to download files is to use the built-in FTP capabilities of the Gnome file manager, midnight commander. You can also use several Gnome-based FTP clients that offer more features, including gFTP and IglooFTP. Check the Gnome Web site at **www.gnome.org** for more. gFTP is included with the current Gnome release. IglooFTP can be downloaded from its Web site at **www.littleigloo.org.** You can link to it through the Gnome software map on the Gnome Web site.

Gnome File Manager

On Gnome, the desktop file manager—*midnight commander*—has a built-in FTP capability much like the KDE file manager. The FTP operation has been seamlessly integrated into standard desktop file operations. Downloading files from an FTP site is as simple as dragging files from one directory window to another, where one of the directories happens to be located on a remote FTP site. Use the Gnome file manager to access a remote FTP site, listing files in the remote directory, just as local files are. Then open another window for the local directory to which you want the remote files copied. In the window showing the FTP files, select those you want to download. Then use a CTRL-click and drag those files to the window for the local directory. A CTRL-click performs a copy operation, not a move. As files are downloaded, a dialog window appears showing the progress (see Chapter 3 for an illustration).

IglooFTP

IglooFTP, shown in Figure 12-2, is designed to be a Linux version of Bullet-proof FTP, used on Windows systems. It has an extensive set of features with an easy-to-use interface. FTP operations can be performed graphically, selecting files with your mouse and clicking a button or menu for a specified task. IglooFTP download features include recursive downloading, queue transfers, and firewall support. You can download a directory with all its subdirectories with only one operation, as well as download from different sites at the same time. Queue transfers feature auto-resume support in case of interruptions. IglooFTP provides operations managing files and directories on your remote site, provided you have the permission to do so. It supports directory creation and deletion, recursive deletion and moving, and **chmod** operations, as well as others.

IglooFTP features a graphical directory browser for both local and remote file systems to locate directories and files easily. The graphical directory browser displays files and directory in a tree-like structure whose directories (folders) can be shrunk or expanded. On your local system, you can use the tree display to locate and open the directory to which you want to download files. You can do the same for the remote system. To activate the directory browser, click the folder icons located above the left corner for each pane. Clicking the folder icon above the left-hand pane displays

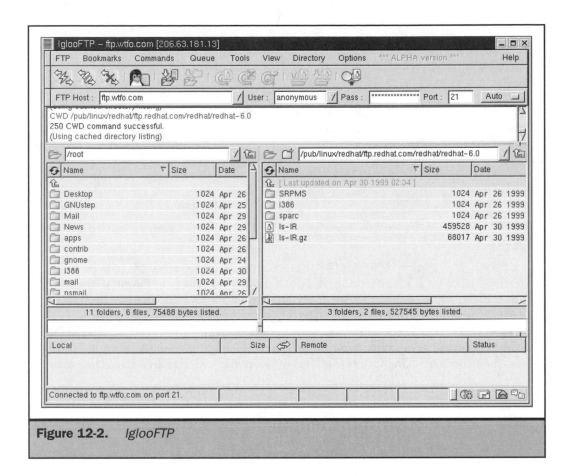

Figure 12-2.   *IglooFTP*

a graphical tree for your local system. You can expand or shrink directories with a preceding + or – symbol. The folder icon above the right-hand pane displays the graphical directory browser for the remote system. Next to this folder icon is an icon for the site manager. Clicking it displays the site manager, and clicking the folder icon returns you to the remote directory.

gFTP

The *gFTP* program is a simpler Gnome FTP client designed to let you make standard FTP file transfers. It has an interface similar to WS_FTP used on Windows. The gFTP window consists of several panes. The top-left pane lists files in your local directory, and the top-right pane lists your remote directory. Subdirectories have a folder icon preceding their name. The parent directory can be referenced by a .. entry with an up-arrow at the top of each list. Double-click a directory entry to access it. The pathnames for all directories are displayed in boxes above each pane. You can enter a new pathname for a different directory to change to it, if you want.

Two buttons between the panes are used for transferring files. The <- button downloads selected files in the remote directory, and the -> button uploads files from the local directory. To download a file, click it in the right-side pane and then click the <- button. When the file is downloaded, its name appears in the left-side pane, your local directory. Menus across the top of the window can be used to manage your transfers. A connection manager enables you to enter login information about a specific site. You can specify whether to perform an anonymous login or to provide a user name and password. Click the Connect button to connect to that site. A drop-down menu for sites enables you to choose the site you want.

ncftp

The *ncftp program,* shown in Figure 12-3, has a screen-based interface that can be run from any shell command line. It does not use a desktop interface. FTP operations are executed using commands you enter at a prompt. Options and bookmarks can be selected using cursor-based menus. To start up ncftp, you enter the **ncftp** command on the command line. If you are working in a window manager, such as KDE, GNOME, or FVWM open a shell terminal window and enter the command at its prompt. The main ncftp screen consists of an input line at the bottom of the screen with a status line above

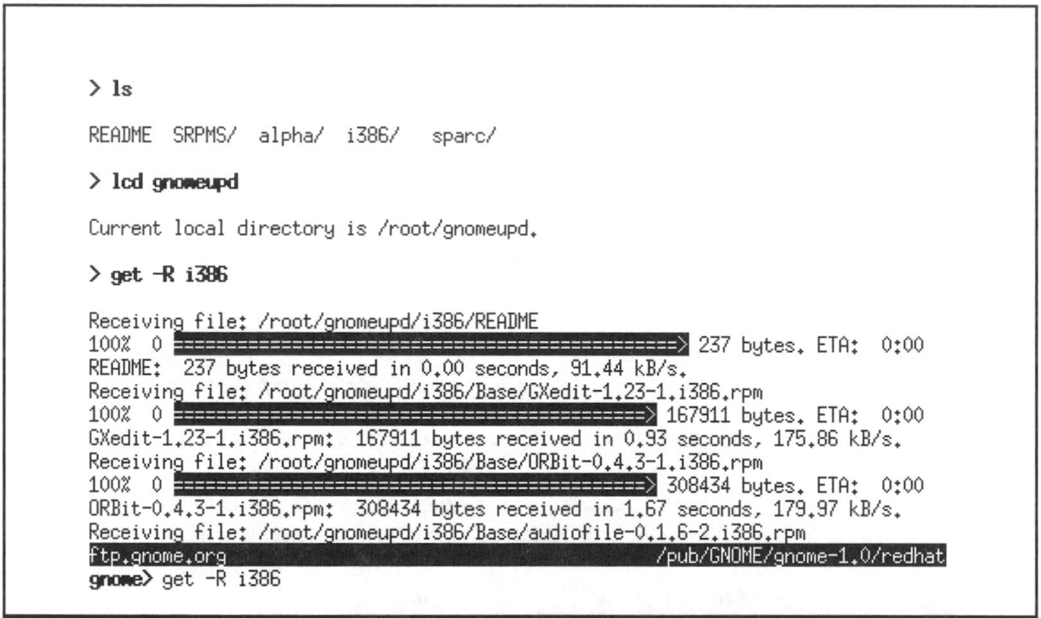

Figure 12-3. *ncftp*

it. The remainder of the screen is used to display commands and responses from remote systems. For example, when you download a file, a message specifying the download files is displayed in the status line. ncftp lets you set preferences for different features, such as anonymous login, progress meters, or a download directory. Enter the **pref** command to open the preferences screen. From there, you can select and modify the listed preferences.

To connect to an FTP site, you enter the open command on the input line, followed by the site's address. The address can be either an IP address or a domain name, such as **ftp.gnome.org**. If you don't supply an address, then a list of your bookmarked sites is displayed, and you can choose one from there. By default, ncftp attempts an anonymous login, using the term "anonymous" as your username and your e-mail address as the password. When you successfully connect, the status bar displays the remote site's name on the left and the remote directory name on the right.

```
open ftp.gnome.org
```

If you want to log into a specific account on a remote site, have yourself prompted for the username and password by using the –u options with the **open** command. The **open** command remembers the last kind of login you performed for a specific site and repeats it. If you want to change back to an anonymous login from a user login, you use the –a option with the **open** command. For busy sites, you may be unable to connect on the first try and you must repeat the open process. ncftp has a redial capability you turn on with the –r option. The –d option sets the delay for the next attempt, and the –g option sets the maximum number of connection attempts. With the **lookup** command, you can obtain the IP and domain name addresses for an FTP site. The **lookup** command takes as an argument either the IP or domain name address, and then displays both. This is useful for finding a site's IP address. With the –v option more information, such as aliases, is retrieved. The ncftp **open** options are shown in Table 12-1.

Option	Description
-a	Connect anonymously
-u	Connect with username and password prompts
-p *num*	Use specified port number when connecting
-r	Redial until connected
-d *num*	Set delay (*num*) in number of seconds for redial option
-g *num*	Specify the maximum number of redials

Table 12-1.   *ncftp* open *Options*

INTERNET

Once connected, you enter commands on the input line to perform FTP operations such as displaying file lists, changing directories, or downloading files. With the **ls** command, you can list the contents of the current remote directory. Use the **cd** command to change to another remote directory. The **dir** command displays a detailed listing of files. With the **page** command you view the contents of a remote file, a screen at a time. To download files, you use the **get** command, and to upload files, you use the **put** command. During a download, a progress meter above the status bar displays how much of the file has been downloaded so far. The **get** command has several features described in more detail in the following section. When you finish, you can disconnect from the site with the **close** command. You can then use **open** to connect to another site, or quit the ncftp program with the **quit** command. The **help** command lists all ncftp commands. You can use the **help** command, followed by the name of a command to display specific information on it.

The ncftp program supports several commands that operate on your local system. These are usually standard FTP command names preceded by an *l*. **lcd** changes your local working directory, **lls** lists the contents of your local directory, **lpage** displays the contents of a remote file a screen at a time, and **lpwd** displays the local directory's full pathname. For any other local commands or scripts you need to execute, use the shell escape command, **!**. Simply precede the shell command or script with a **!**.

The ncftp program also provides commands for managing files and directories on your remote site, provided you have the permission to do so. You can use **mkdir** to create a remote directory, and **rmdir** to remove one. Use the **rm** command to erase remote files. With the **rename** command, you can change their names. The ncftp commands are listed in Table 12-2.

The ncftp program also has a colon mode of operation that enables you to issue a single **ncftp** command to download a file. Enter the **ncftp** command, followed by a URL, for the file you want. You can enter the command on the shell command line or place it within a script. For example, the following command downloads the README file on the Red Hat FTP site.

```
$ ncftp ftp.redhat.com/pub/README
```

In the colon mode, the **-c** option sends the file to the standard output and the **-m** option pipes it to your pager, usually the **more** program.

```
$ ncftp -c ftp.redhat.com/pub/README > ~/redhatinfo/readme
$ ncftp -m ftp.redhat.com/pub/README
```

INTERNET

Command	Description
help [*command*]	Lists names of ncftp commands
cd [*directory*]	Changes the working directory on the remote host
create [*filename*]	Creates an empty file on the remote host, enabling you to use the filename as a message
debug	Turns debugging on or off
version	Displays version information
dir	Displays a detailed directory listing
echo	Displays a string, useful for macros
get	Downloads files from a remote host to your working directory
lcd [*directory*]	Changes the local working directory
lls	Lists files in your local working directory
lookup [*host*]	Looks up entries for remote hosts
lpage [*filename*]	Displays contents of local file, a page at time
lpwd	Displays the local current working directory
mkdir [*directory name*]	Creates a directory on the remote host
mode [*mode*]	Specifies transfer mode (*b* for block mode, *s* for stream mode)
open [*option*] [*hostname*]	Connects to a remote host. If no hostname is specified, then the bookmark editor displays a host list from which you can choose one (**-a** forces anonymous login, **-u** forces user login, **-r** redials automatically, **-d** specifies time delay before redial-used with **-r**, and **-g** specifies the maximum number of redials-used with **-r**)

Table 12-2.   *ncftp Commands*

Command	Description
page *filename*	Displays the contents of a remote file
pdir	Same as dir, but outputs to your pager, enabling you to display remote file list a page at a time. Used for command line interface.
pls	Same as **ls**, but outputs to your pager. Used for command line interface.
redir	Redisplays the last directory listing
predir	Redisplays the last directory listing and outputs to pager if working in command line interface
put *filename*	Uploads a file to a remote host
pwd	Displays the remote current working directory
rename *orig-name new-name*	Changes the name of a remote file
quit	Quits ncftp
quote	Sends an FTP protocol command to the remote server
rhelp [*command*]	Sends a help request to the remote host
rm *filenames*	Erases remote files
rmdir *directories*	Removes remote directories
site *command*	Executes site-specific commands
type *type*	Changes transfer type (ASCII, binary, image)
! *command*	Escapes to the shell and executes the following shell command or script

Table 12-2.   *ncftp Commands* (continued)

ncftp Download Features

The ncftp **get** command differs significantly from the original FTP client's **get** command. Whereas the original FTP client uses two commands, **get** and **mget**, to perform download operations, ncftp uses only the **get** command. However, the ncftp **get** command combines the capabilities of both **mget** and **get** into the **get** command, as well as adding several new features. Table 12-3 lists the various

get command options. By default, the ncftp **get** command performs wildcard matching for filenames. If you enter only part of a filename, the **get** command tries to download all files beginning with that name. You can turn off wildcard matching with the **-G** option, in which case you must enter the full names of the files you want. The following example downloads all files with names beginning with "Xfree86" and is similar to using **mget** Xfree86* in the original FTP.

```
get Xfree86
```

The **get** command checks to see if you already have a file you are trying to download. If so, it skips the download. The **get** command also checks if the file you already have is a newer version, in which case it also skips the download. This is a helpful feature for easily maintaining upgrade files. You can simply access the update directory on the remote site, and then use the **get** command with the * to download to the directory you are using to keep your upgrade file. Only newer versions or newly added upgrade files are download, instead of the entire set. If you want to download a file, even though you have it already, you can force the download with the **-f** option. For example, to download upgrades for Red Hat manually, you can connect to the Red Hat upgrade directory in the Red Hat FTP site and then issue the following **get** command:

```
get *
```

If you were interrupted during a download, you can restart the download from where you left off. This feature is built into ncftp. (On other FTP programs, it can be invoked with the **reget** command.) ncftp checks to see if you have already started to download a file and then continues from where you left off.

Command	Description
-G	Turn wildcard matching for filenames on or off
-R *directory*	Download a directory and all its subdirectories (recursive)
-f *filenames*	Force the download of all specified files, even if older or the same as local ones
-C	Force resumption of a download from where it was interrupted
-z *remote-file local-file*	Rename a remote file on your local system
-n *num*	Download files no older than the specified number of days

Table 12-3. *ncftp* **get** *Options*

INTERNET

Certain features require you to enter an option on the command line after the **get** command. For example, adding the **-R** command specifies a recursive capability, enabling you to download and create subdirectories and their files. This command is particularly helpful in downloading upgrade directories, such as Red Hat's, which contain several subdirectories. The following example downloads the **i386** directory and all its subdirectories.

```
get -R i386
```

If you want to give a file a different name on your local system, use the **-z** option. Enter the local filename you want after the remote filename. The following example downloads the **readme** file and renames it **calinfo**. If you did not use the **-z** option, then both names would be taken as files to be downloaded, instead of only the first.

```
get -z readme calinfo
```

To obtain recent files only, you can use the **-n** option. **-n** takes as its argument a number of days. Files older than the specified number of days are not retrieved. The following example downloads files posted within the last 30 days.

```
get -n 30 *
```

Bookmarks and Macros

When you disconnect (close) from a site, ncftp automatically saves information about it. This includes the site address, the directory you were in, and the login information. This information is placed in a file called **bookmarks** in your **.ncftp** directory. The site information is given a bookmark name you can use to access the site easily again. The bookmark name is usually the key name in the site's address. You can use this name to connect to the site. For example, **ftp.redhat.com** could be named redhat. You could then connect to it with the command

```
open redhat
```

You can edit your bookmark entries using the bookmark editor. Enter the command **bookmarks** to bring up the editor. Remote systems you have accessed are listed on the right side of the screen. Bookmark commands are listed on the left. You can change the bookmark name or edit login information, such as the user name or password, the remote directory, or the transfer mode.

The ncftp program supports macros for simple operations. You create macros by entering macro definitions in the macros file located in your **.ncftp** directory. Initially, no such file will exist, so you have to create one using any text editor. The macros file is a simple text file you can edit with any text editor. The syntax for a macro definition follows:

```
macro macro-name
    ftp-commands
end
```

A macro executes ncftp commands. Remember, however, the ! is an ncftp command that enables you to execute any Linux command or script. With a preceding ! you can define an ncftp macro that executes any shell command or any script you have written. A simple example of a macro is

```
macro ascii
    type ascii
end
```

Macros support parameters similar to those used by shell programs. Arguments entered after a macro name can be referenced in the macro using a $ sign and the number of the argument in the argument list. $1 references the first argument, $2 the second, and so on. $* is a special parameter that references all arguments, and $@ references all arguments, encasing each in double quotes.

```
macro cdls
  cd $1
  ls
end
```

The ncftp program also supports a limited numbers of event macros. These are macros executed when a certain event is detected, such as when the program starts or shuts down. For example, a macro defined with the name **.start.ncftp** has its commands executed every time you start ncftp; **.quit.ncftp** executes its commands when you quit. Site-specific macros also execute whenever it is necessary to access or disconnect from certain sites. These macros begin with either the open or close event, followed by the site's bookmark. For example, a macro defined with the name **.open.redhat** would execute its commands whenever you connected to the Red Hat site. A macro named **.open.any** has its commands executed whenever you connect to any site, and one named **.close.any** executes whenever you disconnect from a site.

ftp

The name **ftp** designates the original FTP client used on UNIX and Linux systems. **ftp** uses a command line interface, and it has an extensive set of commands and options you can use to manage your FTP transfers. You start the **ftp** client by entering the command **ftp** at a shell prompt. If you have a specific site you want to connect to, you can include the name of that site on the command line after the ftp keyword. Otherwise, you need to connect to the remote system with the **ftp** command open. You are then prompted for the name of the remote system with the prompt (to). Upon entering the remote system name, **ftp** connects you to the system and then prompts you for a login name. The prompt for the login name consists of the word "Name" and, in parentheses, the system name and your local login name. Sometimes the login name on the remote system is the same as the login name on your own system. If the names are the same, press ENTER at the prompt. If they are different, enter the remote system's login name. After entering the login name, you are prompted for the password. In the next example, the user connects to the remote system **garnet** and logs into the **robert** account.

```
$ ftp
ftp> open
(to) garnet
Connected to garnet.berkeley.edu.
220 garnet.berkeley.edu FTP server (ULTRIX Version 4.1 Sun May 16
10:23:46 EDT 1996) ready.
Name (garnet.berkeley.edu:root): robert
password required
Password:
user robert logged in
ftp>
```

Once logged in, you can execute Linux commands on either the remote system or your local system. You execute a command on your local system in **ftp** by preceding the command with an exclamation point. Any Linux commands without an exclamation point are executed on the remote system. One exception exists to this rule. Whereas you can change directories on the remote system with the **cd** command, to change directories on your local system, you need to use a special **ftp** command called **lcd** (local cd). In the next example, the first command lists files in the remote system, while the second command lists files in the local system.

```
ftp> ls
ftp> !ls
```

The **ftp** program provides a basic set of commands for managing files and directories on your remote site, provided you have the permission to do so. You can use **mkdir** to create a remote directory, and **rmdir** to remove one. Use the **delete** command to erase a remote file. With the **rename** command, you can change their names. You close your connection to a system with the **close** command. You can then open another connection if you want. To end the **ftp** session, use the **quit** or **bye** command.

```
ftp> close
ftp> bye
Good-bye
$
```

File Transfer

To transfer files to and from the remote system, use the **get** and **put** commands. The **get** command receives files from the remote system to your local system, and the **put** command sends files from your local system to the remote system. In a sense, your local system gets files *from* the remote and puts files *to* the remote. In the next example, the file **weather** is sent from the local system to the remote system using the **put** command.

```
ftp> put weather
PORT command successful.
ASCII data connection
ASCII Transfer complete.
ftp>
```

If a download is ever interrupted, you can resume the download with **reget**. This is helpful for an extremely large file. The download resumes from where it left off, so the whole file needn't be downloaded again. Also, be sure to download binary files in binary mode. For most FTP sites, the binary mode is the default, but some sites might have ASCII (text) as the default. The command **ascii** sets the character mode, and the command **binary** sets the binary mode. Most software packages available at Internet sites are archived and compressed files, which are binary files. In the next example, the transfer mode is set to binary, and the archived software package **mydata.tar.gz** is sent from the remote system to your local system using the **get** command.

```
ftp> binary
ftp> get mydata.tar.gz
PORT command successful.
Binary data connection
Binary Transfer complete.
ftp>
```

You may often want to send several files, specifying their names with wildcard characters. **put** and **get**, however, operate only on a single file and do not work with special characters. To transfer several files at a time, you have to use two other commands, **mput** and **mget**. When you use **mput** or **mget**, you are prompted for a file list. You can then either enter the list of files or a file-list specification using special characters. For example, *.c specifies all the files with a .c extension, and * specifies all files in the current directory. In the case of **mget**, each file is sent, one by one, from the remote system to your local system. Each time, you are prompted with the name of the file being sent. You can type *y* to send the file or *n* to cancel the transmission. You are then prompted for the next file. The **mput** command works in the same way, but it sends files from your local system to the remote system. In the next example, all files with a **.c** extension are sent to your local system using **mget**.

```
ftp> mget
(remote-files) *.c
mget calc.c? y
PORT command successful
ASCII data connection
ASCII transfer complete
mget main.c? y
PORT command successful
ASCII data connection
ASCII transfer complete
ftp>
```

Answering the prompt for each file can be a tedious prospect if you plan to download a large number of files, such as those for a system update. In this case, you can turn off the prompt with the prompt command, which toggles the interactive mode on and off. The **mget** operation then downloads all files it matches, one after the other.

```
ftp> prompt
Interactive mode off.
ftp> mget
(remote-files) *.c
 PORT command successful
ASCII data connection
ASCII transfer complete
PORT command successful
ASCII data connection
ASCII transfer complete
ftp>
```

To access a public FTP site, you have to perform an anonymous login. Instead of a login name, you enter the keyword anonymous. Then, for the password, you enter your Internet address. Once the **ftp** prompt is displayed, you are ready to transfer files. You may need to change to the appropriate directory first or set the transfer mode to binary. The **fpt** client commands are listed in Table 12-4.

Command	Effect
ftp	Invokes **ftp** program
open *site-address*	Opens a connection to another system
close	Closes connection to a system
quit or **bye**	Ends **ftp** session
ls	Lists the contents of a directory
dir	Lists the contents of a directory in long form
get *filename*	Sends file from remote system to local system
put *filename*	Sends file from local system to remote system
mget *regular-expression*	Enables you to download several files at once from a remote system; you can use special characters to specify the files; you are prompted one-by-one, in turn, for each file transfer
mput *regular-expression*	Enables you to send several files at once to a remote system; you can use special characters to specify the files; you are prompted one-by-one for each file to be transferred
runique	Toggles storing of files with unique filenames. If a file already exists with the same filename on the local system, a new filename is generated
reget *filename*	Resumes transfer of an interrupted file from where you left off
binary	Transfers files in binary mode
ascii	Transfers files in ASCII mode
cd *directory*	Changes directories on the remote system
lcd *directory*	Changes directories on the local system

Table 12-4.   *ftp Client Commands*

INTERNET

Command	Effect
help or **?**	Lists **ftp** commands
mkdir *directory*	Creates a directory on the remote system
rmdir	Deletes a remote directory
delete *filename*	Deletes a file on the remote system
mdelete *file-list*	Deletes several remote files at once
rename	Renames a file on a remote system
hash	Displays progressive hash signs during download
status	Displays current status of **ftp**

Table 12-4. *ftp Client Commands* (continued)

Automatic Login and Macros: .netrc

The **ftp** client has an automatic login capability and support for macros. Both are entered in a user's **ftp** configuration file called **.netrc**. Each time you connect to a site, the **.netrc** file is checked for connection information, such as a login name and password. In this way, you needn't enter a login name and password each time you connect to a site. This feature is particularly useful for anonymous logins. Instead of your having to enter the username anonymous and your e-mail address as your password, they can be automatically read from the **.netrc** file. You can even make anonymous login information your default so, unless otherwise specified, an anonymous login is attempted for any FTP site to which you try to connect. If you have sites you must log into, you can specify them in the **.netrc** file and, when you connect, either automatically log in with your username and password for that site or be prompted for them.

Entries in the **.netrc** file have the following syntax. An entry for a site begins with the term "machine," followed by the network or Internet address, and then the login and password information.

```
machine system-address  login  remote-login-name  password  password
```

The following example shows an entry for logging into the **dylan** account on the **turtle.trek.com** system.

```
machine golf.mygames.com  login   dylan  password  legogolf
```

For a site you would anonymously log into, you enter the word "anonymous" for the login name and your e-mail address for the password.

```
machine  ftp.1redhat.com  login anonymous  password dylan@turtle.trek.com
```

In most cases, you are using **ftp** to access anonymous FTP sites. Instead of trying to make an entry for each one, you can make a default entry for anonymous FTP login. When you connect to a site, **ftp** looks for a machine entry for it in the **.netrc** file. If none exists, then **ftp** looks for a default entry and uses that. A default entry begins with the term "default" with no network address. To make anonymous logins your default, enter "anonymous" and your e-mail address as your login and password.

```
default  login anonymous  password  dylan@turtle.trek.com
```

.netrc

```
machine golf.mygames.com  login   dylan  password  legogolf
default  login anonymous  password dylan@turtle.trek.com
```

You can also define macros in your **.netrc** file. With a macro, you can execute several **ftp** operations at once using only the macro name. Macros remain in effect during a connection. When you close a connection, the macros are undefined. Although a macro can be defined on your **ftp** command line, defining them in **.netrc** entries makes more sense. This way, you needn't redefine them again. They are read automatically from the **.netrc** file and defined for you. You can place macro definitions within a particular machine entry in the **.netrc** file or in the default entry. Macros defined in machine entries are defined only when you connect to that site. Macros in the default entry are defined whenever you make a connection to any site.

The syntax for a macro definition follows. It begins with the keyword macdef, followed by the macro name you want to give it, and ends with an empty line. **ftp** macros can take arguments, referenced within the macro with n, where $1 references the first argument, and $2 the second, and so on. If you need to use a $ character in a macro, you have to quote it using the backslash, \$.

```
macdef  macro-name
ftp commands
empty-line
```

The **redupd** macro, defined next, changes to a directory where it then downloads Red Hat updates for the current release. It also changes to a local directory where the update files are to be placed. The **prompt** command turns off the download prompts for each file. The **mget** command then downloads the files. The macro assumes you are connected to the Red Hat FTP site.

```
defmac redupd
cd pub/redhat/current
lcd /root/redupdate
prompt
mget *
```

A sample **.netrc** file follows with macros defined for both specific and default entries. An empty line is placed after each macro definition. You can define several macros for a machine or the default entry. The macro definitions following a machine entry up to the next machine entry are automatically defined for that machine connection.

.netrc

```
machine updates.redhat.com  login   anonymous  password
dylan@turtle.trek.com
defmac redupd
cd pub/redhat/current
lcd /root/redupdate
prompt
mget *

default login anonymous password dylan@turtle.trek.com
defmac lls
!ls
```

Online FTP Resources

The Internet has a great many sites open to public access. They contain files anyone can obtain using file transfer programs, such as **ftp**. Unless you already know where a file is located, however, finding it can be difficult. To search for files on FTP sites, you can use search engines provided by Web sites, such as Yahoo!, Excite, Alta Vista, or Lycos. These usually search for both Web pages and FTP files. Normally, you must use a Web browser to access such sites and perform searches. However, Linux utilities are being developed that can access sites directly and list the results. *Ganesha* is one such utility, which is a Gnome-based application that accesses the Lycos FTP search service at **ftpsearch.lycos.com**, performs a search, and displays the results, as shown in Figure 12-4. You enter the search string and press ENTER. Results are listed showing round-trip times, number of hops, the FTP site, and the full pathname of the file. You can then select items and save them to your disk. The number of hops to a locations indicates how far away the site is. You can also drag Netscape URLs into the Ganesha window to check the round-trip times and number of hops to a Web site.

Another utility you can use for locating files is *Archie. Xarchie* is an X-Windows program that enables you to use menus and list boxes to perform an Archie search

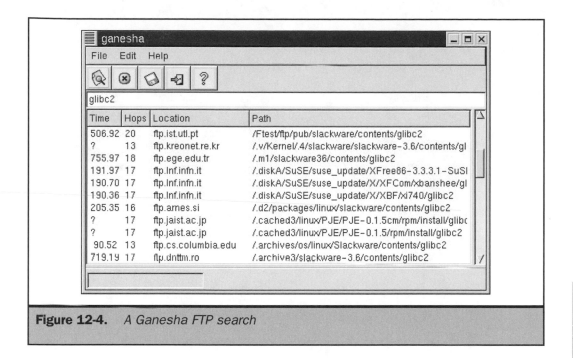

Figure 12-4.   *A Ganesha FTP search*

and to display its results. You can even use Xarchie to perform an FTP operation for a file you select, downloading it to your system. Xarchie has three menus, File, Settings, and Query. The fourth item on the menu bar is an Abort button you can use to stop an Archie search. The last item is a Help button that starts a window displaying various Xarchie help files. Xarchie operates by accessing an Archie server to perform a search and then displays the results. The list of Archie servers is displayed by selecting the Archie Host item in the Settings menu. The Settings menu also contains items for configuring your search, enabling you to determine the sorting sequence or the pattern-matching method. To perform a search, enter the search term in the box labeled Search Term, and then select the Item entry in the Query menu. The display window is separated into several list boxes, the first of which lists the Internet sites found. When you click a particular site, the pathname for the file you are looking for is displayed in the second list box (there can be more than one list box). The third list box shows the item found, which can be either a file or a directory. If it is a directory, you can double-click it to display the list of files in it. To download a file, click the filename and select the Get item from the File menu.

The
Complete
Reference

Chapter 13

The World Wide Web

The World Wide Web (*WWW* or the *Web*) is a hypertext database of different types of information, distributed across many different sites on the Internet. A *hypertext database* consists of items linked to other items, which, in turn, may be linked to yet other items, and so on. Upon retrieving an item, you can use that item to retrieve any related items. For example, you could retrieve an article on the Amazon rain forest and then use it to retrieve a map or a picture of the rain forest. In this respect, a hypertext database is like a web of interconnected data you can trace from one data item to another. Information is displayed in pages known as *Web pages*. On a Web page, certain keywords are highlighted that form links to other Web pages or to items, such as pictures, articles, or files.

The Web links data across different sites on the Internet throughout the world. The Web originated in Europe at CERN research laboratories and CERN remains the original Web server. An Internet site that operates as a Web server is known as a *Web site*. Such Web sites are often dedicated to specialized topics or institutions, for example, the Smithsonian Web site or the NASA Web site. These Web sites usually have an Internet address that begins with www, as in **www.redhat.com**, the Web site for Red Hat, Inc. Once connected to a Web site, you can use hypertext links to move from one Web page to another.

To access the Web, you use a client program called a *browser*. You can choose from many different Web browsers. Browsers are available for use on UNIX, Windows, the Mac, and Linux. Certain browsers, such as Netscape and Mosaic, have versions that operate on all such systems. On your Linux system, you can choose from several Web browsers, including Netscape Navigator. Navigator is available as part of all Linux distributions. Netscape and Mosaic are X-Windows-based browsers that provide full picture, sound, and video display capabilities. Most distributions also include the Lynx browser, a line-mode browser that displays only lines of text. The K Desktop incorporates Web browser capabilities into its file manager, letting a directory window operate as a Web browser. Gnome-based browsers, such as Express and Mnemonic, are also designed to be easily enhanced.

URL Addresses

An Internet resource is accessed using a *Universal Resource Locator* (*URL*). A URL is composed of three elements: the transfer protocol, the hostname, and the pathname. The transfer protocol and the hostname are separated by a colon and two slashes, **://**. The *pathname* always begins with a single slash.

```
transfer-protocol://host-name/path-name
```

The *transfer protocol* is usually **http** (Hypertext Transfer Protocol), indicating a Web page. Other possible values for transfer protocols are **gopher**, **ftp**, and **file**. As their names suggest, **gopher** and **ftp** initiate Gopher and FTP sessions, whereas **file** displays a local file on your own system, such as a text or an HTML file. Table 13-1 lists the various transfer protocols.

The *hostname* is the computer on which a particular Web site is located. You can think of this as the address of the Web site. By convention most hostnames begin with www. In the next example, the URL locates a Web page called **toc.html** on the **home.netscape.com** Web site.

```
http://home.netscape.com/toc.html
```

If you do not want to access a particular Web page, you can leave the file reference out, and then you automatically access the Web site's home page. To access a Web site directly, use its hostname. The default name for a Web site's home page is **index.html**, located in the site's top directory. A Web site can override the default and specify a particular file as the home page. If no file is specified, however, the **index.html** file is taken as the home page. In the next example, the user brings up the Red Hat home page.

```
http://www.redhat.com/
```

The pathname specifies the directory where the resource can be found on the host system, as well as the name of the resource's file. For example, **/pub/Linux/newdat.html** references an HTML document called **newdat** located in the **/pub/Linux** directory. As you move to other Web pages on a site, you may move more deeply into the directory tree. In the following example, the user accesses the **FAQ.html** document in the directory **corp/support/docs/FAQ/FAQ.html**.

Protocol	Description
http	Hypertext Transfer Protocol for Web site access
gopher	Access Gopher site
ftp	File Transfer Protocol for anonymous FTP connections
telnet	Makes a telnet connection
wais	Access WAIS site
news	Reading Usenet news; uses Net News Transfer Protocol (NNTP)

Table 13-1.   *Web Protocols*

```
http://www.redhat.com/corp/support/docs/FAQ/FAQ.html
```

As just explained, if you specify a directory pathname without a particular Web page file, your Web browser looks for a file called **index.html** in that directory. An **index.html** file in a directory operates as the default Web page for that directory. In the next example, the **index.html** Web page in the **/apps/support** directory is displayed.

```
http://www.redhat.com/apps/support/index.html
```

You can use this technique to access local Web pages on your system. For example, once installed, the demo Web pages for Java are located in **/usr/local/java/**. Because this is on your local system, you needn't include a hostname. An **index.html** page in the **/usr/local/java/** directory is automatically displayed when you specify the directory path. You can do the same for your system documentation, which is in Web-page format located in the **/usr/doc/HTML/ldp** directory.

```
file:/usr/local/java
file:/usr/doc/HTML/ldp
```

If you reference a directory that has no **index.html** file, the Web server creates one for you, and your browser then displays it. This index simply lists the different files and directories in that directory. You can click an entry to display a file or to move to another directory. The first entry is a special entry for the parent directory.

The resource file's extension indicates the type of action to be taken on it. A picture has a **.gif** or **.jpeg** extension and is converted for display. A sound file has a **.au** or **.wav** extension and is played. The following URL references a **.gif** file. Instead of displaying a Web page, your browser invokes a graphics viewer to display the picture. Table 13-2 provides a list of the different file extensions.

```
http://www.train.com/engine/engine1.gif
```

Web Pages

A *Web page* is a specially formatted document that can be displayed by any Web browser. You can think of a Web page as a word processing document that can display both text and graphics. Within the Web page, links can be embedded that call up other Internet resources. An Internet resource can be a graphic, a file, a telnet connection, or even another Web page. The Web page acts as an interface for accessing different Internet tools, such as FTP to download files or telnet to connect to an online catalog or other remote service.

Web pages display both text and graphics. Text is formatted with paragraphs and can be organized with different headings. Graphics of various sizes may be placed

File Type	Description
.html	Web page document formatted using HTML, the Hypertext Markup Language
Graphics Files	
.gif	Graphics, using GIF compression
.jpeg	Graphics, using JPEG compression
Sound Files	
.au	Sun (UNIX) sound file
.wav	Microsoft Windows sound file
.aiff	Macintosh sound file
Video Files	
.QT	Quicktime video file, multiplatform
.mpeg	Video file
.avi	Microsoft Windows video file

Table 13-2.   *Web File Types*

INTERNET

anywhere in the page. Throughout the page there are usually anchor points you can use to call up other Internet resources. Each *anchor point* is associated with a particular Internet resource. One anchor point may reference a picture; another, a file. Others may reference other Web pages or even other Web sites. These anchor points are specially highlighted text or graphics that usually appear in a different color from the rest of the text. Whereas ordinary text may be black, text used for anchor points might be green, blue, or red. You select a particular anchor point by moving your mouse pointer to that text or picture, and then clicking it. The Internet resource associated with that anchor point is then called up. If the resource is a picture, the picture is displayed. If it is another Web page, that Web page is displayed. If the Internet resource is on another Web site, that site is accessed. The color of an anchor point indicates its status and the particular Web browser you are using. Both Mosaic and Netscape use blue for anchors you have not yet accessed. Netscape uses the color purple for anchors you have already accessed, and Mosaic uses red. All these colors can be overridden by a particular Web page.

Your Web browser keeps a list of the different Web pages you access for each session. You can move back and forth easily in that list. Having called up another Web page, you can use your browser to move back to the previous one. Web browsers construct their lists according to the sequence in which you displayed your Web pages. They keep track of the Web pages you are accessing, whatever they may be. On many Web sites, however, several Web pages are meant to be connected in a particular order, like chapters in a book. Such pages usually have buttons displayed at the bottom of the page that reference the next and previous pages in the sequence. Clicking Next displays the next Web page for this site. The Home button returns you to the first page for this sequence.

Web Browsers

Most *Web browsers* are designed to access several different kinds of information. Web browsers can access a Web page on a remote Web site or a file on your own system. Some browsers can also access a remote news server or an FTP site. The type of information for a site is specified by the keyword **http** for Web sites, **nntp** for news servers, **ftp** for FTP sites, and **file** for files on your own system.

To access a Web site, you enter **http://** followed by the Internet address of the Web site. If you know a particular Web page you want to access on that Web site, you can add the pathname for that page, attaching it to the Internet address. Then simply press ENTER. The browser connects you to that Web site and displays its home page or the page you specified.

You can just as easily use a Web browser to display Web pages on your own system by entering the term **file** followed by a colon, **file:**, with the pathname of the Web page you want to display. You do not specify an Internet site. Remember, all Web pages have the extension **.html**. Links within a Web page on your own system can connect you to other Web pages on your system or to Web pages on remote systems. When you first start a Web browser, your browser displays a local Web page on your own system. The default page is usually a page for your particular distribution, such as OpenLinux or Red Hat. Such pages have links to a distribution's Web site where you can obtain online support. If you want, you can create your own Web pages, with their own links, and make one of them your default Web page.

Web pages on a Web site often contain links to other Web pages, some on the same site and others at other Web sites. Through these links, you can move from one page to another. As you move from Web page to Web page using the anchor points or buttons, your browser displays the URL for the current page. Your browser keeps a list of the different Web pages you have accessed in a given session. Most browsers have buttons that enable you to move back and forth through this list. You can move to the Web page you displayed before the current one and then move back further to the previous one. You can move forward again to the next page, and so on.

To get to a particular page, you may have moved through a series of pages, using links in each finally to reach the Web page you want. To access any Web page, all you need is its URL address. If you want to access a particular page again, you can enter its URL address and move directly to it, without moving through the intervening pages as you did the first time. Instead of writing down the URL addresses and entering them yourself, most Web browsers can keep a *hotlist*—a list of favorite Web pages you want to access directly. When you are displaying a Web page you want to access later, instruct your browser to place it on the hotlist. The Web page is usually listed in the hotlist by its title, not its URL. To access that Web page later, select the entry in the hotlist.

Most Web browsers can also access FTP and Gopher sites. You may find using a Web browser to access an FTP site is easier than using the FTP utility. Directories and files are automatically listed, and selecting a file or directory is only a matter of clicking its name. First enter **ftp://** and then the Internet address of the FTP site. The contents of a directory are then displayed, listing files and subdirectories. To move to another directory, just click it. To download a file, click its name. You see an entry listed as **. .**, representing the parent directory. You can move down the file structure from one subdirectory to another and move back up one directory at a time by selecting **...** To leave the FTP site, return to your own home page. You can also use your browser to access Gopher sites. Enter **gopher://** followed by the Internet address of the Gopher site. Your Web browser then displays the main Gopher menu for that site, and you can move from one Gopher menu to the next.

Most browsers can connect to your news server to access specified newsgroups or articles. This is a local operation, accessing the news server to which you are already connected. You enter **nntp** followed by a colon and the newsgroup or news article. Some browsers, such as Netscape, have an added newsreader browser that allows them to access any remote news servers.

As noted previously, several popular browsers are available for Linux. Three distinctive ones are described here: Netscape Navigator, Mosaic, and Lynx. Netscape and Mosaic are X-Windows-based Web browsers capable of displaying graphics, video, and sound, as well as operating as newsreaders and mailers. Lynx is a command line–based browser with no graphics capabilities but, in every other respect, it is a fully functional Web browser.

Netscape Navigator

Hypertext databases are designed to access any kind of data, whether it is text, graphics, sound, or even video. Whether you can actually access such data depends to a large extent on the type of browser you use. One of the more popular Web browsers is Netscape Navigator. Versions of Netscape operate on different graphical user interfaces such as X-Windows, Microsoft Windows, and the Macintosh. Using X-Windows, the Netscape browser can display graphics, sound, video, and Java-based programs (you learn about Java a little later in the chapter). You can obtain more information about Netscape on its Web site: **www.netscape.com**.

Netscape Navigator is now included on Red Hat Linux distributions' CD-ROMs. For more recent versions as they come out, you can access the Red Hat FTP site at **ftp.redhat.com**. You can also obtain compressed archive versions (**.tar.gz**) from

Netscape FTP sites such as **ftp8.netscape.com**. A compressed archive version has to be decompressed and unpacked with the `gunzip` and `tar xvf` commands, once the archive has been placed in an install directory such as **/usr/local**.

Netscape Navigator is an X-Windows application you operates from your desktop. Many distributions have a desktop icon for Netscape or an entry for it in the desktop's menu. Netscape Navigator displays an area at the top of the screen for entering a URL address and a series of buttons for various Web page operations. Drop-down menus provide access to Netscape features. To access a Web site, you enter its address in the URL area and press ENTER. The icon bar across the top of the browser holds buttons for moving from one page to another and performing other operations.

Netscape refers to the URLs of Web pages you want to keep in a hotlist as *bookmarks*, marking pages you want to access directly. The Bookmarks menu enables you add your favorite Web pages to a hotlist. You can then view your bookmarks and select one to view. Items in the Windows menu enhance your Web browser operations. In the address book, you can keep a list of Web site URLs. The Bookmark item enables you to edit your list of bookmarks, adding new ones or removing old ones. The History item is a list of previous URLs you have accessed. If you want to return to a Web page you did not save as a bookmark, you can find it in the history list. Additionally, you can use Netscape to receive and send mail, as well as to access Usenet newsgroups.

The Options menu in the Netscape Navigator enables you to set several different kinds of preferences for your browser. You can set preferences for mail and news, the network, and security, as well as general preferences. In general preferences, you can determine your home page and how you want the toolbar displayed. For mail and news, you can enter the mail and news servers you use on the Internet. Netscape can be set to access any number of news servers you subscribe to and that use the NNTP transfer protocols. You can switch from one news server to another if you want.

If you are on a network that connects to the Internet through a firewall, you must use the Proxies screen to enter the address of your network's firewall gateway computer. A *firewall* is a computer that operates as a controlled gateway to the Internet for your network. Several types of firewalls exist. One of the most restrictive uses programs called *proxies,* which receive Internet requests from users and then make those requests on their behalf. There is no direct connection to the Internet. From the Options menu, select Network, and then choose the Proxies screen. Here, enter the IP address of your network's firewall gateway computer.

Through the Mail item in the Windows menu, you can open a fully functional mail client with which you can send and receive messages over the Internet. The News item, also in the Windows menu, opens a fully functional newsreader with which you can read and post articles in Usenet newsgroups. In this respect, your Netscape Navigator is more than just a Web browser. It is also a mail program and a newsreader.

K Desktop File Manager

If you are using the K Desktop, then you can use a file manager window as a Web browser, as shown in Figure 13-1. The K Desktop's file manager is automatically configured to act as a Web browser. It can display Web pages, including graphics and links. The K Desktop's file manager supports standard Web page operation, such as moving forward and backward through accessed pages. Clicking a link accesses and displays the Web page referenced. In this respect, the Web becomes seamlessly integrated into the K Desktop.

Gnome Web Browsers: Express and Mnemonic

Unlike the K Desktop, the Gnome file manager does not support Web access. You use a Web browser such as Netscape, Express, or Mnemonic. Express and Mnemonic are Gnome-based Web browsers that support standard Web operations. Express is

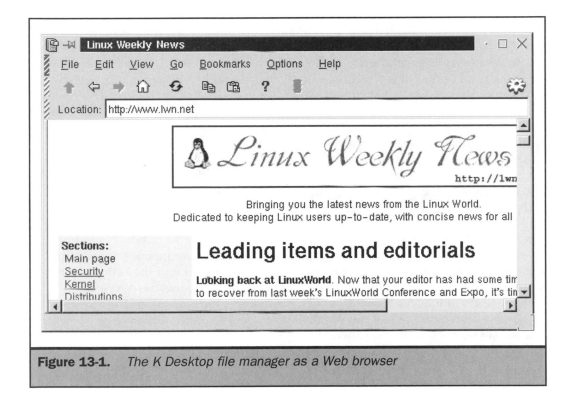

Figure 13-1. *The K Desktop file manager as a Web browser*

designed to rely on plug-ins for Web features. This way, the browser can be made as complex or simple as you want. All major operations, such as viewers and protocols, are handled as plug-ins. This design allows new features to be easily added in this way. Mnemonic is an extensible and modular Web browser that integrates a set of *Object Implementation Libraries (OILs)* into a Web browser with a Gnome interface.

Lynx: Line-Mode Browser

Lynx is a line-mode browser you can use without X-Windows. A Web page is displayed as text only. A text page can contain links to other Internet resources, but does not display any graphics, video, or sound. Except for the display limitations, Lynx is a fully functional Web browser. You can use Lynx to download files or to make telnet connections. All information on the Web is still accessible to you. Because it does not require much of the overhead graphics-based browsers need, Lynx can operate much faster, quickly displaying Web page text. To start the Lynx browser, you enter **lynx** on the command line and press ENTER.

The links are displayed in bold and dispersed throughout the text of the Web page. A selected link is highlighted in reverse video with a shaded rectangle around the link text. The first link is automatically selected. You can then move sequentially from one link to the next on a page by pressing the DOWN ARROW key. The UP ARROW key moves you back to a previous link. To choose a link, first highlight it and then press either ENTER or the RIGHT ARROW key. If you want to go to a specific site, press G. This opens a line at the bottom of the screen with the prompt **URL to open:**. There, you can enter the URL for the site you want. Pressing M returns you to your Home page. The text of a Web page is displayed one screen at a time. To move to the next screen of text, you can either press SPACEBAR or PAGE DOWN. PAGE UP displays the previous screen of text. Pressing DOWN ARROW and UP ARROW moves to the next or previous links in the text, displaying the full screen of text around the link. To display a description of the current Web page with its URL, press the = key.

Lynx uses a set of one-letter commands to perform various browser functions. By pressing the ? key at any time, you can display a list of these commands. For example, pressing the D key downloads a file. The H key brings up a help menu. To search the text of your current Web page, press the / key. This opens a line at the bottom of the screen where you enter your search pattern. Lynx then highlights the next instance of that pattern in the text. If you press N, Lynx displays the next instance. The \ key toggles you between a source and rendered version of the current Web page, showing you the HTML tags or the formatted text.

HotJava

The Linux version of the HotJava browser is currently available. You can download it directly from the **java.sun.com** Web site. It can be easily customized to your particular needs. Its Places menu enables you to collect Web page addresses or use Netscape bookmarks. HotJava can also display both frames and tables. It has a small footprint and can be used to complement Netscape browsers or other software designed to access the Web. HotJava includes support for security features such as signed applets. It is more flexible in its reading of HTML code, allowing the browser to recover successfully from errors.

Mosaic

Mosaic, which can display graphics, sound, and video data, was the first graphics-based browser developed for the Web. Unlike Netscape, it is available free to anyone. Versions of Mosaic exist for different graphical user interfaces, such as X-Windows, Microsoft Windows, and the Macintosh. Mosaic was developed by the National Center for Supercomputing Applications (NCSA) at the University of Illinois, Champaign-Urbana. More information about Mosaic is available at the NCSA Web site: **www.ncsa.uiuc.edu**. You can download a copy of Mosaic from the Mosaic FTP site at **ftp.ncsa.uiuc.edu** in the directory **/Web/Mosaic/Unix**.

Menus across the top of the Mosaic window enable you to manage your Web searches. With the Navigate menu, you maintain a hotlist of favored Web sites. The Options menu has several entries for configuring your Mosaic browser. You can set your home page or specify mail or news servers. You can also set default colors used for the background and for URL links. The News menu enables you to use your Mosaic browser to access Usenet newsgroups, displaying and saving articles. Mosaic also has built-in security features that can protect your system.

JAVA for Linux: Blackdown

To develop Java applications, use Java tools, and run many Java products, you must install the Java Development Kit and the Java Runtime Environment on your system. Sun does not support or develop Linux versions of these products. They have been ported to Linux by the Blackdown project, however, and you can download the Blackdown ports of the JDK and JRE and install them on your system. More information and documentation is available at the Blackdown Web site at **www.blackdown.org**.

Numerous Java-based products and tools are currently adaptable for Linux. Linux versions of the HotJava browser and the Java Web server exist. Tools include IDE development environments, *Just In Time* compilers (*JIT*), and Java virtual machines. Most of the products and some of the tools are free. You can download most of the products and tools through links in the Blackdown Web page located at **www.blackdown.org**. Select the JavaSoft Products entry for a list of links to available Java products; select Java Tools for Linux for a list of tools. Many of the products run directly as provided by Sun. You can download several directly from the Sun Java Web site at **java.sun.com**. A few of the currently available products are listed in Table 13-3.

Java Development Kit (JDK) and Java Runtime Environment (JRE)	A Java development environment with a compiler, interpreters, debugger, and more. Download the Linux port from your distribution's update through **www.blackdown.org.**
HotJava browser 3.0	Sun's HTML 3.2– and JDK 1.1–compliant Web browser. Download the Linux version from **java.sun.com**.
Java Foundation Classes (Swing Set)	Swing is a new set of GUI components being developed by JavaSoft.
The Java Servlet Development Kit	Provides resources for running, testing, and operating servlets with Netscape, Microsoft, and Apache Web servers.
Java Web Server	A Web server implemented with Java. Available at Java Web site at **java.sun.com**.
The JDBC Database Access API	A SQL database access interface for Java.

Table 13-3.   *Java Applications*

The Java Development Kit: JDK and JRE

The *Java Development Kit* (*JDK*) provides tools for creating and debugging your own Java applets and provides support for Java applications, such as the HotJava browser. The kit includes demonstration applets with source code. You can obtain detailed documentation about the JDK from the Sun Web site at **java.sun.com**. Three major releases of the JDK are currently available, 1.0, 1.1.*x*, and 1.2, with corresponding versions for the *Java Runtime Environment* (*JRE*) for 1.1 and 1.2. JDK 1.0 is an earlier version of the JDK that is compatible with older browsers. JDK 1.1.*x* includes standard features, such as JavaBeans and database connectivity. The current version of JDK 1.1.*x* is 1.1.7. JAVA 2 adds capabilities for security, Swing, and running Java enhancements, such as Java3D and Java Sound. JDK 1.2 is also known as JAVA 2 (SDK). All JDK and JRE releases are available for Linux. You can download them from a Java-Linux mirror site that you can link to through the Blackdown Web page (**www.blackdown.org**) mentioned earlier. JDK and JRE 1.1 are not usually included on Linux distribution CD-ROMs. You can, however, download RPM versions from the Red Hat FTP site, at **ftp.redhat.com/pub/contrib**. JDK and JRE 1.2 currently must be downloaded through **www.blackdown.org** as a compressed archive, **.tar.gz** file.

JDK 1.1 includes features such as for Internationalization, signed applets, JAR file format, AWT (window toolkit) enhancements, JavaBeans component model, networking enhancements, Math package for large numbers, *database connectivity* (*JDBC*), Object Serialization, and Inner Classes. Detailed descriptions of these features can be found in the JDK documentation. The JDK package installs the Java applications, libraries, and demos in the specified directory. Java applications include a Java compiler, javac, a Java debugger, jdb, and an applet viewer, appletviewer. To use these applications, you must add the directory to your **PATH** in either the **/etc/profile** or **.profile** initialization files.

JAVA 2 SDK (JDK 1.2)

JAVA 2 offers numerous capabilities over JDK 1.1, such as integrated Swing, Java 2d, the new security model, the Collections framework, CORBA, and JDBC 2.0. The Blackdown port of Java 2 has support for both native threads and green threads, and it includes a Just In Time dynamic bytecode compiler. With JAVA 2, you can run the Blackdown port of Java 3D, Java Advanced Imaging, Java Media Framework, and Java Sound. Detailed descriptions of these features can be found in the JAVA 2 documentation.

The Linux version of JAVA 2 is currently packaged as compressed archives. You need to download, decompress, and unpack the **.tar.gz** file. Once you download the archive, place it in the directory you want the JDK 1.2 installed in, usually a directory, such as **/usr/local**. You then decompress it with gunzip and unpack it with tar xvf, or combine both operations with tar xvzf. A directory is then created for the JDK where you find the **bin** and **lib** subdirectories holding the Java applications and libraries. You should add that directory to your **PATH** in the **/etc/profile** or **.profile** script (**.login** for the TCSH shell). Also, in either **/etc/profile** or **.profile,** you should add an entry that assigns the respective directory to the **JDK_HOME** variable. This variable is used by various Java application, such as HotJava, to locate the Java interpreter. Check the README file for details.

Java Applets

You create a Java applet much as you would create a program using a standard programming language. You first use a text editor to create the source code, which is saved in a file with a **.java** extension. Then you can use the **javac** compiler to compile the source code file, generating a Java applet. This applet file has the extension **.class**. For example, the JDK demo directory includes the Java source code for a Blink applet called **Blink.java**. You can go to that directory and then compile the **Blink.java** file, generating a **Blink.class** file. The **example1.html** file in that directory runs the **Blink.class** applet. Start your browser and access this file to run the Blink applet.

```
# javac Blink.java
```

An applet is called within a Web page using the <applet> HTML tag. This tag can contain several attributes, one of which is required: code. You assign to code the name of the compiled applet. You can use several optional attributes to set features, such as the region used to display the applet and its alignment. You can even access applets on a remote Web site. In the following example, the applet called **Blink.class** is displayed in a box on the Web browser that has a height of 140 pixels and a width of 100 pixels, and is aligned in the center.

```
<applet code="Blink.class" width=100 height=140 align=center></applet>
```

To invoke the debugger, use the appletviewer command with the -debug option and the name of the HTML file that runs the applet.

```
appletviewer -debug mypage.html
```

Numerous *Interface Development Environments* (*IDE*) applications are available for composing Java applets and applications. Although most are commercial, some provide free shareware versions. An IDE provides a GUI interface for constructing Java applets. You can link to and download several IDE applications through the Blackdown Web page.

Web Search Utilities

To search for files on ftp sites, you can use search engines provided by Web sites, such as Yahoo!, Excite, Alta Vista, or Lycos. These usually search for both Web pages and ftp files. To find a particular Web page you want on the Internet, you can use any number of online search sites such as Yahoo!, Excite, Alta Vista, or Lycos. You can use their Web sites or perform searches from any number of Web portals, such as Netscape or Linux online. Web searches have become a standard service of most Web sites. Searches carried out on documents within a Web site, may use local search indexes set up and maintained by indexing programs like ht://Dig and WAIS. Sites using ht://Dig use a standard Web page search interface, where WAIS provides its own specialized client programs like **swais** and **xwais**. See the ht://Dig Web site at **www.htdig.org** for more details and RPM versions to download (also available at **rtp.redhat.com/pub/contrib**). WAIS is an older indexing program currently being supplanted by newer search applications like ht://Dig. You can still obtain a free version of WAIS, called *freeWAIS*, from **ftp.cnidr.org.**

Creating Your Own Web Site

To create your own Web site, you need access to a Web server. Most Linux distributions, such as OpenLinux and Red Hat, automatically install the Apache Web server on their

Linux systems. You can also rent Web page space on a remote server, a service many ISPs provide, some free. On Red Hat and OpenLinux systems, the directory set up by your Apache Web server for your Web site pages is **/home/httpd/html**. Other servers provide you with a directory for your home page. Place the Web pages you create in that directory. You can make other subdirectories with their own Web pages to which these can link. Web pages are not difficult to create. Links from one page to another move users through your Web site. You can even create links to Web pages or resources on other sites. Many excellent texts are available on Web page creation and management.

Web Page Composers

Web pages are created using HTML, the Hypertext Markup Language, which is a subset of *Standard Generalized Markup Language* (*SGML*). Creating an HTML document is a matter of inserting HTML tags in a text file. In this respect, creating a Web page is as simple as using a tag-based word processor. You use the HTML tags to format text for display as a Web page. The Web page itself is a text file you can create using any text editor, such as Vi. If you are familiar with tag-based word processing on UNIX systems, you will find it conceptually similar to nroff. Some HTML tags indicate headings, lists, and paragraphs, as well as to reference Web resources.

Instead of manually entering HTML code, you can use Web page composers. A Web page composer provides a graphical interface for constructing Web pages. The Linux version of WordPerfect can automatically generate a Web page from a WordPerfect document. You can create Web pages using all the word processing features of WordPerfect. Special Web page creation programs, such as Netscape Composer, also can help you easily create complex Web pages without ever having to type any HTML tags explicitly. Remember, though, no matter what tool you use to create your Web page, the Web page itself will be an HTML document.

Many of the standard editors for the K desktop and Gnome include Web page construction features. Many enable you to insert links or format headings. The kedit program supports basic text-based Web page components. You can add headings, links, or lines, but not graphics. gXedit can also compose and edit Web pages. You can easily insert HTTP elements, such as links, image references, or headings. gXedit can then access Netscape to preview the page. gnotepad+ is a simple editor for making small text files. It does, however, have a toolbar for Web page composition containing several of the more common HTML elements. You can insert links, headings, and lists, as well as other basic Web page components.

Common Gateway Interfaces

A *Common Gateway Interface* (*CGI*) script is a program a Web server at a Web site can use to interact with Web browsers. When a browser displays a Web page at a particular Web site, the Web page may call up CGI programs to provide you with certain real-time information or to receive information from you. For example, a Web page may execute the server's date command to display the current date whenever the Web page is accessed.

A CGI script can be a Linux shell script, Perl script, Tcl/Tk program, or a program developed using a programming language, such as C. Two special HTML operations are also considered CGI scripts: query text and forms. Both receive and process interactive responses from particular users. You have seen how a user can use a browser to display Web pages at a given Web site. In effect, the user is receiving information in the form of Web pages from the Web site. A user can also, to a limited extent, send information back to the Web site. This is usually information specifically prompted for in a Web page displayed by your browser. The Web server then receives and processes that information using the CGI programs.

A *form* is a Web page that holds several input fields of various types. These can be input boxes for entering text or check boxes and radio buttons users simply click. The text boxes can be structured, allowing a certain number of characters to be entered, as in a phone number. They can also be unstructured, enabling users to type in sentences as they would for a comment. Forms are referred to as *form-based queries.* After entering information into a form, the user sends it back to the server by clicking a Submit button. The server receives the form and, along with it, instructions to run a specific CGI program to process the form.

The
Complete
Reference

Linux

Chapter 14

Network Tools

You can use a variety of network tools to perform tasks such as obtaining information about other systems on your network, accessing other systems, and communicating directly with other users. Network information can be obtained using utilities such as **ping**, **finger**, and **host**. Talk, ICQ, and IRC clients enable you to communicate directly with other users on your network. Telnet performs a remote login to an account you may have on another system connected on your network. Each has a corresponding K Desktop or Gnome version. These provide a GUI interface, so you no longer have to use the shell command line to run these tools. In addition, your network may make use of older remote access commands. These are useful for smaller networks and enable you to access remote systems directly to copy files or execute commands.

Network Information: ping, finger, and host

You can use the **ping**, **finger**, **traceroute**, and **host** commands to find status information about systems and users on your network. **ping** is used to check if a remote system is up and running. You use **finger** to find out information about other users on your network, seeing if they are logged in or if they have received mail. **host** displays address information about a system on your network, giving you a system's IP and domain name addresses. **traceroute** can be used to track the sequence of computer networks and systems your message passed through on its way to you.

On the Gnome desktop, the Gnetutil utility provides a Gnome interface for entering the **ping**, **finger**, and **host** commands. On the K Desktop, you can use the KDE network utilities to issue **ping** , **finger**, **traceroute**, and **host** commands. Select the appropriate tabbed panel. For the Ping panel, enter the address of the remote system at the box labeled Host and click Go. The results are displayed in the pane below, as shown in Figure 14-1. Also on KDE, the knu program provides a front end to various network utilities.

ping

The **ping** command detects whether a system is up and running. **ping** takes as its argument the name of the system you want to check. If the system you want to check is down, **ping** issues a timeout message, indicating a connection could not be made. The next example checks to see if **www.redhat.com** is up and connected to the network.

```
$ ping www.redhat.com
PING www.portal.redhat.com (206.132.41.202) from 24.0.67.231 : 56(84) bytes of data.
64 bytes from 206.132.41.202: icmp_seq=0 ttl=246 time=10.9 ms
64 bytes from 206.132.41.202: icmp_seq=1 ttl=246 time=15.3 ms
64 bytes from 206.132.41.202: icmp_seq=2 ttl=246 time=19.5 ms
64 bytes from 206.132.41.202: icmp_seq=3 ttl=246 time=36.9 ms
```

```
--- www.portal.redhat.com ping statistics ---
4 packets transmitted, 4 packets received, 0% packet loss
round-trip min/avg/max = 10.9/20.6/36.9 ms
$
```

finger and who

You can use the **finger** command to obtain information about other users on your network and the **who** command to see what users are currently online on your system. The **who** command lists all users currently connected along with when, how long, and where they logged in. It has several options for specifying the level of detail. **who** is meant to operate on a local system or network. **finger** operates on large networks, including the Internet. As shown in Figure 14-2, **finger** checks to see when a user last logged in, the type of shell he is using, the path name of his home directory, and whether any mail has been received. **finger** then checks for a **.plan** file in a user's home directory that may contain information about him. The **.plan** file is a file you create yourself on your own home directory. You can place information you want made publicly available into the **.plan** file. You can enter the command **finger** on the command line with the login name of the user you want to check.

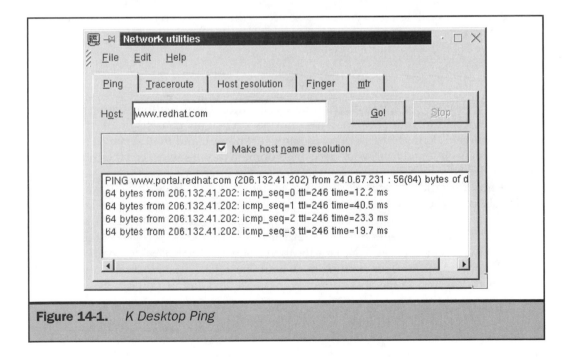

Figure 14-1. *K Desktop Ping*

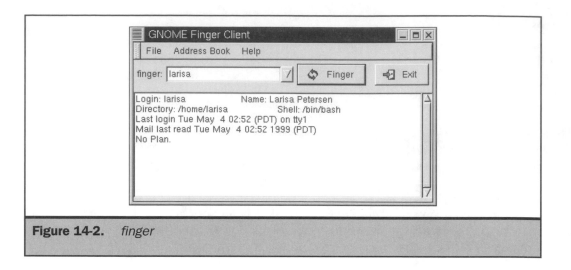

Figure 14-2. *finger*

On the K Desktop, you can use the KDE network utilities to issue finger commands. Click the Finger panel and enter the address of the host you want to check. On the K Desktop, the kfinger tool also provides a GUI for easily sending finger queries. It features entries for users and remote servers. You can search for users on specific remote systems. With kfinger, you can also access the K Desktop talk utility to talk with selected users online. You can start kfinger by selecting the User Information entry in the K Desktop's Internet menu.

host

With the **host** command, you can find network address information about a remote system connected to your network. This information usually consists of a system's IP address, domain name address, domain name nicknames, and mail server. This information is obtained from your network's domain name server. For the Internet, this includes all systems you can connect to over the Internet.

The **host** command is an effective way to determine a remote site's IP address or vice versa. If you have only the IP address of a site, you can use **host** to find its domain name. For network administration, an IP address can be helpful for making your own domain name entries in your **/etc/host** file. That way, you needn't rely on a remote domain name server (DNS) for locating a site. On the K Desktop, you can use the KDE network utilities for running host commands. Click the Host resolution panel and enter the address of the host you want to check. On Gnome, you can use the gHostLookup utility.

```
$ host www.gnome.org
www.gnome.org is a nickname for gnome.labs.redhat.com
```

```
gnome.labs.redhat.com has address 199.183.24.235
gnome.labs.redhat.com mail is handled (pri=10) by mail.redhat.com

$ host 199.183.24.235
235.24.183.199.IN-ADDR.ARPA domain name pointer
gnome.labs.redhat.com
```

The *Xwhois* program is a Gnome-base client that displays information obtained from NIC network services. Xwhois provides an X Windows interface with a list of NIC servers from which to choose. gHostLookup is a simple Gnome application that returns a machines IP address when you give it the hostname.

Network Talk Clients

You may, at times, want to communicate directly with other users on your network. You can do so with talk and IRC utilities, provided the other user is also logged into a connected system at the same time. The *Talk* utility operates like a telephone, enabling you to have a direct two-way conversation with another user. Talk is designed for users on the same system or connected on a local network. *ICQ* (*I Seek You*) is an Internet tool that notifies you when other users are online and enables you to communicate with them. ICQ works much like an instant messenger. With an *Internet Relay Chat* (*IRC*) utility, you can connect to a remote server where other users are also connected and talk with them.

Talk

You can use the **talk** utility to set up an interactive two-way communication between you and another user. **talk** operates more like a phone call—both you and the other user can type in messages simultaneously—where two people are constantly talking back and forth to each other. You initiate the communication by entering the **talk** command followed by the other user's address, usually the login name. This displays a message on the other user's screen asking if she wants to talk and giving your address. The user then responds with a **talk** command of her own, using your address. Both your screen and the other user's screen then split into two segments. The top segment displays what you type and the bottom segment displays what the other user types. Either user can end the session with an interrupt character, usually CTRL-C.

A K Desktop version of **talk** called **ktalk** displays user screens as panes in a K Desktop window. **ktalk** includes an address book and supports word wrap and file transfer features. **ktalkd** is a KDE-aware Talk daemon with answering machine features and forwarding capabilities. *GNU Talk* is a Gnome version of Talk that supports multiple clients, file transfers, encryption, shared applications, autoanswer, and call-forwarding. GNU Talk includes both clients and a daemon. The client can operate using different front ends such as Emacs, *screen-based cursors* (*curses*), X window system, Motif, and Gnome.

INTERNET

Among applications included with GNU Talk is one that enables you to draw pictures with another user.

ICQ Clients

The ICQ protocol enables you to communicate directly with other users online, but like an instant messenger utility. Using an ICQ client, you can send users messages, chat with them, or send files. You can set up a contact list of users who you may want to contact when they are online. You are then notified in real-time when they connect, and you can communicate with them if you wish. Several modes of communication are supported, include chat, message, e-mail, file transfer, or games. To use ICQ, you register with an ICQ server that provides you with an ICQ number, also known as a Universal Internet Number (UIN). You can find out more about the ICQ protocol at **www.mirabilis.com**.

Several Gnome-based ICQ clients are available for your use. Check the Gnome software map at **www.gnome.org** for new versions and recent updates. *GnomeICU* (formerly GtkICQ) is an ICQ client that can communicate with other ICQ users on any platform, whether Linux, Windows, or the Mac. You can find out more about GnomeICU at **gnomeicu.gdev.net**. Currently, GnomeICU features include message history for individual users, chat, messages, and sound events. File transfers will be supported in future updates. *Gicq* is a Gnome ICQ instant messenger client. You can currently use it to send and receive messages and to search for users to add to your client list. *kicq* and *KXicq* are K Desktop ICQ clients currently under development. They will support instant messaging, client lists, and other ICQ features.

Internet Relay Chat

Internet Relay Chat (IRC) operates like a chat room, where you can enter channels and talk to other users already there. First, you select an IRC server to connect to. Various servers are available for different locals and topics. Once connected to a server, you can choose from a list of channels to enter. The interface works much like a chat room. When you connect to the server, you can choose a nickname by which you will be referred. Several Internet Relay Chat clients are available for use on Linux systems. Most operate on either X Windows, KDE, or Gnome platforms. Irssi, X-Chat, and yaggIRC are Gnome IRC clients, though there are versions for other platforms. All have support for multiple concurrent server connections, multiple windows, DCC (Send Chat Voice and Resume), and Perl scripts. X-Chat has a plug-in interface for adding new features (see **xchat.linuxpower.org** for more details). Irssi has an easy-to-use interface with support for the Gnome panel. kvirc and kSirc are K Desktop IRC clients. Kvirc features an alias and events editor, DCC, and scripting. Xirc is an X Windows client.

Telnet

You use the **telnet** command to log in remotely to another system on your network. The system can be on your local area network or available through an Internet connection. Telnet operates as if you were logging into another system from a remote terminal. You will be asked for a login name and, in some cases, a password. In effect, you are logging into another account on another system. In fact, if you have an account on another system, you could use telnet to log into it. You invoke the **telnet** utility with the keyword **telnet**. If you know the name of the site you want to connect with, you can enter **telnet** and the name of the site on the Linux command line. As an alternative, you can use the K Desktop **kTelnet** utility. This provides a GUI interface to connecting and logging into remote systems.

```
$ telnet garnet.berkeley.edu
Connected to garnet
login:
```

The telnet program also has a command mode with a series of commands you can use to configure your connection. You can enter the telnet command mode either by invoking telnet with the keyword **telnet** or by pressing CTRL-] during a session. The telnet **help** command lists all the telnet commands you can use. A comprehensive list is available on the man pages (**man telnet**). In the next example, the user first invokes the **telnet** utility. A prompt is displayed next, indicating the command mode, **telnet>**. The telnet command **open** then connects to another system.

```
$ telnet
telnet> open garnet.berkeley.edu
Connected to garnet.berkeley.edu
login:
```

Once connected, you follow the login procedure for that system. If you are logging into a regular system, you must provide a login name and password. Once logged in, you are provided with the operating system prompt that, in the case of Linux or UNIX, will either be $ or %. You are then directly connected to an account on that system and can issue any commands you want. When you finish your work, you log out. This breaks the connection and returns you to the telnet prompt on your own system. You can then quit telnet with the **quit** command.

```
telnet> quit
```

When using telnet to connect to a site that provides public access, you needn't provide a login name or password. Access is usually controlled by a series of menus that restricts what you can do on that system.

If you are logging into a specific account on another system, you can use the -1 option to specify the login name of that account. This enables you to skip the login prompt. You can use the -1 option either with the telnet invocation on the command line or with the **open** command, as shown in the next examples. Here, the user is logging into a specific account called **dylan** on the **rose.berkeley.edu** system.

```
$ telnet rose.berkeley.edu -l dylan
telnet> open rose.berkeley.edu -l dylan
```

Remote Access Commands: rwho, rlogin, rcp, and rsh

The remote access commands were designed for smaller networks such as intranets. They enable you to log in remotely to another account on another system and to copy files from one system to another. You can also obtain information about another system, such as who is logged on currently. Many of the remote commands have comparable network communication utilities used for the Internet. For example, **rlogin**, which remotely logs into a system, is similar to telnet. The **rcp** command, which remotely copies files, performs much the same function as FTP. As an alternative to these remote commands, you can use the Secure Shell (SSL) commands for more secure connections; ssh scp, and slogin (see Chapter 31).

You can use several commands to obtain information about different systems on your network. You can find out who is logged in, get information about a user on another system, or find out if a system is up and running. For example, the **rwho** command functions in the same way as the **who** command. It displays all the users currently logged into each system in your network.

```
$ rwho
violet     robert:tty1    Sept 10 10:34
garnet     chris:tty2     Sept 10 09:22
```

The **ruptime** command displays information about each system on your network. The information shows how each system has been performing. **ruptime** shows whether a system is up or down, how long it has been up or down, the number of users on the system, and the average load on the system for the last five, ten, and fifteen minutes.

```
$ ruptime
violet     up     11+04:10,     8 users,   load 1.20 1.10     1.00
garnet     up     11+04:10,    20 users,   load 1.50 1.40     1.30
```

Remote Access Permission: .rhosts

You use a **.rhosts** file to control access to your account by users using TCP/IP commands. Users create the **.rhosts** file on their own accounts using a standard editor such as Vi. It must be located in the user's home directory. In the next example, the user displays the contents of a **.rhosts** file.

```
$ cat .rhosts
garnet chris
violet robert
```

The **.rhosts** file is a simple way to allow other people access to your account without giving out your password. To deny access to a user, simply delete the system's name and the user's login name from your **.rhosts** file. If a user's login name and system are in an **.rhosts** file, then that user can directly access that account without knowing the password. This type of access is unnecessary for remote login operations to work (you could use a password instead); the **.rhosts** file is required for other remote commands, such as remotely copying files or remotely executing Linux commands. If you want to execute such commands on an account in a remote system, that account must have your login name and system name in its **.rhosts** file.

The type of access **.rhosts** provides enables you to use TCP/IP commands to access other accounts directly that you might have on other systems. You do not have to log into them first. In effect, you can treat your accounts on other systems as extensions of the one you are currently logged into. Using the **rcp** command, you can copy any files from one directory to another no matter what account they are on. With the **rsh** command, you can execute any Linux command you want on any of your other accounts.

rlogin, rcp, and rsh

You may have accounts on different systems in your network or you may be permitted to access someone else's account on another system. You could access an account on another system by first logging into your own and then remotely logging in across your network to the account on the other system. You can perform such a remote login using the **rlogin** command, which takes as its argument a system name. The command connects you to the other system and begins login procedures.

Login procedures using **rlogin** differ from regular login procedures in that the user is not prompted for a login name. **rlogin** assumes the login name on your local system is the same as the login name on the remote system. Upon executing the **rlogin** command, you are immediately prompted for a password. After entering the password, you are logged into the account on the remote system. Once logged into a remote system, you can execute any command you want. You can end the connection with **exit**, CTRL-D, **~.**, or **logout** (TCSH or C-shell). **rlogin** assumes the login name on the remote system is the same as the one on the local system because most people use **rlogin** to access accounts they have on other systems with their own login name. When the login name on the remote system is different from the one on the local system, however, the **-1** option enables you to enter it. The syntax is shown here:

```
$ rlogin system-name -1 login-name
```

You can use the **rcp** command to copy files to and from remote and local systems. **rcp** is a file transfer utility that operates like the **cp** command, but across a network connection to a remote system. The **rcp** command requires the remote system to have your local system and login name in its **.rhosts** file. The **rcp** command begins with the keyword **rcp** and has as its arguments the source file and copy filenames. To specify the file on the remote system, you need to place the remote system name before the filename, separated by a colon. When you are copying a file on the remote system to your own, the source file is a remote file and requires the remote system's name. The copy file is a file on your own system and does not require a system name:

```
$ rcp remote-system-name:source-file   copy-file
```

In the next example, the user copies the file **wednesday** from the remote system violet to her own system and renames the file **today**.

```
$ rcp violet:wednesday today
```

You can also use **rcp** to copy whole directories to or from a remote system. The **rcp** command with the **-r** option copies a directory and all its subdirectories from one system to another. Like the **cp** command, **rcp** requires source and copy directories. The directory on the remote system requires the system name and colon be placed before the directory name. When you copy a directory from your own system to a remote system, the copy directory is on the remote system and requires the remote system's name. In the next example, the user copies the directory **letters** to the directory **oldnotes** on the remote system violet.

```
$ rcp -r letters violet:oldnotes
```

At times, you may need to execute a single command on a remote system. The **rsh** command executes a Linux command on another system and displays the results on your own. Your system name and login name must, of course, be in the remote system's **.rhosts** file. The **rsh** command takes two general arguments: a system name and a Linux command. The syntax is as follows:

```
$ rsh remote-system-name   Linux-command
```

In the next example, the **rsh** command executes an **ls** command on the remote system violet to list the files in the **/home/robert** directory on violet.

```
$ rsh violet ls /home/robert
```

Special characters are evaluated by the local system unless quoted. This is particularly true of special characters that control the standard output, such as redirection operators or pipes. The next example lists the files on the remote system and sends them to the standard output on the local system. The redirection operator is evaluated by the local system and redirects the output to **myfiles**, which is a file on the local system.

```
$ rsh violet ls /home/robert > myfiles
```

If you quote a special character, it becomes part of the Linux command evaluated on the remote system. Quoting redirection operators enables you to perform redirection operations on the remote system. In the next example, the redirection operator is quoted. It becomes part of the Linux command, including its argument, the file name **myfiles**. The **ls** command then generates a list of filenames that is redirected on the remote system to a file called **myfiles**, also located on the remote system.

```
$ rsh violet ls /home/robert '>' myfiles
```

The same is true for pipes. The first command (shown next) prints the list of files on the local system's printer. The standard output is piped to your own line printer. In the second command, the list of files is printed on the remote system's printer. The pipe is quoted and evaluated by the remote system, piping the standard output to the printer on the remote system.

```
$ rsh violet ls /home/robert | lpr
$ rsh violet ls /home/robert '|' lpr
```

UNIX to UNIX CoPy: UUCP

The UUCP protocols are an alternative set of protocols to those of the Internet (TCP/IP) that provide network communication between Linux and UNIX systems. However, UUCP is an older protocol designed to operate between systems not already connected on a network. With UUCP, one system can connect to another across phone lines at a predetermined time, sending a batched set of communications all at once. UUCP is helpful for making a direct connection to a particular system, transferring data, and then cutting the connection. UUCP enables you to set up direct modem-to-modem communication with another system.

UUCP has its own set of remote access commands: **uuto**, **uupick**, **uucp**, and **uux**. The **uuto** command mails files to other systems, while **uupick** receives those files. These commands are used for sending and receiving large files. The **uucp** command copies files from one system to another. The **uux** command remotely executes a Linux command on another system. Many of the UUCP commands correspond to the TCP/IP remote access commands. **uucp** operates much like **rcp** and **uux** like **rsh**. UUCP commands are subject to the same permission restrictions as your own local commands. Protected files and directories cannot be accessed; only files and directories with the other user permission set can be accessed.

You can think of UUCP commands as referencing files on other Linux systems through a mail system. These commands are designed to operate using point-to-point communication. This is as if you were using the mail capabilities of different systems to implement a network. When you issue a UUCP command for a given system, the command is queued and collected with other commands for that same system. The commands are then mailed to that system for execution. Once that system receives the commands and executes them, it mails back any results. Several systems can arrange to receive and send commands to each other, forming a UUCP network. The entire process then depends on each system in the network sending and receiving commands to and from other systems. In this respect, the network is only as strong as its weakest link. On the other hand, it requires no special structure, only the sending and receiving of what are essentially messages.

The Complete Reference

Linux

Part IV

Servers

The
Complete
Reference

Chapter 15

Internet Servers

Reflecting the close relationship between UNIX and the development of the Internet, Linux is particularly good at providing Internet services, such as the Web, FTP, and e-mail. In the case of the Web, instead of only accessing other sites, you can set up your own Linux system as a Web site. Other people can then access your system using Web pages you created or download files you provide for them. A system that operates this way is called a *server*, and is known by the service it provides. You can set up your system to be a Web server or an ftp server, connecting it to the Internet and turning it into a site others can access. A single Linux system can provide several different services. Your Linux system can be a Web server and an ftp server, as well as a Mail and News server, all at the same time. One user could download files using your ftp services, while another reads your Web pages. All you have to do is install and run the appropriate server software for each service. Each one operates as a continually running daemon looking for requests for its particular services from remote users.

When you install Red Hat, you have the option of installing several Internet servers, including Web and ftp servers. Red Hat was designed with Internet servers in mind. A standard install installs these servers automatically and configures them for you. Every time you start your system, you also start the Web and ftp server daemons. Then, to turn your Linux system into a Web server, all you have to do is create Web pages. For an ftp server, you only have to place the files you want to make available in the ftp directories.

You can operate your Linux system as a server on the Internet, an intranet (local area network), or to service only the users on your own system. To operate servers as Internet servers, you must obtain a connection to the Internet and provide access to your system for remote users. Access is usually a matter of enabling anonymous logins to directories reserved for server resources. Red Hat systems are already configured to enable such access for Web and ftp users. Connections to the Internet that can accommodate server activity can be difficult to find. You may need a dedicated connection or you may need to use a connection set up by an *Internet service provider* (*ISP*). You are no longer connecting only yourself to the Internet, but you are allowing many other users to make what could be a great many connections to you through the Internet. If you only want to provide the services to a *local area network* (*LAN*), you don't need a special connection. Also, you can provide these services to users by allowing them to connect over a modem and to log in directly. Users could dial into your system and use your Web pages or use ftp to download files. Furthermore, users with accounts on your own machine can also make use of the servers. In whatever situation you want to use these services, you need the appropriate server software installed and running. This chapter examines how servers are started and stopped on your system, as well as different ways of accessing the servers.

Starting Servers: Standalone and inetd

A server is a daemon that runs concurrently with your other programs, continuously looking for a request for its services, either from other users on your system or from remote users connecting to your system through a network. When it receives a request from a user, a server starts up a session to provide its services. For example, if users want to download a file from your system, they can use their own ftp client to request your ftp server start a session for them. In the session, they can access and download files from your system. Your server needs to be running for a user to access its services. For example, if you set up a Web site on your system with HTML files, you must have the **httpd** Web server program running before users can access your Web site and display those files. See Chapters 16 and 17 on how to install ftp and Web servers.

You can start a server in several ways. One way is to do it manually from the command line by entering the name of the server program and its arguments. When you press ENTER, the server starts, although your command line prompt reappears. The server runs concurrently as you perform other tasks. To see if your server is running, you can enter the following command to list all currently running processes. You should see a process for the server program you started. To refine the list, you can add a **grep** operation with a pattern for the server name you want. The second command lists the process for the Web server.

```
# ps -aux
# ps -aux | grep 'httpd'
```

On Redhat systems, you can also use special startup scripts to start and stop your server manually. These scripts are located in the **/etc/rc.d/init.d** directory and have the same name as the server programs. For example, the **/etc/rc.d/init.d/httpd** script with the start option starts the Web server. Using this script with the stop option stops it. These scripts are explained in greater detail later in this chapter.

```
/etc/rc.d/init.d/httpd stop
/etc/rc.d/init.d/httpd start
```

Instead of manually executing all the server programs each time you boot your system, your system can automatically start the servers for you. You can do this in two ways, depending on how you want to use a server. You can have a server running continuously from the time you start your system until you shut it down, or you can have the server start only when it receives a request from a user for its services. If a server is being used frequently, you may want to have it running all the time. If it is used rarely, you may only want the server to start when it receives a request. For example, if you are running a Web site, your Web server is receiving requests all the time from remote hosts on the Internet. For an ftp site, however, you may receive requests infrequently, in which case you may want to have the ftp server start only when it receives a request. Of course, certain ftp sites receive frequent requests, which would warrant a continually running ftp server.

A server that starts automatically and runs continuously is referred to as a *standalone* server. Red Hat uses the SysV Init procedure to start servers automatically whenever your system boots. This procedure use special startup scripts for the servers located in the **/etc/rc.d/init.d** directory. Red Hat systems already configured the Web server to start automatically and to run continuously. A script for it is in the **/etc/rc.d/init.d** directory called **httpd**.

To start the server only when a request for its services is received, you configure it using the **inetd** daemon, known as the *Internet Superserver*. **inetd** looks for server requests, and then starts up the server when a request comes through. The Washington University ftp server (**wu-ftpd**), which is installed on Red Hat systems, is configured to run under **inetd**. **wu-ftpd** starts only when someone initiates an ftp session with your system. You can find an entry for the ftp server in the **/etc/inetd.conf** configuration file, but no script for it is in **/etc/rc.d/init.d**, as is for the Web server.

If you add, change, or delete server entries in the **/etc/inetd.conf** file, you will have to restart the **inetd** daemon for these changes to take effect. To restart the **inetd** daemon, you can use the **/etc/rc.d/init.d/inet** script with the **restart** argument, as shown here:

```
# /etc/rc.d/init.d/inet restart
```

You can also use the **inet** script to start and stop the **inetd** daemon. Stopping the daemon effectively shuts down all the servers that **inetd** manages (those listed in the **/etc/inetd.conf** file).

```
# /etc/rc.d/init.d/inet stop
# /etc/rc.d/init.d/inet start
```

Standalone Server Tools

On Red Hat systems, the System V Runlevel Editor, Linuxconf, and the KDE System V Editor all provide simple interfaces you can use to choose what servers you want started up and how you want them to run. You can start up the System V Editor by selecting the System Editor icon in the Red Hat Control Panel, which you can access from the System menu on Gnome or AnotherLevel.

The System V Runlevel Editor features a GUI interface to enable you to manage any daemons on your system easily—Internet servers as well as system daemons, such as print servers. The Runlevel Editor window is divided into three major panes. To the left is a scroll window labeled "available" that lists all the daemons available for use on your system. These include the daemons for Internet servers, such as httpd. Below are buttons for operations you can perform on the server daemons: add, remove, edit, and execute. To the right, taking up most of the window, are an upper pane and a lower pane. The upper pane has four scroll windows, one for each run level. These list the daemons currently configured to run in their respective run levels. The lower pane also holds four scroll windows, one for each run level. These are daemons that will be shut down if you switch to that respective run level. System administrators can switch from one level to another. All the servers that start up under normal processing are listed in the start runlevel 3 scroll window.

To start or stop a server manually, click its entry in the available scroll window, and then click the Execute button. This displays a small window with the various options to start or stop the selected server. To stop the httpd server, click its entry in the available scroll window, and then click the Stop button in the displayed window. Use the same procedure to restart the server, clicking the Start button. You can also configure a server to start automatically when you boot at a certain run level. You can boot your system to operate at certain runlevels, each specified by a given number, such as the standard multiuser level (runlevel 3), a graphical login level (runlevel 5), and an administrative level (runlevel 1). See Chapter 20 for a discussion on runlevels. To have a server start at a given runlevel, select its entry in the available scroll window, and then click the Add button. A window appears where you can select the runlevel and whether you want to start or stop the server. To have a server automatically start up when you boot normally, make sure it is listed in the runlevel 3 start scroll window. If not, click its entry in the available window and select Start and runlevel 3 in the window displayed. The server is then added to the list in the runlevel 3 start scroll window. For example, if you don't want your Web server to start when you boot, click the httpd entry in the runlevel 3 start list and click the Remove button. To have the Web server start again whenever you boot, click its entry in the available window, and then click the Add button, selecting Start and runlevel 3 in the window that appears. httpd is then added to the runlevel 3 start list. Figure 15-1 shows the System V Runlevel Editor with the Execute and Add windows.

Servers that operate under inetd are not listed by the System V Runlevel Editor. The FTP wu-ftpd server is installed by Red Hat to run under inetd, so you won't find entries for them here. The System V Editor reads its list of servers from the server scripts in the **/etc/rc.d/init.d** directory. If you add a new script, you can have the System V Editor rescan that directory and you then see it appear in the available list. Removing a server from a runlevel window only removes its link in the corresponding runlevel **rc.d** directory. It does not touch the startup script in the **init.d** directory. Adding in the server to the Start runlevel window, puts the link back in that runlevel directory. Adding a server to a Stop window adds a *K* link in the corresponding **rc.d** directory, which stops a server when the system switches to that run level. For example, if you

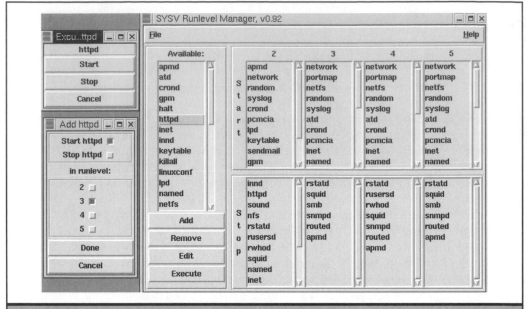

Figure 15-1.   *System V Runlevel Editor with Execute and Add windows*

remove httpd from the runlevel 3 start window, then the **S85httpd** link in the **rc3.d** directory is deleted. Adding **httpd** back to the runlevel 3 start window recreates the **S85htppd** link in the **rc3.d** directory. Adding **httpd** to the runlevel 2 stop directory would create a **K85httpd** link in the **rc2.d** directory, shutting down the server when switching to runlevel 2.

You can also control the startup of a server using Linuxconf. The Control service activity panel, located in the Control panel list, lists various services available on your system (see Figure 15-2). You can click check boxes to enable or disable them. Disabling a service removes its startup link in the **rc.d** directory. For example, disabling the Web server removes the **S85httpd** link in the **rc3.d** directory. Enabling the service restores that link.

If you change the configuration of a server, you may need to start and stop it several times as you refine the configuration. Several servers provide special management tools that enable you to perform this task easily. The **apachectl** utility enables you to start and stop the Apache Web server easily. It is functionally equivalent to using the /tec/rc.d/init.d/httpd script to start and stop the server. For the domain name server, the **ndc** utility enables you to start and stop the named server.

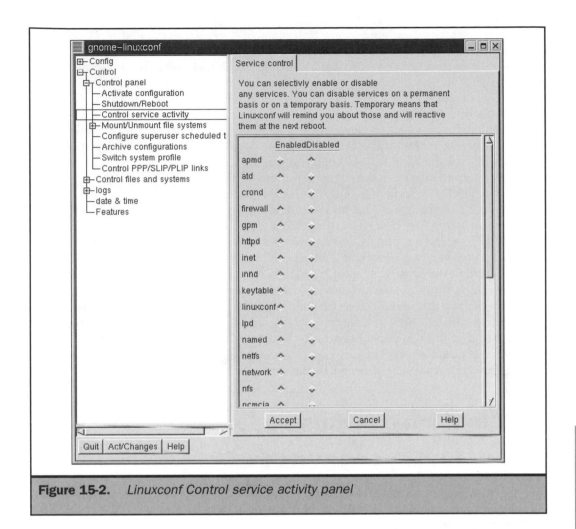

Figure 15-2. *Linuxconf Control service activity panel*

Linuxconf Server Configuration

Linuxconf provides configuration interfaces for most Internet servers. Configuration
interfaces exist for the Apache Web server, the BIND domain name server, the
Washington University ftp server, and the Sendmail mail server, among others.
Linuxconf has both a cursor-based interface, which can be run from a shell command
line, and a Gnome and X-windows interface that uses an expandable tree to display
entries for different panels. On Red Hat Linux, you can find an entry for Linuxconf in

the Gnome start menu under Systems. You can also start it from the Red Hat Control Panel. If no menu entry exists, you can start a terminal window and enter the command **linuxconf**. You can also use a **netconf** command to display a window with panels only for network and server tasks. Click the server panel to display the list of buttons for servers you can configure. When using the main Linuxconf utility, select Server tasks under Networking.

Panels for various configuration components are displayed with entries for different features. Different panels display buttons for basic operations, such as accept, add, delete, and help. Clicking the Help button displays a window providing detailed documentation for the current panel and the configuration process for that server. Once you make your entries and click the Act/changes button to accept the configuration, linuxconf generates the appropriate configuration files for you. For example, if you use linuxconf to configure your Domain Name Service server, it generates the **named.conf** file and any needed zone files. Configuring the wu-ftpd ftp server generates a new **/etc/ftpaccess** file. Configuring the Apache Web server generates new **httpd.conf**, **srm.conf**, and **access.conf** files. Many servers have an extensive set of features that only need to be turned on or off, rather than given a value. For these, linuxconf provides check buttons, enabling you to include a feature by clicking its button. The server configurations currently require certain linuxconf modules to be loaded: Mailconf, dnsconf, apache, and wu-ftpd. Current distributions configure linuxconf to do this automatically. You can manually add modules by selecting the Linuxconf modules panel in the Control files and systems list and entering the module name. Figure 15-3 shows the panel for the ftp server (wu-ftpd) configuration.

SysV Init: init.d Scripts

Red Hat manages the startup and shutdown of server daemons using special startup scripts located in the **/etc/rc.d/init.d** directory. These scripts often have the same name as the server's program. For example, for the **/usr/sbin/httpd** Web server program, a corresponding script is called **/etc/rc.d/init.d/httpd**. This script actually starts and stops the Web server. This method of using **init.d** startup scripts to start servers is called *SysV Init*, after the method used in UNIX System V.

The startup scripts in the **/etc/rc.d/init.d** directory can be executed automatically whenever you boot your system. Be careful when accessing these scripts, however. These start essential programs, such as your network interface and your printer daemon. These init scripts are accessed from links in subdirectories set up for each possible run level. In the **/etc/rc.d** directory, is a set of subdirectories whose names have the format **rc***N*.**d**, where *N* is a number referring to a run level. The **rc** script detects the run level in which the system was started, and then executes only the startup scripts specified in the subdirectory for that run level. The default run level is 3, the multiuser level. When you start your system, the **rc** script executes the startup scripts specified in the **rc3.d** directory. The **rc3.d** directory holds symbolic links to certain startup scripts in the **/etc/rc.d/init.d** directory. So, the **httpd** script in the **/etc/rc.d/init.d** directory is

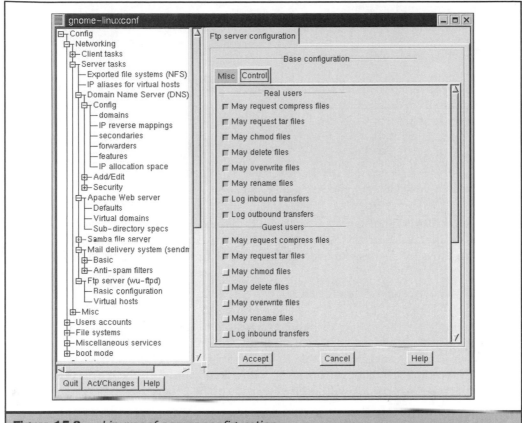

Figure 15-3. *Linuxconf server configuration*

actually called through a symbolic link in the **rc3.d** directory. The symbolic link for the **/etc/rc.d/httpd** script in the **rc3.d** directory is **S85httpd**. The *S* prefixing the link stands for *startup* and calls the corresponding **init.d** script with the start option. **S85httpd** invokes **/etc/rc.d/init.d/httpd** with the option **start**. The numbers in these links are simply there for ordering purposes. If you change the name of the link to start with a *K*, then the script is invoked with the **stop** option, stopping it. To have a server start automatically, first create a startup script for it in the **/etc/rc.d/init.d** directory, and then create a symbolic link to that script in the **/etc/rc.d/rc3.d** directory. The startup script **httpd** used on Red Hat systems is shown here. You can see the different options listed under the case statement: start, stop, status, restart, and reload. If no option is provided (*), then the script use syntax is displayed. The **httpd** script first executes a script to define functions used in these startup scripts. The **daemon** function with **httpd** actually executes the **/usr/sbin/httpd** server program.

```
echo -n "Starting httpd: "
   daemon httpd
   echo
   touch /var/lock/subsys/httpd
```

The **killproc** function shuts down the daemon. The lock file and process ID file (**httpd.pid**) are then deleted.

```
killproc httpd
echo
rm -f /var/lock/subsys/httpd
rm -f /var/run/httpd.pid
```

daemon, **killproc**, and **status** are shell scripts defined in the **functions** script also located in the **inet.d** directory. The **functions** script is executed at the beginning of each startup script to activate these functions. A list of these functions is provided in Table 15-1.

```
. /etc/rc.d/init.d/functions
```

The beginning of the startup script holds tags used to configure the server. These tags begin with an initial # and are used to provide runtime information about the service to your system. The tags are listed in Table 15-1 along with the startup functions. You enter a tag with a preceding # symbol, the tag name with a colon, and then the tag arguments. For example, the processname tag will specify the name of the program being executed, in this example httpd:

```
# processname: httpd
```

If your script starts up more than one daemon, you should have a processname entry for each. For example, the samba service starts up both the **smdb** and **nmdb** daemons.

```
# processname: smdb
# processname: nmdb
```

The end of the tag section is indicated by an empty line. After this line, any line beginning with a # is treated as a comment. The chkconfig line will list the default runlevels that the service should start up on, along with the start and stop priorities. The following entry lists runlevels 3, 4, and 5 with a start priority of 85 and a stop of 15:

```
# chkconfig: 345 85 15
```

With the description you enter a short description of the service, using the \ symbol before a newline to use more than one line. **pidfile** indicates the file where the server process id is held. With config tags, you specify the configuration files the server may use. In the case of the Red Hat Apache Web server, there are three configuration files:

```
# config: /etc/httpd/conf/access.conf
# config: /etc/httpd/conf/httpd.conf
# config: /etc/httpd/conf/srm.conf
```

Init Script Functions	Description
daemon [+/-*nicelevel*] *program* [*arguments*] [&]	Starts a daemon, if it is not already running
killproc *program* [*signal*]	Sends a signal to the program; by default it sends a SIGTERM, and if the process doesn't stop, it sends a SIGKILL. It will also remove any pidfiles if it can.
pidofproc *program*	Used by other function, it determines the pid of a program
status *program*	Displays status information
Init Script Tags	**Description**
# **chkconfig**: *startlevellist startpriority endpriority*	Required. Specifies the default startlevels for this service as well as start and end priorities.
# **description** [*ln*]: *description of service*	Required. The description of the service, continued with '\' characters. Use an initial # for any added lines. With the *ln* option you can specify the language the description is written in.
# **autoreload**: *true*	Optional. If this line exists, the daemon checks its configuration files and reloads them automatically when they change.
# **processname**: *program*	Optional, multiple entries allowed. Name of the program or daemon started in the script.

Table 15-1. *System V Init Script Functions and Tags*

Init Script Tags	Description
# config: *configuration-file*	Optional, multiple entries allowed. Specify a configuration file used by the server. If the filename is unspecified, the server automatically loads the file as the term autoreload.
# pidfile: *pid-file*	Optional, multiple entries allowed. Specifies the pid file.
# probe: *true*	Optional. Used *in place* of autoreload, processname, config, and pidfile entries to automatically probe and start the service.

Table 15-1. *System V Init Script Functions and Tags* (continued)

As an example, the Web server startup script is shown here. It has the same name as the Web server daemon, **httpd**:

```
/etc/rc.d/init.d/httpd

#!/bin/sh
#
# Startup script for the Apache Web Server
#
# chkconfig: 345 85 15
# description: Apache is a World Wide Web server.  It is used to \
#          serve HTML files and CGI.
# processname: httpd
# pidfile: /var/run/httpd.pid
# config: /etc/httpd/conf/access.conf
# config: /etc/httpd/conf/httpd.conf
# config: /etc/httpd/conf/srm.conf


# Source function library.
. /etc/rc.d/init.d/functions

# See how we were called.
case "$1" in
```

```
    start)
     echo -n "Starting httpd: "
     daemon httpd
     echo
     touch /var/lock/subsys/httpd
     ;;
    stop)
     killproc httpd
     echo
     rm -f /var/lock/subsys/httpd
     rm -f /var/run/httpd.pid
     ;;
    status)
     status httpd
     ;;
    restart)
     $0 stop
     $0 start
     ;;
    reload)
     echo -n "Reloading httpd: "
     killproc httpd -HUP
     echo
     ;;
    *)
     echo "Usage: $0 {start|stop|restart|reload|status}"
     exit 1
   esac

   exit 0
```

The RPM packaged versions for an Internet server includes the startup script for that server. Install the RPM package installs the script in the **/etc/rc.d/init.d** directory and creates its appropriate links in the runlevel directories, such as **/etc/rc.h/rc3.d.** If you decide, instead, to create the server using its source code files, you can then manually install the startup script. If no startup script exists, you first make a copy of the **httpd** script, renaming it, and edit it to replace all references to **httpd** with the name of the server daemon program. Then, place the copy of the script in the **/etc/rc.d/init.d** directory and make a symbolic link to the **/etc/rc.d/rc3.d** directory. Or, you could use the System V Runlevel Editor to create the link in the **/etc/rc.d/rc3.d** directory. Have the editor scan the **init.d** directory by selecting Re-scan from the File menu, click the entry in the Available listing, click the Add button, and then select the Runlevel and Start options in the Add window. When you start your system now, the new server is automatically started up, running concurrently and waiting for requests.

If you want to change a server from using inetd to a standalone process, first create a startup script for it in the **/etc/rc.d/init.d** directory with a link to it in the **rc3.d** directory. Then you have to remove or comment out its entry in the **/etc/inetd.conf** configuration file. To change a server from a standalone process to using inetd, you first remove its link in the **/etc/rc.d/rc3.d** directory and any other runlevel directory, and then place an entry for it in the **inetd.conf** file. For example, the ProFTP ftp server can run as a standalone or an inetd server. If it is running as an inetd server, and you want to run it as a standalone server, you first set up a Sys V Init script for it in the **/etc/rc.d/init.d** directory (ProFTP provides one). Place a symbolic link for it in the **rc3.d** directory. The name of the standalone ProFTP server program is **proftpd**. Then disable **inetd** management of the ProFTP server by commenting out or removing its entry in the **inetd.conf** file. The server name used in this file is **in.proftpd**.

inetd Server Management

If your system averages only a few requests for a specific service, you don't need the server for that service running all the time. You only need it when a remote user is accessing its service. The **inetd** daemon manages Internet servers, invoking them only when your system receives a request for their services. **inetd** checks continuously for any requests by remote users for a particular Internet service and, when it receives a request, it then starts the appropriate server daemon. For example, the Washington University ftp daemon, wu-ftpd, is installed by Red Hat to run using inetd, rather than as a standalone daemon. When **inetd** receives a request from a user to access ftp, it starts **in.ftpd**, the ftp daemon. **in.ftpd** then handles the request, enabling the remote user to download files.

For **inetd** to call the appropriate server daemon, it must be configured for that service. You place entries for that server in the **/etc/services** and the **/etc/inetd.conf** files. The **/etc/services** file lists services available on your system. An entry in **/etc/services** consists of the name of the service followed by its port and protocol, separated by a slash. Entries for ftp as they appear in your Red Hat **/etc/service** file are shown here. Other distributions may require only one entry for ftp.

```
ftp-data      20/tcp
ftp           21/tcp
```

The **/etc/inetd.conf** file is the **inetd** configuration file. For this entry, you specify the service, its protocol, and the server program to invoke. An entry for ftp is shown here. Server paths and arguments may vary according to different Linux distributions. Some programs have a special script, link, or alternate program to use for **inet.d** activation, instead of directly using the program file. Such scripts or links begin with the prefix "in" and a period, followed by the program name. For example, the ProFTP server is called **proftpd**, but uses **in.proftpd** as the program name in an **inetd.conf** entry. Other programs, such as the Apache Web server, use the same program name—in this case, **httpd**.

```
#<service> <sock_type> <proto> <flags> <user> <server_path>    <args>
ftp        stream       tcp     nowait  root  /usr/sbin/in.ftpd in.ftpd
```

For some services, the configuration lines may exist, but they may be commented out with a preceding # symbol. Remove the #. If no configuration entries exist, you need to add them. The standard entries in inetd.conf for Internet services are shown here:

```
# These are standard services.
#
ftp     stream  tcp  nowait  root  /usr/sbin/in.ftpd  in.ftpd -l -a
telnet  stream  tcp  nowait  root  /usr/sbin/in.telnetd  in.telnetd
gopher  stream  tcp  nowait  root  /usr/sbin/in.gn  gn
```

tcpd

You can use the **tcpd** daemon to add another level of security to **inetd** managed servers. Set up **tcpd** to monitor a server connection made through **inetd**. **tcpd** verifies remote user identities and checks to make sure they are making valid requests. With **tcpd**, you can also restrict access to your system by remote hosts. Lists of hosts are kept in the **hosts.allow** and **hosts.deny** files. Entries in these files have the format **service:hostname:domain**. The domain is optional. For the service, you can specify a particular service, such as ftp, or you can enter **ALL** for all services. For the hostname, you can specify a particular host or **ALL** for all hosts. In the following example, the first entry allows access by all hosts to the Web service, **http**. The second entry allows access to all services by the **pango1.train.com** host. The third and fourth entries allow **rabbit.trek.com** and **sparrow.com** ftp access.

```
http:ALL
ALL:pango1.train.com
ftp:rabbit.trek.com
ftp:sparrow.com
```

The **hosts.allow** file holds hosts to which you allow access. If you want to allow access to all but a few specific hosts, you can specify **ALL** for a service in the **hosts.allow** file, but list the ones you are denying access to in the **hosts.deny** file. Using IP addresses instead of hostname is more secure because hostnames can be compromised through the DNS records by spoofing attacks where an attacker pretends to be another host. The **tcpd** Man pages (**man tcpd**) provide more detailed information about **tcpd**.

To have **tcpd** monitor a server, you have to place the pathname for **tcpd** in the pathname field of a server's entry for the **inetd.conf** file. This is what has already been done for the **ftpd** server entry in the RedHat inetd.conf file. Instead of the pathname for the **ftpd** program, **/usr/sbin/in.ftpd**, there is the pathname for the **tcpd** daemon, **/usr/sbin/tcpd**. The argument field that follows then lists the **in.ftpd** server program.

```
# <service> <sock_type> <proto> <flags> <user>  <server_path>   <args>
ftp          stream     tcp     nowait  root    /usr/sbin/tcpd  in.ftpd
```

When **inetd** receives a request for an ftp service, it calls the **tcpd** daemon, which then takes over and monitors the connection. Then it starts up the **in.ftpd** server program. By default, **tcpd** allows all requests. To allow all requests specifically for the ftp service, you would enter the following in your **/etc/hosts.allow** file. The entry **ALL:ALL** opens your system to all hosts for all services.

```
ftp:ALL
```

The standard Internet services listed in the Red Hat **/etc/initd.conf** file all use the **tcpd** daemon, as shown here:

```
# These are standard services.
#
ftp     stream tcp nowait root /usr/sbin/tcpd  in.ftpd -l -a
telnet  stream tcp nowait root /usr/sbin/tcpd  in.telnetd
```

The Complete Reference

Chapter 16

FTP Servers

The *File Transfer Protocol* (*FTP*) is designed to transfer large files across a network from one system to another. Like most Internet operations, FTP works on a client/server model. FTP client programs can enable users to transfer files to and from a remote system running an FTP server program. Chapter 12 discusses FTP clients. Any Linux system can operate as an FTP server. It only has to run the server software—an FTP daemon with the appropriate configuration. Transfers are made between user accounts on client and server systems. A user on the remote system has to log in to an account on a server and can then transfer files to and from that account's directories only. A special kind of user account, called *FTP*, that allows any user to log in to it with the user name "anonymous." This account has its own set of directories and files that are considered public, available to anyone on the network who wants to download them. The numerous FTP sites on the Internet are FTP servers supporting FTP user accounts with anonymous login. Any Linux system can be configured to support anonymous FTP access, turning them into network FTP sites. Such sites can work on an intranet or on the Internet. On Red Hat systems, the configuration files for anonymous FTP are in a package beginning with the term anonftp. Installing this package sets up your FTP directories and configures the FTP account.

FTP Daemons

FTP server software consists of an FTP daemon and configuration files. The *daemon* is a program that continuously checks for FTP requests from remote users. When a request is received, it manages a login, sets up the connection to the requested user account, and executes any `ftp` commands the remote user sends. For anonymous FTP access, the FTP daemon allows the remote user to log in to the FTP account using anonymous as the user name. The user then has access to the directories and files set up for the FTP account. As a further security measure, however, the daemon changes the root directory for that session to be the FTP **home** directory. This hides the rest of the system from the remote user. Normally, any user on a system can move around to any directories open to him. A user logging in with anonymous FTP can only see the FTP **home** directory and its subdirectories. The remainder of the system is hidden from that user. By default, the FTP server also requires a user be using a valid shell. It checks for a list of valid shells in the **/etc/shells** file. Most daemons have options for turning off this feature.

Several FTP server daemons are available for use on Linux systems. Most Linux distributions come with the Washington University FTP server called *wu-ftpd*. You can download RPM package updates from **updates.redhat.com**. The daemon software begins with the term wu-ftpd. You can obtain the original compressed archive from the Washington University archive at **http://wuarchive.wustl.edu/packages/wuarchive-ftpd**.

ProFTPD is a newer and popular FTP daemon based on an Apache Web server design. It features simplified configuration and support for virtual FTP hosts. Although not currently included with most distributions, you can download RPM packages from **contrib.redhat.com**. The package begins with the term *proftpd*. The compressed archive of the most up-to-date version, along with documentation, is available at the ProFTPD Web site at **www.proftpd.org**. Another FTP daemon, *ncftpd*, is a commercial product produced by the same programmers who did the ncftp FTP client. ncftpd is free for academic use and features a reduced fee for small networks. Check **www.ncftpd.org** for more information.

The Red Hat distribution currently installs the wu-ftpd server and the **anon** anonymous FTP package during installation. At that time, directories are created where you can place files for FTP access. The directories have already been configured to control access by remote users, restricting use to only the FTP directories and any subdirectories. The directory reserved for your FTP files is **/home/ftp**. Place the files you want to allow access to in the **/home/ftp/pub** directory. You can also create subdirectories and place files there. Once connected to a network, a remote user can connect to your system and download files you placed in **/home/ftp/pub** or any of its subdirectories. The Red Hat FTP server installations implement a default configuration. You can change these if you want. If you are installing an FTP server yourself, you need to know the procedures detailed in the following sections to install an FTP server and create its data directories.

Anonymous FTP: anon

An anonymous FTP site is essentially a special kind of user on your system with publicly accessible directories and files in its **home** directory. Anyone can log in to this account and access its files. Because anyone can log in to an anonymous FTP account, you must be careful to restrict a remote FTP user to only the files on that anonymous FTP directory. Normally, a user's files are interconnected to the entire file structure of your system. Normal users have write access that lets them create or delete files and directories. The anonymous FTP files and directories can be configured in such a way that the rest of the file system is hidden from them and remote users are given only read access. In ProFTPD, this is achieved through configuration directives placed in its configuration file. An older approach used by wu-ftpd involves having copies of certain system configuration, command, and libraries files placed within the FTP **home** directory. These are placed in directories that restrict access by other users. Within the FTP **home** directory, you then have a publicly accessible directory that holds the files you want to make available to remote users. This directory usually has the name **pub**, for public.

An FTP site is made up of an FTP user account, an FTP **home** directory, and certain copies of system directories containing selected configuration and support files. Newer FTP daemons, such as ProFTPD, do not need the system directories and support files. Most distributions, including Red Hat, have already set up an FTP user account when you installed your system. On systems that support RPM package installation, such as

Red Hat, you can use the anon rpm package to set up the **home** directory and the copies of the system directories. If you do not have access to the anon package, you may have to create these system directories yourself.

The FTP User Account: anonymous

To allow anonymous FTP access to your system by other users, you must have a user account named *ftp*. Most distributions, such as Red Hat, have already created this account for you. If your system does not have such an account, you will have to create one. You can then place restrictions on the ftp account to keep any remote FTP users from accessing any other part of your system. You must also modify the entry for this account in your **/etc/passwd** file to prevent normal user access to it. The following is the entry you find in your **/etc/passwd** file on Red Hat systems that sets up an FTP login as an anonymous user:

```
ftp:*:14:50:FTP User:/home/ftp:
```

The asterisk in the password field blocks the account. This prevents any other users from gaining access to it, thereby, gaining control over its files or access to other parts of your system. The user ID, 14, is a unique ID. The comment field is FTP User. The login directory is **/home/ftp**. When FTP users log in to your system, this is the directory in which they are placed. If a **home** directory has not been set up, create one and then change its ownership to the FTP user with the **chown** command.

The group ID is the ID of the **ftp** group, which is set up only for anonymous FTP users. You can set up restrictions on the **ftp** group, thereby restricting any anonymous FTP users. Here is the entry for the **ftp** group you find in the **/etc/group** file. If your system does not have one, you should add it.

```
ftp::50:
```

Anonymous FTP Server Directories

On most distributions, the FTP **home** directory is **/home/ftp**. When users login anonymously, they are placed in this directory. An important part of protecting your system is preventing remote users from using any commands or programs not in the restricted directories. For example, you would not let a user use your **ls** command to list filenames because **ls** is located in your **/bin** directory. At the same time, you want to let the FTP user list filenames using an **ls** command. Newer FTP daemons like ProFTPD solve this problem by creating secure access to needed system commands and files, while restricting remote users to only the FTP site's directories. Another more traditional solution, used by wu-ftpd, is to create copies of certain system directories and files needed by remote users and to place them in the **/home/ftp** directory where users can access them. A **bin** directory is placed in the **/home/ftp** directory and remote users are restricted to it, instead of the system's **bin** directory. Whenever they use the **ls** command, remote users are using the **bin** directory in **/home/ftp/bin**, not the one you use in **/bin**.

On systems that support RPM installation, such as Red Hat, you can use the **anon** rpm package to set up these copies of system directories and files. Otherwise, you may have to create these directories and support files yourself. The **anon** package installs **etc**, **bin**, and **lib** directories in the **/home/ftp** directory. These contain localized versions of system files needed to let an FTP client execute certain FTP commands, such as listing files or changing directories. The **/home/ftp/etc** directory contains versions of the password and group configuration files, the **/home/ftp/bin** directory contains copies of shell and compression commands, and the **lib** directory holds copies of system libraries. The directories set up by the anon package are shown here:

```
/home/ftp
/home/ftp/bin
/home/ftp/etc
/home/ftp/lib
/home/ftp/pub
```

The **/home/ftp/etc** directory holds a copy of your **passwd** and **group** files. Again, the idea is to prevent any access to the original files in the **/etc** directory by FTP users. The **/home/ftp/etc/passwd** file should not include any entries for regular users on your system. All entries should have their passwords set to ***** to block access. The **group** file should not include any user groups and all passwords should be set to *****.

```
/home/ftp/etc/passwd
root:*:0:0:::
bin:*:1:1:::
operator:*:11:0:::
ftp:*:14:50:::
nobody:*:99:99:::

/home/ftp/etc/group
root::0:
bin::1:
daemon::2:
sys::3:
adm::4:
ftp::50:
```

If, for some reason, you do not have access to the anon package, you can set up the anonymous FTP directories yourself. Again, remember, if you are using ProFTPD, you do not need any of these files, except the **home** directory. You must use the **chmod** command to change the access permissions for the directories so remote users cannot access the rest of your system. Create a **/home/ftp** directory and use the **chmod** command with the permission 555 to turn off write access: **chmod** 555 /home/ftp. Next, make a new **bin** directory in the **/home/ftp** directory, and then make a copy of the **ls** command and place it in **/home/ftp/bin**. Do this for any commands you want to make available to FTP users. Then create a **/home/ftp/etc** directory to hold a copy of your **passwd** and **group** files. Again, the idea is to prevent any access to the original files in the **/etc** directory by FTP users. The **/home/ftp/etc/passwd** file should be edited to remove any entries for regular users on your system. All other entries should have their passwords set to ***** to block access. For the **group** file, remove all user groups and set all passwords to *****. Create a **/home/ftp/lib** directory, and then make copies of the libraries you need to run the commands you placed in the **bin** directory. Some libraries make use of the **/dev/zero** file. For these, you have to create a **/home/ftp/dev** directory and use **mknod** to make a copy of the **/dev/zero** device file and place it in this directory.

Anonymous FTP Files

A directory named **/home/ftp/pub** usually holds the files you are making available for downloading by remote FTP users. When FTP users log in, they are placed in the **/home/ftp** directory and they can then change to the **/home/ftp/pub** directory to start accessing those files. Within **/home/ftp/pub**, you can add as many files and directories as you want. You can even designate some directories as upload directories, enabling FTP users to transfer files to your system.

In each directory set up under **/home/ftp/pub** to hold FTP files, you should create a **readme** file and an **index** file as a courtesy to FTP users. The **readme** file contains a brief description of the kind of files held in this directory. The **index** file contains a listing of the files and a description of what each one holds.

Permissions

Technically, any remote FTP user gaining access to your system is considered a user and, unless restricted, could access other parts of your file system, create directories and files, or delete the ones already there. Permissions can be used to restrict remote users to simple read access, and the rest of your file system can be hidden from the FTP directories. The anon package and the ProFTPD daemon already implement these restrictions. If you are manually creating your anonymous FTP files, you must be sure to set the permission correctly to restrict access.

Normally, a Linux file structure interconnects all the directories and files on its system. Except where prevented by permissions set on a directory or file, any user can access any directory or file on your system. Technically, any remote FTP user gaining anonymous access is an anonymous user and, as a user, could theoretically access an unrestricted directory or file on your system. To restrict FTP users to the **/home/ftp** directory and its subdirectories, the rest of the file structure must be hidden from them. In effect, the **/home/ftp** directory should appear to be the root directory, as far as FTP users are concerned. The real root directory, **/**, and the rest of the directory structure remain hidden. The FTP daemon attains this effect by using the **chroot** command to make the **/home/ftp** directory appear as a root directory, with the FTP user as the argument. When a remote FTP user issues a **cd /** command to change to the root, he always changes to the **/home/ftp** directory.

As a further restriction, all the directories that hold commands in **/home/ftp**, as well as the commands themselves, should be owned by the root, not by the FTP user. In other words, no FTP user should have any control over these directories. The root has to own **/home/ftp/bin**, **/home/ftp/etc**, and all the files they contain. The anon package already has set the ownership of these directories to the root. If you need to set them manually, you can use the **chown** command. The following example changes the ownership of the **/home/ftp/bin** directory to the root:

```
# chown root  /home/ftp/bin
```

Permissions for the FTP directories should be set to allow access for FTP users. You recall that three sets of permissions exist—read, write, and execute for the owner, the group, and others. To allow access by FTP users, the group and other permissions for directories should be set to both read and execute. The execute permission allows FTP users to access that directory, and the read permission allows listing the contents of the directory. Directories should not allow write permission by FTP users. You don't want them to be able to delete your directories or make new ones. For example, the **/home/ftp/bin** directory needs both read and execute permissions because FTP users have to access and execute its commands. This is particularly true for directories, such as **/home/ftp/pub**, which hold the files for downloading. It must have both read and execute permissions set.

You, as the owner of the directories, may need write permission to add new files or subdirectories. Of course, you only need this when you are making changes. To add further security, you could set these directories at just read and execute, even for the owner when you are not making changes. You can set all permissions to read and execute with the **chmod** command and the number 555 followed by the directory name. This sets the owner, group, and other permissions to read and execute. The permissions currently in place for the FTP directories set up by the anon package are designated by the number 755, giving the owner write permission.

```
# chmod 555 /home/ftp/bin
```

Permissions for files within the **/home/ftp/bin** and other special FTP directories can be more restrictive. Some files only need to be read, while others must be executed.

Files in the **/home/ftp/bin** or **/home/ftp/lib** directories only have to be executed. These could have their permissions set to 555. Files in the **/home/ftp/etc** directory such as **passwd** and **group** should have their permissions set to 111. They only have to be read. You always use the **chmod** command to set permissions for files, as shown in the following example. The **anon** package sets these permissions at read and execute, 555. For other distributions, you may have to set them yourself.

```
# chmod 111 /home/ftp/etc/passwd
```

FTP Server Tools

Both the wu-ftpd and ProFTPD daemons provide a set of FTP tools you can use to manage your FTP server. With the **ftpshut** command, you can smoothly shut down a running server, warning users of the shutdown well before it happens. **ftpwho** can tell you who is currently connected and what they are doing. **ftpcount** can give you the number of connections currently in effect. Although each daemon has its own set of tools, they perform the same action with much the same set of options. Tools provided by both ProFTPD and wu-ftpd have the same name and options, though ProFTPD provides more information on virtual hosts and has some added options.

ftpshut

With the **ftpshut** command, you can have the FTP server shut down at a given time, rather than suddenly shutting it down by killing its process. This gives you the chance to warn users the server is shutting down and not to start any long downloads. **ftpshut** takes several options for specifying the time and including a warning message. **ftpshut** takes as its arguments the time until the shutdown, followed by the warning message you want sent to users. The time can be a word such as "now" that effects an immediate shutdown, a + sign with the number of minutes remaining, or a specific time of day indicated by an HHMM format, where HH is the hour in a 24-hour cycle and MM is the minute. Shutdown disables new FTP access ten minutes before a scheduled shutdown, though this can be changed using the **-l** option with the number of minutes you want. Five minutes before a scheduled shutdown, all current connections are disconnected. You can adjust the time with the **-d** options. The warning message is formatted at 75 characters and you can use special formatting symbols for in-place substitutions of certain values in the warning message, such as the shutdown time. These symbols are called *magic cookies.* For example, **%s** is the shutdown time, **%r** is the time when new connections are refused, **%d** is the time when current connections are cut, **%M** is the maximum number of users, and **%L** is the local hostname.

ftpwho and ftpcount

With the **ftpwho** command, you can find out who is currently connected to your FTP server. **ftpwho** shows the current process information for each user. The output displays five fields: the process ID, the tty connection, the status of the connection, the amount of CPU time used so far for the process, and the connection details. The status of the connection is *R* for running, *S* for sleeping, and *Z* for crashed. The connection details include the Internet address from where the connection is made, the user making the connection, and the task currently being performed, such as downloading a file. The field begins with the name of the FTP daemon, usually **ftpd**, followed by the different segments separated by colons.

    ftpcount displays the number of users connected to your FTP server, broken down according to the classes specified in your **.ftpaccess** file. Along with the number of users, it shows the maximum number allowed to connect.

The Washington University FTP Daemon: wu-ftpd

The Washington University FTP daemon is currently the most widely used FTP server on Linux systems. It is the FTP server installed by most Linux distributions. The name of the Washington University FTP daemon is wu-ftpd. wu-ftpd options are shown in Table 16-1. wu-ftpd must be running to allow FTP access by remote users. As with other servers, you can start the FTP server at boot time, through **inetd** when a request is received, or directly from the command line. By default, the wu-ftpd server is installed to run using inetd. The use of inetd for the servers is described in detail in the previous chapter. The command name for the FTP server invoked by inetd is **in.ftpd.** This is a link to the wu-ftpd command. If you want to run your server continually (like a Web server), you have to set up an init script for it in the **/etc/rc.d/init.d** directory, so it starts when you boot your system. You can also start the FTP server directly from the command line by entering the **wu-ftpd** command with any options or arguments. The wu-ftpd server can be called with several options. Usually, it is called with the **-l** option that allows logins. The **-t** and **-T** options set timeouts for users, cutting off those that have no activity after a certain period of time. The **-d** option displays debugging information, and **-u** sets the umask value for uploaded files.

wu-ftpd Server Configuration Files

You can use numerous configuration options to tailor your FTP server to your site's particular needs. wu-ftpd makes use of several configuration files located in the **/etc** directory. All begin with the pattern **ftp**. The primary configuration file is named

Option	Effect
-d	Writes debugging information to the syslog
-l	Logs each FTP session in the syslog
-t*seconds*	Sets the inactivity timeout period to specified seconds (default is 15 minutes)
-T*seconds*	The maximum timeout period allowed when timeout is set by user (default is two hours)
-a	Enables use of the **ftpaccess(5)** configuration file
-A	Disables use of the **ftpaccess(5)** configuration file
-L	Logs commands sent to the **ftpd** server to the syslog
-i	Logs files received by **ftpd** to **xferlog**
-o	Logs files transmitted by **ftpd** to the syslog

Table 16-1.   `wu-ftpd` Options

ftpaccess. Here, you provide basic server information and access for specified directories. The **ftphosts**, **ftpusers**, and **ftpgroups** control access by systems, particular users, and groups. **ftpconversions** specifies how archive and compression operations are to be performed on files before or after they are transferred. **xferlog** is the log file that stores a running log of all transactions perform by the server. You can also configure your wu-ftpd server using Linuxconf (see Chapter 21).

ftpaccess

The **ftpaccess** file determines capabilities users have when they gain access to your FTP site. Access, information, permissions, logging, and several miscellaneous capabilities can be designated. You can have entries that create aliases for certain directories, display a message when FTP users login, or prevent anonymous users from deleting files. A **loginfails** entry determines the number of login tries a user can make before being cut off, and the **email** entry specifies the e-mail address of the FTP administrator. The Man page for **ftpaccess** lists the possible entries. The **ftpaccess** file with the configuration used on Red Hat systems is shown in this section. For commonly used **ftpaccess** entries, see Table 16-2. For more detailed information, check the **ftpaccess** Man page and wu-ftpd documentation.

Access Capabilities	Description
`autogroup` *group classglob* [*classglob...*]	This allows access to a groups read-only files and directories by particular classes of anonymous users. *group* is a valid group from **/etc/group**.
`class` *class typelist addrglob* [*addrglob...*]	Defines *class* of users, with source addresses of the form *addrglob. typelist* is a comma-separated list of the user types: anonymous, guest, and real.
`deny` *host-addrglob message_file*	Always deny access to host(s) matching *host-addrglob. message_file* is displayed.
`guestgroup` *groupname* [*groupname...*]	Allow guest access by a real user, where the user is a member of the specified group. A password entry for the guest user specifies a **home** directory within the FTP site directories.
`limit` *class n times message_file*	Limit class to *n* users at times—*times*, displaying *message_file* if access is denied.
`noretrieve` *file-list*	Deny retrieval ability of these files.
`loginfails` *number*	After *number* login failures, terminate the FTP connection. Default value is 5.
`private` *yes*	*no*	The user becomes a member of the group specified in the group access file **ftpgroups**.
Informational Capabilities	
`banner` *file*	The banner is displayed before login. File requires full pathname.
`email` *email-address*	Defines the e-mail address of the FTP manager.

Table 16-2.   */etc/ftpaccess* `wu-ftpd` *Configuration File*

Access Capabilities	Description
message *file* { *when* { *class* ...}}	FTP displays the contents of the *file* at login time or upon changing directories. The **when** parameter may be LOGIN or CWD=*dir*; *dir* specifies the directory that displays the message when entered. Magic cookies can be in the message file that cause the FTP server to replace the cookie with a specified text string, such as the date or the user name.
readme *file* { *when* { *class*}}	The user is notified at login time or upon using a change working directory command (**cd**) that *file* exists and was modified on such-and-such date.
Logging Capabilities	
log commands *typelist*	Enables logging of individual commands by users.
log transfers *typelist directions*	Enables logging of file transfers. *directions* is a comma-separated list of the terms "inbound" and "outbound," and logs transfers for files sent to the server and sent from the server.
Miscellaneous Capabilities	
alias *string dir*	Defines an alias, string, for a directory.
cdpath *dir*	Defines an entry in **cdpath**. This defines a search path used when changing directories.
compress yes | no *classglob* [*classglob* **tar** yes | no *classglob* [*classglob*...]...]	Enables **compress** or **tar** capabilities for any class matching of *classglob*. The actual conversions are defined in the external file **ftconversion**.
shutdown *path*	If the file pointed to by *path* exists, the server checks the file regularly to see if the server is going to be shut down.

Table 16-2.   /etc/ftpaccess **wu-ftpd** Configuration File (continued)

Access Capabilities	Description
virtual *address* root | banner | logfile *path*	Enables the virtual FTP server capabilities.
Permission Capabilities	Allows or disallows the ability to perform the specified function. By default, all users are allowed.
chmod yes | no *typelist*	Allow or disallow changing file permissions.
delete yes | no *typelist*	Allow or disallow deleting files, **rm**.
overwrite yes | no *typelist*	Allow or disallow modifying files.
rename yes | no *typelist*	Allow or disallow renaming files, **mv**.
umask yes | no *typelist*	Allow or disallow file creation permissions.
passwd-check *none* | *trivial* | *rfc822* (*enforce* | *warn*)	Define the level and enforcement of password checking done by the server for anonymous FTP.
path-filter *typelist mesg allowed_charset* { *disallowed regexp*...}	For users in *typelist*, **path-filter** defines regular expressions that control what a filename can or cannot be. Multiple disallowed *regexps* may occur.
upload *root-dir dirglob* yes | no *owner group mode* ["dirs" | "nodirs"]	Define a directory with *dirglob,* which permits or denies uploads.

Table 16-2.   /etc/ftpaccess **wu-ftpd** Configuration File (continued)

In the **ftpaccess** file, you set capabilities for different types of users, called *classes*. Three different types of users exist: anonymous, guest, and real. *Anonymous users* are any users using the anonymous login name. *Guest users* can be those with special guest accounts or access. A *real user* is one who has an account on the system and is using an FTP connection to access it. You can define your own class using the **class** option. In the **ftpaccess** file shown here, a class called **all** is created that consists of all users of the anonymous, guest, and real types.

The message entry specifies a file with the message to be displayed and when that message is to appear. You can have one message appear when users log in and other messages displayed when users enter certain directories. For example, the following entry will display the message in the **/welcome.msg** file when a user logs in:

```
message /welcome.msg          login
```

To set permissions, you use the command followed by a yes or a no and then a list of the user types or classes. In the **ftpaccess** file shown here, all users can perform **tar** and **compress** operations, but anonymous and guest users are prohibited from using **chmod**, **delete**, **overwrite**, and **rename** operations. They also cannot erase files, modify them, or change their names or permissions.

/etc/ftpaccess

```
class    all    real,guest,anonymous    *
email root@localhost
loginfails 5
readme       README*       login
readme       README*       cwd=*
message      /welcome.msg login
message      .message      cwd=*
compress     yes           all
tar          yes           all
chmod        no            guest,anonymous
delete       no            guest,anonymous
overwrite    no            guest,anonymous
rename       no            guest,anonymous

log transfers anonymous,real inbound,outbound
shutdown /etc/shutmsg
passwd-check rfc822 warn
```

ftphosts

You use the **ftphosts** file to allow or deny access by other host computers to your FTP site. When the remote system accesses your systems, it does so by logging in as a registered user. Access is made through a user account already set up on your system. You allow the remote host to log in as a certain specific user or deny access as a certain user. You could use this kind of control to allow or deny anonymous access to the FTP user by a remote host.

The file **ftphosts** has two kinds of entries: one for allowing access and the other for denying access. Entries to allow access begin with the keyword **allow**, then the user account on your system to which the host is allowed access, followed by the address of the remote host. The address can be a pattern that can be used to match several hosts. You can use any of the filename generation symbols (see Chapter 9). Entries to deny access begin with the keyword **deny**, then the user account on your system to which the host is denied access, followed by the address of the remote host. The terms **deny** and **allow** can be misleading. **allow** is a much more restrictive control, whereas **deny** is a much more open control. **allow** only allows access by the remote host to the specified account. No other access is permitted. You could use **allow** to permit a remote host anonymous access only. **deny**, on the other hand, only denies access to the specified account. You could use **deny** to deny anonymous access by a certain system, but not any direct FTP access from one user to another.

ftpusers and ftpgroups

The **ftpusers** files list users that cannot be accessed through FTP. For example, the root user should not be accessible through an FTP connection, even if you knew the password. **ftpgroups** is a group access file that allows FTP users to become members of specified groups on your system. This file lists special group passwords. For these to work, the private entry must be set to yes in the **ftpaccess** file.

ftpconversions

The **ftpconversions** file holds possible FTP conversions for compression and archive operations. It operates as an FTP conversions database, listing all possible conversions. A default **ftpconversions** file is included with the installation package that already has entries for the most common conversion operations. Each line in the file is a record of eight fields, with the fields separated by colons. The fields are strip prefix and postfix, addon prefix and postfix, external command, types, options, and a description. The prefix and postfix fields refer to changes made to the filename after the specified action is performed. The strip postfix removes a specified suffix from a filename, and the add postfix adds a suffix. For example, a gzipped compressed file has a suffix of **.gz**. If the command is to compress a file with gzip, then the add postfix entry should have the **.gz** placed in it. When the file is compressed, **.gz** is added to the end. If you were decompressing a file with gunzip, then you would want to remove the **.gz** suffix. For this, you would place **.gz** in the strip postfix field. The strip and add prefix fields perform the same kind of action, but for prefixes.

The external command is the command you would use to convert the file. You can list command options after the command. The filename you are operating on is specified with **%s**, usually placed after any options. For example, you would use the **tar** command to extract a **.tar** archived file and gunzip to decompress a **.gz** file. The type field lists the type of files that can be operated on by the command. These can be regular files, character files, or directories as indicated by the entries **T_REG**, **T_ASCII**, and **T_DIR**. You can specify more than one entry by placing a | between them. The options field specifies the type of operation the command performs. Currently, options exist for compression, decompression, and use of the **tar** command: **O_COMPRESS**, **O_UNCOMPRESS**, and **O_TAR**. You can list more than one by separating them with a | symbol. The description provides some documentation as to what the conversion operation does. Here is the **ftpconversion** file used on Red Hat systems.

```
:.Z:   :   :/bin/compress -d -c
%s:T_REG|T_ASCII:O_UNCOMPRESS:UNCOMPRESS
:   :   :.Z:/bin/compress -c %s:T_REG:O_COMPRESS:COMPRESS
:.gz:   :   :/bin/gzip -cd %s:T_REG|T_ASCII:O_UNCOMPRESS:GUNZIP
:   :   :.gz:/bin/gzip -9 -c %s:T_REG:O_COMPRESS:GZIP
:   :   :.tar:/bin/tar -c -f - %s:T_REG|T_DIR:O_TAR:TAR
:   :   :.tar.Z:/bin/tar -c -Z -f -


%s:T_REG|T_DIR:O_COMPRESS|O_TAR:TAR+COMPRESS
:   :   :.tar.gz:/bin/tar -c -z -f -


%s:T_REG|T_DIR:O_COMPRESS|O_TAR:TAR+GZIP
```

FTP Log File: xferlog

This file contains log information about connections and tasks performed by your
FTP server. On Red Hat systems, this file is found in the **/var/log** directory. On other
systems, this file may be on the **/usr/adm** directory. The file is made up of server
entries, one on each line. The entry is divided into several fields separated by
spaces. The fields are: current-time, transfer-time, remote-host, file-size, filename,
transfer-type, special-action-flag, direction, access-mode, username, service-name,
authentication-method, and authenticated-user-id. The *transfer-time* is the time in
seconds for the transfer. The *remote-host* is the address of the remote system making
the connection and *username* is the name of the user on that system. The *transfer-type* is
either an *a* for ASCII or *b* for binary. The *access-mode* is the method by which the user
logged in: *a* for anonymous, *g* for guest, and *r* for a real login (to another account on
your system). The direction is either *o* for outgoing or *i* for incoming.

Professional FTP Daemon: ProFTPD

ProFTPD is based on the same design as the Apache Web server, implementing a
similar simplified configuration structure and supporting such flexible features as
virtual hosting. ProFTPD rpm packages are available from the Red Hat contrib site at
contrib.redhat.com and contrib mirror sites. Unlike other FTP daemons, you needn't
include directories of system files for FTP commands. No special **bin** or **etc** files are
needed. You can set it up to alternate automatically between inetd startups or as a
standalone server constantly running, depending on the system load.

ProFTPD's tools operate in the same way as the wu-ftpd tools. **ftpshut** shuts down the
system at specified times with warnings. With ProFTPD, you can shut down a virtual host
while the main server continues to run. **ftpwho** displays a list of all remote users currently
connected, broken down according to virtual hosts and servers. **ftpcount** shows the
number of current connections by server and virtual hosts. See the previous section on
FTP tools for more information.

Install and Startup

If you install ProFTPD using Red Hat RPM packages, the required configuration entries are made in your **proftpd.conf** files. If you installed from compiled source code, you may have to modify the entries in the default **proftpd.conf** file provided. Make sure the FTP user and group specified in the **proftpd.conf** file actually exist.

You can run ProFTPD either as a standalone process or from inetd. Make sure the appropriate entry is made in the ServerType directive in your **proftpd.conf** file. Unlike wu-ftpd, the RPM package, by default, installs proftpd to run as a standalone server, setting the ServerType to standalone. **ProFTPD** options are listed in Table 16-3. A startup script named **proftpd** is placed in the **/etc/inet.d** directory that starts up the daemon when you boot your system. A standalone process is continually running. If you want to run **proftpd** as an inetd process, you first must change the ServerType to inetd and disable the **proftpd** startup script in the **/etc/rc.d/inet.d** directory.

When you run ProFTPD from inetd, make sure the appropriate entry is in the **inetd.conf** file. If you were running wu-ftpd previously, you must change this entry to run proftpd. The RPM package implements an **in.proftpd** link to the **proftpd** daemon. Use this link to invoke ProFTPD in the **inetd.conf** file. The ProFTPD inetd entry looks like this:

```
ftp stream tcp nowait root /usr/sbin/in.proftpd in.proftpd
```

Option	Description
-h, --help	Use description, including options.
-n, --nodaemon	Runs the proftpd process in standalone mode (must also specify standalone as ServerType in the configuration file).
-v, --version	Displays ProFTPD version number.
-d, --debug *debuglevel*	Sets proftpd's internal debug level (1–5).
-c, --config *config-file*	Specifies alternate configuration file.
-p, --persistent 0|1	Disables (0) or enables (1) the default persistent password support, which is determined at configure time for each platform.
-l, --list	Lists all modules compiled into proftpd.

Table 16-3. *ProFTPD Daemon Startup Options*

Red Hat systems use TCP wrappers for their inetd entries. The inetd entry looks like this.

```
ftp stream tcp nowait root  /usr/sbin/tcpd  in.proftpd
```

proftpd.config and .ftpaccess

ProFTPD uses only one configuration file, named **proftpd.conf**, located in the **/etc** directory. Configuration entries take the form of directives. This format is purposely modeled on Apache configuration directives. With the directives, you can enter basic configuration information, such as your server name, or perform more complex operations, such as implementing virtual FTP hosts. The design is flexible enough to enable you to define configuration features for particular directories, users, or groups.

To configure a particular directory, you can use an **.ftpaccess** file with configuration options placed within that directory. These **.ftpaccess** options take precedence over those in the **proftpd.conf** directory. **.fptaccess** files are designed to operate like **.htaccess** files in the Apache Web server that configure particular Web site directories. You can find a complete listing of ProFTPD configuration parameters at the ProFTPD Web site (**www.proftpd.org**) and in the ProFTPD documentation installed in **/usr/doc** as part of the ProFTPD software package. Several of the more commonly used parameters are listed in Table 16-4. When creating a new configuration, you should

Directive	Description
AccessGrantMsg *message*	Response message sent to an FTP client indicating the user has logged in or anonymous access has been granted. The magic cookie **'%u'** is replaced with the username specified by the client. Default: Dependent on login type Context: server config, <VirtualHost>, <Anonymous>, <Global>
Allow ["from"]"all"|"none" *| host	network* [,*host	network* [,...]]	Used inside a <Limit> context to specify explicitly which hosts and/or networks have access to the commands or operations being limited. Used with Order and Deny to create access control rules. Default: Allow from all Context: <Limit>

Table 16-4. *ProFTPD Configuration Directives, proftpd.conf*

Directive	Description
AllowAll	Allows access to a <Directory>, <Anonymous> or <Limit> block Default: Default is to implicitly AllowAll, but not explicitly Context: <Directory>, <Anonymous>, <Limit>, .ftpaccess
AllowForeignAddress *on | off*	Allows clients to transmit foreign data connection addresses that do not match the client's address. Default: AllowForeignAddress off Context: server config, <VirtualHost>, <Anonymous>, <Global>
AllowGroup *group-expression*	List of groups allowed in a limit block. Default: None Context: <Limit>
AllowUser *user-expression*	Users allowed access. Default: None Context: <Limit>
AnonRequirePassword *on | off*	Requires anonymous logins to enter a valid password that must match the password of the user that the anonymous daemon runs as. This is used to create guest accounts that function like anonymous logins, but require a valid password. Default: AnonRequirePassword off Context: <Anonymous>
<Anonymous *root-directory>*	Create an anonymous FTP login, terminated by a matching </Anonymous> directive. The root-directory parameters are the directory proftpd first moves to and then **chroot**, hiding the rest of the file system. Default: None Context: server config,<VirtualHost>

Table 16-4.   *ProFTPD Configuration Directives, proftpd.conf* (continued)

SERVERS

Directive	Description
AuthGroupFile *path*	Alternate group's file with the same format as the system **/etc/group** file. Default: None Context: server config, <VirtualHost>, <Global>
AuthUserFile *path*	Alternate **passwd** file with the same format as the system **/etc/passwd** file. Default: None Context: server config, <VirtualHost>, <Global>
Bind *address*	Allows additional IP addresses to be bound to a main or VirtualHost configuration. Multiple Bind directives can be used to bind multiple addresses. Default: None Context: server config, <VirtualHost>
DefaultRoot *directory* *[group-expression]*	Default root directory assigned to user on login. The group-expression argument restricts the DefaultRoot directive to a group or set of groups. Default: DefaultRoot /Context: server config, <VirtualHost>, <Global>
Deny ["from"]"all"|"none"| *host* | *network* **[,***host* | *network* **[,...]]**	List of hosts and networks explicitly denied access to a given <Limit> context block. **all** indicates all hosts are denied access. **none** indicates no hosts are explicitly denied. Default: None Context: <Limit>
DenyAll	Deny access to a directory, anonymous FTP, or limit block. Default: None Context: <Directory>, <Anonymous>, <Limit>, .ftpaccess

Table 16-4.   *ProFTPD Configuration Directives, proftpd.conf* (continued)

Directive	Description
DenyUser *user-expression*	Users denied access within a limit block. Default: None Context: <Limit>
<Directory *pathname***>**	Directory-specific configuration. Used to create a block of directives that apply to the specified directory and its subdirectories. Default: None Context: server config, <VirtualHost>, <Anonymous>, <Global>
DisplayFirstChdir *filename*	Specifies the text file displayed to a user the first time he changes into a given directory during an FTP session. Default: None Context: server config, <VirtualHost>, <Anonymous>, <Directory>, <Global>
DisplayLogin *filename*	Specifies the text file displayed to a user who logs in. Default: None Context: server config, <VirtualHost>, <Anonymous>, <Global>
<Global>	Global configuration block is used to create a set of configuration directives applied universally to both the main server configuration and all VirtualHost configurations. Default: None Context: server config, <VirtualHost>
<Limit *command*	*command-group* [*command2 ..*] **>**	Access restrictions on FTP commands, within a given context. The *command-group* refers to groupings of commands as defined in the ProFTPD documentation. Default: None Context: server config, <VirtualHost>, <Directory>, <Anonymous>, <Global>, .ftpaccess

Table 16-4.   *ProFTPD Configuration Directives, proftpd.conf* (continued)

SERVERS

Directive	Description
LsDefaultOptions *"options string"*	Default options for directory listings (as in the **ls** command) Default: None Context: server config, <VirtualHost>, <Global>
MaxClients *number* | *none message*	Maximum number of connected clients allowed. The message specified is displayed when a client is refused connection. Default: MaxClients none Context: server config, <Anonymous>, <VirtualHost>, <Global>
MaxLoginAttempts *number*	Maximum number of times a client may attempt to log in to the server during a given connection. Default: MaxLoginAttempts 3 Context: server config, <VirtualHost>, <Global>
Order *allow,deny* | *deny,allow*	Configures the order Allow and Deny directives are checked inside of a <Limit> block. Default: Order allow,deny Context: <Limit>
PersistentPasswd *on* | *off*	When on, proftpd, during login, opens the system-wide **/etc/passwd**, **/etc/group** files, accessing them even during a **chroot** operation that changes the root directory. Default: Platform dependent Context: server config
RequireValidShell *on* | *off*	Allow or deny logins not listed in **/etc/shells**. By default, proftpd disallows logins if the user's default shell is not listed in **/etc/shells**. Default: RequireValidShell on Context: server config, <VirtualHost>, <Anonymous>, <Global>

Table 16-4. *ProFTPD Configuration Directives, proftpd.conf* (continued)

Directive	Description
ScoreboardPath *path*	Directory that holds proftpd run-time Scoreboard files. Default: ScoreboardPath /var/run Context: server config
ServerAdmin *"admin-email-address"*	E-mail address of the server or virtual host administrator. Default: ServerAdmin root@[ServerName] Context: server config, \<VirtualHost\>
ServerType *type-identifier*	The server daemon's operating mode, either inetd or standalone. Default: ServerType standalone Context: server config
TimeoutIdle *seconds*	Maximum number of seconds proftpd allows clients to stay connected without any activity. Default: TimeoutIdle 600 Context: server config
Umask *octal-mask*	Permissions applied to newly created file and directory within a given context. Default: None Context: server config, \<Anonymous\>, \<VirtualHost\>, \<Directory\>, \<Global\>, .ftpaccess
User *userid*	The user the proftpd daemon runs as. Default: None Context: server config, \<VirtualHost\>, \<Anonymous\>, \<Global\>
UserAlias *login-user userid*	Maps a login name used by a client to a user ID on the server. A client logging in as login-user is actually logged in as user ID. Often used inside an \<Anonymous\> block to allow specified login-names to perform an anonymous login. Default: None Context: server config, \<VirtualHost\>, \<Anonymous\>, \<Global\>

Table 16-4.   *ProFTPD Configuration Directives, proftpd.conf* (continued)

SERVERS

Directive	Description
`<VirtualHost address>`	Configuration directives that apply to a particular hostname or IP address. Often used with virtual servers that run on the same physical machine. The block is terminated with a </VirtualHost> directive. By using the Port directive inside a VirtualHost block, creating a virtual server that uses the same address as the master server, but that listens on a separate TCP port is possible. Default: None Context: server config

Table 16-4.   *ProFTPD Configuration Directives, proftpd.conf* (continued)

make a copy of the **proftpd.conf** configuration file and modify it. Then you can test its syntax using the **proftpd** command with the **-c** option and the name of the file.

```
proftpd -c newfile.conf
```

Different kinds of directives exist. Many set values, such as MaxClients, which set the maximum number of clients, or NameServer, which sets the name of the FTP server. Others create blocks that can hold directives that apply to specific FTP server components. Block directives are entered in pairs: a beginning directive and a terminating directive. The terminating directive defines the end of the block and consists of the same name, beginning with a slash. Block directives take an argument that specifies the particular object to which the directives will apply. For the Directory block directive, you must specify a directory name to which it will apply. The <Directory *mydir*> block directive creates a block whose directives within it apply to the *mydir* directory. The block is terminated by a </Directory> directive. <Anonymous *ftp-dir*> configures the anonymous service for your FTP server. You need to specify the directory on your system used for your anonymous FTP service, such as **/home/ftp**. The block is terminated with the </Anonymous> directive. The <VirtualHost *hostaddress*> block directive is used to configure a specific virtual FTP server and must include the IP or the domain name address used for that server. </VirtualHost> is its terminating directive. Any Directives you place within this block are applied to that virtual FTP server. The <Limit *permission*> directive specifies the kind of access you want to limit. It takes as its argument one of several keywords indicating the kind of permission to be controlled: **WRITE** for write access, **READ** for read access, **STOR** for transfer access (uploading), and **LOGIN** to control user login.

A sample of the standard **proftpd.conf** file installed as part of the ProFTPD software package is shown here. Notice the default ServerType is standalone. If you want to use inetd to run your server, you must change this entry to inetd. Detailed examples of **proftpd.conf** files, showing various anonymous FTP and virtual host configurations, can be found with the ProFTPD documentation, located in **/usr/doc**, and on the ProFPTD Web site at **www.proftpd.org**.

proftpd.conf

```
# This is a basic ProFTPD configuration file (rename it to
# 'proftpd.conf' for actual use.  It establishes a single server
# and a single anonymous login.  It assumes that you have a user/group
# "nobody" and "ftp" for normal operation and anon.


ServerName              "ProFTPD Default Installation"
ServerType              standalone
DefaultServer           on


# Port 21 is the standard FTP port.
Port            21
Umask           022
MaxInstances            30


# Set the user and group that the server normally runs at.
User            nobody
Group           nobody


# Normally, we want files to be overwriteable.
<Directory /*>
  AllowOverwrite        on
</Directory>


# A basic anonymous configuration, with one incoming directory.
<Anonymous ~ftp>
  User            ftp
  Group           ftp
  RequireValidShell       off
  MaxClients            10
  # We want clients to be able to login with "anonymous" as well as "ftp"
  UserAlias             anonymous ftp

  # We want 'welcome.msg' displayed at login, and '.message' displayed
  # in each newly chdired directory.
  DisplayLogin          welcome.msg
  DisplayFirstChdir       .message
```

```
# Limit WRITE everywhere in the anonymous chroot except incoming
<Directory *>
  <Limit WRITE>
      DenyAll
  </Limit>
</Directory>

<Directory incoming>
  <Limit WRITE>
    AllowAll
  </Limit>
  <Limit READ>
    DenyAll
  </Limit>
</Directory>

</Anonymous>
```

Anonymous Access

You use the Anonymous configuration directive to create an anonymous configuration block in which you can place directives that configure your anonymous FTP service. The directive includes the directory on your system used for the anonymous FTP service. The ProFTPD daemon executes a **chroot** operation on this directory, making it the root directory for the remote user accessing the service. By default, anonymous logins are supported, expecting users to enter their e-mail address as a password. You can modify an anonymous configuration to construct more controlled anonymous services, such as guest logins and required passwords. For ProFTPD, your anonymous FTP directory does not require any system files. Before ProFTPD executes a **chroot** operation, hiding the rest of the system from the directory, it accesses and keeps open any needed system files outside the directory.

The following example shows a standard anonymous FTP configuration. The initial Anonymous directive specifies **/home/ftp** as the anonymous FTP **home** directory. The User directive specifies the user the Anonymous FTP daemon will run as and Group indicates its group. In both cases, FTP, the standard user name, is used on most systems for anonymous FTP. A Directory directive with the * file matching character then defines a Directory block that applies to all directories and files in **/home/ftp**. The * symbol matches on all filenames and directories. Within the Directory directive is a Limit directive that places restrictions on the **WRITE** capabilities of users. Within the Limit directive, the DenyAll directive denies write permission, preventing users from creating or deleting files, effectively giving them only read access. A second Directory directive creates an exception to this rule for the incoming directory. An incoming directory is usually set up on FTP sites to let users upload files. For this Directory, the first Limit directive prevents both **READ** and **WRITE** access by users with its DenyAll directive, effectively preventing users from deleting or reading files here. The second

Limit directive lets users upload files, however, permitting transfers only (**STOR**) with the AllowAll directive.

One important directive for anonymous FTP configurations is the RequireValidShell. By default, the FTP daemon first checks to see if the remote user is attempting to log in using a valid shell, such as the Bash shell or the C-shell. The FTP daemon obtains the list of valid shells from the **/etc/shells** file. If the remote user does not have a valid shell, a connection is denied. You can turn off the check using the RequireValidShell directive and the `off` option. The remote user can then log in using any kind of shell.

```
<Anonymous /home/ftp>
    User ftp
    Group ftp
    UserAlias anonymous ftp
    RequireValidShell off
 <Directory *>
        <Limit WRITE>
            DenyAll
        </Limit>
    </Directory>
      # The only command allowed in incoming is STOR
      # (transfer file from client to server)
    <Directory incoming>
        <Limit READ WRITE>
            DenyAll
        </Limit>
        <Limit STOR>
            AllowAll
        </Limit>
    </Directory>
</Anonymous>
```

Recall that FTP was originally designed to let a remote user connect to an account of her own on the system. Users can log in to different accounts on your system using the FTP service. Anonymous users are restricted to the anonymous user account. However, you can create other users and their **home** directories that also function as anonymous FTP accounts with the same restrictions. Such accounts are known *as guest accounts.* Remote users are required to know the user name and, usually, the password. Once connected, they only have read access to that account's files; the rest of the file system is hidden from them. In effect, you are creating a separate anonymous FTP site at the same location with more restricted access.

To create a guest account, first create a user and the home directory for it. You then create an Anonymous block in the **proftpd.conf** file for that account. The Anonymous directive includes the **home** directory of the guest user you create. You can specify this directory with a ~ for the path and the directory name, usually the same as the user name. Within the Anonymous block, you use the USER and GROUP directives to specify the user and group name for the user account. Set the AnonRequirePassword directive to on if you want remote users to provide a password. A UserAlias directive defines aliases for the username. A remote user can use either the alias or the original username to login. You then enter the remaining directives for controlling access to the files and directories in the account's **home** directory. An example showing the initial directives is listed here. The USER directive specifies the user as myproject. The **home** directory is **~myproject**, which usually evaluates to **/home/myproject**. The UserAlias lets remote users log in either with the name myproject or mydesert.

```
<Anonymous ~myproject>
    User myproject
    Group other
    UserAlias mydesert myproject
    AnonRequirePassword on
    <Directory *>
```

You could just as easily create an account that requires no password, letting users enter in their e-mail addresses instead. The following example configures an anonymous user named mypics. A password isn't required and neither is a valid shell. The remote user still needs to know the username, in this case mypics.

```
<Anonymous /home/mypics>
    AnonRequirePassword off
    User mypics
    Group nobody
    RequireValidShell off
    <Directory *>
```

The following example provides a more generic kind of guest login. The username is guest with the **home** directory located at **~guest**. Remote users are required to know the password for the guest account. The first Limit directive lets all users log in. The second Limit directive allows write access from users on a specific network, as indicated by the network IP address, and denies write access by any others.

```
<Anonymous ~guest>
  User              guest
  Group             nobody
  AnonRequirePassword        on
```

```
<Limit LOGIN>
  AllowAll
</Limit>

# Deny write access from all except trusted hosts.
<Limit WRITE>
  Order        allow,deny
  Allow        from 10.0.0.
  Deny         from all
</Limit>

</Anonymous>
```

Virtual FTP Servers

The ProFTPD daemon can manage more than one FTP site at once. Using a VirtualHost directive in the **proftpd.conf** file, you can create an independent set of directives that configure a separate FTP server. The VirtualHost directive is usually used to configure virtual servers as FTP sites. You can configure your system to support more than one IP address. The extra IP addresses can be used for virtual servers, not independent machines. You can use such an extra IP address to set up a virtual FTP server, giving you another FTP site on the same system. This added server would use the extra IP address as its own. Remote users could access it using that IP address, instead of the system's main IP address. Because such an FTP server is not running independently on a separate machine but is, instead, on the same machine, it is known as a *virtual FTP server* or *virtual host*. This feature lets you run what appear to others as several different FTP servers on one machine. When a remote user uses the virtual FTP server's IP address to access it, the ProFTPD daemon detects that request and operates as the FTP service for that site. ProFTPD can handle a great many virtual FTP sites at the same time on a single machine. Given its configuration capabilities, you can also tailor any of the virtual FTP sites to specific roles, such as a guest site, anonymous site for a particular group, or an anonymous site for a particular user.

You configure a virtual FTP server by entering a <VirtualHost> directive for it in your **proftpd.conf** file. Such an entry begins with the VirtualHost directive and the IP address, and ends with a terminating VirtualHost directive, </VirtualHost>. Any directives placed within these are applied to the virtual host. For anonymous or guest sites, add anonymous and guest directives. You can even add Directory directives for specific directories. With the Port directive on a standalone configuration, you can create a virtual host that operates on the same system, but connects on a different port.

```
<VirtualHost 10.0.0.1>
  ServerName "My virtual FTP server"
</VirtualHost>
```

Inetd and standalone configurations handle virtual hosts differently. Inetd detects a request for a virtual host, and then hands it off to a FTP daemon. The FTP daemon then examines the address and port specified in the request and processes the request for the appropriate virtual host. In the standalone configuration, the FTP daemon continually listens for requests on all specified ports and generates child processes to handle ones for different virtual hosts as they come in. In the standalone configuration, ProFTPD can support a great many virtual hosts at the same time.

The following example shows a sample configuration of a virtual FTP host. The VirtualHost directives use domain name addresses for its arguments. When a domain name address is used, it must be associated with an IP address in the network's domain name server. The IP address, in turn, has to reference the machine on which the ProFTPD daemon is running. On the **ftp.mypics.com** virtual FTP server, an anonymous guest account named robpics is configured that requires a password to log in. An anonymous FTP account is also configured that uses the **home** directory **/home/ftp/virtual/pics**.

```
<VirtualHost ftp.mypics.com>

  ServerName          "Mypics FTP Server"
  MaxClients          10
  MaxLoginAttempts      1
  DeferWelcome         on
  <Anonymous ~robpics>
    User          robpics
    Group         robpics
    AnonRequirePassword       on

<Anonymous /home/ftp/virtual/pics>

    User         ftp
    Group        ftp
    UserAlias         anonymous ftp


  </Anonymous>

</VirtualHost>
```

The
Complete
Reference

Linux

Chapter 17

Apache Web Server

The Apache Web server is a full-featured free HTTP (Web) server developed and maintained by the Apache Server Project. The aim of the project is to provide a reliable, efficient, and easily extensible Web server, with free open source code. The server software includes the server daemon, configuration files, management tools, and documentation. The Apache Server Project is maintained by a core group of volunteer programmers and supported by a great many contributors worldwide. The Apache Sever Project is one of several projects currently supported by the Apache Software Foundation (formerly known as the Apache Group). This nonprofit organization provides financial, legal, and organizational support for various Apache open-source software projects, including the Apache Server, Java Apache, Jakarta, and XML-Apache. The Web site for the Apache Software Foundation is at **www.apache.org**. Table 17-1 lists various Apache-related Web sites.

Apache was originally based on the NCSA Web server developed at the National Center for Supercomputing Applications, University of Illinois, Champaign-Urbana. Apache has since emerged as a server in its own right and has become one of the most popular Web servers in use. Although originally developed for Linux and UNIX systems, Apache has become a cross-platform application with Windows and OS2 versions. Apache provides online support and documentation for its Web server at **www.apache.org**. An HTML-based manual is also provided with the server installation. Several GUI configuration tools are also available to help configure your Apache server easily. They operate on any X-Windows window manager, including Gnome and KDE. You can link to these Apache GUI configuration tools at **gui.apache.org**.

Other Web servers available for Linux include the Red Hat Secure Server (**www.redhat.com**), Apache-SSL (**www.apache-ssl.org**), Stronghold (**www.c2.net**), and Netscape Enterprise Server (**home.netscape.com**). *Apache-SSL* is an encrypting Web server based on Apache and OpenSSL (**www.openssl.org**). *Stronghold* is a commercial version of the Apache Web server featuring improved security and administration tools. You can also use the original NCSA Web server, though it is no longer supported (**hoohoo.ncsa.uiuc.edu**).

JAVA: Jakarta and Apache-Java

The Java Apache Project develops open source Java software and has its Web site located at **java.apache.org**. Currently, the Java Apache Project supports numerous projects, including the JServ, JSSI, JMeter, and mod_java, among others. The Apache Jserv Project has developed a Java servlet engine compliant with the JavaSoft Java Servlet APIs 2.0 specification. The Apache JSSI project has developed a Java servlet for dynamic servlet output from HTML files through the <SERVLET> tag as designated by the JavaSoft Java Web Server. *JMeter* is a Java desktop application to test performance of server resources, such as servlets and CGI scripts. The MOD_JAVA project has developed a mod_java extension module for Apache Web servers that allows Apache

www.apache.org	Apache Software Foundation
www.apache.org/apache.html	Apache HTTP Serve Project
java.apache.org	Java Apache Project
Jakarta.apache.org	Jakarta Apache Project
gui.apache.org	Apache GUI Project
comanche.com.dtu.dk.	Comanche (Configuration Manager for Apache)
www.redhat.com	Red Hat Linux Distribution
www.apache-ssl.org	Apache-SSL server

Table 17-1.   *Apache-related Web Sites*

modules to be written in JAVA instead of in C. It functions much like mod_perl (which allows modules to be written in Perl).

Jakarta is an Apache project to develop server side Java capabilities on Linux. Jakarta's main product, called *Tomcat*, is an open-source implementation of the Java Servlet 2.2 and JavaServer Pages 1.1 Specifications. Tomcat is designed for use in Apache servers. The Jakarta Web site is at **jakarta.apache.org**.

Linux Distribution Apache Installations

During the installation of Red Hat Linux, you have the option of having the Apache Web server automatically installed on your system, with all the necessary directories and configuration files. Then, whenever you run Red Hat Linux, your system is already a fully functional Web site. Every time you start your system, the Web server also starts up, running continuously. The directory reserved for your Web site data files is **/home/httpd/html**. Place your Web pages in this directory or in any subdirectories. Your system is already configured to operate as a Web server. All you need to do is perform the necessary network server configurations, and then designate the files and directories open to remote users. You needn't do anything else. Once your Web site is connected to a network, remote users can access it.

The Web server installed on Red Hat systems sets up your Web site in the **/home/httpd** directory. It also sets up several directories for managing the site. The **/home/httpd/cgi-bin** directory holds the CGI scripts, and **/home/httpd/html/manual** holds the Apache manual in HTML format. You can use your browser to examine it. Your Web pages are to be placed in the **/home/httpd/html** directory. Place your Web site home page there. Your configuration files are located in a different directory,

/etc/httpd/conf. Table 17-2 lists the various Apache Web server Web site directories and server configuration files.

To upgrade your Apache server, look for the most recent Apache RPM package at the Red Hat update site. For Red Hat, this is at **updates.redhat.com** (many mirror sites exist). Download the package and use the **rpm** command with the **-Uvh** options to install
the upgrade.

```
rpm -Uvh apache-1.3.4-4.i386.rpm
rpm -Uvh apache-docs-1.3.4-4.i386.rpm
```

Other Web servers are also freely available. The NCSA httpd Web server was one of the first servers developed. You can download server software from most Linux FTP sites. Check for RPM package versions, if available. You can download the source code version directly from Apache, as well, and compile it on your system. You must decompress the file and extract the archive. Many of the same directories are created, with added ones for the source code. The server package includes installation instructions for creating your server directories and compiling your software. Make sure the configuration files are set up and installed. If you are installing Apache from the source code, notice versions of the configuration files ending with the extension **.conf-dist** are provided. You have to make copies of these configuration files with the same prefix, but only with the extension **.conf** to set up a default configuration. The Web server reads configuration information only from files with a **.conf** extension.

Starting and Stopping the Web Server

On most systems, Apache is installed as a stand-alone server, continually running. As noted in Chapter 16 in the discussion of **init** scripts, your system automatically starts up the Web server daemon, invoking it whenever you start your system. On Red Hat systems, a startup script for the Web server called **httpd** is in the **/etc/rc.d/init.d** directory. A symbolic link through which the **rc** program runs is in the **/etc/rc.d/rc3.d** directory and is called **S85httpd**.

You can use this **httpd** script in the /etc/rc.d/init.d directory to start and stop the server manually. This may be helpful when you are testing or modifying your server. The **httpd** script with the **start** option starts the server and with the **stop** option stops it. You can also use the SysV Runlevel Manager, available on many systems, to start and stop the httpd daemon. Click the **httpd** entry in the Available list, and then click the Execute button. A menu is displayed with buttons to stop or start the daemon. Simply killing the Web process directly is not advisable.

```
/etc/rc.d/init.d/httpd stop
/etc/rc.d/init.d/httpd start
```

Web Site Directories	Description
/home/httpd	Directory for Apache Web site files on your Red Hat system
/home/httpd/html	Web site Web files
/home/httpd/cgi-bin	CGI program files
/home/httpd/html/manual	Apache Web server manual
Configuration Files	
.htaccess	Directory-based configuration files. An .htaccess file holds directives to control access to files within the directory in which it is located
/etc/httpd/conf	Directory for Apache Web server configuration files
/etc/httpd/conf/httpd.conf	Primary Apache Web server configuration file (from version 1.3.4, it holds all configuration directives)
/etc/httpd/conf/srm.conf	Older configuration file still used on Red Hat 6.0 to handle document specifications, configuring file types and locations
/etc/httpd/conf/access.conf	Older configuration file still used on Red Hat 6.0 is designed to hold directives that control access to Web site directories and files
Startup Scripts	
/etc/rc.d/init.d/httpd	Start up script for Web server daemon
/etc/rc.d/rc3.d/S85httpd	Link in runlevel 3 directory (rc3.d) to the httpd startup script in the /etc/rc.d/init.d directory
Application Files	
/usr/sbin	Location of the Apache Web server program file and utilities
/usr/doc/	Apache Web server documentation
/var/log/http	Location of Apache log files

Table 17-2. *Apache Web Server Files and Directories (RPM Installation)*

Apache also provides a control tool called **apachectl** (Apache control) for managing your Web server. With **apachectl** you can start, stop, and restart the server from the command line. **apachectl** takes several arguments: **start** to start the server, **stop** to stop it, **restart** to shut down and restart the server, and **graceful** to shut down and restart gracefully. In addition, you can use **apachectl** to check the syntax of your configuration files with the **config** argument. You can also use **apachectl** as a system startup file for your server in the **/etc/rc.d** directory.

Remember, **httpd** is a script that calls the actual httpd daemon. You could call the daemon directly using its full pathname. This daemon has several options. The **-d** option enables you to specify a directory for the **httpd** program if it is different from the default directory. With the **-f** option, you can specify a configuration file different from **httpd.conf**. The **-v** option displays the version.

```
/usr/sbin/httpd -v
```

To check your Web server, start your Web browser and enter the Internet domain name address of your system. For the system **turtle.trek.com,** the user enters **http://turtle.trek.com**. This should display the home page you placed in your Web root directory. A simple way to do this is to use **lynx,** the command line Web browser. Start **lynx,** and then press **g** to open a line where you can enter a URL for your own system. Then **lynx** displays your Web site's home page. Be sure to place an **index.html** file in the **/home/httpd/html** directory first.

Once you have your server running, you can check its performance with the **ab** benchmarking tool, also provided by Apache. **ab** shows you how many requests at a time your server can handle. Options include **-v,** which enables you to control the level of detail displayed, **-n,** which specifies the number of request to handle (default is 1), and **-t,** which specifies a time limit.

Red Hat, like most distributions, does not configure the Web server to run from **inetd**. If you want this done, place the appropriate entries in **/etc/services** and **/etc/inetd.conf**. You also must remove your Web server from the list of startup daemons in your system's autostart list (see Chapter 16 for details). If you want to have **httpd** called by the **inetd** daemon, place an entry for **httpd** in the **/etc/services** and **/etc/inetd.conf** files. The **/etc/services** file lists the different services available on your system. For a Web server, you enter **http** with a *port*/tcp specification.

```
http    80/tcp
```

The Web server entry in the **/etc/inetd.conf** file is similar to the entry for the FTP server. Use the pathname for the Web server installed on your system, usually **/usr/sbin/httpd**.

```
http stream tcp nowait nobody /usr/sbin/httpd  /usr/sbin/httpd
```

To have Web server requests monitored and controlled by **tcpd**, you place the
/usr/sbin/tcpd pathname in place of the **/usr/sbin/httpd** pathname.

```
http stream tcp nowait nobody /usr/sbin/tcpd  /usr/sbin/httpd
```

You also have to specify the **inetd** value for the ServerType variable in your Apache
httpd.conf file, **/etc/httpd/conf/httpd.conf**.

```
# ServerType is either inetd, or standalone.
ServerType inetd
```

Apache Configuration Files

Traditionally configuration directives have been placed in their different configuration
files: **httpd.conf**, **srm.conf** and **access.conf**. These files are located in the /etc/httpd/conf
directory. **srm.conf** and **access.conf** are designed to hold directives that configure your
Web site documents. **httpd.conf** is used to configure your server. The **srm.conf** file
handles document specifications, configuring file types and locations. The **access.conf** file
is designed to hold directives that control access to Web site directories and files. This
three-file organization was originally implemented to maintain compatibility with the
NCAA Web server that preceded Apache.

With version 1.3.4, Apache recommends all configuration directives be placed in
one file, the **httpd.conf** file. In fact, if you download the original source code version,
both the **srm.conf** and **access.conf** files will be empty. Only the **httpd.conf** file is
used. Directives even exist that prevent reading the **srm.conf** and **access.conf** files.
By default, Apache still reads both the **srm.conf** and **access.conf** files, in case anything
is in them, though **httpd.conf** is still considered the primary configuration file. The
situation is complicated because most major distributions, including Red Hat, still use
all three configuration files. Placing directives all in one file is an advantage because
you only have to maintain one configuration file.

Apache configuration directives, ordinarily placed in the **srm.conf** or **access.conf**
file, can now be placed in the **httpd.conf** file, and those files can be left empty if you
want. Still, the three-files organization does help to categorize files into primary
directives, resources, and access controls. On the other hand, the Apache's capabilities
have extended to the point that these categories no longer cover the current directives.
For example, directives for virtual hosts are placed in the **httpd.conf** file, along with
their access control directives. Directives should be thought of as independent of any
particular file. Table 17-3 lists the different directives by the different files in which
they are found using the old configuration structure.

Any of the directives in the main configuration files can be overridden on a
per-directory basis using an **.htaccess** file located within a directory. Although originally
designed only for access directives, the **.htaccess** file can also hold any resource directives,

srm.conf Directives	access.conf Directives
AccessFileName	<Directory *pathname*> </Directory>
AddDescription	Directives
AddEncoding *extensions-list*	Options *feature-list*
AddIcon *image file file-extensions*	AllowOverride *feature-list*
AddIconByEncoding	<Limit> </Limit>
AddIconByType	
AddLanguage *language extension*	
AddType *type/subtype extension*	
Alias *alias-name pathname*	
DefaultType	
DefaultIcon	
DirectoryIndex	
DocumentRoot	
FancyIndexing	
HeaderName	
IndexIgnore *file-list*	
IndexOptions	
LanguagePriority *language-list*	
OldScriptAlias	
ReadmeName	
Redirect	
ScriptAlias *alias-name pathname*	
UserDir	

Table 17-3. *Directives Used in srm.conf and access.conf Files*

enabling you to tailor how Web pages are displayed in a particular directory. You can configure access to .htaccess files in the httpd.conf file.

Apache Directives

Apache configuration operations take the form of directives entered into the Apache configuration files. With the directives you can enter basic configuration information, such as your server name, or perform more complex operations, such as implementing virtual hosts. The design is flexible enough to enable you to define configuration features for particular directories and different virtual hosts. Apache has a variety of different directives performing operations as diverse as controlling directory access, assigning file icon formats, and creating log files. Most directives set values such as DirectoryRoot, which holds the root directory for the server's Web pages, or Port, which holds the port on the system that the server listens on for requests. Table 17-4 (later in this chapter) provides a listing of the more commonly used Apache Directives. The syntax for a simple directive is shown here.

```
directive option option …
```

Certain directives create blocks able to hold directives that apply to specific server components. For example, the **Directory** directive is used to define a block within which you place directives that apply only to a particular directory. Block directives are entered in pairs: a beginning directive and a terminating directive. The terminating directive defines the end of the block and consists of the same name beginning with a slash. Block directives take an argument that specifies the particular object to which the directives apply. For the **Directory** block directive, you must specify a directory name to which it will apply. The **<Directory *mydir*>** block directive creates a block whose directives within it apply to the *mydir* directory. The block is terminated by a **</Directory>** directive. The **<VirtualHost *hostaddress*>** block directive is used to configure a specific virtual Web server and must include the IP or domain name address used for that server. **</VirtualHost>** is its terminating directive. Any directives you place within this block are applied to that virtual Web server. The **<Limit *method*>** directive specifies the kind of access method, such as GET or POST, you want to limit. The access control directives located within the block list the controls you are placing on those methods. The syntax for a block directive is as follows.

```
<block-directive option … >
    directive option …
    directive option …
</block-directive>
```

Usually, directives are placed in one of the main configuration files. Directory directives in those files can be used to configure a particular directory. However,

Apache also makes use of directory-based configuration files. Any directory may have its own **.htaccess** file that holds directives to configure only this directory. If your site has many directories or if any directories have special configuration needs, you can place their configuration directives in their **.htaccess** files, instead of filling the main configuration files. You can control which directives in an **.htaccess** file take precedence over those in the main configuration files.

Much of the power and flexibility of the Apache Web server comes from its use of modules to extend its capabilities. Apache is implemented with a core set of directives. Modules can be created that hold definitions of other directives. They can be loaded into Apache, enabling you to use those directives for your server. A standard set of modules is included with the Apache distribution, though you can download others and even create your own. For example, the mod_autoindex module holds the directives for automatically indexing directories (as described in the following section). The mod_mime module holds the MIME type and handler directives. Modules are loaded with the **LoadModule** directive. On Red Hat Linux, you can find **LoadModule** directives in the **httpd.conf** configuration file for most of the standard modules.

```
LoadModule mime_module    modules/mod_mime.so
```

The **apxs** application provided with the Apache package can be used to build Apache extension modules. With the **apxs** application, you can compile Apache module source code in C and create dynamically shared objects that can be loaded with the **LoadModule** directive. The **apxs** application requires the **mod_so** module be part of your Apache application. It includes extensive options such as **-n** to specify the module name, **-a** to add an entry for it in the **httpd.conf** file, and **-i** to install the module on your Web server.

You can find a complete listing of Apache Web configuration directives at the Apache Web site, **www.apache.org**, and in the Apache manual located in your site's Web site root directory. On Red Hat systems, this is located at **/home/httpd/manual**. Many of the more commonly used directives are listed in Table 17-1.

Server Configuration

Certain directives are used to configure your server's overall operations. These directives are placed in the **httpd.conf** configuration file. Some require pathnames, whereas others only need to be turned on or off with the keywords **on** and **off**. On the Red Hat distribution, the **httpd.conf** file already contains these directives. Some are commented out with a preceding # symbol. You can activate a directive by removing its # sign. Many of the entries are preceded by comments explaining their purpose. The following is an example of the **ServerAdmin** directive used to set the address where users can send mail for administrative issues. You replace the you@your.address entry with the address you want to use to receive system administration mail. On Red Hat systems, this is set to root@localhost.

```
# ServerAdmin: Your address, where problems should be e-mailed.
ServerAdmin you@your.address
```

Some directives require specific information about your system. For example, **ServerName** holds the host name for your Web server. Specifying a host name to avoid unnecessary DNS lookup failures that can hang your server is important. Notice the entry is commented with a preceding **#**. Simply remove the **#** and type your Web server's host name in place of **new.host.name**.

```
# ServerName allows you to set a hostname which is sent
# back to clients for your server if it's different than the
# one the program would get (i.e. use
# "www" instead of the host's real name).

#ServerName new.host.name
```

On Red Hat systems, entries have already been made for the standard Web server installation using **/home/httpd** as your Web site directory. You can tailor your Web site to your own needs by changing the appropriate directives. The **DocumentRoot** directive determines the home directory for your Web pages. The **ServerRoot** directive specifies where your Web server configuration, error, and log files are kept.

```
DocumentRoot /home/httpd/html
ServerRoot /etc/httpd
```

The **MaxClients** directive sets the maximum number of clients who can connect to your server at the same time.

```
MaxClients 150
```

Directory-Level Configuration: .htaccess and <Directory>

One of the most flexible aspects of Apache is its capability to configure individual directories. With the **Directory** directive, you can define a block of directives that apply only to a particular directory. Such a directive can be placed in the **httpd.conf** or the **access.conf** configuration file. You can also use an **.htaccess** file within a particular directory to hold configuration directives. Those directives are then applied only to that directory. The name ".htaccess" is actually set with the **AccessFileName** directive. You can change this if you want.

```
AccessFileName .htaccess
```

A *Directory block* begins with a **<Directory *pathname*>** directive, where *pathname* is the directory to be configured. The ending directive uses the same <> symbols, but with a slash preceding the term "Directory": **</Directory>**. Directives placed within this block apply only to the specified directory. The following example denies access to only the **mypics** directory by requests from **www.myvids.com**.

```
<Directory /home/httpd/html/mypics>
    Order Deny,Allow
    Deny from www.myvids.com
</Directory>
```

With the **Options** directive, you can enable certain features in a directory, such as the use of symbolic links, automatic indexing, execution of CGI scripts, and content negotiation. The default is the All option, which turns on all features except content negotiation (multiviews). The following example enables automatic indexing (Indexes), symbolic links (FollowSymLinks), and content negotiation (Multiviews).

```
Options Indexes FollowSymLinks Multiviews
```

Configurations made by directives in main configuration files or in upper-level directories are inherited by lower-level directories. Directives for a particular directory held in **.htaccess** files and Directory blocks can be allowed to override those configurations. This capability can be controlled by the **AllowOverride** directive. With the all argument, **.htaccess** files can override any previous configurations. The none argument disallows overrides, effectively disabling the **.htaccess** file. You can further control the override of specific groups of directives. AuthConfig enables use of authorization directives, FileInfo is for type directives, Indexes is for indexing directives, Limit is for access control directives, and Options is for the **options** directive.

```
AllowOverride all
```

Access Control

With access control directives, such as allow and deny, you can control access to your Web site by remote users and hosts. If you are using three configuration files, such directives are usually placed in the **access.conf** file. The **allow** directive followed by a list of hostnames restricts access to only those hosts. The **deny** directive with a list of hostnames denies access by those systems. The argument "all" applies the directive to all hosts. The **order** directive specifies in what order the access control directives are to be applied. Other access control directives, such as **require,** can establish authentication controls, requiring users to log in. The access control directives can be used globally to control access to the entire site or placed within **Directory** directives to control access to individual directives. In the following example, all users are allowed access.

```
order allow,deny
allow from all
```

You can further qualify access control directives by limiting them to certain HTML access methods. HTML access methods are ways a browser interacts with your Web site. For example, a browser could get information from a page (GET) or send information through it (POST). You can control such access methods using the **<Limit>** directive. **Limit** takes as its argument a list of access methods to be controlled. The directive then pairs with a **</Limit>** directive to define a Limit block within which you can place access control directives. These directives only apply to the specified access methods. You can place such Limit blocks with a Directory block to set up controls of access methods for a specific directory.

On the Red Hat distribution, a Directory block is placed in your **access.conf** file that controls access methods for your Web site's home directory, **/home/httpd/html**.

```
# This should be changed to whatever you set DocumentRoot to.
<Directory /home/httpd/html>
Options Indexes FollowSymLinks
AllowOverride All
<Limit GET>
order allow,deny
allow from all
</Limit>
</Directory>
```

Controls are inherited from upper-level directories to lower-level ones. If you want to control access strictly on a per-directory basis to your entire Web site, you can use the following entry to deny access to all users. Then, in individual directories, you can allow access to certain users, groups, or hosts.

```
<Directory /home/htppd/html>
    Order Deny,Allow
    Deny from All
</Directory>
```

URL Pathnames

Certain directives can modify or complete pathname segments of a URL used to access your site. The pathname segment of the URL specifies a particular directory or Web page on your site. Directives enable you to alias or redirect pathnames, as well as to select a default Web page. With the **Alias** directive, you can let users access resources located in other parts of your system, on other file systems, or on other Web sites. An alias can use a URL for sites on the Internet, instead of a pathname for a directory on your system. With the **Redirect** directive, you can redirect a user to another site.

```
Alias /mytrain /home/dylan/trainproj
```

If Apache is given only a directory to access, rather than a specific Web page, it looks for an index Web page located in that directory and displays it. The possible names for a default Web page are listed by the **DirectoryIndex** directive. The name usually used is index.html, but you can add others. The standard names are shown here. When Apache is given only a Web directory to access, it looks for and displays the **index.html** Web page located in it.

```
DirectoryIndex index.html index.shtml index.cgi
```

Apache also enables a user to maintain Web pages located in a special subdirectory in the user's home directory, rather than in the main Web site directory. Using a ~ followed by the user name accesses this directory. The name of this directory is specified with the **UserDir** directive. The default name is public_html, as shown here. The site turtle.trek.com/~dylan accesses the directory **turtle.trek.com/home/dylan/public_html** on the host turtle.trek.com.

```
UserDir public_html
```

Types

When a browser accesses Web pages on a Web site, it is often accessing many different kinds of objects, including HTML files, picture or sound files, and script files. To display these objects correctly, the browser must have some indication of what kind of object they are. A JPEG picture file is handled differently from a simple text file. The server provides this type information in the form of MIME types. MIME types are the same types used for sending attached files through Internet mailers, such as Pine. Each kind of object is associated with a given MIME type. Provided with the Mime type, the browser can correctly handle and display the object.

The MIME protocol associates a certain type with files of a given extension. For example, files with a **.jpg** extension would have the MIME type image/jpeg. The **TypesConfig** directive holds the location of the **mime.types** file, which lists all the MIME types and their associated file extensions. DefaultType is the default MIME type for any file whose type cannot be determined. AddType enables you to modify the **mime.type** types list without editing the MIME file.

```
TypesConfig /etc/mime.types
DefaultType text/plain
```

Other type directives are used to specify actions to be taken on certain documents. **AddEncoding** lets browsers decompress compressed files on the fly. **AddHandler** maps file extensions to actions, **AddLanguage** enables you to specify the language for a document. The following example marks filenames with the **.gz** extension as gzip-encoded files and files with the **.fr** extension as French language files.

```
AddEncoding x-gzip gz
AddLanguage fr .fr
```

A Web server can display and execute many different types of files and programs. Not all Web browsers are able to display all those files, though. Older browsers are the most limited. Some browsers, such as Lynx, are not designed to display even simple graphics. To allow a Web browser to display a page, the server negotiates with it to determine the type of files it can handle. To enable such negotiation, you need to enable the **multiviews** option.

```
Option multiviews
```

CGI Files

Common Gateway Interface (*CGI*) files are programs that can be executed by Web browsers accessing your site. CGI files are usually initiated by Web pages that execute the program as part of the content they display. Traditionally, CGI programs were placed in a directory called cgi-bin and could only be executed if they resided in such a special directory. Usually, only one cgi-bin directory exists per Web site. Red Hat systems set up a cgi-bin directory in the /home/httpd directory, **/home/httpd/cgi-bin**. Here, you place any CGI programs that can be executed on your Web site. The **ScriptAlias** directive specifies an alias for your cgi-bin directory. Any Web pages or browsers can use the alias to reference this directory.

```
ScriptAlias /cgi-bin/ /home/httpd/cgi-bin/
```

If you want to execute CGI programs that reside anywhere on your Web site, you can specify files with a **.cgi** extension are treated as executable CGI programs. You do this with the **AddHandler** directive. This directive applies certain handlers to files of a given type. The handler directive to do this is included in the default **httpd.conf** file, provided with the Apache source code files, though commented out. You can remove the comment symbol (#) to enable it.

```
AddHandler cgi-script cgi
```

Automatic Directory Indexing

When given a URL for a directory instead of an HTML file, and when no default Web page is in the directory, Apache creates a page on the fly and displays it. This is usually only a listing of the different files in the directory. In effect, Apache indexes the items in the directory for you. You can set several options for generating and displaying such an index. If **FancyIndexing** is turned on, then Web page items are displayed with icons and column headers that can be used to sort the listing.

```
FancyIndexing on
```

Icon directives tells Apache what icon to display for a certain type of file. The **AddIconByType** and **AddIconByEncoding** directives use MIME-type information to determine the file's type, and then associate the specified image with it. **AddIcon** uses the file's extension to determine its type. In the next example, the **text.gif** image is displayed for text files with the extension **.txt**. You can also use **AddIcon** to associate an image with a particular file. The **DefaultIcon** directive specifies the image used for files of undetermined type.

```
AddIcon /icons/text.gif .txt
DefaultIcon /icons/unknown.gif
AddIconByType (VID,/icons/movie.gif) video/*
```

With the **AddDescription** directive, you can add a short descriptive phrase to the filename entry. The description can be applied to an individual file or to filenames of a certain pattern.

```
AddDescription "Reunion pictures" /home/httpd/html/reunion.html
```

Within a directory, you can place special files that can be used to display certain text both before and after the generated listing . The **HeaderName** directive is used to set the name of the file whose text is inserted before the listing. The **ReadmeName** directive sets the name of the file whose text is placed at the end of the listing. You can use these directives in an **.htaccess** files or a **<Directory>** block to select particular files within a directory. The **ReadmeName** directive is usually set to README and **HeaderName**, to HEADER. In that case, Apache searches for files named **HEADER** and **README** in the directory.

```
HeaderName HEADER
ReadmeName README
```

With the **IndexOptions** directive, you can set different options for displaying a generated index. Options exist for setting the height and width of icons and filenames. The **IconsAreLinks** option makes icons part of filename anchors. The **ScanHTMLTitles** read the titles in HTML documents and use those to display entries in the index listing instead of filenames. Various options exist for suppressing different index display features such as sorting, descriptions, and header/readme inserts. You can set options for individual directories using a Directory block or an .**htaccess** file. Normally, options set in higher-level directories are inherited by lower-level ones. If you use an **IndexOption** directive to set any new option, however, all previously inherited options are cleared. If you want to keep the inherited options, you can set the add or remove options using the plus (+) or minus (–) symbols. If you were also to set an option without the + or – symbols, though, all inherited options would be cleared.

```
IndexOptions IconsAreLinks FancyIndexing
IndexOptions +ScanHTMLTitles
```

Authentication

Your Web server can also control access on a per-user or per-group basis to particular directories on your Web site. You can require various levels for authentication. Access can be limited to particular users and require passwords, or expanded to allow access to members of a group. You can dispense with passwords altogether or set up an anonymous type of access, as used with FTP.

To apply authentication directives to a certain directory, you place those directives either within a Directory block or the directory's .**htaccess** file. You use the **require** directive to determine which users can access the directory. You can list particular users or groups. The **AuthName** directive provides the authentication realm to the user, the name used to identify the particular set of resources accessed by this authentication process. The **AuthType** directive specifies the type of authentication, such as basic or digest. A **require** directive requires also **AuthType**, **AuthName**, and directives specifying the locations of group and user authentication files. In the following example, only the users george, robert, and mark are allowed access to the **newpics** directory:

```
<Directory /home/httpd/html/newpics
AuthType Basic
AuthName Newpics
AuthUserFile /web/users
AuthGroupFile /web/groups
<Limit GET POST>
    require users george robert mark
</Limit>
</Directory>
```

The next example allows group access by administrators to the CGI directory:

```
<Directory /home/httpd/html/cgi-bin
AuthType Basic
AuthName CGI
AuthGroupFile /web/groups
<Limit GET POST>
   require groups admin
</Limit>
</Directory>
```

To set up anonymous access for a directory, place the **Anonymous** directive with the user anonymous as its argument in the directory's Directory block or **.htaccess** file. You can also use the **Anonymous** directive to provide access to particular users without requiring passwords from them.

Apache maintains its own user and group authentication files specifying what users and groups are allowed to which directories. These files are normally simple flat files, such as your system's password and group files. They can become large, however, possibly slowing down authentication lookups. As an alternative, many sites have used database management files in place of these flat files. Database methods are then used to access the files, providing a faster response time. Apache has directives for specifying the authentication files, depending on the type of file you are using. The **AuthUserfile** and **AuthGroupFile** directives are used to specify the location of authentication files that have a standard flat file format. The **AuthDBUserFile** and **AuthDBGroupFile** directives are used for DB database files, and the **AuthDBMGUserFIle** and **AuthDBMGGroupFile** are used for DBMG database files.

htdigest, **htpasswd**, and **dbmmanage** are tools provided with the Apache software package for creating and maintaining user authentication files. These are user password files listing users who have access to specific directories or resources on your Web site. **htdigest** and **htpasswd** manage a simple flat file of user authentication records, whereas **dbmmanage** uses a more complex database management format. If your user list is extensive, you may want to use a database file for fast lookups. **htdigest** takes as its arguments the authentication file, the realm, and the username, creating or updating the user entry. **htpasswd** can also employ encryption on the password. **dbmmanage** has an extensive set of options to add, delete, and update user entries. A variety of different database formats are used to set up such files. Three common ones are Berkeley DB2, NDBM, and GNU GBDM. **dbmanage** looks for the system libraries for these formats in that order. Be careful to be consistent in using the same format for your authentication files.

Log Files

Apache maintains logs of all requests by users to your Web site. By default, these logs include records using the *Common Log Format* (*CLF*). The record for each request takes up a line composed of several fields: host, identity check, authenticated user (for logins), the date, the request line submitted by the client, the status sent to the client, and the size of the object sent in bytes. Using the **LogFormat** and **CustomLog** directives, you can customize your log record to add more fields with varying levels of detail. These directives use a format string consisting of field specifiers to determine the fields to record in a log record. You add whatever fields you want, and in any order. A field specifier consists of a percent (%) symbol followed by an identifying character. For example, %h is the field specifier for a remote host, %b, for the size in bytes, and %s, for the status. See the documentation for the **mod_log_config** module for a complete listing. You should quote fields whose contents may take up more than one word. The quotes themselves must be quoted with a backslash to be included in the format string. The following example is the Common Log Format implemented as a **FormatLog** directive:

```
FormatLog "%h %l %u %t \"%r\" %s %b"
```

Instead of maintaining one large log file, you can create several log files using the **CustomLog** or **TransferLog** directive. This is helpful for virtual hosts where you may want to maintain a separate log file for each host. You use the **FormatLog** directive to define a default format for log records. The **TransferLog** then uses this default as its format when creating a new log file. **CustomLog** combines both operations, enabling you to create a new file and to define a format for it.

```
FormatLog "%h %l %u %t \"%r\" %s %b"
TransferLog myprojlog
CustomLog mypicslog "%h %l %u %t \"%r\" %s %b"
```

Certain field specifiers in the log format can be qualified to record specific information. The *%i specifier* records header lines in requests the server receives. The reference for the specific header line to record is placed within braces between the % and the field specifier. For example, User-agent is the header line that indicates the browser software used in the request. To record User-agent header information, use the conversion specifier %{User-agent}i.

To maintain compatibility with NCSA servers, Apache originally implemented **AgentLog** and **RefererLog** directives to record User-agent and Referer headers. These have since been replaced by qualified %i field specifiers used for the **LogFormat** and

CustomLog directives. A referer header records link information from clients, detecting who may have links to your site. The following is an NCSA-compliant log format:

```
"%h %l %u %t \"%r\" %s %b\"%{Referer}i\" \"%{User-agent}i\"".
```

Apache provides two utilities for processing and managing log files. **logresolve** resolves IP addresses in your log file to host names. **rotatelogs** rotates log files without having to kill the server. You can specify the rotation time.

Virtual Hosting

Virtual hosting allows the Apache Web server to host multiple Web sites as part of its own. In effect, the server can act as several servers, each hosted Web site appearing separate to outside users. Apache supports both IP address and name-based virtual hosting. IP address virtual hosts use valid registered IP addresses, whereas name-based virtual hosts use fully qualified domain addresses. These domain addresses are provided by the Host header from the requesting browser. The server can then determine the correct virtual host to use on the basis of the domain name alone. Note, SSL servers require IP Virtual Hosting.

IP-Address Virtual Hosts

In the IP address virtual hosting method, your server must have a different IP address for each virtual host. The IP address you use is already set up to reference your system. Network system administration operations can set up your machine to support several IP addresses. Your machine could have separate physical network connections for each one or a particular connection could be configured to listen for several IP addresses at once. In effect, any of the IP addresses can access your system.

You can configure Apache to run a separate daemon for each virtual host, separately listening for each IP address, or you can have a single daemon running that listens for requests for all the virtual hosts. To set up a single daemon to manage all virtual hosts, use **VirtualHost** directives. To set up a separate daemon for each host, also use the **Listen** and **BindAddress** directives.

A **VirtualHost** directive block must be set up for each virtual host. Within each **VirtualHost** block you place the appropriate directives for accessing a host. You should have **ServerAdmin**, **ServerName**, **DocumentRoot**, and **TransferLog** directives specifying the particular values for that host. You can use any directive within a **VirtualHost** block, except for **ServerType**, **StartServers**, **MaxSpareServers**, **MinSpareServers**, **MaxRequestsPerChild**, **BindAddress**, **Listen**, **PidFile**, **TypesConfig**, **ServerRoot**, and **NameVirtualHost**.

Although you can use domain names for the address in the **VirtualHost** directive, using the actual IP address is preferable. This way, you are not dependent on your domain name service to make the correct domain name associations. Be sure to leave an IP address for your main server. If you use all the available IP addresses for your machine for virtual hosts, then you can no longer access your main server. You could, of course, reconfigure your main server as a virtual host. The following example shows two IP-based virtual host blocks: one using an IP address and the other, a domain name that associates with an IP address:

```
<VirtualHost 192.168.1.23>
    ServerAdmin webmaster@mail.mypics.com
    DocumentRoot /groups/mypics/html
    ServerName www.mypics.com
    ErrorLog /groups/mypics/logs/error_log
    …..
</VirtualHost>

<VirtualHost www.myproj.org>
    ServerAdmin webmaster@mail.myproj.org
    DocumentRoot /groups/myproj/html
    ServerName www.myproj.org
    ErrorLog /groups/myproj/logs/error_log
    ....
</VirtualHost>
```

Name-based Virtual Hosts

With IP-based virtual hosting, you are limited to the number of IP addresses your system supports. With name-based virtual hosting, you can support any number of virtual hosts using no additional IP addresses. With only a single IP address for your machine, you can still support an unlimited number of virtual hosts. Such a capability is made possible by the HTTP/1.1 protocol, which lets a server identify the name by which it is being accessed. This method requires the client, the remote user, to use a browser that supports the HTTP/1.1 protocol, as current browsers do (though older ones may not). A browser using such a protocol can send a host: header specifying the particular host to use on a machine.

To implement name-based virtual hosting, use a **VirtualHost** directive for each host and a **NameVirtualHost** directive to specify the IP address you want to use for the virtual hosts. If your system has only one IP address, you need to use that address. Within the **VirtualHost** directives, you use the **ServerName** directive to specify the domain name you want to use for that host. Using **ServerName** to specify the domain name is important to avoid a DNS lookup. A DNS lookup failure disables the virtual host. The **VirtualHost** directives each take the same IP address specified in the **NameVirtualHost** directive as its argument. You use Apache directives within the

VirtualHost blocks to configure each host separately. Name-based virtual hosting uses the domain name address specified in a host: header to determine the virtual host to use. If no such information exists, the first host is used as the default. The following example implements two name-based virtual hosts. Here **www.mypics.com** and **www.myproj.org** are implemented as name-based virtual hosts, instead of IP-based hosts:

```
  ServerName turlte.trek.com

NameVirtualHost 192.168.1.5

<VirtualHost 192.168.1.5>
    ServerName www.mypics.com
    ServerAdmin webmaster@mail.mypics.com
    DocumentRoot /home/httpd/mypics/html
    ErrorLog /home/httpd/mypics/logs/error_log
    ...
</VirtualHost>

<VirtualHost 192.168.1.5>
    ServerName www.myproj.org
    ServerAdmin webmaster@mail.myproj.org
    DocumentRoot /home/httpd/myproj/html
    ErrorLog /home/httpd/myproj/logs/error_log
     ....
</VirtualHost>
```

If your system has only one IP address, then implementing virtual hosts prevents access to your main server with that address. You could no longer use your main server as a Web server directly; you could only use it indirectly to manage your virtual host. You could configure a virtual host to manage your main server's Web pages. You would then use your main server to support a set of virtual hosts that would function as Web sites, rather than the main server operating as one site directly. If your machine has two or more IP addresses, you can use one for the main server and the other for your virtual hosts. You can even mix IP-based virtual hosts and name-based virtual hosts on your server. You can also use separate IP addresses to support different sets of virtual hosts. You can further have several domain addresses access the same virtual host. To do so, place a **ServerAlias** directive listing the domain names within the selected **VirtualHost** block.

```
ServerAlias www.mypics.com www.greatpics.com
```

Requests sent to the IP address used for your virtual hosts have to match one of the configured virtual domain names. To catch requests that do not match one of these virtual hosts, you can set up a default virtual host using _default_:*. Unmatched requests are then handled by this virtual host.

```
<VirtualHost _default_:*>
```

Server Side Includes

Server Side Include (*SSI*) are designed to provide a much more refined control of your Web site content, namely the Web pages themselves. Server Side Includes are Apache directives placed within particular Web pages as part of the page's HTML code. You can configure your Apache Web server to look for SSI directives in particular Web pages and execute them. First, you have to use the Options directive with the include option to allow SSI directives.

```
Options Includes
```

You need to instruct the server to parse particular Web pages. The easiest way to enable parsing is to instruct Apache to parse HTML files with specified extensions. Usually, the extension .shtml is used for Web pages that have SSI directories. In fact, in the default Apache configuration files, you can find the following entry to enable parsing for SSI directives in HTML files. The **AddType** directive here adds the .shtml type as an HTML type of file and the **AddHandler** directive specifies the .shtml files are to be parsed (server-parsed).

```
# To use server-parsed HTML files
AddType text/html .shtml
AddHandler server-parsed .shtml
```

Or, instead of creating a separate type of file, you can use the **XBitHack** directive to have Apache parse any executable file for SSI directives. In other words, any file with execute permission (see Chapter 9) will be parsed for SSI directives.

SSI directives operate much like a programming language statements. You can define variables, create loops, and use tests to select alternate directives. An SSI directive consists of an element followed by attributes that can be assigned values. The syntax for a SSI directive is shown here.

```
<!--#element attribute=value …  -->
```

You can think of an element as operating much like a command in a programming language and attributes as its arguments. For example, to assign a value to a variable, you use the set element with the variable assignment as its attribute. The if directive displays any following text on the given Web page. The if directive takes as its attribute expr, which is assigned the expression to test. The test is able to compare two strings using standard comparison operators like <=, !=, or =. Variables used in the test are evaluated with the $ operator.

```
<!--#set myvar="Goodbye"  -->
<!--#if expr="$myvar = Hello"  -->
```

Other helpful SSI elements are **exec**, which executes CGI programs, or **shell** commands, which reads the contents of a file into the Web page and also executes CGI files. The **echo** element displays values such as the date, the document's name, and the page's URL. With the config element, you can configure certain values, such as the date or file size.

Apache GUI Configuration Tools: Comanche

The Apache GUI Project (**gui.apache.org**) provides a set of GUI tools for configuring and managing your Apache Web server. Its currently active projects are Comanche and TkApache. An older Comanche module comes with the Red Hat distribution. In the Linuxconf utility, you can also configure your Apache Web server.

Comanche (Configuration Manager for Apache) is an easy-to-use, full-featured Apache configuration utility that runs on any X Windows window manager. (See Figure 17-1.) You can download the current version and documentation from the Comanche Web site at **comanche.com.dtu.dk**. Comanche uses a simple, directory treelike structure to enable you to access and configure your main Web server, and any virtual server you have set up. Currently, Comanche can only configure the server on your local machine but, in the future, it may be able to configure remote servers. The main window is divided into two panes: The upper pane is a tree of Apache servers, and the lower pane is a status display that shows the Apache directives and commands executed by actions you specify using the Comanche interface. Unlike in ordinary programs, the menus are in the form of pop-up menus activated on entries in the server-tree, not from the menu bar at the top of the window. This menu bar only has an entry for quitting the program and accessing help.

The server-tree in the upper pane of the Comanche main window initially only shows one entry, eComanche with a folder icon. Click the folder to expand the tree to show the different machines you can configure. Currently, Comanche can only configure your local machine, so only one entry is there, named Apache Machine, with a computer icon next to it. Double-click the computer icon to expand the tree and to display a Server Management entry and a list of servers. To perform actions on any of

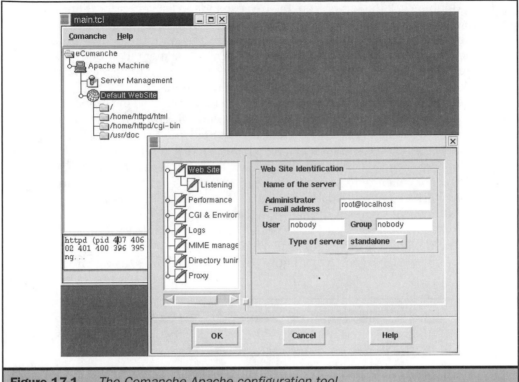

Figure 17-1.   *The Comanche Apache configuration tool*

these entries, you use pop-up menus that you activate by right-clicking the entry. A right-click on the Server Management entry displays a pop-up menu with items to Start, Stop, Restart, and Query the server status, as well as to save your configuration. Any changes you make with Comanche are not made in your Apache configuration files until you explicitly save the configuration by selecting this item in the Server Management pop-up menu. Be sure to save before you quit. To see what actual entries are going to be made in the Apache configuration files, choose the server entry, right-click, and select the Conf entry in the pop-up menu. This displays a version of the **httpd.conf** configuration file that reflects your current configuration selections. When you save your configuration, this version overwrites your **httpd.conf** file.

Initially, only one server is listed, labeled Default WebSite. If you add virtual hosts, they are listed at the same level. Servers have a blue ball icon placed next to them. You can use Comanche to create a virtual host. First, access the pop-up menu for the Apache Machine by right-clicking the computer icon. Then select New on the pop-up menu. This activates a drop-down menu with a Virtual Host entry. Select the Virtual Host entry to create your virtual host.

SERVERS

If you double-click the server icon, the tree expands to list server locations. These are the root directory, your Web server home directory, the CGI program directory, and the documentation directory. To create new directories, right-click the blue ball icon in the Web server entry and select the New item in the menu that pops up. Then select Directory in the drop-down menu displayed. If you want to delete it later, right-click its entry and select Delete from the pop-up menu.

To configure a server or directory, right-click its entry and select the Properties item from the pop-up menu displayed. This opens a new window for configuring your selection, as shown in Figure 17-2. The window is divided into two panes: a left pane that shows a tree of configuration items and a right pane that displays the configuration dialog windows for these items. The structure is similar to the Netscape preferences interface.

On Linuxconf, an entry for Apache Web server is under the Server tasks heading with the Networking entries. Apache has entries for defaults, directory configuration, and virtual domains. A panel is displayed for each entry with fields where you can enter your value or buttons to click to select features. The defaults entry displays a panel listing field for the directives used to configure your main server. The subdirectory entry enables you to configure particular directories, using buttons

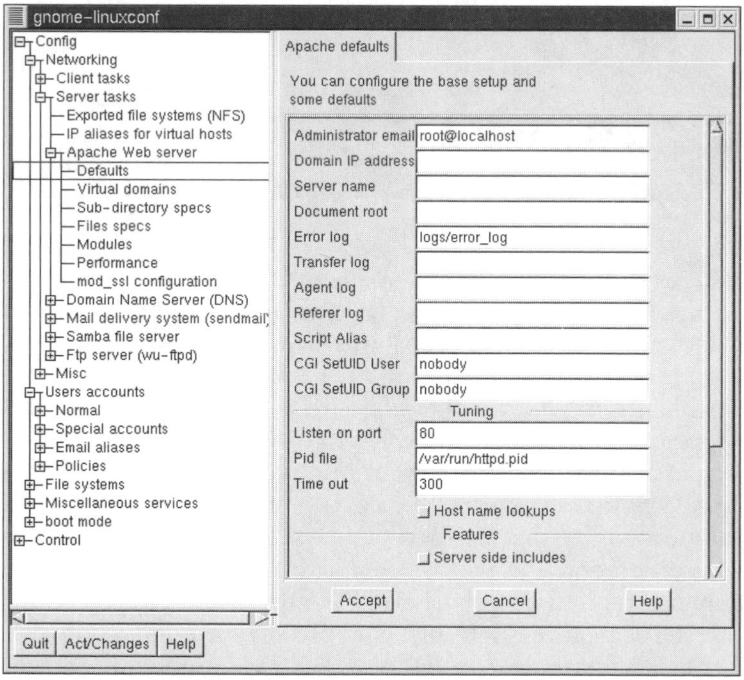

Figure 17-2. *The Linuxconf Apache configuration module*

to select controls you want to place on them. The files entry does the same, but for files. With virtual domains, you can create and configure virtual hosts, entering directive values into displayed fields and selecting controls from a list of buttons. The performance entry lets you set performance features like the maximum number of clients and timeouts. With the modules entry you can add to or edit the list modules to be loaded.

If you installed Apache as part of your Red Hat installation (a standard install), Linuxconf already has its Apache module loaded. Otherwise, to configure your Apache server, you may have to load the Apache module first into the Linuxconf utility. To do this, first select the Control entry, and then select Control files and systems, and, finally, select the Linuxconf modules entry. This displays a panel where you can select various Linuxconf modules you want added, including the one for Apache.

AccessConfig *filename*	File to be read for more directives after reading the ResourceConfig file. *Filename* is relative to the ServerRoot. Default: AccessConfig conf/access.conf Context: server config, virtual host
AccessFileName *filename filename ...*	Default directory configuration filenames located within directories. Default: AccessFileName **.htaccess** Context: server config, virtual host
Action *action-type cgi-script*	Adds an action, which activates *cgi-script* when *action-type* is triggered by the request. Context: server config, virtual host, directory, **.htaccess** Override: FileInfo Module: mod_actions
AddDescription *string file file ...*	Sets the description to display for a file. Can be a file extension, partial filename, wildcard expression, or full filename. String is enclosed in double quotes ("). Context: server config, virtual host, directory, **.htaccess** Override: Indexes Status: Base Module: mod_autoindex

Table 17-4.   *Apache Configuration Directives*

AddHandler *handler-name* *extension extension* ...	Maps the filename extensions *extension* to the handler *handler-name*. Context: server config, virtual host, directory, **.htaccess** Override: FileInfo Status: Base Module: mod_mime
AddIcon *icon name name* ...	Specifies the icon to display next to a file ending in *name*. Context: server config, virtual host, directory, **.htaccess** Override: Indexes Status: Base Module: mod_autoindex
AddIconByEncoding *icon MIME-encoding MIME-encoding* ...	Specifies the icon to display next to files with *MIME-encoding* (FancyIndexing). Context: server config, virtual host, directory, **.htaccess** Override: Indexes Status: Base Module: mod_autoindex
AddIconByType *icon MIME-type MIME-type* ...	Specifies the icon to display next to files of type *MIME-type* (FancyIndexing). Context: server config, virtual host, directory, **.htaccess** Override: Indexes Status: Base Module: mod_autoindex
AddLanguage *MIME-lang extension extension* ...	Maps the given filename extensions to the specified content language. Context: server config, virtual host, directory, **.htaccess** Override: FileInfo Status: Base Module: mod_mime

Table 17-4. *Apache Configuration Directives* (continued)

`AddModule` *module module ...*	Enables use of modules compiled, but not in use. Context: server config
`Alias` *url-path directory-filename*	Enables access to documents stored in the local file system, other than under the DocumentRoot. Context: server config, virtual host Status: Base Module: mod_alias
`allow` *from host host ...*	Determines which hosts can access a given directory: all, partial, or full domain name, or IP address. Context: directory, **.htaccess** Override: Limit Status: Base Module: mod_access
`AllowOverride` *override override ...*	Directives that can be overridden by entries in an **.htaccess** file. All allows overrides, and none denies them. Default: AllowOverride All Context: directory
`Anonymous` *user user ...*	Users who are allowed access without password verification. *User* is usually anonymous (case-sensitive). Default: none Context: directory, **.htaccess** Override: AuthConfig Status: Extension Module: mod_auth_anon
`Anonymous_Authoritative` on | off	When on, there is no fall-through to other authorization methods. Default: Anonymous_Authoritative off Context: directory, **.htaccess** Override: AuthConfig Status: Extension Module: mod_auth_anon

Table 17-4.   *Apache Configuration Directives* (continued)

AddType *MIME-type extension extension ...*	Maps the given filename extensions onto the specified content type. *MIME-type* is the MIME type to use for filenames containing extension. Context: server config, virtual host, directory, **.htaccess** Override: FileInfo Status: Base Module: mod_mime
AuthGroupFile *filename*	Sets the name of the file with the list of user groups for user authentication. Context: directory, **.htaccess** Override: AuthConfig Status: Base Module: mod_auth
AuthDBGroupFile *filename*	DB file containing the list of groups for user authentication. Context: directory, **.htaccess** Override: AuthConfig Status: Extension Module: mod_auth_db
AuthDBUserFile *filename*	DB file containing the list of users and passwords for user authentication. Context: directory, **.htaccess** Override: AuthConfig Status: Extension Module: mod_auth_db
AuthDBMGroupFile *filename*	DBM file containing the list of groups for user authentication. Context: directory, **.htaccess** Override: AuthConfig Status: Extension Module: mod_auth_dbm

Table 17-4. *Apache Configuration Directives* (continued)

`AuthDBMUserFile` *filename*	DBM file containing the list of users and passwords for user authentication. Context: directory, **.htaccess** Override: AuthConfig Status: Extension Module: mod_auth_dbm
`AuthName` *auth-domain*	The authorization realm for a directory. A realm is given to the client so the user knows which username and password to send. Context: directory, **.htaccess** Override: AuthConfig
`AuthType` *type*	Type of user authentication for a directory. Only Basic and Digest are currently implemented. Context: directory, **.htaccess** Override: AuthConfig
`AuthUserFile` *filename*	Sets the name of the file with the list of users and passwords for user authentication. Context: directory, **.htaccess** Override: AuthConfig Status: Base Module: mod_auth
`BindAddress` *saddr*	Binds the server to a specified IP address. If the value is *, then the server listens for connections on every IP address; otherwise, the server only listens on the IP address specified. Only one BindAddress directive can be used. For more control over the address and ports listened to, use the **Listen** directive. Default: BindAddress * Context: server config

Table 17-4.   *Apache Configuration Directives* (continued)

CheckSpelling on	off	Enables or disables spelling module. This module tries to find a matching document by comparing each document name in the requested directory against the requested document name, disregarding case and allowing up to one misspelling. Default: CheckSpelling Off Context: server config, virtual host, directory, **.htaccess** Override: Options Status: Base Module: mod_speling
ClearModuleList	Clears the built-in list of active modules. Context: server config
CustomLog *file-pipe* *format-or-nickname*	Creates a new log file with the specified format. Context: server config, virtual host Status: Base Compatibility: Nickname only available in Apache 1.3 or later Module: mod_log_config
DefaultIcon *url*	Specifies the icon to display for files when no specific icon is known (FancyIndexing). Context: server config, virtual host, directory, **.htaccess** Override: Indexes Status: Base Module: mod_autoindex
DefaultLanguage *MIME-lang*	Specifies *MIME-lang* as the default file language. Context: server config, virtual host, directory, **.htaccess** Override: FileInfo Status: Base Module: mod_mime

Table 17-4. *Apache Configuration Directives* (continued)

DefaultType *MIME-type*	Default type for documents whose type cannot be determined by their MIME types mappings. Default: DefaultType text/html Context: server config, virtual host, directory, **.htaccess** Override: FileInfo
deny *from host host ...*	Determines hosts that can access a given directory: **all**, or partial or full domain name or IP address. Context: directory, **.htaccess** Override: Limit Status: Base Module: mod_access
\<Directory *directory\> ...* **\</Directory\>**	**\<Directory\>** and **\</Directory\>** directives operate as tags that enclose a group of directives applying only to the named directory and subdirectories of that directory. Context: server config, virtual host
\<DirectoryMatch *regex\> ...* **\</DirectoryMatch\>**	**\<DirectoryMatch\>** and **\</DirectoryMatch\>** enclose a group of directives that apply only to the named directory. It operates the same as **\<Directory\>,** but takes a regular expression as an argument. Context: server config, virtual host
DirectoryIndex *local-url* *local-url ...*	Specifies the list of resources to look for when the client requests an index of the directory by specifying a / at the end of a directory name (usually index.html). Default: DirectoryIndex index.html Context: server config, virtual host, directory, **.htaccess** Override: Indexes Status: Base Module: mod_dir

Table 17-4.   *Apache Configuration Directives* (continued)

DocumentRoot *directory-filename*	The directory from which httpd serves files. Default: DocumentRoot /usr/local/ apache/htdocs (/home/httpd/html on Red Hat systems) Context: server config, virtual host
ErrorDocument *error-code document*	Redirects to a local or external URL to handle the problem/error. Context: server config, virtual host, directory, **.htaccess**
ErrorLog *filename* | *syslog*[:*facility*]	The file on which the server logs errors. Default: ErrorLog logs/error_log Context: server config, virtual host
FancyIndexing *Boolean*	Sets the FancyIndexing option for a directory. Boolean can be on or off. Context: server config, virtual host, directory, **.htaccess** Override: Indexes Status: Base Module: mod_autoindex
<Files *filename***>** ... **</Files>**	Provides for access control by filename. Similar to the **<Directory>** directive and **<Location>** directive. **<Files>** sections are processed in the order they appear in the configuration file, after the **<Directory>** sections and **.htaccess** files are read, but before **<Location>** sections. **<Files>** can be nested inside **<Directory>** sections to restrict the portion of the file system to which they apply. Context: server config, virtual host, **.htaccess**
<FilesMatch *regex***>** ... **</FilesMatch>**	Provides for access control by filename like the **<Files>** directive, but uses a regular expression. Context: server config, virtual host, **.htaccess**

Table 17-4. *Apache Configuration Directives* (continued)

Group *unix-group*	Sets the group for the server. The standalone server must be run initially as root. The recommendation is you set up a new group specifically for running the server. Default: Group #-1 Context: server config, virtual host
HeaderName *filename*	Specifies the name of the file to be inserted at the top of the index listing (FancyIndexing). Context: server config, virtual host, directory, **.htaccess** Override: Indexes Status: Base Module: mod_autoindex
HostNameLookups on | off | double	Enables DNS lookups so host names can be logged. Double refers to double-reverse DNS. Default: HostNameLookups off Context: server config, virtual host, directory
IdentityCheck *Boolean*	Enables RFC 1413-compliant logging of the remote user name for each connection. Default: IdentityCheck off Context: server config, virtual host, directory
<IfDefine [!]*parameter-name*> ... **</IfDefine>** Default: NoneContext: all	The **<IfDefine** *test*>...**</IfDefine>** section specifies conditional directives. Directives within an **IfDefine** section are processed if the test is true and are ignored otherwise. The test consists of a parameter name, which is true if the parameter is defined, and false if undefined. A ! placed before the parameter makes the test true if the parameter is undefined (not).
<IfModule [!]*module-name*> ... **</IfModule>**	The **<IfModule** *test*>...**</IfModule>** section specifies conditional directives. The test checks to see if a module is compiled in Apache. It is true if present, and false if not. A !module-name is true if the module is not present.

Table 17-4.   *Apache Configuration Directives* (continued)

SERVERS

Include *filename*	Inclusion of other configuration files. Context: server config
IndexOptions [+ | -]*option* [+ | -]*option* ...	Set options for directory indexing: FancyIndexing, IconHeight, IconsAreLinks, IconWidth, NameWidth, ScanHTMLTitles, SuppressDescription. Context: server config, virtual host, directory, **.htaccess** Override: Indexes Status: Base Module: mod_autoindex
KeepAlive on/off	Enables persistent connections, "Off" to disable. Default: KeepAlive On Context: server config
KeepAliveTimeout *seconds*	The number of seconds Apache waits for another request before closing the connection. Default: KeepAliveTimeout 15 Context: server config
<Limit *method method* ... **>** ... **</Limit>**	**<Limit>** and **</Limit>** specify a group of access control directives that apply only to the specified access methods, any valid HTTP method. Access control directives appearing outside a **<Limit>** directive apply to all access methods. Method names are GET, POST, PUT, DELETE, CONNECT, or OPTIONS
<LimitExcept *method method* ... **>** ... **</LimitExcept>**	**<LimitExcept>** and **</LimitExcept>** specify a group of access control directives, which then apply to any HTTP access method *not* listed in the arguments
LimitRequestBody *number*	Limits the size of an HTTP request message body. Default: LimitRequestBody 0 Context: server config, virtual host, directory, **.htaccess**

Table 17-4. *Apache Configuration Directives* (continued)

LimitRequestFields *number*	Limits the number of request header fields allowed in an HTTP request. Default: LimitRequestFields 100 Context: server config
Listen [*IP address*:]*port number*	Listens to more than one IP address or port. By default, it responds to requests on all IP interfaces, but only on the port given by the Port directive. Context: server config
ListenBacklog *backlog*	The maximum length of the queue of pending connections. Default: ListenBacklog 511 Context: server config
LoadFile *filename filename ...*	Links in the named object files or libraries when the server is started or restarted. Used to load additional code required for some module to work Context: server config Status: Base Module: mod_so
LoadModule *module filename*	Links in the object file or library filename and adds the module structure named *module* to the list of active modules. Context: server config Status: Base Module: mod_so
<Location *URL*> ... **</Location>**	The **<Location>** directive provides for access control by URL. Similar to the **<Directory>** directive. Context: server config, virtual host
<LocationMatch *regex*> ... **</LocationMatch>**	Provides access control by URL, in an identical manner to **<Location>**, using a regular expression as an argument. Context: server config, virtual host

Table 17-4.   *Apache Configuration Directives* (continued)

SERVERS

LockFile *filename*	Path to the lockfile used when Apache is compiled. Default: LockFile logs/accept.lock Context: server config
LogFormat *format* [*nickname*]	Sets the format of the default logfile named by the TransferLog directive Default: LogFormat "%h %l %u %t \"%r\" %s %b" Context: server config, virtual host Status: Base Module: mod_log_config
LogLevel *level*	Adjusts the verbosity of the messages recorded in the error logs. Default: LogLevel error Context: server config, virtual host
MaxClients *number*	Limits the number of simultaneous requests that can be supported. Any connection attempts over the MaxClients limit are normally queued, up to a number based on the **ListenBacklog** directive. Default: MaxClients 256 Context: server config
MaxKeepAliveRequests *number*	Limits the number of requests allowed per connection when KeepAlive is on Default: MaxKeepAliveRequests 100 Context: server config
NameVirtualHost *addr*[*:port*]	Specifies the address a name-based virtual host name resolves. If you have multiple name-based hosts on multiple addresses, repeat the directive for each address. Required for configuring name-based virtual hosts. Although *addr* can be a hostname, the recommendation is for you always to use an IP address. Context: server config

Table 17-4. *Apache Configuration Directives* (continued)

`Options` `[+|-]`*option* `[+|-]`*option* ...	Controls the server features available in a particular directory. If set to None, then none of the extra features are enabled. **All** All options except for MultiViews. This is the default setting. **ExecCGI** Execution of CGI scripts is permitted. **FollowSymLinks** The server follows symbolic links in this directory. **Includes** Server-side includes are permitted. **IncludesNOEXEC** Server-side includes are permitted, but the #exec command and #include of CGI scripts are disabled. **Indexes** Returns a formatted listing of the directory for directories with no DirectoryIndex. **MultiViews** Content negotiated MultiViews are allowed. **SymLinksIfOwnerMatch** The server only follows symbolic links for which the target file or directory is owned by the same user ID as the link. Context: server config, virtual host, directory, **.htaccess** Override: Options
`order` *ordering*	Controls the order in which allow and deny directives are evaluated Default: order deny, allow Context: directory, **.htaccess** Override: Limit Status: Base Module: mod_access

Table 17-4.   *Apache Configuration Directives* (continued)

SERVERS

PidFile *filename*	File in which the server records the process ID of the daemon. Default: PidFile logs/httpd.pid Context: server config
Port *number*	If no **Listen** or **BindAddress** directives exist, then a port directive sets the network port on which the server listens. Ports for a virtual host are set by the **VirtualHost** directive. Default: Port 80 Context: server config
ReadmeName *filename*	Specifies the name of the file to be appended to the end of the index listing. Context: server config, virtual host, directory, **.htaccess** Override: Indexes Status: Base Module: mod_autoindex
Redirect [*status*] *url-path url*	Maps an old URL into a new one. Context: server config, virtual host, directory, **.htaccess** Override: FileInfo Status: Base Module: mod_alias
RemoveHandler *extension extension* ...	Removes handler associations for files with the given extensions. This allows **.htaccess** files in subdirectories to undo any associations inherited from parent directories or the server configuration files. Context: directory, **.htaccess** Status: Base Module: mod_mime

Table 17-4.   *Apache Configuration Directives* (continued)

require *entity-name entity entity ...*	Selects the authenticated users that can access a directory. *entity-name* is either the user or group, followed by a list of users or groups. require user *userid userid* ... require *group group-name group-name* ... Context: directory, **.htaccess** Override: AuthConfig
ResourceConfig *filename*	Server reads this file for more directives after reading the **httpd.conf** file. Default: ResourceConfig conf/srm.conf Context: server config, virtual host
Satisfy *directive*	Access policy if both allow and require are used. The parameter can be either 'all' or 'any'. Syntax: Satisfy 'any' or 'all' Default: Satisfy all Context: directory, **.htaccess**
ScoreBoardFile *filename*	Specifies the ScoreBoardFile file. Default: ScoreBoardFile logs/apache_status Context: server config
Script *method cgi-script*	Adds an action, which activates *cgi-script* when a file is requested using the method of *method,* which can be one of GET, POST, PUT, or DELETE. Context: server config, virtual host, directory Status: Base Module: mod_actions
ScriptAlias *url-path directory-filename*	Marks the target directory as containing CGI scripts. Context: server config, virtual host Status: Base Module: mod_alias
ScriptInterpreterSource 'registry' or 'script'	Finds the interpreter used to run CGI scripts. The default method is to use the interpreter pointed to by the #! line in the script. Default: ScriptInterpreterSource script Context: directory, **.htaccess**

Table 17-4. *Apache Configuration Directives* (continued)

SERVERS

ServerAdmin *e-mail-address*	The e-mail address included in any error messages sent to a client. Context: server config, virtual host
ServerAlias *host1 host2 ...*	Sets the alternate names for a host, for use with name-based virtual hosts. Context: virtual host
ServerName *fully qualified domain name*	Sets the host name of the server. This is only used when creating redirection URLs. If it is not specified, then the server attempts to deduce it from its own IP address. Context: server config, virtual host
ServerPath *pathname*	Sets the legacy URL pathname for a host, for use with name-based virtual hosts. Context: virtual host
ServerRoot *directory-filename*	Sets the directory in which the server resides. Default: ServerRoot /usr/local/apache Context: server config
ServerSignature Off | On | EMail	Configures a trailing footer line under server-generated documents, such as error messages. Default: ServerSignature Off Context: server config, virtual host, directory, **.htaccess**
ServerType *type*	Sets how the server is executed by the system. *type* can be either inetd or standalone. Default: ServerType standalone Context: server config
SetHandler *handler-name*	Forces all matching files to be parsed through the handler given by *handler-name*. Context: directory, **.htaccess** Status: Base Module: mod_mime
StartServers *number*	Sets the number of child server processes created on startup. Default: StartServers 5 Context: server config

Table 17-4. *Apache Configuration Directives* (continued)

TimeOut *number*	Sets the timeout in seconds for receiving GET requests, receipt of POST and PUT requests, and TCP packet transmissions acknowledgments. Default: TimeOut 300 Context: server config
TransferLog *file-pipe*	Adds a log file in the format defined by the most recent **LogFormat** directive or Common Log Format if default is specified. Default: none Context: server config, virtual host Status: Base Module: mod_log_config
TypesConfig *filename*	Sets the location of the MIME types configuration file. Default: TypesConfig conf/MIME.types Context: server config Status: Base Module: mod_mime
User *unix-userid*	Specifies the user ID for the server. The standalone server must be run as root initially. You can use a user name or a user ID number. The user should have no access to system files. The recommendation is for you to set up a new user and group specifically for running the server. Default: User #-1 Context: server config, virtual host
UserDir *directory/filename*	Sets the real directory in a user's home directory to use when a request for a document for a user is received. Default: UserDir public_html Context: server config, virtual host Status: Base Module: mod_userdir

Table 17-4.   *Apache Configuration Directives* (continued)

\<VirtualHost *addr*[:*port*] ...> ... **\</VirtualHost>**	**\<VirtualHost>** and **\</VirtualHost>** specify a group of directives that apply only to a particular virtual host. When the server receives a request for a document on a particular virtual host, it uses the configuration directives enclosed in the **\<VirtualHost>** section. Addr can be an IP address of the virtual host or its fully qualified domain name. Each VirtualHost must correspond to a different IP address, a different port number, or a different host name for the server. Context: server config

Table 17-4.   *Apache Configuration Directives* (continued)

Apache Web Server Configuration Files

The current Red Hat **httpd.conf** and **smf.conf** configuration files are shown here:

httpd.conf

```
##
## httpd.conf -- Apache HTTP server configuration file
##

# This is the main server configuration file. See URL http://www.apache.org/
# for instructions.

# Do NOT simply read the instructions in here without understanding
# what they do, if you are unsure consult the online docs. You have been
# warned.

# Originally by Rob McCool

# ServerType is either inetd, or standalone.

ServerType standalone

# If you are running from inetd, go to "ServerAdmin".

# Port: The port the standalone listens to. For ports < 1023, you will
```

```
# need httpd to be run as root initially.

Port 80

# HostnameLookups: Log the names of clients or just their IP numbers
#   e.g.   www.apache.org (on) or 204.62.129.132 (off)
# The default is off because it'd be overall better for the net if people
# had to knowingly turn this feature on.

HostnameLookups off

# If you wish httpd to run as a different user or group, you must run
# httpd as root initially and it will switch.

# User/Group: The name (or #number) of the user/group to run httpd as.
#   On SCO (ODT 3) use User nouser and Group nogroup
#   On HPUX you may not be able to use shared memory as nobody, and the
#   suggested workaround is to create a user www and use that user.
#   NOTE that some kernels refuse to setgid(Group) or semctl(IPC_SET)
#   when the value of (unsigned)Group is above 60000;
#   don't use Group nobody on these systems!

User nobody
Group nobody

# ServerAdmin: Your address, where problems with the server should be
# e-mailed.

ServerAdmin root@localhost

# ServerRoot: The directory the server's config, error, and log files
# are kept in.
# NOTE!  If you intend to place this on a NFS (or otherwise network)
# mounted filesystem then please read the LockFile documentation,
# you will save yourself a lot of trouble.

ServerRoot /etc/httpd

# BindAddress: You can support virtual hosts with this option. This option
# is used to tell the server which IP address to listen to. It can either
# contain "*", an IP address, or a fully qualified Internet domain name.
# See also the VirtualHost directive.

#BindAddress *

# ErrorLog: The location of the error log file. If this does not start
# with /, ServerRoot is prepended to it.
```

```
ErrorLog logs/error_log

# LogLevel: Control the number of messages logged to the error_log.
# Possible values include: debug, info, notice, warn, error, crit,
# alert, emerg.

LogLevel warn

# Dynamic Shared Object (DSO) Support
#
# To be able to use the functionality of a module
# which was built as a DSO you
# have to place corresponding 'LoadModule' lines at this location so the
# directives contained in it are actually available _before_ they are used.
# Please read the file README.DSO in the Apache 1.3 distribution for more
# details about the DSO mechanism and run 'httpd -l' for the list of already
# built-in (statically linked and thus always available) modules in httpd
# binary.
#
# Example:
# LoadModule foo_module libexec/mod_foo.so
#
# Documentation for modules is in "/home/httpd/manual/mod" in HTML format.

#LoadModule mmap_static_module modules/mod_mmap_static.so
LoadModule env_module          modules/mod_env.so
LoadModule config_log_module   modules/mod_log_config.so
LoadModule agent_log_module    modules/mod_log_agent.so


............................... . .

#LoadModule example_module     modules/mod_example.so
#LoadModule unique_id_module    modules/mod_unique_id.so
LoadModule setenvif_module     modules/mod_setenvif.so

# Extra Modules
#LoadModule php_module          modules/mod_php.so
#LoadModule php3_module         modules/libphp3.so
#LoadModule perl_module         modules/libperl.so

#  Reconstruction of the complete module list from all available modules
#  (static and shared ones) to achieve correct module execution order.
#  [WHENEVER YOU CHANGE THE LOADMODULE SECTION ABOVE UPDATE THIS, TOO]
ClearModuleList
#AddModule mod_mmap_static.c
AddModule mod_env.c
AddModule mod_log_config.c
```

```
.................................. . .
#AddModule mod_example.c
#AddModule mod_unique_id.c
AddModule mod_so.c
AddModule mod_setenvif.c

# Extra Modules
#AddModule mod_php.c
#AddModule mod_php3.c
#AddModule mod_perl.c


# The following directives define some format nicknames for use with
# a CustomLog directive (see below).

LogFormat "%h %l %u %t \"%r\" %>s %b \"%{Referer}i\" \"%{User-Agent}i\"" combined
LogFormat "%h %l %u %t \"%r\" %>s %b" common
LogFormat "%{Referer}i -> %U" referer
LogFormat "%{User-agent}i" agent

# The location of the access logfile (Common Logfile Format).
# If this does not start with /, ServerRoot is prepended to it.

CustomLog logs/access_log common

# If you would like to have an agent and referer logfile uncomment the
# following directives.

#CustomLog logs/referer_log referer
#CustomLog logs/agent_log agent

# If you prefer a single logfile with access, agent and referer information
# (Combined Logfile Format) you can use the following directive.


#CustomLog logs/access_log combined

# PidFile: The file the server should log its pid to
PidFile /var/run/httpd.pid

# ScoreBoardFile: File used to store internal server process information.
# Not all architectures require this.  But if yours does (you'll know because
# this file is created when you run Apache) then you *must* ensure that
# no two invocations of Apache share the same scoreboard file.
ScoreBoardFile /var/run/httpd.scoreboard


# The LockFile directive sets the path to the lockfile used when Apache
```

```
# is compiled with either USE_FCNTL_SERIALIZED_ACCEPT or
# USE_FLOCK_SERIALIZED_ACCEPT. This directive should normally be left at
# its default value. The main reason for changing it is if the logs
# directory is NFS mounted, since the lockfile MUST BE STORED ON A LOCAL
# DISK. The PID of the main server process is automatically appended to
# the filename.
#
#LockFile /var/lock/httpd.lock

# ServerName allows you to set a host name which is sent back to clients for
# your server if it's different than the one the program would get (i.e. use
# "www" instead of the host's real name).
#
# Note: You cannot just invent host names and hope they work. The name you
# define here must be a valid DNS name for your host. If you don't understand
# this, ask your network administrator.

#ServerName new.host.name

# UseCanonicalName:  (new for 1.3)  With this setting turned on, whenever
# Apache needs to construct a self-referencing URL (a url that refers back
# to the server the response is coming from) it will use ServerName and
# Port to form a "canonical" name.  With this setting off, Apache will
# use the hostname:port that the client supplied, when possible.  This
# also affects SERVER_NAME and SERVER_PORT in CGIs.
UseCanonicalName on

# CacheNegotiatedDocs: By default, Apache sends Pragma: no-cache with each
# document that was negotiated on the basis of content. This asks proxy
# servers not to cache the document. Uncommenting the following line disables
# this behavior, and proxies will be allowed to cache the documents.

#CacheNegotiatedDocs

# Timeout: The number of seconds before receives and sends time out

Timeout 300

# KeepAlive: Whether or not to allow persistent connections (more than
# one request per connection). Set to "Off" to deactivate.

KeepAlive On

# MaxKeepAliveRequests: The maximum number of requests to allow
# during a persistent connection. Set to 0 to allow an unlimited amount.
# We recommend you leave this number high, for maximum performance.
```

```
MaxKeepAliveRequests 100

# KeepAliveTimeout: Number of seconds to wait for the next request

KeepAliveTimeout 15

# Server-pool size regulation.  Rather than making you guess how many
# server processes you need, Apache dynamically adapts to the load it
# sees --- that is, it tries to maintain enough server processes to
# handle the current load, plus a few spare servers to handle transient
# load spikes (e.g., multiple simultaneous requests from a single
# Netscape browser).

# It does this by periodically checking how many servers are waiting
# for a request.  If there are fewer than MinSpareServers, it creates
# a new spare.  If there are more than MaxSpareServers, some of the
# spares die off.  These values are probably OK for most sites ---

MinSpareServers 8
MaxSpareServers 20

# Number of servers to start --- should be a reasonable ballpark figure.

StartServers 10

# Limit on total number of servers running, i.e., limit on the number
# of clients who can simultaneously connect --- if this limit is ever
# reached, clients will be LOCKED OUT, so it should NOT BE SET TOO LOW.
# It is intended mainly as a brake to keep a runaway server from taking
# Unix with it as it spirals down...

MaxClients 150

# MaxRequestsPerChild: the number of requests each child process is
#   allowed to process before the child dies.
#   The child will exit so as to avoid problems after prolonged use when
#   Apache (and maybe the libraries it uses) leak.  On most systems, this
#   isn't really needed, but a few (such as Solaris) do have notable leaks
#   in the libraries.

MaxRequestsPerChild 100

# Proxy Server directives. Uncomment the following line to
# enable the proxy server:

#ProxyRequests On
```

```
# To enable the cache as well, edit and uncomment the following lines:

#CacheRoot /var/cache/httpd
#CacheSize 5
#CacheGcInterval 4
#CacheMaxExpire 24
#CacheLastModifiedFactor 0.1
#CacheDefaultExpire 1
#NoCache a_domain.com another_domain.edu joes.garage_sale.com

# Listen: Allows you to bind Apache to specific IP addresses and/or
# ports, in addition to the default. See also the VirtualHost command

#Listen 3000
#Listen 12.34.56.78:80

# VirtualHost: Allows the daemon to respond to requests for more than one
# server address, if your server machine is configured to accept IP packets
# for multiple addresses. This can be accomplished with the ifconfig
# alias flag, or through kernel patches like VIF.

# Any httpd.conf or srm.conf directive may go into a VirtualHost command.
# See also the BindAddress entry.

#<VirtualHost host.some_domain.com>
#ServerAdmin webmaster@host.some_domain.com
#DocumentRoot /www/docs/host.some_domain.com
#ServerName host.some_domain.com
#ErrorLog logs/host.some_domain.com-error_log
#TransferLog logs/host.some_domain.com-access_log
#</VirtualHost>
```

srm.conf

```
##
## srm.conf -- Apache HTTP server configuration file
##

# With this document, you define the name space that users see of your http
# server.  This file also defines server settings which affect how requests are
# serviced, and how results should be formatted.

# See the tutorials at http://www.apache.org/ for
```

```
# more information.

# Originally by Rob McCool; Adapted for Apache


# DocumentRoot: The directory out of which you will serve your
# documents. By default, all requests are taken from this directory, but
# symbolic links and aliases may be used to point to other locations.

DocumentRoot /home/httpd/html

# UserDir: The name of the directory which is appended onto a user's home
# directory if a ~user request is received.

UserDir public_html

# DirectoryIndex: Name of the file or files to use as a pre-written HTML
# directory index.  Separate multiple entries with spaces.

DirectoryIndex index.html index.shtml index.cgi

# FancyIndexing is whether you want fancy directory indexing or standard

FancyIndexing on

# AddIcon tells the server which icon to show for different files or filename
# extensions

AddIconByEncoding (CMP,/icons/compressed.gif) x-compress x-gzip

AddIconByType (TXT,/icons/text.gif) text/*
AddIconByType (IMG,/icons/image2.gif) image/*
AddIconByType (SND,/icons/sound2.gif) audio/*
AddIconByType (VID,/icons/movie.gif) video/*

AddIcon /icons/binary.gif .bin .exe
AddIcon /icons/binhex.gif .hqx
AddIcon /icons/tar.gif .tar
AddIcon /icons/world2.gif .wrl .wrl.gz .vrml .vrm .iv
AddIcon /icons/compressed.gif .Z .z .tgz .gz .zip
AddIcon /icons/a.gif .ps .ai .eps
AddIcon /icons/layout.gif .html .shtml .htm .pdf
AddIcon /icons/text.gif .txt
AddIcon /icons/c.gif .c
AddIcon /icons/p.gif .pl .py
AddIcon /icons/f.gif .for
AddIcon /icons/dvi.gif .dvi
```

```
AddIcon /icons/uuencoded.gif .uu
AddIcon /icons/script.gif .conf .sh .shar .csh .ksh .tcl
AddIcon /icons/tex.gif .tex
AddIcon /icons/bomb.gif core

AddIcon /icons/back.gif ..
AddIcon /icons/hand.right.gif README
AddIcon /icons/folder.gif ^^DIRECTORY^^
AddIcon /icons/blank.gif ^^BLANKICON^^

# DefaultIcon is which icon to show for files which do not have an icon
# explicitly set.

DefaultIcon /icons/unknown.gif

# AddDescription allows you to place a short description after a file in
# server-generated indexes.
# Format: AddDescription "description" filename

# ReadmeName is the name of the README file the server will look for by
# default. Format: ReadmeName name
#
# The server will first look for name.html, include it if found, and it will
# then look for name and include it as plaintext if found.
#
# HeaderName is the name of a file which should be prepended to
# directory indexes.

ReadmeName README
HeaderName HEADER

# IndexIgnore is a set of filenames which directory indexing should ignore
# Format: IndexIgnore name1 name2...

IndexIgnore .??* *~ *# HEADER* README* RCS

# AccessFileName: The name of the file to look for in each directory
# for access control information.

AccessFileName .htaccess

# TypesConfig describes where the mime.types file (or equivalent) is
# to be found.

TypesConfig /etc/mime.types

# DefaultType is the default MIME type for documents which the server
```

```
# cannot find the type of from filename extensions.

DefaultType text/plain

# AddEncoding allows you to have certain browsers (Mosaic/X 2.1+) uncompress
# information on the fly. Note: Not all browsers support this.

AddEncoding x-compress Z
AddEncoding x-gzip gz

# AddLanguage allows you to specify the language of a document. You can
# then use content negotiation to give a browser a file in a language
# it can understand.  Note that the suffix does not have to be the same
# as the language keyword --- those with documents in Polish (whose
# net-standard language code is pl) may wish to use "AddLanguage pl .po"
# to avoid the ambiguity with the common suffix for perl scripts.

AddLanguage en .en
AddLanguage fr .fr
AddLanguage de .de
AddLanguage da .da
AddLanguage el .el
AddLanguage it .it

# LanguagePriority allows you to give precedence to some languages
# in case of a tie during content negotiation.
# Just list the languages in decreasing order of preference.

LanguagePriority en fr de

# Redirect allows you to tell clients about documents which used to exist in
# your server's namespace, but do not anymore. This allows you to tell the
# clients where to look for the relocated document.
# Format: Redirect fakename url


# Aliases: Add here as many aliases as you need (with no limit). The format is
# Alias fakename realname

# Note that if you include a trailing / on fakename then the server will
# require it to be present in the URL.  So "/icons" isn't aliased in this
# example.

Alias /icons/ /home/httpd/icons/

# ScriptAlias: This controls which directories contain server scripts.
# Format: ScriptAlias fakename realname
```

```
ScriptAlias /cgi-bin/ /home/httpd/cgi-bin/

# If you want to use server side includes, or CGI outside
# ScriptAliased directories, uncomment the following lines.

# AddType allows you to tweak mime.types without actually editing it, or to
# make certain files to be certain types.
# Format: AddType type/subtype ext1

# For example, the PHP3 module (not part of the Apache distribution)
# will typically use:
#AddType application/x-httpd-php3 .php3
#AddType application/x-httpd-php3-source .phps
# The following is for PHP/FI (PHP2):
#AddType application/x-httpd-php .phtml

# AddHandler allows you to map certain file extensions to "handlers",
# actions unrelated to filetype. These can be either built into the server
# or added with the Action command (see below)
# Format: AddHandler action-name ext1

# To use CGI scripts:
#AddHandler cgi-script .cgi

# To use server-parsed HTML files
AddType text/html .shtml
AddHandler server-parsed .shtml

# Uncomment the following line to enable Apache's send-asis HTTP file
# feature
#AddHandler send-as-is asis

# If you wish to use server-parsed imagemap files, use
AddHandler imap-file map

# To enable type maps, you might want to use
#AddHandler type-map var

# To enable the perl module (if you have it installed), uncomment
# the following section
#
#Alias /perl/ /home/httpd/perl/
#<Location /perl>
#SetHandler perl-script
#PerlHandler Apache::Registry
#Options +ExecCGI
```

```
#</Location>

# Action lets you define media types that will execute a script whenever
# a matching file is called. This eliminates the need for repeated URL
# pathnames for oft-used CGI file processors.
# Format: Action media/type /cgi-script/location
# Format: Action handler-name /cgi-script/location

# MetaDir: specifies the name of the directory in which Apache can find
# meta information files. These files contain additional HTTP headers
# to include when sending the document

#MetaDir .web

# MetaSuffix: specifies the file name suffix for the file containing the
# meta information.

#MetaSuffix .meta

# Customizable error response (Apache style)
#   these come in three flavors
#
#     1) plain text
#ErrorDocument 500 "The server made a boo boo.
#   n.b.  the (") marks it as text, it does not get output
#
#     2) local redirects
#ErrorDocument 404 /missing.html
#   to redirect to local url /missing.html
#ErrorDocument 404 /cgi-bin/missing_handler.pl
#   n.b. can redirect to a script or a document using server-side-includes.
#
#     3) external redirects
#ErrorDocument 402 http://some.other_server.com/subscription_info.html
#

# mod_mime_magic allows the server to use various hints from the file itself
# to determine its type.
#MimeMagicFile /etc/httpd/conf/magic

# The following directives disable keepalives and HTTP header flushes.
# The first directive disables it for Netscape 2.x and browsers which
# spoof it. There are known problems with these.
# The second directive is for Microsoft Internet Explorer 4.0b2
# which has a broken HTTP/1.1 implementation and does not properly
# support keepalive when it is used on 301 or 302 (redirect) responses.
```

```
BrowserMatch "Mozilla/2" nokeepalive
BrowserMatch "MSIE 4\.0b2;" nokeepalive downgrade-1.0 force-response-1.0

# The following directive disables HTTP/1.1 responses to browsers which
# are in violation of the HTTP/1.0 spec by not being able to grok a
# basic 1.1 response.

BrowserMatch "RealPlayer 4\.0" force-response-1.0
BrowserMatch "Java/1\.0" force-response-1.0
BrowserMatch "JDK/1\.0" force-response-1.0
```

Chapter 18

Domain Name System

The *Domain Name System* (*DNS*) is an Internet service that converts domain names into their corresponding IP addresses. As you may recall, all computers connected to the Internet are addressed using an *Internet Protocol* (*IP*) address. This consists of a number composed of four segments separated by periods. Depending on the type of network, several of the first segments are used for the network address and several of the last segments are used for the host address. In a standard Class C network used in smaller networks, the first three segments are the computer's network address and the last segment is the computer's host ID. For example, in the address 192.168.1.2, 192.168.1 is the network address and **2** is the computer's host ID within that network. Together, they make up an IP address with which the computer can be addressed from anywhere on the Internet. IP addresses, though, are difficult to remember and easy to get wrong. Early on, IP addresses were associated with corresponding names called fully qualified domain names. A *fully qualified domain name* is composed of three or more segments: the first segment is the name to identify the host and the remaining segments are for the network in which the host is located. The network segments of a fully qualified domain name are usually referred to simply as the domain name, while the host part is referred to as the host name (though this is also used to refer to the complete fully qualified domain name). The fully qualified domain name, **www.linux.org**, has an IP address 198.182.196.56, where 198.182.196 is the network address and 56 is the host ID. Computers can be accessed only with an IP address. So, a fully qualified domain name must first be translated into its corresponding IP address to be of any use. See Chapter 30 for a detailed discussion of IP addresses, including network classes and *Classes Interdomain Routing* (*CIDR*).

Any computer on the Internet can maintain a file that manually associates IP addresses with domain names. On Linux and UNIX systems, this file is called the **/etc/hosts** file. Here, you can enter the IP address and domain names of computers you commonly access. Using this method, however, each computer needs a complete listing of all other computers on the Internet, and that listing must be updated constantly. Early on, this became clearly impractical for the Internet, though it is still feasible for small isolated networks. The Domain Name System has been implemented to deal with the task of translating the domain name of any computer on the Internet to its IP address. The task is carried out by interconnecting domain name severs that keep lists of fully qualified domain names and their IP addresses. The Internet is composed of many connected subnets called *domains,* each with its own servers—such as mail servers. Each subnet also has its own domain name servers that keep track of all the fully qualified domain names and IP addresses for all the computers on its network. Domain name servers are hierarchically linked to root servers, which, in turn, connect to other root servers and the domain name servers on their subnets throughout the Internet. The section of a network for which a given domain name server is responsible is called a *zone*. Although a zone may correspond to a domain, many zones may, in fact, be within a domain, each with its own name server. This is true for large domains where too many systems exist for one name server to manage.

When a user enters a fully qualified domain name to access a remote system, a resolver program queries the local network's domain name server requesting the corresponding IP address for that remote system. The names of the domain name servers that service a host's network are kept in the host's **/etc/resolv.conf** file.

If you are setting up a domain name server for a *local area network* (*LAN*) that is not connected to the Internet, you should use a special set of IP numbers reserved for such non-Internet networks (also known as *private networks* or *intranets*). This is especially true if you are implementing IP masquerading, where only a gateway machine has an Internet address, and the others make use of that one address to connect to the Internet. For a class C network (254 hosts or less), these are numbers, which having the special network number 192.168., as used in these examples. If you are setting up a LAN, such as a small business or home network, you are free to use these numbers for your local machines. You can set up a private network, such as an intranet, using network cards such as Ethernet cards and Ethernet hubs, and then configure your machines with IP addresses starting from 192.168.1.1. The host segment can range from 1 to 254, where 255 is used for the broadcast address. If you have three machines on your home network, you could give them the addresses 192.168.1.1, 192.168.1.2, and 192.168.1.3. You can then set up DNS for your network by running a domain name server on one of the machines. This machine becomes your network's domain name server. You can then give your machines fully qualified domain names and configure your domain name server to translate the names to their corresponding IP addresses. For example, you could give the machine 192.168.1.1 the name **turtle.mytrek.com**, and the machine 192.168.1.2 the name **rabbit.mytrek.com**. You can also implement Internet services on your network such as ftp, Web, and mail services by setting up servers for them on your machines. You can then configure your domain name server to let users access those services using fully qualified domain names. For example, for the **mytrek.com** network, the Web server could be accessed using the name **www.mytrek.com**. Instead of a domain name service, you could have the /etc/hosts files in each machine contain the entire list of IP addresses and domain names for all the machines in your network. But, for any changes, you would have to update each machine's /etc/hosts file.

Numbers are also reserved for Class A and Class B non-Internet local networks. Table 18-1 lists these addresses. The possible addresses available span from 0 to 255 in the host segment of the address. For example, Class B network addresses range from 172.16.0.0 to 172.16.255.255, giving you a total of 65,534 possible hosts. The Class C network range from 192.168.0.0 to 192.168.255.255, giving you 254 possible subnetworks, each with 254 possible hosts. The number 127.0.0.0 is reserved for a system's loopback interface, which allows it to communicate with itself, as it enables users on the same system to send messages to each other.

SERVERS

10.0.0.0	Class A Network
172.16.0.0	Class B Network
192.168.0.0	Class C Network
127.0.0.0	Loopback Network (for system self-communication)

Table 18-1. *Non-Internet Private Network IP Addresses*

BIND

The domain name server software currently in use on Linux systems is *Berkeley Internet Name Domain* (*BIND*). BIND was originally developed at the University of California, Berkeley, and is currently maintained and supported by *the Internet Software Consortium* (*ISC*). You can obtain BIND documentation and current software releases from its Web site at **www.isc.org**. The site includes online Web page documentation and manuals, including the *BIND Operations Guide* (*BOG*). RPM packages are available at Red Hat FTP sites. The BIND directory in **/usr/doc** contains extensive documentation, including Web page manuals and examples. The Linux HOW-TO for the Domain Name Service, DNS-HOWTO, provides detailed examples. Documentation, news, and DNS tools can be obtained from the DNS Resource Directory at **www.dns.net/dnsrd**.

The BIND domain name server software consists of a name server daemon called **named**, several sample configuration files, and resolver libraries. As of 1998, a new version of BIND, beginning with the series number 8.*x*, implemented a new configuration file using a new syntax. Older versions, which begin with the number 4.*x*, use a different configuration file with an older syntax. In effect, two versions are now in use with different configuration files. All Linux distributions currently install the newer 8.*x* version of BIND.

To operate your machine as a name server, simply run the **named** daemon with the appropriate configuration. The **named** daemon listens for resolution requests and provides the correct IP address for the requested host name. You can use the **ndc** utility provided with BIND to start, stop, restart, and check the status of the server as you test its configuration. **ndc** with the **stop** command stops **named** and, with the **start** command starts it again, reading your **named.conf** file. **ndc** with the **help** command provides a list of all **ndc** commands. Once your name server is running, you can test it using the **nslookup** utility. **nslookup** queries a name server, providing information about hosts and domains. If you start **nslookup** with no arguments, it enters an interactive mode where you can issue different **nslookup** commands to refine your queries. Numerous other DNS tools are also available, such as Dig and host. Check the DNS Resource Directory at **www.dns.net/dnsrd** for a listing.

On Red Hat systems, the **named** daemon is started using a startup script in the **/etc/rc.d/init.d** directory called **named**. You can use this script to start and stop the daemon using the **stop** and **start** arguments. **named** runs as a standalone daemon, constantly running. If you don't want **named** to run, you can use the System V Runlevel Editor or Linuxconf to change its status.

Domain Name System Configuration

You configure a domain name server using a configuration file, several zone files, and a cache file. The part of a network for which the name server is responsible is called a zone. A *zone* is not the same as a domain because in a large domain, you could have several zones, each with its own name server. You could also have one name server service several zones. In this case, each zone has its own zone file. The zone files hold resource records that provide host name and IP address associations for computers on the network for which the domain name server is responsible. Zone files exist for the server's network and the local machine. The most commonly used zone types are described here.

- **Master zone** This is the primary zone file for a network. It holds the mapping from a domain name to IP addresses for all the hosts on the network.

- **Slave zone** These are references to other domain name servers for your network. Your network can have a master domain name server and several slave domain name servers to help carry the workload. A slave domain name server automatically copies its configuration files, including all zone files, from the master domain name server. Any change to the master configuration files triggers an automatic download of these files to the slave servers. In effect, you only have to manage the configuration files for the master domain name server, as they are automatically copied to the slave servers.

- **Forward zone** The forward zone lists name servers outside your network that should be searched if your network's name server fails to resolve and address.

Zone entries are defined in the **named.conf** file. Here you place zone entries for your master, slave, and forward domain name servers. In addition, you also need to make entries for several special zones, described here.

- **IN-ADDR.ARPA zone** For each master zone entry, a corresponding reverse mapping zone entry named IN-ADDR.ARPA also exists, as well as one for the localhost. This entry performs reverse mapping from an IP address to its domain name. The name of the zone entry uses the domain IP address, which is the IP address with segments listed starting from the host, instead of the network. So, for the IP address 192.168.1.4 where 4 is the host address, the corresponding domain IP address is 4.1.168.192, listing the segments in reverse order. The reverse mapping for the localhost is 0.0.127.

- **. zone**   This zone entry defines a hint zone specifying the root name servers.

As an alternative to making entries in the configuration files manually, you can use the Linuxconf domain name server configuration panels. You can use the **dnsconf** command to start up Linuxconf to perform only the Domain Name configuration tasks. This command displays a window with buttons for the different Domain Name Server configuration panels. If you use the main Linuxconf window, select the Domain Name Server entry in the Servers Tasks list located under Networking. Linuxconf provides panels for primary (master), secondary (slave), reverse mapping, and forwarder zone entries. You can also configure features such as access control and logging. When you finish configuration, Linuxconf generates new **named.conf** and zone files. Use the domain panel to create zone files, and the IP reverse mapping panel to create corresponding reverse mapping zone files. In this panel, be sure to use only the network part of the IP address for the network number. Figure 18-1 shows the domain name server panel.

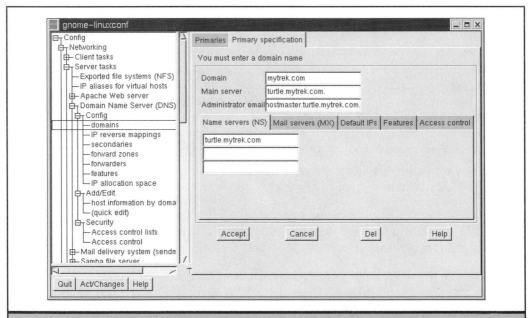

Figure 18-1.   *Linuxconf domain name server configuration*

named.conf

The configuration file for the **named** daemon is **named.conf**, located in the **/etc** directory. It uses a flexible syntax similar to C programs. The format enables easy configuration of selected zones, enabling features such as access control lists and categorized logging. The **named.conf** file consists of BIND configuration commands with attached blocks within which specific options are listed. A `configuration` command is followed by arguments and a block that is delimited with braces. Within the block are lines of option and feature entries. Each entry is terminated with a semicolon. Comments can use the C, C++, or Shell/Perl syntax: enclosing /* */, preceding //, or preceding #. The following example shows a `zone` command followed by the zone name and a block of options that begin with an opening brace, {. Each option entry ends with a semicolon. The entire block ends with a closing brace, also followed by a semicolon.

```
// a caching only nameserver config
//
zone "." {
     type hint;
     file "named.ca";
};
```

The **named.conf** file is a new feature implemented with BIND version 8.*x*. The older BIND 4.*x* versions use a file called **named.boot**. This file is no longer used by version 8.*x*. The syntax used in these configuration files differs radically. If you upgrade to 8.*x*, you can use the **named-bootconf.pl** Perl script provided with the BIND software to convert your **named.boot** file to a **named.conf** file.

The **zone** command is used to specify the domains the name server will service. You enter the keyword **zone,** followed by the name of the domain placed within double quotes. Do not place a period at the end of the domain name. In the following example, a period is within the domain name, but not at the end, **"mytrek.com"**. This differs from the zone file, which requires a period at the end of a complete domain name.

After the zone name, you can specify its class. By default, this is the Internet whose class name is "**in**". Within the zone block, you can place several options. Two essential options are the **type** and the **file**. The **type** option is used to specify the zone's type. The **file** option is used to specify the name of the zone file to be used for this zone. You can choose from several types of zones: master, slave, stub, forward, and hint. Master specifies the zone holds master information and is authorized to act on it. A master server was called a primary server in the older 4.*x* BIND configuration. *Slave* indicates the zone needs to update its data periodically from a specified master name server. A slave is also known as a *secondary server*. You use this entry if your name server is operating as a secondary server for another primary (master) domain name server. A *stub zone* only copies other name server entries, instead of the entire zone. A *forward zone* directs all queries to name servers specified in a forwarders statement. A *hint zone* specifies the set of root name servers used by all Internet domain name servers. You can also specify several options that can override any global options set with the **options** command. Table 18-2 lists the BIND zone types. The following example shows a simple **zone** command for the **mytrek.com** domain. Its class is Internet, "in", and its type is master. The name of its zone file is usually the same as the zone name, in this case, **"mytrek.com"**.

```
zone "mytrek.com" in {
        type master;
        file "mytrek.com";
};
```

Other commands, such as **acl**, **server**, **control**, and **logging**, enable you to configure different features for your name server. The server statement defines the characteristics to be associated with a remote name server, such as the transfer method and key ID for transaction security. The control statement defines special control channels. The key statement defines a key ID to be used in a server statement that associates an authentication method with a particular name server. The logging statement is used to configure logging options for the name server, such as the maximum size of the log file and a severity level for messages. To control access by other hosts, you use the **acl** command. **allow** and **deny** options with access control host lists enable you to deny or allow access by specified hosts to the name server. Table 18-3 lists the **BIND** commands.

The **options** statement defines global options and can be used only once in the configuration file. An extensive number of options cover such components as forwarding, name checking, directory path names, access control, and zone transfers, among others. A complete listing can be found in the BIND documentation. A critically important option found in most configuration files is the **directory** option, which holds the location of the name server's zone and cache files on your system. The following example is taken from the Red Hat **/etc/named.conf** file. This example specifies the zone files are located in

master	Primary DNS zone
slave	Slave (secondary) DNS server. Controlled by a master DNS server.
hint	Set of root DNS Internet servers
forward	Forwards any queries in it to other servers
stub	Like a slave zone, but only holds names of DNS servers

Table 18-2.   *DNS BIND Zone Types*

the **/var/named** directory. In this directory, you can find your zone files, including those used for your local system.

```
options {
        directory "/var/named";
        forwarders { 192.168.1.34;
                     192.168.1.47;
                     };
};
```

Another commonly used global option is the `forwarders` option. With the `forwarders` option, you can list several DNS servers to which queries can be forwarded if they cannot be resolved by the local DNS server. This is helpful for local networks that may need to use a DNS server connected to the Internet. The `forwarders` option can also be placed in forward zone entries.

With the `notify` option turned on, the master zone DNS servers send messages to any slave DNS servers whenever their configuration has changed. The slave servers can then perform zone transfers in which they download the changed configuration files. Slave servers always use the DNS configuration files copied from their master DNS servers. `notify` takes one argument, yes or no, where yes is the default. With the `no`, you can have the master server not send out any messages to the slave servers, in effect, preventing any zone transfers.

The following example is a simple **named.conf** file based on the example provided in the BIND documentation. This example shows samples of several of the configuration commands. The file begins with comments using C++ syntax, //. The `options` command has a directory entry that sets the directory for the zone and cache files to **/var/named**. Here, you find your zone files, such as **named.local** and reverse mapping files, along with the cache file, **named.ca**. The first `zone` command (.) defines a hint zone specifying the root name servers. The cache file listing these servers is **named.ca**. The second `zone` command defines a zone for the **mytrek.com** domain. Its type is master and its zone file is named **"mytrek.com"**. The next zone is used for reverse IP mapping of the previous zone. Its name is made up of a reverse listing of the **mytrek.com** domain's IP address with the term **in-addr.arpa** appended. The domain address for **mytrek.com** is 192.168.1, so the reverse is 1.168.192. The **in-addr.arpa** domain is a special domain that supports gateway location and Internet address to host mapping. The last `zone` command defines a reverse mapping zone for the loopback interface, the method used by the system to address itself and enable communication between local users on the system. The zone file used for this local zone is **named.local**.

named.conf

```
//
// A simple BIND 8 configuration
```

```
//

logging {
        category cname { null; };
};

options {
   directory "/var/named";
   };
};

zone "." {
   type hint;
   file "named.ca";
};

zone "mytrek.com"{
   type master;
   file "mytrek.com";
};
zone "1.168.192.IN-ADDR.ARPA"{
   type master;
   file "192.168.1";
};

zone "0.0.127.in-addr.arpa"{
   type master;
   file "named.local";
};
```

When BIND is initially installed, it creates a default configuration for what is known as a caching only server. A *caching only server* copies queries made by users and saves them in a cache, for use later if the queries are repeated. This can save DNS lookup response times. The cache is held in memory and only lasts as long as **named** runs. The following example is the **named.conf** file initially installed for a caching only server. Only the local and cache zones are defined.

```
named.conf (caching only server)

// generated by named-bootconf.pl

options {
   directory "/var/named";
};
```

```
//
// a caching only nameserver config
//
zone "." {
   type hint;
   file "named.ca";
};

zone "0.0.127.in-addr.arpa" {
   type master;
   file "named.local";
};
```

/ comment */*	BIND comment in C syntax
// comment	BIND comment in C++ syntax
# comment	BIND comment in UNIX shell and Perl syntax
acl	Defines a named IP address matching list
include	Includes a file
key	Specifies key information for use in authentication and authorization
logging	Specifies what the server logs and where the log messages are sent
options	Global server configuration options and defaults for other statements
controls	Declares control channels to be used by the **ndc** utility
server	Sets certain configuration options for the specified server basis
trusted-keys	Defines DNSSEC keys preconfigured into the server and implicitly trusted
zone	Defines a zone

Table 18-3.   *BIND Configuration Commands*

SERVERS

Resource Records

Your name server holds domain name information about the hosts on your network in resource records placed in zone and reverse mapping files. Resource records are used to associate IP addresses with fully qualified domain names. You need a record for every computer in the zone that the name server services. A record takes up one line, though you can use parentheses to use several lines for a record, as is usually the case with SOA records. A resource record uses the Standard Resource Record Format as shown here:

```
name [<ttl>] [<class>] <type> <rdata> [<comment>]
```

name is the name for this record. It can be a domain name for a fully qualified domain name. If you only specify the host name, the default domain is appended. If no name entry exists, then the last specific name is used. If the @ symbol is used, the name server's domain name is used. **ttl** (time to live) is an optional entry that specifies how long the record is to be cached. **class** is the class of the record. The class used in most resource record entries is IN, for Internet. By default, it is the same as that specified for the domain in the **named.conf** file. **type** is the type of the record. **rdata** is the resource record data. The following is an example of a resource record entry. The name is the **rabbit.mytrek.com**, the type is Internet (IN), its type is a host address record (A), and the data is the IP address 192.168.1.2.

```
rabbit.mytrek.com.    IN    A      192.168.1.2
```

Different types of resource records exist for different kinds of hosts and name server operations. See Table 18-4 for a listing of resource record types. A, NS, MX, PTR, and CNAME are the ones commonly used. *A* is used for host address records that match domain names with IP addresses. NS is used to reference a name server. MX specifies the host address of the mail server that services this zone. The name server has mail messages sent to that host. The PTR type is used for records that point to other resource records and is used for reverse mapping. CNAME is used to identify an alias for a host on your system.

A zone and reverse mapping files always begin with a special resource record called the *Start of Authority record* (*SOA*). This record specifies that all the following records are authoritative for this domain. It also holds information about the name server's domain, which is to be given to other name servers. An SOA record has the same format as other resource records, though its data segment is arranged differently. The format for an SOA record follows:

```
name    {ttl}   class   SOA Origin   Person-in-charge (
                                            Serial
                                            Refresh
```

```
Retry
Expire
Minimum )
```

Each zone has its own SOA record. The SOA begins with the zone name specified in the named.conf zone entry. This is usually a domain name. An @ symbol is usually used for the name and acts like a macro expanding to the domain name. The class is usually the Internet class, IN. SOA is the type. Origin is the machine that is the origin of the records, usually the machine running your name server daemon. The Person-in-charge is the e-mail address for the person managing the name server (use dots, not @, for the e-mail address). Several configuration entries are placed in a block delimited with braces. The first is the serial number. You change the serial number when you add or change records, so it is updated by other servers. The serial number can be any number, as long as it is incremented each time a change is made to any record in the zone. A common practice is to use the year-month-day-number for the serial number, where number is the number of changes in that day. For example, 1999120403 would be the year 1999, December 4th, for the third change.

Refresh specifies the time interval for refreshing SOA information. *Retry* is the frequency for trying to contact an authoritative server. *Expire* is the length of time a secondary name server keeps information about a zone without updating it. *Minimum* is the length of time records in a zone live. The times are specified in the number of seconds. The following example shows an SOA record. The machine running the name

A	Host address
NS	Authoritative name server
CNAME	Canonical name for an alias
SOA	Start of a zone of authority
WKS	Well-known service description
PTR	Domain name pointer
HINFO	Host information
MINFO	Mailbox or mail list information
MX	Mail exchange
TXT	Text strings

Table 18-4.   *Domain Name System Resource Record Types*

server is **turtle.mytrek.com,** and the e-mail address of the person responsible for the server is **hostmaster@turtle.mytrek.com**. Notice the periods at the end of these names. For names with no periods, the domain name is appended. **turtle** would be the same as **turtle.mytrek.com**. When entering full host names, be sure to add the period so the domain is not appended.

```
@    IN    SOA    turtle.mytrek.com. hostmaster.turtle.mytrek.com.
(
                                  1997022700 ; Serial
                                  28800      ; Refresh
                                  14400      ; Retry
                                  3600000    ; Expire
                                  86400 )    ; Minimum
```

The name server record specifies the name of the name server for this zone. These have a resource record type of NS. If you have more than one name server, list them in NS records. These records usually follow the SOA record. As they usually apply to the same domain as the SOA record, their name field is often left blank to inherit the server's domain name specified by the @ symbol in the previous **SOA** record.

```
     IN          NS   turtle.mytrek.com.
```

Resource records of type A are address records that associate a fully qualified domain name with an IP address. Often, only their host name is specified. Any domain names without a terminating period automatically have the domain appended to it. Given the domain mytrek.com, the turtle name in the following example is expanded to **turtle.mytrek.com**.

```
rabbit.mytrek.com.   IN    A    192.168.1.2
turtle               IN    A    192.168.1.1
```

Resource records of type MX specify mail exchangers used for this host. The mail exchanger is the machine to which mail for the host is sent. In the following example, mail for **turtle.mytrek.com** is also sent to **turtle.mytrek.com**, but mail for **rabbit.mytrek.com** is sent to **turtle.mytrek.com**. An MX record recognizes an additional field that specifies the ranking for a mail exchanger. You can list several mail exchangers for a host with different rankings where the smaller number has a higher ranking. This way, if mail cannot reach the first mail exchanger, it can be routed to an alternate exchanger to reach the host.

```
turtle.mytrek.com.   IN                    192.168.1.1
                     IN    MX    10        turtle.mytrek.com.
```

```
rabbit.mytrek.com.     IN     A               192.168.1.2
                       IN     MX     10        turtle.mytrek.com.
```

Resource records of type CNAME are used to specify alias names for a host in the zone. Aliases are often used for machines running several different types of servers, such as both Web and FTP servers. They are also used to locate a host when it changes its name. The old name becomes an alias for the new name. In the following example, **ftp.mytrek.com** is an alias for a machine actually called **turtle.mytrek.com**.

```
ftp.mytrek.com.            IN             CNAME   turtle.mytrek.com.
```

A more stable way to implement aliases is simply to create another address record for it. You can have as many host names for the same IP address as you want, provided they are certified. For example, to make **www.mytrek.com** an alias for **turtle.mytrek.com**, you only have to add another address record for it, giving it the same IP address as **turtle.mytrek.com**.

```
turtle.mytrek.com.   IN   A     192.168.1.1
www.mytrek.com.      IN   A     192.168.1.1
```

A PTR record is used to perform reverse mapping from an IP address to a host. PTR records are used in the reverse mapping files. The name entry holds a reversed IP address and the data entry holds the name of the host. The following example maps the IP address 192.168.1.1 to **turtle.mytrek.com**.

```
1.1.168.192     IN   PTR     turtle.mytrek.com.
```

The HINFO, RP, MINFO, and TXT records are used to provide information about the host. The RP record enables you to specify the person responsible for a certain host. The HINFO record provides basic hardware and operating system identification. The TXT record is used to enter any text you want. MINFO provides a host's mail and mailbox information.

Zone Files

A domain name server uses several zone files covering different components of the DNS. Each zone uses two zone files: a zone file and a reverse mapping zone file. The *zone file* contains the resource records for hosts in the zone. A *reverse mapping file* contains records that provide reverse mapping of your domain name entries, enabling you to map from IP addresses to domain names. The name of the file used for the zone file can be any name. The name of the file is specified in the **zone** command's file entry in the **named.conf** file. If your server supports several zones, you may want to use a name that denotes the specific zone. Most systems use the domain name as the name of the zone file. For example, the zone **mytrek.com** would have a zone file also called **mytrek.com**. These could be placed in a subdirectory called **zones** or **master**. The zone file used in the following example is called **mytrek.com**. The reverse mapping file can also be any name, though it is usually the reverse IP address domain specified in its corresponding zone file. For example, in the case of **mytrek.com** zone file, the reverse mapping file might be called **192.168.1**, the IP address of the **mytrek.com** domain defined in the **mytrek.com** zone file. This file would contain reverse mapping of all the host addresses in the domain, allowing their host name addresses to be mapped to their corresponding IP addresses. In addition, BIND sets up a cache file and a reverse mapping file for the localhost. The cache file holds the resource records for the root name servers to which your name server connects. The cache file can be any name, although it is usually called **named.ca**. The localhost reverse mapping file holds reverse IP resource records for the local loopback interface, localhost. Although localhost can be any name, it usually has the name **named.local**.

Zone Files for Internet Zones

A zone file holds resource records that follow a certain format. The file begins with general directives to define default domains or to include other resource record files. These are followed by a single SOA, name server, and domain resource records, and then resource records for the different hosts. Comments begin with a semicolon and can be placed throughout the file. The @ symbol operates like a special macro, representing the domain name of the zone to which the records apply. The @ symbol is used on the first field of resource and SOA records as the zone's domain name. Multiple names can be specified using the * matching character. The first field in a resource record is the name of the domain to which it applies. If the name is left blank, the next previous explicit name entry in another resource record is automatically used. This way, you can list several entries that apply to the same host without having to repeat the host name. Any host or domain name used throughout this file that is not terminated with a period has the zone's domain appended to it. For example, if the zone's domain is **mytrek.com** and a resource record has only the name **rabbit** with no trailing period, the zone's domain is automatically appended to it, giving you **rabbit.mytrek.com.** Be sure to include the trailing period whenever you enter the complete fully qualified domain name as in **turtle.mytrek.com.**. You can also use several directives to set global attributes. $ORIGIN sets a default domain name to append to address names that do not end in a period. $INCLUDE includes a file. $GENERATE can generate records where part of a domain name or IP address differs only by an iterated number.

A zone file begins with an SOA record specifying the machine the name server is running on, among other specifications. The @ symbol is used for the name of the **SOA** record, denoting the zone's domain name. After the SOA, the name server resource records (NS) are listed. Just below the name server record are resource records for the domain itself. Resource records for hosts addresses (A), aliases (CNAME), and mail exchangers (MX) follow. The following example shows a sample zone file, which begins with an SOA record and is followed by an NS record, resource records for the domain, and then resource records for individual hosts.

```
; Authoritative data for turle.mytrek.com
;
@     IN  SOA turtle.mytrek.com. hostmaster.turtle.mytrek.com.(
                                 93071200    ; Serial number
                                 10800       ; Refresh 3 hours
                                 3600        ; Retry   1 hour
                                 3600000     ; Expire  1000 hours
                                 86400 )     ; Minimum 24 hours
            IN    NS             turtle.mytrek.com.
            IN    A              192.168.1.1

            IN    MX      150    turtle.mytrek.com.

turtle      IN    A              192.168.1.1
            IN    IIINFO  PC-686 LINUX
            IN    MX      100    turtle
            IN    MX      150    fast.mytrek.com.
gopher      IN    CNAME          turtle.mytrek.com.
ftp         IN    CNAME          turtle.mytrek.com.
www         IN    A              192.168.1.1

rabbit      IN    A              192.168.1.2
            IN    HINFO   PC-586 LINUX
            IN    MX      100    turtle.mytrek.com.

lizard      IN    A              192.168.1.3
            IN    HINFO   MAC    MACOS
            IN    MX      100    turtle.mytrek.com.
localhost   IN    A              127.0.0.1
```

The first two lines are comments about the server for which this zone file is used. Notice the first two lines begin with a semicolon. The class for each of the resource records in this file is IN, indicating these are Internet records. The SOA record begins with an @ symbol that stands for the zone's domain. In this example, it is **mytrek.com**. Any host or domain name used throughout this file that is not terminated with a period has this domain appended to it. For example, in the following resource record, **turtle** has no period, so it automatically expands to **turtle.mytrek.com**. The same happens for **rabbit** and **lizard**. These are read as **rabbit.mytrek.com** and **lizard.mytrek.com**. Also, in the SOA, notice the e-mail address for host master uses a period instead of an @ symbol. @ is a special symbol in zone files and cannot be used for any other purpose.

The next resource record specifies the name server for this zone. Here, it is **mytrek.com.** Notice the name for this resource record is blank. If the name is blank, a resource record inherits the name from the previous record. In this case, the NS record inherits the value of @ in the SOA record, its previous record. This is the zone's domain and the NS record specifies **turtle.mytrek.com** is the name server for this zone.

```
        IN   NS     turtle.mytrek.com.
```

The following address records set up an address for the domain itself. This is often the same as the name server, in this case 192.168.1.1 (the IP address of **turtle.mytrek.com**). This enables users to reference the domain itself, rather than a particular host in it. A mail exchanger record follows that routes mail for the domain to the name server. Users can send mail to the **mytrek.com** domain and it will be routed to **turtle.mytrek.com.**

The following resource record is an address record (A) that associates an IP address with the fully qualified domain name **turtle.mytrek.com**. The resource record name only holds **turtle** with no trailing period, so it is automatically expanded to **turtle.mytrek.com.** This record provides the IP address to which **turtle.mytrek.com** can be mapped.

```
turtle   IN    A     192.168.1.1
```

Several resource records immediately follow that have blank names. These inherit their name from the previous record, in this case **turtle.mytrek.com.** In effect, these records also apply to that host. Using blank names is an easy way to list additional resource records for the same host (notice an apparent indent occurs). The first record is an information record, providing the hardware and operating system for the machine.

```
        IN   HINFO   PC-686    LINUX
```

The second record is a mail exchanger record listing **turtle.mytrek.com** as also capable of receiving mail for itself. You can have more than one mail exchanger record for host. More than one host may exist through which mail can be routed. These can be listed in mail exchanger records with a priority set where the smaller number ranks higher. In this example, if **turtle.mytrek.com** cannot be reached, its mail is routed through **fast.mytrek.com**, which has been set up also to handle mail from **turtle.mytrek.com.**

```
IN    MX      100    turtle
IN    MX      150    fast.mytrek.com.
```

If you are using the same machine to run several different servers, such as a Web, FTP, and Gopher server, you may want to assign aliases to these servers to make accessing them easier for users. Instead of using the actual domain name, such as **turtle.mytrek.com,** to access the Web server running on it, users may find using the following is easier: **www.mytrek.com**; for the Gopher server, **gopher.mytrek.com**; and for the FTP server, **ftp.mytrek.com**. In the DNS, you can implement such a feature using alias records. In the example zone file, two CNAME alias records exist for the **turtle.mytrek.com** machine: FTP, and gopher. The next record implements an alias for **www** using another address record for the same machine. None of the name entries end in a period, so they are appended automatically with the domain name **mytrek.com**. **www.mytrek.com, ftp.mytrek.com**, and **gopher.mytrek.com** are all aliases for **turtle.mytrek.com**. Users entering those URLs automatically access the respective servers on the **turtle.mytrek.com** machine.

Address and main exchanger records are then listed for the two other machines in this zone: **rabbit.mytrek.com** and **lizard.mytrek.com**. You could add HINFO, TXT, MINFO, or alias records for these entries. The file ends with an entry for localhost, the special loopback interface that allows your system to address itself.

Reverse Mapping File

Reverse name lookups are enabled using a reverse mapping file. *Reverse mapping files* map fully qualified domain names to IP addresses. This reverse lookup capability is unnecessary, but it is convenient to have. With reverse mapping, when users access remote hosts, their domain name address can be used to identify their own host, instead of only the IP address. The name of the file can be anything you want. On most current distributions, it is the zone's domain address (the network part of a zone's IP address). For example, the reverse mapping file for a zone with the IP address of 192.168.1.1 is 192.168.1. Its full pathname would be something like **/var/named/192.168.1**. On some systems using older implementations of BIND, the reverse mapping filename may consist of the root name of the zone file with the extension **.rev**. For example, if the zone file is called **mytrek.com,** the reverse mapping file would be called something like **mytrek.rev**. The zone entry for a reverse mapping in the **named.conf** file uses a special domain name consisting of the IP address in reverse, with an **in-addr.arpa** extension. This reverse IP address becomes the zone domain referenced by the @ symbol in the reverse mapping file. For example, the reverse mapping zone name for a domain with the IP address of **192.168.43** would be **43.168.192.in-addr.arpa**. In the following example, the reverse domain name for the domain address **192.168.1** is **1.168.192.in-addr.arpa**.

```
zone "1.168.192.in-addr.arpa " in {
```

```
        type master;
        file "192.168.1";
};
```

A reverse mapping file begins with an SOA record, which is the same as that used in a forward mapping file. Resource records for each machine defined in the forward mapping file then follow. These resource records are PTR records that point to hosts in the zone. These must be actual hosts, not aliases defined with CNAME records. Records for reverse mapping begin with a reversed IP address. Each segment in the IP address is sequentially reversed. Each segment begins with the host ID, followed by reversed network numbers. If you list only the host ID with no trailing period, the zone domain is automatically attached. In the case of a reverse mapping file, the zone domain as specified in the **zone** command is the domain IP address backwards. The 1 expands to **1.1.168.192**. In the following example, **turtle** and **lizard** inherit the domain IP address, whereas **rabbit** has its explicitly entered.

```
;    reverse mapping of domain names 1.168.192.in-addr.arpa
;
@    IN   SOA turtle.mytrek.com. hostmaster.turtle.mytrek.com.(
                          92050300   ; Serial (yymmddxx format)
                          10800      ; Refresh   3hHours
                          3600     ; Retry     1 hour
                          3600000    ; Expire    1000 hours
                          86400 )    ; Minimum   24 hours
@              IN   NS    turtle.mytrek.com.
1              IN   PTR   turtle.mytrek.com.
2.1.168.192    IN   PTR   rabbit.mytrek.com.
3              IN   PTR   lizard.mytrek.com.
```

Localhost Reverse Mapping

A localhost reverse mapping file implements reverse mapping for the local loopback interface known as *localhost*, whose network address is **127.0.0.1**. This file can be any name. On Red Hat systems, localhost is given the name **named.local**. On other systems, localhost may use the network part of the IP address, **127.0.0**. This file allows mapping the domain name localhost to the localhost IP address, which is always **127.0.0.1** on every machine. The address **127.0.0.1** is a special address that functions as the local address for your machine. It allows a machine to address itself. In the **zone** command for this file, the name of the zone is **0.0.127.IN-ADDR.ARPA**. The domain part of the IP address is entered in reverse order, with **in-addr.arpa** appended to it, **0.0.127.in-addr.arpa**. The **named.conf** entry is shown here:

```
zone "0.0.127.in-addr.arpa" {
   type master;
   file "named.local";
};
```

The name of the file used for the localhost reverse mapping file is usually **named.local**, though it can be any name. The NS record specifies the name server localhost should use. This file has a PTR record that maps the IP address to the localhost. The 1 used as the name expands to append the zone domain—in this case, giving you **1.0.0.127**, a reverse IP address. The contents of the **named.local** file are shown here. Notice the trailing periods for localhost.

```
@       IN      SOA     localhost. root.localhost.  (
                                    1997022700 ; Serial
                                    28800      ; Refresh
                                    14400      ; Retry
                                    3600000    ; Expire
                                    86400 )    ; Minimum
        IN      NS      turtle.mytrek.com.
1       IN      PTR     localhost.
```

Subdomains and Slaves

Adding a subdomain to a DNS server is a simple matter of creating an added master entry in the **named.conf** file, and then placing name server and authority entries for that subdomain in your primary DNS server's zone file. The subdomain, in turn, has its own zone file with its SOA record and entries listing hosts, which are part of its subdomain, including any of its own mail and news servers.

The name for the subdomain could be a different name altogether or a name with the same suffix as the primary domain. In the following example, the subdomain is called **beach.mytrek.com**. It could just as easily be called **mybeach.com**. The name server to that domain is on the host **crab.beach.mytrek.com**, in this example. Its IP address is 192.168.1.33 and its zone file is **beach.mytrek.com**. The **beach.mytrek.com** zone file holds DNS entries for all the hosts being serviced by this name server. The following example shows zone entries for its named.conf.

```
zone "beach.mytrek.com"{
   type master;
   file "beach.mytrek.com";
};
```

```
zone "1.168.192.IN-ADDR.ARPA"{
   type master;
   file "192.168.1";
};
```

On the primary DNS sever, in the example **turtle.mytrek.com**, you would place entries in the master zone file to identify the subdomain server's host and designate it as a name sever. In this example, you would place the following entries in the **mytrek.com** zone file on **turtle.mytrek.com**.

```
beach.mytrek.com.          IN    NS     beach.mytrek.com.
beach.mytrek.com.    IN    A      192.168.1.33
```

URL references to hosts serviced by **beach.mytrek.com** can now be reached from any host serviced by **mytrek.com. mytrek.com** does not need to maintain any information about the **beach.mytrek.com** hosts. It simply refers such URL references to the **beach.mytrek.com** name server.

A slave DNS server is tied directly to a master DNS server and periodically receives DNS information from it. You use a master DNS server to configure its slave DNS servers automatically. Any changes you make to the master server are automatically transferred to its slave servers. This transfer of information is called a *zone transfer*. Zone transfers are automatically initiated whenever the slave zone's refresh time is reached or it receives a notify message from the master. The *refresh time* is the second argument in the zone's SOA entry. A notify message is automatically sent by the master whenever changes are made to the master zone's configuration files and the named daemon is restarted. In effect, slave zones are automatically configured by the master zone, receiving the master zone's zone files and making them their own.

Using the previous examples, suppose you want to set up a slave server on **rabbit.mytrek.com**. Zone entries, as shown in the following example, are set up in the **named.conf** configuration file for the slave DNS server on **rabbit.mytrek.com**. The slave sever is operating in the same domain as the master, and so it has the same zone name, **mytrek.com**. Its SOA file is named **slave.mytrek.com**. The term "slave" in the filename is merely a convention that helps identify it as a slave server configuration file. The masters statement lists its master DNS server, in this case, 192.168.1.1. Whenever the slave needs to make a zone transfer, it transfers data from that master DNS server. The entry for the reverse mapping file for this slave server lists its reverse mapping file as "slave.192.168.1".

```
zone "mytrek.com"{
   type slave;
   file "slave.mytrek.com";
```

```
   masters { 192.168.1.1;
           };
};

zone "1.168.192.IN-ADDR.ARPA"{
   type slave;
   file "slave.192.168.1";
   masters { 192.168.1.1;
           };
};
```

On the master DNS server, the master SOA zone file has entries in it to identify the host that holds the slave DNS server and to designate it as a DNS server. In this example, you would place the following in the **mytrek.com** zone file.

```
   IN   NS   192.168.1.2
```

You would also place an entry for this name server in the **mytrek.com** reverse mapping file.

```
   IN   NS   192.168.1.2
```

The master DNS server can control which slave servers can transfer zone information from it using the **allow-transfer** command. Place the command with the list of IP addresses for the slave servers for which you want to allow access. Also, the master DNS server should be sure the **notify** option is not disabled. The **notify** option is disabled by a "notify no" statement in the options or zone named.conf entries. Simply erase the "no" argument to enable notify.

IP Virtual Domains

IP-based virtual hosting allows more than one IP address to be used for a single machine. If a machine has two registered IP addresses, either one can be used to address the machine. If you want to treat the extra IP address as another host in your domain, you need only create an address record for it in your domain's zone file. The domain name for the host would be the same as your domain name. If you want to use a different domain name for the extra IP, however, you have to set up a virtual domain for it. This entails creating a new **zone** command for it with its own zone file. For example, if the extra IP address is **192.168.1.42** and you want to give it the domain name **sail.com**, you must create a new **zone** command for it in your **named.conf** file with a new **zone** file. The **zone** command would look something like this. The zone file is called **sail.com**.

```
zone "sail.com" in {
        type master;
        file "sail.com";
};
```

In the "**sail.com**" file, the name server name is **turtle.mytrek.com** and the e-mail address is **hostmaster@turtle.mytrek.com**. In the name server record (NS), the name server is **turtle.mytrek.com.** This is the same machine using the original address that the name server is running as. **turtle.mytrek.com** is also the host that handles mail addressed to **sail.com** (MX). An address record then associates the extra IP address **192.168.1.42** with the **sail.com** domain name. A virtual host on this domain is then defined as **jib.sail.com**. **www** and **ftp** aliases are created for that host, creating **www.sail.com** and **ftp.sail.com** virtual hosts.

```
; Authoritative data for sail.com
;
@       IN   SOA    turtle.mytrek.com. hostmaster.turtle.mytrek.com. (

93071200     ; Serial (yymmddxx)
                                10800      ; Refresh 3 hours
                                3600     ; Retry   1 hour
                                3600000    ; Expire   1000 hours
                                86400 )   ; Minimum 24 hours
        IN   NS           turtle.mytrek.com.
        IN   MX    100    turtle.mytrek.com.
        IN   A            192.168.1.42   ;address of the sail.com domain

jib   IN   A            192.168.1.42
www   IN   A            192.168.1.42
ftp   IN   CNAME        jib.sail.com.
```

In your reverse mapping file (**/var/named/192.168.1**), add PTR records for any virtual domains.

```
42.1.168.192   IN    PTR   sail.com.
42.1.168.192   IN    PTR   jib.sail.com.
```

You also have to configure your network connection to listen for both IP addresses on your machine (see Chapter 28).

Cache File

The *cache file* is used to connect the domain name server to root servers on the Internet. The file can be any name. On Red Hat systems, the cache file is called **named.ca**. Other systems may call the cache file **named.cache** or **roots.hints**. The cache file is usually a standard file installed by your BIND software, which lists resource records for designated root servers for the Internet. You can obtain a current version of the **named.ca** file from the rs.internic.net FTP site. The following example shows sample entries taken from the **named.ca** file:

```
; formerly NS.INTERNIC.NET
;
.                         3600000  IN  NS    A.ROOT-SERVERS.NET.
A.ROOT-SERVERS.NET.       3600000      A     198.41.0.4
;
; formerly NS1.ISI.EDU
;
.                         3600000      NS    B.ROOT-SERVERS.NET.
B.ROOT-SERVERS.NET.       3600000      A     128.9.0.107
```

If you are creating an isolated intranet, you need to create your own root domain name server until you connect to the Internet. In effect, you are creating a fake root server. This can be another server on your system pretending to be the root or the same name server.

BIND Version 4.*x*

BIND version 4.*x* uses a different kind of configuration file called the **named.boot** file. The entries in this file consist of one-line records similar to that in a **named** zone file. Records begin with keywords for the type of entry followed by the associated values. For example, the directory record specifies the directory for zone files, just like the directory entry in the **options** command used in the **named.conf** file in BIND 8.*x*. The primary record specifies the zone and the data domain host file used for it. A secondary record specifies the name server operates as a secondary name server in the given domain. The cache record specifies the file name used for the cache. You can always convert a **name.boot** file to a **named.conf** file using the **named-bootconf.pl** Perl script provided with BIND 8.*x*.

SERVERS

You can learn more about BIND version 4.*x* from **www.isc.org** and BIND documentation. A sample **named.boot** file is shown here:

```
;
; nameserver config
;
directory        /var/named
cache            .                       named.ca
primary          mytrek.com              mytrek.com
primary          1.168.192.in-addr.arpa  "192.168.1"
primary          0.0.127.in-addr.arpa    named.local
```

Chapter 19

Mail, News, Proxy, and Search Servers

493

M ail and news servers provide Internet users with electronic mail and Usenet news services. They have their own TCP/IP protocols, just as FTP and Web servers have theirs. Mail servers use the *Simple Mail Transfer Protocol* (*SMTP*) and news servers use the *Network News Transfer Protocol* (*NNTP*). In addition, servers exist that provide better access to Internet resources. Proxy servers speed Web access by maintaining current copies of commonly accessed Web pages, speeding access times by eliminating the need to access the original site constantly. They also perform security functions, protecting servers from unauthorized access. Search servers, such as ht:/Dig and WAIS, enable document searches of Web and FTP sites. They can index documents and provide search engines for carrying out complex search requests.

Mail Servers: SMTP, POP, and IMAP

Messages are sent across the Internet through mail servers that service local domains. A *domain* can be seen as a subnet of the larger Internet, with its own server to handle mail messages sent from or received for users on that subnet. When a user mails a message, it is first sent from her host system to the mail server. The mail server then sends the message to another mail server on the Internet, the one servicing the subnet on which the recipient user is located. The receiving mail server then sends the message to the recipient's host system. At each stage, a different type of operation takes place using different agents (programs). A *Mail User Agent (MUA)* is a mail client program, such as **mail** or **Elm**. With a MUA, a user composes a mail message and sends it. Then a *Mail Transport Agent* (*MTA*) transports the messages over the Internet. MTAs are mail servers that use the *Simple Mail Transfer Protocol* (*SMTP*) to send messages across the Internet from one mail server to another, transporting them from one subnet to another. On Linux and UNIX systems, the commonly used MTA is **sendmail,** a mail server daemon that constantly checks for incoming messages from other mail servers and sends outgoing messages to appropriate servers. Incoming messages received by a mail server are then distributed to a user with *Mail Delivery Agents* (*MDA*). Most Linux systems use **procmail** as their MDA, taking messages received by the mail server and delivering them to user accounts (see **www.procmail.org** for more information).

Red Hat automatically installs and configures **sendmail** for you. On starting your system, you can send and receive messages over the Internet using **sendmail**. You can also set up your Linux system to run a POP server. POP servers hold user's mail until they log in to access their messages, instead of having mail sent to their hosts directly.

Messages exchanged with a system require a loopback interface. Most Linux distributions do this automatically for you during the installation process. A *loopback interface* enables your system to address itself, allowing it to send and receive mail to and from itself. A loopback interface uses the host name **localhost** and a special IP address reserved for use by local systems, **127.0.0.1**. You can examine your **/etc/hosts** file to see if your loopback interface has been configured as the local host. You see **127.0.0.1 localhost** listed as the first entry. If, for some reason, no entry exists for "localhost", you may have to create a loopback interface yourself using the **ifconfig** and **route** commands as shown here. **lo** is the term for *loopback.*

```
ifconfig lo 127.0.0.1
route add -net 127.0.0.0
```

Sendmail

sendmail operates as a server to both receive and send mail messages. sendmail listens for any mail messages received from other hosts and addressed to users on the network hosts it serves. At the same time, sendmail handles messages users are sending out to remote users, determining to what hosts to send them. You can learn more about sendmail at **www.sendmail.org**, including online documentation and current software packages. The sendmail newsgroup is **comp.mail.sendmail**.

The domain name server for your network designates the host that runs the sendmail server. This is your mail host. Messages are sent to this host whose sendmail server then sends the message to the appropriate user and its host. On your domain name server configuration file, the mail host entry is specified with an MX entry. To print the mail queue of messages for future delivery, you can use mailq. This runs sendmail with instructions to print the mail queue.

sendmail supports the use of aliases either for sent or received mail. It checks an aliases database file called **aliases.db** that holds alias names and their associated e-mail addresses. This is often used for administrator mail, where mail may be sent to the system's root user, and then redirected to the mail address of the actual system administrator. You can also alias host addresses, enabling you to address hosts on your network using only their alias. Aliases entries are kept in the **/etc/allases** file. This file consists of one-line alias records, beginning with the address of the user or host followed by a colon and a list of aliases for that entry. You can edit this file to add new entries or to change old ones. They are then stored for lookup in the **aliases.db** file using the command **newaliases,** which runs sendmail with instructions to update the **aliases.db** file. The following is an example of an alias entry for the system administrator address:

```
# Basic system aliases -- these MUST be present.
MAILER-DAEMON:    postmaster
postmaster:    root
# Person who should get root's mail
#root:       richlp
```

Sendmail Configuration

The main sendmail configuration file is **sendmail.cf,** located in the **/etc** directory. This file consists of a sometimes lengthy list of mail definitions that set general options, designate *Mail Transport Agents* (*MTAs*), and define the address rewrite rules. A series of options set features, such as maximum size of mail messages or the name of host files. The MTAs are those mailers through which sendmail routes messages. The rewrite rules 'rewrite' a mail address to route through the appropriate Internet connections to its destination (these rules can be complex). Check the sendmail HOW-TO and the online documentation for a detailed explanation.

The sendmail.cf definitions can be complex and confusing. To simplify the configuration process, sendmail supports the use of macros you can use to generate the **sendmail.cf** file using the m4 preprocessor (this requires installation of the sendmail-cf package). Macros are placed in the **sendmail.mc** file. Here, you can use macros to designate the definitions and features you want for sendmail, and then the macros are used to generate the appropriate definitions and rewrite rules in the **sendmail.cf** file. As part of the Sendmail package, several specialized versions of the **sendmail.mc** file are made available. These begin with a system name and have the suffix "mc". For example, a **redhat.mc** file exists for Red Hat systems and a generic-solaris2.mc for Sun Solaris files. On Red Hat systems, the **redhat.mc** file is already installed as your **sendmail.mc** file.

The **sendmail.mc** file consists of macros with arguments encased in parenthesis. Comments begin with the word **dnl**. Define macros are used to change sendmail default settings. The FEATURE macro is used to turn on or off different Sendmail features. The MAILER macro enables you to designate the MTA mailers that sendmail uses. A standard **sendmail.mc** file is shown here:

```
divert(-1)
dnl This is the macro config file used to generate the
dnl /etc/sendmail.cf file. If you modify their file you will have to
dnl regenerate the /etc/sendmail.cf by running this macro config
dnl through the m4 preprocessor:
dnl
dnl        m4 /etc/sendmail.mc > /etc/sendmail/cf
dnl
dnl You will need to have the sendmail-cf package installed for this
dnl to work.
include('/usr/lib/sendmail-cf/m4/cf.m4')
define('confDEF_USER_ID',''8:12'')
OSTYPE('linux')
undefine('UUCP_RELAY')
undefine('BITNET_RELAY')
define('confAUTO_REBUILD')
define('confTO_CONNECT', '1m')
define('confTRY_NULL_MX_LIST',true)
define('confDONT_PROBE_INTERFACES',true)
define('PROCMAIL_MAILER_PATH','/usr/bin/procmail')
```

```
FEATURE('smrsh','/usr/sbin/smrsh')
FEATURE('virtusertable','hash -o /etc/mail/virtusertable')
FEATURE(redirect)
FEATURE(always_add_domain)
FEATURE(use_cw_file)
FEATURE(local_procmail)
MAILER(procmail)
MAILER(smtp)
FEATURE('access_db')
FEATURE('blacklist_recipients')
dnl We strongly recommend to comment this one out if you want to
dnl protect yourself from spam. However, the laptop and users on
dnl computers that do not have 24x7 DNS do need this.
FEATURE('accept_unresolvable_domains')
dnl FEATURE(`relay_based_on_MX')
```

Once you configure your **sendmail.mc** file, you use the following command to generate a **sendmail.cf** file (be sure first to back up your original **sendmail.cf** file). You can rename the **sendmail.mc** file to reflect the specific configuration. You can have as many different **.mc** files as you want and use them to implement different configurations.

```
m4 sendmail.mc > /etc/sendmail.cf
```

You can also use Linuxconf to configure sendmail. This requires that Linuxconf has its mailconf module loaded. Under the Networking heading, open the Server Tasks listing and select the Mail Delivery System entry. This opens a lengthy list of entries for panels that configure sendmail on your system. Click its entry to display a panel (see Figure 19-1). Once you configure sendmail, you can then have Linuxconf generate a **sendmail.cf** file. You can also use the **mailconf** command to display a window with buttons for the different Linuxconf sendmail panels.

Sendmail Configuration Operators

Table 19-1 lists the basic sendmail configuration operators found in the **sendmail.cf** file. These operators consist of a single uppercase character, some with no spaces separating their arguments. The *D* operator defines macros. These are often used for specific information, such as the name of a host. The macro name usually consists of one character. Lowercase macro names are reserved for use by Sendmail, whereas lowercase macro names are used for user-defined macros. The following example defines a macro called *T* for **turtle.mytrek.com.** You can then reference the macro anywhere in other operations by preceding it with a $, as in $T. To have a macro

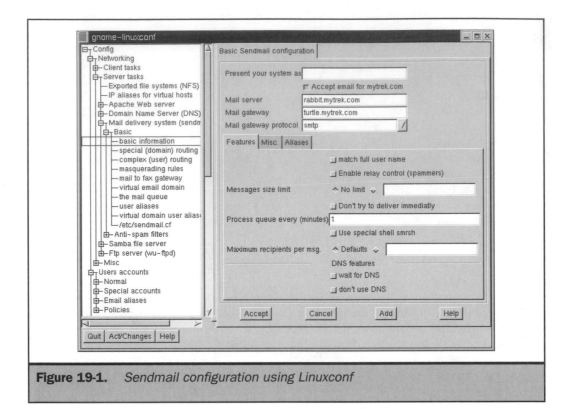

Figure 19-1. *Sendmail configuration using Linuxconf*

name longer than one character, encase the name within braces, as shown here for rabbit. To evaluate the rabbit macro use ${rabbit}.

```
DTturtle.mytrek.com
D{rabbit}rabbit.mytrek.com
```

Much of the **sendmail.cf** file consists of options that are specified by the *O* operator followed by the option and its arguments. For example, the following entries determine the location of the alias file and the maximum size of a message.

```
O AliasFile=/etc/aliases
O HelpFile=/usr/lib/sendmail.hf
O MaxMessageSize=1000000
```

The *H* operator is used to define mail headers. The *P* operator is used to define the priority of mail messages based on keywords, such as the term "bulk" in the mail header. The *K* operator specifies the location of key database files, such as the aliases databases. The *C* operator is used to define a class, such as a collection of hosts, while the *F* operator is used to define a class from names read from a file.

```
# file containing names of hosts for which we receive email
Fw/etc/sendmail.cw
```

The *M* operator is used to define the mailers used by sendmail. The *S* and *R* operators are used to define rulesets and rewriting rules. Rulesets and rewriting rules are used to determine how a message is to be routed and, if necessary, to rewrite its address so sendmail's MTAs can handle it. You can think of *rulesets* as functions in a program, which are called as needed to work on message addresses, and can themselves call yet other rulesets. A ruleset consists of a set of rules, much like a function consists of a set of programming statements. Each ruleset is labeled with a number defined by an initial *S* operator. The rules making up the ruleset are then defined by *R* operators. Sendmail uses the rulesets first to format an address into a standard form. Then, for messages being sent, it determines the MTA to use. Special rules called *rewriting rules* can rewrite the address into a form that can be better handled by the MTA. Rewriting rules consist of a left-hand and a right-hand pattern. An address that matches the pattern on the left-hand side is rewritten in the format of the pattern on the right-hand side.

D	Define a macro
C	Define a class
F	Define a class read from a file
H	Define mail header
O	Set an option
P	Set message precedence
V	Specify version level of sendmail.cf file
K	Specify key file
M	Specify mailer
S	Label and start a ruleset
R	Define a rule
#	Comment

Table 19-1.   *Sendmail Configuration Operators*

SERVERS

POP Servers

The *Post Office Protocol* (*POP*) allows a remote server to hold mail for users who can then log in to access their mail. Unlike sendmail and procmail, which deliver mail messages directly to a user account on a Linux system, the POP protocol holds mail until a user accesses his account on the POP server. Servers are often used by ISPs to provide Internet mail services for users. Instead of sending mail directly to a user's machine, the mail resides in the POP server until it's retrieved.

Qpopper is the current version of the Berkeley POP server (popper). Qpopper is supported by Qualcomm, makers of Eudora e-mail software. The qpopper Web page is **www.eudora.com/free/qpop.html**. You can obtain a current source code version from **ftp.qualcomm.com/eudora/servers/unix**. An RPM package for Red Hat is located in the Red Hat site at **ftp.redhat.com**. You can install Qpopper software on your Linux system and have it operate as a POP server for your network. It consists of both the **qpopper** daemon and the **popauth** program, which manages an authentication database with password encryption for secure user access. **popauth** creates a database file called **/etc/pop.auth**. To add a user, enter the **popauth** command with the options **-user** and **user name**. You are then prompted for a password with which the user can access his POP account.

You can also use the University of Washington POP server (**ftp.cac.washington.edu/imap**), which is part of the University of Washington's imap RPM package. Simply install the package, which is already done as part of the standard install (both POP2 and POP3 servers are installed). The Server daemons are called **ipop2d** and **ipop3d**. Your Linux system then runs as a POP2 and POP3 server for your network. These servers are usually run through inetd and, in the **/etc/inetd.conf** file, you can find the following entries for them.

```
pop-2   stream  tcp     nowait  root    /usr/sbin/tcpd   ipop2d
pop-3   stream  tcp     nowait  root    /usr/sbin/tcpd   ipop3d
```

IMAP

The *Internet Mail Access Protocol* (*IMAP*) is a more advanced version of the POP protocol. Unlike POP, it enables users to create multiple folders on their mail server in which they can save their read mail. IMAP can also enable user's to track read and unread messages. IMAP only downloads headers, and then it downloads select messages only. On Red Hat Linux, you can install the Washington University IMAP server. The RPM software package begins with the name "imap" and the name of the server daemon is also **imap**. The server is run through inetd and you can find a line for it in the **/etc/inetd.conf** file.

```
imap    stream  tcp     nowait  root    /usr/sbin/tcpd   imapd
```

News Servers: INN

The *InterNetNews (INN)* news server accesses Usenet newsfeeds, providing news clients on your network with the full range of newsgroups and their articles. Newsgroup articles are transferred using the *Network News Transfer Protocol (NNTP)*, and servers that support this protocol are known as *NNTP servers*. INN was written by Rich Salz, and is currently maintained and supported by the *Internet Software Consortium (ISC)*. You can download current versions from its Web site at **www.isc.org**. INN is also included with most Linux distributions, including Red Hat, and the documentation directory for INN in **/usr/doc** contains extensive samples. The primary program for INN is the **innd** daemon. Various INN configuration files can be found in **/etc/news**, including **innd, inn.conf, rnews, nnrp.access,** and **hosts.nntp. inn.conf** sets options for INN, and the **hosts.nntp** file holds the hosts from which you receive newsfeeds. Place entries for remote hosts in the **nnrp.access** file to allow them access to your news server. Correct configuration of INN can be a complex and time-consuming process, so be sure to consult references and online resources, such as the HOW-TO documents. A **innd** script is in the **/etc/rc.d/init.d** directory, which has similar arguments to the Web **httpd** script. You can use start and stop arguments with the **innd** script to start and stop the INN server.

Red Hat systems have already created a **news** user with a news group for use by your INN daemon. On other systems, you may have to create the **news** user and group. On all systems, you must create a news home directory, such as **/home/news**. INN software also installs **cron** scripts, which are used to update your news server, removing old articles and fetching new ones. These are placed in the **/etc/cron.daily** directory. **inn-cron-expire** removes old articles and **inn-cron-rnews** retrieves new ones. **inn-cron-nntpsend** sends articles posted from your system to other news servers.

Squid

Squid is a proxy-caching server for Web clients, designed to speed Internet access. It implements a proxy-caching service for Web clients that caches Web pages as users make requests. Copies of Web pages accessed by users are kept in the Squid cache and, as requests are made, Squid checks to see if it has a current copy. If Squid does have a current copy, it returns the copy from its cache, instead of querying the original site. In this way, Web browsers can then use the local Squid cache as a proxy HTTP server. Squid currently handles Web pages supporting the HTTP, FTP, Gopher, SSL, and WAIS protocols (Squid cannot be used with FTP clients). Replacement algorithms periodically replace old objects in the cache.

Squid is supported and distributed under a GNU public license by the *National Laboratory for Applied Network Research (NLANR)* at the University of California, San Diego. The work is based on the Harvest Project. You can obtain current source code versions and online documentation from the Squid homepage at **http://squid.nlanr.net** and the Squid FTP site at **ftp.nlanr.net**. The Squid software package consists of the

SERVERS

Squid server, a domain name lookup program called **dnsserver**, an FTP client called **ftpget**, and a cache manager script called **cachemgr.cgi**. The **dnsserver** resolves IP addresses from domain names, and the **ftpget** program is an FTP client Squid uses to retrieve files from FTP servers.

The Squid configuration file is **squid.conf,** located in the **/etc/squid** directory. The default version provided with Squid software includes detailed explanations of all standard entries, along with commented default entries. Entries consist of tags that specify different attributes. For example, the maximum_object_size and maximum_object set limits on objects transferred.

```
#maximum_object_size 4096 KB
```

Security

You can configure Squid both to provide security to your Web server and to set up your cache hierarchies. In each case, you first define access control lists (ACL) using the **acl** command, in which you create a label for the systems on which you are setting controls. You then use commands, such as **http_access,** to define these controls. You can define a system, or a group of systems, based on several **acl** options, such as the source IP address, the domain name, or even the time and date (see Table 19-2). For example, the **src** option is used to define a system or group of systems with a certain source address. To define a **mylan acl** entry for systems in a local network with the addresses 192.168.1.0 through to 192.168.1.255, use the following ACL definition.

```
acl mylan src 192.168.1.0/255.255.255.0
```

Once defined, you can use an **acl** definition in a Squid option to specify a control you want to place on those systems. For example, to allow access by the mylan group of local systems to the Web through the proxy, use a **http_access** option with the **allow** action specifying **mylan** as the **acl** definition to use, as shown here.

```
http_access allow mylan
```

By defining ACLs and using them in Squid options, you can tailor your Web site with the kind of security you want. The following example allows access to the Web through the proxy by only the mylan group of local systems, denying access to all others. Two **acl** entries are set up: one for the local system and one for all others. **http_access** options first allow access to the local system, and then deny access to all others.

```
acl mylan src 192.168.1.0/255.255.255.0
acl allsystems src 0.0.0.0/0.0.0.0
```

```
http_access allow mylan
http_access deny allsystems
```

The order of the **http_access** options is important. Squid starts from the first and works its way down, stopping at the first **http_access** option with an **acl** entry that matches. In the previous example, local systems that match the first **http_access** command are allowed, whereas other fall through to the second **http_access** command and are denied.

For systems using the proxy, you can also control what sites they can access. For a destination address, you create an **acl** entry with the **dst** qualifier. Then you can create an **http_access** option to control access to that address. The following example denies access by anyone using the proxy to **rabbit.mytrek.com.** If you have a local network accessing the Web through the proxy, you can use such commands to restrict access to certain sites.

```
acl myrabbit dst rabbit.mytrek.com
http_access deny myrabbit
```

You can also qualify addresses by domain. Often Web sites can be referenced using only the domain. For example, a site called **www.mybeach.com** can be referenced using just the **domain mybeach.com.** To create an **acl** entry to reference a domain, use either the **dstdomain** or **srcdomain** options, for destination and source domains, respectively. Remember, such a reference refers to all hosts in that domain. An **acl** entry with the **dstdomain** option for **mybeach.com** restricts access to **www.mybeach.com**, **ftp.mybeach.com**, **surf.mybeach.com**, and so on. The following example restricts access to the **www.mybeach.com** site along with all other **.mybeach.com** sites and any hosts in the **mybeach.com** domain.

```
acl thebeache dstdomain .mybeach.com
http_access deny thebeach
```

You can list several domains or addresses in an **acl** entry to reference them as a group, but you cannot have one domain that is a subdomain of another. The following example restricts access to both **mybeach.com** and **mysurf.com**.

```
acl beaches dstdomain .mybeach.com .mysurf.com
http_access deny beaches
```

An **acl** entry can also use a pattern to specify certain addresses and domains. In the following example, the access is denied to any URL with the pattern "chocolate", and allows access from all others:

```
acl Choc1 url_regex chocolate
http_access deny Choc1
http_access allow all
```

Squid also supports ident and proxy authentication methods to control user access. The following example only allows the users **dylan** and **chris** to use the Squid cache:

```
ident_lookup on
acl goodusers user chris dylan
http_access allow goodusers
http_access deny all
```

Caches

Squid uses the *Internet Cache Protocol* (*ICP*) to communicate with other Web caches. Using the ICP protocols, your Squid cache can connect to other Squid caches or other cache servers, such as Microsoft proxy server, Netscape proxy server, and Novell Bordermanager. This way, if your network's Squid cache does not have a copy of a requested Web page, it can contact another cache to see if it is there, instead of accessing the original site. You can configure Squid to connect to other Squid caches by connecting it to a cache hierarchy. Squid supports a hierarchy of caches denoted by the terms *child*, *sibling*, and *parent*. Sibling and child caches are accessible on the same level and are automatically queried whenever request cannot be located in your own Squib's cache. If these queries fail, then a parent cache is queried, which then searches its own child and sibling caches, or its own parent cache, if needed, and so on. Use cache_host to set up parent and sibling hierarchical connections.

```
cache_host sd.cache.nlanr.net    parent 3128 3130
```

You can set up a cache hierarchy to connect to the main NLANR server by registering your cache using the following entries in your **squid.conf** file.

```
cache_announce 24
announce_to sd.cache.nlanr.net:3131
```

Squid keeps several logs. access.log holds requests sent to your proxy, **cache.log** holds Squid server messages, such as errors and startup messages, and **store.log** holds

src *ip-address/netmask*	Clients IP address
src *addr1-addr2/netmask*	Range of addresses
dst *ip-address/netmask*	Destination IP address
myip *ip-address/netmask*	Local socket IP address
srcdomain *domain*	Reverse lookup, client IP
dstdomain *domain*	Destination server from URL. For dstdomain and dstdom_regex, a reverse lookup is tried if a IP-based URL is used
srcdom_regex [-i] *expression*	Regular expression matching client name
dstdom_regex [-i] *expression*	Regular expression matching destination
time *[day-abbrevs] [h1:m1-h2:m2]*	Time as specified by day, hour, and minutes. Day-abbreviations: S – Sunday, M – Monday, T – Tuesday, W – Wednesday, H – Thursday, F – Friday, A - Saturday
url_regex [-i] *expression*	Regular expression matching on whole URL
urlpath_regex [-i] *expression*	Regular expression matching on URL path
port *ports*	Specify a port or range of ports
proto *protocol*	Specify a protocol, such as HTTP or FTP
method *method*	Specify methods, such as GET and POST
browser [-i] regexp	Pattern match on User-Agent header
ident *username*	String match on ident output
src_as *number*	Used for routing of requests to specific caches
dst_as *number*	Used for routing of requests to specific caches
proxy_auth *username*	List of valid user names
snmp_community *string*	A community string to limit access to your SNMP Agent

Table 19-2.   *Squid ACL Options*

information about the Squid cache, such as objects added or removed. You can use the cache manager (**cachemgr.cgi**) to manage the cache and view statistics on the cache manager as it runs. To run the cache manager, use your browser to execute the **cachemgr.cgi** script (this script should be placed in your Web server's **cgi-bin** directory). You can also monitor Squid using the Multi Router Traffic utility.

Dig Server

Dig, known officially as *ht://Dig*, is a Web-indexing and search system designed for small networks or intranets. Dig is not considered a replacement for full-scale Internet search systems, such as Lycos, Infoseek, or AltaVista. Unlike WAIS-based or Web server-based search engines, Dig can span several Web servers at a site. Dig was developed at San Diego State University and is distributed free under the GNU public license. You can obtain information and documentation at **www.htdig.org**, and you can download software packages—including RPM packages—from **ftp.htdig.org**. An RPM package version for Red Hat can be found at the Red Hat site in the contrib. Directory, **ftp.redhat.com/contrib**.

Dig supports simple and complex searches, including complex Boolean and fuzzy search methods. *Fuzzy searching* supports a number of search algorithms, including exact, soundex, and synonyms. Searches can be carried out on both text and HTML documents. HTML documents can have keywords placed in them for more accurate retrieval and you can also use HTML templates to control how results are displayed.

Searches can be constrained by authentication requirements, location, and search depth. To protect documents in restricted directories, Dig can be informed to request a specific user name and password. You can also restrict a search to retrieve documents in a certain URL, search subsections of the database, or to retrieve only documents that are a specified number of links away.

All the htdig programs use the same configuration file, **htdig.conf**, located in the **/etc/htdig** directory. The configuration file consists of attribute entries, each beginning with the attribute line and followed by the value after a colon. Each program takes only the attributes it needs.

```
max_head_length:     10000
```

You can specify attributes such as allow_virtual_hosts, which index virtual hosts as separate servers, and search_algorithm, which specifies the search algorithms to use for searches.

Dig consist of five programs: htdig, htmerge, htfuzzy, htnotify, and htsearch. *htdig, htmerge,* and *htfuzzy* generate the index, while *htsearch* performs the actual searches. First, htdig gathers information on your database, searching all URL connections in your domain and associating Web pages with terms. The htmerge program use this information to create a searchable database, merging the information from any previously generated database. htfuzzy creates indexes to allow searches using fuzzy algorithms, such as soundex and synonyms. Once the database is created, users can use Web pages that invoke htsearch to search this index. Results are listed on a Web page. You can use META tags in your HTML documents to enter specific htdig keywords, exclude a document from indexing, or provide notification information, such as an e-mail address and an expiration date. htnotify uses the e-mail and expiration date to notify Web page authors when their pages are out-of-date.

htsearch is a CGI program that expects to be invoked by an HTML form, and it accepts both the GET and POST methods of passing data. The htsearch program can accept a search request from any form containing the required configuration values. Values include search features such as config (configuration file), method (search method) , and sort (sort criteria). For the Web page form that invokes htsearch, you can use the default page provided by htdig or create your own. Output is formatted using templates you can modify. Several sample files are included with the htdig software: **rundig** is a sample script for creating a database, **searchform.html** is a sample html document that contains a search form for submitting htdig searches, **header.html** is a sample header for search headers, and **footer.html** is for search footers.

WAIS Server

WAIS (*Wide Area Information Service*) searches a database of documents using keywords and displays the documents it finds with a ranking of their importance. This is a most effective way to make information available throughout a network. WAIS was developed by Thinking Machines and is now managed by WAIS, Inc. A free version of WAIS, called *freeWAIS*, is available through the *Center for Networked Information Discovery and Retrieval* (*CNIDR*). You can obtain a Linux version of freeWAIS from CNIDR and the FTP site (**ftp.cnidr.org**). The freeWAIS package includes clients, a server, and an indexer program. The clients are called **swais**, **xwais**, and **waissearch**. They are used to enter requests and display results. The indexer is called **waisindex**. You use **waisindex** to create indexes of keywords for your WAIS documents, providing fast and effective search capabilities. The server is called **waisserver**. With **waisserver**, you can create your own WAIS site and allow other users to perform searches on your WAIS documents.

SERVERS

The
Complete
Reference

Part V

Administration

Chapter 20

Basic System Administration

L inux is designed to serve many users at the same time, as well as to provide an interface among the users and the computer with its storage media, such as hard disks and tapes. Users have their own shells through which they interact with the operating system, but you may need to configure the operating system itself in different ways. You may need to add new users, printers, and even file systems. Such operations come under the heading of system administration. The person who performs such actions is referred to as either a *system administrator* or a *superuser*. In this sense, two types of interaction with Linux exist: regular users' interaction and the superuser, who performs system administration tasks. The chapters in the Administration section cover operations such as changing system states, managing users, and configuring printers and compiling the kernel. You perform most of these tasks, such as adding a new printer or mounting a file system, rarely. Other tasks, such as adding users, you perform on a regular basis. This chapter covers basic system administration topics, such as superusers, runlevels, configuration files, and performance monitoring.

Although system administration can become complex, basic administration tasks, such as adding users or mounting files systems, are easy to perform, particularly if you use a configuration tool, such as Linuxconf. Red Hat uses Linuxconf as its primary administration tool, though it also still provides the set of older specialized Red Hat tools used in previous Red Hat releases. Both have cursor-based interfaces as well as an X-Windows-based interface that uses menus, windows, and buttons with which you can make entries. You can run the cursor-based interface from the command line, using arrow keys, the SPACEBAR, and the ENTER key to make choices. Both are operated as front ends for making entries in Linux configuration files. You can edit these files and make entries directly, if you want. The underlying administration tasks are the same. Configuration using Linuxconf is discussed throughout the book where appropriate, with Chapter 21 examining how you can better configure and use the Linuxconf utility. The traditional Red Hat administration tools are usually accessed through a control panel entry on your desktop menu. These control panel tools are discussed in Chapter 22.

System Management: Superuser

To perform system administration operations, you must first have the correct password that enables you to log in as the root user, making you the superuser. Because a superuser has the power to change almost anything on the system, such a password is usually a carefully guarded secret given only to those whose job it is to manage the system. With the correct password, you can log in to the system as a system administrator and configure the system in different ways. You can start up and shut down the system, as well as change to a different operating mode, such as a single-user mode. You can also add or remove users, add or remove whole file systems, back up and restore files, and even designate the system's name. To become a superuser, you log in to the root user account. This is a special account reserved for system management operations with unrestricted access to all components of your Linux operating system. When you log in to the system as the root user, you are placed in a shell from which you can issue administrative Linux commands. The prompt for this shell is a sharp sign, **#**. In the next example, the user logs in to the system as the root user. The password is, of course, not displayed.

```
login: root
password:
#
```

As the root user, you can use the **passwd** command to change the password for the root login, as well as for any other user on the system.

```
# passwd root
New password:
Re-enter new password:
#
```

While you are logged in to a regular user account, it may be necessary for you to log in to the root and become a superuser. Ordinarily, you would have to log out of your user account first, and then log in to the root. Instead, you can use the **su** command to log in directly to the root while remaining logged in to your user account. A CTRL-D or **exit** command returns you to your own login. When logged in as the root, you can use **su** to log in as any user, without providing the password. For security reasons, Red Hat Linux does not allow the use of **su** in a Telnet session to access the root user. In the next example, the user is logged in already. The **su** command then logs the user in to the root, making the user a superuser. Some basic superuser commands are shown in Table 20-1.

```
$ pwd
/home/chris
$su
 password:
# cd
# pwd
/root
# exit
$
```

Command	Description
su root	Logs a superuser into the root from a user login; the superuser returns to the original login with a CTRL-D
passwd *login-name*	Sets a new password for the login name
crontab *options filename*	With *filename* as an argument, installs crontab entries in the file to a **crontab** file; these entries are operations executed at specified times **-e** Edits the **crontab** file **-l** Lists the contents of the **crontab** file **-r** Deletes the **crontab** file
init *state*	Changes the system state (see Table 20-2)
lilo *options Config-file*	Reinstalls the Linux Loader (LILO)
shutdown *options time*	Shuts down the system; similar to CTRL-ALT-DEL
date	Sets the date and time for the system

Table 20-1. *Basic System Administration*

System Configuration

Although many different specialized components go into making up a system, such as servers, users, and devices, some operations apply to the system in general. These include setting the system date and time, specifying shutdown procedures, and determining the services to start up and run whenever the system boots. In addition, you can use numerous performance analysis tools to control processes and check on resource use.

System Time and Date

You can use several different tools to set the system time and date, depending on the distribution you use. On all distributions, you can set the system time and date using the shell **date** command. Most users prefer to use a configuration tool. On Red Hat and other distributions, you can use Linuxconf or the control panel timetool. Recall that you set the time and date when you first installed your system. You should not need to do so again. If you entered the time incorrectly or moved to a different time zone, though, you could use this utility to change your time.

You can use the **date** command on your root user command line to set the date and time for the system. As an argument to date, you list (with no delimiters) the month, day, time, and year. In the next example, the date is set to 2:59 P.M., March 6, 2000 (03 for March, 06 for the day, 1459 for the time, and 00 for the year 2000):

```
# date 0306145900
Mon Mar  6 02:59:27 PST 2000
```

To set the system time and date with Linuxconf, select the Time and Date entry under Control. This displays a panel with boxes for the date and time (see Figure 20-1). Linuxconf is configured to read your system's time and date directly from the CMOS, the time and date set on your motherboard's BIOS.

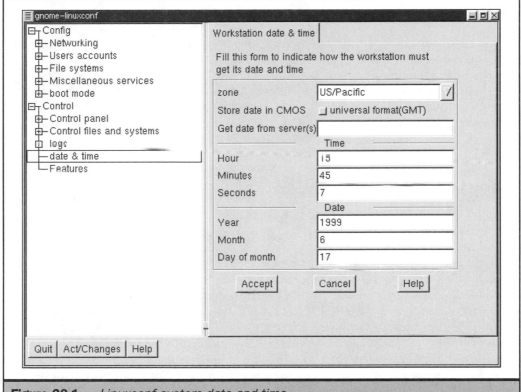

Figure 20-1.   *Linuxconf system date and time*

You can also use the Red Hat TimeTool, included on many distributions. An icon exists for it in the Control panel. Double-click the TimeTool icon or select its menu entry to open the Time Configuration window:

You can make changes to any part of the time you want. Move your mouse pointer to the hour, for example, and then click. The hour is then highlighted. Use the two triangles below the time and date display to increase or decrease the time or date entry. If you select the hour, clicking the upper triangle sets the time forward to the next hour. The bottom inverted triangle moves the hour backward. The same is true for the date. Once you have set the new time and date, click the Set System Clock button at the bottom of the window. Then click the Exit Time Machine button to exit the Time Configuration window.

Scheduling Tasks: crontab

Although it is not a system file, a crontab file is helpful in maintaining your system. A *crontab* file lists actions to take at a certain time. The cron daemon constantly checks the user's crontab file to see if it is time to take these actions. Any user can set up a crontab file of her own. The root user can set up a crontab file to take system administrative actions, such as backing up files at a certain time each week or month.

A crontab entry has six fields: the first five are used to specify the time for an action, while the last field is the action itself. The first field specifies minutes (0–59), the second field specifies the hour (0–23), the third field specifies the day of the month (1–31), the fourth field specifies the month of the year (1–12), and the fifth field specifies the day of the week (0–6), starting with 0 as Sunday. In each of the time fields, you can specify a range, a set of values, or use the asterisk to indicate all values. For example, 1–5 for the day-of-week field specifies Monday through Friday. In the hour field, 8, 12, 17 would specify 8 A.M., 12 noon, and 5 P.M. An * in the month-of-year field indicates every month. The following example backs up the **projects** directory at 2:00 A.M. every weekday.

```
0 2 1-5 * * tar cf  /home/chris/backp   /home/chris/projects
```

You use the **crontab** command to install your entries into a crontab file. To do this, you first create a text file and type your crontab entries. Save this file with any name you want, such as **mycronfile**. Then, to install these entries, enter crontab and the name of the text file. The **crontab** command takes the contents of the text file and creates a crontab file in the **/var/spool/cron** directory, adding the name of the user who issued the command. In the next example, the root user installs the contents of the **mycronfile** as the root's crontab file. This creates a file called **/var/spool/cron/root**. If a user named justin installed a crontab file, it would create a file called **/var/spool/cron/justin**. You can control use of the **crontab** command by regular users with the **/etc/cron.allow** file. Only users with their names in this file can create crontab files of their own.

```
# crontab mycronfile
```

Never try to edit your crontab file directly. Instead, use the **crontab** command with the **-e** option. This opens your crontab file in the **/var/spool/cron** directory with the standard text editor, such as Vi. **crontab** uses the default editor as specified by the EDITOR shell environment variable. To use a different editor for **crontab**, change the default editor by assigning the Editor's program name to the EDITOR variable and exporting that variable. Running **crontab** with the **-l** option displays the contents of your crontab file, and the **-r** option deletes the entire file. Invoking **crontab** with another text file of crontab entries overwrites your current crontab file, replacing it with the contents of the text file.

System States: init and shutdown

Your Linux system has several states, numbered from 0 to 6, and a single-user state represented by the letters s and S. When you power up your system, you enter the default state. You can then change to other states with the **init** command. For example, state 0 is the power down state. The command **init 0** shuts down your system. State 6 stops the system and reboots. Other states reflect how you want the system to be used. State 1 is the administrative state, allowing access only to the superuser. This enables you as administrator to perform administrative actions without interference from others. State s is a single-user state that allows use of the system by only one user. State 2 is a partial multiuser state, allowing access by many users, but with no remote file sharing. State 3, the default state for the command line interface, is the multiuser state that implements full remote file sharing. State 5 is the default state for graphical logins using display managers, such as gdm or xdm. If you choose to use graphical logins during installation, this will be your default state. You can change the default state by editing the **/etc/inittab** file and changing the init default entry. The states are listed in Table 20-2.

No matter what state you start in, you can change from one state to another with the **init** command. If your default state is 2, you power up in state 2, but you can change to, say, state 3 with init 3. In the next example, the **init** command changes to state *s*, the single-user state.

```
# init s
```

Although you can power down the system with the **init** command and the 0 state, you can also use the **shutdown** command or the Shutdown panel in Linuxconf. On Linuxconf, select the Shutdown/Reboot entry in the Control Panel under Control. This displays a panel that shows the entries for entering a shutdown message and specifying how long to wait before shutting down.

The **shutdown** command has a time argument that gives users on the system a warning before you power down. You can specify an exact time to shut down or a period of minutes from the current time. The exact time is specified by *hh:mm* for the hour and minutes. The period of time is indicated by a + and the number of minutes. The shutdown command takes several options with which you can specify how you want your system shut down. The **-h** option simply shuts down the system, whereas the **-r** option shuts down the system, and then reboots it. In the next example, the system is shut down after ten minutes. The shutdown options are listed in Table 20-3.

```
# shutdown -h +10
```

To shut down the system immediately, you can use +0 or the word "now." The following example has the same effect as the CTRL-ALT-DEL method of shutting down your system, as described in Chapter 3. It shuts down the system immediately, and then reboots.

```
# shutdown -r now
```

With the **shutdown** command, you can include a warning message to be sent to all users currently logged in, giving them time to finish what they are doing before you shut them down.

```
# shutdown -h +5  "System needs a rest"
```

If you do not specify either the **-h** or the **-r** options, the shutdown command shuts down the multiuser mode and shifts you to an administrative single-user mode. In effect, your system state changes from 3 (multiuser state) to 1 (administrative single-user state). Only the root user is active, allowing the root user to perform any necessary system administrative operations with which other users might interfere.

Use the **runlevel** command to see what state you are currently running in. In the next example, the system is running in state 3. The word "runlevel" is another term for state.

```
# runlevel
N 3
```

State	Description
init *state*	Changes the system state; you can use it to power up or power down a system, allow multiuser or single-user access; the **init** command takes as its argument a number representing a system state
System States	
0	Halt (do *not* set the default to this); this shuts down the system completely
1	Administrative single-user mode; denies other users access to the system, but allows root access to the entire multiuser file system
2	Multiuser, without NFS (the same as 3, if you do not have networking)
s or S	Single user; only one user has access to the system; used when you want all other users off the system or you have a single-user personal system
3	Full multiuser mode with login to command line interface; allows remote file sharing with other systems on your network
4	Unused
5	Graphical login (X11) for full multiuser mode; allows remote file sharing with other systems on your network (same as 3, but with graphical login)
6	Reboots; shuts down and restarts the system (do *not* set the default to this)

Table 20-2. *Runlevel States*

Command	Description
`shutdown [-rkhncft]` *time [warning-message]*	Shuts the system down after the specified time period, issuing warnings to users; you can specify a warning message of your own after the time argument; if neither **-h** nor **-r** is specified to shut down the system, the system sets to the administrative mode, runlevel state 1
Argument	
Time	Has two possible formats: it can be an absolute time in the format *hh:mm*, with *hh* as the hour (one or two digits) and *mm* as the minute (in two digits); it can also be in the format +*m*, with *m* as the number of minutes to wait; the word now is an alias for +0
Option	
-t *sec*	Tells init to wait *sec* seconds between sending processes the warning and the kill signal, before changing to another runlevel
-k	Doesn't actually shut down; only sends the warning messages to everybody
-r	Reboots after shutdown, runlevel state 6
-h	Halts after shutdown, runlevel state 0
-n	Doesn't call init to do the shutdown; you do it yourself
-f	Does a *fast* reboot
-c	Cancels an already running shutdown; no time argument

Table 20-3. *System Shutdown Options*

System Directories and Files

Your Linux system is organized into directories whose files are used for different system functions. Directories with "bin" in the name are used to hold programs. The **/bin** directory holds basic user programs, such as login, shells (bash, tcsh, and zsh), and file commands (**cp, mv, rm, ln,** and so on). The **/sbin** directory holds specialized system programs for such tasks as file system management (fsck, fdisk, mkfs) and system operations like shutdown and startup (lilo, init). The **/usr/bin** directory holds program files designed for user tasks. The **/usr/sbin** directory holds user-related system operation, such as useradd to add new users. The **/lib** directory holds all the libraries your system makes use of, including the main Linux library, libc, and subdirectories such as **modules**, which holds all the current kernel modules.

```
# ls /
bin boot dev etc home lib lost+found mnt proc root sbin tmp usr var
```

The **/etc** directory holds your system, network, server, and application configuration files. Here you can find the **fstab** file listing your file systems, the **hosts** file with IP addresses for hosts on your system, and **lilo.conf** for the boot systems provided by LILO. This directory includes various subdirectories, such as **apache** for the Apache Web server configuration files and **X11** for the X Window System and window manager configuration files.

The **/mnt** directory is usually used for mount points for your CD-ROM, floppy, or Zip drives. These are file systems you may be changing frequently, unlike partitions on fixed disks. The **/home** directory holds user home directories. When a user account is set up, a home directory for it is set up here, usually with the same name as the user. On Red Hat systems, the **/home** directory also holds server data directories, such as **/home/httpd** for the Apache Web server Web site files or **/home/ftpd** for your FTP site files. The **/var** directory holds subdirectories for tasks whose files change frequently, such as lock files, log files, or printer spool files. The **/tmp** directory is simply a directory to hold any temporary files programs may need to perform a particular task.

The **/usr** directory holds programs for user-related operations. The **/usr/lib** directory holds many of the libraries for particular applications. The **/usr/X11R6** directory holds the X Window System programs and libraries for revision 6 of the X Window System. The **/usr/X11R6/lib/X11** directory is a link to the **/etc/X11** directory, which holds the X Window System configuration files. The **/usr/src** directory holds source files; in particular, **/usr/src/linux** holds the kernel source files you use to update the kernel. The **/usr/doc** directory holds documentation that is usually installed with different applications. Here you can also find HOW-TO documents. The **/usr/local** directory is used for programs meant to be used only on this particular system. The **/usr/opt** directory is where optional packages are installed.

```
# ls /usr
X11R6 bin cgi-bin dict doc etc games include info lib libexec local
man sbin share src tmp
```

Standard system directories and configuration files are shown in Tables 20-4 and 20-5. See Chapter 30 for network configuration files.

Directories	Description
/bin	System-related programs
/sbin	System programs for specialized tasks
/lib	System libraries
/etc	Configuration files for system and network services and applications
/home	The location of user home directories and server data directories, such as Web and FTP site files
/mnt	The location where CD-ROM and floppy disk files systems are mounted
/var	The location of system directories whose files continually change, such as logs, printer spool files, and lock files
/usr	User-related programs and files. Includes several key subdirectories, such as **/usr/bin**, **/usr/X11**, and **/usr/doc**
/usr/bin	Programs for users
/usr/X11	X Window System programs and files
/usr/doc	Documentation for applications
/tmp	Directory for system temporary files

Table 20-4. *System Directories*

File	Description
/etc/inittab	Sets the default state, as well as terminal connections
/etc/passwd	Contains user password and login configurations
/etc/shadow	Contains user encrypted passwords
/etc/group	Contains a list of groups with configurations for each
/etc/fstab	Automatically mounts file systems when you start your system

Table 20-5. *Configuration Files*

File	Description
/etc/lilo.conf	The LILO configuration file for your system
/etc/conf.modules	Modules on your system to be automatically loaded
/etc/printcap	Contains a list of each printer and its specifications
/etc/termcap	Contains a list of terminal type specifications for terminals that could be connected to the system
/etc/gettydefs	Contains configuration information on terminals connected to the system
/etc/skel	Directory that holds the versions of initialization files, such as **.bash_profile,** which are copied to new users' home directories
/etc/ttys	List of terminal types and the terminal devices to which they correspond
/etc/services	Services run on the system and the ports they use
/etc/profile	Default shell configuration file for users
/etc/shells	Shells installed on the system that users can use
/etc/motd	System administrator's message of the day

Table 20-5.   *Configuration Files* (continued)

System Startup Files: /etc/rc.d

Each time you start your system, it reads a series of startup commands from system initialization files located in your **/etc/rc.d** directory. These initialization files are organized according to different tasks. Some are located in the **/etc/rc.d** directory itself, while others are located in a subdirectory called **init.d**. You should not have to change any of these files. The organization of system initialization files varies among Linux distributions. The Red Hat organization is described here. Some of the files you find in **/etc/rc.d** are listed in Table 20-6.

The **/etc/rc.d/rc.sysinit** file holds the commands for initializing your system, including the mounting of your file systems. Kernel modules for specialized features or devices can be loaded in an **rc.modules** file. The **/etc/rc.d/rc.local** file is the last initialization file executed. You can place commands of your own here. If you look at this file, you see the message displayed for you every time you start the system. You can change that message if you want. When you shut down your system, the **halt** file, which contains the commands to do this, is called. The files in **init.d** are then called to shut down daemons, and the file systems are unmounted. In the current distribution of Red Hat, **halt** is located in the **init.d** directory. For other distributions, it may be called **rc.halt** and located in the **/etc/rc.d** directory.

The **/etc/rc.d/init.d** directory is designed primarily to hold scripts that both start up and shut down different specialized daemons. Network and printer daemons are started up here. You also find files here to start font servers and Web site daemons. These files perform double duty, starting a daemon when the system starts up and shutting down the daemon when the system shuts down. The files in **init.d** are designed in a way to make it easy to write scripts for starting up and shutting down specialized applications. Many of these files are set up for you automatically. You needn't change them. If you do change them, be sure you know how these files work first. Chapter 15 describes this process in detail.

When your system starts up, several programs are automatically started and run continuously to provide services such as Web site operations. Depending on what kind of services you want your system to provide, you can add or remove items in a list of services to be automatically started. In the installation process, you could determine what services those would be. For example, the Web server is run automatically when your system starts up. If you are not running a Web site, you would have no need, as yet, for the Web server. You could have the service not started, removing an extra task the system does not need to perform. Several of the servers and daemons perform necessary tasks. The sendmail process enables you to send messages across networks, while the lpd server performs printing operations.

When your system starts up, it uses links in special runlevel directories in the **/etc/rc.d/** directory to run the startup scripts in the **/etc/rc.d/init.d** directory. A runlevel directory bears the number of its runlevel, as in **/etc/rc.d/rc3.d** for runlevel 3. To have a service not start up, remove its link from that runlevel directory. You can use any of these scripts to start and stop a daemon manually at any time by using the stop argument to stop it, the start argument to start it again, and the restart argument to restart the daemon.

You can use a System V Init utility to determine which servers and daemons are to start and stop at what runlevel. You can choose from several System V Init utilities. Sys V Init Manager is an X-based utility that provides an easy-to-use GUI interface for managing the servers and daemons in your **/etc/rc.d/init.d** directory. You can stop, start, and assign servers to different runlevels. There is also a KDE System V init utility called the Sys V Init Editor, with many of the same features (see Figure 20-2). The Sys V Init Editor is easier to use because it supports drag-and-drop operations. To assign a server to a particular runlevel, drag its entry from the Services box to the appropriate Runlevel box. To remove it from a particular runlevel, drag its entry out of that Runlevel box to the Trash icon. To start and stop a daemon manually, right-click it and select either the stop or start entry from the pop-up menu.

Most administration tools provide interfaces displaying a simple list of services from which you can select the ones you want to start up. On Linuxconf, the Control

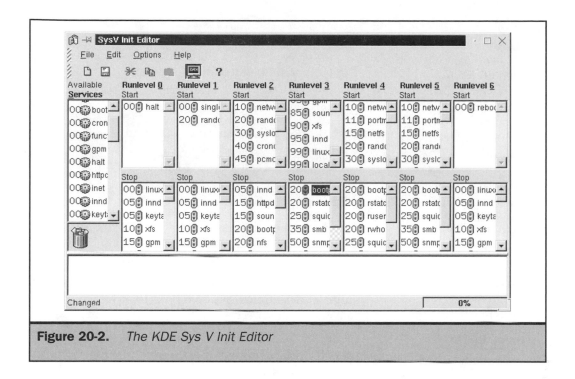

Figure 20-2. *The KDE Sys V Init Editor*

Service Activity panel lists different daemons and servers you can have start by clicking a check box (see Chapter 15 for more details). On the Red Hat Setup menu, select System Services, and then choose from the list of servers and daemons provided. Toggle an entry on or off with the SPACEBAR.

System Logs: /var/log and syslogd

Various system logs kept for tasks performed on your system are kept in the **/var/log** directory. Here you can find logs for mail, news, and all other system operations. The **/var/log/messages** file is a log of all system tasks not covered by other logs. This usually includes startup tasks, such as loading drivers and mounting file systems. If a driver for a card failed to install at start up, you find an error message for it here. Logins are also logged in this file, showing you who attempted to log in to what account. The **/var/log/maillog** file logs mail message transmissions and news transfers.

Logs are managed by the **syslogd** daemon. This daemon will manage all the logs on your system as well as coordinating with any logging operation of other systems on your network. Configuration information for **syslogd** is held in the **/etc/syslog.conf** file. This file contains the names and locations of your system log files. Here you find entries for **/var/log/messages** and **/var/log/maillog**, among others. An entry consists of two fields, a selector, and an action. The selector is the kind of service to be logged,

ADMINISTRATION

File	Description
/etc/rc.d	Directory that holds system startup and shutdown files
/etc/rc.d/rc.sysinit	Initialization file for your system
/etc/rc.d/rc.local	Initialization file for your own commands; you can freely edit this file to add your own startup commands; this is the last startup file executed
/etc/rc.d/rc.modules	Loads kernel modules (not implemented by default on Red Hat Linux)
/etc/rc.d/init.d	Directory that holds many of the daemons, servers, and scripts such as httpd for Web servers and networks to start up network connections
/etc/rc.d/rc*num*.d	Directories for different runlevels where *num* is the runlevel. The directories hold links to scripts in the **/etc/rc.d/init.d** directory
/etc/rc.d/init.d/halt	Operations performed each time you shut down the system, such as unmounting file systems; called **rc.halt** in other distributions
/etc/rc.d/init.d/lpd	Start up and shut down the lpd daemon
/etc/rc.d/init.d/inet	Operations to start up or shut down the inetd daemon
/etc/rc.d/init.d/network	Operations to start up or shut down your network connections
/etc/rc.d/init.d/httpd	Operations to start up or shut down your Web server daemon, httpd

Table 20-6. *System Startup Files*

such as mail or news, and the action is the location where messages are to be placed. The action is usually a log file, but it can also be a remote host or a pipe to another program. The kind of service is referred to as a *facility*. **syslog** has several terms it uses to specify certain kinds of services (see Table 20-7). A facility can be further qualified by a priority. A priority specifies the kind of message generated by the facility. **syslog** uses several designated terms to indicate different priorities (see Table 20-7). A sector is constructed from both the facility and priority separated by a period. For example, to save error messages generated by mail systems, you use a sector consisting of the mail facility and the err priority, as shown here:

mail.err

To save these messages to the **/var/log/maillog** file, you specify that file as the action, giving you the following entry:

```
mail.err                        /var/log/maillog
```

syslog also supports the use of * as a matching character to match either all the facilities or prorities in a sector. **cron.*** would match all cron messages no matter what the priority, *****.err** would match error messages from all the facilities, and *****.*** would match all messages. The following example saves all mail messages to the **/var/log/maillog** file and all critical messages to the **/var/log/mycritical** file:

```
mail.*                          /var/log/maillog
*.crit                          /var/log/mycritical
```

When you specify a priority for a facility, that will in fact include all the messages with a higher priority. So the **err** priority also includes the **crit**, **alret**, and **emerg** priorities. If you just want to select the message for a specific priority, you qualify the priority with the = operator. For example, **mail.=err** will select only error messages, not **crit**, **alert**, and **emerg** messages. You can also restrict priorities with the ! operator. This will eliminate all messages with the specified priority and higher. For example, **mail.!crit** will exclude **crit** messages and the higher **alert** and **emerg** messages. To specifically exclude all the messages for an entire facility, you use the **none** priority. **mail.none** excludes all mail messages. This is used usually when you are defining several sectors in the same entry.

You can list several priorities or facilities in a given sector by separating them with commas. You can also have several sectors in the same entry by separating them with semicolons. The first example below saves to the **/var/log/messages** file all messages with **info** priority, excluding all mail, news, and authentication messages (authpriv). The second saves to the **/var/log/spooler** file all **crit** messages and higher for the **uucp** and **news** facilities:

```
*.info;mail.none;news.none;authpriv.none    /var/log/messages
uucp,news.crit                              /var/log/spooler
```

For the action field you can specify files, remote systems, users, or pipes. An action entry for a file must always begin with a / and specify its full pathname, such as **/var/log/messages**. To log messages to a remote host you simply specify the host

name, preceded by an @ sign. The following example saves all kernel messages on
rabbit.trek.com:

```
kern.*                          @rabbit.trek.com
```

For users, you list the login names of just the users you want to receive the messages.
The following example will send critical news messages to the consoles for the user's **chris**
and **aleina**:

```
news.=crit                              chris,aleina
```

You can also output messages to a named pipe (FIFO). The pipe entry for the action
field begins with a |. The following example pipes kernel debug messages to the name
pipe |/usr/adm/debug:

```
kern.=debug             |/usr/adm/debug
```

Facilities	Description
auth–priv	Security/authorization messages (private)
cron	Clock daemon (cron and at) messages
daemon	Other system daemon messages
kern	Kernel messages
lpr	Line printer subsystem messages
mail	Mail subsystem messages
mark	Internal use only
news	USENET news subsystem messages
syslog	syslog internal messages
user	Generic user-level messages
uucp	UUCP subsystem messages
local0 through local7	Reserved for local use

Table 20-7.   *syslogd Facilities, Priorities, and Operators*

Priorities	Description
debug	7, Debugging messages; lowest priority
info	6, Informational messages
notice	5, Notifications; normal, but significant, condition
warning	4, Warnings
err	3, Error messages
crit	2, Critical conditions
alert	1, Alerts that action must be taken immediately
emerg	0, Emergency messages; system is unusable; highest priority
Operators	**Description**
*	Matches all facilities or priorities in a sector
=	Restricts to a specified priority
!	Excludes specified priority and higher ones
/	A file to save messages to
@	A host to send messages to
		FIFO pipe to send messages to

Table 20-7.   *syslogd Facilities, Priorities, and Operators* (continued)

The default **/etc/syslog.conf** file for Red Hat systems is shown here. Messages are logged to various files in the **/var/log** directory.

```
# Log all kernel messages to the console.
# Logging much else clutters up the screen.
#kern.*                                        /dev/console

# Log anything (except mail) of level info or higher.
# Don't log private authentication messages!
*.info;mail.none;news.none;authpriv.none        /var/log/messages
```

```
# The authpriv file has restricted access.
authpriv.*                              /var/log/secure

# Log all the mail messages in one place.
mail.*                                  /var/log/maillog

# Everybody gets emergency messages, plus log them on another
# machine.
*.emerg                                         *

# Save mail and news errors of level err and higher in a
# special file.
uucp,news.crit                          /var/log/spooler

# Save boot messages also to boot.log
local7.*                                /var/log/boot.log

#
# INN
#
news.=crit                              /var/log/news/news.crit
news.=err                               /var/log/news/news.err
news.notice                             /var/log/news/news.notice
```

Performance Analysis Tools and Processes

Each task performed on your system is treated by Linux as a process, and is assigned a number and a name. You can examine these processes and even stop them. From the command line, you can use the **ps** command to list processes. With the **-aux** command, you can list all processes. Piping the output to a **grep** command with a pattern enables you to search for a particular process. The following command lists all X Window System processes.

```
ps -aux | grep 'X'
```

A number of utilities on your system provide detailed information on your processes, as well as other system information, such as CPU and disk use. Although these tools were designed to be used on a shell command line, displaying output in text lines, several now have KDE and Gnome versions that provide a GUI interface for displaying results and managing processes. The **vmstat** command outputs a detailed listing indicating the performance of different system components, including CPU, memory, I/O, and swap operations. A report is issued as a line with fields for the different components. If you provide a time period as argument, it repeats at the specified interval, usually a few seconds. The top command provides a listing of the processes on your system that are the most CPU intensive, showing what processes are using most of your resources. The listing is in real-time and updated every few seconds. Commands are provided for changing a process's status, such as its priority. The **free** command lists the amount of free RAM memory on your system, showing how much is used and how much is free, as well as what is used for buffers and swap memory. Xosview is a X Window System tool showing the load, CPU, and memory. You can also use Linuxconf to display basic system information, such as memory and disk use. Select Viewing System State under Control.

The K desktop provides two utilities for viewing and managing your processes: the KDE Task Manager (KTop, shown in Figure 20-3) and the KDE Process Manager (kpm). On both utilities, you can sort the processes according to their fields by clicking the field's button at the top of the process list. If you select a process, you can then choose to perform several different actions on it, such as ending it (killing the process) or suspending it (putting it to sleep). A right-click on a process entry displays a pop-up menu with the different actions you can take. You can further refine your process list by choosing to view only your own processes, system processes, or all processes.

KTop provides both list and tree views. With the tree view, you can see what processes are dependent on others. For example, the desktop relies on the X Window System process. A Performance Meters panel displays system information, such as memory use and CPU load.

On the Gnome System Manager (GTop), you can also sort the processes according to their fields by clicking the field's button at the top of the process list. If you right-click an entry, a pop-up menu displays with actions you can perform on it (see Figure 20-4). System statistic summary graphs are displayed at the top of the window showing the CPU load, memory use, and disk use. You can add more graphs or change their display features, such as the colors used. The GTop window displays three tabbed panels for detailed reports showing processes, memory use, and file system use. You can add more, showing customized reports, such as only the user processes. Process lists can be further refined to show user, system, or all processes. To configure GTop, you select the Preferences entry in the Settings menu. This displays a menu with tabbed panels for specifying the update frequency for different statistics, determining the summaries you want displayed, and what process fields to show. You can find the Gnome System Manager in the Utilities menu.

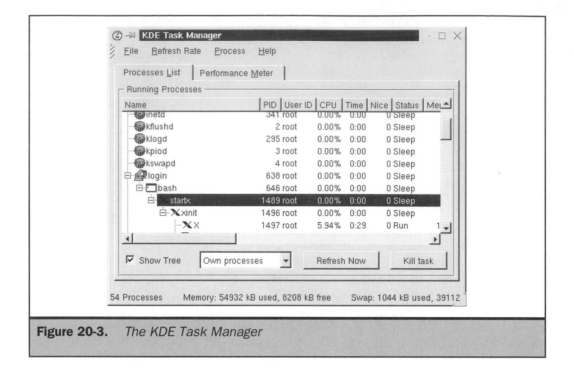

Figure 20-3. *The KDE Task Manager*

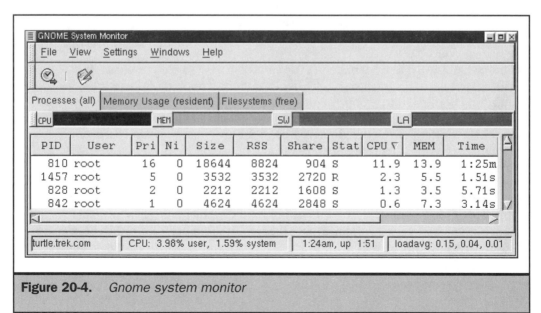

Figure 20-4. *Gnome system monitor*

LILO

If you have installed two or more operating systems on your computer's hard disks, you need to use a boot manager to enable you to choose the one you want to use whenever your computer starts up. As shown in Chapter 2, Red Hat Linux provides the *Linux Loader* (*LILO*) as its boot manager, which you can install as part of the Red Hat installation process. LILO currently has one important limitation: on hard disks greater than 8 gigs, any operating system boot partitions need to be located within the first 8 gigs of the hard disk. Other partitions can then be located anywhere else, including the gigs after the first 8 gigs. Boot partitions can be relatively small. For example, on a 30-gig hard drive, you could have a 1-gig partition for the Linux boot partition somewhere in the first 8 gigs and another 10 gig Linux partition anywhere else. The same is true for Windows. You could have a 3-gig primary partition in the first 8 gigs and a large extended partition located anywhere else. Also, depending on your computer's BIOS, LILO can also be limited to a partition size of 1,024 cylinders. For large hard disks, you would specify the LINEAR global option in the **lilo.conf** file to insure LILO can access vary large partitions.

If you need to change your LILO configuration, you can easily do so by modifying the **/etc/lilo.conf** configuration file and executing the command **lilo.** If you examine your **/etc/lilo.conf** file, you find it organized into different segments called *stanzas*, one for each operating system that LILO is to start up. If your Linux system shares your computer with a DOS system, you should see two stanzas listed in your **/etc/lilo.conf** file: one for Linux and one for DOS. Each stanza indicates the hard disk partition on which the respective operating system is located. It also includes an entry for the label. This is the name you enter at the LILO prompt to start that operating system.

You can, if you want, make changes directly to the **/etc/lilo.conf** file using a text editor. Whenever you make a change, you must execute the **lilo** command to have it take effect. Type **lilo** and press ENTER.

```
# lilo
```

You can also configure LILO using the LILO panels in Linuxconf. You can add segments and specify options there. When you activate your changes in Linuxconf, the **/etc/lilo.conf** file is updated and the **lilo** command is run.

/etc/lilo.conf
```
# general section
boot = /dev/hda
# wait 20 seconds (200 10ths) for user to select the entry to load
timeout = 200
message = /boot/message
```

```
prompt
linear
 # default entry
default = win
vga = normal
map=/boot/map
install=/boot/boot.b
image = /boot/vmlinuz-2.2.5-15
        label = linux
        root = /dev/hda4
        read-only
other = /dev/hda1
        label = win
        table=/dev/had
```

Unless specified by the default entry, the default operating system LILO boots the one whose segment is the first listed in the **lilo.conf** file. Because the Linux stanza is the first listed, this is the one LILO boots if you don't enter anything at the LILO prompt. If you want to have your DOS system be the default, you can use **lilo** with the **-D** option to reset the default or you can edit the **lilo.conf** file to assign a value to **default**. You could also use a text editor to place the DOS stanza first, before the Linux stanza. Be sure to execute **lilo** to have the change take effect. The next time you start your system, you could press ENTER at the LILO prompt to have DOS loaded, instead of typing DOS.

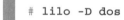

```
 # lilo -D dos
```

You can set a number of LILO options using either command line options or options in the **lilo.conf** file. These options are listed in Table 20-8.

Command Line Options	lilo.conf options	Description
-b *bootdev*	boot=*bootdev*	Boot device
-c	compact	Enable map compaction. Speeds up booting.
-d *dsec*	delay=*dsec*	Timeout delay to wait for you to enter the label of an operating system at the LILO prompt when you boot up

Table 20-8. *LILO Options for Command Line and lilo.conf*

Command Line Options	lilo.conf options	Description
-D *label*	default=*label*	Use the kernel with the specified label, instead of the first one in the list, as the default kernel to boot
-I *bootsector*	install=*bootsector*	File to be used as the new boot sector
-f *file*	disktab=*file*	Disk geometry parameter file
-l	linear	Generate linear sector addresses, instead of sector/head/cylinder addresses for large hard disks. (This option can cause a conflict with compact.)
-m *mapfile*	map=*mapfile*	Use specified map file instead of the default
-P fix	fix-table	Fix corrupt partition tables
-P ignore	ignore-table	Ignore corrupt partition tables
-s *file*	backup=*file*	Alternate save file for the boot sector
-S *file*	force-backup=*file*	Allow overwriting of existing save file
-v	verbose=*level*	Increase verbosity
-u		Uninstall LILO, by copying the saved boot sector back
-V		Print version number
-t		Test only. Do not actually write a new boot sector or map file. Use together with -v to learn what LILO is about to do.
-I *label*		Display label and pathname of running kernel. Label is held in BOOT_IMAGE shell variable
	timeout=*dsec*	Timeout delay to wait for you to enter the label of an operating system at the LILO prompt when you boot up

Table 20-8. *LILO Options for Command Line and lilo.conf* (continued)

Command Line Options	lilo.conf options	Description
	image=*Linux-kernel*	Pathname for boot image of a Linux kernel
	other=*os-boot-image*	Pathname for boot image of a non-Linux operating system
	read-only	Boot Linux kernel as read-only (system startup remounts as read/write)

Table 20-8.   *LILO Options for Command Line and lilo.conf* (continued)

If you are booting an operating system from a location other than the first hard disk, you need to include a loader line for the **chain.b** file in its stanza.

```
loader=/boot/chain.b
```

The
Complete
Reference

Chapter 21

Linuxconf

Linuxconf is a comprehensive configuration tool for almost all your administrative tasks, including user and file system management, as well as network services (see the list of features in Table 21-1). Linuxconf is designed to work on any Linux distribution, and is currently, compatible with Caldera, Red Hat, SuSE, Slackware, and Debian. Both compressed archive and RPM versions of the software are provided. You can download the current version from the Linuxconf Web site at **www.solucorp.qc.ca/linuxconf**. Here you can also find documentation and links to any added packages.

Linuxconf currently has three interfaces: text, GUI, and HTML. The *text interface* provides cursor-based full screens that can be run from any shell command line. You use the TAB key to move between boxes, lists, and buttons, and you use the arrow keys to select entries in a list. The text mode also operates as a command line mode, enabling you to place Linuxconf commands in the shell scripts. The *GUI interface* is an X Window System interface that runs on any window manager or desktop, including Gnome and KDE. It provides a menu tree with which you can easily select panels for different configuration tasks. The *HTML interface*, shown in Figure 21-1, is a Web page interface that lists options as links to other Web pages. It provides boxes and check boxes with which you can make your entries. To access the HTML interface, enter your system's hostname with the port 98, written as :98 attached to the end of the hostname, for example http://turtle.mytrek.com:98. Be sure to first permit access by setting permissions for the user you want to use (such as **root**) in the Linuxconf Network Access panel in the Misc list under Networking. All the interfaces provide context-level help. On each screen, panel, or page is a Help button that displays detailed information about the current task.

In the GUI interface, the main Linuxconf window displays a window with two frames. On the left is a list of all the system administration operations. The list is

Features	Description
User accounts and groups	User configuration, passwords, and permissions
Networking	TCP/IP, NIS, PPP, IPX, DHCP, DNS, IP-aliasing, UUCP, hosts, routing, and gateways
Servers	Apache, Squid, ProFTP, wu-ftpd, DHCPD, Samba, DNS, and sendmail
File systems	fstab, NFS
LILO	LILO boot options and entries

Table 21-1. *Linuxconf Configuration Features*

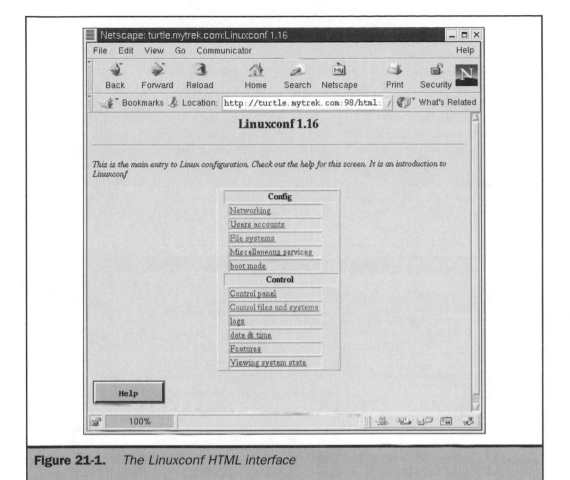

Figure 21-1.   *The Linuxconf HTML interface*

organized into categories and subcategories you can expand to list entries or shrink to show only the category heading. Small boxes to the left of the category headings show small minus (–) signs when expanded and plus (+) signs when entries are not displayed. Initially, all entries for each category are displayed. Clicking a category box displays or hides the entries. Two major categories are shown: Config and Control. You use the Config entries to configure almost all components on your systems, including users, file systems, networking, servers, and LILO. Among the servers supported are Apache, Squid, wu-ftpd, DHCPD, Samba, and sendmail. The Control entries enable you to perform tasks such as setting the time, adding modules, selecting servers to start up, and mounting file systems.

Using the main window shown in Figure 21-2, you select an administration task by clicking its entry. A panel for that task is then displayed on the right frame. Most tasks have several panels with panel tabs displayed at the top of the window. Click a tab to display that panel. If you do not close the window before selecting another administration task, then a new window is opened on top of the current one. You can move from one task to another by clicking the respective entries.

Much of the configuration support for specific components, such as the Apache Web server or Squid, is implemented using modules. You can add or remove modules as you choose. Modules are usually included with the Linuxconf software package. You can then select which modules to load into Linuxconf using the Configure Linuxconf Modules panel in the Control Files And Systems list under Control panel. In version 1.16, this panel shows all the available modules with check boxes you can use to toggle whether a module should be loaded. For example, to add firewall configuration panels to Linuxconf, make sure the firewall module check box is selected. On earlier versions of Linuxconf (as in 1.14 used on Red Hat 6.0), this panel shows

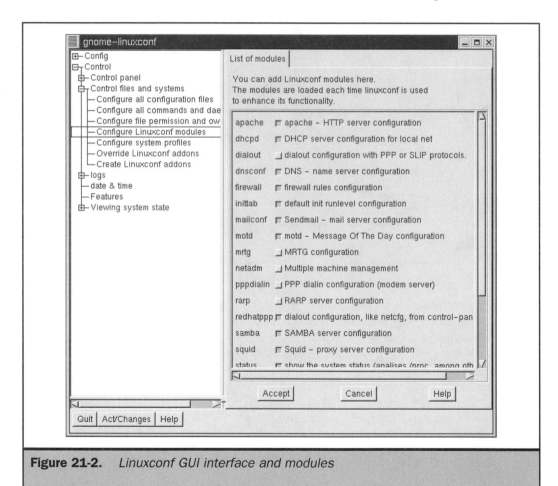

Figure 21-2.   *Linuxconf GUI interface and modules*

boxes where you can type in the name of the modules to add. Table 21-2 shows a list of current Linuxconf modules. Those listed as core modules are included in the Linuxconf package. Those listed as pkg are packages installed separately and usually located at different sites. Links are available on the Linuxconf Web site and most are also kept on the FTP site, **ftp.solucorp.qc.ca/pub/linuxconf/modules**.

Module	Status	Description
apache	core	Configuration of the Apache Web server
dhcpd	core	Configuration of the ISC dhcpd server
dialout	core	PPP dialout configuration. Alternative to redhatppp.
dnsconf	core	Configuration of bind 4 and 8 DNS
firewall	core	Configuration of the kernel 2.0 packet filter, including support for masquerading, port redirection, and accounting
inittab	core	Control editing of the **/etc/inittab** file
isdnadmin	pkg	Manages an ISDN adapter, www.terminator.net/isdnadmin
ldapconf	pkg	Configures an ldap server and clients, www.terminator.net/ldapconf
mailconf	core	Configuration of sendmail
managerpm	pkg	Manipulates RPM packages
mgettyconf	pkg	Configuration of the mgetty serial port manager
motd	core	Edits the message of the day file
mrtg	core	Configuration for the mrtg package
netadm	core	Configures PPP connections
pppdialin	core	Configures a PPP session
proftpd	pkg	Manages the pro-ftp daemon, http://lie-br.conectiva.com.br/~marcelo
rarp	core	Configures the kernel RARP table

Table 21-2.   *Linuxconf Modules*

Module	Status	Description
redhatppp	core	PPP/SLIP/PLIP configuration compatible with Red Hat netcfg utility
samba	core	Configuration of the Samba SMB file server
shellmod	pkg	Writes Linuxconf modules and standalone utilities using the shell (**/bin/sh**)
squid	core	In development. Provides basic support for the configuration of the squid.
status	core	Reports various items of information about the system
treemenu	core	Pulls all menu/submenu options into a single large tree
updpass	pkg	Updates password
userinfo	pkg	Adds custom fields to the user account dialog box
usermenu	core	Custom views of the Linuxconf menu access privileges
usersbygroup	pkg	Enables user account management by group
virtual	pkg	In development. Provides a unified view of all services supporting virtual hosting, to configure a virtual host in one dialog box.
wuftpd	core	Configuration of the wu-ftpd FTP server
xterminals	core	Management of Linux-based X terminals

Table 21-2.   *Linuxconf Modules* (continued)

You can also access Linuxconf using specialized windows for the particular service you want to configure: **userconf**, **fsconf**, **dnsconf**, **netconf**, and **mailconf**. These are special Linuxconf commands that call Linuxconf using an interface listing option for a particular service. For example, to add a new user to your system, you could use the **userconf** command to display a special Linuxconf window. This window displays buttons and icons for accessing the different Linuxconf user and group configuration panels. These are the same panels you can access through the main Linuxconf interface. The **netconf** command displays a window listing the icons for the different network configuration panels. Another panel on this same window lists icons for the different server configuration panels. The **dnsconf** command displays a window with buttons for accessing the Domain Name Service (named) configuration panels. The **mailconf** command enables you to access panels directly for configuring your mail server (sendmail). The `liloconf` command provides a window with buttons for panels that enable you to configure LILO, adding new boot entries and editing current ones. Currently, the Red Hat 6.1 distribution includes no menu entries for these specialized windows. You have to open a terminal window, and then enter and execute their commands at the prompt.

Linuxconf saves its configuration information in files located in the **/etc/linuxconf/archive** directory. When you activate changes with new configuration information, Linuxconf both updates your system configuration files and saves the information in its own files. In effect, Linuxconf maintains its own set of your system's configuration files and can detect if its information does not correspond to your system's configuration files. Linuxconf also includes a sophisticated translation system that enables you to implement Linuxconf in the language of your choice.

Linuxconf enables you to create multiple system configurations that you can load, activating or deactivating features and services. You could have one set of configurations for your office and one for home, or even one for, say, Web server. A home configuration might have your Web server turned off, whereas a Web server configuration might have it running. If you have Linux running on a portable PC, you could switch networking configurations just by switching Linuxconf system configurations. Different configurations are placed in subdirectories in the **/etc/linuxconf/archive** directory. Their names are the same as those subdirectories. Linuxconf provides two for you by default: Office and Home-Office. Various Linuxconf startup commands appear in Table 21-3.

Command	Description
linuxconf	Start Linuxconf in the main window
netconf	Network configuration window for configuring your network and servers, accesses network and server panels directly
userconf	User configuration window, accesses user and group configuration panels directly
fsconf	File system configuration window, accesses file system configuration panels directly
dnsconf	Domain Name Service configuration window, accesses DNS configuration panels directly
mailconf	Mail (sendmail) configuration window, accesses sendmail configuration panels directly

Table 21-3. *Linuxconf Startup Commands*

System Profile Versioning

With system profile versioning you can create customized configurations for your entire system. Linuxconf enables you to switch easily from one configuration to another. You can even set up shared configurations where you can partially switch from one to another. A history of changes is kept for each configuration.

A specific configuration consists of a set of configuration files collected into a subsystem. In effect, a *subsystem* is a particular system configuration. A subsystem consists of a key name and a description. The configuration files Linuxconf uses are located in the subsystem for the configuration currently in use. Subsystems are the archiving unit for Linuxconf, holding all configuration files.

Configuration files are connected to a subsystem dynamically, where the configuration file consists of the subsystem key name. You can even define a module to include configuration files for specific subsystems.

You can set up archiving families where different subsystems can form families and create their own subsystems that they can share. A profile version specifies the families in which each subsystem is to be archived. The profile has a default family in which added subsystems are placed. If you do not want a subsystem archived, you give it the family "none".

You can switch from one version to another at any time during a session or when you boot up. When you switch, the version currently in use is archived and the new one is activated. If the new one shares subsystems in the same family, those subsystems are left alone. The original subsystems remain. A log of all operations is maintained for you to check.

An archive is saved in the /etc/linuxconf/archive/ and given the name of the profile version. Within the directory is a directory tree of standard Linux configuration directories and files. Directories like etc, var, and dev are listed. The configuration files have the extension ,v, the extension for an RCS file. Configuration files are actually archived with the **cfgarchive** command. **cfgarchive** normally used the RCS system to archive a file, provided RCS is installed on your Linux system. If not, then the most recent file is simply stored on disk.

Boot Time Control

Linuxconf has the boot time control feature that enables users to select the kind of interface they want to boot to, such as the command line or the graphical user interface, such as Gnome. With boot time control, users can easily select an interface, boot to administration level, select a Linuxconf profile version, or view the boot messages. With the boot time control feature installed, Linuxconf runs an **askrunlevel** command at boot time. This command is located in the /etc/rc.d/rc.sysinit startup file on RedHat systems.

```
/sbin/askrunlevel
```

The **runlevel** command offers a menu to users (timed out by default at 20 seconds). The menu lists the following options:

```
Start graphic & network
Start graphic only
Start in X terminal mode
Start in text mode & network
Start in text mode only
System maintenance (single user mode)
Configure the workstation
Select configuration version
View the boot logs
```

The graphic mode starts the GUI interface (runlevel 5), whereas the text mode starts with the command line interface (runlevel 3). The Configure the workstation entry lets the user login as the root user and perform configurations before the boot process finishes. This is helpful when installing a computer on a different network. The Select configuration version enables you to switch at startup to a different system profile version. You can choose from a list of available profile versions. The "View the boot logs" entry lists the boot messages that normally scroll by onscreen at startup.

Creating Your Own Linuxconf Modules

Creating your own Linuxconf module is a fairly simple process. Modules are written in C++ and automatically make use of the Linuxconf API. The API interface is already set up for you by Linuxconf. Any Linuxconf module you create can take advantage of any Linuxconf features. The module is fully translatable, can work in any of the Linuxconf interfaces (text, html, or GUI), can be operated remotely, can be part of system profile versions, and can partake in multiple machine management.

The simplest way to create a module is to use the setupmod.sh script provided with Linuxconf. The setupmod.sh script prompts you with some basic questions, and then creates a directory for that module and generates the template source files. You can then build on this basic structure, adding or changing elements as you want.

Each module has its own directory located in the Linuxconf module directory. In the directory on your system where Linuxconf configuration files are installed, you can find a directory named *modules*, and within it, different subdirectories for each module your version of Linuxconf currently supports. For a new module, **setupmod.sh** creates a subdirectory for you. You can also create one manually. Within this directory is the source code for your module, along with a **makefile** for compiling it. A simple way to create the **makefile** is to copy one from one of the other module directories (**setupmod.sh** can generate one for you). You then edit the **makefile** to enter the name of your source files and module name. The following example shows the entries for a **mymod** module.

```
CURDIR=mymod
LOCAL_CLEAN=std_local_clean
LOCAL_INSTALL=std_local_install
all: $(CURDIR).so
OBJS =  mymod.o mrtgedit.o _dict.o

include ../rules.mak

include ../stdmod.mak

# Test program
```

A module needs to include a file named **_dict.cc** as one of its source code files. It is a simple file, as shown here, and it provides hooks to the translation system. **_dict.cc** compiles to a **_dict.o** object file, which is then linked into your module. Be sure to include the .m file for your module in the **_dict.cc** file, such as **mymod.m** for the **mymod** module.

```
#include "mymod.m"
#include <translat.h>
DICTIONARY_REQUEST;
```

The module program you write is a C++ program that links to the Linuxconf libraries. You need to set it up to inherit the class definitions from Linuxconf. To create the source for your own module, you define your own C++ class, which you derive from the Linuconf base class, LINUXCONF_MODULE. Throughout the program, you use Linuxconf-defined classes to create objects that you can use to interface with Linuxconf. For example, the CONFIG_FILE object is used to hold configuration file names and the SSTRING object is used to define string variables you want to use. Table 21-4 lists several of the major Linuxconf classes for which you can define objects. These classes include numerous functions listed in detail in the Linuxconf documentation.

Your module source file should begin with the following directives:

```
#pragma implementation
#include <stdio.h>
#include <translat.h>
#include "mymod.h"
#include "mymod.m"
```

You then add the following line to allow Linuxconf to check version compatibility:

```
MODULE_DEFINE_VERSION;
```

You can define your own constructor and destructor functions which are derived from the LINUXCONF_MODULE base class.

To insert a module in a Linuxconf menu, use the setmenu function. The domenu function then executes the module whenever it is selected. Both setmenu and domenu are member functions inherited from the Linuxconf base class. The menus that you can insert your module into are defined in the MENU_CONTEXT list in the dialog_def.h header file. The following list shows the currently allowed menus that you can insert your module into:

```
MENU_NETWORK_CLIENT,      // Client section of the network menu
MENU_NETWORK_SERVER,      // Server section of the network menu
MENU_NETWORK_MISC,        // Misc section of the network menu
MENU_MAIN_CONFIG,         // Config section of the main linuxconf menu
MENU_MAIN_CONTROL,        // Control section of the main linuxconf menu
MENU_CONTROL,             // Control panel
MENU_NETWORK_BOOT,        // Boot services section of the network menu
```

You need to redefine the setmenu function in your program to install the module into a specific menu. Linuxconf will automatically call each module and insert it into the menu that the setmenu function assigns it to. The following example shows a simple setmenu function that will insert mymod into the miscellaneous menu:

```
static const char *keymenu=NULL;

PUBLIC void mymod::setmenu ( DIALOG &dia, MENU_CONTEXT context)
{
if (context == MENU_NETWORK_MISC){
        keymenu = MSG_U(M_MYMOD,"My very own module (mymod)");
        dia.new_menuitem ("mymod","",keymenu);
        }
}
```

The following example will insert the module into the miscellaneous section:

```
Setmenu(MENU_NETWORK_MISC);
```

You then redefine the domenu function to call the function you will use when the menu entry is selected:

```
PUBLIC int mymod::domenu (
    MENU_CONTEXT context,
        const char *key)
      {
```

```
        if (context == MENU_NETWORK_SERVER){
            if (key == keymenu){
                mymodtask();
            }
        }
        return 0;
    }
```

Linuxconf executes a probe operation to check the current configuration of your system and determine if anything needs to be done to bring it up to date. You can define a probe function in your module that Linuxconf's probe operation will call. In your function, you can specify any particular tasks to be performed to update the configuration files your module is managing. net_prtlong will prompt the user if probe reports that there is any update to be performed.

A module will usually contain the following elements:

- A menu
- Configuration files definitions
- Help screens definitions
- User privilege definitions
- A user interface

To specify configuration files you use the CONFIG_FILE object. This object will also support system profiling operations. Help screens are defined with the HELP_FILE object. The PRIVELEGES object allows ordinary users the ability to manage certain configurations. Throughout the module code you may make use of several string handling objects such as SSTRING, which can hold varying size strings, and SSTRINGS to hold arrays of strings.

To set up a user interface in Linuxconf, you use the DIALOG object. The following example is derived from the Linuxconf technical documentation. It defines a DIALOG object and several new fields for name, phone, fax, and e-mail. The results are stored in the corresponding name, phone, fax, and e-mail strings.

```
void mymodtask()
    {
        DIALOG dia;
        SSTRING name,phone,fax,email;
        dia.newf_str ("Name Prompt",name);
        dia.newf_str ("Phone number",phone);
        dia.newf_str ("Fax number",fax);
        dia.newf_str ("email",email);
        int nof = 0;
```

```
while (1){
    MENU_STATUS code = dia.edit ("Mymod Title"
        ,"Description of mymod task\n"
         "which can use several lines"
        ,help_nil    // Help file objects
        ,nof);
    if (code == MENU_ESCAPE || code == MENU_CANCEL){
        break;
    }else{
        // Now validate the input
        // The SSTRING variables now contain the input
        if (all is fine){
            break;
        }
    }
}
```

Object	Description
LINUXCONF_MODULE	Module operations such as setmenu, domenu, and probe
ARRAY_OBJ	Holds the data managed by modules
ARRAY	An extensible table of ARRAY_OBJ pointers
CONFDB	Manages a configuration database. Designed to support the /etc/conf.linuxconf file.
CONFIG_FILE	Manages configuration files that are maintained or used by Linuxconf
HELP_FILE	Specifies and manages help files
SSTRING	A string of any size
VIEWITEMS	Used to parse a configuration file with comments and a continuation line
POPEN	Manages processes
DICTIONARY	An array where each entry is indexed by a name instead of a number, like an associative array

Table 21-4.   *Linuxconf Objects*

Object	Description
SSTREAM	Allows writing and reading to a stream
VIRTDB	Virtualizes access to different configuration files
PRIVILEGE	Allows user privileges
USER	Deals with user accounts, including virtual e-mail accounts
GROUP	Deals with groups
USERACCT_COMNG	Extends the user account dialog with added fields

Table 21-4.   *Linuxconf Objects* (continued)

Network Administration System

With its network administration system, you can use Linuxconf to administer Linux systems on remote machines. You first define an admin group that consists of the machines sharing configuration files. In effect, they are sharing subsystems, parts of the Linuxconf configuration. And, in effect, each machine has its own system profile version.

The configuration files and directories for a particular machine are placed in an administration tree. This is a subdirectory in the Linuxconf admtrees directory. These files and directories include copies of the machine's configuration files and directories, such as **/etc/passwd, /etc/hosts**, and **/etc/ppp**. Linuxconf works entirely within this admtree, as these files are the same as those on the machine.

To manage a remote machine, you use the netadm module. Currently, this connects to the remote host with a GUI front end. The command line version of netadm has several options you can use. The –import option installs configuration files received for an administration host. The –remadm option enables remote administration. A GUI front end starts up and connects to Linuxconf on a remote host. If you do not specify a host on the command line, then a menu is displayed of the different hosts you can access.

The Complete Reference

Linux

Chapter 22

Control Panel and Setup Administration Tools

ed Hat has traditionally provided several easy-to-use configuration interfaces for most system administration tasks. Most of these task have been superceded by Linuxconf, which is now the official Red Hat administration tool. The older Red Hat tools described in this chapter, however, are still included with Red Hat distributions and many user prefer them. Some provide an easy way to perform simple tasks, such as selecting a new keyboard and changing the time zone.

Two sets of administration tools exist, classified by the type of interface: X Window System–based configuration tools and cursor-based command-line tools. Each set is commonly identified by the utility through which it is ordinarily accessed. The X Window System–based configuration tools are normally accessed through the Control Panel utility, which displays a button for each tool (see Table 22-1). The cursor-based command line tools are normally accessed through the Setup utility, which displays a menu listing for each tool (see Table 22-2). Each tool can also be accessed using its command name. For Control Panel tools, you can enter their command in a terminal window. You can run the cursor-based interface from the command line using arrow keys, the SPACEBAR, and the ENTER key to make choices. The tools are simple front ends for making entries in Linux configuration files. You can edit these files and make entries directly if you want. The underlying administration tasks are the same.

These tools are only available to the root user. You first must log in as the root user and provide the password. You can run most of these tools either from the desktop or from a shell command line. On the shell command line, a screen-based interface is used from which you can select entries using the arrow keys and the TAB key. From a

Configuration Tool	Command	Description
Linuxconf	`linuxconf`	The Linuxconf configuration tool providing comprehensive configuration for users, networks, file systems, servers, and LILO. The official Red Hat administration tool.
Control Panel	`control-panel`	Red Hat collection of X configuration tools for networking, modules, printers, time settings, and so forth
Setup	`setup`	Collection of Red Hat setup utilities for specifying device types, time zone, and X Window configuration (screen-based only)

Table 22-1.   *Red Hat Linux Configuration Tools*

Tools	Description
tksysv	Starts and stops servers and daemons
timetool	Sets the system date and time
printtool	Configures a printer, creating a printer device and printcap entry for the printer
netcfg	Configures your network interfaces (see Chapter 21)
kernelcfg	Kernel Configurator: loads and configures kernel modules
modemtool	Selects your modem's device name (sets the /etc/modem link to the modem's port)
helptool	Searches for documentation, man pages, and info pages
Linuxconf	Linuxconf configuration tool for user, networking, LILO, servers, file systems, and so forth

Table 22-2.   *Red Hat Control Panel*

window manager or desktop, most tools provide an X Window interface with menus, icons, and buttons.

Red Hat Control Panel

You can access the X Window–based configuration tools using the Control Panel window on your root user desktop. An entry for the Control Panel is in a window manager or the desktop's main menu under System or Administration. As shown next, the Control Panel provides icons for accessing a variety of configuration tools.

Currently, tools exist for such tasks as setting the time and date, network administration, and kernel module management. Many of these tools have their own entries in the System or Administration menus. You can also invoke them from a terminal window using their command names. The netcfg utility enables you to configure your network interfaces (discussed in detail in Chapter 25). With timetool, you can set the system time and date (see Chapter 20). Using printtool, you can configure new printers, interfacing them with your system (see Chapter 26). The helptool enables you to search for documentation on your system using a keyword search (see this chapter). The helptool displays man, HOW-TO, and info documentation. The Sys V Init Editor enables you to start and stop servers and daemons (see Chapter 15). With the Kernel Configurator you can manually add and remove modules. Many system tasks, including user, server, and file system management, are provided by the Linuxconf, which is accessible by clicking the icon labeled System, which shows a picture of a music conductor waving a baton. Table 22-2 lists these tools.

tksysv

The tksysv tool is used to configure the System V daemon configuration, enabling you to determine what daemons to start up at boot time. It also enables you to start or stop daemons manually. Daemons include your Internet daemons, such as the FTP or Web servers, as well as services, such as your printer daemon. See Chapter 15 for a more detailed discussion and figure.

timetool

With timetool, you can configure all aspects of the system date and time (see Chapter 20 for a figure). For example, select the hour entry to change the hour. You use the two triangles below the time and date display to increase or decrease the time or date entry. If you select the hour, clicking the upper triangle sets the time forward to the next hour. The bottom inverted triangle moves the hour backward. The same is true for the date. Once you set the new time and date, click the Set System Clock button at the bottom of the window. Then click the Exit Time Machine button to exit the Time Configuration window.

printtool

printtool is an easy interface for setting up and managing your printers (see Chapter 26 for more details and a figure). Using only printtool, you can easily install a printer on your Linux system. You can start printtool either by selecting its entry in the System menu or clicking its icon in the Red Hat Control Panel. In the printtool window, select the Add button. This opens an Edit window that displays several fields in which you enter printer configuration information. In the Names field, you enter the names you want to use for the printer. Each name is separated by a |. A default name for your first printer is lp. In the Spool directory fields, the default spool directory is already entered for you. You can change this to another directory if you want. For the Device field, enter the name of the device your printer uses. Four devices have already been set up for parallel printers: **/dev/lp0**, **/dev/lp1**, **/dev/lp2**, and **/dev/lp4**. These correspond to first, second, third, and fourth parallel ports. If you have a serial device, you must use a serial device name, such as /dev/ttyS1, for the second serial port.

For the Input Filter, you can click Select to display a window with three fields. Each field has a Select button by it that displays a set of currently available options. The Select button for the PrinterType field opens a menu of printers from which you can choose. The Select button for the Resolution field lists several possible resolutions. The Select button for the PaperSize field lists paper sizes, such as letter and legal. When you finish, click OK to close the window and do the same for the Edit window. You then see your printer listed in the PrintTool window. Choose the Quit item from the PrintTool menu to quit PrintTool. You are now ready to print. For a detailed explanation of printer installation, see the **Printing-HOWTO** file in **/usr/doc/HOWTO**.

netcfg

Red Hat provides an easy-to-use network configuration tool called netcfg (see Chapter 25 for more details and a figure). On the Red Hat control panel, an icon is labeled Network Configuration. You can also start it from the desktop or window manager's program menus, usually with the entry Network Configuration. The netcfg window consists of four panels and a button bar at the top for each one: Name, Hosts, Interfaces, and Routing. Clicking a button displays its panel. Basic configuration of your network requires you to specify the hostname and IP address of your own system, the IP addresses of your network's name servers and gateway, the network netmask, and your network interfaces. Using the netcfg tool, you can enter all this information easily. The Name panel is where you enter your own system's hostname and your network's name server addresses. The Hosts panel lists host IP addresses and their domain names, including those for your own system. On the Interfaces panel, you add and configure your network interfaces, such as an Ethernet or PPP interface. The Routing panel is where you specify special routing hosts, including your gateway system. If you already configured your network during installation, entries are now in these panels.

kernelcfg

The kernelcfg utility provides an interface for **kerneld** or **kmod** daemons with which you can load and unload kernel modules. You use kernel modules to add different capabilities to your system, particularly support for hardware devices (see Chapter 26 for a figure of kernelcfg). The modules your system needs are usually determined during installation, based on the kind of configuration information you provided. For example, if your system uses an Ethernet card whose type you specified during installation, then the system loads the module for that card. You can, however, manually control what modules are to be loaded for your system. This, in effect, enables you to customize your kernel any way you want. Be careful not to remove any necessary modules. *Modules* are essentially extensions of the kernel and they are often critical for providing the needed support for your system.

ADMINISTRATION

modemtool

For a modem, you should make sure there is a link by the name of **/dev/modem** to your modem device, which is usually one of the **/dev/ttyS**num devices, where num is in the range of 0–3. For example, a modem on the second serial port would have a device name of **/dev/ttyS1**, and **/dev/modem** would be a link to the **/dev/ttyS1** device file. This is usually done for you during installation. You can use the modem configuration tool modemtool to create this link. Many modem programs and PPP configuration programs look for the **/dev/modem** file by default. modemtool provides a simple way to create this link. It displays four entries, one for each serial port. Click the one that applies to your system (see Chapter 22), as shown here:

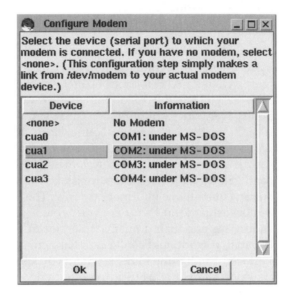

helptool

The helptool, shown next, enables you to search for documentation on your system using a keyword search. It displays man, HOW-TO, and info documentation. Any user can use helptool. It is not limited to system administration.

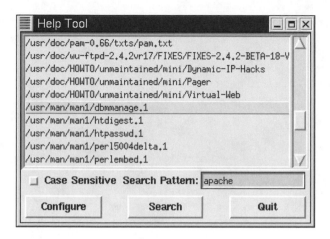

linuxconf

Many system tasks, including user, server, and file system management, are provided by the Linuxconf, which is accessible by clicking the icon labeled System (see Chapter 21). The icon shows a picture of a music conductor waving a baton.

Setup Configuration Tools

Red Hat also provides a Setup utility with which you can configure different devices and system settings, such as your keyboard, mouse, and time zone. Setup is useful if you have changed any of your devices—say, installed a new mouse, keyboard, or sound card. Start the Setup utility with the command **setup**, which you enter at a shell command line. On the desktop, you can open a terminal window and enter the command. A menu of configuration choices is displayed. Use the arrow keys to select one, and then press the TAB key to move to the Run Tool and Quit buttons. Figure 22-1 Shows the initial Setup menu.

Setup is actually an interface for running several configuration tools (see Table 22-3). You can call any of these tools separately using their commands. For example, the **kbdconfig** command starts the keyboard configuration utility that enables you to select the type of keyboard, while the **mouseconfig** command enables you to select type of mouse. Table 22-3 lists the different Setup configuration tools.

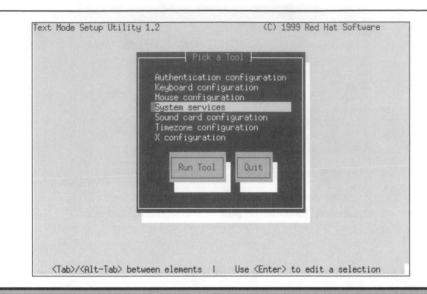

Figure 22-1. *Red Hat Setup*

Tools	Description
setup	Red Hat Setup interface listing configuration tools for system and device setting
authconfig	Authentication options, such as enabling NIS, shadow passwords, and MD5 passwords
kbdconfig	Selects the keyboard type
mouseconfig	Selects the mouse type
ntsysv	Selects servers and daemons to start up at boot time
sndconfig	Detects and configures your sound card
timeconfig	Selects the time zone
Xconfigurator	Configures your X Window System for your video card and monitor

Table 22-3. *Setup Tools*

authconfig

Authentication configuration displays a simple dialog box, shown next, for enabling the *Network Information Service* (*NIS*) and Password encryption. You find an entry for NIS, and entries for the shadow and MD5 password security methods.

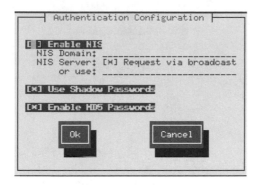

kbdconfig

With kbdconfig, you can select the type of keyboard you are using. A cursor-based dialog box appears with a list of different keyboard types:

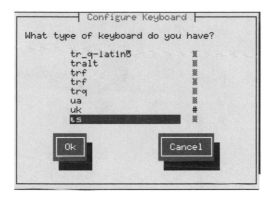

mouseconfig

With mouseconfig you can select the type of mouse you are using. A cursor-based dialog box, shown next, appears with a list of different mouse device types. Your system is automatically probed for the type of mouse connected to your system and the cursor is positioned at that entry. If you have a two button mouse, you can select the three-button emulation option to let a simultaneous click on both the left and the right mouse buttons emulate a third mouse button. Changes are made to the X Window system configuration file, **/etc/x11/xF86 config** (see Chapter 27).

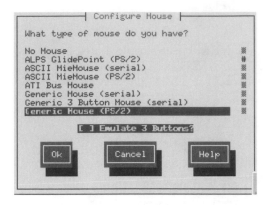

ntsysv

ntsysv is a simple utility for specifying which servers and services should be automatically started at boot time (see Chapter 15). The dialog box, shown next, lists the possible servers and services to choose from. Move to the entry you want and use the spacebar to toggle it on or off. An entry with an asterisk next to it is selected and is started automatically the next time you boot your system.

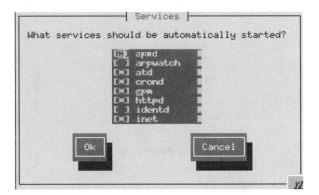

sndconfig

The sndconfig utility enables you to select and configure your sound card. It initially tries to detect your sound card automatically. If the automatic detection fails, a dialog box appears with a listing of different sound cards. Select the one on your system. Another dialog box appears where you need to enter the setting for your sound card. sndconfig then tries to play sample sound and MIDI files to test the card. As an alternative to sndconfig, you can obtain, load, and configure sound drivers yourself (see Chapter 25).

timeconfig

timeconfig is a simple time zone utility you can use to specify your system's time zone. The following dialog box lists different time zones from which you can select one. This is useful if your system moved to a different time zone.

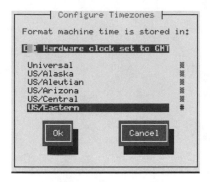

Xconfigurator

One important utility is the X Window System setup provided by Xconfigurator. If you have trouble with your X Window System configuration, you can use the Xconfigurator command to configure it again. Xconfigurator is also helpful for updating X Windows if you change your video card. Run Xconfigurator again and select the card. When you download a new version of XFree86, the packages includes a compatible version of Xconfigurator. See Chapter 3 for more details and figures.

The Complete Reference

Chapter 23

Managing Users

L inux is designed to serve many users at the same time, as well as provide an interface between the users and the computer with its storage media, such as hard disks and tapes. Users have their own shells through which they interact with the operating system. As a system administrator, you can manage user logins on your system. You can add or remove users, as well as add and remove groups. You also have access to system initialization files you can use to configure all user shells. And you have control over the default initialization files copied into an account when it is first created. With them, you can decide how accounts should initially be configured.

You can find out which users are currently logged in with the **who** command. Add the **-u** option to display information about each connected user, such as from where they have logged in and how long they have been inactive. The command displays the login name, the login port, the date and time of login, the length of inactivity (if still active), and the process ID for the login shell. For example:

```
# who -u
root         console        Oct 12 10:34        .        1219
valerie      tty1           Oct 12 22:18       10        1492
```

Any utility to add a user, such as Linuxconf, makes use of certain default files, configuration files, and directories to set up the new account. A set of path names is used to locate these default files or to know where to create certain user directories. For example, **/etc/skel** holds initialization files for a new user. A new user's home directory is placed in the **/home** directory. A list of the path names is shown in this table:

/home	Location of the user's own home directory
/etc/skel	Holds the default initialization files for the login shell, such as **.bash_profile** and **.cshrc**
/etc/shells	Holds the login shells, such as BASH or TCSH
/etc/passwd	Holds the password for a user
/etc/group	Holds the group to which the user belongs

The /etc/passwd File

When you add a user, an entry for that user is made in the **/etc/passwd** file, commonly known as the *password file*. Each entry takes up one line that has several fields separated by colons. The fields are shown here:

Username	Login name of the user
Password	Encrypted password for the user's account

user ID	Unique number assigned by the system
group ID	Number used to identify the group to which the user belongs
Comment	Any user information, such as the user's full name
home directory	The user's home directory
login shell	Shell to run when the user logs in; this is the default shell, usually **/bin/bash**

The following is an example of a **/etc/passwd** entry. The entry for **chris** has a * in its password field, indicating a password has not yet been created for this user. For such entries, you must use **passwd** to create a password. Notice also, user IDs, in this particular system, start at 500 and increment by one.

```
dylan:YOTPd3Pyy9hAc:500:500:User:/home/dylan:/bin/bash
chris:*:501:501:User:/home/chris:/bin/bash
```

The **/etc/passwd** file is a text file you can edit using a text editor. You can change fields in entries and even add new entries. The only field you cannot effectively change is the password, which must be encrypted. To change the password field, you should always use the **passwd** command.

Although you can make entries directly to the **/etc/passwd** file, an easier and safer way is to use the **userconf**, **adduser**, and **useradd** utilities. These programs not only make entries in the **/etc/passwd** file, but they also create the home directory for the user and install initialization files in the user's home directory.

The **/etc/passwd** file is a simple text file and is vulnerable to security breaches. If anyone gains access to the **/etc/password** file, they might be able to decipher the passwords. On current Linux systems, the shadow suite of applications implements a greater level of security. These include versions of **useradd, groupadd,** and their corresponding update and delete programs. Most other user configuration tools support shadow security measures. With shadow security, passwords are no longer kept in the **/etc/password** file. Instead, passwords are kept in a separate file called **/etc/shadow** and are heavily encrypted. Access is restricted to the root user. A corresponding password file, called **/etc/gshadow,** is also maintained for groups that require passwords.

Managing User Environments: /etc/skel

Each time a user logs in, two profile scripts are executed. A system profile script is the same for every user and each user has the **.bash_profile** script in his home directory. The system profile script is located in the **/etc** directory and named **profile** with no preceding period. As superuser, you can edit the profile script and put in any commands you want executed for each user when she logs in. For example, you may want to define a default path for commands, in case the user has not done so. Or, you may want to notify the user of recent system news or account changes.

When you first add a user to the system, you must provide the user with a skeleton **.bash_profile** file. The **useradd** command does this automatically by searching for a **.bash_profile** file in the directory **/etc/skel** and copying it to the user's new home directory. The **/etc/skel** directory contains a skeleton initialization file for **.bash_profile** files or, if you are using the C-shell as your login shell, **.login** and **.logout** files. It also provides initialization files for BASH and C-shell: **.bashrc** and **.cshrc**. The **/etc/skel** directory also contains default files and directories for your desktops. These include an **.Xdefaults** file for the X Window system, a **.kderc** file for the KDE desktop, and a Gnome Desktop directory that contains default configuration files for the Gnome desktop.

As superuser, you can configure the **.bash_profile** file in the **/etc/skel** any way you want. Usually, basic system variable assignments are included that define path names for commands, system prompts, mail path names, and terminal default definitions. In short, the **PATH**, **TERM**, **MAIL**, and **PS1** variables are defined. Once users have their own **.bash_profile** files, they can redefine variables or add new commands as they choose.

Login Access

You can control user login access to your system with the **/etc/login.access** file. The file consists of entries listing users, whether they are allowed access, and from where they can access the system. A record in this file consists of three colon-delimited fields: a plus (+) or minus (–) sign indicating whether users are allowed access, user login names allowed access, and the remote system (host) or terminal (tty device) from which they are trying to log in. The following enables the user dylan to access the system from the **rabbit.mytrek.com** remote system.

```
+:chris:rabbit.mytrek.com
```

You can list more than one user or location. You can also use the ALL option in place of either users or locations to allow access by all users and locations. The ALL option can be qualified with the EXCEPT option to allow access by all users except certain specified ones. The following entry allows any user to log in to the system using the console, except for the users larisa and aleina.

```
+:ALL EXCEPT larisa aleina:console
```

Other access control files are used to control access for specific services such as the **hosts.deny** and **hosts.allows** files used with tcpd daemon for inetd-supported servers.

Managing Users with Linuxconf

You can easily add, remove, or change users with Linuxconf. Currently, for Red Hat distributions, it is recommended you use Linuxconf to manage user accounts. You can access Linuxconf user configuration panels either through the main Linuxconf interface or through a special user-configuration interface invoked with the **usexconf** command. With the main Linuxconf interface, select the User Accounts entry in the Normal list under the User Accounts heading under Config. This displays a panel listing all your user accounts, including those used for special system purposes, such as FTP and news (see Figure 23-1). Each entry has four fields: the account name, the login name, the account ID, and the group to which it belongs. With the **usexconf** command, you are first presented with a window showing icons for user, group, and password configuration. Click the User icon to display a window with several tabbed panels, the first being a list of all users on the system.

To add a new user, click Add on this panel. This displays a User Information panel with tabbed Base Info and Privileges panels. In the Base Info panel, you can enter the login name, the group the user will belong to, the user's home directory, and the login shell (command interpreter). The home directory has the default consisting of **/home** and the user's login name, as in **/home/aliena**. Both the group and the shell have drop-down menus listing available groups and shells from which to choose. To give the user an initial password, click Passwd. A Changing Password panel is displayed

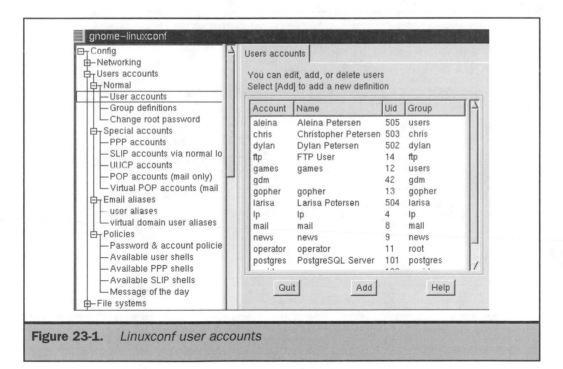

Figure 23-1. *Linuxconf user accounts*

where you can enter the new password. On the Privileges panel, you can set certain user privileges, including giving the user superuser access, or permission to use Linuxconf or to shut down the system.

When you finish, click Accept. You now see the new user displayed in the User accounts panel. If you need to change or delete a user, double-click its entry in this panel to display its User Information panel. To remove the user, click Del. If you want to make some changes, such as adding the user to a different group or giving the user a different home directory, edit the appropriate entries and click Accept. The user information is then updated.

From the User Information panel, shown in Figure 23-2, you can also schedule certain tasks you want performed for this user at specific times, such as backup or printing operations. Click Tasks to display the Schedule Jobs panel. You can then create job definitions. In the Schedule Job Definitions panel, you can enter the command, along with the time and date for the command to be executed. Boxes are there for the month, day, hour, and minute. The scheduling operation works much like the UNIX at command.

You can also deactivate an account, denying all access to it and its files. The files for this account remain intact, and when you decide to reactivate the account, the files can then be accessed. The check box labeled The account in the user's User Information panel is a toggle that activates and deactivates the user account. When recessed and dark, the user account is activated.

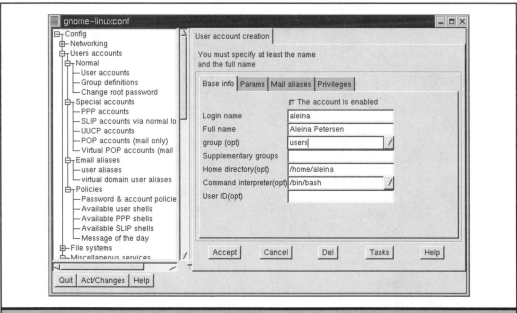

Figure 23-2. *Linuxconf user information*

The K Desktop also provides a simple user management utility called kuser that works much like Linuxconf (see Figure 23-3). You can use it to manage both users and groups. The window is divided into two panes: one for users and the other for groups. Add, Edit, and Delete icons easily enable you to add new users, change their configuration, or remove them. When you add a new user, a new window opens with entries such as the shell and home directory. To add the password, click Password and enter the password in the window displayed.

Adding Users with adduser

You can also add a new user to the system with the **adduser** command. This command is entered on your command line and is easy-to-use. Different versions of **adduser** exist. The one on Red Hat Linux comes from the Debian Linux distribution and operates somewhat differently from other distributions, such as Slackware. This version of **adduser** takes as its argument the user name for the account you are creating. When you press ENTER, it then creates the new account using default values. You can use **passwd** to create a password for the new account. This **adduser** program is a shell script located in the **/usr/sbin** directory. If you are familiar with shell programming, you can edit this script to change its default values.

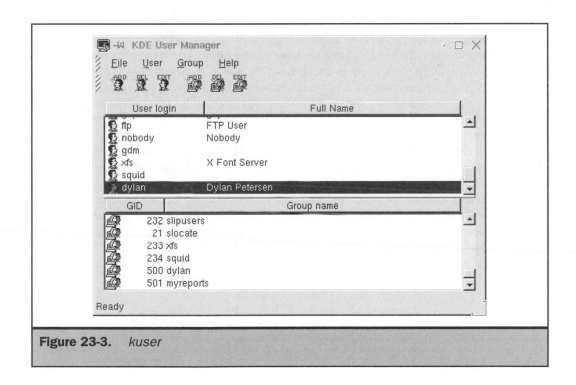

Figure 23-3.   *kuser*

With different versions of **adduser** found on other Linux distributions, it is best to enter the **adduser** command without any arguments. You are then prompted for each piece of information needed to set up a new user. At the end of each prompt, within brackets, **adduser** displays a default value. To accept this default value as your entry, press ENTER. After you type all your entries, **adduser** creates the new account. Once you add a new user login, you need to give the new login a password. The login is inaccessible until you do.

Adding and Removing Users with useradd, usermod, and userdel

Most distributions of Linux also provide the **useradd**, **usermod**, and **userdel** commands to manage user accounts. All these commands take in all their information as options on the command line. If an option is not specified, they use predetermined default values. With the **useradd** command, you enter values as options on the command line, such as the name of a user to create a user account. It then creates a new login and directory of that name using all the default features for a new account.

```
# useradd chris
```

The **useradd** utility has a set of predefined default values for creating a new account. The default values are the group name, the user ID, the home directory, the **skel** directory, and the login shell. The *group name* is the name of the group in which the new account is placed. By default, this is *other*, which means the new account belongs to no group. The user ID is a number identifying the user account. This starts at 1 with the first account and increments automatically for each new account. The **skel** directory is the system directory that holds copies of initialization files. These initialization files are copied into the user's new home directory when it is created. The login shell is the path name for the particular shell the user plans to use. You can display these defaults using the **useradd** command with the -D option. The **useradd** command has options that correspond to each default value. Table 23-1 holds a list of all the options you can use with the **useradd** command. You can use specific values in place of any of these defaults when creating a particular account. Once you add a new user login, you need to give the new login a password. The login is inaccessible until you do. In the next example, the group name for the chris account is set to intro1 and the user ID is set to 578.

```
# useradd chris -g intro1 -u 578
```

The **usermod** command enables you to change the values for any of these features. You can change the home directory or the user ID. You can even change the username for the account.

When you want to remove a user from the system, you can use the **userdel** command to delete the user's login. In the next example, the user chris is removed from the system.

```
# userdel -r chris
```

Command	Description
adduser *username*	Adds a new user, creating a password file entry and home directory with initialization files; uses **passwd** command to create a password for the user
useradd *username options*	Adds new users to the system
usermod *username options*	Modifies a user's features
userdel -r *username*	Removes a user from the system
useradd, usermod Options	
-u *userid*	Sets the user ID of the new user; the default is the increment of the highest number used so far
-g *group*	Sets a group or name
-d *dir*	Sets the home directory of the new user
-s *shell*	Sets the login shell directory of the new user
-c *str*	Adds a comment to the user's entry in the system password file: **/etc/passwd**
-k *skl-dir*	Sets the skeleton directory that holds skeleton files, such as **.profile** files, which are copied to the user's home directory automatically when it is created; the default is **/etc/skel**
-D	Displays defaults for all settings
Group Management Commands	
groupadd	Creates a new group
groupdel	Removes a group
groupmod *option*	Modifies a group **-g** Changes a group ID **-n** Changes a group name

Table 23-1.   *User and Group Management Commands*

Managing Groups

You can manage groups using either shell commands or window utilities like Linuxconf. The system file that holds group entries is called **/etc/group**. The file consists of group records, with one record per line and its fields separated by colons. A group record has four fields: a group name, a password, its ID, and the users who are part of this group. The password field can be left blank. The fields for a group record are shown here:

group name	Name of the group; must be unique
password	Usually an asterisk to allow anyone to join the group; a password can be added to control access
group ID	Number assigned by the system to identify this group
users	List of users that belong to the group

Here is an example of an entry in an **/etc/group** file. The group is called engines, there is no password, the group ID is 100, and the users who are part of this group are chris, robert, valerie, and aleina.

```
engines::100:chris,robert,valerie,aleina
```

As in the case of the **/etc/passwd** file, you can edit the **/etc/group** file directly using a text editor. Instead of using either Linuxconf or groupdel, you could simply delete the entry for that group in the **/etc/group** file. This can be risky, however, if you make accidental changes.

Managing Groups Using Linuxconf

You can add, remove, and modify any groups easily with the Linuxconf utility on your root user desktop. To manage groups using Linuxconf, select the Group Definitions entry in the Normal list under User Accounts in Config. This displays a User Groups panel that lists all the groups currently on your system (see Figure 23-4). Each entry has three fields: the group name, the group ID, and the list of users who are part of this group. To add a new group, click Add. This displays a Group Specification panel where you can enter the name for the new group and the group ID. A default group ID is already listed.

You can edit or delete any group by first double-clicking its entry in the User Groups panel to display its Group Specification panel. To remove the group, click Del. For changes, edit any of the entries and click Accept. For example, to add certain users to a group, bring up the group's Group Specification panel and enter the users you want to add.

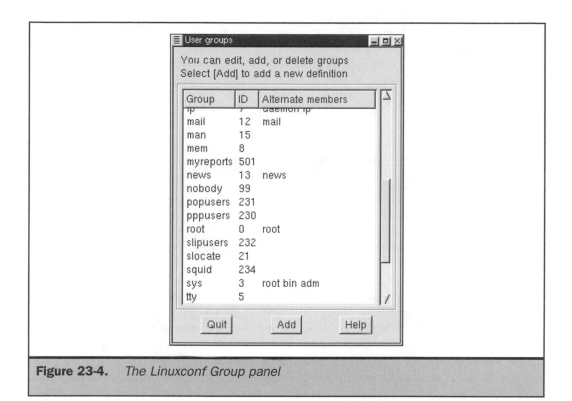

Figure 23-4. *The Linuxconf Group panel*

Managing Groups Using groupadd, groupmod, and groupdel

On many Linux distributions you can manage groups with the **groupadd**, **groupmod**, and **groupdel** commands. With the **groupadd** command you can create new groups. When you add a group to the system, the system places the group's name in the **/etc/group** file and gives it a group ID number. The **groupadd** command only creates the group category. Users are individually added to the group. In the next example, the **groupadd** command creates the engines group.

```
# groupadd engines
```

You can delete a group with the **groupdel** command. In the next example, the engines group is deleted.

```
# groupdel engines
```

You can change the name of a group or its ID using the **groupmod** command. Enter **groupmod -g** with the new ID number and the group name. To change the name of a group, you use the **-n** option. Enter **groupmod -n** with the new name of the group, followed by the current name. In the next example, the engines group has its name changed to trains.

```
# groupmod -n trains engines
```

Disk Quotas

With disk quotas you can control how much disk space a particular user makes use of on your system. On your Linux system, unused disk space is held as a common resource that each user can access as needed. As users create more files, they take the space they need from the pool of available disk space. In this sense, all the users are sharing this one resource of unused disk space. However, if one user were to use up all the remaining disk space, then none of the other users would be able to create files or even run programs. To counter this problem, you can create disk quotas on particular users, limiting the amount of available disk space they can use.

Quotas are enabled using the **quotacheck** and **quotaon** programs. In Red Hat, they are executed in the **/etc/rc.d/rc.sysinit** script, which is run whenever you start up your system. Each partition then needs to be mounted with the quota options, **usrquota** or **grpquota**. **usrquota** enables quota controls and users, and **grpquota** works for groups. These options are usually placed in the mount entry in the **/etc/fstab** file for a particular partition. For example, to mount the **/dev/hda6** hard disk partition to the **/home** directory with support for user and group quotas, you would require a entry like the following:

```
/dev/hda6    /home    ext2    defaults,usrquota,grpquota    1    1
```

You also need to create **quota.user** and **quota.group** files for each partition for which you enable quotas. These are the quota databases used to hold the quota information for each user and group. You can create these files by running the **quotacheck** command with the **-a** option or the device name of the file system where you want to enable quotas.

The limit you set for a quota can be hard or soft. A hard limit will deny a user the ability to exceed his or her quota, whereas a soft limit will just issue a warning. For the soft limit you can designate a grace period during which time the user has the chance to reduce his or her disk space below the limit. If the disk space still exceeds the limit after the grace period expires, then the user can be denied access to his or her account.

You can set disk quotas using the **edquota** command or the user account panels in Linuxconf. In Linuxconf, select a user from the User accounts listing, and then select that user's Disk quota panel. Here you can enter the hard and soft limits along with the grace period. You can also select a default for these limits. The default is set using the Set quota defaults panel in the File system menu. There are entries for both group and user soft and hard defaults. Linuxconf will allow you to place limits on both the disk size and the number of files.

The **edquota** command is run from the command line. With it you can access the quota record for a particular user and group, which is maintained in the disk quota database. You can also set default quotas that will be applied to any user or group on the file system for which quotas have not been set. **edquota** will open the record in your default editor and you can use your editor to make any changes. To open the record for a particular user, use the **-u** option and the user name as an argument for **edquota** (see Table 23-2). The following example opens the disk quota record for the user **larisa**.

```
edquota -u larisa
```

The quota record begins with the hard disk device name and the blocks of memory and inodes in use. The limits segments have parameters for soft and hard limits. If these entries are 0, then there are no limits in place. You can set both hard and soft limits, using the hard limit as a firm restriction. Blocks in Linux are currently about 1,000 bytes. The inodes are used by files to hold information about the memory blocks making up a file. To set the time limit for a soft limit, you use the **edquota** command with the **-t** option. The following example displays the quota record for **larisa**.

```
Quotas for user larisa:
/dev/hda3: blocks in use: 9000, limits (soft = 40000, hard = 60000)
           inodes in use: 321, limits (soft = 0, hard = 0)
```

These records are maintained in the quota database for that partition. Each partition that has quotas enabled will have its own quota database. You can check the validity of your quota database with the **quotacheck** command. You can turn quotas on and off using the **quotaon** and **quotaoff** commands, respectively. When you start up your system, **quotacheck** is run to check the quota databases, and then **quotaon** is run to turn on quotas.

As the system administrator, you can use the **repquota** command to generate a summary of memory usage, checking to see what users are approaching or exceeding quota limits. Individual users can use the **quota** command to check their memory use and how much disk space they have left in their quota (see Table 23-2).

Command	Description
edquota	
-u	Edits the userquota. This is the default.
-g	Edits the groupquota
-p	Duplicates the quotas of the prototypical user specified for each user specified. This is the normal mechanism used to initialize quotas for groups of users.
-t	Edits the soft time limits for each file system
quota	
-g	Prints group quotas for the group of which the user is a member
-u	Prints the user's quota
-v	Displays quotas on filesystems where no storage is allocated
-q	Prints information on filesystems where usage is over quota

Table 23-2.   *edquota* and *quota* Commands and Options

Chapter 24

File System
Administration

Files reside on physical devices such as hard drives, CD-ROMs, or floppy disks. The files on each device are organized into a file system. To access files on a device, you attach its file system to a specified directory. This is called *mounting* the file system. For example, to access files on a floppy disk, you first mount its file system to a particular directory. This chapter discusses how you can access CD-ROMs, floppy disks, and hard disk partitions. You can even access an MS-DOS hard drive partition or floppy disk, as well as file systems on a remote server (see Chapter 25). Archives are used to back up files or to combine them into a package, which can then be transferred as one file over the Internet or posted on an FTP site for easy downloading. The standard archive utility used on Linux and UNIX systems is **tar**, for which several GUI front ends exist. You have several compression programs to choose from, including GNU zip (gzip), Zip, bzip, and compress.

Local File Systems

Your Linux system is capable of handling any number of storage devices that may be connected to it. You can configure your system to access multiple hard drives, partitions on a hard drive, CD-ROM disks, floppy disks, and even tapes. You can elect to attach these storage components manually or to have them automatically mount when you boot. For example, the main partition holding your Linux system programs is automatically attached whenever you boot, whereas a floppy disk must be manually attached when you put one in your floppy drive. You can configure this access to different storage devices either by manually editing configuration files, such as **/etc/fstab**, or by using a file system configuration tool such as the Linuxconf's **fsconf**. Currently, Red Hat uses Linuxconf to configure the file system.

File Systems

Although all the files in your Linux system are connected into one overall directory tree, the files themselves reside on storage devices such as hard drives or CD-ROMs. The Linux files on a particular storage device are organized into what is referred to as a *file system*. Your Linux directory tree may encompass several file systems, each on different storage devices. On a hard drive with several partitions, you would have a file system for each partition. The files themselves are organized into one seamless tree of directories, beginning from the root directory. Although the root may be located in a file system on a hard drive partition, a pathname leads directly to files located on the file system for your CD-ROM.

The files in a file system remain separate from your directory tree until you specifically connect them to it. A file system has its files organized into its own directory tree. You can think of this as a *subtree* that must be attached to the main directory tree. For example, a floppy disk with Linux files has its own tree of directories. You need to attach this subtree to the main tree on your hard drive partition. Until they are attached, you cannot access the files on your floppy disk.

Attaching a file system on a storage device to your main directory tree is called *mounting the device.* The mount operation attaches the directory tree on the storage device to a directory you specify. You can then change to that directory and access those files. The directory in the file structure to which the new file system is attached is referred to as the *mountpoint.* For example, to access files on a CD-ROM, first you have to mount the CD-ROM.

Currently, Linux systems have several ways to mount a file system. You can use Linuxconf to select and mount a file system easily. If you are using either Gnome or the K Desktop, you can use special desktop icons to mount a file system. From a shell command line, you can use the **mount** command. Mounting file systems can only be done as the root user. This is a system administration task and cannot be performed by a regular user. To mount a file system, be sure to login as the root user (or use the **su** operation). As the root user, you can, however, make a particular device like a CD-ROM user mountable. In this way, any user could put in a CD-ROM and mount it. You could do the same for a floppy drive.

For a file system to be accessible, it must be mounted. Even the file system on your hard disk partition must be mounted with a **mount** command. When you install your Linux system and create the Linux partition on your hard drive, however, your system is automatically configured to mount your main file system whenever it starts. Floppy disks and CD-ROMs must be explicitly mounted. Remember, when you mount a CD-ROM or floppy disk, you cannot then simply remove it to put in another one. You first have to unmount it. In fact, the CD-ROM drive remains locked until you unmount it. Once you unmount a CD-ROM, you can then take it out and put in another one, which you then must mount before you can access it. When changing several CD-ROMs or floppy disks, you are continually mounting and unmounting them.

The file systems on each storage device are formatted to take up a specified amount of space. For example, you may have formatted your hard drive partition to take up 300MB. Files installed or created on that file system take up part of the space, while the remainder is available for new files and directories. To find out how much space you have free on a file system, you can use the **df** command or, on Gnome, you can use Gnome disk free. *Gnome disk free* displays a list of meters showing how much space is used on each partition and how much space you have left.

The **df** command lists all your file systems by their device names, how much memory they take up, and the percentage of the memory used, as well as where they are mounted. The **df** command is also a safe way to obtain a listing of all your partitions, instead of using **fdisk**. **df** only shows mounted partitions, however, whereas **fdisk** shows all partitions.

```
$ df
Filesystem      1024-blocks  Used  Available Capacity Mounted on
/dev/hda3          297635   169499   112764     60%    /
/dev/hda1          205380   182320    23060     89%    /mnt/dos
/dev/hdc           637986   637986        0    100%    /mnt/cdrom
```

You can also use **df** to tell you to what file system a given directory belongs. Enter **df** with the directory name or **df .** for the current directory.

```
$ df .
Filesystem      1024-blocks  Used Available Capacity Mounted on
/dev/hda3          297635   169499    112764     60%    /
```

To make sure nothing is wrong with a given file system, you can use the **fsck** command to check it. Enter **fsck** and the device name that references the file system. Table 24-1 lists the **fsck** options. The following example checks the disk in the floppy drive and the primary hard drive:

```
# fsck   /dev/fd0
# fsck   /dev/hda1
```

Device Files: /dev

To mount a file system, you have to specify its device name. The interfaces to devices that may be attached to your system are provided by special files known as *ad device* files. The names of these device files are the device names. Device files are located in the **/dev** directories and usually have abbreviated names ending with the number of device. For example, **fd0** may reference the first floppy drive attached to your system. On Linux

Options	Description
file-system	Specifies the file system to be checked. Use file system's device name, such as **/dev/hda3**
-A	Checks all file systems listed in **/etc/fstab** file
-V	Verbose mode. List actions that **fsck** takes
-t *file-system-type*	Specifies the type of file system to be checked
-a	Automatically repairs any problems
-l	Lists the names of all files in the file system
-r	Asks for confirmation before repairing file system
-s	Lists superblock before checking file system

Table 24-1.   *The* fsck *Options for Checking and Repairing File Systems*

systems operating on PCs, the hard disk partitions have a prefix of **hd,** followed by an alphabetic character that labels the hard drive, and then a number for the partition. For example, **hda2** references the second partition on the first hard drive. In most cases, you can use the **man** command with a prefix to obtain more detailed information about this kind of device. For example, **man sd** displays the Man pages for SCSI devices. A complete listing of all device names can be found in the **devices** file located in the **linux/doc/device-list** directory at the **www.kernel.org** Web site. Table 24-2 lists several of the commonly used device names.

The device name for your floppy drive is **fd0** and is located in the directory **/dev**. **/dev/fd0** references your floppy drive. Notice the numeral **0** after **fd**. If you have more than one floppy drive, they are represented by **fd1, fd2,** and so on.

IDE hard drives use the prefix **hd**, while SCSI hard drives use the prefix **sd**. The prefix for a hard disk is followed by an alphabetic character that labels the hard drive

Device Name	Description
hd	IDE hard drives, 1–4 are primary partitions, and 5 and up are logical partitions
sd	SCSI hard drives
sr	SCSI CD-ROM drives
fd	Floppy disks
st	SCSI tape drives
ht	IDE tape drives
tty	Terminals
lp	Printer ports
pty	Pseudoterminals (used for remote logins)
js	Analog joy sticks
midi	Midi ports
ttyS	Serial ports
cua	Callout devices (COM ports)
cdrom	Link to your CD-ROM device file
modem	Link to your modem device file

Table 24-2. *Device Name Prefixes*

and a number for the partition. For example, **hda2** references the second partition on the first IDE hard drive, and **sdb3** refers to the third partition on the second SCSI hard drive. To find the device name, you can use **df** to display your hard partitions or examine the **/etc/fstab** file.

The device name for your CD-ROM drive varies depending on the type of CD-ROM you have. The device name for an IDE CD-ROM has the same prefix as an IDE hard disk partition, **hd**, and is identified by a following character that distinguishes it from other IDE devices. For example, an IDE CD-ROM connected to your secondary IDE port may have the name **hdc**. An IDE CD-ROM connected as a slave to the secondary port may have the name **hdd**. The actual name is determined when the CD-ROM is installed, as happened when you installed your Linux system. SCSI CD-ROM drives use a different nomenclature for their device names. They begin with **sd** for SCSI drive and are followed by a distinguishing character. For example, the name of a SCSI CD-ROM could be **sdb** or **sda**. The name of your CD-ROM was determined when you installed your system. You can find out what it is either by examining the **/etc/fstab** file or using **Linuxconf** on your root user desktop.

Mount Configuration: /etc/fstab

Although you can mount a file system directly with only a **mount** command, you can simplify the process by placing mount information in the **/etc/fstab** configuration file. Using entries in this file, you can have certain file systems automatically mounted whenever your system boots. For others, you can specify configuration information, such as mountpoints and access permissions, which can be automatically used whenever you mount a file system. You needn't enter this information as arguments to a **mount** command as you otherwise must. This feature is what allows mount utilities on Gnome, KDE, and Linuxconf to enable you to mount a file system simply by clicking a button. All the mount information is already in the **/etc/fstab** file. For example, when adding a new hard disk partition to your Linux system, you most likely want to have it automatically mounted on startup, and then unmounted when you shut down. Otherwise, you must mount and unmount the partition explicitly each time you boot up and shut down your system. To have Linux automatically mount the file system on your new hard disk partition, you only need to add its name to the **fstab** file. You can do this by directly and carefully editing the **/etc/fstab** file to type in a new entry, or you can use the **Linuxconf** as described in the next section.

An entry in a **fstab** file contains several fields, each separated by a space or tab. The first field is the name of the file system to be mounted. This usually begins with **/dev**, such as **/dev/hda3** for the third hard disk partition. The next field is the directory in your file structure where you want the file system on this device to be attached. The third field is the type of file system being mounted. Table 24-3 provides a list of all the different types you can mount. The type for a standard Linux hard disk partition is

Types	Description
Minux	Minux file systems (filenames are limited to 30 characters)
ext	Earlier version of Linux file system, no longer in use
ext2	Standard Linux file system supporting large filenames and file sizes
xiaf	**Xiaf** file system
msdos	File system for MS-DOS partitions (16-bit)
vfat	File system for Windows partitions (32-bit)
hpfs	File system for OS/2 high-performance partitions
proc	Used by operating system for processes
nfs	NFS file system for mounting partitions from remote systems
umsdos	UMS-DOS file system
swap	Linux swap partition or swap file
sysv	UNIX System V file systems
iso9660	File system for mounting CD-ROM.

Table 24-3.   *File System Types*

ext2. The next example shows an entry for the main Linux hard disk partition. This entry is mounted at the root directory, **/**, and has a file type of **ext2**.

```
/dev/hda3   /   ext2   defaults   0   1
```

The field after the file system type lists the different options for mounting the file system. You can specify a default set of options by simply entering **defaults**. You can list specific options next to each other separated by a comma (no spaces). The **defaults** option specifies a device is read/write, asynchronous, block, ordinary users cannot mount on it, and programs can be executed on it. By contrast, a CD-ROM only has a few options listed for it: **ro** and **noauto**. **ro** specifies this is read-only; and **noauto** specifies this is not automatically mounted. The **noauto** option is used with both CD-ROMs and floppy drives, so they won't automatically mount because you do not know if you have anything in them when you start up. At the same time, the entries for both the CD-ROM and the floppy drive specify where they are to be mounted when you decide to mount them. Table 24-4 lists the options for mounting a file system. An example of CD-ROM and floppy drive entries follows. Notice the type for a CD-ROM file system is different from

Options	Description
`async`	All I/O to the file system should be done asynchronously
`auto`	Can be mounted with the -a option
`defaults`	Use default options: `rw`, `suid`, `dev`, `exec`, `auto`, `nouser`, and `async`
`dev`	Interpret character or block special devices on the file system
`noauto`	Can only be mounted explicitly. The -a option does not cause the file system to be mounted
`exec`	Permit execution of binaries
`nouser`	Forbid an ordinary (that is, nonroot) user to mount the file system
`remount`	Attempt to remount an already mounted file system. This is commonly used to change the mount flags for a file system, especially to make a read-only file system writable
`ro`	Mount the file system read-only
`rw`	Mount the file system read-write
`suid`	Allow set-user-identifier or set-group-identifier bits to take effect
`sync`	All I/O to the file system should be done synchronously
`user`	Enable an ordinary user to mount the file system. Ordinary users always have the following options activated: `noexec`, `nosuid`, and `nodev`
`nodev`	Do not interpret character or block special devices on the file system
`nosuid`	Do not allow set-user-identifier or set-group-identifier bits to take effect

Table 24-4.   *Mount Options for File Systems: -o and /etc/fstab*

a hard disk partition, **iso9660**. The floppy drive also has all the **default** options of the hard disk partitions.

```
/dev/fd0    /mnt/floppy   ext2    defaults,noauto  0  0
/dev/hdc    /mnt/cdrom    iso9660 ro,noauto         0  0
```

The last two fields consist of an integer value. The first one is used by the **dump** command to determine if a file system needs to be dumped, backing up the file system. The last one is used by **fsck** to see if a file system should be checked and in what order. If the field has a value of 1, it indicates a boot partition. The 0 value means the **fsck** needn't check the file system.

A copy of an **/etc/fstab** file is shown here. Notice the first line is comment. All comment lines begin with a **#**. The entry for the **/proc** file system is a special entry used by your Linux operating system for managing its processes, and it is not an actual device. To make an entry in the **/etc/fstab** file, you can either edit the **/etc/fstab** file directly or use Linuxconf, which prompts you for information, and then makes the correct entries into your **/etc/fstab** file. You can use the **/etc/fstab** example here as a guide to show how your entries should look. The **/proc** and **swap** partition entries are particularly critical.

/etc/fstab

```
# <device>    <mountpoint>   <filesystemtype>  <options>        <dump><fsck>
/dev/hda3     /              ext2              defaults          0     1
/dev/hdc      /mnt/cdrom     iso9660           ro,noauto         0     0
/dev/fd0      /mnt/floppy    ext2              defaults,noauto   0
/proc         /proc          proc              defaults
/dev/hda2     none           swap              sw
/dev/hda1     /mnt/dos       vfat              defaults          0     0
```

You can mount MS-DOS partitions used by your MS-DOS operating system onto your Linux file structure, just as you would mount any Linux file system. You only have to specify the file type of **vfat**. You may find it convenient to have your MS-DOS partitions automatically mounted when you start up your Linux system. To do this, you need to put an entry for your MS-DOS partitions in your **/etc/fstab** file. You make an entry for each MS-DOS partition you want to mount, and then specify the device name for that partition followed by the directory in which you want to mount it. The **/mnt/dos** directory would be a logical choice (be sure the **dos** directory has already been created in **/mnt**). For the file system type, enter **vfat**. The next example shows a standard MS-DOS partition entry for an **/etc/fstab** file. Notice the last entry in the **/etc/fstab** file example was an entry for mounting an MS-DOS partition.

```
/dev/hda1 /mnt/dos  vfat  defaults  0  0
```

If your **/etc/fstab** file ever becomes corrupt—say, a line gets deleted accidentally or changed—then your system will boot into a maintenance mode, giving you read-only access to your partitions. To gain read/write access so you can fix your **/etc/fstab** file, you have to remount your main partition. The following command performs such an operation:

```
# mount -n -o remount,rw  /
```

File systems listed in the **/etc/fstab** file are automatically mounted whenever you boot, unless this feature is explicitly turned off with the **noauto** option. Notice the CD-ROM and floppy disks have a **noauto** option. Also, if you issue a **mount** -a command, all the file systems without a **noauto** option are mounted. If you would want to make the CD-ROM user mountable, add the **user** option.

```
/dev/hdc    /mnt/cdrom    iso9660   ro,noauto,user   0    0
```

Linuxconf Configuration for Local File Systems

Unless you are familiar with the **fstab** file, using Linuxconf to add and edit entries is better, instead of editing entries directly. Linuxconf is available on RedHat systems and can be installed on any major distribution. With Linuxconf, you can choose many of the configuration options using drop-down menus and check boxes. Once you finish making your entries, you can have Linuxconf generate a new **/etc/fstab** file incorporating your changes.

You can start Linuxconf from a window manager, a desktop, or a shell command line. The figures here show Linuxconf panels as they are displayed in Gnome. Other desktops and window managers show the same display. A Linuxconf shell command shows cursor-based lists and boxes. To access the Linuxconf file system configuration panels, you can select its entry in the main Linuxconf interface or you can use the **fsconf** command to invoke a specialized window showing only file system options (see Chapter 4 for an example of the **fsconf** interface). Using the main Linuxconf interface, you select the Access local drive entry in the file systems list under the Config heading. This displays the information about the different file systems accessible on your local system. The source is the device name for the storage device. The name begins with **/dev**, the directory where device files are kept. For example, the name given to the first partition on the first hard drive is **hda1**. Its device filename is **/dev/hda1**. On most Linux distributions, a CD-DROM is given the device name **/dev/cdrom**. Names for additional CD-ROMS vary, depending on whether they are SCSI or IDE devices. On PCs, a second IDE CD-ROM could have the name **/dev/hdd**. The mountpoint and file system type are shown along with the size, partition type, and whether it is mounted. Figure 24-1 shows the Linuxconf Access local drive panel.

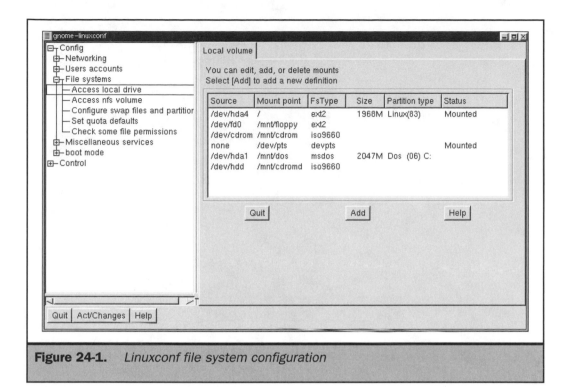

Figure 24-1. *Linuxconf file system configuration*

To add a new entry, click the Add button. This displays panels for file system information and options. The Base tab prompts you to enter in the file system's device name, its file system type, and its mountpoint, as shown in Figure 24-2. The box labeled Partition is where you enter the file system's device name. This box holds a drop-down menu listing the different hard disk partitions on your hard drive. If you are making an entry for one of those partitions, you can select it from there. If you are making an entry for a CD-ROM or floppy drive, you must enter the name yourself. The Type box is where you enter the file system type. The box contains a drop-down menu that lists the different file system types from which you can choose. Select the type from this menu. See Table 24-3 for a listing of file system types supported. The *Mount point* box is where you enter the mountpoint—the directory on your main file system where you attach this file system. For example, a floppy disk is usually attached to the **/mnt/floppy** directory. When you mount a floppy disk, you find its files in that directory. The directory can actually be any directory on your file system. If the directory does not exist, then Linuxconf asks to create it for you. Figure 24-2 shows an example of the Base tab for adding a second CD-ROM. The device name in this example is **/dev/hdd**, the file system type is **iso9660** (standard for CD-ROMs), and the mountpoint is **/mnt/cdromd**. If you were mounting a Linux file system, you would use the **ext2** type, and for DOS partitions you would use **msdos**.

ADMINISTRATION

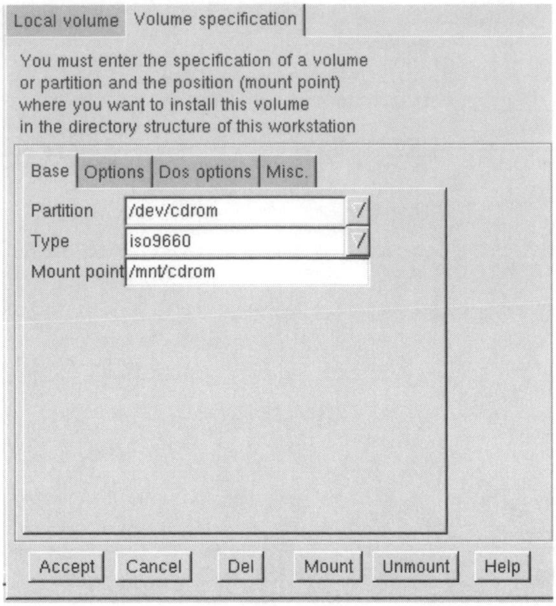

Figure 24-2.   *Linuxconf Base tab for adding or editing file systems*

The Options tab lists different mount options in the form of check boxes. You can select options, such as whether you don't want the file system automatically mounted at boot, or if you want to let normal users mount it. The Options tab, shown next, displays the entries you may make for a CD-ROM. The CD-ROM is read-only, not mounted at boot time, and can be mounted by any user.

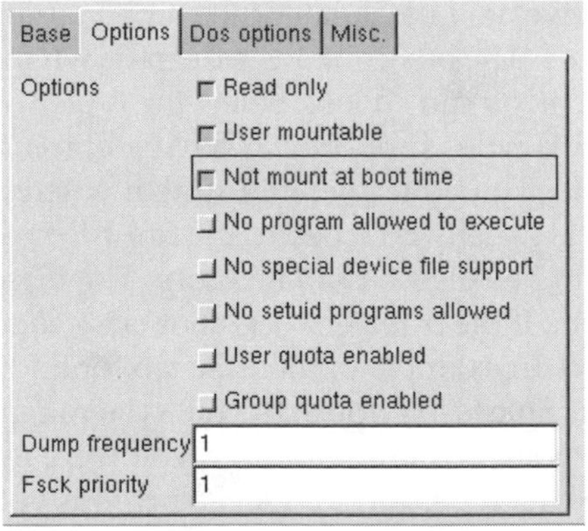

If your Linux system shares a hard drive with a Windows system, then you may want to add mount entries for the Windows partition. This way, those partitions would be accessible by your Linux system. Linux can access any file on a Windows partition, though it cannot run its programs. For example, files could be downloaded by your Linux system and saved directly on a Windows partition. To create a mount entry for a Windows partition, you would enter its hard disk partition name in the Partition box, and enter **vfat** for its file system type. Here is a sample configuration:

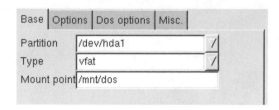

When you finish, click the Accept button. This returns you to the Local volume panel and you then see the new entry displayed. Linuxconf does not actually implement these changes on your system until you click the Act/Changes button in the lower-left corner. When you do this, Linuxconf generates a new **/etc/fstab** file, replacing the previous one.

You can change any of the current entries by simply double-clicking its entry. This displays the Volume specification panel for that entry. You can then change any of the options or the base configuration. For example, to use a different mountpoint, type in a new directory in the Mount point box. If you want to delete the entry, click the DEL button.

Mounting File Systems Using Linuxconf, KDE, and Gnome

Once you enter a new file system configuration and activate the changes to implement it on your system, you can then actually mount the file system. By default, file systems are mounted automatically, though certain file systems, such as CD-ROMs and floppy disks, are normally mounted manually. To mount a file system manually with Linuxconf, select the Control configured local drives in the Mount/Unmount file systems list under the Control Panel located in Config. This displays a listing of your local file systems, as shown in Figure 24-3. When you click an entry, you are then asked if you want to mount the file system. You can also use this panel to unmount a file system. If a file system is already mounted, clicking it displays a dialog box asking if you want to unmount the file system. Remember, when you mount a CD-ROM or floppy disk, you cannot then simply remove it to put in another one. You first have to unmount the CD or floppy disk before you can take it out and put in another one.

Using the Access local drive configuration panel to mount a file system is possible (see Figure 24-2). Click the Mount button in a file system's Volume specification panel.

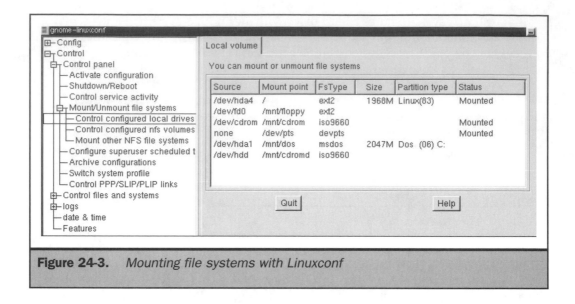

Figure 24-3.   *Mounting file systems with Linuxconf*

An Unmount button also unmounts it. You can use this method when checking to see if a new system mounts correctly.

Both the Gnome and K Desktop provide easy-to-use desktop icons for mounting and unmounting your file systems. Normally, these are used for manually mounted devices, such as CD-ROMs, tapes, and floppy disks. Hard disk partitions are usually mounted automatically at boot time. On Gnome, an icon is automatically generated for your CD-ROM devices. Right-clicking the icon displays a menu from which you can select an entry to mount or unmount the CD-ROM. You can also install a Mount applet in a Gnome panel that enables you to mount a floppy, CD-ROM, or partition by simply clicking its Panel icon (see Chapter 4 for more details).

On the K Desktop, you can create a KDE kdelink file for a particular file system device. Right-click the desktop and select File System from the New entry in the pop-up menu. Enter a name for the KDE link file with the extension **.kdelink**. Then, a Properties dialog box is displayed for the link file. In the Device tab, enter the device name, mountpoint, and file system type. You can also select a mount and unmount icon. A Device tab for a CD-ROM is shown next. The device name, in this example, could also be **/etc/cdrom**.

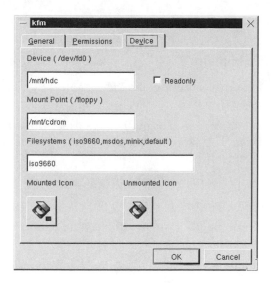

The mount and umount Commands

You can also mount or unmount any file system using the **mount** and **umount** commands. You enter these commands on a shell command line. In a window manager or desktop, you can open a Terminal window and enter the command there, or you can simply use your login shell. The mount operations discussed in the previous sections use the **mount** command to mount a file system. Normally, mounting file systems can only be done as the root user (unless the device is user mountable). This is a system administration task and cannot be performed by a regular user. To mount a file system, be sure to log in as the root user. Table 24-5 list the different options for the **mount** command.

The **mount** command takes two arguments: the storage device through which Linux accesses the file system, and the directory in the file structure to which the new file system is attached. The *mountpoint* is the directory on your main directory tree where you want the files on the storage device attached. The *device* is a special device file that connects your system to the hardware device. The syntax for the **mount** command follows

```
# mount device mountpoint
```

Mount Options	Description
-f	Fakes the mounting of a file system. You use it to check if a file system can be mounted
-v	Verbose mode. Mount displays descriptions of the actions it is taking. Use with -f to check for any problems mounting a file system, -fv
-w,	Mount the file system with read and write permission
-r	Mount the file system with only read permission
-n	Mount the file system without placing an entry for it in the **mstab** file
-t *type*	Specify the type of file system to be mounted. See Table 24-3 for valid file system types
-a	Mount all file systems listed in **/etc/fstab**
-o *option-list*	Mount the file system using list of options. This is a comma-separated list of options following -o. See Table 24-4 for a list of the options and the **Man** pages for mount for a complete listing

Table 24-5.   *The mount Command*

Device files are located in the **/dev** directories and usually have abbreviated names ending with the number of the device. For example, **fd0** may reference the first floppy drive attached to your system. On Linux systems operating on PCs, the hard disk partitions have a prefix of **hd,** followed by an alphabetic character that labels the hard drive, and then a number for the partition. For example, **hda2** references the second partition on the first hard drive. In most cases, you can use the **man** command with a prefix to obtain more detailed information about that kind of device. For example, **man sd** displays the Man pages for SCSI devices. The following example mounts a floppy disk in the first floppy drive device (**fd0**) to the **/mydir** directory.

```
# mount /dev/fd0   /mydir
```

For any partition with an entry in the **/etc/fstab** file, you can mount it using only the mount directory specified in its **fstab** entry. You needn't enter the device filename.

The **mount** command looks up the entry for it in the **fstab** file, using the directory to identify the entry and, in that way, finds the device name. For example, to unmount the **/dev/hda1** DOS partition in the previous example, the **mount** command only needs to know the directory it is mounted to, in this case, **/mnt/dos**.

```
# mount /mnt/dos
```

If you want to replace one mounted file system with another, you must first explicitly unmount the one already mounted. Say, you have mounted a floppy disk, and now you want to take it out and put in a new one. You must unmount that floppy disk before you can put in and mount the new one. You unmount a file system with the **umount** command. The **umount** command can take as its argument either a device name or the directory where it was mounted. Here is the syntax:

```
# umount device-or-mountpoint
```

The following example unmounts the floppy disk mounted to the **/mydir** directory:

```
# umount /dev/fd0
```

Using the example where the device was mounted on the **/mydir** directory, you could use that directory to unmount the file system.

```
# umount /mydir
```

One important constraint occurs on the **umount** command. You can never unmount a file system in which you are currently working. If you change to a directory within a file system that you then try to unmount, you receive an error message saying the file system is busy. For example, suppose you mount the Red Hat CD-ROM on the **/mnt/cdrom** directory, and then change to that **/mnt/cdrom** directory. If you decide to change CD-ROMs, you first have to unmount the current one with the **umount** command. This will fail because you are currently in the directory in which it is mounted. You first have to leave that directory before you can unmount the CD-ROM.

```
# mount  /dev/hdc  /mnt/cdrom
# cd /mnt/cdrom
# umount /mnt/cdrom
umount: /dev/hdd: device is busy
# cd  /root
# umount /mnt/cdrom
```

If other users are using a file system you are trying to unmount, you can use the **lsof** or **fuser** commands to find out who they are.

Mounting Floppy Disks

To access a file on a floppy disk, you first have to mount that disk onto your Linux system. The device name for your floppy drive is **fd0**, and it is located in the directory **/dev**. Entering **/dev/fd0** references your floppy drive. Notice the number **0** after **fd**. If you have more than one floppy drive, they are represented by **fd1**, **fd2**, and so on. You can mount to any directory you want. Red Hat creates a convenient directory to use for floppy disks, **/mnt/floppy**. The following example mounts the floppy disk in your floppy drive to the **/mnt/floppy** directory:

```
# mount /dev/fd0   /mnt/floppy
```

Remember, you are mounting a particular floppy disk, not the floppy drive. You cannot simply remove the floppy disk and put in another one. The **mount** command has attached those files to your main directory tree, and your system expects to find those files on a floppy disk in your floppy drive. If you take out the disk and put another one in, you get an error message when you try to access it.

To change disks, you must first unmount the floppy disk already in your disk drive; then, after putting in the new disk, you must explicitly mount that new disk. To do this, use the **umount** command. Notice no *n* is in the **umount** command.

```
# umount    /dev/fd0
```

For the **umount** operation, you can specify either the directory it is mounted on or the **/dev/fd0** device.

```
# umount   /mnt/floppy
```

You can now remove the floppy disk, put in the new one, and then mount it.

```
# mount    /mnt/floppy
```

When you shut down your system, any disk you have mounted is automatically unmounted. You do not have to unmount it explicitly.

Mounting CD-ROMs

You can also mount CD-ROM disks to your Linux system using the **mount** command. On Red Hat, the directory **/mnt/cdrom** has been reserved for CD-ROM file systems. You see an entry for this in the **/etc/fstab** file. With such an entry, to mount a CD-ROM, all you have to do is enter the command **mount** and the directory **/mnt/cdrom**. You needn't specify the device name. Once mounted, you can access the CD-ROM through the **/mnt/cdrom** directory.

```
# mount /mnt/cdrom
```

As with floppy disks, remember you are mounting a particular CD-ROM, not the CD-ROM drive. You cannot just remove the CD-ROM and put in a new one. The **mount** command has attached those files to your main directory tree, and your system expects to find them on a disc in your CD-ROM drive. To change discs, you must first unmount the CD-ROM already in your CD-ROM drive with the **umount** command. Your CD-ROM drive will not open until you issue this command. Then, after putting in the new disc, you must explicitly mount that new CD-ROM. You can then remove the CD-ROM and put in the new one. Then, issue a **mount** command to mount it.

```
# umount  /mnt/cdrom
```

If you want to mount a CD-ROM to another directory, you have to include the device name in the **mount** command. The following example mounts the disc in your CD-ROM drive to the **/mydir** directory. The particular device name for the CD-ROM in this example is **/dev/hdc**.

```
# mount /dev/hdc  /mydir
```

To change discs, you have to unmount the CD-ROM already in your CD-ROM drive, and then, after putting in the new disc, you must explicitly mount that new CD-ROM.

```
# umount  /mydir
```

You can now remove the CD-ROM and put in the new one. Then, issue a **mount** command to mount it.

```
# mount   /dev/hdc    /mydir
```

Mounting Hard Drive Partitions: Linux and MS-DOS

You can mount either Linux or MS-DOS hard drive partitions with the **mount** command. However, it is much more practical to have them mounted automatically using the **/etc/fstab** file as described in the next section. The Linux hard disk partitions you created during installation are already automatically mounted for you. To mount a Linux hard disk partition, enter the **mount** command with the device name of the partition and the directory to which you want to mount it. IDE hard drives use the prefix **hd**, and SCSI hard drives use the prefix **sd**. The next example mounts the Linux hard disk partition on **/dev/hda4** to the directory **/mnt/mydata**.

```
# mount -t ext2  /dev/hda4  /mnt/mydata
```

You can also mount an MS-DOS partition and directly access the files on it. As with a Linux partition, you use the **mount** command, but you also have to specify the file system type as MS-DOS. For that, use the **-t** option, and then type **vfat**. In the next example, the user mounts the MS-DOS hard disk partition **/dev/hda1** to the Linux file structure at directory **/mnt/dos**. The **/mnt/dos** directory is a common designation for MS-DOS file systems, though you can mount it in any directory. Be sure you have already created the directory.

```
# mount -t vfat  /dev/hda1  /mnt/dos
```

Formatting File Systems: mkfs

If you want to mount a new partition from either a new hard drive or your current drive, you must first create that partition using the Linux **fdisk** and format it with **mkfs**. Once created and formatted, you can then mount it on your system. To start **fdisk**, enter **fdisk** on the command line. This brings up an interactive program you can use to create your Linux partition. Be careful using Linux **fdisk**. It can literally erase your entire hard disk if you are not careful. The Linux **fdisk** operates much as described in the installation process discussed in Chapter 2. The command *n* creates a new partition, and the command *t* enables you to set its type to that of a Linux type, 83. Table 24-6 lists the **fdisk** commands.

Hard disk partitions are named with **hd** (IDE drive) or **sd** (SCSI drives), followed by an alphabetic letter indicating the hard drive, and then a number for the partition on the hard drive. They can belong to any operating system, such as MS-DOS, OS/2, or Windows NT, as well as Linux. The first partition created is called **hda1**—the first partition on the first IDE hard drive, *a*. If you add another partition, it will have the name **hda2**. If you add a new IDE hard drive, its first partition will have the name **hdb1**.

Once you create your partition, you have to format it. For this, use the **mkfs** command and the name of the hard disk partition. A hard disk partition is a device with its own device name in the **/dev** directory. You must specify its full pathname with the **mkfs** command. For example, the second partition on the first hard drive has

Commands	Description
A	Sets and unsets the bootable flag for a partition
C	Sets and unsets the DOS compatibility flag
D	Deletes a partition
L	Lists partition types
M	Displays a listing of **fdisk** commands
N	Creates a new partition
P	Prints the partition table, listing all the partitions on your disk
Q	Quits without saving changes. Use this to abort an **fdisk** session if you made a mistake
T	Select the file system type for a partition
V	Verify the partition table
W	Write partition table to disk and exit. At this point the changes are made, irrevocably
X	Display a listing of advanced fdisk commands. With these, you can set the number of cylinders, sectors, and heads; print raw data; and change the location of data in the partition table

Table 24-6.   *The* fdisk *Commands*

the device name **/dev/hda4**. You can now mount your new hard disk partition, attaching it to your file structure. The next example formats that partition:

```
# mkfs -t ext2   /dev/hda4
```

To format a floppy disk, use the **mkfs** command. This creates a Linux file system on that disk. Be sure to specify the **ext2** file system type with the **-t ext2** option (see Table 24-7). Once formatted, you can then mount that file system. The **mkfs** command takes as its arguments the device name and the number of memory blocks on the disk. At 1,000 bytes per block, 1,400 formats a 1.44MB disk. You do not first mount the blank disk; you simply put it in your floppy drive and enter the **mkfs** command with its arguments. The next example formats a 1.44MB floppy disk:

```
# mkfs -t ext2 /dev/fd0  1400
```

If you have the K Desktop installed, you can use the kfloppy utility to format your floppy disks. Kfloppy, shown next, enables you to choose an MS-DOS or Linux file system type. For MS-DOS disks, you can choose a quick or full format:

Options	Description
Blocks	Number of blocks for the file system. There are 1,440 blocks for a 1.44MB floppy disk
-t *file-system-type*	Specify the type of file system to format. The default is the standard Linux file system type, ext2
fs *–options*	Options for the type of file system specified
-v	Verbose mode. Displays description of each action **mkvfs** takes

Table 24-7. *The* mkfs *Options*

Options	Description
-v	Instructs the file system builder program that **mkvfs** invokes to show actions it take.
-c	Check a partition for bad blocks before formatting it (may take some time)
-l *filename*	Read list of bad blocks

Table 24-7.   *The* mkfs *Options* (continued)

CD Images

With the **mkisofs** command, you can create a CD image file, which you can then write to a CD write device. A CD image can be written to either a CDR or a CDR/W device. A CDR device is like a CD-ROM, but can only write once to a CD disk, whereas a CDR/W can overwrite a CD disk. Each uses special CD media: CDR disks that can be written to only once and special CD read/write disks that can be overwritten like a floppy disk. Once you create your CD image file, you can write it to a CD-write device, using the cdrecord or cdwrite applications. The cdrecord application is a more powerful application with many options. You could also copy the CD image file to an MS-DOS partition, and then use Windows CD-write software to create the CD-ROM.

One important use for a CD image is to create a CD-ROM for a Linux distribution's new release, though Red Hat currently posts an ISO CD image file you can download and burn onto a CD-R directly. You can also download the collection of files making up a release and use them to generate a CD image. For example, the Red Hat distribution includes files for different systems, such as Sun SPARC workstations, DEC alphas, and PCs. Their PC distribution will be under a directory labeled **i386** or **i686** (as in the Intel CPU). Use an FTP client such as IglooFTP, gftp, or even the KDE file manager. If you use **ftp**, be sure to disable the prompt with the prompt command, and use the **mget *** to download the entire directory and all its subdirectories at once. This way, you needn't download individual files and subdirectories. The Red Hat-CD Mini-HOWTO provides a simple shell script to change these permissions.

You may have to make one important change to these files. Certain files must have execute permission set for them. Sometimes, when files are downloaded with an FTP client, the original permissions are note preserved. *Note preserved* means a file with execute permission on the remote system may have only read permission for the copy on your system. Certain install programs need to have execute permission to run off the CD-ROM during the installation process. The Linux Red Hat CD-ROM Mini-HOWTO provides a simple script you can use to change these permissions. You can find the Mini-HOWTOs at **www.linux.org**. Another change is required if you decide to incorporate any updated

RPM packages in the distribution RPMS files, replacing ones from the original set. In this case, you need to generate a new **RedHat/base/hdlist**. This list contains the names of the original set of RPM packages. You need to have a new list generated with the new names to have them installed. The Mini-HOWTO provides another script to do this for Red Hat distributions. The `misc/src/install/genhdlist` command scans your RPMS files and creates an updated list. It expects to find only RPM files in the **RPMS** directory. Remove any others, such as **ls-lR.gz**.

Once you have the distribution files, you can use `mkisofs` to create an ISO CD image of them. You need to include several important options with `mkisofs` to create a distribution CD properly. The `-o` option is used to specify the name of the CD image file. This can be any name you want to give it. The `-r` option specifies Rockridge CD protocols, and the `-J` option provides for long Windows 95 names. The last argument is the directory that contains the files for which you want to make the CD image. For this, you can specify a directory. If you downloaded the **i386** directory, this would be `i386`. The top directory in the CD image is the subdirectories of **i386**, not **i386** itself. You can also change to that directory and then use `.` to indicate the current directory. One other important part of creating a distribution CD image is to specify the boot image and boot catalogue. Red Hat CDs are boot CDs, enabling users to boot directly from the CD-ROM. With the `-c` option, you specify the boot catalogue. For Red Hat distributions, this is the **boot.cat** file. With the `-b` option, you specify the boot image. The *boot image* is a boot disk image, like that used to start up an installation procedure. On Red Hat systems, this is located in the images directory, **images/boot.img**. On other distributions, the boot catalogue and image files may be located in other directories and have different names.

```
mkisofs -v -r -T -J -V "Red6" -b images/boot.img -c boot.cat -o rd6.iso .
```

To test the CD image, you can mount it to a directory, and then access it as if it were simply another file system. Be sure to unmount it when you finish.

```
mount -t iso9660 -o ro,loop=/dev/loop0 redhat6.iso /mnt/cdrom
```

Once `mkisofs` has created the CD image file, you can use **cdrecord** or **cdwrite** to write it to a CD write disk. If your system mounts an MS-DOS partition, you could copy the CD image file to that partition and use Windows CD-write software to write to a CD-write disk. The `mkisofs` command creates an image of type ISO, and you may need to specify that type.

The mtools Utilities: msdos

Your Linux system provides a set of utilities, known as *mtools,* that enable you to easily access a floppy disk formatted for MS-DOS (see Table 24-8) . The **mcopy** command enables you to copy files to and from an MS-DOS floppy disk in your floppy drive. No special operations, such as mounting, are required. With mtools, you needn't mount an MS-DOS partition to access it. For an MS-DOS floppy disk, place the disk in your floppy drive, and you can then use mtool commands to access those files. For example, to copy a file from an MS-DOS floppy disk to your Linux system, use the **mcopy** command. You specify the MS-DOS disk with **a:** for the A drive. Unlike normal DOS pathnames, pathnames used with mtool commands use forward slashes instead of backslashes. The directory **docs** on the A drive would be referenced by the pathname **a:/docs**, not **a:\docs**. Unlike MS-DOS, which defaults the second argument to the current directory, you always need to supply the second argument for mcopy. The next example copies the file **mydata** to the MS-DOS disk, and then copies the **preface** file from the disk to the current Linux directory. Notice that, unlike DOS, mtools uses forward slashes instead of backward slashes.

```
$ mcopy mydata a:
$ mcopy a:/preface  .
```

You can use the **mdir** command to list files on your MS-DOS disk, and you can use the **mcd** command to change directories on it. The next example lists the files on the MS-DOS disk in your floppy drive, and then changes to the **docs** directory on that drive.

```
$ mdir a:
$ mcd a:/docs
```

Most of the standard MS-DOS commands are available as mtool operations. You can create MS-DOS directories with **mmd** and erase MS-DOS files with **mdel**. A list of mtool commands is provided in Table 24-8. For example, to display a file on drive **b:** on an MS-DOS 5 1/4-inch floppy drive, use **mtype** and the name of the file preceded by **b:/**.

```
$ mtype b:/readme
```

Access to MS-DOS partitions is configured by the **/etc/mtools.conf** file. This file lists several different default MS-DOS partitions and disk drives. Each drive or partition is identified with a particular device name. Entries for your floppy drives are already entered, using the device names **/dev/fd0** and **/dev/fd1** for the first and second floppy drives. An entry in the **/etc/mtools.conf** file takes the form of the drive label followed by the term "file" and the equal sign, and then the device name of the drive or partition you want identified with this label. The device name is encased in quotes. For example, assuming the first hard disk partition is an MS-DOS partition and has the device name of **/dev/hda1**, the following entry would identify this as the **c:** drive on an MS-DOS system:

```
drive c: file="/dev/hda1"
```

Commands	Execution
mcopy *filename filename*	Copies a file to and from an MS-DOS disk, or your Linux system. The following copies a file from an MS-DOS floppy disk to your Linux system: **mcopy a:/***filename directory-or-filename* The following copies a file from Linux for an MS-DOS floppy disk in your floppy drive: **mcopy** *filename* **a:/***filename*
mcd *directory-name*	Changes directory on your MS-DOS file system
mdir	Lists the files on an MS-DOS disk in your floppy drive
mattrib	Change the attribute of a MS-DOS file
mdel *filename*	Delete an MS-DOS file
mformat	Add an MS-DOS file system to a floppy disk
mlabel	Make a volume label
mmd *directory-name*	Make an MS-DOS directory
mrd *directory-name*	Remove an MS-DOS directory
mread *filename filename*	Low-level read (copy) an MS-DOS file to UNIX
mren *filename filename*	Rename an MS-DOS file
mtype *filename*	Display contents of an MS-DOS file
mwrite *filename filename*	Low-level write (copy) a UNIX file to MS-DOS

Table 24-8.   *The mtools Access Commands*

You must have the correct device name for your partition. These device names are listed in the **/etc/fstab** file and can also be viewed with the Linuxconf Local drive access panel on your root user desktop. If you have a SCSI hard disk, the hard disk partitions have the form of **sd,** followed by a character for the hard drive and a number for the partition in it. For example, **sda1** refers to the first partition on the SCSI hard drive. IDE hard drives have the form of **hd**, also followed by a character and a partition number—**hda1** refers to the first partition on an IDE hard drive.

On most distributions, a default **/etc/mtools.conf** file is installed for you. This file has commented entries for the **c:** drive: one for a SCSI hard disk partition and one for an IDE partition. Both are commented out with a preceding **#**. If you have an IDE hard drive (as most users do), you need to remove the preceding **#** symbol from the entry for the IDE hard disks partition and leave the preceding **#** symbol in front of the entry for the SCSI partition. Also, if your MS-DOS partition on your IDE hard drive is not the first partition, you must change the device name. For example, if the MS-DOS partition is the second partition, the device name will be **/dev/hda2**. If you have several MS-DOS partitions, you can add entries for each one, assigning a different label to each. The following example assigns the **d:** label to the fourth hard disk partition on an IDE drive:

```
drive d: file="/dev/hda4"
```

/etc/mtools.conf

```
# Linux floppy drives
drive a: file="/dev/fd0" exclusive 1.44m
drive b: file="/dev/fd1" exclusive 1.44m
# First SCSI hard disk partition
#drive c: file="/dev/sda1"
# First IDE hard disk partition
drive c: file="/dev/hda1"
drive d: file="/dev/hda5"
#dosemu floppy image
drive m: file="/var/lib/dosemu/diskimage"
#dosemu hdimage
drive n: file="/var/lib/dosemu/diskimage" offset=3840
#Atari ramdisk image
drive o: file="/tmp/atari_rd" offset=136
mtools_lower_case=1
```

Once the DOS hard disk partitions are referenced, you can then use their drive letters to copy files to and from them to your Linux partitions. The following command copies the file **mydoc.html** to the **c:** partition in the directory **webstuff** and renames it **mydoc.htm**. Notice the use of forward slashes instead of backward slashes.

```
$ mcopy mypage.html c:/webstuff/mypag.htm
```

Because of the differences in the way DOS and Linux handle newlines in text files, you should use the **−t** option whenever copying a DOS text file to a Linux partition. The following command copies the **mydoc.txt** file from the **c:/project** directory to the **/newdocs** directory.

```
$ mcopy -t c:/project/mydoc.txt   /newdocs
```

ADMINISTRATION

Archive Files and Devices: tar

The **tar** utility creates archives for files and directories. With **tar**, you can archive specific files, update them in the archive, and add new files, as you want, to that archive. You can even archive entire directories with all their files and subdirectories, all of which can be restored from the archive. The **tar** utility was originally designed to create archives on tapes. The term *tar* stands for tape archive. You can create archives on any device, such as a floppy disk, or you can create an archive file to hold the archive. The **tar** utility is ideal for making backups of your files or combining several files into a single file for transmission across a network.

On Linux, **tar** is often used to create archives on devices or files. You can direct **tar** to archive files to a specific device or a file by using the **f** option with the name of the device or file. The syntax for the **tar** command using the **f** option is shown in the next example. The device or filename is often referred to as the archive name. When creating a file for a **tar** archive, the filename is usually given the extension **.tar**. This is a convention only, and is not required. You can list as many filenames as you want. If a directory name is specified, then all its subdirectories are included in the archive.

```
$ tar optionsf archive-name.tar directory-and-file-names
```

To create an archive, use the **c** option. Combined with the **f** option, **c** creates an archive on a file or device. You enter this option before and right next to the **f** option. Notice no preceding dash is before a **tar** option. Table 24-9 lists the different options you can use with **tar**. In the next example, the directory **mydir** and all its subdirectories are saved in the file **myarch.tar**.

```
$ tar cf myarch.tar mydir
```

The user can later extract the directories from the tape using the **x** option. The **xf** option extracts files from an archive file or device. The **tar** extraction operation generates all subdirectories. In the next example, the **xf** option directs **tar** to extract all the files and subdirectories from the tar file **myarch.tar**.

```
$ tar xf myarch.tar
```

You use the **r** option to add files to an already-created archive. The **r** option appends the files to the archive. In the next example, the user appends the files in the **letters** directory to the **myarch.tar** archive.

```
$ tar rf myarch.tar letters
```

If you change any of the files in your directories you previously archived, you can use the **u** option to instruct **tar** to update the archive with any modified files. The **tar**

Commands	Execution
tar *options files*	Backs up files to tape, device, or archive file
tar *options*f *archive_name filelist*	Backs up files to a specific file or device specified as *archive_name. filelist*; can be filenames or directories

Options

c	Creates a new archive
t	Lists the names of files in an archive
r	Appends files to an archive
u	Updates an archive with new and changed files; adds only those files modified since they were archived or files not already present in the archive
w	Waits for a confirmation from the user before archiving each file; enables you to update an archive selectively
x	Extracts files from an archive
m	When extracting a file from an archive, no new time stamp is assigned
M	Creates multiple-volume archive that may be stored on several floppy disks
f *archive-name*	Saves the tape archive to the file *archive-name*, instead of to the default tape device; when given an archive-name, the **f** option saves the **tar** archive in a file of that name
f *device-name*	Saves a **tar** archive to a device such as a floppy disk or tape, **/dev/fd0** is the device name for your floppy disk; the default device is held in **/etc/default/tar-file**
v	Displays each filename as it is archived
z	Compresses or decompresses archived files using gzip

Table 24-9.   *File Backups: tar*

command compares the time of the last update for each archived file with those in the user's directory and copies into the archive any files that have been changed since they were last archived. Any newly created files in these directories are also added to the archive. In the next example, the user updates the **myarch.tar** file with any recently modified or newly created files in the **mydir** directory:

```
tar uf myarch.tar mydir
```

If you need to see what files are stored in an archive, you can use the **tar** command with the **t** option. The next example lists all the files stored in the **myarch.tar** archive:

```
tar tf myarch.tar
```

To back up the files to a specific device, specify the device as the archive. For a floppy disk, you can specify the floppy drive. Be sure to use a blank floppy disk. Any data previously placed on it will be erased by this operation. In the next example, the user creates an archive on the floppy disk in the **/dev/fd0** device and copies into it all the files in the **mydir** directory:

```
$ tar cf /dev/fd0 mydir
```

To extract the backed-up files on the disk in the device, use the **xf** option:

```
$ tar xf /dev/fd0
```

If the files you are archiving take up more space than would be available on a device such as a floppy disk, you can create a **tar** archive that uses multiple labels. The **M** option instructs **tar** to prompt you for a new storage component when the current one is filled. When archiving to a floppy drive with the **M** option, **tar** prompts you to put in a new floppy disk when one becomes full. You can then save your **tar** archive on several floppy disks.

```
$ tar cMf /dev/fd0 mydir
```

To unpack the multiple-disk archive, place the first one in the floppy drive, and then issue the following **tar** command using both the **x** and **M** options. You are then prompted to put in the other floppy disks as they are needed.

```
$ tar xMf /dev/fd0
```

The **tar** operation do not perform compression on archived files. If you want to compress the archived files, you can instruct **tar** to invoke the **gzip** utility to compress them. With the lowercase **z** option, **tar** first uses **gzip** to compress files before archiving them. The same **z** option invokes **gzip** to decompress them when extracting files.

```
$ tar czf  myarch.tar mydir
```

Remember, a difference exists between compressing individual files in an archive and compressing the entire archive as a whole. Often, an archive is created for transferring several files at once as one **tar** file. To shorten transmission time, the archive should be as small as possible. You can use the compression utility **gzip** on the archive **tar** file to compress it, reducing its size, and then send the compressed version. The person receiving it can decompress it, restoring the **tar** file. Using **gzip** on a **tar** file often results in a file with the extension **.tar.gz**. The extension **.gz** is added to a compressed **gzip** file. The next example creates a compressed version of **myarch.tar** using the same name with the extension **.gz**:

```
$ gzip myarch.tar
$ ls
$ myarch.tar.gz
```

If you have a default device specified, such as a tape, and you want to create an archive on it, you can simply use **tar** without the **f** option and a device or filename. This can be helpful for making backups of your files. The name of the default device is held in a file called **/etc/default/tar**. The syntax for the **tar** command using the default tape device is shown in the following example. If a directory name is specified, all its subdirectories are included in the archive.

```
$ tar option directory-and-file-names
```

In the next example, the directory **mydir** and all its subdirectories are saved on a tape in the default tape device:

```
$ tar c mydir
```

In this example, the **mydir** directory and all its files and subdirectories are extracted from the default tape device and placed in the user's working directory:

```
$ tar x  mydir
```

Midnight Commander (Gnome) and Kfm (KDE)

Both file managers in Gnome and the K Desktop have the capability to display the contents of a **tar** archive file automatically. The contents are displayed as though they were files in a directory. Figure 24-4 shows the KDE file manager displaying files in a **tar** archive. You can list the files as icons or with details, sorting them by name, type, or other fields. You can even display the contents of files. Clicking a text file opens it with a text editor and an image is displayed with an image viewer. If the file manager cannot determine what program to use to display the file, it prompts you to select an application. Both file managers can perform the same kind of operation on archives residing on remote file systems, such as **tar** archives on FTP sites. You can obtain a listing of their contents and even read their README files. The Midnight Commander file manager (Gnome) can also extract an archive. Right-click the Archive icon and select extract.

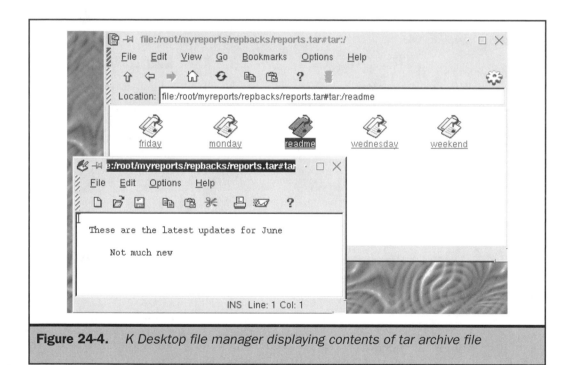

Figure 24-4. *K Desktop file manager displaying contents of tar archive file*

Desktop Archivers: guiTar, Ark, KDAT, and Xtar

Several desktop applications provide a GUI interface for creating and extracting archives. These archivers provide simple methods for managing archives, enabling you to select files and set options easily. The guiTAR archiver is Gnome-based. When creating an archive, you can choose from several compression methods, including **tar**, rar, and zip. You can open an archive with a drag-and-drop operation, dragging an archive file from the file manager window to the guiTAR window (see Figure 24-5). Files listed in an archive can be sorted by different fields by clicking the buttons across the top of the list.

Ark is a K Desktop archiver. To open a new archive, you enter a name with the **.tar.gz** extension. Once an archive is open, you can add to it by dragging files from a file manager window to the Ark window. To extract an archive, first open it, and then select Extract. KDAT is a tape archiver for the K Desktop. You can use it to back up files to a tape drive. You can specify a root directory or create a tape profile listing specific files and directories. The Xtar archiver is an X Window System application that can run on any file manager and provides much the same functionality as the other archivers. Once you select the **tar** archive to open, all the files making up the **tar** archive are then listed in the main window.

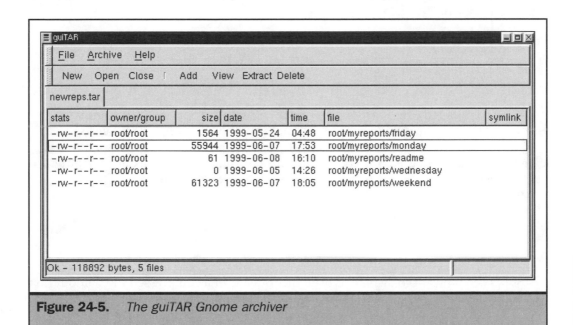

Figure 24-5.   *The guiTAR Gnome archiver*

With XTar, you have the option of either unpacking the entire **tar** archive or only a few files within it. Options also has a View item for displaying short text files, such as a README file.

File Compression: gzip. bzip2, and zip

Several reasons exist for reducing the size of a file. The two most common are to save space or, if you are transferring the file across a network, to save transmission time. You can effectively reduce a file size by creating a compressed copy of it. Anytime you need the file again, you decompress it. Compression is used in combination with archiving to enable you to compress whole directories and their files at once. Decompression generates a copy of the archive file, which can then be extracted, generating a copy of those files and directories.

Several compression utilities are available for use on Linux and UNIX systems. Most software for Linux systems use the GNU **gzip** and **gunzip** utilities. The **gzip** utility compresses files and **gunzip** decompresses them. To compress a file, enter the command **gzip** and the filename. This replaces the file with a compressed version of it, with the extension **.gz**.

```
$ gzip mydata
$ ls
mydata.gz
```

To decompress a gzip file, use either **gzip** with the **-d** option or the command **gunzip**. These commands decompress a compressed file with the **.gz** extension and replace it with a decompressed version with the same root name, but without the **.gz** extension. When you use **gunzip**, you needn't even type in the **.gz** extension. **gunzip** and **gzip -d** assumes it. Table 24-10 lists the different **gzip** options.

```
$ gunzip mydata.gz
$ ls
mydata
```

Suppose you want to display or print the contents of a compressed file without first having to decompress it. The command **zcat** generates a decompressed version of a file and sends it to the standard output. You can then redirect this output to a printer or display a utility such as **more**. The original file remains in its compressed state.

```
$ zcat mydata.gz | more
```

Option	Execution
-c	Sends compressed version of file to standard output; each file listed is separately compressed: **gzip -c** mydata preface > myfiles.gz
-d	Decompresses a compressed file; or, you can use gunzip: **gzip -d** myfiles.gz **gunzip** myfiles.gz
-h	Displays help listing
-l *file-list*	Displays compressed and uncompressed size of each file listed: **gzip -l** myfiles.gz
-r *directory-name*	Recursively searches for specified directories and compresses all the files in them; the search begins from the current working directory; when used with **gunzip**, compressed files of a specified directory are uncompressed
-v *file-list*	For each compressed or decompressed file, displays its name and the percentage of its reduction in size
-*num*	Determines the speed and size of the compression; the range is from -1 to -9. A lower number gives greater speed, but less compression, resulting in a larger file that compresses and decompresses quickly; -1 gives the quickest compression, but with the largest size; -9 results in a very small file that takes longer to compress and decompress. The default is −6

Table 24-10. *The gzip Options*

You can also compress archived **tar** files. This results in files with the extensions **.tar.gz**. Compressed archived files are often used for transmitting extremely large files across networks.

```
$ gzip myarch.tar
$ ls
myarch.tar.gz
```

You can compress **tar** file members individually using the **tar z** option that invokes **gzip**. With the **z** option, **tar** invokes **gzip** to compress a file before placing it in an archive. Archives with members compressed with the **z** option, however, can neither be updated nor is it possible to add to them. All members must be compressed and all must be added at the same time.

You can also use the **compress** and **uncompress** commands to create compressed files. They generate a file that has a **.Z** extension and use a different compression format than **gzip**. The **compress** and **uncompress** commands are not that widely used, but you may run across **.Z** files occasionally. You can use the **uncompress** command to decompress a **.Z** file. The **gzip** utility is the standard GNU compression utility and should be used instead of **compress**.

Another popular compression utility is **bzip2.** It compresses files using the Burrows-Wheeler block-sorting text compression algorithm and Huffman coding. The command line options are similar to **gzip** by design, but they are not exactly the same. See the **bzip2** Man page for a complete listing. You compress files using the **bzip2** command and decompress with **bunzip2**. The **bzip2** command creates files with the extension **.bz2**. You can use **bzcat** to output compressed data to the standard output. The **bzip2** command compresses files in block and enables you to specify their size (larger blocks give you greater compression). Like **gzip**, you can use **bzip2** to compress **tar** archive files. The following example compresses the **mydata** file into a **bzip** compressed file with the extension **.bz2**.

```
$ bzip2 mydata
$ ls
mydata.bz2
```

To decompress, use the **bunzip2** command on a **bzip** file.

```
$ bunzip2 mydata.bz2
```

Zip is a compression and archive utility modeled on **pkzip,** which was used originally on DOS systems. Zip is a cross-platform utility used on Windows, Mac, MSDOS, OS/2, UNIX, and Linux systems. Zip commands can work with archives created by PKZIP and PKZIP programs and can use Zip archives. You compress a file using the **zip** command. This creates a Zip file with the **.zip** extension. If no files are listed, Zip outputs the compressed data to the standard output. You can also use the –

argument to have Zip read from the standard input. To compress a directory, you include the **-r** option. The first example archives and compresses a file:

```
$ zip mydata
$ ls
mydata.zip
```

The next example archives and compresses the **reports** directory.

```
$ zip -r reports
```

A full set of archive operations is supported. With the **-f** option, you can update a particular file in the zip archive with a newer version. The **-u** option replaces or adds files, and the **-d** option deletes files from the zip archive. Options also exist for encrypting files, and DOS to UNIX end-of-line translations, and including hidden files.

To decompress and extract the Zip file, you use the **unzip** command.

```
$ unzip mydata.zip
```

ADMINISTRATION

The Complete Reference

Linux

Chapter 25

Devices

All the devices, such as printers, terminals, and CD-ROMs, are connected to your Linux operating system through special files called *device files.* Such a file contains all the information your operating system needs to control the specified device. This design introduces great flexibility. The operating system is independent of the specific details for managing a particular device; the specifics are all handled by the device file. The operating system simply informs the device what task it is to perform, and the device file tells it how. If you change devices, you only have to change the device file, not the whole system.

To install a device on your Linux system, you need a device file for it, software configuration such as provided by a configuration tool, and kernel support, usually supplied by a module or already built into the kernel. A extensive number of device files is already set up for different kinds of devices. You usually only need to choose one of these. For kernel support, you may have to load a kernel module or recompile the kernel, both simple procedures. In most cases, support is already built into the kernel. Configuration of your device may be provided by desktop configurations tools, such as the Gnome Control Center, system configuration tool like Linuxconf, or a module configuration interface such as that provided for sound modules.

Device Files

The name of a device file is designed to reflect the task of the device. Printer device files begin with **lp** for "line print." Because you could have more than one printer connected to your system, the particular printer device files are distinguished by two or more numbers or letters following the prefix **lp**, such as **lp0**, **lp1**, **lp2**. The same is true for terminal device files. They begin with the prefix **tty**, for "teletype," and are further distinguished by numbers or letters such as **tty0**, **tty1**, **ttyS0**, and so on. You can obtain a complete listing of the current devices filenames and the devices for which they used from the **kernel.org** Web site at

    http://www.kernel.org/pub/linux/docs/device-list/devices.txt

All of these filenames will be implemented as device files in your **/dev** directory. Here you can find printer, CD-ROM, hard drive, SCSI, and sound device files, along with many others. Certain link files bear common device names that are often linked to the actual device file used. For example, a **/dev/cdrom** symbolic link links to the actual device used for your CD-ROM. If your CD-ROM is an IDE device, it may use the device file **hdc**. In this case, **/dev/cdrom** would be a link to **/dev/hdc**. In effect, **/dev/cdrom** is another name for **/dev/hdc**. You can use **/dev/cdrom** to reference your CD-ROM's device file, instead of **/dev/hdc**. A **/dev/modem** link file also exists for your modem. If your modem is connected to the second serial port, its device file would be **/dev/ttyS1**. In this case, **/dev/modem** would be a link to that device file. Applications can then use **/dev/modem** to access your modem, instead of having to know the actual device file used. A listing of commonly used device links is shown in Table 25-1.

Two types of devices are in Linux: block and character. A *block device*, such as a hard disk, transmits data a block at a time. A *character device,* such as a printer or modem, transmits data one character at a time, or rather as a continuous stream of data, not as separate blocks. Device driver files for character devices have a *c* as the first character in the permissions segment displayed by the `ls` command. Device driver files for block devices have a *b*. In the next example, **lp0** (the printer) is a character device and **hda1** (the hard disk) is a block device.

```
# ls -l hda1 lp0
brw-rw----   1 root      disk      3,   1 Sep  7  1994 hda1
crw-r-----   1 root      daemon    6,   0 Dec 31  1979 lp0
```

Although most distributions include an extensive set of device files already set up for you, you can create your own. You use the **mknod** command to create a device file, either a character or block type. The **mknod** command has the following syntax:

```
mknod   options   device   device-type   major-num   minor-num
```

The device type can be either *b, c, p,* or *u.* As already mentioned, the *b* indicates a block device, and *c* is for a character device. The *u* is for an unbuffered character device, and the *p* is for a FIFO device. Devices of the same type often have the same name, for example, Serial interfaces all have the name *ttyS.* Devices of the same type are then uniquely identified by a number attached to the name. This number has two components: the major number and the minor number. Devices may further have the same major number but, if so, the minor number is always different. This major and minor structure is designed to deal with situations in which several devices may be dependent on one larger device, such as several modems connected to the same I/O card. All would have the same major number that would reference the card, but each modem would have a unique minor number. Both the minor and major numbers are required for block and character devices (*b, c,* and *u*). They are not used for FIFO devices, however.

For example, Linux systems usually provide device files for three parallel ports (lp0–2). If you need more, you can use the **mknod** command to create a new one. Printer devices are character devices and must be owned by the root and daemon. The permissions for printer devices are read and write for the owner and the group, 660 (see Chapter 9 for a discussion of file permissions). The major device number is set to 6, while the minor device number is set to the port number of the printer, such as 0 for LPT1 and 1 for LPT2. Once the device is created, you use **chown** to change its ownership to **root.daemon**. In the next example, a parallel printer device is made on a fourth parallel port, **/dev/lp3**. The **-m** option specifies the permissions, in this case, 660. The device is a character device, as indicated by the *c* argument following the device name. The major number is 6, and the minor number is 3. If you were making a device at **/dev/lp4**, the major number would still be 6, but the minor number would be 4. Once the device is made, the **chown** command then changes the ownership of the parallel printer device to **root.daemon**. Be sure to check if a spool directory has been created for your device. If not, you need to make one.

```
# mknod -m 660 /dev/lp3 c 6 3
# chown root.daemon /dev/lp3
```

Installing and Managing Printers

Setting up a printer interface is fairly simple: determine which device file to use and place printer configuration entries in your **printcap** file. You may also have to set up printing filters. You can use several configuration tools to enable you to set up and configure your printer easily. Red Hat systems provide the **PrintTool** utility.

Most distributions of Linux create three device names for parallel printers automatically during installation: **lp0**, **lp1**, and **lp2**. The number used in these names corresponds to a parallel port on your PC. **lp0** references the LPT1 parallel port usually located at address 0x03bc. **lp1** references the LPT2 parallel port located at 0x0378, and **lp2** references LPT3 at address 0x0278. For a detailed explanation of printer installation, see the **Printing-HOWTO** file in **/usr/doc/HOWTO**.

/dev/mouse	Current mouse device
/dev/tape	Current tape device
/dev/cdrom	Current CD-ROM device
/dev/cdwriter	Current CD-writer device
/dev/scanner	Current scanner device
/dev/modem	Current dialout device, modem port
/dev/root	Current root file system
/dev/swap	Current swap device

Table 25-1. *Device Links*

The Red Hat Print Manager: PrintTool

The **PrintTool** utility provided on Red Hat distributions is an easy interface for setting up and managing your printers. Using only **PrintTool**, you can easily install a printer on your Linux system. You can start **PrintTool** either by selecting its entry in the System menu or clicking its icon in the Red Hat Control Panel. In the PrintTool window, select the Add button. This opens an Edit window that displays several fields in which you enter printer configuration information. In the Names field, enter the names you want to use for the printer. Each name is separated by a |. You should include lp as one of your names. The **lpr** command used without a specified printer name uses the printer named lp (actually the first entry in the **/etc/printcap** file). In the Spool directory fields, the default spool directory is already entered for you. You can change it to another directory if you want. For the Device field, entering **/dev/lp0** specifies the first parallel port, which most printers today use. If you have a serial device, you must use a different device name.

For the Input Filter, you can click Select to display a configure filter window. The PrinterType panel lists printers from which you can choose. A description of the selected driver is displayed in the upper right corner. The Resolution panel lists several possible resolutions. The PaperSize panel lists paper sizes, such as letter and legal. The color depth panel lets you select from the color depths available for that printer. When you finish, click OK to close the window and do the same for the Edit window. You then see your printer listed in the PrintTool window, as shown in Figure 25-1. Choose the Quit item from the

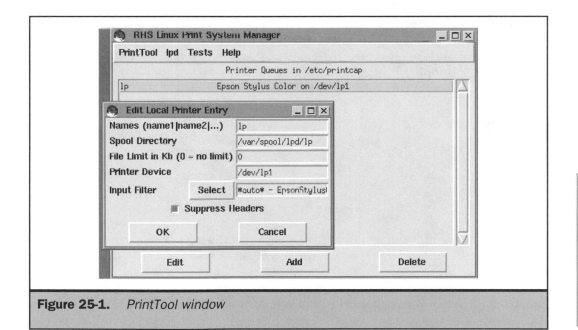

Figure 25-1.   *PrintTool window*

ADMINISTRATION

PrintTool menu to quit **PrintTool**. You are now ready to print. For a detailed explanation of printer installation, see the **Printing-HOWTO** file in **/usr/doc/HOWTO**.

Printer Devices and /etc/printcap

When your system prints a file, it makes use of special directories called *spool directories*. A print job is a file to be printed. When you print a file to a printer, a copy of it is made and placed in a spool directory set up for that printer. The location of the spool directory is obtained from the printer's entry in the **/etc/printcap** file. In the spool directory, two files are made for each print job. One file, which begins with **df,** is the data file containing the copy of the file to be printed. The other file begins with **cf** and is the control file for the print job. This second file contains information about the print job, such as the user to whom it belongs.

The **/etc/printcap** file holds entries for each printer connected to your system. A *printcap entry* holds information, such as the pathname for a printer's spool directory and the device name of the printer port the printer uses. The first field in a printcap entry is a list of possible names for the printer. These are names you can make up yourself, and you can add others if you want. Each name is separated by a |. You use these names to identify the printer when entering various printer commands or options, such as the **-P** option. These names are also used for special shell variables, such as the **PRINTER** variable, used in many initialization scripts.

The fields following the list of names set different fields for your printer. The fields have two-letter names and are usually assigned a value using **=**. These assignments are separated by colons. Three of the more important fields are **lp**, **sd**, and **of**. The **lp** field is set to the device name the printer uses. The **sd** field is set to the pathname of the spool directory, and **of** is set to the particular filter used for this printer. Some have Boolean values and simply list the field name with no assignment for a true value. You can find a complete listing of the printcap fields in the printcap man pages: man 8 printcap. An example of a printcap entry follows.

```
##PRINTTOOL## LOCAL djet500c 600x600 letter {}
 hp1|lp:\
    :sd=/var/spool/lpd/lp:\
    :mx#0:\
    :lp=/dev/lp1:\
    :if=/var/spool/lpd/lp/filter:
```

Instead of making your own entries in the **/etc/printcap** file, you can use the Red Hat **PrintTool** utility, located on your root user desktop, to make them for you automatically.

Printing on your system is handled by a print daemon called lpd, which is constantly running, waiting for print jobs, and then managing their printing procedures. The **lpd** daemon takes its print jobs from a print queue, which you can list using the **lpq** command. The **lpq** command places a job on the print queue, and **lpq** then takes it in turn and prints it. As noted in Chapter 5, **lpq** takes as its argument the name of a file. You can also feed data to **lpq** through the standard input, piping in the data to be printed from another operation. The **-P** option enables you to specify a particular printer. In the next example, the user first prints the file **preface**. Then she uses the **cat** command to generate combined output of the files **intro** and **digest**. This is piped to the **lpq** command, which then prints it. Finally, the user prints the file **report** to the printer with the name **hp1**.

```
$ lpr preface
$ cat intro digest | lpr
$ lpr -Php1 report
```

You can also print directly to the printer by simply redirecting output to the printer's device file. This does not place anything on the print queue. The print operation becomes a command to be immediately executed. However, your system is occupied until the file completes printing. The following example uses this technique to print the **report** file to a printer connected to device **lp1**.

```
$ cat report > /dev/lp1
```

Remote Printers

To install a remote printer, you place remote entries for the printer host and device in the printer's /etc/printcap file entry. An :rm entry identifies the remote host that controls the remote printer and a :rp entry specifies the device name of the remote printer. In the following example, the remote printer is located at **rabbit.mytrek.com** and is called **lp1**.

```
:rm=rabbit.mytrek.com
:rp=lp1
```

You can also use **PrintTool** to set up a remote printer, as shown here:

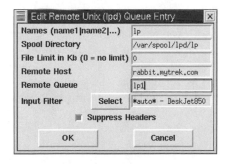

ADMINISTRATION

When you add a printer, you are presented with a dialog box listing several types of printers: Local, Remote UNIX Queue, SMB, and NetWare. For a remote printer, select Remote Queue. This displays a dialog box for configuring the remote printer with entries for the Remote Host and the Remote Queue. For the Remote Host, enter the host name for the system that controls the printer. For the Remote Queue, enter the device name on that host for the printer.

The Linux system controlling the printer should, in turn, list the hosts permitted access to its printer in the **/etc/hosts.lpd** file. For example, the **/etc/hosts.lpd** file on **rabbit.mytrek.com** should hold the host name **turtle.mytrek.com** to enable users on **turtle.mytrek.com** to use its printer.

An SMB remote printer is one located on Windows network. To access an SMB remote printer, you need to install Samba and have the Sever Message Block services enabled using the smbd daemon. Printer sharing must, in turn, be enabled on the Windows network. In the PrintTool SMB configuration dialog box you need to enter the remote system's name, its IP address, the name of the printer, and the printer user name and password. You can then use the **smbclient** (Samba) command to send print jobs to the Window printer.

The Print Queue

To manage the printing jobs on your printer or printers, enter the command **lpc** and press ENTER. You are then given an LPC> prompt at which you can enter **lpc** commands to manage your printers and their jobs. The status command with the name of the printer displays whether the printer is ready, how many print jobs it has, and so on. The **stop** and **start** commands can stop a printer and start it back up.

```
# lpc
lpc> status hp1
hp1|lp1:
    queuing is enabled
    printing is enabled
    1 entry in spool area
```

You can manage the print queue using the **lpq** and **lprm** commands. The **lpq** command lists the printing jobs currently on the print queue. With the **-P** option and the printer name you can list the jobs for a particular printer. If you specify a user name, you can list the print jobs for that user. With the **-l** option, **lpq** displays detailed information about each job. If you want information on a specific job, simply use that job's ID number with **lpq**.

With the **lprm** command, you can remove a printing job from the queue, erasing the job before it can be printed. The **lprm** command takes many of the same options as **lpq**. To remove a specific job, use **lprm** with the job number. To remove all printing jobs for a particular user, enter **lprm** with the user name. To remove all printing jobs for a particular printer, use the **-P** option with the printer name.

The **lprm** command has a special argument indicated by a dash, -, that references all print jobs for the user who issues the command. For example, to remove all your own print jobs, enter **lprm -**. If you logged in as the root user, then **lprm -** removes all print jobs for all printers and users from the print queue, emptying it completely.

You should not use **lprm** to kill a printing job that has already started printing. Instead, you may have to use the **kill** command on the print job process. You can display processes using the **ps -ax** command, and then use **kill** and the number of the process to end it. For a job that is already printing, you see a process for its filter. This is the process to kill.

Table 25-2 shows various printer commands; Table 25-3 includes **lpc** commands.

Printer Management	Description
lpr *options file-list*	Prints a file; copies the file to the printer's spool directory and places it on the print queue to be printed in turn **-P***printer* Prints the file on the specified printer
lpq *options*	Displays the print jobs in the print queue **-P***printer* Prints queue for the specified printer **-l** Prints a detailed listing
lprm *options Printjob-id or User-id*	Removes a print job from the print queue; you identify a particular print job by its number as listed by lpq; if you use *User-id*, it removes all print jobs for that user **-** Removes all print jobs for the logged-in user; if the logged-in user is the root, it refers to all print jobs **-P***printer* Removes all print jobs for the specified printer
lpc	Manages your printers; at the **LPC>** prompt, you can enter commands to check the status of your printers and take other actions

Table 25-2. *Printer Commands*

ADMINISTRATION

Commands	Operation
help [command ...]	Prints a short description of each command
abort printers	Terminates an active spooling daemon on the local host immediately, and then disables printing for the specified printers; use all to indicate all printers
clean printers	Removes any temporary files, data files, and control files that cannot be printed
disable printers	Turns the specified printer queues off; new jobs are not accepted
down printers message	Turns the specified printer queue off, disables printing, and puts message in the printer status file
enable printers	Enables spooling for the listed printers; allows new jobs into the spool queue
quit or exit	Exits from lpc
restart printers	Starts a new printer daemon; used if the printer daemon, lpd, dies, leaving jobs yet to be printed
start printers	Enables printing and starts a spooling daemon for the listed printers
status printers	Displays the status of daemons and queues on the local machine
stop printers	Stops a spooling daemon after the current job completes and disables printing
topq printer [jobnum ...] [user ...]	Places the jobs in the order listed at the top of the printer queue
up printers	Enables everything and starts a new printer daemon; undoes the effects of down

Table 25-3.   *lpc Commands*

Installing and Managing Terminals and Modems

With a multiuser system such as Linux, you might have several users logged in at the same time. Each user would, of course, need his or her own terminal through which to access the Linux system. The monitor on your PC acts as a special terminal called the *console,* but you can add other terminals either through the serial ports on your PC or a special multiport card installed on your PC. The other terminals can be standalone terminals or PCs using terminal emulation programs. For a detailed explanation of terminal installation, see the **Term-HOWTO** file in **/usr/doc/HOWTO**. A brief explanation is provided here.

The serial ports on your PC are referred to as COM1, on up to COM4. These serial ports correspond to the terminal devices **/dev/ttyS0** through **/dev/ttyS3**. Note, several of these serial devices may already be used for other input devices, such as your mouse, and for communications devices, such as your modem. If you have a serial printer, one of these serial devices is already used for that. If you installed a multiport card, you have many more ports from which to choose. For each terminal you add, you must create a character device on your Linux system. As with printers, you use the **mknod** command to create terminal devices. The permissions for a terminal device are 660. *Terminal devices* are character devices with a major number of 4 and minor numbers usually beginning at 64.

Terminal devices are managed by your system using the getty program and a set of configuration files. When your system starts, it reads a list of connected terminals in the **inittab** file, and then executes a **/etc/getty** program for each one. The getty program sets up the communication between your Linux system and a specified terminal. It obtains from the **/etc/gettydefs** file certain parameters, such as speed and the login prompt, as well as any special instructions.

```
# Format: <speed># <init flags> # <final flags> #<login
   string>#<next-speed>
# 38400 fixed baud Dumb Terminal entry
DT38400# B38400 CS8 CLOCAL # B38400 SANE -ISTRIP CLOCAL #@S login:
   #DT38400
```

The **/etc/inittab** file holds instructions for your system on how to manage terminal devices. A line in the **/etc/inittab** file has four basic components: an ID, runlevel, action, and process. Terminal devices are identified by ID numbers, beginning with 1 for the first device. The runlevel at which the terminal operates is usually 1. The action is usually *respawn,* which says to run the process continually. The process is a call to **/etc/getty** with the baud rate and terminal device name. The **/etc/ttys** file associates the type of terminal used with a certain device.

The **/etc/termcap** file holds the specifications for different terminal types. These are the different types of terminals users could use to log in to your system. Your **/etc/termcap** file is already filled with specifications for most of the terminals currently produced. An entry in the **/etc/termcap** file consists of various names that can be used for a terminal separated by a | , and then a series of parameter specifications, each ending in a colon. You find the name used for a specific terminal type here. You can use more to display your **/etc/termcap** file, and then use a search, /, to locate your terminal type. You can set many options for a terminal device. To change these options, use the **stty** command instead of changing configuration files directly. The **stty** command with no arguments lists the current setting of the terminal.

When a user logs in, having the terminal device initialized using the **tset** command is helpful. Usually the **tset** command is placed in the user's **.bash_profile** file and is automatically executed whenever the user logs into the system. You use the **tset** command to set the terminal type and any other options the terminal device requires. A common entry of **tset** for a **.bash_profile** file follows. The **–m** dialup: option prompts the user to enter a terminal type. The type specified here is a default type that is displayed in parentheses. The user presses ENTER to choose the default. The prompt looks like this: TERM=(vt100)?

```
eval `tset -s -Q -m dialup:?vt00`
```

Input Devices

Input devices, such as mice and keyboards, are displayed on several levels. Initial configuration is performed during installation where you select the mouse and keyboard types. You can change that configuration with your administration configuration tool, such as Red Hat Setup (see Chapter 23). Red Hat provides a keyboard configuration tool called **kbdconfig** and a mouse configuration tool called **mouseconfig**. Both can be run from any command line interface. Special configurations also exist for mice and keyboards for X Window Systems, and the KDE and Gnome desktops. You select the keyboard layout and language, as well as configure the speed and display of the mouse.

Installing Sound, Network, and Other Cards

For you to install a new card, your kernel must be configured to support it. Support for most cards is provided in the form of modules that can be dynamically loaded in and attached to the kernel, running as its extension. Installing support for a card is usually a simple matter of loading a module that includes the drives for it. For example, drivers for the SoundBlaster sound card are in the module **sb.o**. Loading this module makes your sound card accessible to Linux. Most distributions automatically detect the cards installed on your system and load the needed modules. If you change cards, you may have to manually load the module you need, removing an older, conflicting one. For example, if you change your Ethernet card, you may have to unload the module for your previous card and load in the one for your new card. Certain utilities, such as **Linuxconf** and **netcfg,** enable you to choose a new Ethernet card and have the module loaded for you. On Red Hat, the **sndconfig** utility provides an interface for selecting a new sound card and loads the module for it automatically. You can, however, load modules manually. The modules section later in this chapter describes this process.

Devices files for most cards are already set up for you in the **/dev** directory. For example, the device name for your sound card is **/dev/audio**. The device name for your Ethernet card begins with **eth,** with the numbering starting from 0, as in **eth0** for the first Ethernet card on your system.

Multimedia Devices: Sound, Video, and DVD

Currently, most Linux sound drivers are developed as part of the Open Sound System and freely distributed as OSS/Free. These are installed as part of Linux distributions, including Red Hat. The OSS device drivers are intended to provide a uniform API for all UNIX platforms, including Linux. They support Sound Blaster and Windows Sound System compatible sound cards (ISA and PCI). OSS is a commercial version called the *Open Sound System* (*OSS*). OSS is also available for a nominal fee and features configuration interfaces for device setup. A listing of the different OSS/Free sound devices is provided in Table 25-4. On Red Hat, you can use the `sndconfig` utility to install most sound cards on Linux. Some sound cards may require more specialized support (see Table 25-5). For sound cards, you can tell what your current sound configuration is by listing the contents of the **/dev/sndstat** file. You can test your card by simply redirecting a sound file to it, as shown here:

```
cat sample.au  >  /dev/audio.
```

The Linux *Musical Instrument Digital Interface* (*MIDI*) and Sound Pages currently at **www.xdt.com/ar/linux-snd** holds links to Web and FTP sites for Linux sound drivers for various sound cards. It also includes links to sites for Linux MIDI and Sound

/dev/sndstat	Sound driver status
/dev/audio	Audio output device
/dev/dsp	Sound sampling device
/dev/mixer	Control mixer on sound card
/dev/music	High-level sequencer
/dev/sequ3encer	Low-level sequencer
/dev/midi	Direct MIDI port

Table 25-4.   *Sound Devices*

software. Currently most Linux sound drivers have been developed as part of the Open Sound System and freely distributed as OSS/Free. These are installed as part of most Linux distributions, including Red Hat. The OSS device drivers are intended to provide a uniform API for all UNIX platforms, including Linux. They support Sound Blaster and Windows Sound System compatible sound cards (ISA and PCI).

The *Advanced Linux Sound Architecture (ALSA)* project is developing a modular sound driver, API, and configuration manager that aims to be a better alternative to OSS, while maintaining compatibility with it. ALSA is a GNU project and is entirely free and its Web site at **www.alsa-project.org** contains extensive documentation, applications, and drivers. Currently under development is the ALSA sound driver, the ALSA Kernel API, the ALSA library to support application development, and the ALSA manager to provide a configuration interface for the driver. ALSA evolved from the Linux Ultra Sound Project.

The Linux Ultra Sound Project has developed drivers for Gravix Ultrasound sound cards. Although Gravis Ultrasound is supported by OSS/Free, the Linux Ultra Sound Project drivers offer many more features. See Table 25-5 for a listing of sites providing sound drivers. Included are drivers for Turtle Beach sound cards and SoundBlaster AWE native support.

Driver Site	Description
Linux MIDI and Sound Pages	Information and links to Linux Sound projects and site: **www.xdt.com/ar/linux-snd**
Advanced Linux Sound Architecture (ALSA)	The Advanced Linux Sound Architecture project (ALSA) is developed on Linux under the GPL: **www.alsa-project.org**
Open Sound System/Free	The standard Linux sound drivers formerly known as USS/Lite, TASD, and Voxware are now called OSS/Free: **www.opensound.com**
Open Sound System/Linux	OSS/Linux is a commercial version of the Linux sound drivers: **www.opensound.com**
Linux Ultra Sound Project	Drivers for the Gravis Ultrasound: **www.perex.cz/~perex/ultra**
Turtle Beach Linux Driver	Unified driver for the Turtle Beach Classic, Pinnacle, Fiji, Tahiti, and Monterey sound cards under Linux

Table 25-5. *Linux Sound Driver Sites*

Driver Site	Description
PC Serial Port MIDI Driver	Linux MIDI driver for IBM-PC serial ports: **http://crystal.apana.org.au/ghansper/midiaxis.html**
Linux AWE 32 Sound Driver	Native support for the SoundBlaster AWE 32/64 soundcards: **http://bahamut.mm.t.u-tokyo.ac.jp/~iwai/midi.html**

Table 25-5. *Linux Sound Driver Sites* (continued)

Several projects are underway to provide TV, Video, and DVD support for Linux (see Table 25-6). The site **linuxtv.org** provides detailed links to DVD, Digital TV (DVD), and Analogue TV Linux projects. The XFree86 version 4.0 with the Xv extensions will include support for video in a window for selected platforms. Several projects have already developed applications. The Video 4 Linux project has created the Video4Linux software package, which enables you to play Mpeg1 video sources on Linux. Video4Linux is included with Linux distributions, including Red Hat. Currently under development is Video for Linux Two (V4L2). This is a separate project that established a set of APIs and standards for handling video devices on Linux, providing a common API for video and tuning sources, teletext, and other TV-related VBI data. V4L2 includes a suite of related driver specifications for different types of video devices and video-related data. It is intended as a replacement for Video for Linux.

Device Name	Type of Device
/dev/video	Video capture interface
/dev/vfx	Video effects interface
/dev/codec	Video codec interface
/dev/vout	Video output interface
/dev/radio	AM/FM radio devices
/dev/vtx	Teletext interface chips
/dev/vbi	Data services interface

Table 25-6. *Video Devices (V4L and V4L2)*

ADMINISTRATION

Drivers for DVD and TV decoders are also under development (see Table 25-7). mga4linux is developing video support for the Matrox Multimedia cards like the Marvel G200. The *General ATI TV and Overlay Software* (*GATOS*) is developing drivers for the currently unsupported features of ATI video cards, specifically TV features. The BTTV Driver Project has developed drivers for the Booktree video chip. Creative Labs sponsors Linux drivers for the Creative line of DVD DXR2 decoders (**opensource.creative.com**).

Modules

Beginning with Linux kernel 2.0, the Linux kernel adopted a modular structure. In earlier kernel versions, support for specific features and devices had to be included directly into the kernel program. Adding support for a new device, say, a new kind of sound card, required you to create a new version of your kernel program that included the code for supporting that device. This involved a sometimes lengthy configuration, followed by compiling and installing the new kernel program, as well as making sure it was called properly when your system booted up.

linuxtv.org	Links to Video, TV, and DVD sites
video4linux	Video for Linux
video4linux 2	Video for Linux Two **millennium.diads.com/bdirks/v4l2.htm**
LiViD	The Linux Video and DVD Project **www.linuxvideo.org**
LinuxDVD	The LinuxDVD Project **linuxdvd.corepower.com**
LSDVD	LSDVD Linux Player Project **www.csh.rit.edu/lsdvd/**
mga4linux	Driver for Matrox Multimedia Cards **www.cs.brandeis.edu/~eddie/mga4linux/**
GATOS	The General ATI TV and Overlay Software **www.core.binghamton.edu/~insomnia/gatos**
BTTV	BTTV Driver Project for cards with Booktree video chips
DVD DXR2	Drivers for Creative DVD DXR2 decoders **opensource.creative.com**.

Table 25-7.   *Video, TV, and DVD Projects and Drivers*

As an alternative to this rebuilding of the kernel, Linux now supports the use of modules. *Modules* are components of the Linux kernel that can be loaded and attached to it as needed. To add support for a new device, you can now simply instruct a kernel to load its module. In some cases, you may have to recompile only that module to provide support for your device. The use of modules has the added advantage of reducing the size of the kernel program. The kernel can load modules in memory only as they are needed. For example, the module for the PPP network interface used for a modem only needs to be used when you connect to an ISP.

The modules your system needs are usually determined during installation, based on the kind of configuration information you provided. For example, if your system uses an Ethernet card whose type you specified during installation, then the system loads the module for that card. You can, however, manually control what modules are to be loaded for your system. This, in effect, enables you to customize your kernel the way you want it to be. You can use several commands, configuration tools, and daemons to manage kernel modules. The 2.2 Linux kernel includes the Kernel Module Loader, which has the capability to load modules automatically as they are needed. In addition, several tools enable you to load and unload modules manually, if you must. Red Hat provides a user interface called kernelcfg that enables you to load and unload modules manually. The Kernel Module Loader uses certain kernel commands to perform the task of loading or unloading modules. The **modprobe** command is a general-purpose command that calls **insmod** to load modules and **rmmod** to unload them. These commands are listed in **Table 25-8**.

The filename for a module has the extension **.o**. Modules reside in the **/lib/modules/***version* directory, where *version* is the version number for your current module. The directory for the 2.2 kernel is **/lib/modules/2.2.5-15**. As you install new kernels on your system, new module directories are generated for them. One trick to access the directory for the current kernel is to use the **uname -r** command to generate the kernel version number. This command needs to have backquotes.

```
cd /lib/modules/'uname -r'
```

In this directory, several subdirectories are where the modules reside. These subdirectories serve to categorize your modules, making them easier to locate. For example, the **net** directory holds modules for your Ethernet cards and the **misc** directory contains sound card modules.

Managing Modules with Red Hat Kernel Configurator

The Red Hat Kernel Configurator utility shown next provides an X interface for loading and unloading modules.

On the Red Hat Control Panel, select the icon that looks like a heart. This opens the Kernel Configurator window that lists all the modules currently loaded. Each entry has three fields: its type, module name, and its arguments. For example, the module 3c59x, which provides support for 3c59x 3Com Ethernet cards, has the type eth0 (the Ethernet interface), 3c59x (its name), and no arguments. You can add new entries by clicking Add. A window opens where you can enter the module type, name, and any arguments. A new entry is not immediately loaded to the kernel. Entries are saved to the **/etc/modules.conf** file. To load the new entry, click Restart to read the **/etc/modules.conf** file, which now has the new entry (replaces the kerneld daemon). To remove a module, select its entry and click Remove. To edit an entry, say, to add arguments, select its entry and click Edit.

Managing Modules with the Module Commands

The **lsmod** command lists the modules currently loaded into your kernel. You can add a new one using the **insmod** command and the module name. With **rmmod,** you can unload a module. See Table 25-8 for kernel module commands. It is often the case, however, that a given module requires other modules to be loaded. For example, the module for the SoundBlaster sound card, **sb.o**, requires the **sound.o** module to be loaded also. Instead of manually trying to determine what modules a given module depends on, you use the **modep** command to detect the dependencies for you. The **modep** command generates a file that lists all the modules on which a given module depends. The **modep** command generates a hierarchical listing, noting what modules should be loaded first and in what order. Then, to load the module, you use the **modprobe** command using that file. **modprobe** reads the file generated by **modep** and loads any dependent modules in the correct order, along with the module you want. You need to execute **modep** with the **-a** option once, before you ever use **modprobe**. Entering **modep -a** creates a complete listing of all module dependencies. This command creates a file called **modules.deb** in the module directory for your current kernel version, **/lib/modules/***version.*

```
modep -a
```

To install a module, you use the **modprobe** command and the module name. You can add any parameters the module may require. The following command installs the SoundBlaster sound module with the IO, IRQ, and DMA values. **modprobe** also supports the use of the * character to enable you to use a pattern to select several modules.

```
modprobe sb io=0x220 irq=5 dma=1
```

You can use the **-l** option to list modules and the **-t** option looks for modules in a specified subdirectory. In the next example, the user lists all modules that begin with 'sound' in the **misc** directory.

```
# modprobe -l -t misc sound*
/lib/modules/2.2.5-15/misc/soundlow.o
/lib/modules/2.2.5-15/misc/soundcore.o
/lib/modules/2.2.5-15/misc/sound.o
```

Options for the **modprobe** command are placed in the **/etc/conf.modules** file. Here, you can enter configuration options, such as default directories and aliases. An alias provides a simple name for a module. For example, the following entry enables you to reference the 3c59x.o Ethernet card module as eth0.

```
alias eth0 3c59x
```

Installing New Modules for the Kernel

The source code for your Linux kernel contains an extensive set of modules, of which only a few are actually used on your system. When you install a new device, you may have to install the kernel module that provides the drivers for it. This involves selecting the module you need from a listing, and then regenerating your kernel modules with the new module included. Then the new module is copied into the module library, installing it on your system. Then you can use **modprobe** to install it manually or to place an entry for it in **modules.conf** to have it loaded automatically. First, make sure you have installed the kernel source code in the **/usr/src/linux** directory (see Chapter 26). If not, simply use **rpm** or an RPM utility like **kpackage** or **gnomerpm** to install the kernel source RPM packages. You can find them in the RPMS directory on your Red Hat CD-ROM. The following command installs the kernel sources.

```
rpm -i kernel-source-2.2.12-20.i386.rpm
```

Now change to the **/usr/src/linux** directory. Then use the **make** command with the xconfig or menuconfig arguments to display the kernel configuration menus, invoking them with the following commands. The **make xconfig** command starts an X Window System interface that needs to be run on your desktop from a terminal window.

```
make xconfig
make menuconfig
```

Using the menus, as described in the next section, select the modules you need. Make sure each is marked as a module, clicking the Module check box in **xconfig** or pressing M for menuconfig. Once the kernel is configured, save it and exit from the configuration menus. Then you create the modules with the following command:

```
make modules
```

This places the modules in the kernel source modules directory: **/usr/src/linux/modules**. You can copy the one you want to the modules directory, **/lib/modules/***version*, where *version* is the version number of your Linux kernel. A simpler approach is to reinstall all your modules, using the following command. This copies all the compiled modules to the **/lib/modules/***version* directory.

```
make modules-install
```

For example, if you want to provide AppleTalk support and your distribution did not create an AppleTalk module or incorporate the support into the kernel directly, then you can use this method to create and install the AppleTalk module. First, check to see if your distribution has already included it. The **appletalk.o** module should be in the **/lib/modules/***version***/misc** directory. If not, you can move to the **/usr/src/linux** directory, run make xconfig, and select AppleTalk as a module. Then generate the modules with the **make modules** command. You could then use the **make modules-install** command to install the new module, along with your other modules. Or, you can use the following command to copy **appletalk.o** to the module directory (**uname -r** is used here to generate the version number for the installed kernel).

```
cp /usr/src/linux/modules/appletalk.o   /lib/modules/'uname -r'/misc
```

Command	Description
lsmod	List modules currently loaded
insmod	Loads a module into the kernel
rmmod	Unloads a module currently loaded
depmod	Creates a dependency file listing all other modules on which the specified module may rely
modprobe	Loads a module with any dependent modules it may also need. Uses the file of dependency listing generated by depmod

Table 25-8. *Kernel Module Commands*

Chapter 26

Red Hat Kernel
Administration

The *kernel* is the core of the operating system, the program that performs operating system functions. The version number for a Linux kernel consists of three segments: the major, minor, and revision numbers. The *major number* increments with major changes in the kernel. The *minor number* indicates stability. *Even numbers* are used for stable releases, whereas *odd numbers* are reserved for development releases, which may be unstable. New features first appear in the development versions. If stability is a concern, waiting for the stable version is best. The *revision number* refers to the corrected versions. As bugs are discovered and corrected, new revisions of a kernel are released. A development kernel may have numerous revisions. For example, kernel 2.2.14 has a major number of 2 and a minor number of 2, with a revision number of 14. On Red Hat systems, another number is added that refers to a Red Hat–specific set of patches applied to the kernel. For Red Hat 6.2, this is 2.2.14-5.0, with 5.0 being the patched number. On systems that support RPM packages, you can use a RPM query to learn what version is installed.

```
rpm -q kernel
```

The Linux kernel is being worked on constantly, with new versions released when they are ready. Red Hat includes the most up-to-date kernel in its releases. Linux kernels are kept at **www.kernel.org**. Also, RPM packages for a new kernel often are available at distribution update sites, such as **ftp.redhat.com**. One reason you may need to upgrade your kernel is to provide support for new hardware or for features not supported by the distribution's version. For example, you may need support for a new device not provided in the distribution's version of the kernel. Certain features may not be included in a distribution's version because they are considered experimental or a security risk. Note, you probably don't need to install a new kernel only to add support for a new device. Kernels provide most device support in the form of modules, of which only those needed are installed with the kernel. Most likely your current kernel has the module you need. You simply have to install it. For this task, see the previous section on Installing New Modules for the Kernel.

You can learn more about the Linux kernel from **www.kernel.org**, the official repository for the current Linux kernels. The most current source code, as well as documentation, is here. For Red Hat systems, **www.redhat.com** also provides online documentation for installing and compiling the kernel on its systems. Several Linux HOWTOs also exist on the subject. You can find the HOWTOS online at **www.linux.org** and at distribution Web sites. The kernel source code software packages also include extensive documentation. Kernel source code files are always installed in the **/usr/src/linux** directory. In this directory, you can find a subdirectory named **Documentation,** which contains an extensive set of files and directories documenting kernel features, modules, and commands. You can also consult the Web site **kernelnotes.org** for the latest information on kernel developments.

To install a new kernel, you need to download the software packages for that kernel to your system. You can download them either from your Linux distribution's FTP sites or from **www.kernel.org**. You can install a new kernel either by downloading a binary version from your distribution's Web site and installing it, or by downloading the source code, compiling the kernel, and then installing the resulting binary file. For Red Hat, the binary version of the kernel is provided in the RPM package. You can install a new kernel using the Red Hat Package Manager, just as you would any other RPM software package. The source code version is available either from your distribution site, such as **ftp.redhat.com** for Red Hat, or from **www.kernel.org**. Wherever you download a kernel version from, it is always the same. The source code downloaded for a particular kernel version from Red Hat is the same as the one for **www.kernel.org**. Patches for that version can be applied to any distribution.

Precautionary Steps

You should retain a copy of your current kernel, so you can use it again in case something goes wrong with the new one. This simply involves making a backup copy of the kernel file. The kernel file has different names on various distributions. On Red Hat, it is called **vmlinuz** with the version number attached as in **vmlinuz2.2.14-5.0,** but others may call it **zImage**. On Red Hat, **vmlinuz2.2.14-5.0** is located in the **/boot** directory. Also there is a file called **/boot/vmlinuz,** which is only a symbolic link to the actual kernel file (on other distributions, the **vmlinuz** file may be the actual boot file). The new kernel is installed with a filename using its own version number. To be on the safe side, however, making a backup copy may be advisable. You should also make a backup of the System.map file. In the case of kernel 2.2.14-5.0, this would be System.map-2.2.14-5.0. If you are going to compile the same version of the kernel, making a few changes, then you should also back up your modules located in the **/lib/modules**/*version* directory, where version is the version number of the kernel. For version 2.2.14-5.0, the libraries are located in **/lib/modules/2.2.14-5.0.** If you are compiling a different version, those libraries are placed in a new directory named with the new version number.

```
cp /boot/vmlinuz2.2.14-5.0  /boot/vmlinuz2.2.14-5.0.back
```

If you are using LILO, you should create a new entry for the old kernel in the **lilo.conf** file. You then make an entry for the new kernel in the **lilo.conf** file. Leaving the entry for the old kernel is advisable, in case something goes wrong with the new kernel. This way, you can always reboot and select the old kernel. In **lilo.conf,** add a new entry, similar to the one for the old kernel, which references the new kernel in its image line. The **lilo.conf** entry would look something like the following code. Be sure to execute the lilo command to update LILO with the new **lilo.conf** entries. You could then use the label oldlinux2.2-20 at the LILO prompt to launch the old kernel.

```
image = /boot/vmlinuz2.2-20.back
    label = oldlinux2.2-20
```

```
root = /dev/hda3
read-only
```

Also advisable is to have a boot disk ready, just in case something goes wrong with the installation. On Red Hat systems, you can create a boot disk using the **mkbootdisk** utility. Examine your **lilo.conf** file to learn the name of the boot image you are currently loading. The boot image is in the line beginning with image= as in the following code. On Red Hat systems, the name of the boot file is **/boot/vmlinuz** (which is a link to the boot file) but, on other systems, the name of the boot file may be **/vmlinuz** or **zImage**. Use the boot image file to create your boot disk.

```
mkbootdisk --device /boot/vmlinuz
```

Installing a Distribution Kernel Binaries and Source: RPM

You can obtain RPM packages for the Linux kernel from your distribution's update sites. For example, to download a new kernel for Red Hat, locate the kernel RPM packages from **updates.redhat.com** or its mirror sites. A series of RPM packages are there, all beginning with the term *kernel*. There are also nonkernel packages you may need, which contain updated system configuration files used by the new kernel. As an example, the kernel packages for the 2.2 kernel are listed in the following code. Only install one of the **kernel-*version*-i*x*86** packages. Choose the one for your machine, for example, i686 for a Pentium II, i586 for a Pentium, and i386 for other PCs.

```
kernel-2.2.14-5.0.i386.rpm
kernel-2.2.14-5.0.i586.rpm
kernel-2.2.14-5.0.i686.rpm
kernel-BOOT-2.2.14-5.0.i386.rpm
kernel-doc-2.2.14-5.0.i386.rpm
kernel-headers-2.2.14-5.0.i386.rpm
kernel-ibcs-2.2.14-5.0.i386.rpm
kernel-pcmcia-cs-2.2.14-5.0.i386.rpm
kernel-smp-2.2.14-5.0.i386.rpm
kernel-smp-2.2.14-5.0.i586.rpm
kernel-smp-2.2.14-5.0.i686.rpm
kernel-source-2.2.14-5.0.i386.rpm
kernel-utils-2.2.14-5.0.i386.rpm
kernelcfg-0.5-5.i386.rpm
initscripts-5.00-1.i386.rpm.
```

```
mkinitrd-2.4.1-2.i386.rpm
SysVinit-2.78-5.i386.rpm.
```

To make sure a kernel RPM package was downloaded without any errors, you can use the **rpm** command with the **-K «—nopgp** options to check it.

```
rpm -K --nopgp *rpm
```

You are now ready to install the new kernel. First, install any nonkernel support packages. In Red Hat, these currently include mkinitrd, SysVinit, and iniscripts. Use the **-Uvh** option to update those packages.

```
# rpm -Uvh mkinitrd*rpm SysVinit*rpm initscripts*rpm
```

Installing the source code and headers for the kernel is also essential. You use the source code to generate any modules and tailor the kernel to your own needs. For example, you can use the source code to generate modules containing devices drivers for any uncommon devices you may have installed.

```
# rpm -Uvh kernel-headers-2.2.14-5.0.i386.rpm \
    kernel-source-2.2.14-5.0.i386.rpm
```

You can now install the kernel. On Red Hat systems, you install the kernel, kernel-ibcs, and the kernel-pcmia-cs packages. As a safety precaution, it is advisable to preserve your old kernel, in case the new one does not work out for some reason. This involves installing with the install (**-i**) instead of the update(**-U**) option, creating a separate RAM disk for the new kernel, and then modifying **lilo.conf** to have LILO start up using the new kernel.

```
# rpm -ivh kernel-2.2.14-5.0.i386.rpm kernel-ibcs 2.2.14-5.0.i386.rpm \
    kernel-pcmcia-cs-2.2.14-5.0.i386.rpm
```

On Red Hat Linux, kernels are installed in the **/boot** directory. Performing an **ls -l** operation on this directory lists all the currently installed kernels. A file for your old kernel and a file for your new one now exist, as well as a link file called **vmlinuz,** which links to the new kernel file. If you took the precautions described in the previous section, you may have already renamed the older kernel. On Red Hat, if you are using LILO, you needn't change the **lilo.conf** file because the entry to invoke the kernel still references the **/boot/vmlinuz** link, which now points to the new kernel. Red Hat boots the kernel using the **/boot/vmlinux** link to the kernel file. In your **lilo.conf** file, the image line for the kernel file references this link.

```
image = /boot/vmlinuz
```

Installing Compressed Archives: tar.gz

You can also download the compressed archive from **www.kernel.org** and its mirror sites. In this case, you first decompress and extract the archive with the following commands. *vnum* is the version number.

```
cd /usr/src
gzip -cd linux-2.2.vnum.tar.gz | tar xfv -
```

For some releases, you can simply update your current kernel source code files using patches. A *patch* modifies a source code file, making required changes. To install a patch, download the patch file, and then execute the following command. The patch file is first decompressed, and then the **patch** command implements the changes.

```
cd /usr/src
gzip -cd patchvnum.gz | patch -p0
```

You may have to implement several patches, depending on how out-of-date your kernel is. In this case, you must execute a patch operation for each patch file needed. Patches need to be applied in sequence. The latest patch does not include any previous ones. So to apply patch 2.2.12, you would first have to apply patch 2.2.11. Or, you can use the patch-kernel script, which determines your kernel version and applies the patches needed.

```
cd /usr/src
linux/scripts/patch-kernel
```

Before you can install the kernel, you have to configure and compile it, as discussed in the next section.

Compiling the Kernel

You can compile a kernel using the Linux kernel source code. One advantage to compiling the kernel is you are able to customize its configuration, selecting particular devices you want supported by the kernel or the kind of networking support you want.

You can have more control over exactly what your operating system can support. You can obtain the most recent version of the source code from **www.kernel.org** or **www.linuxhq.com**. RPM packages of kernel sources are also available. If you are downloading a compressed archive (**.tar.gz**) package, be sure to unpack it in the **/usr/src** directory. The archive extracts a directory named **linux** that holds the source code files. This way, the files are located in the **/usr/src/linux** directory. Links are already set up in the **/usr/include** directory to source files in the **/usr/src/linux** directory. They expect to find the source code in **/usr/src/linux**.

Once the source is installed, then you must configure the kernel. Configuration consists of determining the features for which you want to provide kernel-level support. This includes drivers for different devices, such as sound cards and SCSI devices. This process is referred to as *configuring the kernel*. You can configure features as directly included in the kernel itself or as modules the kernel can load as they are needed. You can also specifically exclude features. Features incorporated directly into the kernel make for a larger kernel program. Features set up as separate modules can also be easily updated. Documentation for many devices that provide sound, video, or network support can be found in the **/usr/doc** directory. Check the kernel-doc package to find a listing of the documentation provided.

```
rpm -ql kernel-doc
```

You can configure the kernel using one of several available configuration tools: config, menuconfig, and xconfig. They perform the same configuration tasks, but use different interfaces. The *config* tool is a simple configure script providing line-based prompts for different configuration options. The *menuconfig* tool provides a cursor-based menu, which you can still run from the command line. Menu entries exist for different configuration categories, and you can pick and choose the ones you want. To mark a feature for inclusion in the kernel, move to it and press the SPACEBAR. An asterisk appears in the empty parenthesis to the left of the entry. If you want to make it a module, press M and an *M* appears in the parenthesis. The *xconfig* tool runs on a window manager and provides a window interface with buttons and menus. You can use your mouse to select entries. A menu of configuration categories are listed as buttons you can click.

You start a configuration tool by preceding it with the **make** command. Be sure you are in the **/usr/src/linux** directory. The process of starting a configuration tool is a **make** operation that uses the Linux kernel Makefile. The xconfig tool should be started from a Terminal window on your window manager. The menuconfig and config tools are started on a shell command line. The following example lists commands to start xconfig, menuconfig, or config.

```
make xconfig
make menuconfig
make config
```

The xconfig tool opens a Linux Kernel Configuration window listing the different configuration categories (see Figure 26-1). Buttons at the right of the screen are used to save the configuration or to copy it to a file, as well as to quit. Clicking an entry opens a window that lists different features you can include. Three check boxes to the left of each entry enable you to choose to have a feature compiled directly into the kernel, created as a separate module that can be loaded at run time, or not included at all. As a rule, features in continual use, such as network and file system support, should be compiled directly into the kernel. Features that could easily change, such as sound cards, or features used less frequently, should be compiled as modules.

The xconfig and menuconfig tools provide excellent context-sensitive help for each entry. To the right of an entry is a Help button. Click it to display a detailed explanation of what that feature does and why you would include it either directly or as a module, or even exclude it. When in doubt about a feature, always use the Help button to learn exactly what it does and why you would want to use it.

In most cases, you should make sure your kernel can load modules. Click the Loadable Modules Support button to display a listing of several module management options (see Figure 26-2). Make sure Enable Loadable Module Support is Yes. This feature allows your kernel to load modules as they are needed. Kernel Daemon Support should also be Yes, as this allows your daemons, like your Web server, to load any modules they

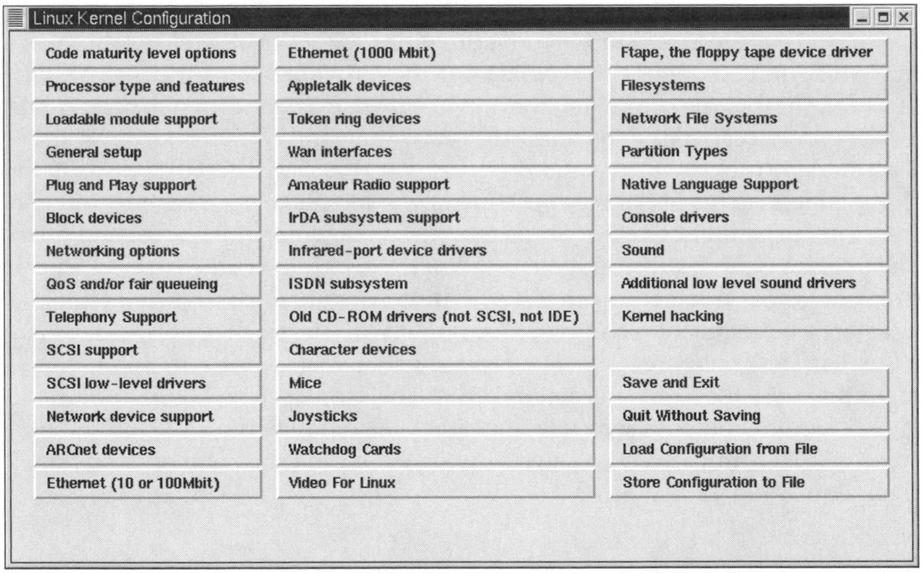

Figure 26-1. *The xconfig Linux kernel configuration tool*

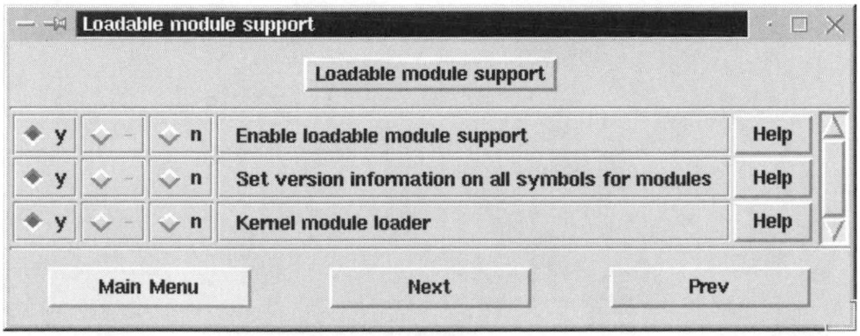

Figure 26-2. *Loadable modules support*

may need. The Set Version Information entry enables you to use any modules set up for previous kernels.

The Processor type and features window enables you to set up support for your particular system. Here, you select the type of processor you have (486, 586, 686, and so forth), as well as the amount of maximum memory your system supports (see Figure 26-3). You also select support for math emulation and systems with multiple processors here.

The General Setup window enables you to select general features, such as math emulation, networking, and PCI BIOS support, Parallel Port device support, as well as support for ELF and a.out binaries (see Figure 26-4).

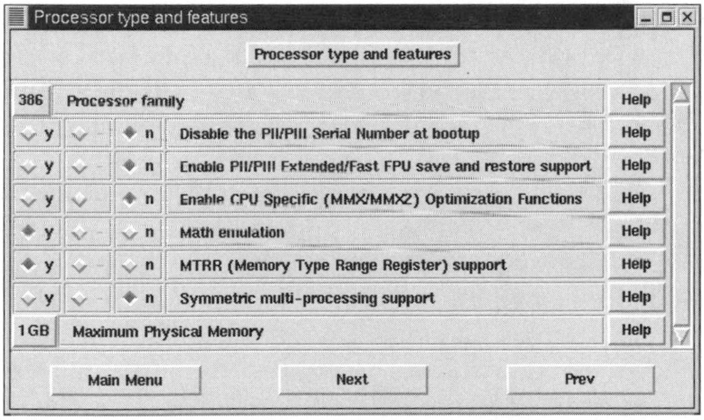

Figure 26-3. *Processor*

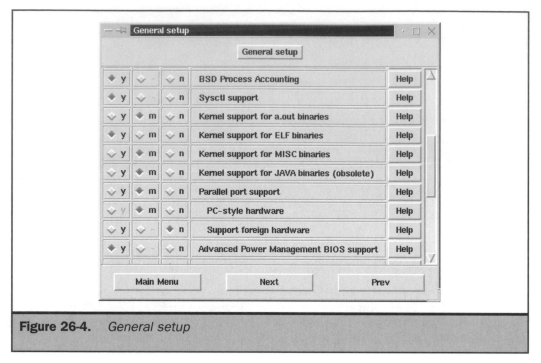

Figure 26-4.   *General setup*

The Block Devices window lists entries that enable support for your IDE floppy and hard drive. Special features, such as RAM disk support and the loopback device for mounting CD-ROM image files, are also there.

The Networking Options window, shown in Figure 26-5, lists an extensive set of networking capabilities. The TCP/IP Networking entry must be set to enable any kind of Internet networking. Here, you can specify features that enable your system to operate as a gateway, firewall, or router. Network Aliasing enables support for IP aliases. Support also exists for other kinds of networks, including AppleTalk and IPX. AppleTalk must be enabled if you want to use NetaTalk to connect to a Macintosh system on your network.

If you have any SCSI devices on your system, make sure the entries in the SCSI support window are set to Yes. You enable support for SCSI disks, tape drives, and CD-ROMs here. The SCSI Low-Level Drivers window displays an extensive list of SCSI devices currently supported by Linux. Be sure the ones you have are selected.

The Network Device Support window lists several general features for network device support. The following windows list support for particular types of network devices, including Ethernet (10 or 100Mbit) devices, Token Ring devices, WAN interfaces, and AppleTalk devices. Many of these devices are created as modules you can load as needed. You can elect to rebuild your kernel with support for any of these

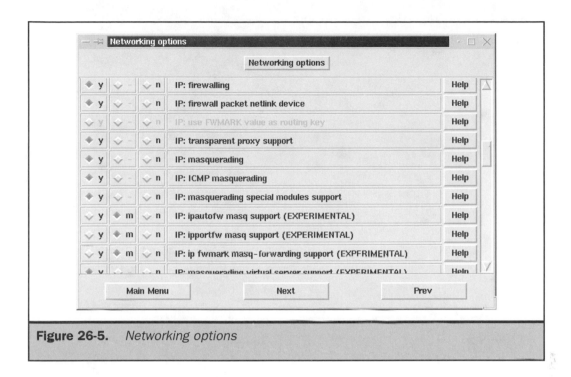

Figure 26-5. *Networking options*

devices built directly into the kernel. Figure 26-6 shows the Ethernet (10 or 100Mbit) window listing Ethernet devices. Notice they are built as separate modules.

The Filesystems window, shown in Figure 26-7, lists the different types of file systems Linux can support. These include DOS, VFAT (Windows 95), and ISO9660 (CD-ROM) file systems. Network file systems, such as NFS, SMB (Samba), and NCP (NetWare), HFS (Macintosh), and NTFS (Windows NT—read-only with 2.2) are also listed. Note, the Linux file system type, ext2fs, must be included in the kernel, not compiled as a module.

The Character Devices window lists features for devices such as your keyboard, mouse, and serial ports. Support exists for both serial and bus mice. The Video For Linux window includes the Video for Linux support for TV and video display for several Video PC cards and chipsets (see Chapter 26). The Sound window lists different sound cards supported by the kernel. Select the one on your system. You also must provide the IRQ, DMA, and Base I/0 your sound card uses. These are compiled as separate modules, some of which you could elect to include directly in the kernel if you want (see Figure 26-8). The Kernel Hacking window lists features of interest to programmers who want to modify the kernel code. You can have the kernel include debugging information.

Once you set your options, save your configuration. You can also make a backup copy by clicking Save To File. Now that the configuration is ready, you can compile

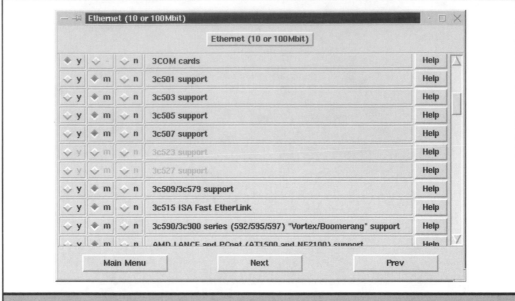

Figure 26-6. *Ethernet (10 or 100Mbit)*

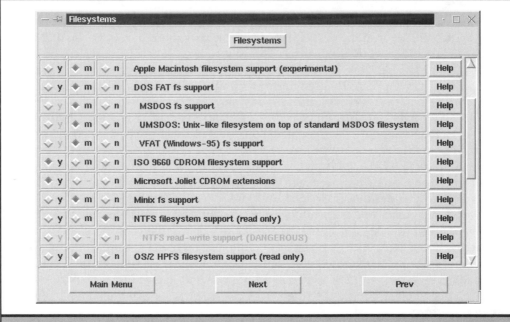

Figure 26-7. *Filesystems window*

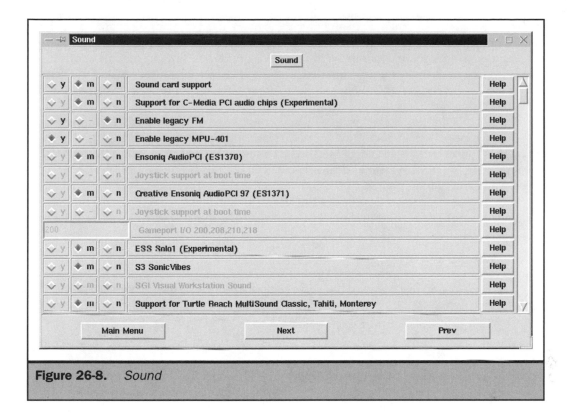

Figure 26-8.   *Sound*

your kernel. You first need to generate a dependency tree to determine what part of the source code to compile, based on your configuration. Use the following command:

```
make dep
```

A good idea is also to clean up any stale object and dependency files that may remain from a previous compilation. Use the following command to remove such files:

```
make mrproper
```

You can use several options to compile the kernel. The **zImage** option simply generates a kernel file called **zImage** and places it in the **/usr/src/linux/arch** directory. For Intel systems, you find **zImage** in the i386/boot subdirectory, **/user/src/linux/arch/ i386/boot**. The install option both generates the kernel file and installs it on your system, as either **vmlinuz** or **zImage**. The **zlilo** option installs the kernel file, as well, but also runs LILO to update LILO. The **zlilo** option is designed for use with systems that run LILO. To install a kernel file generated by zImage manually, copy the **zImage** file to the directory where the kernel resides and give it the name used on your distribution, such as **/vmlinuz** for Red Hat. Remember to first back up the old kernel file.

The `compile` options operate slightly differently depending on the distribution kernel source packages you downloaded. The Red Hat kernel sources install the kernel file to the boot directory and set up a link to **/boot/vmlinuz** for both the `install` and `zlilo` options.

In addition, another set of corresponding options are available that enable you to generate a more efficient and larger kernel. These options begin with the letter *b*. The `bzImage` option creates a kernel file called **bzImage**. The `bzlilo` option both install the kernel file on your system and runs LILO. You should use these options if you receive an error saying your kernel is too large.

The following command compiles the kernel, installs it on your system, and runs LILO for you. To install and update LILO, use the following.

```
make zlilo
```

If you receive an error saying the kernel is too large, try using a *b* version of the option, such as **bzlilo**.

```
make bzlilo
```

This creates the kernel, but not the modules—those features of the kernel to be compiled into separate modules. To compile your modules, use the **make** command with the modules argument.

```
make modules
```

To install your modules, use the **make** command with the **modules_install** option. This installs the modules in the **/lib/modules/***version-num* directory, where *version-num* is the version number of the kernel. Making a backup copy of the old modules before you install the new ones may be advisable.

```
make modules_install
```

Other **make** options are listed in Table 26-1.

LILO Configurations

If you are using LILO, you can configure your system to enable you to start any of your installed kernels. As seen in the "Precautionary Steps" section, you can create an added entry in the **lilo.conf** file for your old kernel. As you install new kernel versions, you

Configuration Tools	Description
config	Line-based interface for kernel configuration
menuconfig	Screen-based interface for kernel configuration
xconfig	X Window System interface for kernel configuration
Maintenance Options	
checkhelp	Checks configuration for options not documented
checkconfig	Checks source tree for missing header files
clean	Removes old object files and dependencies
mrproper	Removes old object files and dependencies
Compiling Options	
zImage	Creates the kernel file called **zImage** located in the **/usr/src/linux/arch** or **arch/i386/boot** directory
install	Creates the kernel and installs it on your system
zlilo	Creates the kernel, installs it on your system, and runs lilo
zdisk	Creates a kernel file and installs it on a floppy disk (creates a boot disk)
bzImage	Creates the kernel file and calls it **bzImage**
bzlilo	Creates and installs the kernel and runs lilo
bzdisk	Creates the kernel and installs it on a floppy disk (creates a boot disk)
Module Options	
modules	Creates kernel modules
modules-install	Installs kernel modules in the **/lib/modules** directory

Table 26-1. *Kernel Compile Options, Use As Arguments to the Make Command in /usr/src/linux*

could simply add more entries, enabling you to use any of the previous kernels. For example, you could install a developmental version of the kernel, along with a current stable version, while keeping your old version. In the image line for each entry, you would specify the filename of the kernel. Whenever you add a new entry, be sure to execute the `lilo` command to update LILO. Whenever you install the kernel on Red Hat using the RPM kernel package, the /boot/vmlinuz link is automatically changed to the new kernel. You can still create another LILO entry for your older kernel. In the next example, the **lilo.conf** file contains entries for two Linux kernels, one using the standard /boot/vmlinuz link, as well as windows.

/etc/lilo.conf

```
boot = /dev/hda
install = /boot/boot.b
message = /boot/message
prompt
timeout = 200
default = win
image = /boot/vmlinuz
        label = linux
        root = /dev/hda3
        read-only
image = /boot/vmlinuz-2.0.36
        label = linux-2.0
        root = /dev/hda3
        read-only
other = /dev/hda1
        label = win
        table = /dev/hda
```

Module RAM Disks

If your system requires certain modules to be loaded when you boot, then you may have to create a RAM disk for them. For example, if you have SCSI hard drivers or CD-ROMs, the SCSI drivers for them are often held in modules that are loaded whenever you start up your system. These modules are stored in a RAM disk from which the startup process reads. If you create a new kernel that needs to load modules to start up, then you must create a new RAM disk for those modules. When you create a new kernel, you also need to create its modules. You place the modules needed for startup, such as SCSI hard drive modules, in a new RAM disk. In the **lilo.conf** file, add an entry to load this RAM disk. You only need to create a new RAM disk if your kernel has to load modules at startup. If, for example, you use a SCSI hard drive, but you incorporated SCSI hard drive and CD-ROM support (including support for the specific model) directly into your kernel, you needn't set up a RAM disk. Support for IDE hard drives and CD-ROMs is already incorporated directly into the kernel.

If you need to create a RAM disk, you can use the **mkinitrd** command to create a RAM disk image file or create a RAM disk device. See the man pages for **mkinitrd** and RAM disk documentation for more details. In the **lilo.conf** segment for the new kernel, you would place a initrd entry specifying the new RAM disk.

```
# mkinitrd /boot/initrd-2.2.14-5.0.img 2.2.14-5.0
```

In your **lilo.conf** file, a initrd entry would exist for the kernel, specifying the RAM disk to use.

```
image=/boot/vmlinuz-2.2.14-5.0
          label=linux
          root=/dev/hda3
          initrd=/boot/initrd-2.2.14-5.0.img
          read-only
```

Chapter 27

The X Window System
and XFree86

653

Linux and UNIX systems use the same standard underlying graphics utility known as the *X Window System,* also known as *X* or *X11.* This means, in most cases, an X-based program can run on any of the window managers and desktops. X-based software is often found at Linux or UNIX FTP sites in directories labeled **X11**. You can download these packages and run them on any window manager running on your Linux system. Some may already be in the form of Linux binaries that you can download, install, and run directly. Netscape is an example. Others are in the form of source code that can easily be configured, compiled, and installed on your system with a few simple commands. Some applications, such as Motif applications, may require special libraries.

The X Window System is designed for flexibility—you can configure it in various ways. You can run the X Window System on almost all the video cards currently available. The X Window System is not tied to any specific desktop interface. It provides an underlying set of graphical operations that user interface applications such as window managers, file managers, and even desktops can use. A window manager uses these operations to construct widgets for manipulating windows, such as scroll bars, resize boxes, and close boxes. Different window managers can construct them to appear differently, providing interfaces with different appearances. All window managers work on the X Window System. You can choose from variety of different window managers, and each user on your system can run a different window manager, each using the same underlying X Window System graphic operations. You can even run X programs without any window or file managers.

To run the X Window System, you need to install an X-Windows server that works for your video card. A free version of X-Windows server software, known as *XFree86,* is used on most Linux systems, though commercial versions are available from MetroLink (**www.metrolink.com**) and Accelerated X. Once you install the XFree86 server appropriate for your system's video card, you must provide configuration information about your monitor, mouse, and keyboard. This information is then used in a configuration file called **/etc/X11/XF86Config**, which includes technical information best generated by an X Window System configuration program, such as Xconfigurator or XF86Setup. When you configured the X Window System when you installed your system, this file was automatically generated. On Red Hat systems, you can access Xconfigurator through the Red Hat Setup utility (see Chapter 3).

You can also configure your own X interface using the **.xinitrc** and **/etc/X11/xinit/xinitrc** configuration files where window managers, file managers, and initial X applications can be selected and started. And, you can use a set of specialized X commands to configure your root window, load fonts, or configure X Window System resources, such as setting the color of window borders. You can also download X utilities from online sources that serve as Linux mirror sites, usually in their **/pub/Linux/X11** directory. If you have to compile an X application, you may have to use special procedures, as well as install support packages. An official source for X Window System news, tools, and window managers is **www.X11.org.** Here you can find detailed information about X Window System features, along with compliant desktops and window managers.

The X Window System was developed and is maintained by *The Open Group* (*TOG*), a consortium of over a hundred companies including Sun, HP, IBM, Motorola, Intel, and Microsoft (**www.opengroup.org**). Development is currently managed by the X.org group (**www.X.org**) on behalf of the TOG. *X.org* is a nonprofit organization that maintains the existing X Window System code. X.org periodically provides free official Window System update releases to the general public. It controls the development of the X11R6 specifications, working with appropriate groups to revise and release updates to the standard, as required. The newest release is currently X11R6.4. *XFree86* is a free distributed version of X Window System servers used on most Linux systems. XFree86 has plans to incorporate X11R6.4 into its XFree86-4.0 release.

The X Protocol

The *X protocol* was developed for UNIX systems in the mid-1980s to provide a network-transparent graphical user interface. The X protocol organizes display operations into a client and server relationship, in which a client submits display requests to a server. The client is known as an *X client,* and the server, as an *X server.* The client, in this case, is an application and the server is a display. This relationship separates an application from the server. The application acts as a client sending requests to the server, which then does the actual work of performing the requested display operation. This has the advantage of letting the server interact with the operating system and its devices, whereas the application need know nothing of those details. An application operating as an X client can display on any system that uses an X server. In fact, a remote X client can send requests to have an X server on a local machine perform certain display operations. In effect, the X server/client relationship is, in a sense, inverted from the way we normally think of servers. Usually, several client systems access a single server. In the X server model, you would have each system operating as an X server who could access a single system that holds X client programs.

XFree86

The *XFree86 Project* (**www.xfree86.org**) is a nonprofit organization that provides free X Window System servers and supporting materials for several operating systems on PCs and other microcomputers. The X servers, client programs, and documentation supplied by the XFree86 Project are commonly referred to as *XFree86.* The XFree86 servers are available free and include source code. The project is funded entirely by donations.

The XFree86 servers support a wide range of video cards and monitors. Servers exist for Monochrome, VGA and Super VGA, and accelerated video cards. In addition, a series of servers is designed for accelerated video cards, a server for each chipset.

Table 27-1 lists XFree86 directories, and Table 27-2 lists the current XFree86 servers. For current updated information, access the XFree86 Web site at **www.xfree86.org** or **www.x11.org**. You can also consult the XFree86 documentation in the **/usr/X11R6/ lib/X11/doc** directory, which contains files for the specific servers available, as well as types of cards supported. The **AccelCards** file lists all the hardware currently supported, including chipsets, while the **Monitors** file lists monitor configurations. Also, you can consult the man pages for the different driver types. The driver types and the associated man pages are listed in the man pages. XFree86 configuration tools, such as Xconfigurator, XF86Setup, and SaX, make configuring your video card and monitor a simple process. They keep on hand an extensive list of video cards and monitors provided by Xfree86 from which you can select your own. If your video card or monitor are quite new, however, they may not be on this list. If this is the case, you need to enter certain hardware specifications, such as horizontal sync. If you must do this, be careful to enter the correct information. The wrong settings could damage both your card and your monitor.

Video Cards	**Man Pages**
Accelerated cards	XF86_Accel
Monochrome cards	XF86_Mono
VGA cards	XF86_VGA16
SVGA cards	XF86_SVGA

The XFree86 servers you specified when you installed your system are automatically installed. Most standard and accelerated graphics cards are supported by the SVGA server, XF86_SVGA. If you are using a simple monochrome or VGA card, you use the XF86_Mono or XF86_VGA generic server. A few accelerated graphics cards are supported by specialized servers, such as the S3 and ATI's Mach64 chips. For these, you first must determine what chipset is used. Consult the manual or documentation that comes with the card. For example, if you have an S3 chipset on your graphics video card, you would use the XFree86_S3 package. In a few cases, you may need to install such a server manually, say, if you change your card. On distributions such as Red Hat, which support RPM packages, you can use an RPM package manager, such as kpackage or GnomeRPM. You can also use the **rpm -i** command to install the package from a shell command line. Compressed tar archives are also available. Each package that contains an XFree server starts with the term XFree86 and you have to install the package appropriate for your graphics card. Most recent video cards are included in the XF86_SVGA server, while older video cards are continually being integrated into this server with new releases. For example, the S3 ViRGE chip (Diamond Stealth 3-D series) now uses the SVGA server, instead of the separate S3V server it once used. You can obtain a current listing of the graphics cards supported by

XFree86 organized by the different server packages at the X11 and XFree86 Web sites, **www.X11.org** and **www.xfree86.org**.

```
rpm -i XFree86_S3-3.3-3.i386.rpm
```

Be sure to check for new releases of XFree86 servers periodically at the XFree86 Web site. You can download the new releases from there or from your distribution's update sites, such as **updates.redhat.com**. If you have a recent card not yet supported by XFree86, you may find a server for it at the XSuSE Web site, at **www.suse.de/en/support/xsuse/.** XSuSE is a special service provided by the SuSE Linux distributor in close association with XFree86 to develop XFree86 servers for cards not yet supported by a current XFree86 release. When a new XFree86 release comes out, these servers are then incorporated into it. The server packages begin with the name Xfcom, as in Xfcom_Matrox for Matrox graphics cards. You can obtain a current listing of these servers and the cards they support at the X11 and XSuSE Web sites.

In addition to the servers, XFree86 includes support programs and development libraries. The entire XFree86 collection is installed in various directories, beginning with the pathname **/usr/X11R6**. Directories are here for X programs, development files, libraries, man pages, and documentation. Configuration files are placed in the **/etc/X11** directory. Applications written to support *X* usually install in the **/usr/X11R6/bin** directory. You can also find the XFree86 servers and support programs here.

/usr/X11R6/bin	Programs (X Window System clients and servers)
/usr/X11R6/include	Development files
/usr/X11R6/lib	Libraries
/usr/X11R6/man	man pages
/usr/X11R6/lib/X11/doc	Documentation
/etc/X11	Configuration files
/usr/X11R6/lib/X11/	Contains subdirectories for window manager program functions

Table 27-1.   *XFree86 Directories*

Server	Type
Xfree86_SVGA	Color SVGA server. Includes drivers for most video cards.
Xfree86_VGA16	16-color SVGA and VGA nonaccelerated server
Xfree86_Mono	Monochrome nonaccelerated server
Xfree86_S3	S3 accelerated server
Xfree86_S3V	Use SVGA
Xfree86_I128	Number 9 Imagine 128 accelerated server
Xfree86_8514	8514/A accelerated server
Xfree86_Mach8	ATI Mach8 accelerated server
Xfree86_Mach32	ATI Mach32 chipset accelerated server
Xfree86_P9000	Weitek accelerated server
Xfree86_W32	ET4000/W32 accelerated server
Xfree86_AGX	IIT AGX accelerated server
Xfree86_Mach64	ATI Mach64 chipset accelerated server
Xfree86_3Dlabs	3Dlabs server

Table 27-2.   *XFree86 Servers (Version 3.3.3)*

XFree86 Configuration: /etc/X11/XF86Config

The XFree86 servers provide a wide range of hardware support, but it can be challenging to configure. You can consult the XFree86-HOWTO document at **www.linux.org** or in the **/usr/doc/HOWTO** directory for most distributions. There are also man pages for XFree86 and XF86Config, and documentation and FAQs are available at **www.xfree86.org**. The configuration file used for your XFree86 server is called **XF86Config**, located in the **/etc/X11** directory. **XF86Config** contains all the specifications for your graphics card, monitor, keyboard, and mouse. To configure the **XF86Config** file, you need specific information on hand about your hardware. For your monitor, you must know the horizontal and vertical sync frequency ranges and bandwidth. For your graphics card, you have to know the chipset and you may even need to know the clocks. For your mouse, you should know whether it is Microsoft-compatible or some other brand, such as Logitech. Also, know the port to which your mouse is connected.

Although you could create and edit the file directly, using a configuration utility, such as Xconfigurator, XF86Setup, or XF86Config is better. (Table 27-3 lists these various configuration tools.) With these, you simply answer questions about your hardware or select options on the dialog window, and the program generates the appropriate **/etc/X11/XF86Config** file. XF86Config provides line mode prompts where you type responses or enter a menu selection, and it provides explanations of each step. You can run it from any shell command line. Xconfigurator uses a cursor-based screen that also operates on a shell command line. You can use arrow keys, TAB, and the ENTER key to make your selections. XF86Config also attempts to detect your card automatically or you can select your monitor from a predetermined list. XF86Setup provides you with a full-screen interface where you can easily select features for your mouse, keyboard, graphics card, and monitor. You need the horizontal and vertical frequency for your monitor. XF86Setup is described in detail in Chapter 4. If you have problems configuring with XF86Setup, however, you can use XF86Config, which presents you with a command-line interface that prompts you for different settings. SaX (SuSE Advanced X Configuration) is another GUI X Window System configuration tool provided by the SuSE Linux distribution. It provides windows similar to XF86Setup for your mouse, keyboard, video card, and monitor. The monitor window lists supported monitor models.

The **/etc/X11/XF86Config** file is organized into several parts, as shown here. You can find a detailed discussion of all these sections and their entries in the XF86Config man page. All of these are set by the XF86Setup program. For example, the Monitor screen generates the Monitor section in the **XF86Config** file, the Mouse screen generates the Pointer section, and so on. A section in the file begins with the keyword **Section,** followed by the name of the section in quotes. The section ends with the term **EndSection**. Comments have a # sign at the beginning of the line. Entries for each section begin with a data specification, followed by a list of values. For example, in the

XF86Setup	GUI X Window System configuration tool. Use after installation process
Xconfigurator	Screen-based X Window System configuration tool (used in Red Hat install procedure)
XF86Setup	Command line X Window System configuration tool. Requires no screen-based support.
/etc/X11/XF86Config	The X Window System configuration file; edited by the configuration tools

Table 27-3. *X Window System Configuration Tools*

ADMINISTRATION

Files section where the **rgb** color data is listed, a line begins with the data specification **RgbPath,** followed by the pathname for that **rgb** color data file.

Files	Directories for font and **rgb** files
Module	Dynamic module loading
ServerFlags	Miscellaneous options
Keyboard	Keyboard specifications
Pointer	Mouse configuration
Monitor	Monitor configuration (set horizontal and vertical frequency)
Device	Video card configuration
Screen	Configures display, setting virtual screen, display colors, screen size, and other features

Although you can directly edit the file using a standard text editor, relying on the setup programs, such as XF86Setup to make changes, is always best. You won't ever have to touch most of the sections but, in some cases, you want to make changes to the Screen section, located at the end of the file. To do so, you would edit the file, and add or change entries in the Screen section. In the Screen section, you can configure your virtual screen display and set the number of colors supported. Because the Screen section is the one you would most likely change, it is discussed first, even though it comes last, at the end of the file.

Screen

A Screen section begins with a Driver entry that specifies the driver name. There are five driver names, one for each type of XFree86 server: Accel, Mono, SVGA, VGA2, and VGA16. The *Accel* driver name is used for all accelerated X servers, such as S3_XFree86. *Mono* is for non-VGA mono drivers supported by the XF86_Mono server. *VGA2* and *VGA16* are used for the VGA server, while *SVGA* is used for the XF86_SVGA server. If you are using the XFree86_SVGA server, the Driver entry would have **svga**. If you are using any of the accelerated servers, this entry would be Accel. Setup programs, such as XF86Setup, generate Screen sections for each of these. If you are using the SVGA server, you would use the SVGA screen section.

After the Driver entry, the Device and Monitor entries specify the monitor and video card you are using. The name given in the Identifier entry in these sections is used to reference those components. A monitor given the Identifier name Nec3v has the entry **Monitor Nec3v** in the Screen section.

```
Section "Screen"
   Driver          "Accel"
   Device          "Primary Card"
   Monitor         "Primary Monitor"
   DefaultColorDepth  16
   SubSection "Display"
      Depth        8
      Modes        "1152x864" "1024x768" "800x600" "640x480"
"640x400" "480x300" "400x300" "320x240" "320x200"
      Virtual 800 600
   EndSubSection
   SubSection "Display"
```

The Screen section has Display subsections, one for each depth supported. Whereas the previous sections were configuring hardware, the Display subsection configures display features, such as the number of colors displayed and the virtual screen size. Three main entries exist: Depth, Modes, and Virtual. The *Depth* entry is the screen resolution: 8, 16, and 24. You can add the DefaultColorDepth entry to set the default color depth to whatever your X server supports: 8 for 256K, 16 for 32K, and 24 for 16M. *Modes* are the modes allowed given the resolution. *Virtual* is the size of the virtual screen. You can have a virtual screen larger than your display area. When you move your mouse to the edge of the displayed screen, it scrolls to that hidden part of the screen. This way, you can have a working screen much larger than the physical size of your monitor. The usual setting for a virtual screen is 1,024 × 768, a 17-inch monitor size. You could also set it to 1,152 × 864, a 21-inch monitor size. For a 15-inch monitor, the virtual screen is usually set to 1,024 × 768. If you want to disable the virtual screen, you can set the Virtual entry to 800 × 600, making the display the same size as the physical screen.

Virtual 1,024 768	17-inch virtual screen
Virtual 1,152 864	21-inch virtual screen
Virtual 800 600	15-inch screen (disable virtual screen)

Any of these features in this section can be safely changed. In fact, to change the virtual screen size, you must modify this section. Other sections in the **XF86Config** file should be left alone, however, unless you are certain of what you are doing.

Files, Modules, ServerFlags, and Keyboard

The Files section lists different directories for resources that XFree86 needs. These are mostly the fonts available on your system. A font entry begins with the data specification **FontPath** and is followed by the pathname for that font. A sample of these entries is shown here:

```
RgbPath      "/usr/X11R6/lib/X11/rgb"
FontPath     "/usr/X11R6/lib/X11/fonts/misc:unscaled"
```

The Module section specifies modules to be dynamically loaded and the **Load** entry loads a module. See the XF86Config man page for more details.

Several flags can be set for the XFree86 server. You can find a complete listing in the XF86Config man page. For example, the **NoTrapSignals** enables the core to be dumped for debugging purposes. **DontZap** disables the use of CTRL-ALT-BACKSPACE to shut down the server. **DontZoom** disables switching between graphic modes.

The keyboard section determines your keyboard type and sets the layout, model, and protocol used. For example, the following entry sets the layout. A large number of options exist for this section. Consult the XF86Config man pages for a complete listing.

```
XkbLayout        "us"
```

Pointer

The *Pointer* section configures your mouse and any other pointer devices. This section has only a few entries, with some tailored for specific types of mice. The *Protocol* entry specifies the protocol your mouse uses, such as Microsoft or Logitech. The *Device* entry is the pathname for the mouse device. You can also use Red Hat's mouseconfig program to select a mouse and have its setting automatically entered into this section of the **/etc/X11/XF86Config** file. The following example shows a standard Pointer section for a Microsoft mouse at 1200 baud. The device file is **/dev/mouse**.

```
Section "Pointer"
    Protocol      "Microsoft"
    Device        "/dev/mouse"
    BaudRate      1200
EndSection
```

The following is a listing of the Pointer section entries.

Protocol	Mouse protocol (do man XF86Config for complete listing)
Device	Device path such as **/dev/mouse** or **/dev/cua0**
BaudRate	Baud rate for serial mouse
Emulate3Buttons	Enables two-button mouse to emulate a third button by pressing both left and right buttons at once

ChordMiddle	Three-button mouse configuration on some Logitech mice
ClearDTR and ClearRTS	Clear DTR and RTS lines, valid only for Mouse Systems mice
SampleRate	Set the sampling rate (Logitech)

Monitor

A Monitor section should exist for each monitor used on your system. The vertical and horizontal frequencies must be accurate or you can damage your monitor. A *Monitor* section begins with entries that identify the monitor, such as vendor and model names. The HorizSync and VerRefresh entries are where the vertical and horizontal frequencies are specified. Most monitors can support a variety of resolutions. Those resolutions are specified in the Monitor section by ModeLine entries. A ModeLine entry exists for each resolution. The ModeLine entry has five values, the name of the resolution, its dot clock value, and then two sets of four values, one for the horizontal timing and one for the vertical timing, ending with flags. The flags specify different characteristics of the mode, such as Interlace, to indicate the mode is interlaced, and +hsync and +vsync to select the polarity of the signal.

```
ModeLine "name"  dotclock  horizontal-freq  vertical-freq  flags
```

A sample of a ModeLine is shown here. Leaving the entire Monitor section alone is best, rely, instead, on the entries generated by XF86Setup.

```
Modeline  "800x600"    50.00 800 856 976 1040 600 637 643 666 +hsync +vsync
```

Commonly used entries for the Monitor section are listed here.

Identifier	A name to identify the monitor
VendorName	Manufacturer
ModelName	The make and model
HorizSync	The horizontal frequency; can be a range or series of values
VerRefresh	Vertical refresh frequency; can be a range or series of values
Gamma	Gamma correction
ModeLine	Specifies a resolution with dotclock, horizontal timing, and vertical timing for that resolution

Device

The *Device* section specifies your video card. It begins with entries that identify the card, such as VendorName, BoardName, and Chipset. The amount of video RAM is indicated in the VideoRam entry. The *Clocks* entry lists your clock values. Many different entries can be made in this section, such as Ramdac for a Ramdac chip, if the board has one, and MemBase for the base address of a frame buffer, if it is accessible. See the XF86Config man pages for a detailed list and descriptions.

Although you could safely change the VideoRam entry—for example, if you added more memory to your card—changing the Clocks entry is not safe. If you get the clock values wrong, you could easily destroy your monitor. Rely on the clock values generated by XF86Setup or other XFree86 setup programs. If the clock values are missing, it means that the server will automatically determine them. This may be the case for newer cards.

X Window System Command Line Arguments

You can start up any X Windows application either within an **.xinitrc** or an **.xsession** script, or on the command line in an Xterm window. Some distributions, including Red Hat, place X Windows startup applications in an **.Xclients** file that is read by the **.xinitrc** script. Most X Windows applications take a set of standard X Windows arguments used to configure the window and display the application uses. You can set the color of the window bars, give the window a specific title, and specify the color and font for text, as well as position the window at a specific location on the screen. Table 27-4 lists these X Windows arguments. They are discussed in detail in the X man pages, man X.

One commonly used argument is **-geometry**. This takes an additional argument that specifies the location on the screen where you want an application's window displayed. In the next example, the xclock X-Windows application is called with a geometry argument. A set of up to four numbers specifies the position. The value +0+0 references the upper left-hand corner. There, you see the clock displayed when you start up the X Window System. The value –0–0 references the upper right-hand corner.

```
& xclock -geometry +0+0 &
```

With the **-title** option, you can set the title displayed on the application window. Notice the use of quotes for titles with more than one word. You set the font with the **-fn** argument, and the text and graphics color with the **-fg** argument. **-bg** sets the background color. The following example starts up an Xterm window with the title "My New Window" in the title bar. The text and graphics color is green and the background color is gray. The font is Helvetica.

```
$ xterm -title "My New Window"  -fg green -bg gray  -fn /usr/fonts/helvetica  &
```

X-Windows Application Configuration Arguments	See X man pages for detailed explanations
-bw *num*	Borderwidth of pixels in frame
-bd *color*	Border color
-fg *color*	Foreground color (for text or graphics)
-bg *color*	Background color
-display *display-name*	Displays client to run on; displays name consisting of hostname, display number, and screen number (see X man pages)
-fn *font*	Font to use for text display
-geometry *offsets*	Location on screen where X-Windows application window is placed; offsets are measured relative to screen display
-iconic	Starts application with icon, not with open window
-rv	Switches background and foreground colors
-title *string*	Title for the window's title bar
-name *string*	Name for the application
xrm *resource-string*	Specifies resource value

Table 27-4.   *Configuration Options for X Window System–Based Applications*

X Window System Commands and Configuration Files

The X Window System uses several configuration files, as well as X commands to configure your X Window System. Some of the configuration files belong to the system and should not be modified. Each user can have her own set of configuration files, however, such as **.xinitrc**, **.xsession**, and **.Xresources** that can be used to configure a personalized X Windows interface. Some distributions, like Red Hat, also use an **.Xclients** file to hold X Window startup applications. These configuration files are automatically read and executed when the X Window System is started up with either the **startx** command or an X display manager, such as xdm, kdm, or gdm. Within these configuration files, you can execute X commands used to configure your system. With commands such as **xset** and **setroot**, you can add fonts or control the display of your root window. Table 27-5 provides a list of X Window System configuration files and commands. You can obtain a complete description of your current X configuration using the **xdypinfo** command. The X man page provide a detailed introduction to the X commands and configuration files.

X Resources

Several X commands, such as **xrdb** and **xmodmap,** configure your X-Windows interface. X-Windows graphic configurations are listed in a resource file called **.Xresources**. Each user can have a customized **.Xresources** file in his home directory, configuring the X Window System to particular specifications. The **.Xresources** file contains entries for configuring specific programs, such as the color of certain widgets. A systemwide version called **/etc/X11/xinit/.Xresources** also exists. (Notice, unlike **/etc/X11/xinit/xinitrc**, a period is before Xresources in the **/etc/X11/xinit/.Xresources** filename.) The **.Xdefaults** file is a default configuration loaded by all programs, which contains the same kind of entries for configuring resources as **.Xresources**. An **.Xdefaults** file is accessible by programs on your system, but not by those running on other systems. The **/usr/X11R6/lib/X11/app-defaults** directory holds files that contain default resource configurations for particular X applications, such as Xterm, Xclock, and Xmixer. The Xterm file holds resource entries specifying how an Xterm window is displayed. You can override any of these defaults with alternative entries in an **.Xresources** file in your home directory. You can create an **.Xresources** file of your own in your home directory and add resource entries to it. You can also copy the **/etc/X11/xinit/.Xresources** file and edit the entries there or add new ones of your own.

Configuration is carried out by the **xrdb** command, which reads both the system's **.Xresources** file and any **.Xresources** or **.Xdefaults** file in your home directory. The **xrdb** command is currently executed in the **/etc/X11/xinit/xinitrc** script and the **/etc/X11/xdm/Xsession** script. If you create your own **.xinitrc** script in your home directory, be sure it executes the **xrdb** command with at least your own **.Xresources** file or the **/etc/X11/xinit/.Xresources** file (preferably both). You can ensure this by simply using a copy of the system's **xinitrc** script as your own **.xinitrc** file, and then modifying that copy as you want. See the man pages on **xrdb** for more details on resources. Also, you can find a more detailed discussion of Xresources, as well as other X commands, in the man pages for X.

An entry in the **.Xresources** file consists of a value assigned to a resource, class, or resources for an application. Usually, resources are used for widgets or classes of widgets in an application. The resource designation typically consists of three elements separated by a period: the application, an object in the application, and the resource. The entire designation is terminated by a colon, and the value follows. For example, suppose you want to change the color of the hour hand to blue in the oclock application. The application is oclock, the object is clock, and the resource is hour: oclock.clock.hour. This entry looks like this:

```
oclock.clock.hour: blue
```

The object element is actually a list of objects denoting the hierarchy leading to a particular object. In the oclock example, only one object exists but, in many applications, the object hierarchy can be complex. This requires a lengthy set of objects listed to specify the one you want. To avoid this complexity, you can use the asterisk notation to reference the object you want directly, using an asterisk in place of the period. You only need to know the name of the resource you want to change. The following example sets the oclock minute and hour hands to green.

```
oclock*hour: green
oclock*minute: green
```

You can also use the asterisk to apply a value to whole classes of objects. Many individual resources are grouped into classes. You can reference all the resources in a class by their class name. Class names begin with an uppercase character. For example, in the Xterm application, the background and pointer color resources are both part of the Background class. The reference **XTerm*Background** would change all these resources in an Xterm window. However, any specific references always override the more general ones.

You can also use the asterisk to change the values of a resource in objects for all your applications. In this case, you place an asterisk before the resource. For example, to change the foreground color to red for all the objects in every application, you enter

```
*foreground: red
```

If you want to change the foreground color of the scroll bars in all your applications, you use

```
*scrollbar*foreground: blue
```

The **showrgb** command lists the different colors available on your system. You can use the descriptive name or a hexadecimal form. Values can also be fonts, bitmaps, and pixmaps. You could change the font displayed by certain objects in, or for, graphic applications, change background, or border graphics. Resources vary with each application. Applications may support different kinds of objects and the resources for them. Check the man pages and documentation for an application to learn what resources it supports and the values accepted for it. Some resources take Boolean

ADMINISTRATION

values that can turn features on or off, while others can specify options. Some applications have a default set of resource values that is automatically placed in your system's **.Xresources** or **.Xdefaults** files.

The **Xmodmap** file holds configurations for your input devices, such as your mouse and keyboard (for example, you can bind keys such as BACKSPACE or reverse the click operations of your right and left mouse buttons). The **Xmodmap** file used by your display manager is in the display manager configuration directory, such as **/etc/X11/xdm**, whereas the one used by **startx** is located in **/etc/X11/xinit**. Each user can create a custom **.Xmodmap** file in her home directory to configure the system's input devices. This is helpful if users connect through their own terminals to your Linux system. The **.Xmodmap** file is read by the **xmodmap** command, which performs the configuration. The **xmodmap** command first looks for an **.Xmodmap** file in the user's home directory and uses that. If no **.Xmodmap** is in the home directory, it uses the one for your display manager or **startx** command. You see entries for the **xmodmap** command in the **/etc/X11/xinit/xinitrc** file and the display manager's **Xsession** file. If you have your own **.xinitrc** or **.xsession** script in your home directory, it should execute the **xmodmap** command with either your own **.Xmodmap** file or the system's **Xmodmap** file. See the man pages on **xmodmap** for more details.

X Commands

Usually, an **.xinitrc** or **.xsession** script has X Window System commands, such as **xset** and **xsetroot,** used to configure different features of your X-Windows session. The **xset** command sets different options, such as turning on the screen saver or setting the volume for the bell and speaker. You can also use **xset** to load fonts. See the **xset** man pages for specific details. With the **b** option and the **on** or **off** argument, **xset** turns your speaker on or off. The following example turns on the speaker.

```
xset b on
```

You use **xset** with the **-s** option to set the screen saver. With the **on** and **off** arguments you can turn the screen saver on or off. Two numbers entered as arguments specify the length and period in seconds. The length is the number of seconds the screen saver waits before activating and the period is how long it waits before regenerating the pattern.

The **xsetroot** command enables you to set the features of your root window (setting the color or displaying a bitmap pattern—you can even use a cursor of your own design). Table 27-5 lists the different **xsetroot** options. See the man pages for **xsetroot** for options and details. The following **xsetroot** command uses the **-solid** option to set the background color of the root window to blue.

```
xsetroot -solid blue
```

Fonts

Your X Window System fonts are located in a directory called **/usr/X11R6/lib/ X11/fonts**. X Window System fonts are loaded using the **xfs** command. **xfs** reads the **/etc/X11/fs/config** configuration file that lists the font directories in an entry for the term **catalogue**. The X man pages provide a detailed discussion on fonts. To install a set of fonts automatically, place them in a directory whose path you can add to the catalogue entry. You can also separately install a particular font with the **xset** command and its **+fp** option. Fonts for your system are specified in a font path. The *font path* is a set of filenames, each holding a font. The filenames include their complete path. An example of the catalogue entry in the **/etc/X11/config** file follows. This is a comma-delimited list of directories. These are directories where the X Window System first looks for fonts.

```
catalogue = /usr/X11R6/lib/X11/fonts/misc/,
/usr/X11R6/lib/X11/fonts/Speedo/,/usr/X11R6/lib/X11/fonts/Type1/,
/usr/X11R6/lib/X11/fonts/75dpi/,/usr/X11R6/lib/X11/fonts/100dpi/
```

Before you can access newly installed fonts, you must first index them with the **mkfontdir** command. From within the directory with the new fonts, enter the **mkfontdir** command. You can also use the directory path as an argument to **mkfontdir**. After indexing the fonts, you can then load them using the **xset** command with the **fp rehash** option. To have the fonts automatically loaded, add the directory with the full pathname to the catalogue entry in the **xfs** configuration file. The following shows how to install a new font, and then load it:

```
$ cp newfont.pcf  ~/myfonts
$ mkfontdir ~/myfonts
$ xset fp rehash
```

Within a font directory, several special files hold information about the fonts. The **fonts.dir** file lists all the fonts in that directory. In addition, you can set up a **fonts.alias** file to give other names to a font. Font names tend to be long and complex. A **fonts.scale** file holds the names of scalable fonts. See the man pages for **xfs** and **mkfontdir** for more details.

With the **xset +fp** and **-fp** options, you can specifically add or remove particular fonts. The **fn** option with the **rehash** argument then loads the fonts. With the default argument, the default set of fonts are restored. The **+fp** adds a font to this font path. For your own fonts, you can place them in any directory and specify their filenames, including their complete path. The next example adds the **myfont** font in the **/usr/local/fonts** directory to the font path. Then the **fp** option with the **rehash** argument loads the font.

ADMINISTRATION

```
xset +fp  /usr/local/fonts/myfont
xset fp rehash
```

To remove this font, use **xset -fp** /usr/home/*myfont* and follow it with the **xset fp rehash** command. If you want to reset your system to the set of default fonts, enter the following:

```
xset fp default
xset fp rehash
```

With **xlsfonts**, you can list the fonts currently installed on your system. To display an installed font to see what it looks like, use **xselfonts**. You can browse through your fonts, selecting the ones you like.

Table 27-5 lists common X Window System commands, whereas Table 27-6 lists the configuration files and directories associated with the X Window System.

X Window System Startup Methods: startx and Display Managers

You can start up your X Window System in two different ways. You can start Linux with the command line interface and then, once you log in, use the **startx** command to start the X Window System and your window manager and desktop. You can also use a display manager that automatically starts the X Window System when you boot your computer, displaying a login window and a menu for selecting the window manager or desktop you want to use. Options for shutting down your system are also there. Currently, you can use three display managers. The K Display Manager is a display manager provided with the KDE. The Gnome Display Manager comes with the Gnome desktop. The X Display Manager is the original display manager used on Linux system.

Each method uses its own startup script. The **startx** command uses the **xinit** command to start the X Window System; its startup script is **/etc/X11/xinit/xinitrc**. Startup scripts for display managers are found in their respective directories. For **xdm** the startup script is **/etc/X11/xdm/Xsession.** kdm and gdm have their own configuration directories, **/etc/X11/kdm** and **/etc/X11/gdm**. Here you find files for configuring their login window and menus. The gdm application as currently implemented on Red Hat uses the Xdm **Xsession** script, whereas kdm uses an **Xsession** script in its own directory.

As an enhancement to either **startx** or a display manager, you can use the X *session manager* (*xsm*). You can use it to launch your X Window System with different sessions. A *session* is a specified group of X applications. Starting with one session might start Gnome and Netscape, while starting with another might start KDE and

X Window Commands	Explanation
xterm	Opens a new terminal window
xset	Sets X Windows options; see man pages for complete listing **-b** Configures bell **-c** Configures key click **+fp** *fontlist* Adds fonts **-fp** *fontlist* Removes fonts **led** Turns on or off keyboard LEDs **m** Configures mouse **p** Sets pixel color values **s** Sets the screen saver **q** Lists current settings
xsetroot	Configures the root window **-cursor** *cursorfile maskfile* Sets pointer to bitmap pictures when pointer is outside any window **-bitmap** *filename* Sets root window pattern to bitmap **-gray** Sets background to gray **-fg** *color* Sets color of foreground bitmap **-bg** *color* Sets color of background bitmap **-solid** *color* Sets background color **-name** *string* Sets name of root window to string
xmodmap	Configures input devices; reads the **.Xmodmap** file **-pk** Displays current keymap **-e** expression Sets key binding keycode NUMBER = KEYSYMNAME Sets key to specified key symbol keysym KEYSYMNAME = KEYSYMNAME Sets key to operate the same as specified key pointer = NUMBER Sets mouse button codes
xrdb	Configures X Windows resources; reads the **.Xresources** file
xdm	X Windows Display Manager; runs the XFree86 server for your system; usually called by **xinitrc**
startx	Starts X Windows by executing **xinit** and instructing it to read the **.Xclients** file

Table 27-5.   *X Window System Commands*

X Window Commands	Explanation
xfs *config-file*	The X Windows font server
mkfontdir *font-directory*	Index new fonts, making them accessible by the font server
xlsfonts	Lists fonts on your system
xfontsel	Displays installed fonts
xdpyinfo	Lists detailed information about your X Windows configuration
xinit	Starts X Windows, first reading the system's **xinitrc** file; when invoked from **startx**, it also reads the user's **.Xclients** file; **xinit** is not called directly, but through **startx**
xmkmf	Creates a Makefile for an X Windows application using the application's Imakefile; invokes **imake** to generate the Makefile (never invoke **imake** directly)
xauth	Reads **.Xauthority** file to set access control to a user account through xdm from remote systems
Desktops, Window and File Managers	
lg	The Caldera Desktop
fvwm	The FVWM window manager
olvwm	The Xview window manager (OpenLook)
fvwm95	The FVWM95 (Windows 95) window manager
qvwm	The QVWM (Windows 95) window manager
mwm	The LessTif window manager
xfm	The XFM file manager
aftersetp	The AfterStep window manager
mlvwm	A Macintosh window manager
mfm	The Motif window manager

Table 27-5.   *X Window System Commands* (continued)

Configuration Files	Explanation
.Xmodmap	User's X Windows input devices configuration file
.Xresources	User's X Windows resource configuration file
.Xdefaults	User's X Windows resource configuration file
.xinitrc	User's X Windows configuration file read automatically by **xinit**, if it exists)
.Xclients or .Xsessions	User's X Windows configuration file (used on Red Hat and other Linux distributions)
.Xauthority	User's access controls through xdm GUI login interface
/usr/X11R6/	Directory where the X Window System release 6 commands, applications, and configuration files are held
/usr/X11R6/lib/X11/	Directory that holds X Window System release 6 configuration file and subdirectories. This is a link to the **/etc/X11/** that always holds the configuration files and subdirectories for the currently installed release
/usr/X11R6/lib/X11/	Directory that holds X Window System configuration files and subdirectories for the version currently installed on your system. On Red Hat, this is a link to the **/etc/X11** directory
/etc/X11/xinit/xinitrc	System X Windows initialization file; automatically read by **xinit**
/etc/X11/xinit/Xclients	System X Windows configuration file (used on Red Hat and other Linux distributions)
/etc/X11/xinit/.Xresources	System X Windows resources file; read by **xinitrc**
/etc/X11/xinit/.Xmodmap	System X Windows input devices file; read by **xinitrc**
/etc/X11/rgb.txt	X Windows colors. Each entry has four fields: the first three fields are numbers for red, green, and blue; the last field is the name given to the color

Table 27-6.   *X Window System Configuration Files*

KOffice. You can save your session either while you are using it or when you shut down. The applications you are running become part of a saved session. When you start, xsm displays a session menu for you to choose from, listing previous sessions you saved. For xsm to work, it must be the last entry in your **.xsessions** or **.Xclients** file and you shouldn't have any other applications started in these files.

startx, xinit, and .xinitrc

The X Window System can be started from the command line interface using the **xinit** command. You do not invoke the **xinit** command directly, but through the **startx** command, which you always use to start the X Window System. Both of these commands are found in the **/usr/X11R6/bin** directory, along with many other X-based programs. The **startx** command is a shell script that executes the **xinit** command. The **xinit** command, in turn, first looks for an X Window System initialization script called **.xinitrc**, in the user's home directory. If no **.xinitrc** script is in the home directory, **xinit** uses **/etc/X11/xinit/xinitrc** as its initialization script. Both **.xinitrc** and **/etc/X11/xinit/xinitrc** have commands to configure your X windows server and to execute any initial X commands, such as starting up the window manager. You can think of the **/etc/X11/xinit/xinitrc** script as a default script. In addition, many systems use a separate file named **Xclients,** where particular X applications, desktop, or window manager can be specified. These entries can be directly listed in an **xinitrc** file, but a separate file makes for a more organized format. The Xclients files are executed as shell scripts by the **xinitrc** file. A user version, as well as a system version, exists: **.Xclients** and **/etc/X11/init/Xclients**. On Red Hat systems, the user's home directory is checked for the **.Xclients** file and, if missing, the **/etc/X11/xinit/Xclients** file is used.

Most distributions, including Red Hat, do not initially set up any **.xinitrc** or **.Xclients** scripts in any of the home directories. These must be created by a particular user who wants one. Each user can create a personalized **.xinitrc** script in her home directory, configuring and starting up the X Window System as wanted. Until a user sets up an **.xinitrc** script, the **/etc/X11/xinit/xinitrc** script is used and you can examine this script to see how the X Window System starts. Certain configuration operations required for the X Window System must be in the **.xinitrc** file. For a user to create his own **.xinitrc** script, copying the **/etc/X11/xinit/xinitrc** first to his home directory and naming it **.xinitrc** is best. Then each user can modify the particular **.xinitrc** file as required. (Notice the system **xinitrc** file has no preceding period in its name, whereas the home directory **.xinitrc** file set up by a user does have a preceding period.) The following example shows a simple system **xinitrc** file that starts the Window Maker window manager and an Xterm window. System and user .Xresources and .Xmodmap files are executed first to configure the X Window System.

/etc/X11/xinit/xinitrc

```
#!/bin/sh
userresources=$HOME/.Xresources
usermodmap=$HOME/.Xmodmap
```

```
sysresources=/usr/X11R6/lib/X11/xinit/.Xresources
sysmodmap=/usr/X11R6/lib/X11/xinit/.Xmodmap

# merge in defaults and keymaps
if [ -f $sysresources ]; then
    xrdb -merge $sysresources
fi
if [ -f $sysmodmap ]; then
    xmodmap $sysmodmap
fi
if [ -f $userresources ]; then
    xrdb -merge $userresources
fi
if [ -f $usermodmap ]; then
    xmodmap $usermodmap
fi
# start some nice programs
xterm &
exec wmaker &
```

On Red Hat, if a user only wants to add startup applications, then the user can simply create an **.Xclients** file, instead of a complete **.xinitrc** file. Be sure commands are in the system **xinitrc** file to check for and run a user's **.Xclients** file. The following example shows the code used in the Red Hat **xinitrc** file to execute a user's **.Xclients** script and, failing that, the system **Xclients** script. If this fails, the FVWM2 window manager is started and, if that fails, then the twm file manager is started.

```
if [ -f $HOME/.Xclients ]; then
    exec $HOME/.Xclients
elif [ -f /etc/X11/xinit/Xclients ]; then
    exec /etc/X11/xinit/Xclients
else
        # failsafe settings.  Although we should never get here
        xclock -geometry 100x100-5+5 &
        xterm -geometry 80x50-50+150 &
        if [ -f /usr/X11R6/bin/fvwm2 ]; then
                exec fvwm2
        else
                exec twm
        fi
fi
```

Display Managers: xdm, kdm, and gdm

When a system configured to run a display manager starts up, the X Window System starts up immediately and displays a login dialog box. The dialog box prompts the user to enter a login name and a password. Once they are entered, a selected X windows interface starts up, say with Gnome, KDE, or some other desktop or window manager. When the user quits the window manager or desktop, the system returns to the login dialog box and remains there until another user logs in. You can shift to a command line interface with the CTRL-ALT-F1 keys and return to the display manager login dialog box with CTRL-ALT-F7. A display manager can do much more than provide a GUI login window. You can also use it to control access to different hosts and users on your network. The **.Xauthority** file in each user's home directory contains authentication information for that user. A display manager like xdm supports the *X Display Manager Control Protocol* (*XDMCP*). They were originally designed for systems like workstations that are continually operating, but are also used to start up X Windows automatically on single user systems when the system boots.

A display manager is automatically run when your system starts up at runlevel 5. Recall that your system can run at different runlevels, for example, runlevel 3 is the standard multiuser level, whereas runlevel 2 is a nonnetwork user level, and runlevel 1 is a system administration level. Runlevel 5 is the same as the standard multiuser level (runlevel 3), except it automatically starts up the X Window System on connected machines and activates the display manager's login screen.

During installation on Red Hat systems, you could choose whether you wanted to start with the display manager (runlevel 5). In this case, your system automatically starts at runlevel 5, activating the display manager. If, instead, you are starting with a standard line-mode login prompt (runlevel 3), you can change to the display manager by changing your default runlevel. To do this, you can edit the system's /etc/inittab file. The entry for your default runlevel should look like the following:

```
id:3:initdefault:
```

You can change the 3 to a 5:

```
id:5:initdefault:
```

To test your display manager you can change to runlevel 5 with the **init** command as shown here:

```
init 5
```

Xsession

A display manager refers to a user's login and startup of a window manager and desktop as a session. When the user quits the desktop and logs out, the session ends. When another user logs in, a new session starts. The X Window System never shuts down; only desktop or window manager programs shut down. Session menus on the display manager login window list different kinds of sessions you can start, in other words, different kinds of window managers or desktops. For each session, the **Xsession** script is the startup script used to configure a user's X Window System display and to execute the selected desktop or window manager. Although this script is unnecessary for gdm, it is still used in the gdm Red Hat implementation.

    Xsession is the display manager session startup script used by xdm, kdm, and also by the Red Hat implementation of gdm. It contains many of the X commands also used in the **xinitrc** startup script. **Xsession** usually executes the same **xmodmap** and **xrdb** commands using the **.Xmodmap** and **.Xrsources** files in the **/etc/X11/xinit** directory. Shown here is the **Xsession** script used by gdm on Red Hat systems, which is located in the **/etc/X11/xdm** directory.

```
#!/bin/bash -login
# (c) 1999 Red Hat Software, Inc.

xsetroot -solid #356390

# redirect errors to a file in user's home directory if we can for
# errfile in "$HOME/.xsession-errors" "${TMPDIR-/tmp}/xses-$USER"
# "/tmp/xses-$USER"
do
    if ( cp /dev/null "$errfile" 2> /dev/null )
    then
    chmod 600 "$errfile"
    exec > "$errfile" 2>&1
    break
    fi
done

# clean up after xbanner
if [ -f /usr/X11R6/bin/freetemp ]; then
    freetemp
fi

userresources=$HOME/.Xresources
usermodmap=$HOME/.Xmodmap
sysresources=/usr/X11R6/lib/X11/xinit/.Xresources
```

```
sysmodmap=/usr/X11R6/lib/X11/xinit/.Xmodmap

# merge in defaults and keymaps
if [ -f $sysresources ]; then
    xrdb -merge $sysresources
fi

if [ -f $sysmodmap ]; then
    xmodmap $sysmodmap
fi

if [ -f $userresources ]; then
    xrdb -merge $userresources
fi

if [ -f $usermodmap ]; then
    xmodmap $usermodmap
fi

#see if xdm/gdm/kdm has asked for a specific environment case $# in 1
    case $1 in
    failsafe)
    exec xterm -geometry 80x24-0-0
    ;;
    gnome)
    exec gnome-session
    ;;
    kde)
    exec startkde
    ;;
    anotherlevel)
        # we assume that switchdesk is installed.
    exec /usr/share/apps/switchdesk/Xclients.anotherlevel
    ;;
    esac
esac
```

If users want to set up their own startup files, you can reprogram the kdm **Xsession** file first to check for an *.xsession* file in the user's home directory and execute that. A user could copy the **Xsession** file to her own **.xsession,** and then edit it, as well as replace the case statement with a single invocation of the desktop she wants. The following example shows a simple **Xsession** script that executes the user's **.xsession** script if it exists. The user's **.xsession** script is expected to start a window manager or desktop.

```
#
# Xsession
#
# This is the program that is run as the client
# for the display manager.


startup=$HOME/.xsession
resources=$HOME/.Xresources

if [ -f "$startup" ]; then
        exec "$startup"
   else
       if [ -f "$resources" ]; then
           xrdb -load "$resources"
       fi
       fvwn2 &
       exec xterm -geometry 80x24+10+10 -ls
 fi
```

The following example shows a simple **.xsession** script to start Window Maker:

```
wmaker &
xrdb -merge "$HOME/.Xresources"
xterm -geometry -0+50 -ls
```

The X Display Manager (xdm)

The *X Display Manager* (*xdm*) manages a collection of X displays either on the local system or remote servers. xdm's design is based on the *X Consortium standard X Display Manager Control Protocol* (*XDMCP*). The xdm program manages user logins, providing authentication and starting sessions. For character-based logins, a session is the lifetime of the user shell that is started up when the user logs in from the command line interface. For xdm and other display managers, the session is determined by the session manager. The session is usually the duration of a window manager or desktop. When the desktop or window manager terminates, so does the session.

The xdm program displays a login window with boxes for a login name and password. The user logs in, and a window manager or desktop starts up. When the user quits the window manager, the X Window System restarts automatically, displaying the login window again. Authentications to control access for particular users are kept in their **.Xauthority** file.

ADMINISTRATION

The xdm configuration files are located in the **/usr/X11R6/lib/X11/xdm/** directory, although on Red Hat this is a link to the **/etc/X11/xdm** directory. The main xdm configuration file is **xdm-config**. Files such as **Xresources** configure how the dialog box is displayed and **Xsetup** enables you to specify a root-window image or other windows to display. You can use the **xbanner** program to choose a graphic to display with the login dialog box. When the user starts up a session, the **Xsession** script is run to configure the user's X Window System and execute the user's window manager or desktop. This script usually calls the **.xsession** script in the user's home directory, if there is one (though this is not currently the case for RedHat Xsession scripts). It holds any specific user X commands.

If you want to start xdm from the command line interface you can enter it with the **–nodaemon** option. CTRL-C then shuts down xdm:

```
xdm -nodaemon
```

Table 27-7 lists the configuration files and directories associated with xdm.

Filenames	Description
/usr/X11R6/lib/X11/xdm	xdm configuration directory. On Red Hat, this is **/etc/X11/xdm**.
xdm-config	xdm configuration file
Xsession	Startup script for user session
Xresource	Resource features for xdm login window
Xsetup	Sets up the login window and xdm login screen
Xstartup	Session startup script
xdm-errors	Errors from xdm sessions
.xsession	User's session script in the home directory. Usually executed by **Xsession**
Xreset	Resets the X Window System after a session ends
.Xauthority	User authorization file where xdm stores keys for clients to read

Table 27-7. *The xdm Configuration Files and Directories*

The Gnome Display Manager

The *Gnome Display Manager* (*gdm*) manages user login and GUI interface sessions. gdm can service several displays and generates a process for each. The main gdm process listens for XDMCP requests from remote displays and monitors the local display sessions. gdm displays a login window with boxes for entering a login name and password, and also displays a pop-up menu labeled options with entries for Sessions and Shutdown submenus. The Sessions menu displays different window managers and desktops you can start up. On Red Hat, you can find entries for Gnome, kde, and AnotherLevel (fvwm2). You can easily add entries to this menu by adding files for them in the gdm configuration directory, **/etc/X11/gdm/Sessions**.

The gdm configuration files are located in the **/etc/X11/gdm** directory. Its main configuration file is **gdm.conf**, where you can set various options, such as the logo image and welcome text to display. The **gdm** directory also contains four directories: **Init**, **Sessions**, **PostSession**, and **PreSession**. You can easily configure gdm by placing or editing files in these different directories. The **Init** directory contains scripts that are executed when gdm starts up. On Red Hat, this directory contains a Default script that holds X commands, such as setting the background. These are applied to the screen showing the gdm login window.

The Sessions directory holds session scripts. These become entries in the session menu displayed on the gdm login window options menu. For example, you could have a script called **kde** that contains the command **startkde** to run the KDE desktop. The term kde appears in the gdm session menu. Selecting kde executes this script and starts KDE. Currently on Red Hat, these scripts contain calls to the **/etc/X11/xdm/Xsession** script, using the filename as its argument. In the **Xsession** script, this name is used to start that particular kind of session. For example, when you select kde, the term kde is passed to the **Xsession** script, which then uses it to execute the **kde** command to start KDE. For example, the **gnome** script consists of only the following lines. The term gnome is passed to the **Xsession** script, which then uses it to execute the **gnome-session** command to start Gnome. This design has the advantage of not having to repeat any X configuration commands, such as **xmodmap**.

```
#!/bin/bash -login
/etc/X11/xdm/Xsession gnome
```

The **PreSession** directory holds any presession commands to execute, while the **PostSession** directory holds scripts for commands you want executed whenever a session ends. Neither the **Init**, **PreSession**, nor the **PostSession** scripts are necessary (Red Hat currently does not include **PreSession** or **PostSession** scripts).

For gdm, the login window is generated by a program called *the greeter*. Initially, the greeter looks for icons for every user on the system, located in the **.gnome/photo** file in users' home directories. Clicking the icon automatically displays the name of the user in the login box. The user can then enter the password and click the Login button to log in.

Table 27-8 lists the configuration files and directories associated with gdm.

The K Display Manager (kdm)

The *K Display Manager (kdm)* also manages user logins and starts X Window System sessions. kdm is derived from the xdm Display Manager, using the same configuration files. The kdm login window displays a list of user icons for users on the system. A user can click his icon and that user's name then appears in the login box. Enter the password and click Go to log in. The session menu is a drop-down menu showing possible sessions. Click the Shutdown button to shut down the system.

You configure kdm using the KDM Configuration Manager located on the KDE root user desktop (see Chapter 4). Log in as the root user, and then start the KDM Configuration Manager by selecting KDM login manager in the Applications menu located in the Settings menu. Panels exist for configuring the background, logo, and welcome message, as well as for adding icons for users on the system. To add a new session entry in the session menu, enter the name for the entry in the New Type box on the Sessions panel and click Add. The name you enter is then passed as an argument to the kdm **Xsession** script.

When you select a session and click Go, kdm runs the **/etc/X11/kdm/Xsession** script, passing the name of the session as an argument. In the **Xsession** script, this name is used to start that particular kind of session. For example, when you select kde, the term kde is passed to the **Xsession** script, which then uses it to execute the `kde` command to start KDE. The kdm program uses the same configuration files as xdm. A directory called **/etc/X11/kdm** is created with kdm versions of the xdm files. Here, you find an **xdm.conf** file along with **Xsession**, **Xresources**, and **Xsetup**, among others. The resources used to control how the kdm login window is displayed are set in the **/opt/kde/share/config/kdmrc** file.

Starting Window Managers

As noted in Chapter 4, the X Window System is started either automatically using a display manager with a login window or from the command line by entering the `startx` command. Your X Window System server then loads, followed immediately by the window manager. You exit the window manager by choosing an exit or quit entry in the desktop workspace menu. The display manager and some window managers, such as FVWM2 and Window Maker, give you the option of starting other window managers. If you get into trouble and the window manager hangs, you can forcibly exit the X Window System with the keys CTRL-ALT-BACKSPACE.

The window manager you start is the default window manager set up by your Linux distribution when you installed your system. Many distributions now use either Gnome or KDE as their default. For Gnome and the K Desktop, different window

File Names	Description
/etc/X11/gdm	gdm configuration directory
gdm.conf	gdm configuration file
Init	Startup scripts for configuring gdm display
Sessions	Holds session scripts whose names appear in session menu
PreSession	Scripts execute at start of session
PostSession	Scripts execute when session ends

Table 27-8.   *The gdm Configuration Files and Directories*

managers are used: kwm for the K Desktop and Enlightenment for Gnome. You can run Gnome or KDE applications on most window managers. To have Gnome use a particular window manager, you need to select it using the Gnome Control Center. You can also use a window manager in place of kwm for KDE. Check the window manager's Web site for current information on Gnome and KDE compatibility. Currently, Enlightenment is fully Gnome compliant, and AfterStep and Window Maker are nearly so. Normally, distributions include several window managers on their CD-ROM, which you can install and run on your system. Red Hat provide Window Maker, Enlightenment, AfterStep, kwm, and FVWM2, with FVWM2 as the default.

To use a different window manager, first install it. RPM packages install with a default configuration for the window manager. If you are installing from source code you compiled, follow the included installation instructions. You can then configure Gnome or KDE to use that window manager, provided it is compliant with them. See Chapters 5 and 6 on how to configure the KDE and Gnome desktops. Or, you can configure your system to start a particular window manager without either desktop. To do this, you have to place an entry for your window manager in an X Window System startup file. Different startup files exist for the display manager and the `startx` command.

startx and .xinitrc

The system X Window System startup file is called **/etc/X11/xinit/xinitrc**. For the `startx` command, users can also set up their own **.xinitrc** files in their home directories in place of the system's **xinitrc** file. To create your own **xinitrc** file, you can copy the one from the system. In addition, Red Hat enables users to specify their own X clients, such as window managers and desktops, in a startup file called **.Xclients**.

ADMINISTRATION

This way, you needn't bother with a complex **.xinitrc** file. These startup files are discussed in more detail earlier in this chapter.

The following command generates a user's **.xinitrc** file using the system's **xinitrc** file. Be sure you are in your home directory. Notice the **.xinitrc** file has a preceding dot as part of its name, whereas the system's **xinitrc** file does not.

```
$ cp /etc/X11/xinit/xinitrc  .xinitrc
```

The invocation of the window manager is always the last command in the **.xinitrc** script. The X Window System exits after finishing the execution of whatever the last command in the **.xinitrc** script is. By making the window manager the last command, exiting the window manager shuts down your X-Windows session. Any other programs you want to start up initially should be placed before the window manager command. You must place the command to start the window manager you want at the end of your **.xinitrc** file. Be sure to comment out any other window managers by placing a # at the beginning of the lines that hold their commands or simply remove them. Also best is to use the full pathname of a window manager program. These pathnames are usually located in the **/usr/X11R6/bin** directory or in the **/usr/bin** directory. Leave the rest of the file alone. The following example runs Window Maker:

```
exec /usr/X11R6/bin/wmaker
```

If you also want to load other programs automatically, such as a file manager, you can place their commands before the command for the window manager. Put an ampersand (&) after the command. The following example starts the Xterm window when the Window Maker window manager starts up:

```
xterm &
exec /usr/X11R6/bin/wmaker
```

If you are planning extensive changes, making them a few at a time is advisable, testing as you go. A simple **.xinitrc** file is shown here:

.xinitrc

```
#!/bin/sh

userresources=$HOME/.Xresources
usermodmap=$HOME/.Xmodmap
sysresources=/usr/X11R6/lib/X11/xinit/.Xresources
sysmodmap=/usr/X11R6/lib/X11/xinit/.Xmodmap
```

```
# merge in defaults and keymaps

if [ -f $sysresources ]; then
    xrdb -merge $sysresources
fi

if [ -f $sysmodmap ]; then
    xmodmap $sysmodmap
fi

if [ -f $userresources ]; then
    xrdb -merge $userresources
fi

if [ -f $usermodmap ]; then
    xmodmap $usermodmap
fi


if [ -f /usr/X11R6/bin/wmaker ]; then
            exec /usr/X11R6/bin/wmaker
    else
            exec fvwm2
    fi
```

Red Hat uses a rather complex startup procedure designed to configure window managers automatically with the complete set of Red Hat menus for applications installed by its distribution. Support exists for FVWM2, Window Maker, and AfterStep. Red Hat's global **Xclients** file searches for a file called **.wm_style** in a user's home directory. This is where the name of your preferred window manager is placed if you select an alternative from the FVWM2 or AfterStep menus. You can also manually edit this file with a text editor and type in one. The **.wm_style** file holds a single name, such as FVWM2, AfterStep, Window Maker, or LessTiff. Xclients then calls the **/usr/X11R6/bin/RunWM** script with an option for the window manager to start. The RunWM script checks to see if the window manager is installed, and then starts it up with helpful options. As the system administrator, you can edit this file to add new entries, if you want. Or, you can create your own **.xinitrc** file to bypass this procedure.

Display Managers and Xsession

To invoke a window manager using a display manager like xdm, kdm, or gdm, you first have to create an entry for it in the login window's session menu. You can do this in different ways for kdm and gdm. You then must edit the session startup script, and add code to select and start up that window manager. The startup script used for the Red Hat implementation of gdm is **/etc/X11/xdm/Xsession**.

Gnome Display Manager: gdm

First, create an entry for the window manager in the session menu displayed in the gdm login window's option's menu. Here you find files for other items listed in this menu. Simply create a file with the name of the entry you want displayed in the **/etc/X11/gdm/Sessions** directory (you can copy one of the scripts already there). On Red Hat, these scripts invoke the **/etc/X11/xdm/Xsession** script with an option for the particular window manager or desktop chosen. For example, to create an entry for Window Maker, you can create a file called WinMaker as shown here.

/etc/X11/gdm/Sessions/winmaker

```
#!/bin/bash -login

/etc/X11/xdm/Xsession wmaker
```

You then must edit the **/etc/X11/xdm/Xsession** file to insert the code for selecting and starting the new window manager. **Xsession** contains detailed code, most of which you can ignore. In it is a case statement that lists the different window managers and desktops. Here you can enter

```
# now, we see if xdm/gdm/kdm has asked for a specific environment
case $# in
1)
    case $1 in
    failsafe)
        exec xterm -geometry 80x24-0-0
        ;;
    gnome)
        exec gnome-session
    ;;
    kde)
    exec startkde
    ;;
wmaker)
exec wmaker
;;
anotherlevel)
        # we assume that switchdesk is installed.
    exec /usr/share/apps/switchdesk/Xclients.anotherlevel
```

```
    ;;
    esac
esac
```

KDE Display Manager: kdm

To start a new window manager or desktop from the kdm login window, you first must add an entry for it to the session menu. You do this using the kdm configuration tool, described in Chapter 4. Log in as the root user and start the KDM Configuration Manager by selecting KDM login manager in the Applications menu located in the Settings menu, and then display the Sessions panel. Enter the new session entry in the box labeled New Type and click Add. The entry is added to the session menu on the kdm login window. The name you give the session entry is the argument passed to the kdm **Xsession** script.

You then need to edit the kdm **Xsession** script and add code that checks for the name of this new session, and then execute your new window manager. The KDE display manager (kdm) uses its own **Xsession** file, **/etc/X11/kdm/Xsession**. The code is added to the case statement in the **Xsession** script that chooses which window manager or desktop to run for the user. The following example shows an entry for Window Maker added to the kdm **Xsession** script.

```
case $# in
1)
   case $1 in
   kde)
       KDEDIR=/opt/kde; export KDEDIR
       PATH=$KDEDIR/bin:$PATH
       exec /etc/X11/xinit/kdeinitrc
       ;;
wmaker)
exec wmaker
;;
failsafe)
       exec xterm -geometry 80x24-0-0
       ;;
   esac
esac
```

Compiling X Window System Applications

To compile X Window System applications, you should first make sure the XFree86 development package is installed, along with any other development package you may need. These contain header files and libraries used by X Window System programs. The name of such packages contain the term **devel**, for example, **XFree86-devel**. Also, many X-Windows applications may need special shared libraries. For example, some applications may need the **xforms** library or the **qt** library. Gnome applications require the Gnome development libraries, while KDE applications require the KDE development libraries. You may have to obtain some of these from online sites, though most are available as part of the standard Red Hat installation.

Many X Window System applications use configure scripts that automatically detect your system's configuration and generate a Makefile, which can then be used to compile and install the program. An applications configure script is locate in its source code directory. Simply change to that directory and execute the **configure** command. Be sure to include a preceding ./ to specify the configure script in that directory. Afterward, the command **make** compiles the program, and **make install** installs the program on your system. Check an application's README and INSTALL files for any special instructions.

```
./configure
make
make install
```

For older applications that do not have configure scripts, use the **xmkmf** command. A Makefile must be generated that is configured to your system. This is done using an Imakefile provided with the application source code. The **xmkmf** command installed on your system can take an Imakefile and generate the appropriate Makefile. Once you have the Makefile, you can use the **make** command to compile the application. The **xmkmf** command actually uses a program called **imake** to generate the Makefile from the Imakefile; however, you should never use **imake** directly. Consult the man pages for **xmkmf** and **make** for more details.

The Complete Reference

Linux

Part VI

Network Administration

The Complete Reference

Chapter 28

Configuring Network Connections

Most distributions, including Red Hat, enable you to configure your network during installation. If you did so, then your system is ready to go. If you need to change your configuration later, you may find the information in this chapter helpful. Administering and configuring a TCP/IP network on your Linux system is not particularly complicated. Your system uses a set of configuration files to set up and maintain your network. Table 31-2 in Chapter 31 provides a complete listing.

Instead of manually editing configuration files, many distributions provided GUI or cursor-based configuration tools that prompt you for network information. Many distributions incorporate this kind of network configuration into the installation process. If you chose not to configure your network during configuration or you need to make changes to it, you may find it easier and safer to use a network configuration tool. On Red Hat, you can use either Linuxconf or netcfg to configure your network.

Many networks now provide a service that automatically configures a system's network interface. They use a protocol called DHCP (Dynamic Host Configuration Protocol). If your network is configuring your system with DHCP, you will not have to configure it manually. All necessary information will be automatically entered into your network configuration files.

If your system does not have a direct hardware connection to a network, such as an Ethernet connection, and you dial into a network through a modem, you will probably have to set up a PPP connection. Several GUI tools are available for use with Red Hat Linux that you can use to configure your PPP connection. These include Linuxconf, netcfg, and kppp. You can even initiate PPP connections from the command line.

Network Startup Script

On Red Hat, your network interface is started up using the network script in the **/etc/rc.d/init.d** directory. You can manually shut down and restart your network interface using this script, and the **start** or **stop** options. The following commands shut down, and then start up your network interface:

```
/etc/rc.d/init.d/network stop
/etc/rc.d/init.d/network start
```

To test if your interface is working, use the **ping** command with an IP address of a system on your network, such as your gateway machine. The **ping** command continually repeats until you stop it with a CTRL-C. For example, if you have a host on your network with the IP address 192.168.1.42, you could enter:

```
ping 192.168.1.42
```

Hardware Specifications

In addition to your configuration files, you may also have to configure support for your networking hardware, such as Ethernet cards and modems. Ethernet cards use different modules. During installation, most Linux systems automatically detect your Ethernet card type and have the appropriate module loaded whenever you boot up. If you change your Ethernet card, you may have to change the module. On most Linux distributions, you can use Linuxconf to select a new Ethernet module. You can also manually load a module using the `insmod` command.

For a modem, you should make sure a link by the name of **/dev/modem** exists to your modem device, which is usually one of the **/dev/ttyS**num devices, where num is in the range of 0–3. For example, a modem on the second serial port has a device name of **/dev/ttyS1**, and **/dev/modem** is a link to the **/dev/ttyS1** device file. On most distributions, this is usually done for you during installation. On many systems, you can use a modem configuration tool called *modemtool* to create this link for you. Many modem programs and PPP configuration programs look for the **/dev/modem** file by default.

Dynamic Host Configuration Protocol (DHCP)

The *Dynamic Host Configuration Protocol* (*DHCP*) provides configuration information to systems connected to a TCP/IP network, whether the Internet or an intranet. The machines on the network operate as DHCP clients, obtaining their network configuration information from a DHCP server on their network. A machine on the network runs a DHCP client daemon that automatically downloads its network configuration information from its network's DHCP server. The information includes its IP address, along with the network's name server, gateway, and proxy addresses, including the netmask. Nothing has to be entered manually on the local system. This has the added advantage of centralizing control over network configuration for the different systems on the network. A network administrator can manage the network configurations for all the systems on the network from the DHCP server.

A DHCP server also supports several methods for IP address allocation: automatic, dynamic, and manual. *Automatic allocation* assigns a permanent IP address for a host. *Manual allocation* assigns an IP address designated by the network administrator. With *dynamic allocation,* a DHCP server can allocate an IP address to a host on the network only when the host actually needs to use it. Allocation can be made from a pool of IP addresses that hosts can use when needed and release when they are finished.

A variety of DHCP servers and clients are available for different operating systems. For Linux, you can obtain DHCP software from the *Internet Software Consortium* (*ISC*) at **www.isc.org**. The software package includes a DHCP server, client, and relay agent. Red Hat Linux includes a DHCP server and client. The DHCP client is called dhcpcd and the server is called dhcpd. The network information a DHCP client downloads is kept in its own network configuration files in the **/etc/dhcpc** directory. For example, here you can find a **resolv.conf** file for your network's name servers.

Linuxconf Network Configuration

Linuxconf provides panels for entering network configuration information that are saved to the appropriate network configuration files when you activate the changes. You use the Basic host information panel to enter your system's hostname and interface information. Select the panel from the Client tasks list under the Networking heading under Config. This panel has several tabbed subpanels for the hostname and for different adapters. On the Hostname panel, enter your system's fully qualified domain name (see Figure 28-1). You can also enter the **netconfig** command in a terminal window to display a Linuxconf window for only the network configuration panels (see Chapter 3).

You then use a different Adapter panel for each network interface on your system. Most systems have only one interface, usually an Ethernet or a PPP interface. To configure an interface, click an Adapter tab to display an Adapter panel (see Figure 28-2). On the Adapter panel, you can use a BOOTP, DHCP, or manual configuration. If the network to which this interface connects provides BOOTP or DHCP configuration

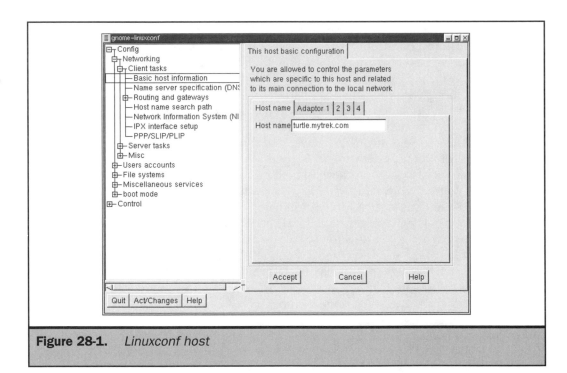

Figure 28-1.   *Linuxconf host*

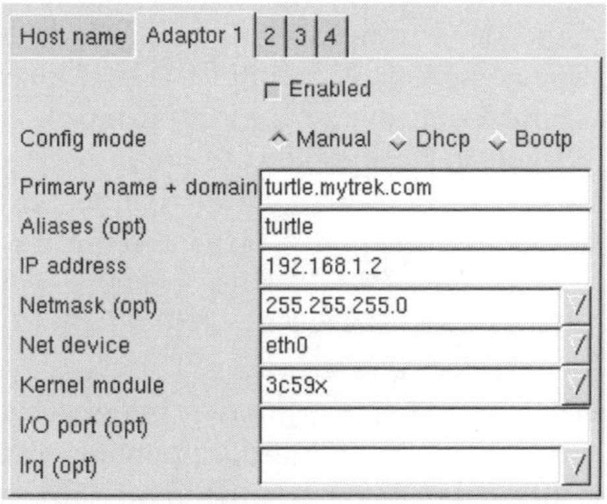

Figure 28-2. *Linuxconf Adaptor panel*

services, then your network information is automatically set up for you. Your system is configured with an IP address, name server and gateway addresses, and the network netmask. If such configuration services are not provided, you must enter your network information manually.

On the Adaptor panel, several boxes are for network interface information, some of which have drop-down menus for selecting entries. In the Primary name + domain box, enter your system's fully qualified domain name and, in the IP Address box, enter your system's IP address. In the Aliases box, you can enter nicknames (these are not IP aliases). For the Netmask box, include your network's netmask. In the Net Device box, enter the name of your network interface. The Net Device box has a drop-down menu listing the different interface devices available. You can select an entry from this menu to make your entry. For example, for an Ethernet card, you can select eth0 from the drop-down menu or, for a modem, you could select **ppp0**. The Kernel module box is where you enter the name of the module used for your interface's device. This is usually used for the many modules available for different Ethernet cards. This box has a long drop-down menu listing all the kernel modules available for your system. Choose the one appropriate for your card and, when you finish, click the Accept button. If the interface is active, the check box labeled Enabled at the top of the panel is darkened and recessed. If the interface is inactive, the check box is lighter and stands out. Click this check box to toggle the interface on and off.

You also must specify your network's domain name servers and search domains. Enter this information in the Resolver configuration panel. Select Name server specification (DNS) from the Client tasks list under the Networking heading. You then find three boxes for name server Internet addresses, starting with the first name server for your network (see Figure 28-3). Enter the IP address for your primary name server in the nameserver1 box, and enter the secondary name sever in the nameserver2 box. Enter your search domains in the search domains box. If your network is connected to the Internet, it has a gateway system. You enter the IP address for the gateway in the default gateway box on the Defaults panel in the Routing and gateways list. This is located in the Client tasks list under the Networking heading.

If you use a modem instead of an Ethernet card to connect to a network, you need to configure a dial-up interface. With Linuxconf, you can configure a PPP, SLIP, or PLIP interface. Most *Internet service providers* (*ISPs*) set up connections over a modem using PPP interfaces. To configure such an interface, click the PPP/SLIP/PLIP entry in the Routing and gateways list under Client tasks in Networking. This displays a PPP/SLIP/PLIP panel. When you add an interface, it displays another panel where you can choose the interface you want. If you select PPP, a PPP interface panel is displayed with boxes for the dial-up phone number, the interface device, and the login name and password you use to connect to your ISP (see Figure 28-4). If you click the Customize button, four more tabbed panels are displayed for Hardware, Communications, Networking, and Pap. On the Hardware panel, you can set communication speeds and the modem port, along with PPP options. The Communications panel enables you to set the modem initialization string, phone number, and dial-up command, as well as the Expect/Send script used for the ISP login operation. Here, you can specify what password and login prompt to expect. When you finish, click Accept. When you click the Linuxconf Activate/Changes button, it

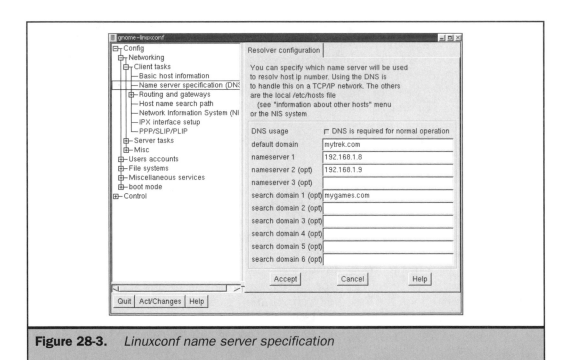

Figure 28-3. *Linuxconf name server specification*

saves your dial-up configuration to appropriate files, generating any needed scripts. For a PPP connection, it generates a chat script to dial the connection and an Expect/Send script for login. To use Linuxconf to connect to your ISP, click the Control PPP/SLIP/PLIP links entry in the Control panel list under Control (not Config). This displays a panel in which you can click a Connect button to have your modem dial up and connect to the ISP. You can also use the PPP/SLIP/PLIP entry in the Routing and gateways list under Client tasks in Networking. For a PPP connection, select the PPP interface panel and click the Connect button. When you finish, click the Disconnect button.

Red Hat Network Configuration Tool: netcfg

Red Hat provides an easy-to-use network configuration tool called netcfg. Other systems may also have this tool. On the Red Hat control panel, an icon is labeled Network Configuration. You can also start netcfg from the desktop or window manager's program menus, usually with the entry Network Configuration. The netcfg window consists of four panels and a button bar at the top for each one: Name, Hosts, Interfaces, and Routing (see Figure 28-5). Clicking a button displays its panel. Basic configuration of your network requires you to specify the hostname and IP address of your own system, the IP addresses of your network's name servers and gateway, the network netmask, and your network interfaces. Using the netcfg tool, you can easily enter all this information. The Name panel is where you enter your own system's hostname and your network's name server addresses. The Hosts panel lists host IP addresses and their domain names, including those for your own system. On the Interfaces panel, you add and configure your network interfaces, such as an Ethernet or PPP interface. The Routing panel is where you specify special routing hosts, including your gateway system. If you already configured your network during installation, your entries are already in these panels.

The Names panel has two boxes at the top, labeled Hostname and Domain. Here, you enter your system's fully qualified domain name and your network's domain

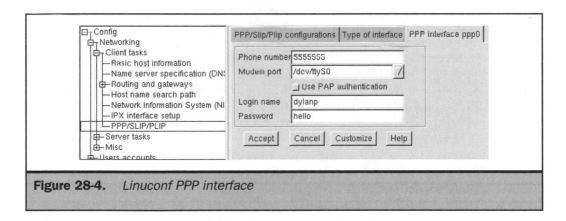

Figure 28-4. *Linuconf PPP interface*

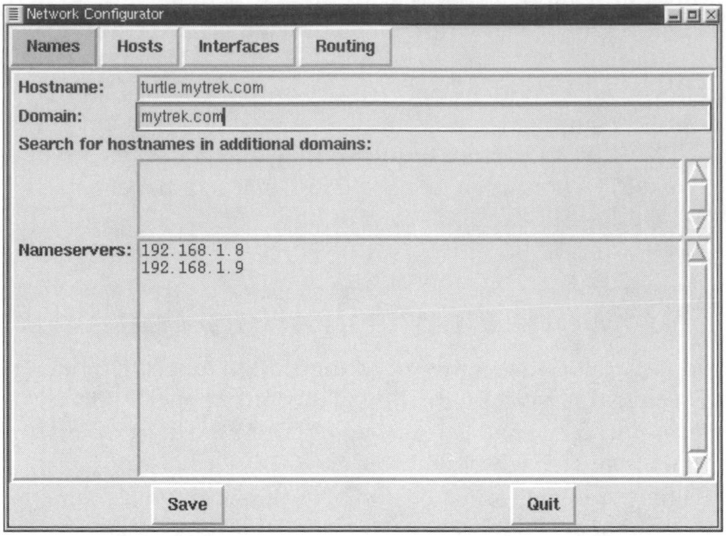

Figure 28-5. *netcfg Names panel*

name. For example, **turtle.mytrek.com** is the fully qualified domain name and **mytrek.com** is the domain name. The panel has two panes, one for search domains and another for name server addresses. For the search domain, you enter specific domains you want searched for an Internet address. In the name server pane, you enter the IP addresses for your network's name servers. Both the search domain and the name server addresses are saved in the **/etc/resolv.conf** file. The hostname is saved to your **/etc/HOSTNAME** file.

The Hosts panel has a single pane with Add, Edit, and Remove buttons (see Figure 28-6). This panel lists entries that associate hostnames with IP addresses. You can also add aliases (nicknames). The Hosts panel actually displays the contents of the **/etc/hosts** file and saves any entries you make to that file. To add an entry, click the Add button. A window opens with boxes for the hostname, IP address, and nicknames. When you click OK, the entry is added to the Hosts list. To edit an entry, click the Edit button and a similar window opens, enabling you to change any of the fields. To delete an entry, select it and click the Remove button.

The Interfaces panel lists configured network interfaces on your system (see Figure 28-7). Making entries here performs the same function as ifconfig. An entry shows the interface name, its IP address, preferences, whether it is made active whenever you boot, and whether it is currently active. Use the Add, Edit, Alias, and Remove buttons to manage the interface entries. You use the Activate and Deactive buttons to connect or disconnect the interface with the network. To add an interface,

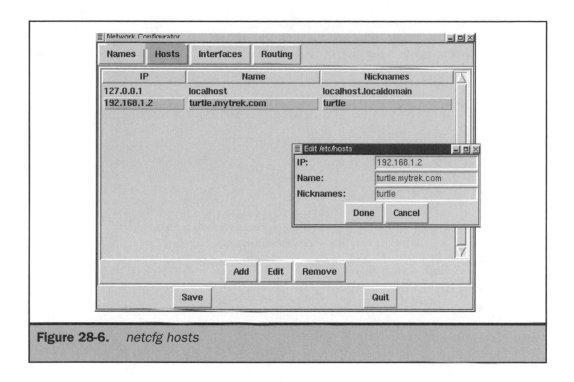

Figure 28-6. *netcfg hosts*

click the Add button. A window opens—the Choose Interface window—listing possible interfaces, including Ethernet or PPP. Select one and its appropriate interface window appears. For example, if you choose Ethernet, the Edit Ethernet Interface window appears. Here, you enter the IP address for your machine and your network's netmask. You can choose further if you want the interface to start automatically at boot time and whether you want to use the BOOTP or DHCP protocols to configure the interface. When you finish, you see your new entry displayed on the Interfaces panel. To activate your new entry, click the Activate button. To make any changes, select it and click the Edit button. The Alias button enables you to create IP aliases for the interface. This enables you to assign two IP addresses to the same interface, instructing your system to listen on that interface for packets and messages addressed to either IP address. In effect, you are giving your system two IP addresses.

The Routing panel has boxes at the top for your network's gateway system. In the Default Gateway box, enter the IP address of the gateway system and, in the Default Gateway Device box, specify the interface through which you connect to the network serviced by that gateway. This is usually the same interface you use to connect to your network. For example, the device for an Ethernet card would be eth0. If your network uses more than one gateway, you can add the others here by clicking the Add button. If you are on a *local area network* (*LAN*) with no connection to the Internet, you do not have a gateway and needn't make any entries here.

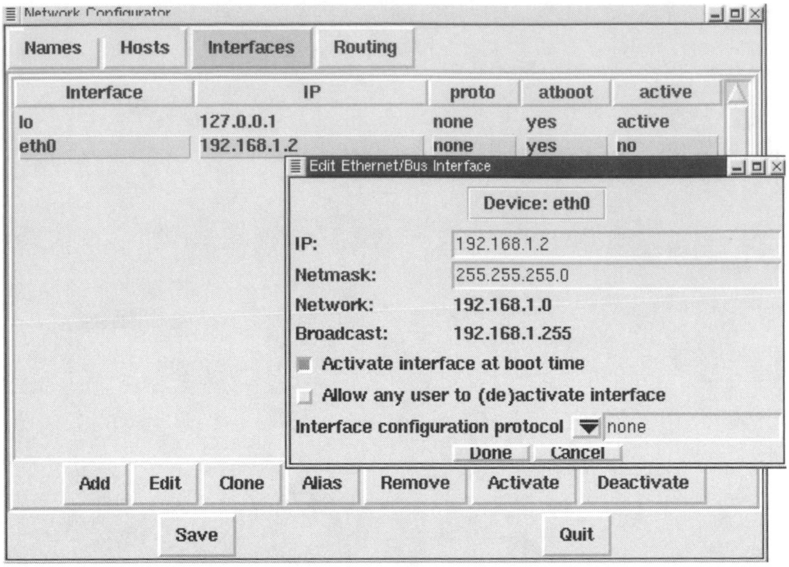

Figure 28-7.   *netcfg interfaces*

When you finish and are ready to save your configuration, click the Save button. If you want to abandon the changes you made, you can Quit without saving. You can run netcfg at any time to make changes in your network configuration or to connect or disconnect manually from a network using the Activate or Deactivate buttons on the Interfaces panel.

You can also use netcfg to configure a PPP interface. When you click Add and select PPP as the interface, a window opens with four panels: Hardware, Communications, Networking, and Pap (see Figure 28-8). The Hardware panel enables you to set hardware specifications, such as the modem speed and the port used. Select the Communications panel to display entries for your ISP's dial-up phone number, your Expect/Send script entries, and modem initializations. To add or change an Expect/ Send entry, click the Append, Insert, or Edit buttons. A window opens where you can enter the Expect and Send strings. When you finish, you can have your modem dial up a connection by simply selecting the PPP interface entry, usually ppp0, and then clicking the Activate button. Click the Deactivate button to disconnect. If you need to edit your PPP configuration, double-click the ppp0 interface entry in the Interfaces panel to display the PPP window.

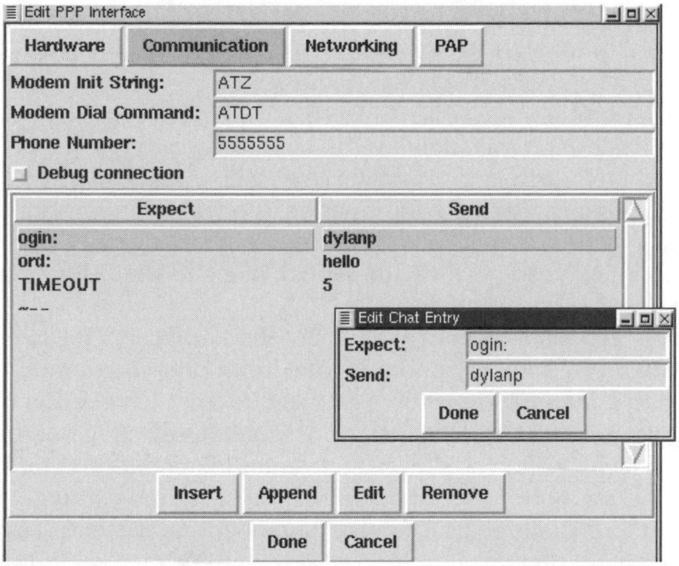

Figure 28-8.   *The netcfg PPP configuration*

PPP and SLIP

As an alternative to hardwired network connections such as Ethernet, you can use a
modem with telephone lines to connect to a network. Two protocols can transmit IP
communications across the telephone lines. These are the *Serial Line Internet Protocol*
(*SLIP*) and the *Point-to-Point Protocol* (*PPP*). SLIP is an older protocol, whereas PPP
is newer and has become predominant. Most high-speed connections used by current
ISPs use PPP. The SLIP and PPP protocols are especially designed for users who
connect their systems to the Internet over a modem and telephone line. Usually, a
connection is made to an ISP, which then connects the system to the Internet through
its own systems. An ISP supports either SLIP or PPP on a given line. Find out which
protocol your ISP supports. You need to use one or the other. Setting up a SLIP or PPP
connection can be a complicated process. For more detailed explanations, see the
PPP-HOWTO and the Net-2-HOWTO documents in **/usr/doc/HOWTO**. Web page
instructions are in **/usr/doc/HTML**, and you can also, check the **/usr/doc/ppp-***version*
where version is the PPP package version.

PPP Connection Utilities: kppp, gnomeppp, and rp3

You can use several graphical PPP configuration utilities on your Linux desktop to create and manage a PPP connection. For a simple PPP connection you can use the Red Hat PPP Dialer utility known as *rp3*. For more complex connections, you can use the KDE PPP tool called *kppp*, a Gnome PPP tool called *gnomeppp*, as well as several X-Windows-based tools such as *xisp* and *easyppp*. All the tools offer the same kind of interface, providing panels for login information, modem configuration, and dial-up connections. You can also use netcfg and Linuxconf to manage a PPP connection. Although their interface is somewhat different, netcfg and Linuxconf do perform many of the same tasks as described here for kppp.

For simple connections, you only need to use the Red Hat PPP Dialer (rp3). Select its entry in the Internet submenu on the Gnome desktop. If you do not have any Internet connections set up already, the Add New Internet Connection dialog box starts up. First, you are asked to configure your modem, selecting its serial device, speed, and sound level. Next, you are asked to enter ISP connection information, such as your login name, password, and phone number. Each time you want to connect, select the Red Hat PPP Dialer entry from the Gnome Internet menu. To change your setting or to add a new connection, select the Red Hat Dialup Configuration Tool entry in the Internet menu. The Edit button opens a window with panels for modifying connection and modem information. These tools are covered in more detail in Chapter 3.

This section discusses the **kppp** PPP utility in detail. You can use **kppp** as a model for using the other PPP tools. During **kppp** configuration, you are presented with a set of tabbed panels in which you enter Internet and modem information. Once configured, connecting is simply a matter of clicking a button labeled Connect. The kppp tool runs fine from the root user, but it needs permission set on certain files to allow use by other users on your system. See the documentation in the **/usr/doc/kppp*** directory, which also includes a detailed tutorial you can view with your Web browser. The main screen appears, as shown here:

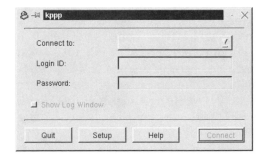

To configure a connection, click the Setup button. This brings up the Configuration window, which has several panels. One panel appears in the front, with tabs for the others

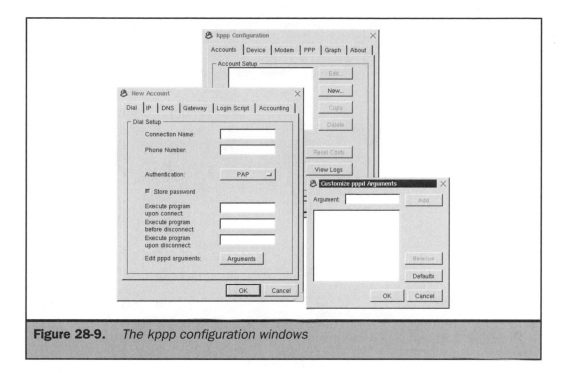

Figure 28-9.   *The kppp configuration windows*

showing at the top. Six panels are in the Configuration window: one for accounts, other panels for device and modem settings, and one for PPP features. Accounts hold your Internet information. You can have more than one account, depending on how many different ISPs you subscribe to (most users have only one). To create an account, click the New button. This brings up a New Accounts window with a set of panels for Internet information. The Dial panel is where you enter connection information, such as the phone number you use to connect to the provider. Be sure to enter a name for the connection, which can be anything you want. The Arguments button brings up another window for entering PPP arguments. These are options for the PPP daemon. Figure 28-9 shows the Configuration, New Accounts, and Arguments windows.

The IP panel is where you enter any local and remote IP addresses, as well as a netmask. Each entry has Dynamic and Static check buttons; the Dynamic check buttons are already set by default. If your ISP gives you dynamic addresses and a netmask, as most do these days, you can leave this panel alone. If, on the other hand, you have a static local or remote address, you must bring up the panel and enter the address(s). Click the tab labeled DNS to bring up the Domain Name Server panel. Here, you enter in the IP addresses of your ISP's domain name servers. Click the box labeled IP Address and type the address. Then, click Add to add the address to the list of name servers.

You then have to create a login script in which you provide the user name and password you use to connect to your ISP. To do this, click the Login Script tab to bring up the Script panel. You then see a frame called Edit Script with several buttons and boxes:

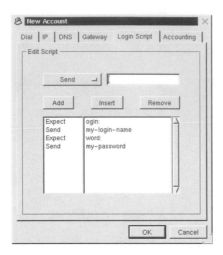

You need to create a simple script that performs the following task using two instructions: send and receive:

```
receive      ogin:
send         username
receive      word:
send         password
```

You see a button labeled Expect. This is actually a pop-up menu with several entries listing possible login instructions. The entry you select is shown when the pop-up menu collapses. Five entries exist: Expect, Send, Pause, Hangup, and Answer. The instructions usually used to send a string or to expect receiving a string are Send and Expect. If you want a send instruction, select the Send entry. If you want a receive instruction, select the Expect entry. The box to the right of this button is where you enter text on which the instruction operates. For example, for the instruction to receive the text ogin:, select the Expect entry and type **ogin:** into this box. To place it in the script, click the Add button. Both the term expect and the text ogin: appear in the script frame below the Add button. If you make a mistake, you can click the entry, and then click the Remove button to delete it. If you need to insert an instruction instead of having it placed at the end, use the Insert button.

Most login scripts only need two pairs of Send and Expect instructions: one for the login name and one for the password. The first instruction expects the text ogin: and the second instruction sends text consisting of the login name. The third instruction expects the text word: and the fourth sends the text consisting of the password. This may vary depending on how you connect to your ISP. The last illustration shows a

sample login script, where my-login-name is your user name and my-password is the
password you use.

After you finish entering the Internet information, click OK to close the Script and
New Accounts windows. At the Configure window, click the Modem tab to bring up
the Modem panel. Make sure the modem port is correct. Usually, this is **/dev/modem**,
where modem is a link to the actual modem port device. In most cases, you needn't
change this. Modem port devices begin with the name **/dev/ttyS** with an attached
number from 0 to 3. On your PC, you have four ports from which to choose: 1 through
4. Usually, a modem is connected to either port 2 or port 4. The names for these would
be **/dev/ttyS1** and **/dev/ttyS3** (the count is from 0, so port 1 is ttyS0 and port 2 is ttyS1).
If you already set up a modem alias for the port, you can use **/dev/modem**.

You then need to check the dialing prefix, as well as any special settings you may
need for your modem. You can click the Edit button to bring up a window with a long
list of boxes with settings for your modem. They should already have default settings
entered. The first box is where you enter your modem initialization string, adding such
instructions as M0 to turn off the connection sound. The third box, labeled Dial String,
is where you enter your dialing prefix. ATDT is the default already entered, which
most people use. Check also the Connect response entry and the Hangup string. The
default connect response is CONNECT, which is valid for most ISPs. The *Hangup string*
is a standard hang-up instruction for most modems.

After you finish, close the Configuration window by clicking the OK button. You
are then ready to use kppp. Click the Connect button in the main window. If you have
problems, click the show log window, and this brings up a window that displays the
connection process and any errors that occur. When kppp makes a connection, it
displays the amount of time connected and the speed at which it connected. The
Connect button is changed to Disconnect. To end your session, click Disconnect.
Clicking Quit ends the kppp program. Each individual user creates his or her own
accounts, using the steps described previously. This information is held in a **.kppprc**
file in the user's **home** directory. In fact, different users could use kppp to connect to
different ISPs.

Manual PPP Connections

You can manually create your own PPP connection, invoking the PPP program directly
on the command line with **chat** scripts to make the appropriate dial-up connections. The
PPP program is called **pppd** (**wvdial** is an alternative dialer discussed in Chaper 3).
The **pppd** program neither makes the initial connection nor does it dial up through your
modem and provide login and password information. To use **pppd**, you first must
establish the connection to the remote host. You can make such a connection using the
chat program, which has its own options and format. The chat program first makes the
connection, and then **pppd** configures it. You needn't call chat first, and then call **pppd**,
however. The **pppd** program is designed to take as its argument a program that can make
the connection—in this case, **chat**. You simply specify **chat** along with its options on the
command line with **pppd**.

Static and dynamic IP addresses are distinguished by **pppd** by whether you include a set of IP addresses as an argument on the command line and by the use of the **noipdefault** option. If you do include the IP addresses, then **pppd** assumes you have a static connection and these are the remote and local addresses to use to establish that connection. If you do not specify any addresses as arguments, then **pppd** assumes a default remote and local address. The default local address is the IP address of your systems, as specified in your **/etc/hostname** file. A default remote address tries to be determined from remote addresses in your **/etc/hosts** file. The **pppd** program assumes you use dynamic addresses and looks for them when a connection is made. To have **pppd** assume dynamic addresses, you use the **noipdefault** option and you do not specify any addresses. The **noipdefault** option instructs **pppd** not to use default addresses. With no address is specified, **pppd** then assumes dynamic addresses are going to be received from the remote host.

The local and remote static addresses are entered next to each other, separated by a colon. The local address is entered first. The following example specifies a local address of **192.168.1.72** and remote address of **163.179.4.22**.

```
192.168.1.72:163.179.4.22
```

If you use a dynamic remote address, but your own local address, you can specify only your local address, followed by the colon. The **pppd** program then uses your local address and dynamically receives your remote address.

```
192.168.1.72:
```

Because your local address as specified in your **/etc/hostname** file is your default local address, you needn't even enter it on the command line. You could enter only the **pppd** command with no addresses. The **pppd** program uses your hostname address as your local address and receives a remote address from the remote host.

Most ISPs that use dynamic addresses provide you with both the local and remote address. In this case, you do not enter any addresses at all and you do have to specify the **noipdefault** option. The **noipdefault** option prevents the use of the hostname address as the default local address. Lacking any addresses, **pppd** obtains both from the remote host.

Chat Scripts

The best way to use chat is to invoke a **chat** script. To make a connection, **chat** has to specify all the connection information: the telephone number, login prompt and user ID, password prompt and password, and any connect strings. You could enter this as a string after the **chat** command on the command line, but this makes for a long and complex command line. Instead, you can create a file with the chat information in it, and then use the **-f** option and the filename with the **chat** command. Such files are called **chat** scripts.

A *chat script* consists of one line organized into different segments for the parts of the connection procedure. Each segment consists of an expect-reply pair of strings. The first string is what you expect to receive, while the second string is what you are sending. If you expect to receive nothing, then you use a null string, *""*. Each expect-reply pair performs a specific task in the login process. You can start with an initialization of your modem, if you need to do this. Many users can simply use the default settings. Then, the number is dialed to make the connection and you can check to see if the connection was made. A login name is provided at the login prompt. And, finally, a password is sent at the password prompt.

If you decide to initialize your modem, you need to start with an expect-reply entry to perform this task. You expect nothing at first, so the expect string is only an empty string, two double quotes, *""*. For the reply string, you specify the codes for your modem initialization. When entering the codes for your initialization string, you need to escape any code beginning with **&**. For chat, the **&** is a break and stops the process. See Table 28-1 for a list of **chat** options and special characters.

The next expect-reply entry dials the phone number. If you have an initialization string before the next expect-reply entry, then its expect string is the word OK. This is the response from your modem indicating no problem occurred initializing your modem. You usually receive a connect string indicating you have connected to the remote system. This can vary from system to system, and there may not even be a connect string at all. On many systems, the connect string is the word CONNECT; on others, the connect string is the baud rate, or speed. In this example, the user receives the speed as the connect string. The response to a connect string is usually nothing, though it can also be a newline. Recall that you represent no response with an empty string—two double quotes, *""*. The newline is represented in a **chat** script with a **\n**.

After the connect string, the remote system usually sends the login prompt. This is often the word "login" with a colon. You only need the last few characters, **ogin:** and don't forget the colon. In reply, you send your user ID. Depending on your ISP, you may have to add **\n** to the user ID to enter a newline, as in **mylogin\n**.

```
ogin:  mylogin
```

After the login, you can expect the password prompt. Again, you only need the last few characters, **word:**. In response, you send your password. If needed, be sure to add the **\n** to enter the newline.

```
word:  mypass
```

All this fits together on just one line. You have a sequence of words that indicate alternating received and sent text:

```
"" AT\&F2V1L0 OK   ATDT8888888 CONNECT \n ogin: mylogin  word: mypass
```

If you did not initialize your modem, it looks slightly different:

```
"" ATDT8888888 CONNECT  \n  ogin:   mylogin  word:   mypass
```

If your ISP does not require you to send a return character on receiving the connect string, you can leave that out, reducing the **chat** script as shown here:

```
"" ATDT8888888 ogin:   mylogin  word:   mypass
```

In a **chat** script, you can break the expect and reply pairs into separate lines, one pair to a line, with the strings for each pair separated by a space or tab. You could also put it all on the first line if you want. The filename for the script has the extension **.chat**. The next example shows the **/etc/ppp/ppp.chat** script with pairs entered on separate lines.

ppp.chat

```
"  "          AT\&F2V1L0
OK            ATDT4448888
CONNECT       \n
ogin:         mylogin
word:         mypass
```

You can then call the **chat** script with the **chat** command and the **-f** option, as shown here. The chat program uses the information in the **chat** script to initialize your modem, to dial up your remote host, and then to log in with your user ID and password.

```
chat -f  /etc/ppp/ppp.chat
```

Many remote systems and modes send error messages if something goes wrong in the connection process. You can use the special expect string, ABORT, followed by a key term to detect such an error message. If such a term is received, chat cancels the connection procedure. If you are using a command line only, you can enter abort strings either where you would expect them to occur in the connection process or at the beginning. Within a **chat** script, as shown here, the abort strings are placed at the beginning. The next example would expect a NO CARRIER or a BUSY response before the login prompt. In either case, an initial connection failed, and **chat** will cancel the remaining steps. Notice the quotes around NO CARRIER. If a string has a space in it, you have to quote it.

ppp.chat

```
ABORT       'NO CARRIER'
ABORT       BUSY
" "         AT\&F2V1L0
OK          ATDT5558888
CONNECT     \n
ogin:       mylogin
word:       mypass
```

You need to incorporate the **chat** operation into your invocation of the **pppd** command. The entire **chat** operation is encased in single quotes and entered on the same line as the **pppd** command. The **chat** program uses the information in the **chat** script to initialize your modem, dial up your remote host, and then log in with your user ID and password. The **chat** script makes the connection, and then **pppd** configures it. The Point-to-Point Protocol daemon (**pppd**) is invoked with several possible options. Its standard syntax is

pppd *options serial-device-name speed local:remote-addresses ppp-options*

The *serial-device-name* is the device name for your modem. This is likely to be **/dev/ttyS** with a number attached, usually from 0 to 3, depending on the port you are using for your modem. Port 1 is ttyS0, port 2 is ttyS2, and so on. The *speed* is the baud rate. For a 14.4 modem, this is 14400. For a v.28 modem, this is 38400, or even 56700. Check with your ISP and your modem documentation for the highest speed you can support.

The options specify configuration features, such as your MTU size and whether you are receiving a dynamic IP address. The **connect** option instructs **pppd** to make a connection and takes as its argument a Linux command that can actually make the connection—usually the **chat** command. You enter **pppd,** followed by the **connect** option, and the **chat** command with its **-f** option and **chat** script filename. The **chat** command and its **-f** option with the chat filename are all enclosed in quotes to distinguish them from other **pppd** options. In the next example, the user invokes **pppd** with the **chat** command using the **mycon.chat chat** script. The modem is connected to port 4, **/dev/ttyS1**, and the speed is 57600 baud.

```
# pppd connect  'chat -f  /etc/ppp/ppp.chat'  /dev/ttyS1   57600
```

To disconnect your PPP connection, you invoke **pppd** with the **disconnect** option. You must use **chat** to instruct your modem to hang up. For this, you may have to send a modem command, such as **H0**. You can also use the **ppp-off** script to disconnect. You might find a chat file is a more convenient to place the **chat** commands, as shown here:

```
# pppd disconnect  'chat  -f  turnoff.chat'
```

turnoff.chat

```
—  \d+++\d\c     OK
ATH0   OK
```

Option	Description
-f *filename*	Executes **chat** commands in the **chat** script with name *filename*
-l *lockfile*	Makes UUCP style like file using *lockfile*
-t *num*	Timeout set to *num* seconds
-v	A description of all chat actions are output to the **/log/messages** file; use tail, cat, or more on this file to display the descriptions: tail /log/messages

Special Characters

BREAK	Sends break to modem
''	Sends null string with single newline character
\b	BACKSPACE
\c	Suppresses newline sent after reply string
\d	Makes chat wait for one second
\K	Sends break; when specifying string for modem initialization, and codes beginning with *K* may have to be escaped
\n	Sends newline characters
\N	Sends null character
\p	Pauses for 1/10 of a second
\q	String does not appear in **syslog** file
\r	Sends or expects a new line
\s	Sends or expects a space
\t	Sends or expects a tab
\\	Sends or expects a backslash
nnn	Specifies a character in octal
^C	Specifies a control character

Table 28-1.   *The* Chat *Options and Special Characters*

PPP Options

The **pppd** command has a great many options. The more commonly used ones are listed in Table 28-2. See the **pppd** man pages for a complete list. For example, the **mru** option sets the maximum receive unit size. The **pppd** command instructs the remote system to send packets no larger than this size. The default is 1,500, and 296 or 542 is recommended for slower modems. The **defaultroute** option instructs **pppd** to set up the PPP connection as the default route. The lack of any addresses combined with the **noipdefault** option instructs **pppd** to detect and use a dynamic IP address from the ISP remote system. You have to specify this option if you have an ISP that supplies dynamic IP addresses. The **crtscts** option uses hardware flow control, while the **modem** option uses the modem control lines. You can list the options after the speed on the command line, as shown here:

```
# pppd connect  'chat -f  /etc/ppp/ppp.chat'  /dev/ttyS1   57600
    mru 1500  defaultroute noipdefault crtscts modem
```

In the following command, the presence of addresses instructs **pppd** to use these addresses to establish a static connection. The local address is **192.168.1.72** and the remote address is **163.179.4.22**.

```
# pppd connect  'chat -f  /etc/ppp/ppp.chat'  /dev/ttyS1   57600
192.168.1.72:163.179.4.22 mru 1500 defaultroute crtscts modem
```

This can make for a lengthy and complex command line, depending on how many options you need. As an alternative, **pppd** enables you to enter options in the file **/etc/ppp/options,** as well as in a **.ppprc** file. The **pppd** option automatically reads and uses the options specified in these files each time it is invoked. You can specify as many options as you want, entering each on a separate line. With the **#** symbol, you can also enter comments, explaining the options and their settings. The **/etc/ppp/options** file contains system default options for **pppd**. You create this file as the root user, and it is the first options file called when **pppd** is invoked. Each user can have a **.ppprc** file in her own **home** directory. These options are specified by a particular user and are read after the system's **/etc/ppp/options** file.

/etc/ppp/options

```
crtscts
defaultroute
modem
mru 1500
asyncmap 0
netmask 255.255.255.0
noipdefault
```

Now when you invoke **pppd**, you needn't enter any of these options on the command line. With your options specified in the **/etc/ppp/options** file, you then only need to enter the **pppd** command with the **chat** invocation, the device name for your modem, and the modem speed.

```
$ pppd connect 'chat -f /etc/ppp/ppp.chat' /dev/ttyS1  57600
```

You can reduce your entry even further by placing the **pppd** invocation in a shell script, and then executing the shell script. Recall that a shell script is a text file you create with any text editor. You type the command invocation with all its arguments as you would on the command line. Be sure to precede the **pppd** command with an **exec** command. The **exec** command runs **pppd** from your command line shell, not the script's shell. You then make the script executable with the command **chmod 755** *script-name*. Now, to execute your **pppd** operation, enter the script name on the command line and press ENTER. In the next example, the **pppd** connect operation is placed in a shell script called **pppcon**, and the user simply enters **pppcon** to invoke **pppd**.

pppcon
```
exec pppd connect 'chat -f /etc/ppp/ppp.chat' /dev/ttyS1 57600
$ pppcon
```

You are now ready to try **pppd** to connect to your remote system. Any number of things may go wrong. You may not have the right connect string or the modem may be initializing wrong. The **pppd** command logs descriptions of all the steps it is taking in the **/var/log/messages** file. You can use **tail** to list these descriptions even as **pppd** is operating. For a successful connection, you see the local and remote IP addresses listed at the end, as shown here:

```
$ tail /var/log/messages
```

To receive an ongoing display of messages as they are entered in the **/var/log/messages** file, use the **tail** command with the **-f** option, as shown here. Use a CTRL-C to end the process.

```
$ tail -f /var/log/messages
Mar 23 20:01:03 richlp pppd[208]: Connected...
Mar 23 20:01:04 richlp pppd[208]: Using interface ppp
Mar 23 20:01:04 richlp kernel: ppp: channel ppp mtu=1500, mru=1500
Mar 23 20:01:04 richlp kernel: ppp: channel ppp open
Mar 23 20:01:04 richlp pppd[208]: Connect: ppp ~/dev/ttyS3
Mar 23 20:01:09 richlp pppd[208]: local  IP address 204.32.168.68
Mar 23 20:01:09 richlp pppd[208]: remote IP address 163.179.4.23
```

The ppp RPM package installed on Red Hat systems includes a sample login PPP script called **ppp-on** in the **/usr/doc/ppp-***version***/scripts** directory, where version is the pppd version. You can use a text editor to set the correct values to certain variables, such as TELEPHONE, ACCOUNT, and PASSWORD. You also must be careful to set the correct arguments and options for both the **chat** and the **pppd** commands. If you have already set options in the **/etc/ppp/options** file, you can remove most of the options you would normally specify on the command line. Also, be sure to set the correct speed and device name for the modem. The default used on the script is 38400. For a 56K modem, change it to 57600. Once working, all you must enter then is **ppp-on** to establish your PPP connection. If you have trouble disconnecting, try the **ppp-off** command.

You can also configure your system to be a PPP server, allowing remote systems to dial into yours and make PPP connections. You only need to create one special account and a script to invoke **pppd** with the **-detach** and **silent** options. The script is usually called **ppplogin**—here is an example:

/etc/ppp/ppplogin
```
exec pppd -detach silent modem crtscts
```

With the **-detach** option, **pppd** won't detach itself from the line on which it is located. The **silent** option makes **pppd** wait for a remote system to make a link to your system. The **modem** option monitors the modem lines, and **crtscts** uses hardware flow control. The special account has the name ppp. The **/etc/passwd** entry for the ppp account appears as follows:

```
ppp:*:501:300:PPP Account:/tmp:etc/ppp/ppplogin
```

PPP Security: CHAP

To ensure security for PPP connections, you have to use additional protocols. Two have been developed for PPP: the *Password Authentication Protocol* (*PAP*) and the *Challenge Handshake Authentication Protocol* (*CHAP*). CHAP is considered a more secure protocol because it uses an encrypted challenge system that requires the two connected systems to authenticate each other continually. The keys for the encryption are kept in the **/etc/ppp/chap-secrets** file. To use CHAP in your PPP connections, you include the **auth** option when you invoke **pppd**. Also, you must enter the required information for the remote host into the **/etc/ppp/chap-secrets** file. The following is an example of a **/etc/ppp/chap-secrets** entry. Entries for the PAP in **/etc/ppp/pap-secrets** have the same format.

etc/ppp/chap-secrets

pango1.train.com	turtle.trek.com	"my new hat"
*	turtle.trek.com	"confirmed tickets"
turtle.trek.com	pango1.train.com	"trek on again"

Option	Description
device-name	Uses the specified device; if the device name does not have **/dev** preceding it, pppd adds it for you
speed *num*	Sets the modem speed (baud rate)
asyncmap *map*	Sets the async character map that specifies what control characters cannot be sent and should be escaped
auth	Requires the remote host to authenticate itself
connect *Connection-operation*	Uses the connection operations to set up the connection; the Linux command here is usually chat, which makes the actual connection
crtscts	Uses hardware flow control
xonxoff	Uses software flow control
defaultroute	**pppd** sets a default route to the remote host
disconnect *Linux-command*	Runs the specified command after **pppd** cuts its connection; usually a chat operation
escape *c,c,...*	Causes the specified characters to be escaped when transmitted
file *filename*	Reads **pppd** options from the specified file
lock	Uses UUCP-style locking on the serial device
mru *num*	Sets the maximum receive units to *num*
netmask *mask*	Sets the PPP network interface mask
noipdefault	For dynamic IP addresses provided by ISP; searches the incoming data stream from the remote host for both the local and remote IP addresses assigned to your system for that Internet session; must have this option to connect with a dynamic IP address
passive	Makes **pppd** wait for a valid connection instead of failing when it can't make the connection immediately
silent	**pppd** waits for a connection to be made by a remote host

Table 28-2.   *The pppd Options*

A CHAP secrets entry has up to four fields: the client's host name, the server's host name, a secret key, and a list of IP possible addresses. For a particular computer trying to make a connection to your system, you can specify that it supply the indicated secret key. Instead of specifying a particular computer, you can use a ***** to indicate any computer. Any system that knows the designated secret key can connect to your system. In the first entry in the following example, the server is the user's own system, **turtle.trek.com**. The server allows **pango1.train.com** to connect to it if it provides the secret key specified. In the next entry, any remote system can connect to **turtle.trek.com** if it knows the secret key "confirmed tickets".

```
pango1.train.com    turtle.trek.com   "my new hat"
   *                turtle.trek.com   "confirmed tickets"
```

You also have to make entries for remote systems you want to access. In that case, the remote system is the PPP server and you are the client. In the next example, **turtle** can connect to **pango1** with the secret key "trek on again".

```
turtle.trek.com pango1.train.com "trek on again"
```

SLIP: dip

Two types of SLIP connections exist: the standard one referred to simply as *SLIP*, and the newer *Compress SLIP* (*CSLIP*). Be sure you know which type of connection your ISP is giving you. You must specify one or the other as your protocol mode when you connect. Except for specifying the mode, the connection procedure is the same for both. References to SLIP apply to both SLIP and CSLIP, unless specifically noted. You use the dip program to manage and set up your SLIP connection. The *dip program* operates like an interpreter. In a file called a **dip** script, you specify certain commands needed to log in to the ISP and make the connection. The dip program then reads the commands in this file, executing them one by one. With Linux, not only can you make a SLIP connection to a remote system, but other systems can also make their own SLIP connections to your system. Another system can dial into your system and make a SLIP connection. If you have provided an account for a user on that remote system, then the user could dial in a SLIP connection and log in to that account. Such remote dial-up SLIP connections are managed by **dip** with the **-i** option. This places dip in a dial-in mode to receive incoming connections. In the dial-in mode, dip prompts a remote user for a user ID and a password, and then makes the SLIP connection.

The Complete Reference

Linux

Chapter 29

Samba, NFS, NIS, and Appletalk

L inux provides several tools for accessing files on remote systems connected to a network. The *Network File System* (*NFS*) enables you to connect to and directly access resources, such as files or devices like CD-ROMs that reside on another machine. The *Network Information Service (NIS)* maintains configuration files for all systems on a network. With Samba, you can connect your Windows clients on a Microsoft Windows network to services such as shared files, systems, and printers controlled by the Linux Samba server. Netatalk enables you to connect your Linux systems to an AppleTalk network, enabling you to access remote Macintosh file systems directly, as well as to access any Apple printers, such as LaserWriters.

Network File Systems: NFS and /etc/exports

The NFS enables you to mount a file system on a remote computer as if it were local to your own system. You can then directly access any of the files on that remote file system. This has the advantage of allowing different systems on a network to access the same files directly, without each having to keep its own copy. Only one copy would be on a remote file system, which each computer could then access.

NFS operates over a TCP/IP network. The remote computer that holds the file system makes it available to other computers on the network. It does so by exporting the file system, which entails making entries in an NFS configuration file called **/etc/exports**, as well as by running three daemons to support access by other systems: **rpc.mountd, rpc.nfsd,** and **rpc.portmapper.rpc.nfsd** receives NFS requests from remote systems and translates them into requests for the local system. **rpc.mountd** performs requested mount and unmount operations. **rpc.portmapper** maps remote requests to the appropriate NFS daemon. You can use the **rpcinfo** command with the **-p** options to see if the daemons are running.

An entry in the **/etc/exports** file specifies the file system to be exported and the computers on the network that can access it. For the file system, enter its *mountpoint*, the directory to which it was mounted. This is followed by a list of computers that can access this file system. A comma-separated list of mount options placed within a set of parentheses may follow each computer. For example, you might want to give one computer read-only access and another read and write access. If only the options are listed, they are applied to anyone. A list of mount options is provided in Table 29-1. Examples of entries in an **/etc/exports** file are shown here. Read-only access with no security check is given to all computers to the file system mounted on the **/pub** directory, a common name used for public access. Read and write access is given to the **ant.trek.com** computer for the file system mounted on the **/home/foodstuff** directory. The next entry would allow access by **butterfly.trek.com** to your CD-ROM. The last entry denies anyone access to **/home/richlp**.

/etc/exports

```
/pub                      (ro,insecure,all_squash)
/home/foodstuff           ant.trek.com(rw)
/mnt/cdrom                butterfly.trek.com(ro)
/home/richlp              (noaccess)
```

Instead of editing the **/etc/exports** file directly, you can use Linuxconf's Exported file systems panel in the Server tasks list under the Networking heading in Config. Click the Add button to add a new entry. Figure 29-1 shows the panel with the **butterfly** example.

Once an NFS file system is made available, different computers on the network must first mount it before they can use the file system. You can mount an NFS file system either by an entry in the **/etc/fstab** file or by an explicit **mount** command. An NFS entry in the **/etc/fstab** file has a mount type of NFS. An NFS file system name consists of the hostname of the computer it is located on, followed by the pathname of the directory where it is mounted. The two are separated by a colon. For example, **rabbit.trek.com:/home/project** specifies a file system mounted at **/home/project** on the **rabbit.trek.com** computer.

You can also include several NFS-specific mount options with your NFS entry. You can specify the size of datagrams sent back and forth, and the amount of time your computer waits for a response from the host system. You can also specify whether a file system is to be hard-mounted or soft-mounted. For a *hard-mounted file system,* your computer continually tries to make contact if, for some reason, the remote system fails to respond. A *soft mounted file system,* after a specified interval, gives up trying to make contact and issues an error message. A hard mount is the default. Table 29-2 and the man pages for **mount** contain a listing of these NFS client options. They differ from the NFS server options indicated previously.

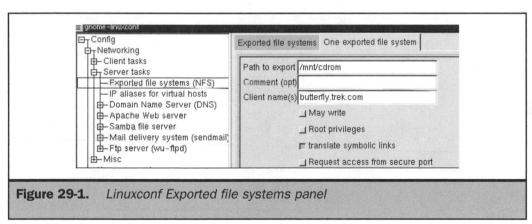

Figure 29-1.   *Linuxconf Exported file systems panel*

An example of an NFS entry follows. The remote system is **rabbit.trek.com** and the file system is mounted on **/home/projects**. This file system is to be mounted on the local system's **/home/dylan** directory. The type of system is NFS and the `timeo` option specifies the local system waits up to 20-tenths of a second (two seconds) for a response.

```
rabbit.trek.com:/home/projects      /home/dylan      nfs    timeo=20
```

You can also use the `mount` command with the `-t nfs` option to mount an NFS file system explicitly. To mount the previous entry explicitly, use the following command:

```
# mount -t nfs -o timeo=20    rabbit.trek.com:/home/projects    /home/dylan
```

Instead of editing the **/etc/fstab** file directly, you can use Linuxconf's Access nfs volume in the File systems list under Config. Figure 29-2 shows the Access NFS volume panel.

Clicking the Add button displays Volume specification panels for Base entries, standard file options, and NFS options. In the Base tab, boxes exist for the remote server, the remote directory (volume), and the directory on your local system where the remote directory is to be attached (mountpoint). Figure 29-3 shows the Volume specification panel where the remote server is **rabbit.trek.com** and the remote directory is **/home/projects**. The local mountpoint directory is **/home/dylan**.

NFS file systems are mounted automatically by **/etc/fstab**. If you want to mount and unmount all the NFS file systems manually, you can do so with the **/etc/rc.d/init.d/ netfs** script. This script reads the **/etc/fstab** file and copies the NFS entries, using them

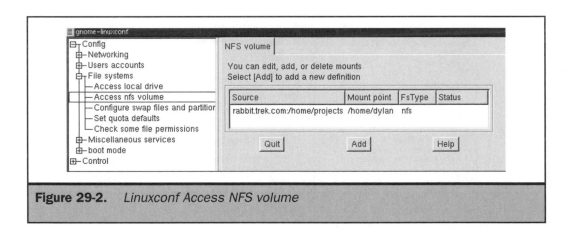

Figure 29-2.   *Linuxconf Access NFS volume*

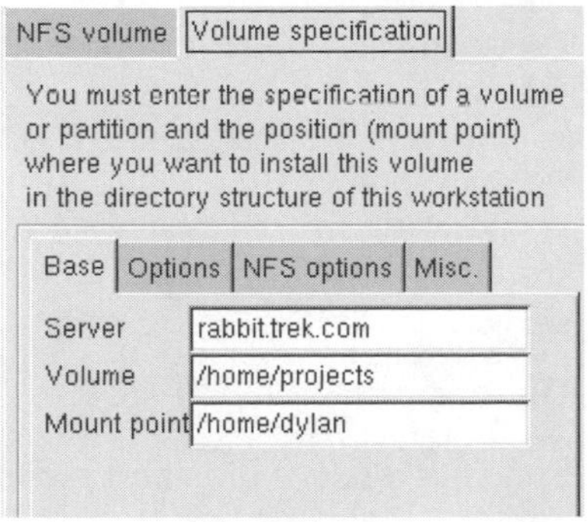

Figure 29-3. *Linuxconf Volume specification for NFS*

to manage the file systems. Using the stop argument unmounts the file systems and, with the start argument, you mount them again. The restart argument first unmounts, and then remounts the file systems.

```
/etc/rc.d/init.d/netfs stop
```

General Options	Description
secure	Requires authentication. This is on by default.
ro	Allows only read-only access.
rw	Allows read-write access. This is the default.
noaccess	Makes everything below the directory inaccessible for the named client.
link_absolute	Leaves all symbolic links as they are. This is the default operation.

Table 29-1. *The /etc/exports Options*

General Options	Description
link_relative	Converts absolute symbolic links (where the link contents start with a slash) into relative links by prepending the necessary number of slashes (/) to get from the directory containing the link to the root on the server.

User ID Mapping	Description
squash_uids squash_gids	Specifies a list of uids and gids that should be subject to anonymous mapping.
all_squash	Maps all uids and gids to the anonymous user. Useful for NFS-exported public FTP directories, news spool directories, and so forth.
no_all_squash	The opposite option to **all_squash**, and is the default setting.
root_squash	Maps requests from uid/gid 0 to the anonymous uid/gid.
no_root_squash	Turns off root squashing. Does not map requests from uid/gid 0. This is the default.
anonuid anongid	Set explicitly the uid and gid of the anonymous account. Primarily useful for PC/NFS clients, where you might want all requests to appear to be from one user.
map_daemon	Turns on dynamic uid/gid mapping. The uids in NFS requests are translated to the equivalent server uids. The uids in NFS replies are mapped the other way. The default setting is map identity, which leaves all uids untouched.

Table 29-1.   *The /etc/exports Options* (continued)

Options	Description
rsize=*n*	The number of bytes NFS uses when reading files from an NFS server. The default is 1,024 bytes.
wsize=*n*	The number of bytes NFS uses when writing files to an NFS server. The default is 1,024 bytes.
timeo=*n*	The value in tenths of a second before sending the first retransmission after a timeout. The default value is seven-tenths of a second.
retry=*n*	The number of times to retry a backgrounded NFS **mount** operation before giving up. The default is 10,000 times.
soft	Mount system using soft mount.
hard	Mount system using hard mount. This is the default.
intr	Allow NFS to interrupt the file operation and return to the calling program. The default is not to allow file operations to be interrupted.
bg	If the first mount attempt times out, continue trying the mount in the background. The default is to fail without backgrounding.
tcp	Mount the NFS file system using the TCP protocol, instead of the default UDP protocol.

Table 29-2.   *NFS Options*

Network Information Service: NIS

On networks supporting NFS, many resources and devices are shared by the same systems. Normally, each system would need its own configuration files for each device or resource. Changes would entail updating each system individually. However, NFS provides a special service called *Network Information Service* (*NIS*) that maintains such configuration files for the entire network. For changes, you only need to update the NIS files. NIS works for information required for most administrative tasks, such as those relating to users, network access, or devices. For example, you can maintain password information with an NIS service, having only to update those NIS password files.

NIS was developed by Sun Microsystems and was originally known as Sun's *Yellow Pages* (*YP*). NIS files are kept on an NIS server (NIS servers are still sometimes referred to as *YP servers*). Individual systems on a network use NIS clients to make requests from the NIS server. The NIS server maintains its information on special database files called *maps*. Linux versions exist for both NIS clients and servers. Linux NIS clients easily connect to any network using NIS.

Most Linux distributions contain both the Linux NIS client and server software in RPM packages that install with default configurations. The NIS client is installed as part of the initial installation on most Linux distributions. You can use Linuxconf Network Information Service panel in the Client tasks list under Networking to specify the remote NIS server on your network. NIS client programs are ypbind (the NIS client daemon), ypwhich, ypcat, yppoll, ypmatch, yppasswd, and ypset. Each has its own man page with details of its use. The NIS server programs are ypserv, ypinit, yppasswd, yppush, ypxfr, and netgroup—each also with its own man page. A detailed NIS-HOWTO document is available in the **/usr/doc/HOWTO** directory.

Samba

Two different kinds of networks have evolved: one centered around Microsoft Windows operating systems and the other around UNIX operating systems. Whereas most UNIX systems use the TCP/IP protocol for networking, Microsoft Windows uses a different protocol, called the *Session Message Block* (*SMB*) protocol, that implements a *local area network* (*LANs*) of PCs running Windows. SMB makes use of a network interface called *Network Basic Input Output System* (*NetBIOS*) that allows Windows PCs to share resources, such as printers and disk space. One Windows PC on such a network can access part of another Windows PC's disk drive as if it were its own. SMB was originally designed for small LANs. To connect it to larger networks, including those with UNIX systems, Microsoft developed the *Common Internet File System* (*CIFS*). CIFS still uses SMB and NetBIOS for Windows networking. Andrew Tridgell wrote a version of SMB he called *Samba*. Samba also allows UNIX and Linux systems to connect to such a Windows network, as if they were Windows PCs. UNIX systems can share resources on Window's systems as if they were just another Windows PC. Windows PCs can also access resources on UNIX systems as if they were Windows systems. Samba, in effect, has become a professional level, open source, and free version of CIFS. It also runs twice as fast. Samba effectively enables you to use a Linux or UNIX server as a network server for a group of Windows machines operating on a Windows network. You can also use it to share files on your Linux system with other Windows PCs or to access files on a Windows PC from your Linux system, as well as between

Windows PCs. On Linux systems, an **smbfs** file system enables you, in effect, to mount a remote SMB-shared directory on to your own file system. You can then access it as if it were a directory on your local system.

You can obtain extensive documentation and current releases from the Samba Web and FTP sites at **www.samba.org** and **ftp.samba.org**. RPM packages can be obtained from respective distribution FTP sites, such as **ftp.redhat.com**. Samba is also included on most Linux distributions, including Red Hat. Other information can be obtained from the SMB newsgroup, **comp.protocols.smb**. Extensive documentation is provided with the software package and installed on your system, usually in the **/usr/doc** directory under a subdirectory bearing the name of the Samba release. Here, you can find extensive documentation in HTML and text format, as well as numerous examples and the current FAQs. The examples include sample **smb.conf** files for different kinds of configuration. The home page of the SWAT configuration utility also provides Web page-based Samba documentation, as well as context level Help for different features.

The Samba software package consists of two server daemons and several utility programs: **smbd**, **nmbd**, **smbclient**, **smbstatus**, and **testparm** (see Table 29-3). One daemon, smbd, provides file and printer services to SMD clients and other systems, such as Windows, that support SMD. The **nmbd** utility is a daemon that provides NetBIOS name resolution and service browser support. The **smbclient** utility provides FTP-like access by Linux clients to Samba services. **smbmount** and **smbumount** enable Linux clients to mount and unmount Samba-shared directories. The **smbstatus** utility displays the current status of the smb server and who is using it. You use **testparm** to test your Samba configuration. smbtar is a shell script that backs up SMB/CIFS-shared resources directly to a UNIX tape drive. You use **nmblookup** to map the NetBIOS name of a Windows PC to its IP address. Included also with the package is the *Samba Web administration tool* (*SWAT*). This enables you to use a Web page interface to create and maintain your Samba configuration file, **smb.conf**.

Samba provides four main services: file and printer services, authentication and authorization, name resolution, and service announcement. The SMB daemon, smbd, provides the file and printer services, as well as authentication and authorization for those services. This means users on the network can share files and printers. You can control access to these services by requiring users to provide a password. When users try to access a shared directory, they are prompted for a password. Control can be implemented in share mode or user mode. The *share mode* sets up one password for the shared resource, and then enables any user who has that password to access it. The *user mode* provides a different password for each user. Samba maintains its own password file for this purpose, **smbpasswords**.

Name resolution and service announcements are handled by the **nmbd** server. Name resolution essentially resolves NetBIOS names with IP addresses (Microsoft plans to have this handled by DNS in the future). Service announcement, also known as *browsing*, is the way a list of services available on the network is made known to the connected Windows PCs (and Linux PCs connected through Samba).

Application	Description
smbd	Samba server daemon that provides file and printer services to SMD clients
nmbd	Samba daemon that provides NetBIOS name resolution and service browser support
smbclient	Provides FTP-like access by Linux clients to Samba services
smbmount	Mounts Samba share directories on Linux clients
smbumount	Unmounts Samba share directories mounted on Linux clients
smbpasswd	Changes SMB-encrypted passwords on Samba servers
smbstatus	Displays the current status of the SMB network connections
smbrun	Interface program between smbd and external programs
testparm	Tests the Samba configuration file, **smb.conf**
smbtar	Backs up SMB/CIFS-shared resources directly to a UNIX tape drive.
nmblookup	Maps the NetBIOS name of a Windows PC to its IP address
SWAT	Samba Web administration tool for configuring smb.conf with a Web browser. Enables you to use a Web page interface to create and maintain your Samba configuration file, **smb.conf**

Table 29-3.   *Samba Applications*

Setting Up Samba

For a simple Samba setup, you should be able to use the default **smb.conf** file installed with the Red Hat Linux RPM package of Samba. If you need to make changes, however, you must restart the Samba server to have the changes take effect. You can do so using the smb startup script, as shown here:

```
/etc/rec.d/init.d/smb restart
```

To test your connection from a Linux system, you can use the **smbclient** command to query the Samba server. To access the home directory of a user on the Samba server, use the IP or hostname address of the Samba server, along with the homes section. With the **–U** option, specify a user to connect to on the system, as shown here:

```
smbclient  '//turtle.mytrek.com/homes'  -U dylan
```

You are then prompted for a password. If the client password is different from the server password, use the server password. Once connected, you are presented with the smbclient prompt as shown here. You can then access the files on the user's home directory.

```
smb: \>
```

To set up a connection for a Window client, you need to specify the Windows workgroup name and configure the password. The workgroup name is the name that appears in the Entire Network window in the Network Neighborhood on the Windows desktop. In the **smb.conf** file, you specify the workgroup name in the **workgroup=** entry in the **global** section. The workgroup name should be uppercase, no more than eight characters, and with no spaces.

You can then restart the Samba server. On a Windows client, you see the workgroup name appear in the Entire Network folder in your Network Neighborhood. Within the workgroup is an icon for the Samba server and, within that, is an icon for the user directory, as specified in the homes section of the **smb.conf** file.

Samaba configuration options are kept in the **/etc/smb.conf** file. You edit this file to make changes to the configuration. Once you finish making any changes, you should test your **smb.conf** file using the **testparm** program. The **testparm** program checks the validity of your configuration entries. By default, **testparm** uses the **/etc/smb.conf** file, although you can supply a different configuration file as an argument.

```
testparm
```

To check your network connections, use the **smbstatus** command. This command returns a listing of all active smb connections.

Samba Configuration: smb.conf

You configure the Samba daemon using the **smb.conf** file located in the **/etc** directory. The file is separated into two basic parts: one for global options and the other for shared services. A *shared service*, also know as *shares*, can either be filespace services (used by clients as an extension of their native file systems) or printable services (used by clients to access print services on the host running the server). The *filespace service* is a directory to which clients are given access and can use the space in it as an extension of their local file system. A printable service provides access by clients to print services, such as printers managed by the Samba server.

The **/etc/smb.conf** file holds the configuration for the various shared resources, as well as global options that apply to all resources. Red Hat Linux installs an **smb.conf** file in your **/etc** directory. The file contains default settings used for the Red Hat distribution. You can edit the file to customize your configuration to your own needs. Many entries are commented with either a semicolon or a # sign, and you can remove the initial comment symbol to make them effective. Instead of editing the file directly, you may want to use the SWAT configuration utility, which provides an easy-to-use, full-screen Web-page interface for entering configurations for shared resources. The SWAT configuration utility also provides extensive help features and documentation. For a complete listing of the Samba configuration parameters, check the man page for **smb.conf**. An extensive set of sample **smb.conf** files is located in the **/usr/doc/samba*** directory in the examples subdirectory.

In the **smb.conf** file, global options are set first, followed by each shared resource's configuration. The basic organizing component of the **smb.conf** file is a section. Each resource has its own section that holds its service name and definitions of its attributes. Even global options are placed in a section of their own: label global. For example, each section for a filespace share consists of the directory and the access rights allowed to users of the filespace. The section of each share is labeled with the name of the shared resource. Special sections, called **printers** and **homes**, provide default descriptions for user directories and printers accessible on the Samba server. Following the special sections, sections are entered for specific services, namely access to specific directories or printers. The basic organizing component is a section. Global options are placed in a section of their own labeled **global**.

A section begins with a section label consisting of the name of the shared resource encased in brackets. Other than the special sections, the section label can be any name you want to give it. Following the section label, on separate lines, different parameters for this service are entered. The parameters define the access rights to be granted to the user of the service. For example, for a directory, you may want it to be browsable, but read-only and to use a certain printer. Parameters are entered in the format *parameter name = value*. You can enter a comment by placing a semicolon at the beginning of the comment line.

A simple example of a section configuration follows. The section label is encased in brackets and followed by two parameter entries. The **path** parameter specifies the directory to which access is allowed. The **writable** parameter specifies whether the user has write access to this directory and its filespace.

```
[foo]
    path = /home/bar
    writable = true
```

A printer service has the same format, but requires certain other parameters. The path parameters specify the location of the printer spool directory. The **read-only** and **printable** parameters are set to true, indicating the service is read-only and printable. Public indicates anyone can access it.

```
[aprinter]
        path = /var/spool/samba
        read only = true
        printable = true
        public = true
```

Parameter entries are often synonymous, different entries that have the same meaning. For example, **read only = no, writable = yes**, and **write ok = yes**, all means the same thing, providing write access to the user.

SWAT

SWAT is a network-based Samba configuration tool that uses a Web page interface to enable you to configure your **smb.conf** file. SWAT is, by far, the easiest and simplest way to configure your Samba server. SWAT provides a simple-to-use Web page interface with buttons, menus, and text boxes for entering values. A simple button bar across the top enables you to select the sections you want to configure. A button bar is even there to add passwords. To see the contents of the **smb.conf** file as SWAT changes it, click the View button. The initial screen (HOME) displays the index for Samba documentation (see Figure 29-1). One of SWAT's more helpful features is its context-sensitive help. For each parameter and option SWAT displays, you can click a help button to display a detailed explanation of the option and examples of its use.

On Red Hat Linux, SWAT in installed with Samba. SWAT is an inetd service, listed in the **/etc/services** and **/etc/inetd.conf** files. In the **/etc/inetd.conf** file, the entry for SWAT will be commented. You will have to edit this file and remove the preceding # comment symbol. The SWAT entry looks like this.

```
swat       stream  tcp     nowait.400      root /usr/sbin/swat swat
```

Once you remove the comment, you must restart the inetd server to have the change take effect. You can do this simply using the **inet** script, as shown here.

```
/etc/rc.d/init.d/inet restart
```

The SWAT program uses port 901, as designated in the **/etc/services** file. Before you use SWAT, back up your current **smb.conf** file. SWAT overwrites the original,

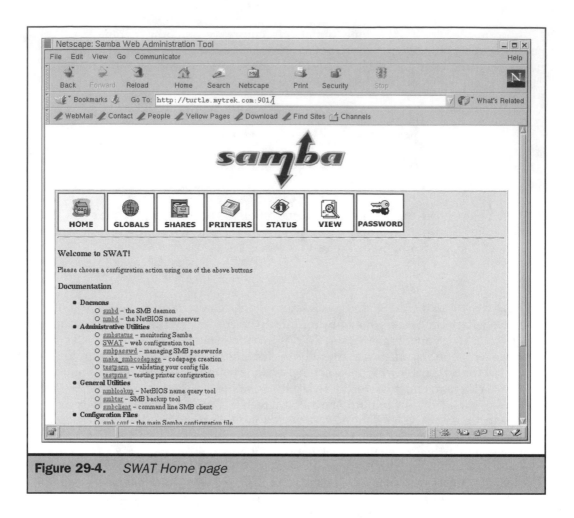

Figure 29-4. SWAT Home page

replacing the Red Hat version with a shorter and more concise version of its own. The **smb.conf** file originally installed by Red Hat lists an extensive number of options with detailed explanations. This is a good learning tool, with excellent examples for creating various kinds of printer and directory sections. Simply make a backup copy.

```
cp /etc/smb.conf   /etc/smb.bk
```

You start up SWAT by entering the address of the Samba server it is running on, along with its port, 901, into a Web browser. The following URL entered into a Web

browser, such as Netscape, displays the Web page interface for SWAT on the
turtle.mytrek.com Samba server.

```
http://turtle.mytrek.com:901
```

If you are logged in to the Linux system that is operating the Samba server, you
could simply use localhost as the URL.

```
http://localhost:901
```

You are first asked to enter a user name and a password. To configure Samba, you
need to enter **root** and the root password. (If you are connecting from a remote system,
it is NOT advisable to enter the root password in clear text, see Chapter 31.) The main
SWAT page is displayed with a button bar, with buttons for links for HOME, GLOBAL,
SHARES, PRINTERS, STATUS, VIEW, and PASSWORD. You can use STATUS to list
your active SMB network connections.

For the various sections, SWAT can display either a basic or advanced version.
The basic version shows only those entries needed for a simple configuration, whereas
the advanced version shows all the possible entries for that type of section. A button—
labeled Advanced View or Basic View—is at the top of the section page for toggling
between the advanced or basic versions.

Section pages for Printers and Shares have added buttons and a menu for selecting
the particular printer or share you want to configure. The term share, as it's used here,
refers to directories you want to make available through Samba. When you click the
SHARES button, you initially see only a few buttons displayed at the top of the SHARES
page. You use these buttons to create new sections or to edit sections already set up
for shares. For setting up a new share section, you enter its name in the box next to
Create Share button, and then click that button. The new share name appears in the
drop-down menu next to the Choose Share button. Initially, this button is blank. Click
it to display the list of current share sections. Select the one you want, and then click
the Choose Share button. The page then displays the entries for configuring a share.
For a new share, these are either blank or hold default values. For example, to select
the homes section that configures the default setting for user home directories, click
the drop-down menu where you find a homes entry (see Figure 29-5). Select it, and
then click the Choose Share button. The entries for the homes section are displayed.
The same process works for the Printers page, where you can select either the printers
section or create sections for particular printers.

In Figure 29-6, notice the Help links next to each entry. Such a link displays a Web
page showing the Samba documentation for smb.conf, positioned at the appropriate
entry. In this figure, the **guest ok** part of the documentation is displayed after the user
clicks the Help link next to the **guest ok** entry.

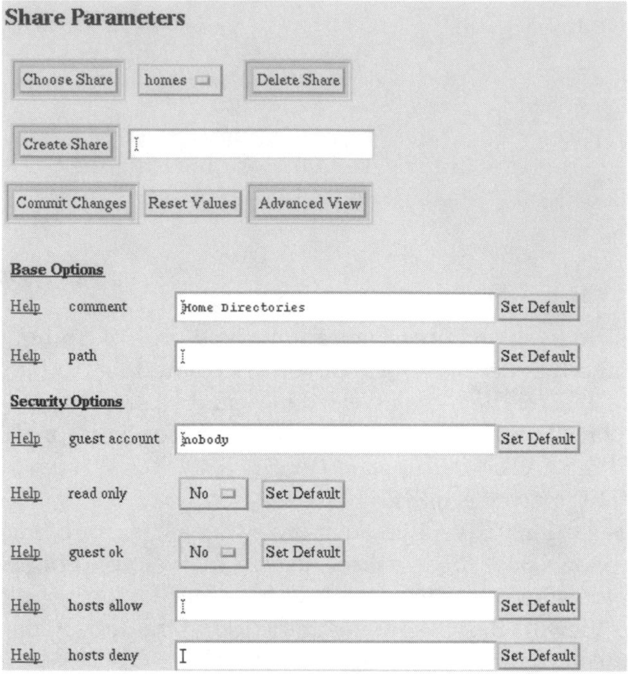

Share Parameters

Choose Share   homes   Delete Share

Create Share   [   ]

Commit Changes   Reset Values   Advanced View

Base Options

Help   comment   Home Directories   Set Default

Help   path   [   ]   Set Default

Security Options

Help   guest account   nobody   Set Default

Help   read only   No   Set Default

Help   guest ok   No   Set Default

Help   hosts allow   [   ]   Set Default

Help   hosts deny   [   ]   Set Default

Figure 29-5.   *SWAT Share page showing homes section*

When you finish working on a section, click the Commit Changes button on its page to save your changes. Do this for each separate page you work on, including the GLOBALS page. Clicking the Commit Changes button generates a new version of the **smb.conf** file. To have the Samba server read these changes, you then have to restart it.

```
/etc/rec.d/init.d/smb restart
```

You can, of course, edit the **/etc/smb.conf** file directly. This is a simple text file you can edit with any text editor. You still must restart the smb server to have the changes take effect.

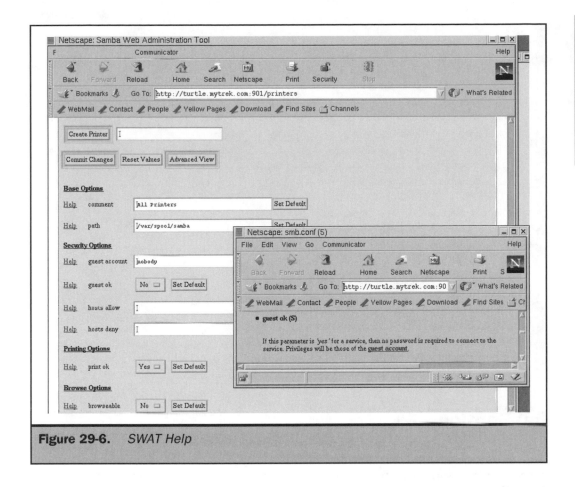

Figure 29-6. *SWAT Help*

The following example shows a **smb.conf** file generated by SWAT for a simple configuration. This is much smaller than the comment intensive versions originally installed by Red Hat.

```
# Samba config file created using SWAT
# from UNKNOWN (24.0.67.231)
# Date: 2000/02/11 01:08:09
```

```
# Global parameters
[global]
      workgroup = MYGROUP
      server string = Samba Server
      username map = /etc/smbusers
      log file = /var/log/samba/log.%m
      max log size = 50
      socket options = TCP_NODELAY SO_RCVBUF=8192 SO_SNDBUF=8192
      dns proxy = No

[homes]
      comment = Home Directories
      read only = No
      browseable = No

[printers]
      comment = All Printers
      path = /var/spool/samba
      print ok = Yes
      browseable = No
```

Global Section

The *global section* determines configuration for the entire server, as well as specifying default entries to be used in the home and directory segments. In this section, you find entries for the workgroup name, password configuration, and directory settings. Several of the more important entries are discussed here. Figure 29-7 shows the Global variables page on the SWAT you can use to set global options. The Basic View of this page lists the options you would most likely need.

The workgroup entry specifies the workgroup name you want to give to your network. This is the workgroup name that appears on the Windows' clients Network

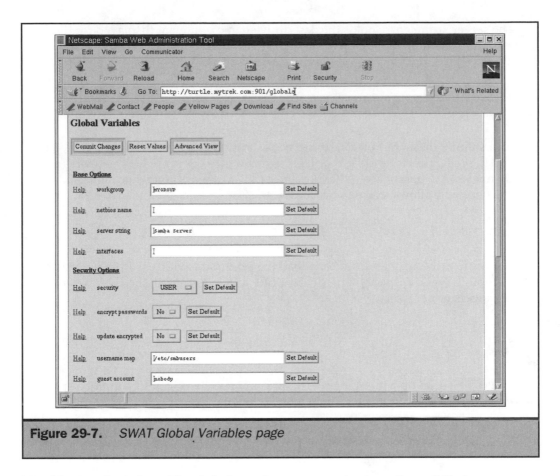

Figure 29-7. SWAT Global Variables page

Neighborhood window. The default workgroup entry in the **smb.conf** file is
shown here:

```
[global]

# workgroup = NT-Domain-Name or Workgroup-Name
   workgroup = MYGROUP
```

The server string entry holds the descriptive name you want displayed for the server on the client systems. On Windows systems, this is the name displayed on the Samba server icon.

```
# server string is the equivalent of the NT Description field
   server string = Samba Server
```

As a security measure, you can restrict access to SMB services to certain specified local networks. On the host's network, type the network addresses of the local networks for which you want to permit access. The localhost (127) is always automatically included. The next example allows access to two local networks.

```
hosts allow = 192.168.1. 192.168.2.
```

To enable printing, allow Samba to load the printer descriptions from your printcap file. Although you can specify a particular print system type with the printing entry, this usually is unnecessary.

```
   printcap name = /etc/printcap
load printers = yes
```

You can also set up a guest login to handle any users who log in without a specific account. Be sure to add the guest login to the password file.

```
   guest account = pcguest
```

Passwords

The global section also handles password configuration. You then need to configure password encryption. Samba can use either clear text or encrypted passwords. For Windows, releases starting from Windows 95 OSR2 and Windows NT Service Pack 3 use encrypted passwords. For such clients, you need to be sure encryption is set of passwords on the Samba server. If you want to use clear text passwords, you must manually configure each such Windows client to use them. To enable password encryption, you can simply remove the comment symbol from the following password entries in the global section in the **smb.conf** file. On SWAT, simply toggle the Encrypt Passwords entry to Yes.

```
encrypt passwords = yes
```

Users are usually prompted for a password when they try to access a client. You can have Samba maintain a list of default passwords in the **/etc/smbpasswd** file, however. If you want, you can use the **smb passwd** file entry to specify a different password file.

```
# smb passwd file = /etc/smbpasswd
```

To add a password for a particular user, you use the **smbpasswd** command with the **–a** option and the user's name.

```
smbpasswd –a dylan
```

On SWAT, you manage passwords on the Server Password Management page, as shown in Figure 29-8. Click Add New User to add a new user. As the root user on the Samba server, you can add new passwords, as well as enable or disable current ones. Users can also use the PASSWORD page to change their own passwords.

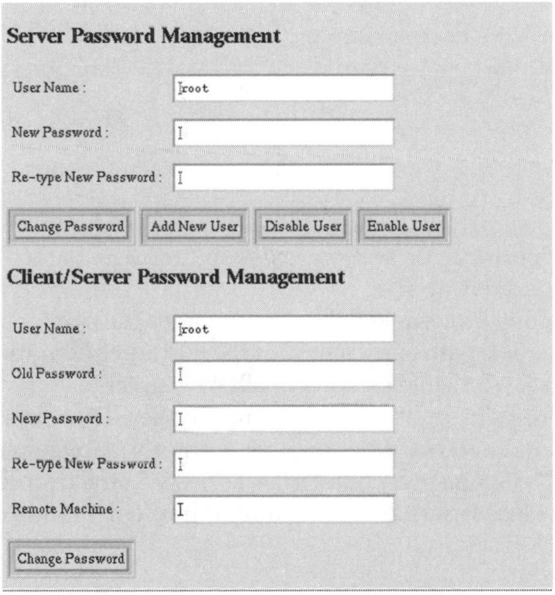

Figure 29-8.   *SWAT Server Password Management page*

If, instead, you want to use clear text passwords, you must manually edit the Windows registry of each Windows client. In the registry, change the EnablePlainTextPassword entry to 1. For Windows 95 and 98, it is located in HKEY_LOCAL_MACHINES\System\CurrentContorlSet\Services\VxD\ VNETSUP. If this entry is not there, you must make one. Select Edit/New/ DWORD Value from the regedit menu bar and rename the entry from New Value #1 to EnablePlainTextPassword. For Window 2000 and NT, check the .reg files in the /usr/doc/Samba*version* directory, in the docs subdirectory.

Homes Section

The *homes* section specifies default controls for accessing a user home directory through the SMB protocols by remote users. Setting the browsable entry to No prevents the client from listing the files with the browser, such as that used by a file manager to display files and directories (for example, Explorer on Windows). The writable entry specifies whether users have read and write control over files in their home directory. On SWAT, you simply select the SHARES page, select the homes entry from the drop-down menu, and click Choose Share (see Figure 29-5).

```
[homes]
  comment = Home Directories
  browseable = no
  writable = yes
```

Printer Section

The *printer* section specifies the default controls for accessing printers. These are used for printers for which no specific sections exist. In this case, Samba uses printers defined in the server's printcap file.

In this context, setting browsable to No simply hides the printer section from the client, not the printers. The path entry specifies the location of the spool directory Samba will use for printer files. To enable printing at all, the printable entry must be set to Yes. To allow guest users to print, set the **guest ok** entry to Yes. The writable entry set to No prevents any kind of write access, other than the printer's management of spool files. On SWAT, select the PRINTER page and the printer's entry in the drop-down menu, and then select Choose Printers (see Figure 29-6). A standard implementation of the printers section is shown here.

```
[printers]
comment = All Printers
  path = /var/spool/samba
  browseable = no
```

```
# Set public = yes to allow user 'guest account' to print
   guest ok = no
   writable = no
   printable = yes
```

If you can't print, be sure to check the **default print** entry. This specifies the command the server actually uses to print documents.

Shares

Sections for specific shared resources, such as directories on your system, are usually placed after the homes and printers sections. For a section defining a shared directory, enter a label for the system. Then, on separate lines, enter options for its pathname and the different permissions you want to set. In the **path =** options, specify the full pathname for the directory. **The comment =** option holds the label to be given the share. You can make a directory writable, public, or read-only. You can control access to the directory with the valid users entry. With this entry, you can list those users permitted access. For those options not set, the defaults entered in the global, home, and printer segments are used.

On SWAT, you use the SHARES page to create and edit shared directories. Select the one you want to edit from the drop-down menu and click Choose Share. The Basic View shows the commonly used entries. For entries such as Valid Users, you need to select the Advanced View. Be sure to click Commit Changes before you move on to another share or printer section.

The following example is found in the Red Hat **smb.conf** file and shows a simple share section for a directory **fredsdir** where only the user **fred** has access.

```
[fredsdir]
comment = Fred's Service
   path = /usr/somewhere/private
   valid users = fred
   public = no
   writable = yes
   printable = no
```

For public access, set public entry to Yes, with no valid user's entry. If you want guest users to have access, you can also set the **only guest** entry to Yes.

```
 [public]
path = /usr/somewhere/else/public
   public = yes
```

```
    only guest = yes
    writable = yes
    printable = no
```

To set up a directory that can be shared by more than one user, where each user has
control of the files she creates, simply list the users in the valid users entry. Permissions for
any created files are specified by the create mask entry. In this example, the permissions
are set to 765, which provides read/write/execute access to owners, read/write access
to members of the group, and only read/execute access to all others.

```
[myshare]
comment = my stuff
    path = /usr/somewhere/shared
    valid users = aleina larisa
    public = no
    writable = yes
    printable = no
    create mask = 0765
```

Printers

For a printer, you need to include the printer and printable entries. With the printer
entry, you name the printer, and by setting the printable entry to Yes, you allow it to
print. You can control access to specific users with the valid users entry and by setting
the public entry to No. For public access, set the public entry to Yes. On SWAT, you can
create individual printer sections on the PRINTER page. Default entries are already set
up for you.

The following example sets up a printer accessible only by the user **fred** (you could
add other users if you want). User's need to have write access to the printer's spool
directory. In this example, **fred**'s home directory is used.

```
[fredsprn]
comment = Fred's Printer
    valid users = fred
    path = /homes/fred
    printer = freds_printer
    public = no
    writable = no
    printable = yes
```

Linuxconf

Or, you can edit the **smb.conf** file using the Linuxconf Samba file server panel in the
Server tasks list under Networking in Config. Five entries correspond to global options:
(Default), the homes section (Default setup for user home directories), the printers
section (Default setup for printers), net login (Netlogon setup), and individual shared
resources (Disk shares).

Linuxconf uses a set of panels for each kind of section, organizing parameters into
different categories. For example, Figure 29-9 shows the Share setup panel for configuring
a shared resource. The panel contains several tabbed panels for configuring access, users,
and features. Entries here correspond to the possible parameters you can enter in share's
section in the **smb.conf** file.

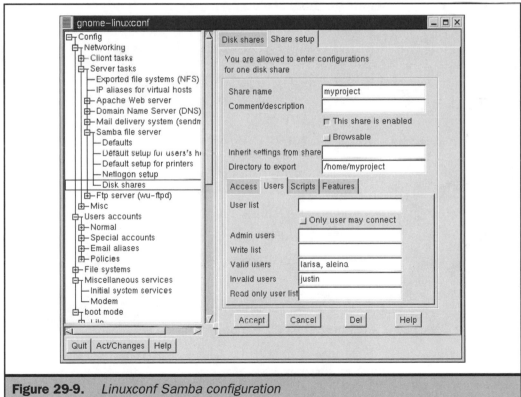

Figure 29-9.   *Linuxconf Samba configuration*

Variable Substitutions

For string values assigned to parameters, you can incorporate substitution operators. This provides greater flexibility in designating values that may be context-dependent, such as user names. For example, suppose a service needs to use a separate directory for each user who logs in. The path for such directories could be specified using the %u variable that substitutes in the name of the current user. The string path = /tmp/%u would become path = /tmp/justin for the **justin** user and "/tmp/dylan" for the **dylan** user. Table 29-4 lists several of the more common substitution variables.

Variable	Description
%S	Name of the current service
%P	Root directory of the current service
%u	Username of the current service
%g	Primary group name of the user
%U	Session username (the username the client wanted)
%G	Primary group name of Session user
%H	Home directory of the user
%v	Samba version
%h	Internet hostname on which Samba is running
%m	NetBIOS name of the client machine
%L	NetBIOS name of the server
%M	Internet name of the client machine
%N	Name of your NIS home directory server
%p	Path of the service's home directory
%d	Process ID of the current server process
%a	Architecture of the remote machine
%I	IP address of the client machine
%T	Current date and time

Table 29-4.   *Samba Substitution Variables*

NETWORK
ADMINISTRATION

Testing the Samba Configuration

After you make your changes to the **smb.conf** file, you can then use the **testparm** program to see if the entries are correctly entered. **testparm** checks the syntax and validity of Samba entries. By default, **testparm** checks the **/etc/smb.conf** file. If you are using a different file as your configuration file, you can specify it as an argument to **testparm**. You can also have **testparm** check to see if a particular host has access to the service setup by the configuration file.

With the **smbstatus** command, you can check on current Samba connections on your network.

To check the real-time operation of your Samba server, you can log in to a user account on the Linux system running the Samba server and connect to the server.

Domain Logons

Samba also supports domain logons whereby a user can log on to the network. Logon scripts can be set up for individual users. To configure such netlogin capability, you need to set up a netlogon share in the **smb.conf** file. The following sample is taken from the Red Hat **smb.conf** file. This share holds the netlogon scripts, in this case, the /home/netlogon directory, which should not be writable, but it should be accessible by all users (guest ok).

```
[netlogon]
    comment = Network Logon Service
    path = /home/netlogon
    guest ok = yes
    writable = no
    share modes = no
```

The **global** section would have the following parameters enabled:

```
domain logons = yes
logon script = %U.bat
```

The logon scripts would be DOS batch scripts (.bat), which you should edit on a DOS or a Windows system.

Accessing Samba Services with Clients

Client systems connected to the SMB network can access the shared services provided by the Samba server. Windows clients should be able to access shared directories and services automatically through the Network Neighborhood and the Entire Network icons on a Windows desktop. For other Linux systems connected to the same network, Samba services can be accessed using special Samba client programs. With **smbclient,** a local Linux system can connect to a shared directory on the Samba server and transfer files, as well as run shell programs. With **smbmount,** directories on the Samba server can be mounted to local directories on the Linux client.

smbclient

smbclient operates like FTP to access systems using the SMB protocols. Whereas with an FTP client you can access other FTP severs or UNIX systems, with **smbclient** you can access SMB-shared services, either on the Samba server or on Windows systems. Many **smbclient** commands are similar to FTP, such as `mget` to transfer a file or `del` to delete a file. The **smbclient** program has several option for querying a remote system, as well as connecting to it (see Table 29-5). See the **smbclient** man page for a complete list of options and commands. The **smbclient** program takes as its argument a server name and the service you want to access on that server. A double slash precedes the server name and a single slash separates it from the service. The service can be any shared resource, such as a directory or a printer. The server name is its NetBIOS name, which may or may not be the same as its IP name. For example, to specify the **myreports** shared directory on the server named **turtle.mytrek.com**, use **//turtle.mytrek.com/myreports**. If you must specify a pathname, use backslashes for Windows files and forward slashes for UNIX/Linux files.

```
//server-name/service
```

You can also supply the password for accessing the service. Enter it as an argument following the service name. If you do not supply the password, you are prompted to enter it.

You can then add several options, such as the remote username or the list of services available. With the **–I** option, you can specify the system using its Domain Name Service name. You use the **–U** option and a login name for the remote login name you want to use on the remote system. Attach **%** with the password if a password is required. With the **–L** option, you can obtain a list of the services provided on a server, such as shared directories or printers. To access a particular directory on a remote system, enter the directory as an argument to the **smbclient** command, followed by any options. For Windows files, you use backslashes for the pathnames, and for UNIX/Linux files you use forward slashes.

Once connected, an **smb** prompt is displayed and you can use **smbclient** commands such as `get` and `put` to transfer files. The `quit` or `exit` commands quit the **smbclient**. In the following example, **smbclient** accesses the directory **myreports** on the **turtle.mytrek.com** system, using the **dylan** login name:

```
smbclient  //turtle.mytrek.com/myreports  -I 192.168.0.1 -U dylan
```

In most cases, you can simply use the server name to reference the server, as shown here:

```
smbclient  //turtle.mytrek.com/myreports -U dylan
```

If you are accessing the home directory of a particular account on the Samba server, you can simply specify the **homes** service. In the next example, the user accesses the home directory of the **aleina** account on the Samba server, after being prompted to enter that account's password.

```
smbclient  //turtle.mytrek.com/homes -U aleina
```

Option	Description
password	The password required to access the specified service on the server. If no password is supplied, the user is prompted to enter one
-s *smb.conf*	Specify the pathname to **smb.conf** file
-B *IP_address*	Specify the broadcast IP address
-O *socket_options*	List the socket options
-R *name resolve order*	Use these name resolution services only
-M *host*	Send a winpopup message to the host
-i *scope*	Use this NetBIOS scope
-N	Don't ask for a password
-n *netbios name*	Use this name as my netbios name
-d *debuglevel*	Set the debuglevel
-P	Connect to the service as a printer
-p *port*	Connect to the specified port

Table 29-5.   *smbclient Options*

Option	Description
-l *log basename*	Base name for log/debug files
-h	Print this help message
-I *IP_address*	Specify the IP address to connect to
-E	Write messages to stderr instead of stdout
-U *username*	Specify the user to log in to on the remote system
-L *host*	List the shares available on the specified host
-t *terminal code*	Terminal i/o code used {sjis l euc l jis7 l jis8 l junet l hex}
-m *max protocol*	Set the max protocol level
-W *workgroup*	Set the workgroup name
-T<c l x>	Command line **tar** operation
-D *directory*	Start from this directory
-c *command_string*	Execute semicolon-separated commands
-b *xmit/send buffer*	Changes the transmit/send buffer (default: 65520)

Table 29-5.   *smbclient Options* (continued)

Once logged in, you can execute **smbclient** commands to manage files and change directories. The **smbclient** commands are listed in Table 29-6. **Shell** commands can be executed with the ! operator. To transfer files, you can use the **mget** and **mput** commands, much as they are used in the ftp program. The **recurse** command enables you to turn on recursion to copy whole subdirectories at a time. You can use file-matching operators, referred to here as *masks,* to select a certain collection of files. The file-matching (mask) operators are *, [], and ? (see Chapter 7). The default mask is * which matches everything. The following example uses **mget** to copy all files with a .c suffix, as in myprog.c.

```
smb> mget *.c
```

During transfers, you can have **smbclient** either prompt you on each individual file, or simply transfer all the selected ones. The **prompt** command toggles this file, prompting on and off.

? [command]	With no command argument, lists of all available commands are displayed. Use command argument to display information about a particular command.
! [shell command]	With no shell command argument, runs a local shell. If a shell command is provided, executes that command.
cd [directory name]	Change directory on server. With no directory specified, the name of the current working directory is displayed.
del mask	Request the server delete all files matching "mask" from the current working directory on the server.
dir mask	A list of the files matching the "mask" in the current working directory on the server are retrieved from the server and displayed.
exit	Terminate the connection with the server and exit from the program.
get remote filename [local filename]	Copy a file from the server to the local system. You can rename the local system copy. Transfer is binary.
help [command]	With no command argument, lists of all available commands are displayed. Use command argument to display information about a particular command. Same as !.
lcd [directory name]	Change directories on the local system. With no argument, the local directory name is displayed.
lowercase	Toggle lowercasing of filenames for the **get** and **mget** commands. When lowercasing is toggled ON, local filenames are converted to lowercase when using the **get** and **mget** commands. This is often useful when copying (say) MS-DOS files from a server because lowercase filenames are the norm on UNIX systems.
ls mask	A list of the files matching the "mask" in the current working directory on the server are retrieved from the server and displayed. Same as dir.

Table 29-6.   *smbclient Commands*

mask *mask*	This command enables the user to set up a mask that is used during recursive operation of the **mget** and **mput** commands. The masks specified to the **mget** and **mput** commands act as filters for directories, rather than files when recursion is toggled ON. The value for mask defaults to blank (equivalent to "*") and remains so until the **mask** command is used to change it.
md *directory name*	Create a new directory on the server (user access privileges permitting) with the specified name. Same as mkdir.
mget *mask*	Copy all files matching mask from the server to the machine running the client. Note, mask is interpreted differently during recursive operation and nonrecursive operation—refer to the recurse and mask commands for more information. Transfers are binary.
mkdir *directory name*	Create a new directory on the server (user access privileges permitting) with the specified name.
mput *mask*	Copy all files matching mask in the current working directory on the local system to the current working directory on the server. Transfers in are binary.
print *filename*	Print the specified file from the local machine through a printable service on the server.
printmode *graphics or text*	Set the print mode for either binary data (graphics) or text. Subsequent print command uses the currently set print mode.
prompt	Toggle prompting for filenames during operation of the **mget** and **mput** commands.
put *local filename [remote filename]*	Copy a file on the local system to the server. You can rename the server copy. Transfers are binary.
queue	Displays the print queue, showing the job ID, name, size, and current status.
quit	Terminate the connection with the server and exit from the program. Same as exit command.

Table 29-6.   *smbclient Commands* (continued)

rd *directory name*	Delete the specified directory (user access privileges permitting) from the server. Same as **rmdir** command.
recurse	Toggle directory recursion for the commands **mget** and **mput**. When toggled ON, the **mget** and **mput** commands will copy any subdirectories and files. Files can be selected by a mask specified with the **mget** and **mput** commands. The mask for directories is specified with the **mask** command. When toggled OFF, only files from the current working directory are copied.
rm *mask*	Delete all files matching "mask" from the current working directory on the server.
rmdir *directory name*	Delete the specified directory (user access privileges permitting) from the server.
tar *c | x [IXbgNa]*	Performs a **tar** operation. See the **-T** command-line option in Table 25-5. Behavior may be affected by the **tarmode** command.
blocksize *blocksize*	Specify blocksize. Must be followed by a valid (greater than zero) blocksize. Causes **tar** file to be written out in blocksize*TBLOCK (usually 512 byte) blocks.
tarmode *full | inc | reset | noreset*	Changes **tar**'s behavior regarding archive bits. In full mode, **tar** backs up everything, regardless of the archive bit setting (this is the default mode). In incremental mode, **tar** only backs up files with the archive bit set. In reset mode, **tar** resets the archive bit on all files it backs up (implies read/write share).
setmode *filename perm=[+ | \-]rsha*	A version of the DOS **attrib** command to set file permissions. For example: setmode myfile +r would make myfile read-only.

Table 29-6.   *smbclient Commands* (continued)

smbmount

With the **smbmount** command, a Linux or a UNIX client can mount a shared directory onto its local system. The syntax for the **smbmount** command is similar to the **smbclient** command, with many corresponding options. The **smbmount** command takes as its arguments the Samba server and shared directory, followed by the local directory to where you want to mount the directory. The following example mounts the **myreports** directory onto the **/mnt/myreps** directory on the local system.

```
smbmount  '//turtle.mytrek.com/myreports' '/mnt/myreps' -U dylan
```

To unmount the directory, use the **smbumount** command with the local directory name, as shown here:

```
smbumount  /mnt/myreps
```

To mount the home directory of a particular user on the sever, specify the **homes** service and the user's login name. The following example mounts the home directory of the user **larisa** to the **/home/chris/larisastuff** directory on the local system.

```
smbmount  '//turtle.mytrek.com/homes' '/home/chris/larisastuff' -U larisa
```

Red Hat smb.conf

A listing of the **/etc/smb.conf** file provided by Red Hat is listed in the following pages. The file includes extensive comments for each entry, but it is still only a simple configuration, with most entries commented with a semicolon. To activate an entry, remove its preceding semicolon. Default values are already assigned to the entries. You can change them as you want. Several sections, such as the fredsdir section, are meant only to be examples. Use them as a guide for making your own sections for shared services. Most global entries may be left as is. The essential ones are already uncommented.

```
# This is the main Samba configuration file. You should read the
# smb.conf(5) manual page in order to understand the options listed
# here. Samba has a huge number of configurable options (perhaps too
# many!) most of which are not shown in this example
#
# Any line which starts with a ; (semi-colon) or a # (hash)
# is a comment and is ignored. In this example we will use a #
# for commentary and a ; for parts of the config file that you
# may wish to enable
#
# NOTE: Whenever you modify this file you should run the command
# "testparm" to check that you have not many any basic syntactic
# errors.
#======================= Global Settings =======================
[global]
```

```
# workgroup = NT-Domain-Name or Workgroup-Name
   workgroup = MYGROUP

# server string is the equivalent of the NT Description field
   server string = Samba Server

# This option is important for security. It allows you to restrict
# connections to machines which are on your local network. The
# following example restricts access to two C class networks and
# the "loopback" interface. For more examples of the syntax see
# the smb.conf man page
;   hosts allow = 192.168.1. 192.168.2. 127.

# if you want to automatically load your printer list rather
# than setting them up individually then you'll need this
   printcap name = /etc/printcap
   load printers = yes

# It should not be necessary to spell out the print system type unless
# yours is non-standard. Currently supported print systems include:
# bsd, sysv, plp, lprng, aix, hpux, qnx
;   printing = bsd

# Uncomment this if you want a guest account, you must add this to
# /etc/passwd otherwise the user "nobody" is used
;  guest account = pcguest

# this tells Samba to use a separate log file for each machine
# that connects
   log file = /var/log/samba/log.%m

# Put a capping on the size of the log files (in Kb).
  max log size = 50

# Security mode. Most people will want user level security. See
# security_level.txt for details.
   security = user
# Use password server option only with security = server
;   password server = <NT-Server-Name>

# Password Level allows matching of _n_ characters of the password
# for all combinations of upper and lower case.
;  password level = 8
;  username level = 8

# You may wish to use password encryption. Please read
# ENCRYPTION.txt, Win95.txt and WinNT.txt in the Samba documentation.
```

```
# Do not enable this option unless you have read those documents
;   encrypt passwords = yes
;   smb passwd file = /etc/smbpasswd

# The following are needed to allow password changing from Windows to
# update the Linux system password also.
# NOTE: Use these with 'encrypt passwords' and 'smb passwd file'
# above.
# NOTE2: You do NOT need these to allow workstations to change only
#        the encrypted SMB passwords. They allow the Unix password
#        to be kept in sync with the SMB password.
;   unix password sync = Yes
;   passwd program = /usr/bin/passwd %u
;   passwd chat = *New*UNIX*password* %n\n *ReType*new*UNIX*password*
%n\n *passwd:*all*authentication*tokens*updated*successfully*

# Unix users can map to different SMB User names
;   username map = /etc/smbusers

# Using the following line enables you to customize your
# configuration on a per machine basis. The %m gets replaced with the
# netbios name of the machine that is connecting
;    include = /etc/smb.conf.%m

# Most people will find that this option gives better performance.
# See speed.txt and the manual pages for details
    socket options = TCP_NODELAY SO_RCVBUF=8192 SO_SNDBUF=8192

# Configure Samba to use multiple interfaces
# If you have multiple network interfaces then you must list them
# here. See the man page for details.
;    interfaces = 192.168.12.2/24 192.168.13.2/24

# Configure remote browse list synchronization here
#  request announcement to, or browse list sync from:
#  a specific host or from / to a whole subnet (see below)
;    remote browse sync = 192.168.3.25 192.168.5.255
# Cause this host to announce itself to local subnets here
;    remote announce = 192.168.1.255 192.168.2.44

# Browser Control Options:
# set local master to no if you don't want Samba to become a master
# browser on your network. Otherwise the normal election rules apply
;    local master = no

# OS Level determines the precedence of this server in master browser
# elections. The default value should be reasonable
```

```
;    os level = 33

# Domain Master specifies Samba to be the Domain Master Browser. This
# allows Samba to collate browse lists between subnets. Don't use
# this if you already have a Windows NT domain controller doing this
# job
;    domain master = yes

# Preferred Master causes Samba to force a local browser election on
# startup and gives it a slightly higher chance of winning the
# election
;    preferred master = yes

# Use only if you have an NT server on your network that has been
# configured at install time to be a primary domain controller.
;    domain controller = <NT-Domain-Controller-SMBName>

# Enable this if you want Samba to be a domain logon server for
# Windows95 workstations.
;    domain logons = yes

# if you enable domain logons then you may want a per-machine or
# per user logon script
# run a specific logon batch file per workstation (machine)
;    logon script = %m.bat
# run a specific logon batch file per username
;    logon script = %U.bat

# Where to store roving profiles (only for Win95 and WinNT)
#         %L substitutes for this servers netbios name, %U is username
#         You must uncomment the [Profiles] share below
;    logon path = \\%L\Profiles\%U

# All NetBIOS names must be resolved to IP Addresses
# 'Name Resolve Order' allows the named resolution mechanism to be specified
# the default order is "host lmhosts wins bcast". "host" means use the unix
# system gethostbyname() function call that will use either /etc/hosts OR
# DNS or NIS depending on the settings of /etc/host.config, /etc/nsswitch.conf
# and the /etc/resolv.conf file. "host" therefore is system configuration
# dependant. This parameter is most often of use to prevent DNS lookups
# in order to resolve NetBIOS names to IP Addresses. Use with care!
# The example below excludes use of name resolution for machines that are NOT
# on the local network segment
# - OR - are not deliberately to be known via lmhosts or via WINS.
;  name resolve order = wins lmhosts bcast

# Windows Internet Name Serving Support Section:
```

```
# WINS Support - Tells the NMBD component of Samba to enable it's WINS Server
;   wins support = yes

# WINS Server - Tells the NMBD components of Samba to be a WINS Client
#Note: Samba can be either a WINS Server, or a WINS Client, but NOT both
;   wins server = w.x.y.z

# WINS Proxy - Tells Samba to answer name resolution queries on
# behalf of a non WINS capable client, for this to work there must be
# at least oneWINS Server on the network. The default is NO.
;   wins proxy = yes

# DNS Proxy - tells Samba whether or not to try to resolve NetBIOS names
# via DNS nslookups. The built-in default for versions 1.9.17 is yes,
# this has been changed in version 1.9.18 to no.
   dns proxy = no

# Case Preservation can be handy - system default is _no_
# NOTE: These can be set on a per share basis
;   preserve case = no
;   short preserve case = no
# Default case is normally upper case for all DOS files
;   default case = lower
# Be very careful with case sensitivity - it can break things!
;   case sensitive = no

#============================ Share Definitions ==============================
[homes]
   comment = Home Directories
   browseable = no
   writable = yes

# Un-comment the following and create the netlogon directory for Domain Logons
; [netlogon]
;   comment = Network Logon Service
;   path = /home/netlogon
;   guest ok = yes
;   writable = no
;   share modes = no

# Un-comment the following to provide a specific roving profile share
# the default is to use the user's home directory
;[Profiles]
;    path = /home/profiles
;    browseable = no
;    guest ok = yes
```

```
# NOTE: If you have a BSD-style print system there is no need to
# specifically define each individual printer
[printers]
   comment = All Printers
   path = /var/spool/samba
   browseable = no
# Set public = yes to allow user 'guest account' to print
   guest ok = no
   writable = no
   printable = yes

# This one is useful for people to share files
;[tmp]
;    comment = Temporary file space
;    path = /tmp
;    read only = no
;    public = yes

# A publicly accessible directory, but read only, except for people in
# the "staff" group
;[public]
;    comment = Public Stuff
;    path = /home/samba
;    public = yes
;    writable = yes
;    printable = no
;    write list = @staff

# Other examples.
#
# A private printer, usable only by fred. Spool data will be placed in fred's
# home directory. Note that fred must have write access to the spool directory,
# wherever it is.
;[fredsprn]
;    comment = Fred's Printer
;    valid users = fred
;    path = /homes/fred
;    printer = freds_printer
;    public = no
;    writable = no
;    printable = yes

# A private directory, usable only by fred. Note that fred requires write
# access to the directory.
;[fredsdir]
;    comment = Fred's Service
;    path = /usr/somewhere/private
```

```
;    valid users = fred
;    public = no
;    writable = yes
;    printable = no

# a service which has a different directory for each machine that connects
# this allows you to tailor configurations to incoming machines. You could
# also use the %u option to tailor it by user name.
# The %m gets replaced with the machine name that is connecting.
;[pchome]
;   comment = PC Directories
;   path = /usr/pc/%m
;   public = no
;   writable = yes

# A publicly accessible directory, read/write to all users. Note that all files
# created in the directory by users will be owned by the default user, so
# any user with access can delete any other user's files. Obviously this
# directory must be writable by the default user. Another user could of course
# be specified, in which case all files would be owned by that user instead.
;[public]
;    path = /usr/somewhere/else/public
;    public = yes
;    only guest = yes
;    writable = yes
;    printable = no

# The following two entries demonstrate how to share a directory so that two
# users can place files there that will be owned by the specific users. In this
# setup, the directory should be writable by both users and should have the
# sticky bit set on it to prevent abuse. Obviously this could be extended to
# as many users as required.
;[myshare]
;    comment = Mary's and Fred's stuff
;    path = /usr/somewhere/shared
;    valid users = mary fred
;    public = no
;    writable = yes
;    printable = no
;    create mask = 0765
```

Netatalk: AppleTalk

Netatalk implements the AppleTalk network protocol on UNIX and Linux systems. It provides support for sharing files' systems, accessing printers, and routing AppleTalk. Netatalk allows a Mac machine connected to an AppleTalk network to access a Linux system as if it were an AppleTalk file and print server. Linux systems can also use Netatalk to access Mac machines connected to an AppleTalk network. AppleTalk is the network protocol used for Apple Macintosh computers. AppleTalk supports file sharing and network printing, where different Macs can share each other's file systems and printers. For example, if you have a LaserWriter connected to a Macintosh, you can have your Linux system access it and print on that LaserWriter. You can also access any shared file systems that may be set up on the Macintoshes on the network. The current Netatalk Web site is **www.umich.edu/~rsug/netatalk/**, with a FAQ site at **threepio.hitchcock.org/netatalk/**.

The name of the Netatalk daemon is atalkd. It performs much the same function as routed and ifconfig. Several programs manage printing. The *papd* program lets Macs spool to a Linux printer. The *pap* program lets Linux systems print to an AppleTalk printer. The *psf* program is a PostScript printer filter for pap, and psorder enables you to print PostScript pages in reverse. The *apfd* program provides an interface to the Linux file system, while the *nbplkup* program lists all AppleTalk objects on the network. For example, **nbplkup :LaserWriter** lists the LaserWriters available. You would use the pap program to access and print to a LaserWriter. To use Linux commands to access a printer, you need to make an entry for the command in the **/etc/printcap** file, and create spool, status, and lock files for it.

Netatalk requires kernel-level support for the AppleTalk Datagram Delivery Protocol (DDP). If your kernel does not currently support it, you either must rebuild the kernel including AppleTalk support or use a loadable module for AppleTalk. Current kernels for most distributions include AppleTalk support.

Netatalk uses five configuration files, as shown in Table 29-7. The software package includes default versions you can modify. The RPM packages include the **config** file that contains documented default entries for use by the **atalk** startup script. Check the variable entries for any parameters you may want to change, such as the maximum number of allowed simultaneous users (default is 5).

Configuration files are automatically installed for you by the RPM package versions of Netatalk, such as those for Red Hat or OpenLinux. If you are installing from the source distribution, you need to install these from default files in the source directory. Also, make sure the following lines are in your **/etc/services** file (RPM packages add these automatically):

```
rtmp 1/ddp # Routing Table Maintenance Protocol
nbp 2/ddp # Name Binding Protocol
echo 4/ddp # AppleTalk Echo Protocol
zip 6/ddp # Zone Information Protocol
```

Netatalk is started using a startup script called **atalk**. RPM packages, such as those for Red Hat and OpenLinux, install **atalk** in the **/etc/rc.d/init.d** directory. You can also

Filename	Description
AppleVolumes.default	List of shared directories, including optional names.
AppleVolumes.system	Maps of file extensions to Mac OS types.
afpd.conf	Configuration file for afpd daemon (AppleTalk File system and printer daemon).
atalkd.conf	Controls the interfaces to which Netatalk binds, enabling you to specify network numbers or zones. If empty, Netatalk detects the interfaces itself.
papd.conf	Provides AppleTalk access to Linux print queues. If empty, uses **/etc/printcap**.

Table 29-7.   *Netatalk Configuration Files*

use a System V Init run-level editor to manage startup and shutdown operations. A link is set up to start the **atalk** script when you boot. You can also use **start** and **stop** arguments directly with **atalk**. The source code distribution uses a startup script called **rc.atalk** and installs it in the **/usr/local/atalk/etc** directory.

```
/etc/rc.d/init.d/atalk  start
```

The Complete Reference

Linux

Chapter 30

Administering TCP/IP Networks

L inux systems are configured to connect into networks that use the TCP/IP protocols. These are the same protocols that the Internet, as well as many *local area networks* (*LANs*), use. In Chapter 12, you were introduced to TCP/IP, a robust set of protocols designed to provide communications among systems with different operating systems and hardware. The TCP/IP protocols were developed in the 1970s as a special DARPA project to enhance communications between universities and research centers. These protocols were originally developed on UNIX systems, with much of the research carried out at the University of California, Berkeley. Linux, as a version of UNIX, benefits from much of this original focus on UNIX. Currently, the TCP/IP protocol development is managed by the *Internet Engineering Task Force* (*IETF*), which, in turn, is supervised by the *Internet Society* (*ISOC*). The ISOC oversees several groups responsible for different areas of Internet development, such as the *Internet Assigned Numbers Authority* (*IANA*), which is responsible for Internet addressing (see Table 30-1). Over the years, TCP/IP protocol standards and documentation have been issued in the form of *Requests for Comments (RFC)* documents. Check the most recent ones for current developments at the IETF Web site at **www.ietf.org**.

The TCP/IP protocols actually consist of different protocols, each designed for a specific task in a TCP/IP network. The three basic protocols are the *Transmission Control Protocol* (*TCP*), which handles receiving and sending communications, and

ISOC	Internet Society	Professional membership organization of Internet experts that oversees boards and task forces dealing with network policy issues **www.isoc.org**
IESG	The Internet Engineering Steering Group	Responsible for technical management of IETF activities and the Internet standards process **www.ietf.org/iseg.html**
IANA	Internet Assigned Numbers Authority	Responsible for Internet Protocol (IP) addresses **www.iana.org**
IAB	Internet Architecture Board	Defines the overall architecture of the Internet, providing guidance and broad direction to the IETF **www.iab.org**
IETF	Internet Engineering Task Force	Protocol engineering and development arm of the Internet **www.ietf.org**

Table 30-1.   *TCP/IP Protocol Development Groups*

the *Internet Protocol* (*IP*), which handles transmitting communications, and the *User Datagram Protocol* (*UPD*), which handles receiving and sending packets. The IP protocol, which is the base protocol that all others use, handles the actual transmissions, handling the packets of data with sender and receiver information in each. The TCP protocol is designed to work with cohesive messages or data. This protocol checks received packets and sorts them into their designated order, forming the original message. For data sent out, the TCP protocol breaks the data into separate packets, designating their order. The UDP protocol, meant to work on a much more raw level, also breaks down data into packets, but does not check their order.

Other protocols provide various network and user services. The *Domain Name Service* (*DNS*) provides address resolution. The *File Transfer Protocol* (*FTP*) provides file transmission, and *Network File Systems* (*NFS*) provides access to remote file systems. Table 30-2 lists the different protocols in the TCP/IP protocol suite. These protocols make use of either TCP or the UDP protocols to send and receive packets, which, in turn, use the IP protocol for actually transmitting the packets.

In a TCP/IP network, messages are broken into small components, called *datagrams*, which are then transmitted through various interlocking routes and delivered to their destination computers. Once received, the datagrams are reassembled into the original message. Datagrams themselves can be broken down into smaller packets. The *packet* is the physical message unit actually transmitted among networks. Sending messages as small components has proved to be far more reliable and faster than sending them as one large, bulky transmission. With small components, if one is lost or damaged, only that component must be resent, whereas, if any part of a large transmission is corrupted or lost, the entire message has to be resent.

The configuration of a TCP/IP network on your Linux system is implemented using a set of network configuration files. Table 30-4 provides a complete listing. Many of these can be managed using administrative programs, such as Linuxconf or **netcfg**, on your root user desktop (see Chapter 29). You can also use the more specialized programs, such as **netstat**, **ifconfig**, and **route**. Some configuration files are easy to modify yourself using a text editor.

TCP/IP networks are configured and managed with a set of utilities: **ifconfig**, **route**, and **netstat**. The **ifconfig** utility operates from your root user desktop and enables you to configure your network interfaces fully, adding new ones and modifying others. The **ifconfig** and **route** utilities are lower-level programs that require more specific knowledge of your network to use effectively. The **netstat** utility provides you with information about the status of your network connections.

TCP/IP Network Addresses

As explained in Chapter 12, a TCP/IP address is organized into four segments, consisting of numbers separated by periods. This is called the *IP address*. Part of this address is used for the network address and the other part is used to identify

Transport	Description
TCP	Transmission Control Protocol; places systems in direct communication
UDP	User Datagram Protocol
IP	Internet Protocol; transmits data
ICMP	Internet Control Message Protocol; status messages for IP
Routing	**Description**
RIP	Routing Information Protocol; determines routing
OSPF	Open Shortest Path First; determines routing
Network Addresses	**Description**
ARP	Address Resolution Protocol; determines unique IP address of systems
DNS	Domain Name Service; translates hostnames into IP addresses
RARP	Reverse Address Resolution Protocol; determines addresses of systems
User Services	**Description**
FTP	File Transfer Protocol; transmits files from one system to another using TCP
TFTP	Trivial File Transfer Protocol; transfers files using UDP
TELNET	Remote log in to another system on the network
SMTP	Simple Mail Transfer Protocol; transfers e-mail between systems
RPC	Remote Procedure Call; allows programs on remote systems to communicate
Gateway	**Description**
EGP	Exterior Gateway Protocol; provides routing for external networks
GGP	Gateway-to-Gateway Protocol; provides routing between Internet gateways

Table 30-2. *TCP/IP Protocol Suite*

Gateway	Description
IGP	Interior Gateway Protocol; provides routing for internal networks
Network Services	**Description**
NFS	Network File Systems; allows mounting of file systems on remote machines
NIS	Network Information Service; maintains user accounts across a network
BOOTP	Boot Protocol; starts system using boot information on server for network
SNMP	Single Network Management Protocol; provides status messages on TCP/IP configuration
DHCP	Dynamic Host Control Protocol; automatically provides network configuration information to host systems

Table 30-2.   *TCP/IP Protocol Suite* (continued)

a particular interface on a host in that network. Realizing IP addresses are assigned to interfaces—such as Ethernet cards or modems and not to the host computer—is important. Often a computer has only one interface and is accessed using only that interface's IP address. In that regard, an IP address can be thought of as identifying a particular host system on a network and, as such, the IP address is usually referred to as the host address.

In fact, though, a host system could have several interfaces, each with its own IP address. This is the case for computers that operate as gateways and firewalls from the local network to the Internet. One interface usually connects to the LAN and another to the Internet, as in two Ethernet cards. Each interface (such as an Ethernet card) has its own IP address. For example, when you use Linuxconf to specify an IP address for an Ethernet card on your system, the panel for entering your IP address is labeled as Adapter 1 and three other panels are there for different adapters. These are for other Ethernet cards that have their own IP address. Currently, the Linux kernel can support up to four network adapters. If you use a modem to connect to an ISP, then you would set up a PPP interface that would also have its own IP address (usually dynamically assigned by the PPP). Remembering this distinction is important if you plan to use Linux to set up a local or a home network, using Linux as your gateway machine to the Internet (see the section "IP Masquerading" in Chapter 31).

Network Address

The IP address is divided into two parts: one part identifies the network and the other part identifies a particular host. The network address identifies the network of which a particular interface on a host is a part. Two methods exist for implementing the Network and Host parts of an IP address: the original class-based IP addressing and the current *Classless Interdomain Routing addressing* (*CIDR*). Class-based IP addressing designates officially predetermined parts of the address for the network and host addresses, whereas CIDR addressing allows the parts to be determined dynamically using a netmask.

Originally IP addresses were organized according to classes. On the Internet, networks are organized into three classes depending on their size—classes A, B, and C. A class A network uses only the first segment for the IP address and the remaining three for the host, allowing a great many computers to be connected to the same network. Most IP addresses reference smaller, class C, networks. For a class C network, the first three segments are used to identify the network, and only the last segment identifies the host. Altogether, this forms a unique address with which to identify any network interface on computers in a TCP/IP network. For example, in the IP address **192.168.1.72**, the network part is **192.168.1** and the interface/host part is **72**. The interface/host is a part of a network whose own address is **192.168.1.0**. Currently, a new version of the IP protocol called IPv6 is replacing the older IPv4 version. IPv6 expands the number of possible IP addresses and provides greater security. It is fully compatible with systems still using IPv4.

In a class C network, the first three numbers identify the network part of the IP address. This part is divided into three network numbers, each identifying a subnet. Networks on the Internet are organized into subnets, beginning with the largest and narrowing to small subnetworks. The last number is used to identify a particular computer referred to as a *host*. You can think of the Internet as a series of networks with subnetworks; these subnetworks have their own subnetworks. The rightmost number identifies the host computer, and the number preceding it identifies the subnetwork of which the computer is a part. The number to the left of that identifies the network the subnetwork is part of, and so on. The Internet address 192.168.187.4 references the fourth computer connected to the network identified by the number 187. Network 187 is a subnet to a larger network identified as 168. This larger network is itself a subnet of the network identified as 192. Here's how it breaks down:

192.168.187.4	IP address
192.168.187	Network identification
4	Host identification

Netmask

Systems derive the network address from the host address using the netmask. You can think of an IP address as a series of 32 binary bits, some of which are used for the network and the remainder for the host. The *netmask* is the network set of bits set to 1s, with the host bits set to 0s (see Figure 30-1). In a standard class-based IP address, all the numbers in the network part of your host address are set to **255**, and the host part is set to **0**. This has the effect of setting all the binary bits making up the network address to 1s. This, then, is your netmask. So, the netmask for the host address **192.168.1.72** is **255.255.255.0**. The network part, **192.168.1**, has been set to **255.255.255**, and the host part, **72**, has been set to **0**. Systems can then use your netmask to derive your network address from your host address. They can determine what part of your host address makes up your network address and what those numbers are.

For those familiar with computer programming, a bitwise AND operation on the netmask and the host address results in zeroing the host part, leaving you with the network part of the host address. You can think of the address as being implemented as a four-byte integer with each byte corresponding to a segment of the address. In a class C address, the three network segments corresponds to the first three bytes and the host segment corresponds to the fourth byte. A netmask is designed to mask out the host part of the address, leaving the network segments alone. In the netmask for a standard class C network, the first three bytes are all 1 and the last byte consists of 0. The 0s in the last byte mask out the host part of the address, and the 1s in the first three bytes leave the network part of the address alone. Figure 30-1 shows the bit-wise operation of the netmask on the address 192.168.1.72. This is a class C address to the mask, which consists of twenty-four 1s making up the first three bytes and eight 0s making up the last byte. When applied to the address 192.168.1.72, the network address remains (192.168.1) and the host address is masked out (72), giving you 192.168.1.0 as the network address.

The Netmask as used in *classless interdomain routing* (*CIDR*) is much more flexible. Instead of having the size of the network address and its mask determined by the network class, it is determined by a number attached to the end of the IP address. This number simply specifies the size of the network address, how many bits in the address it takes up. For example, an IP address whose network part takes up the first three bytes (segments), the number of bits used for that network part is 24—eight bits to a byte (segment). Instead of using a netmask to determine the network address, the attached number for the network size is used. This number is attached to the end of the address with a slash, as shown here:

```
192.168.1.72/24
```

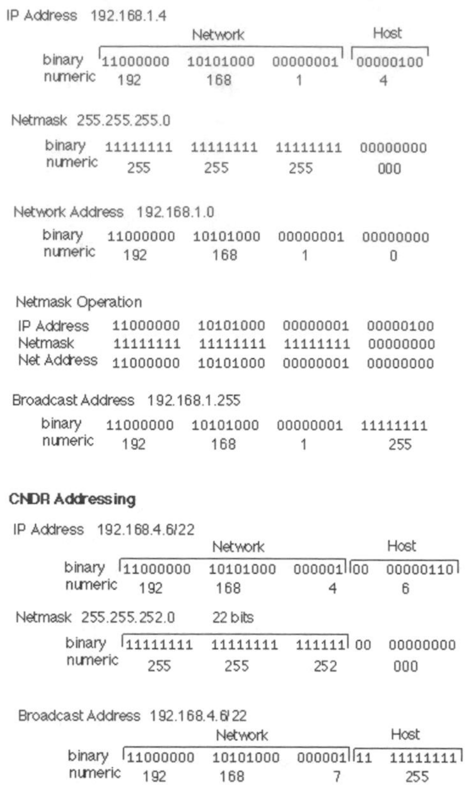

Figure 30-1. *Netmask operation*

CIDR gives you the advantage of specifying networks that are any size bits, instead of only three possible segments. You could have a networks whose addresses takes up 14 bits, 22 bits, or even 25 bits. The host address can use whatever bits are left over. A network with a 21-bit address can range host addresses using the remaining 11 bits, 0 to 2047.

Classless Interdomain Routing (CIDR)

Currently, the class-based organization of IP addresses is being replaced by the CIDR format. CIDR was designed for mid-size networks, those between a class C and classes with hosts greater than 256 and smaller than 65,534. A class C network-based IP address using only one segment for hosts uses only one segment, an 8-bit integer, with a maximum value of 256. A class B network-based IP address uses two segments, which make up a 16-bit integer whose maximum value is 65,534. You can think of an address as a 32-bit integer taking up four bytes, where each byte is eight bits. Each segment conforms to one of the four bytes. A class C network uses three segments, or 24 bits, to make up its network address. A class B network, in turn, uses two segments, or 16 bits, for its address. With this scheme, allowable host and network addresses are changed an entire byte at a time, segment to segment. With CIDR addressing, you can define host and network addresses by bits, instead of whole segments. For example, you can use CIDR addressing to expand the host segment from eight bits to nine, rather than having to jump it to a class B 16 bits (two segments). CIDR addressing notation achieves this by incorporating netmask information in the IP address (the netmask is applied to an IP address to determine the Network part of the address). In the CIDR notation, the number of bits making up the network address are placed after the IP address, following a slash. For example, the CIDR form of the class C 192.168.187.4 IP address is

```
192.168.187.4/24
```

The network address for any standard class C IP address takes up the first three segments, 24 bits. If you want to create a network with a maximum of 512 hosts, you could give them IP addresses where the network address is 23 bits and the host address takes up 9 bits (0–511). The IP address notation remains the same, however, using the four eight-bit segments. This means a given segment's number could be used for both a network and a host address. Segments are no longer either wholly part of the host or the network address. Assigning a 23-bit network address and a 9-bit host address means the number in the third segment is part of both the network and the host address, the first seven bits for the network and the last bit for the host. In this following example, the third number, 145, is used as the end of the network address and as the beginning of the host address.

```
192.168.145.67/23
```

This situation complicates CIDR addressing and, in some cases, the only way to represent the address is to specify two or more network addresses. Check RFC 1520 at **www.ietf.org** for more details.

Obtaining IP Addresses

IP addresses are officially allocated by IANA, which manages all aspects of Internet addressing (**www.iana.org**). IANA oversees *Internet Registries* (IR), which, in turn, maintain Internet addresses on a regional and local level. The Internet Registry for the Americas is the *American Registry for Internet Numbers* (*ARIN*), whose Web site is at **www.arin.net.** These addresses are provided to users by *Internet service providers* (*ISPs*). You can obtain your own Internet address from an ISP or, if you are on a network already connected to the Internet, your network administrator can assign you one. If you are using an ISP, the ISP may temporarily assign one from a pool it has on hand with each use.

Certain numbers are reserved. The numbers 127, 0, or 255 cannot be part of an official IP address. The address 127.0.0.0 is the loopback address that enables users on your computer to communicate with each other. For class-based IP addressing, the number 255 is a special broadcast identifier you can use to broadcast messages to all sites on a network. Using 255 for any part of the IP address references all nodes connected at that level. For example, 192.168.255.255 broadcasts a message to all computers on network 192.168, all its subnetworks, and their hosts. The address 192.168.187.255 broadcasts to every computer on the local network. If you use 0 for the network part of the address, the host number references a computer within your local network. For example, 0.0.0.6 references the sixth computer in your local network. If you want to broadcast to all computers on your local network, you can use the number 0.0.0.255. For CIDR IP addressing, the broadcast address may appear much like a normal IP address. As indicated in the previous section, CIDR addressing allows the use of any number of bits making up the IP address for either the network or the host part. For a broadcast address, the host part must have all its bits set to 1 (see Figure 30-1).

A special set of numbers is reserved for use on non-Internet LANs (RFC 1918). These are numbers that begin with the special network number 192.168 (for class C network), as used in these examples. If you are setting up a LAN, such as a small business or a home network, you are free to use these numbers for your local machines. You can set up an intranet using network cards, such as Ethernet cards and Ethernet hubs, and then configure your machines with IP addresses starting from 192.168.1.1. The host segment can go up to 256. If you have three machines on your home network, you could give them the addresses 192.168.1.1, 192.168.1.2, and 192.168.1.3. You can implement Internet services, such as FTP, Web, and mail services on your local machines and use any of the Internet tools to make use of those services. They all use the same TCP/IP protocols as used on the Internet. For example, with FTP tools, you can transfer files among the machines on your network, with mail tools you can send messages from one machine to another, and, with a Web browser, you can access local Web sites that may be installed on a machine running its own Web servers. If you want to have one of your machines connected to the Internet or some other network, you can set it up to be a gateway machine. By conventions, the gateway machine is usually given the address 192.168.1.1. With a method called *IP masquerading*, you can have any of the non-Internet machines use a gateway to connect to the Internet.

Numbers are also reserved for class A and class B non-Internet local networks. Table 30-3 lists these addresses. The possible addresses available span from 0 to 255 in the host segment of the address. For example, class B network addresses range from 172.16.0.0 to 172.31.255.255, giving you a total of 32,356 possible hosts. The class C network ranges from 192.168.0.0 to 192.168.255.255, giving you 256 possible subnetworks, each with 256 possible hosts. The number 127.0.0.0 is reserved for a

10.0.0.0	Class A Network
172.16.0.0 to 172.31.255.255	Class B Network
192.168.0.0	Class C Network
127.0.0.0	Loopback Network (for system self-communication)

Table 30-3. *Non-Internet Local Network IP Addresses*

system's loopback interface, which allows it to communicate with itself, enabling users on the same system to send messages to each other.

Broadcast Address

The *broadcast address* allows a system to send the same message to all systems on your network at once. With class-based IP addressing, you can easily determine the broadcast address using your host address: the broadcast address has the host part of your address set to **255**. The network part remains untouched. So, the broadcast address for the host address **192.168.1.72** is **192.168.1.255** (you combine the network part of the address with **255** in the host part). For CIDR IP addressing, you need to know the number of bits in the netmask. The remaining bits are set to 1 (see Figure 30-1). For example, an IP address of 192.168.4.6/22 has a broadcast address of 192.168.7.255/22. In this case, the first 22 bits are the network address and the last ten bits are the host part set to the broadcast value (all 1s). In fact, you can think of a class C broadcast address as merely a CIDR address using 24 bits (the first three segments) for the network address, and the last eight bits (the fourth segment) as the broadcast address. The value 255 expressed in binary terms is simply eight bits that are all 1s. 255 is the same as 11111111.

Gateway Address

Some networks have a computer designated as the gateway to other networks. Every connection to and from a network to other networks passes through this gateway computer. Most local networks use gateways to establish a connection to the Internet. If you are on this type of network, you must provide the gateway address. If your network does not have a connection to the Internet, if you use a standalone system, or if you dial into an ISP, you may not need a gateway address. The *gateway address* is the address of the host system providing the gateway service to the network. On many networks, this host is given a host ID of **1**: the gateway address for a network with the address **192.168.1** would be **192.168.1.1**, but this is only a convention. To be sure of your gateway address, ask your network administrator.

Name Server Addresses

Many networks, including the Internet, have computers that provide a Domain Name Service (DNS) that translates the domain names of networks and hosts into IP addresses. These are known as the network's *domain name servers*. The DNS makes your computer identifiable on a network, using only your domain name, rather than your IP address. You can also use the domain names of other systems to reference them, so you needn't know their IP addresses. You must know the IP addresses of any domain name servers for your network, however. You can obtain the addresses from your system administrator (often more than one exists). Even if you are using an ISP, you must know the address of the domain name servers your ISP operates for the Internet.

TCP/IP Configuration Files

A set of configuration files in the **/etc** directory, shown in Table 30-4, are used to set up and manage your TCP/IP network. These configuration files specify such network information as host and domain names, IP addresses, and interface options. The IP addresses and domain names of other Internet hosts you want to access are entered in these files. If you configured your network during installation, you can already find that information in these files. The **netcfg**, Linuxconf, and the **netconfig** configuration tools described in the next section provide easy interfaces for entering the configuration data for these files.

Identifying Hostnames: /etc/hosts

Without the unique IP address the TCP/IP network uses to identify computers, a particular computer cannot be located. Because IP addresses are difficult to use or remember, domain names are used instead. For each IP address, a domain name exists. When you use a domain name to reference a computer on the network, your system translates it into its associated IP address. This address can then be used by your network to locate that computer.

Originally, every computer on the network was responsible for maintaining a list of the hostnames and their IP addresses. This list is still kept in the **/etc/hosts** file. When you use a domain name, your system looks up its IP address in the **hosts** file. The system administrator is responsible for maintaining this list. Because of the explosive growth of the Internet and the development of more and more large networks, the responsibility for associating domain names and IP addresses has been taken over by domain name servers. The **hosts** file is still used to hold the domain names and IP addresses of frequently accessed hosts, however. Your system normally checks your **hosts** file for the IP address of a domain name before taking the added step of accessing a name server.

The format of a domain name entry in the **hosts** file is the IP address followed by the domain name, separated by a space. You can then add aliases for the hostname.

After the entry, on the same line, you can enter a comment. A comment is always preceded by a # symbol. You can already find an entry in your **hosts** file for localhost with the IP address **127.0.0.1**. *Localhost* is a special identification used by your computer to enable users on your system to communicate locally with each other. The IP address **127.0.0.1** is a special reserved address used by every computer for this purpose. It identifies what is technically referred to as a *loopback device*.

/etc/hosts

```
127.0.0.1           turtle.trek.com                 localhost
192.168.1.72        turtle.trek.com
192.168.196.56      pango1.train.com
202.211.234.1       rose.berkeley.edu
```

Network Name: /etc/networks

The **/etc/networks** file holds the domain names and IP addresses of networks you are connected to, not the domain names of particular computers. Networks have shortened IP addresses. Depending on the type of network, they use one, two, or three numbers for their IP addresses. You also have your localhost network IP address **127.0.0.0**. This is the network address used for the loopback device.

The IP addresses are entered, followed by the network domain names. Recall that an IP address consists of a network part and a host part. The network part is the network address you find in the **networks** file. You always have an entry in this file for the network portion of your computer's IP address. This is the network address of the network to which your computer is connected.

/etc/networks

```
loopback 127.0.0.0
trek.com 192.168.1.0
```

/etc/HOSTNAME

The **/etc/HOSTNAME** file holds your system's hostname. To change your hostname, you change this entry. The **netcfg** program enables you to change your hostname and places the new name in **/etc/HOSTNAME**. Instead of displaying this file to find your hostname, you can use the **hostname** command.

```
$ hostname
turtle.trek.com
```

/etc/services

The **/etc/services** file lists network services available on your system, such as FTP and Telnet, and associates each with a particular port. Here, you can find out what port your Web server is checking or what port is used for your FTP server. You can give a service an alias, which you specify after the port number. You can then reference the service using the alias.

/etc/protocols

The **/etc/protocols** file lists the TCP/IP protocols currently supported by your system.

/etc/sysconfig/network

The **/etc/sysconfig/network** file contains system definitions for your network configuration. These include definitions for your domain name, gateway, and hostname, among others.

Domain Name Service (DNS)

Each computer connected to a TCP/IP network, such as the Internet, is identified by its own IP address. An *IP address* is a set of four numbers specifying the location of a network and of a host (a computer) within that network. IP addresses are difficult to remember, so a domain name version of each IP address is also used to identify a host. As described in Chapter 10, a domain name consists of two parts, the hostname and the domain. The hostname is the computer's specific name, and the domain identifies the network of which the computer is a part. The domains used for the United States usually have extensions that identify the type of host. For example, **.edu** is used for educational institutions and **.com** is used for businesses. International domains usually have extensions that indicate the country they are located in, such as **.de** for Germany or **.au** for Australia. The combination of a hostname, domain, and extension forms a unique name by which a computer can be referenced. The domain can, in turn, be split into further subdomains.

As you know, a computer on a network can still only be identified by its IP address, even if it has a hostname. You can use a hostname to reference a computer on a network, but this involves using the hostname to look up the corresponding IP address in a database. The network then uses the IP address, not the hostname, to access the computer. Before the advent of large TCP/IP networks, such as the Internet, it was feasible for each computer on a network to maintain a file with a list of all the hostnames and IP addresses of the computers connected on its network. Whenever a hostname was used, it was looked up in this file and the corresponding IP address was located. You can still do this on your own system for remote systems you access frequently.

As networks became larger, it became impractical—and, in the case of the Internet, impossible—for each computer to maintain its own list of all the domain names and IP addresses. To provide the service of translating domain addresses to IP addresses, databases of domain names were developed and placed on their own servers. To find the IP address of a domain name, a query is sent to a name server, which then looks up the IP address for you and sends it back. In a large network, several name servers can

Address	Description
Host address	IP address of your system; it has a network part to identify the network you are on and a host part to identify your own system
Network address	IP address of your network
Broadcast address	IP address for sending messages to all hosts on your network at once
Gateway address	IP address of your gateway system, if you have one (usually the network part of your host IP address with the host part set to **1**)
Domain name server addresses	IP addresses of domain name servers your network uses
Netmask	Used to determine the network and host parts of your IP address

Files	Description
/etc/hosts	Associates hostnames with IP addresses
/etc/networks	Associates domain names with network addresses
/etc/host.conf	Lists resolver options
/etc/nsswitch.conf	Name Service Switch Configuration
/etc/resolv.conf	Lists domain name server names, IP addresses (nameserver), and domain names where remote hosts may be located (search)
/etc/protocols	Lists protocols available on your system
/etc/services	Lists available network services, such as FTP and telnet, and the ports they use
/etc/HOSTNAME	Holds the name of your system
/etc/sysconfig/network	Network configuration information

Table 30-4. *TCP/IP Configuration Addresses and Files*

cover different parts of the network. If a name server cannot find a particular IP address, it sends the query on to another name server that is more likely to have it.

If you are administering a network and you need to set up a name server for it, you can configure a Linux system to operate as a name server. To do so, you must start up a name server daemon, and then wait for domain name queries. A name server makes use of several configuration files that enable it to answer requests. The name server software used on Linux systems is the *Berkeley Internet Name Domain* (*BIND*) distributed by the Internet Software Consortium (**www.isc.org**). Chapter 18 describes the process of setting up a domain name server in detail.

Name servers are queried by resolvers. These are programs specially designed to obtain addresses from name servers. To use domain names on your system, you must configure your own resolver. Your local resolver is configured with your **/etc/host.conf** and **/etc/resolv.conf** files. **/etc/nsswitch** is used in place of **/etc/host.conf** for libc6.

host.conf

Your **host.conf** file lists resolver options (shown in the following table). Each option can have several fields, separated by spaces or tabs. You can use a **#** at the beginning of a line to enter a comment. The options tell the resolver what services to use. The order of the list is important. The resolver begins with the first option listed and moves on to the next ones in turn. You can find the **host.conf** file in your **/etc** directory, along with other configuration files.

Option	Description
order	Specifies sequence of name resolution methods:
	hosts Checks for name in the local **/etc/host** file
	bind Queries a DNS name server for address
	nis Uses Network Information Service protocol to obtain address
alert	Checks addresses of remote sites attempting to access your system; you turn it on or off with the on and off options
nospoof	Confirms addresses of remote sites attempting to access your system
trim	Checks your local host's file; removes the domain name and checks only for the hostname; enables you to use only a hostname in your host file for an IP address
multi	Checks your local hosts file; allows a host to have several IP addresses; you turn it on or off with the on and off options

In the next example of a **host.conf** file, the **order** option instructs your resolver first to look up names in your local **/etc/hosts** file, and then, if that fails, to query domain name servers. The system does not have multiple addresses.

/etc/host.conf

```
#  host.conf file
#  Lookup names in host file and then check DNS
order bind host
# There are no multiple addresses
multi off
```

/etc/nsswitch.conf: Name Service Switch

Different functions in the standard C Library must be configured to operate on your Linux system. Previously, database-like services, such as password support and name services like NIS or DNS, directly accessed these functions, using a fixed search order. For GNU C Library 2.*x*, used on current versions of Linux, this configuration is carried out by a scheme called the *Name Service Switch* (*NSS*), which is based on the method of the same name used by Sun Microsystems Solaris 2 OS. The database sources and their lookup order are listed in the **/etc/nsswitch.conf** file.

The **/etc/nsswitch.conf** file holds entries for the different configuration files that can be controlled by NSS. The system configuration files that NSS supports are listed in Table 30-5. An entry consists of two fields: the service and the configuration specification. The service consists of the configuration file followed by a colon. The second field is the configuration specification for that file, which holds instructions on how the lookup procedure will work. The configuration specification can contain service specifications and action items. Service specifications are the services to search. Currently, valid service specifications are nis, nis-plus, files, db, dns, and compat (see Table 30-6). Not all are valid for each configuration file. For example, the dns service is only valid for the hosts file, whereas nis is valid for all files. An action item specifies the action to take to the lookup results for a specific service. An action item is placed within brackets after a service. A configuration specification can list several services, each with its own action item. In the following example, the entry for the network file has a configuration specification that says to check the NIS service and, if not found, to check the **/etc/networks** file.

```
networks:       nis [NOTFOUND=return] files
```

An action consists of a status and an action. The status holds a possible result of a service lookup and the action is the action to take if the status is true. Currently, the possible status values are SUCCESS, NOTFOUND, UNAVAIL, and TRYAGAIN (service temporarily unavailable). The possible actions are **return** and **continue**. **return** stops the lookup process for the configuration file, whereas **continue** continues on to the next listed service. In the previous example, if the record is not found in NIS, the lookup process ends.

Shown here is a copy of the current Red Hat **/etc/nsswitch.conf** file. Comments and commented-out entries begin with a # sign.

File	Description
aliases	Mail aliases, used by sendmail
ethers	Ethernet numbers
group	Groups of users
hosts	Host names and numbers
netgroup	Network-wide list of hosts and users, used for access rules. C libraries before glibc 2.1 only support netgroups over NIS
network	Network names and numbers
passwd	User passwords
protocols	Network protocols
publickey	Public and secret keys for SecureRPC used by NFS and NIS+
rpc	Remote procedure call names and numbers
services	Network services
shadow	Shadow user passwords

Table 30-5.   *NSS Supported Files*

Service	Description
files	Check corresponding **/etc** file for the configuration (for example, **/etc/hosts** for hosts). This service is valid for all files.
db	Check corresponding **/var/db** databases for the configuration. Valid for all files except netgroup.
compat	Valid only for passwd, group, and shadow files.
dns	Check the DNS service. Valid only for hosts file.
nis	Check the NIS service. Valid for all files.
nisplus	NIS version 3.
hesoid	Use hesoid for lookup.

Table 30-6.   *NSS Configuration Services*

/etc/nsswitch.conf

```
#
# /etc/nsswitch.conf
#
# An example Name Service Switch config file. This file should be
# sorted with the most-used services at the beginning.
#
# The entry '[NOTFOUND=return]' means that the search for an
# entry should stop if the search in the previous entry turned
# up nothing. Note that if the search failed due to some other reason
# (like no NIS server responding) then the search continues with the
# next entry.
#
# Legal entries are:
#
#       nisplus or nis+         Use NIS+ (NIS version 3)
#       nis or yp               Use NIS (NIS version 2), also called YP
#       dns                     Use DNS (Domain Name Service)
#       files                   Use the local files
#       db                      Use the local database (.db) files
#       compat                  Use NIS on compat mode
#       hesiod                  Use Hesiod for user lookups
#       [NOTFOUND=return]       Stop searching if not found so far
#

# To use db, put the "db" in front of "files" for entries you want to
# be looked up first in the databases
#
# Example:
#passwd:    db files nisplus nis
#shadow:    db files nisplus nis
#group:     db files nisplus nis

passwd:     files nisplus nis
shadow:     files nisplus nis
group:      files nisplus nis

hosts:      files nisplus nis dns

# Example - obey only what nisplus tells us...
#services:  nisplus [NOTFOUND=return] files
#networks:  nisplus [NOTFOUND=return] files
#protocols: nisplus [NOTFOUND=return] files
#rpc:       nisplus [NOTFOUND=return] files
#ethers:    nisplus [NOTFOUND=return] files
#netmasks:  nisplus [NOTFOUND=return] files

bootparams: nisplus [NOTFOUND=return] files

ethers:     files
netmasks:   files
networks:   files
protocols:  files
rpc:        files
```

```
services:    files

netgroup:    nisplus

publickey:   nisplus

automount:   files nisplus
aliases:     files nisplus
```

Network Interfaces and Routes: ifconfig and route

Your connection to a network is made by your system through a particular hardware interface, such as an Ethernet card or a modem. Data passing through this interface is then routed to your network. The **ifconfig** command configures your network interfaces and the **route** command routes them accordingly. If you configure an interface with a network configuration tool, such as **netcfg**, Linuxconf, or YaST, you needn't use **ifconfig** or **route**. If you are using another Linux system, the **netconfig** utility also performs the same configuration as **netcfg**. However, you can directly configure interfaces using **ifconfig** and **route**, if you want. Every time you start your system, the network interfaces and their routes must be established. This is done automatically for you when you boot up by **ifconfig** and **route** commands executed for each interface by the **/etc/rc.d/init.d/network** initialization file, which is executed whenever you start your system. If you are manually adding your own interfaces, you must set up the network script to perform the **ifconfig** and **route** operations for your new interfaces.

On Red Hat, your network interface is started up using the network script in the **/etc/rc.d/init.d** directory. You can manually shut down and restart your network interface using this script and the **start** or **stop** options. The following commands shut down, and then start up your network interface:

```
/etc/rc.d/init.d/network stop
/etc/rc.d/init.d/network start
```

To test if your interface is working, use the **ping** command with an IP address of a system on your network, such as your gateway machine. The **ping** command continually repeats until you stop it with a CTRL-C.

```
ping 192.168.1.42
```

ifconfig

The **ifconfig** command takes as its arguments the name of an interface and an IP address, as well as options. The **ifconfig** command then assigns the IP address to the interface. Your system now knows such an interface exists and that it references a particular IP address. In addition, you can specify whether the IP address is a host or a network address. You can use a domain name for the IP address, provided the domain name is listed along with its IP address in the **/etc/hosts** file. The syntax for the **ifconfig** command is as follows:

```
# ifconfig   interface  -host_net_flag   address   options
```

The *host_net_flag* can be either **-host** or **-net** to indicate a host or network IP address. The **-host** flag is the default. The **ifconfig** command can have several options, which set different features of the interface, such as the maximum number of bytes it can transfer (**mtu**) or the broadcast address. The **up** and **down** options activate and deactivate the interface. In the next example, the **ifconfig** command configures an Ethernet interface:

```
# ifconfig eth0  204.32.168.56
```

For a simple configuration such as this, **ifconfig** automatically generates a standard broadcast address and netmask. The standard broadcast address is the network address with the number **255** for the host address. For a class C network, the standard netmask is **255.255.255.0**, whereas for a class A network, the standard netmask is 255.0.0.0. If you are connected to a network with a particular netmask and broadcast address, however, you must specify them when you use **ifconfig**. The option for specifying the broadcast address is **broadcast**; for the network mask, it is **netmask**. Table 30-7 lists the different **ifconfig** options. In the next example, **ifconfig** includes the netmask and broadcast address:

```
# ifconfig eth0 204.32.168.56   broadcast 204.128.244.127  netmask 255.255.255.0
```

Once you configure your interface, you can use **ifconfig** with the **up** option to activate it and with the **down** option to deactivate it. If you specify an IP address in an **ifconfig** operation, as in the previous example, the **up** option is implied.

```
# ifconfig eth0 up
```

Point-to-point interfaces such as *Parallel IP* (*PLIP*), *Serial Line IP* (*SLIP*), and *Point-to-Point Protocol* (*PPP*) require you to include the **pointopoint** option. A PLIP interface name is identified with the name plip with an attached number. For example, plip0 is the first PLIP interface. SLIP interfaces use slip0. PPP interfaces start with ppp0. Point-to-point interfaces are those that usually operate between only two hosts, such as two computers connected over a modem. When you specify the **pointopoint** option, you need to include the IP address of the host. In the next example, a PLIP interface is configured that connects the computer at IP address **192.168.1.72** with one at **204.166.254.14**. If domain addresses were listed for these systems in **/etc/hosts**, those domain names could be used in place of the IP addresses.

```
# ifconfig  plip0  192.168.1.72  pointopoint 204.166.254.14
```

If you need to, you can also use **ifconfig** to configure your loopback device. The name of the loopback device is lo, and its IP address is the special address **127.0.0.1**. The following example shows the configuration:

```
# ifconfig lo 127.0.0.1
```

The **ifconfig** command is useful for checking on the status of an interface. If you enter the **ifconfig** command, along with the name of the interface, information about that interface is displayed.

```
# ifconfig eth0
```

To see if your loopback interface is configured, you can use **ifconfig** with the loopback interface name, lo.

```
# ifconfig lo

lo          Link encap:Local Loopback
            inet addr:127.0.0.1  Bcast:127.255.255.255  Mask:255.0.0.0
            UP BROADCAST LOOPBACK RUNNING  MTU:2000  Metric:1
            RX packets:0 errors:0 dropped:0 overruns:0
            TX packets:12 errors:0 dropped:0 overruns:0
```

Routing

A packet that is part of a transmission takes a certain *route* to reach its destination. On a large network, packets are transmitted from one computer to another until the destination computer is reached. The route determines where the process starts and to what computer your system needs to send the packet for it to reach its destination. On small networks, routing may be static—that is, the route from one system to another is fixed. One system knows how to reach another, moving through fixed paths. On larger networks and on the Internet, however, routing is dynamic. Your system knows the first computer to send its packet off to, and then that computer takes the packet from there, passing it on to another computer, which then determines where to pass it on. For dynamic routing, your system needs to know little. Static routing, however, can become complex because you have to keep track of all the network connections.

Your routes are listed in your routing table in the **/proc/net/route** file. To display the routing table, enter **route** with no arguments.

```
# route
Kernel routing table
Destination       Gateway    Genmask        Flags Metric  Ref   Use Iface
loopback          *          255.0.0.0      U     0       0      12 lo
pango1.train.com  *          255.255.255.0  U     0       0       0 eth0
```

Option	Description
Interface	Name of the network interface, such as eth0 for the first Ethernet device or ppp0 for the first PPP device (modem)
aftype	Address family for decoding protocol addresses; default is inet, currently used by Linux
up	Activates an interface. Implied if IP address is specified
down	Deactivates an interface
-arp	Turns ARP on or off; preceding—turns it off
-trailers	Turns on or off trailers in Ethernet frames; preceding—turns it off
-allmulti	Turns on or off the promiscuous mode; preceding - turns it off. This allows network monitoring
metric *n*	Cost for interface routing (not currently supported)
mtu *n*	Maximum number of bytes that can be sent on this interface per transmission
dstaddr *address*	Destination IP address on a point-to-point connection
netmask *address*	IP network mask; preceding—turns it off
broadcast *address*	Broadcast address; preceding—turns it off
point-to-point *address*	Point-to-point mode for interface; if address is included, it is assigned to remote system
hw	Sets hardware address of interface
Address	IP address assigned to interface

Table 30-7.   *The* `ifconfig` *Options*

Each entry in the routing table has several fields, providing information such as the route destination and the type of interface used. The different fields are listed in the following table.

Field	Description
Destination	Destination IP address of the route
Gateway	IP address or hostname of the gateway the route uses; * indicates no gateway is used
Genmask	The netmask for the route
Flags	Type of route: U = up, H = host, G = gateway, D = dynamic, M = modified
Metric	Metric cost of route
Ref	Number of routes that depend on this one
Window	TCP window for AX.25 networks
Use	Number of times used
Iface	Type of interface this route uses

You should have at least one entry in the routing table for the loopback interface. If not, you must route the loopback interface using the **route** command. The IP address for an interface has to be added to the routing table before you can use that interface. You add an address with the **route** command and the **add** option.

```
route  add  address
```

The next example adds the IP address for the loopback interface to the routing table:

```
route add 127.0.0.1
```

With the **add** argument, you can add routes either for networks with the **−net** option or with the **−host** option for IP interfaces (hosts). The **−host** option is the default. In addition, you can then specify several parameters for information, such as the netmask (**netmask**), gateway (**gw**), interface device (**dev**), and the default route (**default**). If you have more than in IP interface, such as several Ethernet cards, you must specify the name of the interface using the **dev** parameter. If your network has a gateway host, you use the **gw** parameter to specify it. If your system is connected to a network, at least one entry should be in your routing table that specifies the default route. This is the route taken by a message packet when no other route entry leads to its destination. The following example is the routing of an Ethernet interface:

```
# route add 192.168.1.2 dev eth0
```

If your system has only the single Ethernet device as your IP interface, you could leave out the **dev eth0** parameter.

```
# route add 192.168.1.2
```

You can delete any route you establish by invoking **ifconfig** with the **del** argument and the IP address of that route, as in this example:

```
# route del 192.168.1.2
```

You also need to add routes for networks that an IP interface can access. For this, you use the **–net** option. In this example, a route is set up for a system's LAN at **192.168.1.0**:

```
# route add -net  192.168.1.0 dev eth0
```

For a gateway, you first add a route to the gateway interface, and then add a route specifying it is a gateway. The address of the gateway interface in this example is **192.168.1.1**:

```
# route add 192.168.1.1
# route add default gw  192.168.1.1
```

If you are using the gateway to access a subnet, add the network address for that network (in this example, **192.168.23.0**).

```
 # route add -net 192.168.23.0 gw dev eth1
```

To add another IP address to a different network interface on your system, use the **ifconfig** and **route** commands with the new IP address. The following command configures a second Ethernet card (eth1) with the IP address **192.168.1.3**.

```
ifconfig eth1 192.168.1.3
route add 192.168.1.3 dev eth1
```

Network Startup Script: /etc/rc.d/init.d/network

On OpenLinux and Red Hat systems, the **/etc/rc.d/init.d/network** file performs the startup operations for configuring your network. The network script uses a script called **ifup** to activate a network connection, and **ifdown** to shut it down. These scripts make use of special configuration files located in the **/etc/sysconfig/network-scripts** directory that bear the names of the network interfaces currently configured. These files define shell variables that hold information on the interface, such as whether to start them at boot time. The **ifdown** and **ifup** scripts hold the **ifconfig** and **route** commands to activate scripts using these special variables. As noted previously, you can use the network script to activate and deactivate your network interfaces at any time. Use the **start** option to activate interfaces, and **stop** to deactivate them.

Monitoring Your Network: ping and netstat

With the ping program, you can check to see if you can actually access another host on your network. The ping program sends a request to the host for a reply. The host then sends a reply back, and it is displayed on your screen. The ping program continually sends such a request until you stop it with a **break** command, a CTRL-C. You see one reply after another scroll by on your screen until you stop the program. If ping cannot access a host, it issues a message saying the host is unreachable. If ping fails, this is an indication your network connection is not working. It may only be the particular interface, a basic configuration problem, or a bad physical connection. To use ping, enter **ping** and the name of the host. You can also use the KDE network utilities on the KDE desktop and gfinger on the Gnome desktop (see Chapter 15).

```
$ ping pang01.mytrain.com
```

The netstat program provides real-time information on the status of your network connections, as well as network statistics and the routing table. The netstat program has several options you can use to bring up different information about your network (see Table 30-8).

```
# netstat
Active Internet connections
Proto Recv-Q Send-Q Local Address        Foreign Address        (State)        User
tcp      0      0 turtle.mytrek.com:01  pango1.mytrain.com.:ftp ESTABLISHED dylan
Active UNIX domain sockets
Proto RefCnt Flags     Type         State        Path
unix  1      [ ACC ]   SOCK_STREAM  LISTENING    /dev/printer
unix  2      [ ]       SOCK_STREAM  CONNECTED    /dev/log
unix  1      [ ACC ]   SOCK_STREAM  LISTENING    /dev/nwapi
```

```
unix    2       [ ]         SOCK_STREAM     CONNECTED       /dev/log
unix    2       [ ]         SOCK_STREAM     CONNECTED
unix    1       [ ACC ]     SOCK_STREAM     LISTENING       /dev/log
```

The **netstat** command with no options lists the network connections on your system. First, active TCP connections are listed, and then the active domain sockets are listed. The domain sockets contain processes used to set up communications among your system and other systems. The various fields are described in the following table. You can use **netstat** with the **-r** option to display the routing table, and **netstat** with the **-i** option displays the use for the different network interfaces.

IP Aliasing

In some cases, you may want to assign a single Linux system that has only one network interface to two or more IP addresses. For example, you may want to run different Web

Option	Description
-a	Displays information about all Internet sockets, including those sockets that are only listening
-I	Displays statistics for all network devices
-c	Displays network status continually every second until the program is interrupted
-n	Displays remote and local address as IP addresses
-o	Displays timer states, expiration times, and backoff state for network connections
-r	Displays the kernel routing table
-t	Displays information about TCP sockets only, including those that are listening
-u	Displays information about UDP sockets only
-v	Displays version information
-w	Displays information about raw sockets only
-x	Displays information about UNIX domain sockets

Table 30-8. *The* netstat *Options*

sites on this same system that can be accessed with separate IP addresses. In effect, you are setting up an alias for your system, another address by which it can be accessed. In fact, you are assigning two IP addresses to the same network interface, for example, assigning a single Ethernet card two IP addresses. This procedure is referred to as and is used to set up multiple IP-based virtual hosts for Internet servers. This method enables you to run several Web servers on the same machine using a single interface (or more than one on each of several interfaces). See Chapters 16 and 17 for FTP and Web server information about virtual hosts, and Chapter 18 for Domain Name Service configuration.

Setting up an IP alias is a simple matter of configuring a network interface on your system to listen for the added IP address. Your system needs to know what IP addresses it should listen for and on what network interface. You set up IP aliases using either Linuxconf or the **ifconfig** and **route** commands. For Linuxconf, select the IP aliases for virtual hosts under Server tasks. This opens a panel that lists available interfaces. Click one to open a panel where you can enter added IP addresses for it.

To add another address to the same interface, you need to qualify the interface by adding a colon and a number. For example, if you are adding another IP address to the first Ethernet card (eth0), you would add a **:0** to its interface name, eth0:0. The following example shows the **ifconfig** and **route** commands for the Ethernet interface **192.168.1.2** and two IP aliases added to it: **192.168.1.100** and **192.168.1.101**. To add yet another IP address to this same interface, you would use **eth0:1**, incrementing the qualifier, and so on. The first **ifconfig** command assigns the main IP address, **192.168.1.2**, to the first Ethernet device, eth0. Then, two other IP addresses are assigned to that same device. In the first **route** command, the network route is set up for the Ethernet device, and then routes are set up for each IP interface. The interfaces for the two aliases are indicated with **eth0:0** and **eth0:1**.

```
ifconfig eth0 192.168.1.2
ifconfig eth0:0 192.168.1.100
ifconfig eth0:1 192.168.1.101
route add -net 192.168.1.0 dev eth0
route add -host 192.168.1.2 dev eth0
route add -host 192.168.1.100 dev eth0:0
route add -host 192.168.1.101 dev eth0:1
```

IP aliasing must be supported by the kernel before you can use it. If your kernel does not support it, you may have to rebuild the kernel, including IP aliasing support, or use loadable modules to add IP aliasing.

Chapter 31

Network Security:
Firewalls and Encryption

787

Most systems currently connected to the Internet are open to attempts by outside users to gain unauthorized access. Outside users can try either to gain access directly by setting up an illegal connect or to intercept valid communications from users remotely connected to the system. Firewalls and encryption are ways of protecting against such attacks. A firewall prevents any direct unauthorized attempts at access and encryption protects transmissions from authorized remote users. The current Linux kernel incorporates support for firewalls. The firewall package is called *ipchains.* You simply provide a series of rules to govern what kind of access you want to allow on your system. If that system is also a gateway for a private network, then the system's firewall capability can effectively protect the network from outside attacks. To protect remote communications, transmission can be simply encrypted. For Linux systems, you can use the *Secure Shell* (*SSH*) suite of programs to encrypt any transmissions, preventing them from being read by anyone else.

Outside users may also try to gain unauthorized access through any Internet services you may be hosting, such as a Web site. In such a case, you can set up a proxy to protect your site from attack. Linux systems use Squid proxy software to set up a proxy to protect your Web server (see Chapter 15).

Firewalls: IP-Chains

To provide security for your network, you can set up a Linux system to operate as a firewall for your network, protecting it from unauthorized access. You can use a firewall to implement either packet-filtering or proxies. *Packet-filtering* is simply the process of deciding whether a packet received by the firewall host should be passed on into the local network. It checks the address of the packet and sends the packet on, if it's allowed. Even if your system is not part of a network, but it connects directly to the Internet, you can still use the firewall feature to control access to your system. Of course, this also provides you with much more security. With proxies, you can control access to specific services, such as Web or FTP servers. You need a proxy for each service you want to control. The Web server has its own Web proxy, while an FTP server has an FTP proxy. Proxies can also be used to cache commonly used data, such as Web pages, so users needn't constantly access the originating site. The proxy software commonly used on Linux systems is Squid, discussed in Chapter 15.

The tool used to implement packet-filtering on firewalls is ipchains. The Linux Web site for ipchains is currently **www.rustcorp.com/linux/ipchains**. *ipchains* is the successor to ipfwadm used on older versions of Linux. Support for ipchains is already implemented on current Red Hat versions of Linux (from kernel 2.2). For earlier versions, you must enable support in the kernel, rebuilding it with Network Firewalls and IP Firewalling features (see Chapter 26). The IP-chains HOWTO, located in your **/usr/doc/ipchains-1.3.9** directory, provides an excellent introduction and tutorial to ipchains, and how you use it to implement a firewall. The HOWTO is in Web-page format and can be viewed with any Web browser. The HOWTO features specific examples on how to guard against several standard attacks, such as IP spoofing, the ping of death, and teardrop.

The process of setting up and maintaining firewall chains can be complex. To simplify the process, you can use a GUI-based firewall configuration tool, such as Linuxconf or **fwconfig**. You can download fwconfig from its current site at **www.mindstorm.com/~sparlin/fwconfig.shtml**.

Linuxconf provides a configuration interface for maintaining simple chain rules, as well as loading special kernel ipchains modules for services such as FTP, Quake, and IRC. You may have to load the Linuxconf's own firewall module. Select Firewalling under Networking, and then choose the panel for the kind of chain rules you want to configure: Blocking, Forward, and Output.

IP-Chain Rules

The kernel uses chains to manage packets it receives. A *chain* is simply a checklist of rules. These rules specify what action to take for packets containing certain headers. The rules operate with an if-then-else structure. If a packet does not match the first rule, the next rule is then checked, and so on. If the packet does not match any rules, then it consults chain policy. Usually, at this point the packet is rejected. If the packet does match a rule, it is passed to its target, which determines what to do with the packet. The standard targets are listed in the following table. If a packet does not match any of the rules, then it is passed to the chain's default target. Table 31-1 is a list of targets.

Target	Function
ACCEPT	Allow packet to pass through the firewall
DENY	Deny access by the packet
REJECT	Deny access and notify the sender
MASQ	Masquerade the packet. Used only in the forward chain or chains called from the forward chain. Replaces sender's address with firewall host address
REDIRECT	Redirect the packet to a local socket or process on the firewall. Used only in the input chain or chains called from the forward chain
RETURN	Jump to the end of the chain and let the default target process it

Table 31-1.   *ipchains Targets*

A *target* could, in turn, be another chain of rules, even a chain of user-defined rules. A packet could be passed through several chains before finally reaching a target. In the case of user-defined chains, the default target is always the next rule in the chains from which it was called. This sets up a procedure or function-call-like flow of control found in programming languages. When a rule has a user-defined chain as its target, then, when activated, that user-defined chain is executed. If no rules are matched, execution returns to the next rule in the originating chain.

The kernel uses three firewall chains: input, output, and forward. When a packet is received through an interface, the input chain is used to determine what to do with it. The kernel then uses its routing information to decide where to send it. If the kernel sends the packet to another host, then the forward chain is checked. Before the packet is actually sent, the output chain is also checked.

You add and modify chain rules using the **ipchains** commands. An **ipchains** command consists of the keyword **ipchains**, followed by an argument denoting the command to execute. For example, **ipchains -A** is the command to add a new rule, whereas **ipchains -D** is the command to delete a rule. The **ipchains** commands are listed in Table 31-2. The following command simply lists the chains along with their rules currently defined for your system. The output shows the default values created by **ipchains** commands for Red Hat.

```
ipchains -L
Chain input (policy ACCEPT):
Chain forward (policy ACCEPT):
Chain output (policy ACCEPT):
```

Following the command, list the chain to which the rule applies, such as the input, output, forward, or a user defined chain. Next, list different options that specify the actions you want taken. Options exist to specify the address a rule is to match on (**-s**, **-r**) and an option to specify the target the rule is to execute (**-j**). Table 31-3 lists the available options. In the following example, the user adds a rule to the input chain to accept all packets with the address 192.168.1.55. The **-s** option specifies the address attached to the packet, while the **-j** option specifies the target. Any packets that received (input), whose source address (**-s**) matches 192.168.1.55, are accepted and passed through.

```
ipchains -A input -s 192.168.1.55 -j ACCEPT
```

To deny access from a particular site, simply specify the DENY target. In the following example, any packet received from **www.myjunk.com** is rejected.

```
ipchains -A input -s www.myjunk.com -j DENY
```

Command	Function
-A *chain*	Append a rule to a chain
-D *chain*	Delete matching rule from a chain
-D *chain rulenum*	Delete rule *rulenum* (1 = first) from chain
-I *chain* [*rulenum*]	Insert in chain as *rulenum* (default 1= first)
-R *chain rulenum*	Replace rule *rulenum* (1 = first) in chain
-L [*chain*]	List the rules in a chain or all chains
-F [*chain*]	Delete all rules in chain or all chains
-Z [*chain*]	Zero counters in chain or all chains
-C chain	Test this packet on chain
-N *chain*	Create a new user-defined chain
-X *chain*	Delete a user-defined chain
-P *chain target*	Change policy on chain to target
-M –L	List current masquerading connections
-M –S *tcp tcpfin udp*	Set masquerading timeout values
-h	Display list of commands
--*version*	Display version

Table 31-2.   *ipchains Commands*

You can specify an individual address using its domain name or its IP number. For a range of addresses, you can use the IP number of their network and the network IP mask. The IP mask can be an IP number or simply the number of bits making up the mask. For example, all of the address in network 192.168.0 can be represented by 192.168.0.0/225.255.255.0 or by 192.168.0.0/24. To specify any address, you can use 0.0.0.0/0.0.0.0 or simply 0/0. By default, rules reference any address if no **-s** or **-d** specification exists. The following example accepts messages coming in that are from (source) any host in the 192.168.0 network and that are going (destination) anywhere at all (the **-d** option is left out or could be written as **-d** 0/0).

```
ipchains –A input –s 192.168.0.0/24  –j ACCEPT
```

If your system is hosting an Internet service, such as a Web or FTP server, you can use ipchains to control access to it. You can specify a particular service by specifying the port it uses. For a Web server, the port would be www. The names of services and the ports they use are listed in the **/etc/services** file, which maps ports to particular services. For a domain name server, the port would be **domain**. You can also use the port number if you want, preceding the number with a colon. The following example accepts all messages to the Web server located at 192.168.0.43.

```
ipchains -A input -d 192.168.0.43 www -j ACCEPT
```

Inverse Operations

With the ! operator you can change the effect of a rule to its inverse. The ! operator works like a "not" logical operator in programming languages. Placing a ! operator before a –s entry matches on any address that is not the specified address. **! –s 192.168.1.66** matches on any packet whose address is not 192.168.1.66. The operator is helpful if you want to restrict by only a few selected sites. The following example restricts access to 192.168.1.66, denying access to all others.

```
ipchains -A input ! -s 192.168.1.66 -t DENY
```

The inverse can apply also to ports, protocols, and devices. For example, to allow access to any port except the Ethernet device eth2, you would use

```
ipchains -A input ! eth2 -t ACCEPT
```

The following example denies access to any port except the Web server.

```
ipchains -A input ! www -t DENY
```

SYN Packets

If you are designing a firewall that is meant to protect your local network from any attempts to penetrate it from an outside network, you may want to restrict packets coming in. Simply denying access by all packets is unfeasible because users connected to outside servers, say, on the Internet, must receive information from them. You can, instead, deny access by a particular kind of packet used to initiate a connection. The idea is that an attacker must initiate a connection from the outside. The headers of these kinds of packets have their SYN bit set on and their FIN and ACK bits empty. The **ipchains -y** option matches on any such SYN packet. By specifying a DENY target for such packets, you deny access by any packet that is part of an attempt to make a connection with your system. Anyone trying to connect to your system from the outside is unable to do so. Users on your local system who have initiated connections with outside hosts can still communicate with them.

```
ipchains -A input -y -j DENY
```

You make this a qualification of a rule with an ACCEPT target by preceding the **–y** with a ! symbol. This turns the rule into its inverse. For example, to accept all messages except the SYN messages, you could use the following rule. This says to accept all input messages except those that are

```
ipchains -A input ! -y -j ACCEPT
```

Option	Function
-b	Execute the rule bidirectionally (whether a packet is coming in or going out). Actually insert two rules where the second one has the sender (-s) and destination (-d) reversed.
-p [!] *proto*	Specify a protocol, such as TCP, UDP, ICMP, or ALL.
-s [!] *address*[/*mask*] [!] [*port*[:*port*]]	Source address to match. With the port argument, you can specify the port.
--source-port [!] [*port*[:*port*]]	Source port specification. You can specify a range of ports using the colon, *port:port*.
-d [!] *address*[/*mask*] [!] [*port*[:*port*]]	Destination address to match. With the port argument, you can specify the port.
--destination-port [!][*port*[:*port*]]	Destination port specification.
--icmp-type [!] *typename*	Specify ICMP type.
-i [!] *name*[+]	Specify a network interface using its name (for example, eth0). The + symbol functions as a wildcard. The + attached to the end of the name matches all interfaces with that prefix (eth+ matches all Ethernet interfaces).

Table 31-3. *ipchains options*

Option	Function
-j *target* [port]	Specify the target for a rule (specify [port] for REDIRECT target).
-m [+-]*mark*	Number to mark on matching packet.
-n	Numeric output of addresses and ports.
-l	Turn on kernel logging for matching packets, logging them in the syslog.
-o [*maxsize*]	Output matching packet to netlink device.
-t and **xor**	Specify and/xor masks for Type of Service (TOS) field.
-v	Verbose mode.
-x	Expand numbers (display exact values).
[!] **-f**	Match second through the last fragments of a fragmented packet.
[!] **-y**	Match SYN TCP packets only (TCP packets requesting connections). A ! placed before **-y** rejects an SYN TCP packets.
[!] **-V**	Print package version.
!	Negates an option or address.

Table 31-3.   `ipchains` *Options* (continued)

Firewalls often block certain *Internet Control Message Protocol* (*ICMP*) messages. ICMP redirect messages in particular can take control of your routing tasks. You need to enable some ICMP messages, however, such as those needed for ping, traceroute, and particularly destination-unreachable operation. In most cases, you always need to make sure destination-unreachable packets are allowed; otherwise, domain name queries could hang. Some of the more common ICMP packet types are listed in Table 31-4. You can enable an ICMP type of packet with the **-icmp-type** option, which takes as its argument a number or a name representing the message. The following example enables the use of echo-reply messages, which have the number 3 and the name destination-unreachable.

```
ipchains -A input -icmp-type destination-unreachable -t ACCEPT
```

Number	Name	Required by
0	echo-reply	Ping
3	destination-unreachable	Any TCP/UDP traffic
5	Redirect	Routing if not running routing daemon
8	echo-request	Ping
11	time-exceeded	Traceroute

Table 31-4.   *Common ICMP Packets*

IP-Chains Scripts

You can enter **ipchains** commands from the shell command line. When you shut down your system, however, these commands will be lost. To save your commands, you can use the **ipchains-save** script to save them to a file. The recommended file to use is **/etc/ipchains.rules**. The **ipchains-save** command outputs rules to the standard output. To save them in a file, you must redirect the output to a file with the redirection operator, >, as shown here:

```
ipchains-save > /etc/ipchains.rules
```

Then, to restore the rules, use the **ipchains-restore** script to read the **ipchains** commands from that saved file.

```
ipchains-restore < /etc/ipchains.rules
```

An example of the output from the **ipchains-save** script is shown here.

```
[root@turtle /root]# cat /etc/ipchains.rules
:input DENY
:forward DENY
:output DENY
-A input -s ! 192.168.1.0/255.255.255.0 -d 0.0.0.0/0.0.0.0 -i eth1 -j DENY -l
-A input -s 192.168.1.0/255.255.255.0 -d 0.0.0.0/0.0.0.0 -i ! eth1 -j DENY -l
-A input -s 127.0.0.0/255.0.0.0 -d 0.0.0.0/0.0.0.0 -i ! lo -j DENY -l
-A input -s 24.0.67.231/255.255.255.255 -d 0.0.0.0/0.0.0.0 -i lo -j ACCEPT
-A input -s 0.0.0.0/0.0.0.0 -d 10.0.0.2/255.255.255.255 80:80 -i eth0 -p 6 -j ACCEPT
-A input -s 0.0.0.0/0.0.0.0 -d 10.0.0.1/255.255.255.255 -i eth0 -p 6 -j ACCEPT ! -y
-A input -s 0.0.0.0/0.0.0.0 -d 10.0.0.1/255.255.255.255 -i eth0 -p ! 1 -j ACCEPT
-A input -s 192.168.1.0/255.255.255.0 -d 0.0.0.0/0.0.0.0 -i eth1 -j ACCEPT
```

```
-A input -s 0.0.0.0/0.0.0.0 0:0 -d 10.0.0.1/255.255.255.255 -i eth0 -p 1 -j ACCEPT
-A input -s 0.0.0.0/0.0.0.0 8:8 -d 10.0.0.1/255.255.255.255 -i eth0 -p 1 -j ACCEPT
-A input -s 0.0.0.0/0.0.0.0 3:3 -d 10.0.0.1/255.255.255.255 -i eth0 -p 1 -j ACCEPT
-A input -s 0.0.0.0/0.0.0.0 -d 10.0.0.1/255.255.255.255 -p 6 -l -y
-A forward -s 0.0.0.0/0.0.0.0 -d 0.0.0.0/0.0.0.0 -i eth0 -j MASQ
-A output -s 24.0.67.231/255.255.255.255 -d 0.0.0.0/0.0.0.0 -i lo -j ACCEPT
-A output -s 10.0.0.2/255.255.255.255 80:80 -d 192.168.1.0/255.255.255.0 -i eth0 -p 6 -j ACCEPT ! -y
-A output -s 10.0.0.2/255.255.255.255 80:80 -d 0.0.0.0/0.0.0.0 -i eth0 -p 6 -j ACCEPT
-A output -s 10.0.0.1/255.255.255.255 -d 0.0.0.0/0.0.0.0 -i eth0 -p ! 1 -j ACCEPT
-A output -s 0.0.0.0/0.0.0.0 -d 192.168.1.0/255.255.255.0 -i eth1 -j ACCEPT
-A output -s 10.0.0.1/255.255.255.255 0:0 -d 0.0.0.0/0.0.0.0 -i eth0 -p 1 -j ACCEPT
-A output -s 10.0.0.1/255.255.255.255 8:8 -d 0.0.0.0/0.0.0.0 -i eth0 -p 1 -j ACCEPT
-A output -s 10.0.0.1/255.255.255.255 3:3 -d 0.0.0.0/0.0.0.0 -i eth0 -p 1 -j ACCEPT
```

To have ipchains start up automatically at boot time, you can create a packetfilter script and place it in the **/etc/rc.d/init.d** directory. Make a symbolic link to it, such as **S39packetfileter**, in the appropriate rc*n*.d directory.

packetfilter

```
#! /bin/sh
# Script to control packet filtering.

# If no rules, do nothing.
[ -f /etc/ipchains.rules ] || exit 0

case "$1" in
        start)
            echo -n "Turning on packet filtering:"
            /sbin/ipchains-restore < /etc/ipchains.rules || exit 1
            echo 1 > /proc/sys/net/ipv4/ip_forward
            echo "."
            ;;
        stop)
            echo -n "Turning off packet filtering:"
            echo 0 > /proc/sys/net/ipv4/ip_forward
            /sbin/ipchains -X
            /sbin/ipchains -F
            /sbin/ipchains -P input ACCEPT
            /sbin/ipchains -P output ACCEPT
            /sbin/ipchains -P forward ACCEPT
            echo "."
            ;;
        *)
            echo "Usage: /etc/init.d/packetfilter {start|stop}"
            exit 1
            ;;
    esac

    exit 0
```

Using this startup script, you can then manually start and stop **ipchains** with the start and stop arguments.

```
/etc/init.d/packetfilter start
/etc/init.d/packetfilter stop
```

Instead of manually typing in each **ipchains** command on the command line, you can create a shell script of these commands, and then simply run the script. This technique is useful if you want to create several different firewall configurations, each with different levels of control. Running the script is the same as entering the rules, one by one. Once you run the script, the rules take effect. If you are using the **packetfilter** startup script, you can then use **ipchains-save** to make those ipchains script rules for your startup configuration.

The following example shows a simple ipchains script called **mychains**. It configures a simple firewall for a private network (check the ipchains HOWTO for a more complex example). In this configuration, all remote access initiated from the outside is blocked, but two-way communication is allowed for connections that users in the network make with outside systems. In this example, the firewall system functions as a gateway for a private network whose network address is 192.168.1.0. The Internet address is, for the sake of this example, 10.0.0.1. The system has two Ethernet devices: one for the private network (eth1) and one for the Internet (eth0). The gateway firewall system also supports a Web server at address 10.0.0.2. Entries in this example that are too large to fit on one line are continued on a second line, with the newline quoted with a backslash.

mychains

```
# Firewall Gateway system IP address is 10.0.0.1 using Ethernet device eth0
# Private network address is 192.168.1.0 using Ethernet device eth1

# turn off IP forwarding
echo 0 > /proc/sys/net/ipv4/ip_forward

# Flush chain rules
ipchains -F input
ipchains -F output
ipchains -F forward

# set default rules
ipchains -P input DENY
ipchains -P output DENY
ipchains -P forward DENY

# IP spoffing, deny any outside packets with internal address
ipchains -A input -j DENY  -i eth1 \! -s 192.168.1.0/24 -l
# IP spoofing, deny any internal address source packets
# not on the internal Ethernet interface (eth1)
ipchains -A input -j DENY \! -i eth1 -s 192.168.1.0/24 -l
# IP spoofing, deny any outside packets with localhost address
ipchains -A input -j DENY  -i \! lo  -s  127.0.0.0/255.0.0.0 -l
```

```
# allow all incoming outgoing messages for users on firewall gateway
ipchains -A input -j ACCEPT  -i lo  -s localhost
ipchains -A output -j ACCEPT -i lo -s localhost

# allow  communication to the Web server (address 10.0.0.2), port www
ipchains -A input  -j ACCEPT -p tcp -i eth0  -d 10.0.0.2 www
# Allow  established connections from Web servers to internal network
ipchains -A output -j ACCEPT -p tcp -i eth0 \! -y -s 10.0.0.2 www  -d
192.168.1.0/24
# Allow communication from Web server
ipchains -A output  -j ACCEPT -p tcp -i eth0  -s 10.0.0.2 www

# prevent outside initiated connections, allow established ones
ipchains -A input -j ACCEPT -p tcp -i eth0 \! -y -d 10.0.0.1
# allow outside communication to the firewall, except for ICMP packets
ipchains -A input -j ACCEPT -p \! icmp -i eth0  -d 10.0.0.1
# allow all firewall communication to the outside,
# except for ICMP packets
ipchains -A output -j ACCEPT -p \! icmp -i eth0 -s 10.0.0.1

# allow all local communication to and from the firewall
ipchains -A input -j ACCEPT -p all -i eth1 -s 192.168.1.0/24
ipchains -A output -j ACCEPT -p all -i eth1 -d 192.168.1.0/24

# Set up masquerqading to allow internal machines access
# to outside network
ipchains -A forward -j MASQ -p all -i eth0

# Accept ICMP Ping (0 and 8) and Destination ureachable (3)  messages
# Others will be rejected by input and output DENY policy
ipchains -A input -j ACCEPT  -p icmp -i eth0 --icmp-type \
   echo-reply -d 10.0.0.1
ipchains -A output -j ACCEPT  -p icmp -i eth0 --icmp-type \
   echo-reply  -s 10.0.0.1
ipchains -A input -j ACCEPT  -p icmp -i eth0 --icmp-type \
   echo-request -d 10.0.0.1
ipchains -A output -j ACCEPT  -p icmp -i eth0 --icmp-type \
    echo-request -s 10.0.0.1
ipchains -A input -j ACCEPT -p icmp -i eth0 --icmp-type \
   destination-unreachable -d 10.0.0.1
ipchains -A output -j ACCEPT -p icmp -i eth0 --icmp-type \
   destination-unreachable -s 10.0.0.1

# Log attempts to initiate access from outside
ipchains -A input -p tcp -y -l  -d 10.0.0.1

# Turn on IP Forwarding
echo 1 > /proc/sys/net/ipv4/ip_forward
```

Initially, in the script you would clear your current ipchains with the flush command (**-F**), and then set the policies (default targets) for the nonuser-defined rules. IP Forwarding should also be turned off while the chain rules are being set.

```
echo 0 > /proc/sys/net/ipv4/ip_forward
```

One way to protect the private network from IP spoofing any packets is to check for any outside addresses on the Ethernet device dedicated to the private network. In this example, any packet on device eth1 (dedicated to the private network) whose source address is not that of the private network (**! –s 192.168.1.0**) is denied. Also, check to see if any packets coming from the outside are designating the private network as their source. In this example, any packets with the source address of the private network on any Ethernet device other than for the private network (eth1) are denied. The same strategy can be applied to the local host.

```
# IP spoofing, deny any outside packets with internal address
ipchains -A input -j DENY  -i eth1 \! -s 192.168.1.0/24 -1
# IP spoofing, deny any internal address source packets
# not on the internal Ethernet interface (eth1)
ipchains -A input -j DENY \! -i eth1 -s 192.168.1.0/24 -1
# IP spoofing, deny any outside packets with localhost address
ipchains -A input -j DENY  -i \! lo  -s  127.0.0.0/255.0.0.0 -1
```

Then you would set up rules to allow all packets sent and received within your system (localhost) to pass: one for input and one for output.

```
ipchains -A input -j ACCEPT  -i lo  -s localhost
ipchains -A output -j ACCEPT -i lo -s localhost
```

For the Web server, you want to allow access by outside users, but to block access by anyone attempting to initiate a connection from the Web server into the private network. In the next example, all messages are accepted to the Web server, but the Web server cannot initiate contact with the private network (**! –y**). Established connections are allowed, permitting the private network to use the Web server.

```
#allow communication to the Web server (address 10.0.0.2), port www
ipchains -A input  -j ACCEPT -p tcp -i eth0  -d 10.0.0.2 www
#Allow established communication from Web servers to internal network
ipchains -A output -j ACCEPT -p tcp -i eth0 \! -y -s 10.0.0.2 \
        www   -d 192.168.1.0/24
ipchains -A output  -j ACCEPT -p tcp -i eth0  -s 10.0.0.2 www
```

To prevent outsiders from initiating any access to your system, create a rule to block access by SYN packets from the outside. The following rules use the ! –y inverse to allow everything but SYN packets. Notice the ! is escaped with a backslash (\). ! is also a shell operator and, as part of the shell script, needs to be quoted with a \ to prevent the shell from executing it instead of ipchains.

```
ipchains -A input -j ACCEPT -p tcp -i eth0 \! -y -d 10.0.0.1
```

To allow access by the firewall to outside networks, you allow output and input by all packets except for ICMP packets. These are handled later. The firewall address is designated as the input destination and output source.

```
ipchains -A input -j ACCEPT -p \! icmp -i eth0  -d 10.0.0.1
ipchains -A output -j ACCEPT -p \! icmp -i eth0 -s 10.0.0.1
```

To allow interaction by the internal network with the firewall, you allow output and input by all packets on the internal Ethernet connection, eth1. The valid internal network addresses are designated as the input source and output destination.

```
ipchains -A input -j ACCEPT -p all -i eth1 -s 192.168.1.0/24
ipchains -A output -j ACCEPT -p all -i eth1 -d 192.168.1.0/24
```

To implement masquerading, where systems on the private network can use the gateway's Internet address to connect to Internet hosts, you simply create a MASQ target for the forward rule.

```
ipchains -A forward -j MASQ -p all -i eth0
```

In addition, to allow ping and destination-reachable ICMP packets, you enter input and output rules with the firewall as the destination and the source, respectively. To enable ping operations you use both echo-reply and echo-request icmp types, and for destination unreachable, you use the destination-unreachable type.

```
ipchains -A input -j ACCEPT  -p icmp -i eth0 --icmp-type \
   echo-reply -d 10.0.0.1
ipchains -A output -j ACCEPT  -p icmp -i eth0 --icmp-type \
   echo-reply  -s 10.0.0.1
ipchains -A input -j ACCEPT  -p icmp -i eth0 --icmp-type \
   echo-request -d 10.0.0.1
 ipchains -A output -j ACCEPT  -p icmp -i eth0 --icmp-type \
   echo-request -s 10.0.0.1
ipchains -A input -j ACCEPT -p icmp -i eth0 --icmp-type \
```

```
    destination-unreachable -d 10.0.0.1
ipchains -A output -j ACCEPT -p icmp -i eth0 --icmp-type \
    destination-unreachable -s 10.0.0.1
```

The final rule logs all attempts to initiate a connection to the firewall by an outside host:

```
ipchains -A input -p tcp -y -l  -d 10.0.0.1
```

At the end, IP forwarding is turned on again:

```
echo 1 > /proc/sys/net/ipv4/ip_forward
```

A listing of these **ipchains** commands shows the different rules for each command, as shown here:

```
[root@turtle /root]# ipchains -L
Chain input (policy DENY):
target      prot opt    source                destination   ports
DENY        all  ----l- !192.168.1.0/24       anywhere      n/a
DENY        all  ----l- 192.168.1.0/24        anywhere      n/a
DENY        all  ----l- 127.0.0.0/8           anywhere      n/a
ACCEPT      all  ------ localhost.localdomain anywhere      n/a
ACCEPT      tcp  ------ anywhere              10.0.0.2      any ->   www
ACCEPT      tcp  !y---- anywhere              10.0.0.1      any ->   any
ACCEPT      !icmp ------ anywhere             10.0.0.1      any ->   any
ACCEPT      all  ------ 192.168.1.0/24        anywhere      n/a
ACCEPT      icmp ------ anywhere              10.0.0.1      echo-reply
ACCEPT      icmp ------ anywhere              10.0.0.1      echo-request
ACCEPT      icmp ------ anywhere              10.0.0.1      destination-unreachable
-           tcp  -y--l- anywhere              10.0.0.1      any ->   any
Chain forward (policy DENY):
target      prot opt    source                destination   ports
MASQ        all  ------ anywhere              anywhere      n/a
Chain output (policy DENY):
target      prot opt    source                destination    ports
ACCEPT      all  ------ localhost.localdomain anywhere       n/a
ACCEPT      tcp  !y---- 10.0.0.2              192.168.1.0/24 www ->   any
ACCEPT      tcp  ------ 10.0.0.2              anywhere       www ->   any
ACCEPT      !icmp ------ 10.0.0.1             anywhere       any ->   any
ACCEPT      all  ------ anywhere              192.168.1.0/24 n/a
ACCEPT      icmp ------ 10.0.0.1             anywhere       echo-reply
ACCEPT      icmp ------ 10.0.0.1             anywhere       echo-request
ACCEPT      icmp ------ 10.0.0.1             anywhere       destination-unreachable
```

IP Masquerading

On Linux systems, you can set up a network in which you can have one connection to the Internet, which several systems on your network can use. This way, using only one IP address, several different systems can connect to the Internet. This method is called *IP masquerading*, where a system masquerades as another system, using that system's IP address. In such a network, one system is connected to the Internet with its own IP address, while the other systems are connected on a *local area network* (*LAN*) to this system. When a local system wants to access the network, it masquerades as the Internet-connected system, borrowing its IP address.

IP masquerading is implemented on Linux using the ipchains firewalling tool. In effect, you set up a firewall, which you then configure to do IP masquerading. Currently, IP masquerading—as does ipchains firewalling—supports all the common network services, such as Web browsing, telnet, ping, and gopher. Other services, such as IRC, FTP, and Real Audio require the use of certain modules. Any services you want local systems to access must also be on the firewall system because request and response are actually handled by services on that system.

You can find out more information on IP masquerading at the IP Masquerade Resource Web site at **http://ipmasq.cjb.net/**. In particular, the Linux IP Masquerade mini-HOWTO provides a detailed, step-by-step guide to setting up IP masquerading on your system. IP masquerading must be supported by the kernel before you can use it. If your kernel does not support it, you may have to rebuild the kernel including IP masquerade support or use loadable modules to add it. In addition, certain services require their own modules, such as ip_masq_ftp for FTP, ip_masq_irc for IRC, and ip_masq_raudio for Real Audio. See the IP Masquerade mini-HOWTO for more information.

With IP masquerading, as implemented on Linux systems, the machine with the Internet address is also the firewall and gateway for the LAN of machines that use the firewall's Internet address to connect to the Internet. Firewalls that also implement IP masquerading are sometimes referred to as *MASQ gates*. With IP masquerading, the Internet-connected system (the firewall) listens for Internet requests from hosts on its LAN. It then replaces the requesting local host's IP address with the Internet IP address of the firewall, and then passes the request out to the Internet, as if the request were its own. Replies from the Internet are then sent to the firewall system. The replies the firewall receives are addressed to the firewall using its Internet address. The firewall then determines the local system to whose request the reply is responding. It then strips off its IP address and sends the response on to the local host across the LAN. The connection from the perspective of the local machines is transparent. They appear to be connected directly to the Internet.

You need to specify forwarding rules for use by **ipchains** to implement IP masquerading. See the **mychains** file in the previous section for another example of an ipchains masquerade entry. The following example assumes the Internet connect host, the firewall, uses its first Ethernet device to connect to the Internet, eth0. If you are using a modem to dial up a connection to an ISP, then the interface used would probably be the first PPP interface, ppp0. The second command appends (**-A**) the forward rule to the target (**-j**) **MASQ** (masquerade) for the interface (**-i**) eth0. The host machines on the LAN must specify the connected system as their gateway machine. The last command enables IP forwarding. To enable IP masquerading using Linuxconf's firewalling entries, select Forward Firewalling and click the "Do masquerade" check box for any firewall forwarding rules you add that you want to apply to IP masquerading.

```
ipchains -P forward DENY
ipchains -A forward -i eth0 -j MASQ
echo 1 > /proc/sys/net/ipv4/ip_forward
```

IP masquerading is often used to allow machines on a private network to access the Internet. These could be machines in a home network or a small LAN, say, for a small business. Such a network might have only one machine with Internet access and, as such, only the one Internet address. The local private network would have IP addresses chosen from the Private Network allocations (**10.**, **172.16.**, or **192.168.**). Ideally, the firewall has two Ethernet cards: one for an interface to the LAN (say, **eth1**) and one for an interface to the Internet, such as **eth0** (for dial-up ISPs, this would be **ppp0** for the modem). The card for the Internet connection (**eth0**) would be assigned the Internet IP address. The Ethernet interface for the local network (**eth1**, in this example) is the firewall Ethernet interface. Your private LAN would have a network address like **192.168.1**. Its Ethernet firewall interface (**eth1**) would be assigned the IP address **192.168.1.1**. In effect, the firewall interface lets the firewall operate as the local network's gateway. The firewall is then configured to masquerade any packets coming from the private network. Your LAN needs to have its own domain name server, identifying the machines on your network, including your firewall. Each local machine needs to have the firewall specified as its gateway. Try not to use IP aliasing to assign both the firewall and Internet IP addresses to the same physical interface. Use separate interfaces for them, such as two Ethernet cards, or an Ethernet card and a modem (**ppp0**).

Secure Shell (SSH)

Although a firewall can protect a network from attempts to break in to it from the outside, the problem of securing legitimate communications to the network from outside sources still exists. A particular problem is one of users who want to connect to your network remotely. Such connections could be monitored, and information such as passwords and user IDs used when the user logs in to your network could be copied and used later to break in. One solution is to use the SSH for remote logins. The SSH encrypts any communications between the remote user and a system on your network.

SSH encryption makes use of two keys: a public key and a private key. The *public key* is used to encrypt data, while the *private key* decrypts it. Each host or user has her own public and private keys. The public key is freely distributed to other hosts, who can then use it to encrypt data that only the host's private key can decrypt. For example, when a host sends data to a user on another system, the host encrypts the data with a public key, which it previously received from that user. The data can only be decrypted by the user's corresponding private key. The public key can safely be sent in the open from one host to another, allowing it to be installed safely on different hosts. You can think of the process as taking place between a client and server. The client (a user) connects to a server (a remote system). Each has his own pair of public and private keys. To enable an SSH connection, the client and server have to exchange their public keys, though each always retains their private keys. The client needs the server's public key, and the server needs the client's public key. When the client sends data to the server, it first encrypts the data using the server's public key. The server can then decrypt the data using its own private key. The server, in turn, can encrypt data using the client's public key, which the client can then decrypt using the client's private key.

SSH uses strong encryption methods for which reexporting from the United States may be illegal. Currently, SSH can deal with the following kinds of attacks:

- IP spoofing, where a remote host sends out packets that pretend to come from another, trusted host.

- IP-source routing, where a host can pretend an IP packet comes from another, trusted host.

- DNS spoofing, where an attacker forges name server records.

- Interception of clear text passwords and other data by intermediate hosts.

- Manipulation of data by people in control of intermediate hosts.

- Attacks based on listening to X authentication data and spoofed connection to the X11 server.

The official developer of SSH is SSH Communication's Security, whose Web site is **www.ssh.fi**. It actually supports several security products, including the IPSEC and IKE toolkits. IPsec is an *Internet Engineering Task Force* (*IETF*) standard for protecting IP transmission using cryptography on IP packets. The *Internet Key Exchange (IKE)* protocol is a method for managing keys used in an encrypted transmission.

The site for SSH Communication Security's Secure Shell product is **www.ssh.org**. Here, you can find links to download a free version of SSH for use on a variety of platforms. You can also find a link to the SSH FAQ that answers most questions (**www.ssh.org/faq.html**). The FAQ also provides a list of links to the SSH tutorials, such as Purdue University's SSH tutorial currently located at **csociety.ecn.purdue.edu/ ~sigos/projects/ssh/**.

SSH Communication Security provides SSH free for noncommercial use and sells SSH for commercial use through Datafellows. Numerous alternative free versions of SSH are being developed or are currently available for several different platforms, including MAC, Windows, JAVA, and, of course, Linux. All use the SSH protocols as supported by SSH Communication's Security. See the FAQ for a current listing.

SSH1 and SSH2

Two different implementations of SSH currently use what is, in effect, two different and incompatible protocols. The first version of SSH, known as SSH1, uses the original SSH protocol, whereas version 2.0, known as SSH2, uses a completely rewritten version of the SHH protocol. Encryption is performed in different ways, encrypting different parts of a packet. SSH1 uses server and host keys to authenticate systems, whereas SSH2 only uses host keys. Furthermore, certain functions, such as **sftp**, are only supported by SSH2.

Although SSH2 is more secure, it has stronger licensing restrictions. SSH1 is available free to anyone for noncommercial purposes. For SSH1, the term noncommercial is interpreted broadly and businesses can use it for their private networks. SSH2, on the other hand, is free only for educational and personal use. All other uses require a license to be purchased from Datafellows, which controls commercial distribution for SSH Communications Technology. For this reason, most networks still make use of SSH1.

SSH Applications

The official distribution site for SSH is at the Helsinki University of Technology at **ftp.cs.hut.fi/pub/ssh/**, though you can easily download it from a variety of mirror sites or use the SSH Web site at **www.ssh.org**. From these sites, you can download a compressed archive (.tar.gz) of the most recent version, either version 1 or version 2. Decompress and unpack with the **gunzip** and **tar xvf** commands, and then check the README file for detailed instructions on creating and installing the SSH applications. Be sure your development libraries and C compiler are installed on your system. The **./configure**, **make**, and **make install** commands generate the applications and install them by default on the /usr/local/bin directory. You can either place this directory in your **PATH** in the **/etc/profile** file or simply copy the applications to the **/usr/bin** directory.

The SSH applications are listed in Table 31-5. They include several client programs and the SSH server. The SSH server (**sshd**) provides secure connections to anyone from the outside using the SSH client to connect. With SSH, users can remotely log in and execute commands using encrypted transmissions. In the same way, with **scp**, users can copy files from one host to another securely. The SSH server can also invoke the **sftp-server** to provide encrypted ftp transmissions to those using the sftp client. sftp only works with SSH version 2.0 and it operates much like ftp, with many of the same commands (see Chapter 12). Several configuration utilities are also included such as **ssh-add,** which adds valid hosts to the authentication agent and **ssh-keygen,** which generates the keys used for encryption.

SSH was originally designed to replace remote access operations, such as rlogin, rcp, and telnet (see Chapter 15). The SSH clients package contains corresponding SSH clients to replace these applications. With slogin or SSH, you can log in from a remote host to execute commands and run applications, much like rlogin and **rsh**. With **scp**, you can copy files between the remote host and a network host, just like rcp.

For version 2.0, names of the actual applications have a '2' suffix to indicate they are version 2.0 programs. For version 1.0 applications, they have a '1' as their suffix.

During installation, however, links are set for each application to use only the name with the suffix. For example, if you have installed version 2.0, there is a link called **scp** to the scp2 application. You can then use the link to invoke the application. Using **scp** starts scp2. Table 31-5 specifies only the link name, as these are the same for each version. Remember, though, some applications, such as sftp, are only available with version 2.0.

SSH Setup

Each user who intends to use SSH applications first needs to create the public and private keys to use for the encryption process. You do this using the **ssh-keygen** command. The **ssh-keygen** command prompts you for a pass-phrase, which it will use as a kind of password to protect your private key. The pass-phrase should be several words long. The **ssh-keygen** command generates the public key and places it in your .ssh/identity.pub file; it places the private key in the .ssh/identity file. If you need to change your pass-phrase, you can do so with the **ssh-keygen** command and the **–p** option. Each user will have her own SSH configuration directory, called **.ssh**, located in her own home directory. The public and private keys, as well as SSH configuration files, are placed here. Table 31-6 lists the SSH configuration files.

Application	Description
ssh	SSH client
sshd	SSH server (daemon)
sftp	sftp client. Version 2 only. Use **?** to list sftp commands
sftp-server	sftp server. Version 2 only
scp	scp client
ssh-keygen	Utility for generating keys. **-h** for help
ssh-add	Add identities to the authentication agent
ssh-agent	SSH authentication agent
ssh-askpass	X Window System utility for querying passwords
ssh-signer	Signs "hostbased"-authentication packets. Version 2 only. Must be suid root (performed by installation)
slogin	Remote login (Version 1)

Table 31-5.   *SSH Applications*

File	Description
$HOME/.ssh/known_hosts	Records host keys for all hosts the user has logged in to (that are not in /etc/ssh/ssh_known_hosts).
$HOME/.ssh/random_seed	Used for seeding the random number generator.
$HOME/.ssh/identity	Contains the RSA authentication identity of the user.
$HOME/.ssh/identity.pub	Contains the public key for authentication (public part of the identity file in human-readable form). The contents of this file should be added to $HOME/.ssh/authorized_keys on all machines where you want to log in using RSA authentication.
$HOME/.ssh/config	The per-user configuration file.
$HOME/.ssh/authorized_keys	Lists the RSA keys that can be used for logging in as this user.
/etc/ssh/ssh_known_hosts	System-wide list of known host keys.
/etc/ssh/ssh_config	System-wide configuration file. This file provides defaults for those values not specified in the user's configuration file.
$HOME/.rhosts	This file is used in .rhosts authentication to list the host/user pairs permitted to log in. Note, this file is also used by rlogin and **rsh**, which makes using this file insecure.
$HOME/.shosts	This file is used exactly the same way as .rhosts. The purpose for having this file is to use orhosts authentication with SSH without permitting login with rlogin or **rsh**.
/etc/hosts.equiv	This file is used during .rhosts authentication. It contains canonical hosts' names, one per line. If the client host is found in this file, login is automatically permitted, provided client and server user names are the same.

Table 31-6.   *SSH Configuration Files (SSH2 files are placed in /etc/ssh2 and .ssh2 directories)*

/etc/ssh/shosts.equiv	This file is processed exactly as /etc/hosts.equiv. This file may be useful to permit logins using SSH but not using rsh/rlogin.
/etc/ssh/sshrc	System default. Commands in this file are executed by SSH when the user logs in just before the user's shell (or command) is started.
$HOME/.ssh/rc	Commands in this file are executed by SSH when the user logs in just before the user's shell (or command) is started.

Table 31-6.   *SSH Configuration Files (SSH2 files are placed in /etc/ssh2 and .ssh2 directories)* (continued)

A public key is used to identify a user and its host. You use the public key on a remote system to allow that user access. The public key is placed in the remote user account's .ssh/authorized_keys file. Recall the public key is held in the .ssh/identity.pub file. If a user wants to log in remotely from a local account to an account on a remote system, he would first place his public key in the .ssh/authorized_keys file in the account on the remote system he wants to access. If the user larisa on **turtle.mytrek.com** wants to access the aleina account on **rabbit.mytrek.com,** larisa's public key from /home/larisa/.ssh/ identity.pub first must be placed in aleina's authorized_keys file, /home/aleina/.ssh/ authorized_keys.

If you regularly make connections to a variety of remote hosts, you can use the **ssh-agent** command to place private keys in memory where they can be accessed quickly to decrypt received transmissions. The **ssh-agent** command is intended for use at the beginning of a login session. If you are using a shell in your work, use that shell as the argument for the **ssh-agent** command. If you are using the X Window System (Gnome or KDE), use the **startx** command as your argument. That way, any applications you start inherit a connection to **ssh-agent**. For a graphical login, such as GDM, place the **ssh-agent** command in your .xsession file.

Although the **ssh-agent** command enables you to use private keys in memory, you also must specifically load your private keys into memory using the **ssh-add** command. **ssh-add** with no arguments loads your private key from your .ssh/identity file. You are prompted for your pass-phrase for this private key. To remove the key from memory, use **ssh-add** with the **−d** option. If you have several private keys, you can load them all into memory. **ssh-add** with the **−l** options lists those currently loaded.

SSH also supports the original rhosts form of authentication where hosts and users that are permitted access are placed in a .rhosts or .shosts file. However, this method is not considered secure.

ssh

With **ssh** you can remotely log in from a local client to a remote system on your network operating as the SSH server. The term *local client* here refers to one outside the network such as your home computer, and the term *remote* refers to a host system on the network to which you are connecting. In effect, you connect from your local system to the remote network host. It is designed to replace rlogin, which performs remote logins, and **rsh**, which executes remote commands. With **ssh**, you can log in from a local site to a remote host on your network, and then send commands to be executed on that host. **ssh** is also capable of supporting X Window System connections. This feature is automatically enabled if you make an **ssh** connection from an X Window System environment, such as Gnome or KDE. A connection is set up for you between the local X server and the remote X server. The remote host sets up a dummy X server and sends any X Window System data through it to your local system to be processed by your own local X server.

The **ssh** log in operation function is much like the **rlogin** command. You enter the **ssh** command with the address of the remote host, followed by an **-1** option and the login name (user name) of the remote account you are logging in to. The following example logs in to the **rabbit.mytrek.com** host to the aleina user account.

```
ssh rabbit.mytrek.com -l aleina
```

A variety of options are available to enable you to configure your connection (see Table 31-7). Most have corresponding configuration options that can be set in the configuration file. For example, with the **-c** option, you can designate which encryption method you want to use. With the **-i** option, you can select a particular private key to use. The **-C** option enables you to have transmissions compressed at specified levels.

scp

You use **scp** to copy files from one host to another on a network. It is designed to replace rcp. **scp** actually uses **ssh** to transfer data and employs the same authentication and encryption (see Table 31-8). If authentication requires it, **scp** requests a password or pass-phrase. **scp** operates much like rcp. Directories and files on remote hosts are specified using the user name and the host address before the filename or directory. The user name specifies the remote user account the **scp** is accessing and the host is the

Option	Description
-a	Disables forwarding of the authentication agent connection.
-c *idea	des	3des	blowfish	arcfour	none*	Selects the cipher to use for encrypting the session. idea is used by default and is believed to be secure. none disables encryption entirely; it is only intended for debugging and renders the connection insecure.
-e *ch	^ch	none*	Sets the escape character for sessions with a pty (default: ~). The escape character is only recognized at the beginning of a line. The escape character followed by a dot (.) closes the connection, followed by CTRL-Z suspends the connection, and followed by itself sends the escape character once. Setting the character to "none" disables any escapes and makes the session fully transparent.
-f	Requests **ssh** to go to background after authentication is done and forwardings are established.
-i *identity_file*	Selects the file from which the identity (private key) for RSA authentication is read. Default is .ssh/identity in the user's home directory.
-k	Disables forwarding of the kerberos tickets.
-l *login_name*	Specifies the user to log in as on the remote machine.
-n	Redirects stdin from /dev/null (actually, prevents reading from stdin). Used when **ssh** is run in the background. Used to run X11 programs in a remote machine.
-o *option*	Specify options.
-p *port*	Port to connect to on the remote host.
-q	Quiet mode, suppresses warning and diagnostic messages.
-P	Use nonprivileged port.
-t	Force pseudo-tty allocation.
-v	Verbose mode.
-V	Display version number.

Table 31-7.   `ssh` *Command Options*

Option	Description
-g	Allows remote hosts to connect local port forwarding ports.
-x	Disables X11 forwarding.
-C	Requests compression of all data. The compression algorithm is the same used by gzip and the level can be controlled by the CompressionLevel option.
-L *port:host:hostport*	Specifies the given port on the local (client) host is to be forwarded to the given host and port on the remote side.
-R *port:host:hostport*	Specifies the given port on the remote (server) host is to be forwarded to the given host and port on the local side.

Table 31-7.   *ssh Command Options* (continued)

remote system where that account is located. You separate the user from the host address with an @, and you separate the host address from the file or directory name with a colon, :. The following example copies the file **party** from a user current directory to the user **aleina**'s **birthday** directory, located on the **rabbit.mytrek.com** host.

```
scp party aleina@rabbit.mytrek.com:/birthday/party
```

Of particular interest is the **-r** option, which enables you to copy whole directories. In the next example, the user copies the entire **reports** directory to the user **justin**'s **projects** directory.

```
scp -r reports justin@rabbit.mytrek.com:/projects
```

Port Forwarding

If, for some reason, you can only connect to a secure host by going through an unsecure host, **ssh** provides a feature called port forwarding. With *port forwarding,* you can secure the unsecure segment of your connection. This involves simply specifying the port at which the unsecure host is to connect to the secure one. This sets up a direct connection between the local host and the remote host, through the intermediary unsecure host. Encrypted data is passed through directly.

You can set up port forwarding to a port on the remote system or your local system. To forward a port on the remote system to a port on your local system, use the **ssh -R**

Option	Description
-q	Turn off statistics display
-Q	Turn on statistics display
-r	Recursively copy entire directories
-v	Verbose mode
-B	Selects batch mode (prevents asking for passwords or pass-phrases)
-C	Compression-enabled
-P *port*	Specifies the port to connect to on the remote host
-S *path-to-ssh*	Specifies the path to **ssh** program

Table 31-8.   *scp Options*

option, followed by an argument holding the local port, the remote host address, and the remote port to be forwarded, each separated by a colon. This works by allocating a socket to listen to the port on the remote side. Whenever a connection is made to this port, the connection is forwarded over the secure channel, and a connection is made to a remote port from the local machine. In the following example, port 22 on the local system is connected to port 23 on the **rabbit.mytrek.com** remote system.

```
ssh -R 22:rabbit.mytrek.com:23
```

To forward a port on your local system to a port on a remote system, use the **ssh –L** option, followed by an argument holding the local port, the remote host address, and the remote port to be forwarded, each separated by a colon. A socket is allocated to listen to the port on the local side and, whenever a connection is made to this port, the connection is forwarded over the secure channel and a connection is made to the remote port on the remote machine. In the following example, the port 22 on the local system is connected to port 23 on the **rabbit.mytrek.com** remote system.

```
ssh -L 22:rabbit.mytrek.com:23
```

You can use the **LocalForward** and **RemoteForward** options in your **.ssh/config** file to set up port forwarding for particular hosts or to specify a default for all hosts you connect to.

SSH Session

An SSH session can be implemented as a pseudo-terminal, much like a Telnet connection, or it can be transparent, as is the case with X server connections. With a psuedoterminal, the user can control the connection with a set of escape characters, each beginning with a tidle (~). To end the connection, use a "~." escape sequence. A **~Ctrl-z** suspends the session. The escape sequence must be entered in a line of its own. The **~?** lists the available escape sequences you can use.

If no pseudoterminal is set up, the session is transparent. Usually, setting the escape character to "none" makes the session transparent. Binary data can safely be transmitted during transparent sessions. A transparent session ends when the shell or command on the remote system ends and all connections have been closed. X Window System connections are automatically set up as transparent connections. SSH sets up a proxy X server on the remote system.

SSH Configuration

The SSH configuration file for each user is in her **.ssh/config** file. The **/etc/sys_config** file is used to set sitewide defaults. In the configuration file, you can set various options, as listed in Table 31-9. The configuration file is designed to specify options for different remote hosts to which you might connect. It is organized into segments where each segment begins with the keyword HOST, followed by the IP address of the host. The following lines hold the options you have set for that host. A segment ends at the next HOST entry. Of particular interest are the **User** and **Ciper** options. Use the **User** option to specify the names of users on the remote system that are allowed access. With the **Cipher** option, you can select which encryption method to use for a particular host (see Table 31-10). The following example allows access from larisa at **turtle.mytrek.com** and uses blowfish encryption for transmissions.

```
Host turtle.mytrek.com
     User larisa
     Compression no
     Cipher blowfish
```

To specify global options that apply to any host you connect to, create a HOST entry with the asterisk as its host, HOST *. This entry must be placed at the end of the configuration file because an option is changed only the first time it is set. Any subsequent entries for an option are ignored. Because a host matches on both its own entry and the global one, its specific entry should come before the global entry. The asterisk, *, and the question mark, ?, are both wildcard matching operators that can enable you to specify a group of hosts with the same suffix or prefix.

```
Host *
  FallBackToRsh yes
  KeepAlive no
  Cipher idea
```

Option	Description
Host *hostname*	Specifies the host to which the following options apply. All options apply to this host until the next Host entry. You can specify a range of hosts by using the * and ? pattern-matching wildcard symbols. A host specified as only '*' matches on all hosts and can be used to specify global options.
BatchMode (*yes* | *no*)	If set to "yes", pass-phrase/password querying is disabled. This option is useful in scripts and other batch jobs where you have no user to supply the password. The argument must be yes or no.
Cipher *cipher*	Specifies the cipher to use for encrypting the session, such as idea, des, 3des, blowfish, arcfour, and none. The default is idea (or 3des if idea is not supported by both hosts). Using "none" (no encryption) is intended only for debugging, and renders the connection unsecure.
ClearAllForwardings (*yes* | *no*)	Clears all forwardings after reading all config files and the parsing command line. This is useful to disable forwardings in config file when you want to make a second connection to the host having forwardings in the config file. **scp** sets this on by default so it does not fail, even if you have some forwardings set in config file.
Compression (*yes* | *no*)	Specifies whether to use compression.
CompressionLevel (*1 - 9*)	Specifies the compression level. The argument must be an integer from 1 (fast) to 9 (slow, best). The default level is 6.

Table 31-9. *SSH Configuration Options*

Option	Description
ConnectionAttempts *num*	Specifies the number of tries (one per second) to make.
EscapeChar	Sets the escape character (default: ~). The argument should be a single character, ^, followed by a letter or "none" to disable the escape character entirely (making the connection transparent for binary data).
FallBackToRsh (*yes* | *no*)	Specifies if connecting with **ssh** fails because no **sshd** is on the remote host, **rsh** should automatically be used instead.
ForwardAgent (*yes* | *no*)	Specifies whether the connection to the authentication agent should be forwarded to the remote machine.
ForwardX11 (*yes* | *no*)	Specifies whether X11 connections should be automatically redirected over the secure channel and DISPLAY set.
GatewayPorts (*yes* | *no*)	Specifies remote hosts may connect to locally forwarded ports.
GlobalKnownHostsFile *file*	Specifies a file to use instead of /etc/ssh/ssh_known_hosts.
HostName *hostname*	Specifies the real host name to log in to. This can be used to specify nicknames or abbreviations for hosts.
IdentityFile *file*	Specifies the file from which the user's RSA authentication identity is read (default .ssh/identity in the user's home directory).
KeepAlive (*yes* | *no*)	Specifies whether the system should send keepalive messages to the other side. Used to detect if connection fails.
KerberosAuthentication (*yes* | *no*)	Specifies whether Kerberos V5 authentication should be used.

Table 31-9.   *SSH Configuration Options* (continued)

Option	Description
KerberosTgtPassing (*yes* | *no*)	Specifies whether a Kerberos V5 TGT is to be forwarded to the server.
LocalForward *host host:port*	Specifies a TCP/IP port on the local machine be forwarded over the secure channel to given host:port from the remote machine. The first argument must be a port number, and the second must be host:port.
NumberOfPasswordPrompts *num*	Specifies the number of password prompts before giving up.
PasswordAuthentication (*yes* | *no*)	Specifies whether to use password authentication.
PasswordPromptHost (*yes* | *no*)	Specifies whether to include the remote host name in the password prompt.
PasswordPromptLogin (*yes* | *no*)	Specifies whether to include the remote login name in the password prompt.
Port	Specifies the port number to connect on the remote host. Default is 22.
ProxyCommand *command*	Specifies the command to use to connect to the server.
RemoteForward *host host:port*	Specifies a TCP/IP port on the remote machine be forwarded over the secure channel to given host:port from the local machine. The first argument must be a port number, and the second must be host:port.
RhostsAuthentication (*yes* | *no*)	Specifies whether to try rhosts based authentication.
RhostsRSAAuthentication (*yes* | *no*)	Specifies whether to try rhosts based authentication with RSA host authentication.
RSAAuthentication (*yes* | *no*)	Specifies whether to try RSA authentication.

Table 31-9. *SSH Configuration Options* (continued)

Option	Description
StrictHostKeyChecking (*yes* | *no* | *ask*)	If this flag is set to "yes", **ssh** never automatically adds host keys to the $HOME/.ssh/known_hosts file and refuses to connect hosts whose host key has changed.
TISAuthentication (*yes* | *no*)	Specifies whether to try TIS authentication.
UsePrivilegedPort (*yes* | *no*)	Specifies whether to use privileged port when connecting to other end.
User *username*	Specifies the user to log in.
UserKnownHostsFile *file*	Specifies a file to use instead of $HOME/.ssh/known_hosts.
UseRsh (*yes* | *no*)	Specifies rlogin/rsh should be used for this host if it does not support the **ssh** protocol.
XAuthLocation *path*	Specifies the path to xauth program.

Table 31-9.   *SSH Configuration Options* (continued)

Method	Description
idea	Believed to be secure.
des	The data encryption standard, but this is breakable by governments, large corporations, and major criminal organizations.
3des (triple-des)	Encrypt-decrypt-encrypt triple with three different keys. Presumably more secure than DES and used as the default if both sites do not support IDEA.
blowfish	128-bit keys encryption algorithm invented by Bruce Schneier.

Table 31-10.   *SSH2 Encryption Methods*

Method	Description
arcfour	Equivalent with the RC4 cipher from RSA Data Security (RC4 is a trademark of RSA Data Security). This is the fastest algorithm currently supported.
Twofish	Version 2 only
Arcfour	Version 2 only
Cast128-cbc	Version 2 only

Table 31-10. *SSH2 Encryption Methods* (continued)

The Complete Reference

Part VII

Applications

The Complete Reference

Linux

Chapter 32

Software Management

Installing or updating software packages has always been a simple process in Red Hat Linux due to Red Hat's use of the Red Hat Package Manager. Instead of using a standard tar archive, software is packaged in a special archive for use with the Red Hat Package Manager. These archives have become known as RPMs, where *RPM* stands for *Red Hat Package Manager.* An RPM archive contains all the program files, configuration files, data files, and even documentation that constitute a software application. With one simple operation, the Red Hat Package Manager installs all these for you from an RPM software package. You can even create your own RPM packages. You can use any of several RPM window-based utilities to manage your RPM packages, installing new ones or uninstalling ones you have. These utilities provide an easy-to-use interface for managing your packages, enabling you to obtain detailed information on a package easily, including a complete listing of the files it installs. Also, as part of their administration tools, distributions like Red Hat also provide software management for packages on their CD-ROMs.

You can also download source code versions of applications, and then compile and install them on your system. Where this process once was complex, it has been significantly streamlined with the addition of configure scripts. Most current source code, including GNU software, is distributed with a configure script. The *configure script* automatically detects your system configuration and generates a Makefile with which a binary, created compatible to your system, is created. With three simple commands, you can compile and install complex source code on any system.

Extensive online sources exist for downloading Linux software. Sites are available for particular kinds of applications, such as Gnome and KDE, as well as for particular distributions, such as Red Hat. Some are repositories for RPM packages, such as **rpmfind.net,** while others like **freshmeat.net** refer you to original development sites where you can download software packages. The **freshmeat.net** and **www.linuxapps.com** sites are useful for finding out about new available software. For particular database and office applications, you can download software packages directly from the company's Web site, such as **www.sun.com** for the StarOffice office suite and **www.oracle.com** for the Oracle database (see Chapters 22 and 23). For RPM packages for Red Hat, which are not part of its distribution, you can check the **contrib** directory on the **ftp.redhat.com** site. Here, you can find Red Hat RPM packages for applications, such as ProFTPD and htDig. Table 32-1 lists several popular Linux software sites.

ftp and Web sites	Applications
ftp.redhat.com	Software packaged in RPM packages for Red Hat. Check the **contrib** directory for contributed software

Table 32-1. *Linux Software Sites*

ftp and Web sites	Applications
freshmeat.net	New Linux software
linuxapps.com	New Linux software
rpmfind.net	RPM package repository
www.gnome.org	Gnome software
www.kde.org	KDE software
http://www.xnet.com/~blatura/linapps.shtml	Linux Applications and Utilities Page
www.filewatcher.org	Linux FTP site watcher
www.gnu.org	GNU Archive
www.helixcode.com	Helix Code, Office Applications for Gnome
koffice.kde.com	The KDE KOffice Suite of Office Applications
www.xdt.com/ar/linux-snd	Linux MIDI and Sound Pages
www.linuxvideo.org	The Linux Video and DVD Project, LiViD
www.opensound.com	Open Sound System drivers
www.uk.linux.org/Commercial.html	Linux Commercial Vendors Index
linuxwww.db.erau.edu/	Linux archive
metalab.unc.edu	Extensive Linux archive (formerly **sunsite.unc.edu**)
happypenquin.org	Linux Game Tome
www.linuxgames.org	Linux games
www.linuxquake.com	Quake

Table 32-1.   *Linux Software Sites* (continued)

Red Hat Package Manager (RPM)

Several Linux distributions, including Red Hat, OpenLinux, and SuSE, use RPM to organize Linux software into packages you can automatically install or remove. An

RPM software package operates as its own installation program for a software application. A Linux software application often consists of several files that need to be installed in different directories. The program itself is, most likely, placed in a directory called **/usr/bin**, online manual files go in another directory, and library files, in yet another directory. In addition, the installation may require modification of certain configuration files on your system. The RPM software packages performs all these tasks for you. Also, if you later decide you don't want a specific application, you can uninstall packages to remove all the files and configuration information from your system. RPM works similarly to the Windows install wizard, automatically installing software, including configuration, documentation, image, sample, and program files, along with any other files an application may use. All are installed in their appropriate directories on your system. RPM maintains a database of installed software, keeping track of all the files installed. This enables you to use RPM also to uninstall software, automatically removing all files that are part of the application.

To install and uninstall RPM packages, you can use the **rpm** command on a shell command line or any available RPM window-based program, such as kpackage or GnomeRPM. Also, distribution install and management utilities, such as COAS, Lisa, and YaST, enable you to install or uninstall your distribution software packages. These are usually the RPM packages on your CD-ROM. Although you should download RPM packages for your particular distribution using, numerous RPM software packages are designed to run on any Linux system. Many of these are located at distribution contrib sites or directories, such as **contrib.redhat.com**. You can learn more about RPM at its Web site at **www.rpm.org**. The site contains up-to-date versions for RPM, documentation, and RPM support programs, such as rpm2html and rpm2cpio. rpm2html takes a directory containing RPM packages and generates Web pages listing those packages as links that can be used to download them. rpm2cpio is Perl script to extract RPMs.

The RPM packages on your CD-ROMs only represent a small portion of the software packages available for Linux. You can download additional software in the form of RPM packages from distribution contrib sites, such as **contrib** directory in Red Hat FTP site at **ftp.redhat.com**. In addition, these packages are organized into **lib5** and **lib6** directories. **lib5** refers to the packages using the older libraries, whereas **lib6** refers to those using the new GNU 2.*x* libraries. For Red Hat 6.0 and later, you should use the **lib6** versions, though **lib5** versions also work.

An extensive repository for RPM packages is also located at **http://rpmfind.net/ linux/RPM**. Packages here are indexed according to distribution, group, and name. It includes packages for every distribution, including previous versions of those distributions. From **http://rpmfind.net,** you can download the **rpmfind** command that enable you to search for RPM packages, either on your local system or on the RPM repository at **rpmfind.net**. You can even use **rpmfind** to download and update packages. **rpmfind** detects your system's distribution and lists RPM packages for it.

Search results also tell on what other packages a given RPM can depend. With the **--apropos** option, you can use more general terms to locate a package, instead of filename patterns. With the **--upgrade** option, you can download and install newer versions of installed packages. The **rpmfind** command also sets up a **.rpmfind** configuration file, where you can specify such features as a download directory, the remote servers to search, and the location of local RPM packages on your system.

Your Red Hat distribution includes an extensive set of applications located in a **RedHat/RPMS** directory on the Red Hat CD-ROM. You can install or uninstall any of these packages using an **rpm** command, a GUI RPM utility, or the software manager screen on your distribution administration tool. To install a software package from your CD-ROM using the **rpm** command, it is easier to move first to the **RPMS** directory, and then install the package you want. Be sure to mount the CD-ROM first before you try to access it.

You have to download additional RPM packages not located on your CD-ROM from distribution sites, such as **ftp.redhat.com**. Web sites for the particular software you want may also have RPM packages already set up for you for your distribution. For example, you can obtain the ProFTPD RPM package for Red Hat from **ftp.redhat.com**, and the current Red Hat or Linuxconf RPM packages from the Linuxconf Web site (see Chapter 21). You could place these packages in a directory on your system, and then use either **rpm** or a GUI RPM utility, such as GnomeRPM to install it. Normally, you should always try to use the version of the RPM package set up for your distribution. In many cases, attempting to install an RPM meant for a different distribution fails. Some exceptions exist, though. Popular RPM package managers are listed here:

Kpackage	K Desktop RPM package manager
GnomeRPM	Gnome RPM package manager
Rpm	The shell command to manage RPM packages
Xrpm	X Window System RPM package manager
Glint	Older X Window System RPM package manager

The K Desktop Package Manager: kpackage

The KDE desktop provides a powerful and easy-to-use RPM package manager called *kpackage* (see Figure 30-1). You run kpackage under any window manager or desktop (including Gnome), as long as you have installed the K Desktop on your system. You can start kpackage by selecting its entry in the K menu utility menu or by entering the **kpackage** command in a terminal window.

The right side of kpackage contains two tabbed panels: one for Properties and the other for the File List. The Properties panel displays information about the software in the

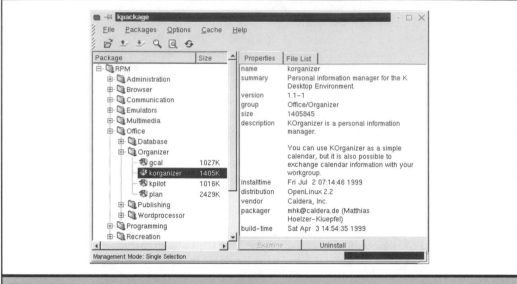

Figure 32-1.   *The RPM package manager called kpackage*

currently selected RPM package, including the version number and the authors. The File List lists all the files contained in the software package, including README files. If you are using kpackage on the K Desktop, you can click any text file in the File List and it is displayed by the text editor. This is a convenient way to read installation files, such as README or INSTALL files. To uninstall a package, select it and click Uninstall.

The list of installed packages is often extensive. To locate a particular package, select the Find entry in the File menu. If the Substring check box is selected, you can use a pattern to search for your package instead of a complete name. The package list in the left pane moves to the first package found, highlighting it. If you use a pattern and more choices exist, you can move to the next one by selecting the Find menu item again. The kpackage application also enables you to search for a particular file in a package. Select the Find File entry in the File menu and enter the name of the file to locate. You have to use the full pathname for the file. Patterns are not supported.

You can also use kpackage to install RPM packages. You must know where on the system the packages are located. For example, on Red Hat systems, they are in the **RedHat/RPMS** directory. If you mounted the CD-ROM at **/mnt/cdrom**, then the full pathname should be **/mnt/cdrom/RedHat/RPMS**. Packages you download from FTP sites would be in whatever directory you downloaded them to, say, **/root/download**. To install a package, select Open from the File menu. This opens a file browser dialog box where you can move to the directory you want and select the RPM package. An Installation dialog box is displayed with options that include updating and testing the package. You select Update for packages that are updated versions of ones already installed. With the **Test** option, you can test an installation without actually having to install it.

GnomeRPM

Although not written by Red Hat, GnomeRPM provides an effective and easy-to-use interface for managing RPM packages on your Gnome desktop. It runs on any window manager, provided Gnome is installed on your system. As Figure 30-2 shows, the GnomeRPM window displays two panes, the left one showing a tree listing categories of different installed RPM packages. Expand a category to display the packages in the right pane. You can query a package by selecting it and clicking the Uninstall icon in the icon bar, or by right-clicking it and selecting Uninstall from the pop-up menu. You can use the same method for querying packages and for displaying information and file listings. You can select several packages at once from different categories by CTRL-clicking their icons. A selected package darkens. When you select uninstall, all those packages are uninstalled. CTRL-click the package again to deselect it. Click Unselect to deselect all the packages you selected. The number of selected packages is shown in the lower-left corner of the window. The GnomeRPM package also features a **find** utility, which you can use to locate RPM packages easily. In the find window, you can then query or uninstall the package.

To install new packages with GnomeRPM, click the Install icon. This opens a window that displays the selected packages to install. You then click Add to open a window for locating packages on your system. You can add as many windows as you want to the list. Click Install to install the packages. To upgrade a package that is already installed, click Upgrade and follow the same procedure.

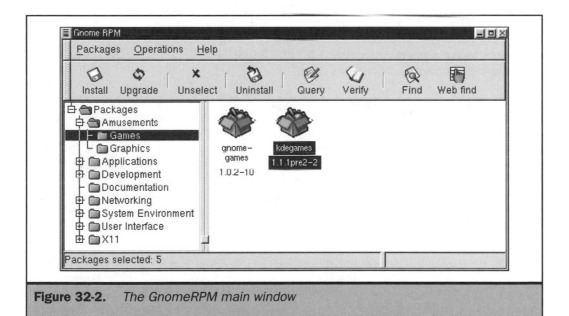

Figure 32-2.   *The GnomeRPM main window*

GnomeRPM supports drag-and-drop operations from the desktop and file manager. You can drag one or more RPM packages from a file manager window to the GnomeRPM install dialog window. You can then install or query selected packages. GnomeRPM also enables you to browse through packages available with the rpmfind system. Click the Web Find button. The listing of packages is then downloaded and displayed in the treemenu. Use the treemenu to navigate to the package you want.

KDE and Gnome File Managers

On Gnome, you can install RPM packages directly from the file manager, without using any special utility such as GnomeRPM. Use the file manager window to access the directory with your package, such as your distribution CD-ROM. Then right-click the package name or icon. In the pop-up menu, you can select the **Install** option to install the package. You can use this same method for FTP sites. The Gnome file manager is Internet-aware. You can enter a URL for an FTP site in its location box to access the site. Be sure to include the FTP protocol in the URL, ftp://. When you locate the package, right-click it, and select Install or Update. The file is downloaded, and then automatically installed on your system.

The KDE file manager also enables you to install RPM packages, though it uses kpackage to perform the actual installation. Locate an RPM file on your system using the file manager, and then single-click its icon or name. This automatically opens kpackage with the RPM package loaded, which is then displayed on a window with panels for the package information and the list of files in it. At the bottom of the panels is an install button. Click it to install the package. Because the KDE file manager is Internet-aware, you can use this same method both to download and install RPM packages from FTP sites. Locate the FTP site with the file manager (enter its URL in the location box), and then locate your package. Once your package is listed in the file manager window, click it. The package is then automatically downloaded and kpackage starts up, showing the package. Click the Install button to install it.

Command Line Installation: rpm

If you do not have access to the desktop or you prefer to work from the command line interface, you can use the **rpm** command to manage and install software packages. **rpm** is the command that actually performs installation, removal, and queries of software packages. In fact, GnomeRPM and kpackage use the **rpm** command to install and remove packages. An RPM package is an archive of software files that include information about how to install those files. The file names for RPM packages end with .rpm, indicating software packages that can be installed by the Red Hat Package Manager.

With the **rpm** command, you can maintain packages, query them, build your own, and verify the ones you have. Maintaining packages involves installing new ones, upgrading to new versions, and uninstalling packages. The **rpm** command uses a set of options to determine what action to take. In addition, certain tasks, such as installing or querying packages, have their own options that further qualify the kind of action they take. For example, the **−q** option queries a package, but when combined with the **−l** option, it lists all the files in that package. Table 32-2 lists the set of **rpm** options.

You use the **−i** option to install a new software package and the **−U** option to update a currently installed package with a newer version. With an **−e** option, **rpm** uninstalls the package. The **q** option tells you if a package is already installed, and the **qa** option displays a list of all installed packages. Piping this output to a pager utility, such as more, is best.

```
rpm -qa | more
```

In the next example, the user checks to see if **xv** is already installed on the system. Notice the full filename of the rpm archive is unnecessary. If the package is installed, your system has already registered its name and where it is located.

```
# rpm -q xv
```

You can combine the **q** options with the **i** or **l** options to display information about the package. The options **−qi** display information about the software, such as the version number or author (**−qpi** queries an uninstalled package file). The option **−ql** displays a listing of all the files in the software package. The **−−h** option provides a complete list of **rpm** options. The syntax for the **rpm** command is as follows (*rpm-package-name* is the name of the software package you want to install):

```
rpm options rpm-package-name
```

The software package name is usually lengthy, including information about version and release date in its name. All end with **.rpm**.

If you are installing from a CD-ROM, you can change to the CD-ROM's RedHat/ RPMS directory, which holds the RPM packages. An **ls** command lists all the software packages. If you know how the name of a package begins, you should include that with the **ls** command and an attached *. The list of packages is extensive and does not all fit on one screen. This is helpful for displaying the detailed name of the package. The following example lists most X Window System packages:

```
# ls x*
```

You use the **−i** option to install new packages and the **−U** option to update currently installed packages with new versions. If you try to use the **−i** option to install a newer version of an installed package, you receive an error saying the package is already installed. In the next example, the user first installs a new package with the **−i** option, and then updates a package with the **-U** option. Including the -v and -h options is customary. Here, **-v** is the verbose option that displays all files as they are installed, and **-h** displays a cross-hatch symbol periodically to show RPM is still working.

In the following example, the user installs the software package for ht:/Dig (see Chapter 21). Notice the full filename is entered. To list the full name, you can use the **ls** command with the first few characters and an asterisk, ls htdig*. The **h** option displays # symbols as the installation takes place. The **rpm** command with the **-q** option is then used to check that the software was installed. For installed packages only, the software name needs to be used, in this case, htdig.

```
[root@turtle mypackages]# ls ht*
htdig-3.1.2-0glibc.i386.rpm
[root@turtle mypackages]# rpm -ivh htdig-3.1.2-0glibc.i386.rpm
htdig                       ######################################
[root@turtle mypackages]# rpm -q htdig
htdig-3.1.2-0glibc
```

To display information about the installed package, use **-qi**, and **-ql** displays a listing of the files a given RPM package contains.

```
# rpm -qi htdig
# rpm -ql htdig
```

To display information taken directly from an RPM package, you add the p qualifier to the **q** options. The **-qpi** combination displays information about a specific package, and **-qpl** displays a listing of the files a given RPM package contains. In this case, you must specify the entire filename of the RPM package. You can avoid having to enter the entire name simply by entering a unique part of the name and using the * filename matching character to generate the rest.

```
[root@turtle mypackages]# ls proftp*
proftpd-1.2.0pre3-2.i386.rpm
[root@turtle mypackages]# rpm -qp proftpd-1.2.0pre3-2.i386.rpm
proftpd-1.2.0pre3-2
[root@turtle mypackages]# rpm - qpi proftpd-1.2*.rpm
Name        : proftpd                      Relocations: (not relocateable)
Version     : 1.2.0pre3                         Vendor: (none)
.....................................
[root@turtle mypackages]# rpm -qpl proftpd*
/etc/logrotate.d/proftpd
/etc/pam.d/ftp
/etc/proftpd.conf
.....................................
```

Remember, if you are installing an upgrade, you need to use the **–U** option instead of the **–I** option. If you try to use **–I** to upgrade a package, you receive an error saying the package is already installed. If you receive an error stating dependency conflicts exist, the package may require other packages or their updated versions to be installed first. In some cases, you may have to install with the no dependency check options, **--nodeps** (notice the two dashes before the option). In some rare cases, installation instructions for a particular package may require you to use **--nodeps**. Another risky option is the **--force** option. This forces installation, overwriting any current files. This is a brute-force approach that should be used with care.

To remove a software package from your system, first use **rpm -q** to make sure it is actually installed. Then, use the **–e** option to uninstall it. You needn't use the full name of the installed file. You only need the name of the application. For example, if you decide you do not need ht://Dig, you can remove it using the **–e** option and the software name, as shown here.

```
# rpm  -e  htdig
```

If direct conflicts occur with another software package, you may have to uninstall the other package first. This is the case with wu-ftpd and ProFTP on many distributions. Red Hat currently installs wu-ftpd as the default FTP server. You must first uninstall the wu-ftpd with the **–e** option before you can install ProFTP. However, when you try to do this, you receive a dependency error. You can overcome this error by using the **--nodeps** option. Once wu-ftpd is removed, you can install ProFTP.

```
[root@turtle mypackages]# rpm -e --nodeps wu-ftpd
[root@turtle mypackages]# rpm -ivh proftpd-1.2*rpm
proftpd         #############################################
[root@turtle mypackages]# rpm -q proftpd
proftpd-1.2.0pre3-2
```

You can use the verify option (**–V**) to check to see if any problems occurred with the installation. RPM compares the current attributes of installed files with information about them placed in the RPM database when the package was installed. If no discrepancies exist, RPM outputs nothing. Otherwise, RPM outputs a sequence of eight characters, one for each attribute, for each file in the package that fails. Those that do not differ have a period. Those that do differ have a corresponding character code, as shown here:

5	MD5 Checksum
S	File Size
L	Symbolic link

T	File modification time
D	Device
U	User
G	Group
M	Mode (includes permissions and file types)

The following example verifies the proftpd package.

```
[root@turtle mypackages]# rpm -V proftpd
```

To compare the installed files directly with the files in an RPM package file, you use the **-Vp** option, much like the **-qp** option. To check all packages, use the **-Va** option as shown here.

```
rpm -Va
```

If you want to verify a package, but only know the name of a file in it, you can combine verify with the **-f** option. The following example verifies the RPM package containing the **ftp** command.

```
rpm -Vf  /bin/ftp
```

A complete description of **rpm** and its capabilities is provided in the online manual.

```
# man rpm
```

RPM maintains a record of the packages it has installed in its RPM database. You may, at times, have to rebuild this database to ensure RPM has current information on what is installed and what is not. Use the **--rebuilddb** options to rebuild your database file.

```
rpm --rebuilddb
```

To create a new RPM database, use the **-initdb** option. This can be combined **with -dbpath** to specify a location for the new database.

APPLICATIONS

Mode of Operation	Effect
rpm –i*options package-file*	Installs a package; the complete name of the package file is required
rpm –e*options package-name*	Uninstalls (erases) a package; you only need the name of the package, often one word
rpm –q*options package-name*	Queries a package; an option can be a package name or a further option and package name, or an option applied to all packages
rpm –U*options package-name*	Upgrade; same as install, but any previous version is removed
rpm –b*options package-specifications*	Builds your own rpm package
rpm –F*options package-name*	Upgrade, but only if package is currently installed
rpm –verify*options*	Verifies a package is correctly installed; uses same options as query; you can use **–V** or **–y** in place of **–verify**
--nodeps	Installs without doing any dependency checks
--force	Forces installation despite conflicts
--percent	Displays percentage of package during installation
--test	Tests installation; does not install, only checks for conflicts
-h	Displays # symbols as package is installed
--excludedocs	Excludes documentation files

Table 32-2.   *Red Hat Package Manager (RPM) Options*

Mode of Operation	Effect
Uninstall Options (to be used with -e)	
`--test`	Tests uninstall; does not remove, only checks for what is to be removed
`--nodeps`	Uninstalls without checking for dependencies
`--allmatches`	Removes all version of package
Query Options (to be used with -q)	
package-name	Queries package
`-a`	Queries all packages
`-f` *filename*	Queries package that owns *filename*
`-R`	List packages on which this package depends
`-p` *package-name*	Queries an uninstalled package
`-I`	Displays all package information
`-l`	Lists files in package
`-d`	Lists only documentation files in package
`-c`	Lists only configuration files in package
`--dump`	Lists only files with complete details
General Options (to be used with any option)	
`-vv`	Debug; displays descriptions of all actions taken
`--quit`	Displays only error messages
`--version`	Displays rpm version number
`--help`	Displays detailed use message
`--root`*directory*	Uses directory as top-level directory for all operations (instead of root)
`--dbpath`*directory*	Uses RPM database in the specified directory

Table 32-2. *Red Hat Package Manager (RPM) Options* (continued)

APPLICATIONS

Mode of Operation	Effect
--dbpath *cmd*	Pipes output of RPM to the command *cmd*
--rebuilddb	Rebuilds the RPM database; can use with **–root** and **–dbpath** options
--initdb	Builds a new RPM database; **–root** and **–dbpath** options
Other Sources of Information	
RPM-HOWTO on **www.RedHat.com**	More detailed information, particularly on how to build your own rpm packages
man rpm	Detailed list of options

Table 32-2.   *Red Hat Package Manager (RPM) Options* (continued)

Updating Red Hat

In the period between major releases, distributions post RPM package updates for software installed from your CD-ROM. Red Hat posts these packages at their update dircctory at their FTP site at **ftp.redhat.com**. Such updates may range from single software packages to whole components, for instance, all the core, applications, and development packages issued when a new release of Gnome, KDE, or XFree86 are made available.

With version 6.1, Red Hat now provides an Update Agent, which automatically locates, downloads, and installs any updates for your Red Hat system:

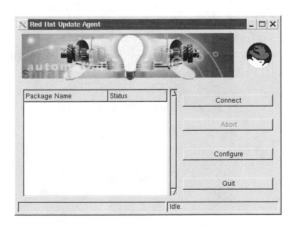

To use Update Agent, however, you must first register your copy of Red Hat at the Red Hat Web site at **www.redhat.com**. You are then provided with a user name and password with which you can configure Update Agent to access Red Hat's special secure server at **priority.redhat.com.** To start Update Agent, select its entry in the System menu in the Gnome main menu. Upon starting Update Agent, you are asked for your root user password as an added precaution.

The first time you use Update Agent, you must configure it, providing information about your system. Click the Configure button to display the Configuration dialog box with three tabbed panels: there is one panel for user, retrieval, and exceptions. The user panel holds your registration information and your e-mail address. The retrieval panel is where you enter the server you want to use (for example, **priority.redhat.com**) as well as download instructions and the download directory you want to use. The exception panel holds the names of any packages you don't want to update automatically.

To use Update Agent, click the Connect button. Update Agent connects to the FTP server, and then opens your Web browser (such as Netscape) and display a Web page listing the possible updates it found. You can then select individual packages by clicking the check boxes next to them. Then click the Request Selected packages button. To select all packages, click the Request ALL packages button. Once you select your packages, you can click the Request Packages button. The browser closes and the Update Agent begins downloading the selected packages. The packages are listed with a Status icon. They are first downloaded, during which the Status icon is a button, and then they are installed, which is indicated by a red arrow. When finished, the Status icon becomes a check mark.

Or, you can upgrade manually by first downloading all the packages and installing them yourself. For example, to install new releases of the K Desktop, you can download distribution versions of their packages from the KDE FTP site at **ftp.kde.org** or from distribution FTP sites. You can use an FTP client, such as ncftp, to download them all at once, including any subdirectories (see Chapter 12). Then change to that directory and use the **rpm -Uvh** command to install the packages.

For single packages, you can download them from the distribution FTP site, and then use the **rpm** command with the **-U** option to install them. You could also use an RPM utility such as **kpackage**. In fact, you can use both **kpackage** and GnomeRPM to access the distribution FTP sites directly, download the package, and automatically install it on your system. Just enter the FTP URL for the site in the Location box. In the following example, the **rpm** command with the **-Uvh** option installs an upgrade for Linuxconf.

```
$ rpm -Uvh   linuxconf-1.16r-1-1.i386.rpm
```

Installing Software from Compressed Archives: .tar.gz

Linux software applications in the form of source code are available at different sites on the Internet. You can download any of this software and install it on your system. You download software using an FTP client as described in Chapter 12. Recent and older software is usually downloaded in the form of a compressed archive file. This is particularly true for the recent versions of Gnome or KDE packages. RPM packages are only intermittently generated. A *compressed archive* is an archive file created with **tar**, and then compressed with gzip. To install such a file, you must first decompress it with the gunzip utility, and then use **tar** to extract the files and directories making up the software package. Instead of the gunzip utility, you could also use **gzip -d**. The next example decompresses the **ganesha-0.6.tar.gz** file, replacing it with a decompressed version called **ganesha-0.6.tar**.

```
$ ls
 ganesha-0.6.tar.gz
$ gunzip ganesha-0.6.tar.gz
$ ls
ganesha-0.6.tar
```

First, use **tar** with the **t** option to check the contents of the archive. If the first entry is a directory, that directory is created and the extracted files are placed in it. If the first entry is not a directory, you should first create one, and then copy the archive file to it. Then extract the archive within that directory. If no directory exists as the first entry, files are extracted to the current directory. You must create a directory yourself to hold these files.

```
$ tar tvf ganesha-0.6.tar
```

Now you are ready to extract the files from the tar archive. You use **tar** with the **x** option to extract files, the **v** option to display the pathnames of files as they are extracted, and the **f** option, followed by the name of the archive file:

```
$ tar xvf ganesha-0.6.tar
```

APPLICATIONS

You can combine the decompressing and unpacking operation into one **tar** command by adding a **z** option to the option list, **xzvf**. The following command both decompresses and unpacks the archive:

```
$ tar xzvf ganesha-0.6.tar.gz
```

Installation of your software may differ for each package. Instructions are usually provided along with an installation program.

Downloading Compressed Archives from Online Sites

Many software packages under development or designed for cross-platform implementation may not be in an RPM format. Instead, they may be archived and compressed. The filenames for these files end with the extensions **.tar.gz** or **.tar.Z**. In fact, most software with an RPM format also has a corresponding **.tar.gz** format. After you download such a package, you must first decompress it with gunzip, and then unpack it with the **tar** command. Many RPM packages only contain binary versions of software applications. If you want the source code for the application, you must download and unpack the compressed archive for that application.

In the next example, the user uses FTP to connect to the **metalab.unc.edu** Linux FTP site. For the login ID, the user enters anonymous and, for the password, the user enters her Internet address. The download mode can be set to binary by entering in the keyword binary. With the **cd** command, the user changes to the **pub/Linux/libs/X/xview** directory, where the Xview window manager software is located (see Chapter 3). The **get** command then downloads the package. The **close** command cuts the connection and the **quit** command leaves the **ftp** utility.

```
ftp> get xview-3.2p1.4.bin.tar.gz
>local: xview-3.2p1.4.bin.tar.gz remote: xview-3.2p1.4.bin.tar.gz
200 PORT command successful.
150 Opening BINARY mode data connection for
xview-3.2p1.4.bin.tar.gz .
226 Transfer complete.
2192197 bytes received in 728 secs (2.9 Kbytes/sec)
ftp>
```

Or, you could use Netscape or another Web Browser to access, browse through, and download software without having to bother with all the ftp commands. Be sure to precede an FTP site name with the term ftp:// instead of the usual http://. For Sunsite, you would enter: **ftp://sunsite.unc.edu.** Once you selected the software you want, hold down the SHIFT key and click it to download it.

Once downloaded, any file that ends with a **.Z** , **bz**, **.zip**, or **.gz** is a compressed file that must be decompressed. Use the **gunzip** command, followed by the name of the file.

```
# gunzip xview-3.2p1.4.bin.tar.gz
```

If the file then ends with **.tar**, it is an archived file that must be unpacked using the **tar** command. Before you unpack the archive, move it to the directory where you want it. Source code you intend to compile is usually placed in the **/usr/src** directory. Most archives unpack to a subdirectory they create, placing all those files or directories making up the software package into that subdirectory. For example, the file **xview-3.2p1.4.bin.tar** unpacks to a subdirectory called **usr**. To check if an archive unpacks to a directory, use **tar** with the **t** option to list its contents and to see if the names are prefixed by a directory. If so, that directory is created and the extracted files are placed in it. If no directory name exists, create one, and then copy the archive file to it. Then extract the archive within that directory.

```
# tar tf xview-3.2p1.4.bin.tar
```

Now you are ready to extract the files from the tar archive. You use **tar** with the **x** option to extract files, the **v** option to display the pathnames of files as they are extracted, and the **f** option, followed by the name of the archive file:

```
# tar xvf xview-3.2p1.4.bin.tar
```

Installation of your software may differ for each package. Instructions are usually provided, along with an installation program. Downloaded software usually includes README files or other documentation. Be sure to consult them.

Compiling Software

Some software may be in the form of source code that you need to compile before you can install it. This is particularly true of programs designed for cross-platform implementations. Programs designed to run on various UNIX systems, such as Sun, as well as on Linux, may be distributed as source code that is downloaded and compiled in those different systems. Compiling such software has been greatly simplified in recent years by the use of configuration scripts that automatically detect a given system's configuration and compile the program accordingly. For example, the name of the C compiler on a system could be gcc or cc. Configurations scripts detect which is present and use it to compile the program.

Before you compile software, first read the README or INSTALL files included with it. These give you detailed instructions on how to compile and install this particular program. If the software used configuration scripts, then compiling and installing usually involves only the following three simple commands:

```
#  ./configure
#  make
#  make install
```

The `./configure` command performs configuration detection. The **make** command performs the actual compiling, using a Makefile script generated by the ./configure operation. The **make install** command installs the program on your system, placing the executable program in a directory, such as **/usr/local/bin,** and any configuration files in **/etc**. Any shared libraries it created may go into **/usr/lib**.

If you are compiling an X-, Gnome-, or KDE-based program, be sure their development libraries have been installed. For X applications, be sure the xmkmf program is also installed. If you chose a standard install when you installed your distribution system, these most likely were not installed. For distributions using RPM packages, these come in the form of a set of development RPM packages, usually having the word "development" or "develop" in their name. You need to install them using either RPM, kpackage, or gnomeRPM. Gnome, in particular, has an extensive set of RPM packages for development libraries. Many X applications may need special shared libraries. For example, some applications may need the xforms library or the qt library. Some of these you need to obtain from online sites.

Some older X applications use xmkmf directly instead of a configure script to generate the needed Makefile. In this case, enter the command **xmkmf** in place of ./configure. Be sure to consult the INSTALL and README files for the software. Usually, you only need to issue the following commands within the directory that contains the source code files for the software.

```
xmkmf
make
make install
```

If no configure script exists and the program does not use **xmkmf,** you may have to enter the **make** command, followed by a **make install** operation. Check the README or INSTALL files for details.

```
make
make install
```

Be sure to check the documentation for such software to see if any changes must be made to the Makefile. Only a few changes may be necessary, but more detailed changes require an understanding of C programming and how **make** works with it. If you successfully configure the Makefile, you may only have to enter the **make** and **make install** operations. One possible problem is locating the development libraries for C and X-Windows. X-Windows libraries are in the **/usr/X11R6/lib** directory. Standard C libraries are located in the **/usr/lib** directory.

Command and Program Directories: PATH

Programs and commands are usually installed in several standard system directories, such as **/bin**, **/usr/bin**, **/usr/X11R6/bin**, or **/usr/local/bin**. Some packages place their commands in subdirectories, however, which they create within one of these standard directories or in an entirely separate directory. In such cases, you may be unable to run those commands because your system may be unable to locate them in the new subdirectory. Your system maintains a set of directories that searches for commands each time you execute one. This set of directories is kept in a system variable called PATH that is created when you start your system. If a command is in a directory that is not in this list, then your system will be unable to locate and run it. To use such commands, you first need to add the new directory to the set of directories in the PATH variable.

On RedHat systems, the PATH variable is assigned its set of directories in the **/etc/profile** file, which is a script run when your system starts and is used to configure user's working environments. In this file, you can find a line that begins with PATH, followed by an = sign, and then a list of directories, each separated by a colon. These are the directories that contain commands and programs.

To add a directory, carefully edit the **/etc/profile** file using a text editor, such as kedit, gedit, Emacs, or Vi (you may want to make a backup copy first with the **cp** command). At the end of the list of directories, add the new directory with its full pathname before the closing double quote. Be sure a colon separates the new directory from the last one. You should also have a colon at the end. For example, if you install the MH mail utility, the **MH** commands are installed in a subdirectory called **mh** in the **/usr/bin** directory. The full pathname for this directory is **/usr/bin/mh**. You need to add this directory to the list of directories assigned to PATH in the **/etc/profile** script. (The command **rpm -qpl** *package-name* lists all the directories where commands in an RPM software package are installed.) The following example shows the PATH variable with its list of directories and the **/usr/bin/mh** directory added (shown in boldface).

```
PATH="/bin:/usr/bin:/opt/bin:/usr/X11R6/bin:/usr/openwin/bin:/usr/
local/bin:/usr/bin/mh"
```

The **/etc/profile** script is a system script executed for each user when the user logs in. Individual users can customize their PATH variables by placing a PATH assignment in either their **.bashrc** or **.profile** files. In this way, users can access commands and programs they create or install for their own use in their own user directories (see Chapter 15 for more details). The following entry in the **.profile** file adds a user's **mybin** directory to the PATH variable. Use of $PATH keeps all the directories already listed in the **/etc/profile** script. Notice both the colon placed before the new directory and the use of the $HOME variable to specify the pathname for the user's home directory.

```
PATH=$PATH:$HOME/mybin
```

Packaging Your Software: Autoconf and RPM

Once you finish developing your software, you may then want to distribute it to others. Ordinarily, you would pack your program into a tar archive file. People would then download the file and unpack it. You would have to include detailed instructions on how to install it and where to place any supporting documentation and libraries. If you were distributing the source code, users would have to determine how to adapt the source code to their systems. Any number of variations might stop compilation of a program.

The RPM and Autoconf are designed to automate these tasks. The Autoconf program is used to automatically configure source code to a given system. RPM automatically installs software on a system in the designated directories, along with any documentation, libraries, or support programs. Both have complex and powerful capabilities, and can handle the most complex programs. Simple examples of their use are provided here.

Autoconf

A UNIX system can compile any software written in the C programming language. Different UNIX systems have different configurations, however, some using different compilers or placing programs and libraries in different system directories. Different types of support libraries may be present. In the past, to compile software on different systems, the software had to be configured manually for each system. For example, if your system has the gcc compiler instead of the cc compiler, you would have to set that feature in the software's Makefile.

The Autoconf program is designed to automate the configuration process. It automatically detects the configuration of the current UNIX system and generates an appropriate Makefile that can then be used to compile that software on this particular system. Much of the current software on the Internet in source form uses Autoconf. A detailed manual on Autoconf can be found in the **/usr/info** directory and is called **autoconf.info**. You can use the **info** command to view it. (You can also view the text with any text editor.) The general operations are described here.

Software that uses Autoconf performs the configuration without any need of the actual Autoconf software. Special shell scripts included with the software detect the different system features the software needs. The **./configure** command usually automatically configures the software for your system. As the configuration is performed, it checks for different features one by one, displaying the result of each check. The operation is entirely automatic and doesn't even require the identity of the system on which it is working.

To create a configuration script for your own software, you use special Autoconf commands. The Autoconf applications package is available on your Red Hat CD-ROM. Generating the configurations involves several stages, using several intermediate configuration files. Autoconf has many options designed to handle the requirements of a complex program. For a simple program, you may only need to follow the basic steps.

The goal is to create a **configure** script. Two phases are in this process, using the **autoscan** and **autoconf** commands. The first phase creates a **configure.scan** file, using the **autoscan** command. The **autoscan** command is applied directly to your source code files. Next, check the **configure.scan** file for any errors, make any changes or additions you want, and then rename it as the **configure.in** file. This file is used as input for the **autoconf** command, which then generates the **configure** script. The autoscan step is an aid in the creation of the **configure.in** file, but autoscan and the **configure.scan** file it generates are optional. You can create your own **configure.in** file, entering various Autoconf macros. These are described in detail in the Autoconf info file.

In addition, you need to create a version of the Makefile for your program named **makefile.in**. This is essentially your original Makefile, with reference to special Autoconf variables. When the software is compiled on another system, the **configure.in** detects the system's features, and then uses this information with the **makefile.in** file to generate a Makefile for that particular system. This new Makefile is then used to compile the program.

Autoconf is designed to create values for different features, which can then be used with **makefile.in** to create a new Makefile containing those features. The feature values are placed in special shell variables called *output* variables. You should place references to these shell variables in the **makefile.in** file wherever you want to use these values. For example, the **CC** variable holds the name of the C compiler on your system (cc or gcc). The **AC_PROG_CC** macro in the **configure** script detects the C compiler in use and places its name in the **CC** variable. A reference to this variable should be placed in the **makefile.in** file wherever you invoke the C compiler. The variable name is bounded by two @ symbols. For example, **@CC@** in **makefile.in** references the **CC** variable and its value is substituted in that place.

Once you have the **configure** file, you no longer need the **configure.in** file. You only need **configure**, **makefile.in**, and the source code files along with any header files. The **configure** file is a shell script designed to execute on its own. It does not need Autoconf.

Once another user has received the software package and unpacked all the source code files, you only need to take three steps: configuration, compilation, and installation. The **./configure** command generates a customized Makefile for the user's system, the **make** command compiles the program using that Makefile, and the **make install** command installs the program on the user's system.

```
./configure
make
make install
```

Creating RPM Packages

The package creation process is designed to take the program through several stages, starting with unpacking it from an archive, and then compiling its source code, and, finally, generating the RPM package. You can skip any of these stages, up to the last one. If your software is already unpacked, you can start with compiling it. If your software is compiled, you can start with installation. If it is already installed, you can go directly to creating the RPM package.

RPM makes use of three components to build packages: the build tree, the **/etc/rpmrc** configuration file, and an **rpm** spec script. The build tree is a set of special instructions used to carry out the different stages of the packaging process. The **rpm** spec script contains instructions for creating the package, as well as the list of files to be placed in it. The **/etc/rpmrc** file is used to set configuration features for RPM. RPM has several options you can set in the **/etc/rpmrc** file. To obtain a listing, enter

```
$ rpm -showrc
```

The build tree directories, listed in the following table, are used to hold the different files generated at each stage of the packaging process. The **SOURCES** directory holds the compressed archive. The **BUILD** directory holds the source code unpacked from that archive. The **RPMS** directory is where the RPM package containing the executable binary program is placed, and **SRPMS** is where the RPM package containing the source code is placed. If you are creating a package from software stored in a compressed archive, such as a **tar.gz** file, you first must copy that file to the build tree's **SOURCES** directory.

Directory Name	Description
BUILD	The directory where RPM does all its building
SOURCES	The directory where you should put your original source archive files and your patches
SPECS	The directory where all spec files should go
RPMS	The directory where RPM puts all binary RPMs when built
SRPMS	The directory where all source RPMs are put

The following example copies the compressed archive for the bookrec software to the **SOURCES** directory:

```
# cp bookrec-1.0.tar.gz  /usr/src/Red Hat/SOURCES
```

The **topdir:** entry in the **/etc/rpmrc** file specifies the location of the build tree directories. In this file, you can find an entry for **topdir:**. Currently, the Red Hat system has already set this directory to **/usr/src/redhat**. You can find the **SOURCES, BUILD, RPMS,** and **SRPMS** directories here. You can specify a different directory for these subdirectories by changing the entry for **topdir:** in the **/etc/rpmrc** file.

```
topdir: /usr/src/Red Hat
```

By default, RPM is designed to work with source code placed in a directory consisting of its name and a release number, separated by a hyphen. For example, a program with the name *bookrec* and *release 1.0* should have its source-code files in a directory called **bookrec-1.0**. If RPM needs to compile the software, it expects to find the source code in that directory within the **BUILD** directory, **BUILD/bookrec-1.0**. The same name and release number also must be specified in the **spec** file.

RPM Spec File

To create a package, first create an **rpm spec** file for it. The **rpm spec** file specifies the files to be included, any actions to build the software, and information about the package. The **spec** file is designed to take the program through several stages, starting with unpacking it from an archive, compiling its source code, and generating the RPM package. In the **spec** file are segments for the different stages and special RPM macros that perform actions at these stages. These are listed here:

File Segment or Macro	Description
%description	A detailed description of the software
%prep	The prep stage for archives and patches
%setup	The prep macro for unpacking archives. A **-n** *name* option resets the name of the build directory
%patch	The prep macro for updating patches
%build	The build stage for compiling software
%install	The install stage for installing software
%files	The files stage that lists the files to be included in the package. A **-f** *filename* option specifies a file that contains a list of files to be included in the package
%config *file-list*	A file macro that lists configuration files to be placed in the **/etc** directory
%doc *file-list*	A file macro that lists documentation files to be placed in the **/usr/doc** directory with the subdirectory of the name-version-release

APPLICATIONS

%dir *directory-list*	The specification of a directory to be included as being owned by a package. (A directory in a file list refers to all files in it, not only the directory)
%pre	A macro to do preinstall scripts
%preun	A macro to do preuninstall scripts
%post	A macro to do postinstall scripts
%postun	A macro to do postuninstall scripts

A **spec** file is divided into five basic segments: header, prep, build, install, and files. These segments are separated in the file by empty lines. The header segment contains several lines of information, each preceded by a tag and a semicolon. For example, the following tag is used for a short description of the software.

```
Summary: bookrec program to manage book records
```

The Name, Version, and Release tags are used to build the name of the RPM package. The name, version, and release are separated with hyphens. For example, the name *bookrec* with the *version 1.0* and *release 2* have the following name:

```
bookrec-1.0-2
```

The Group entry is a list of categories for the software and is used by the Red Hat **glint** utility to place the software in the correct glint display folder. The Source entry is the compressed archive where the software is stored on your system. Description is a detailed description of the software.

Following the header are the three stages for creating and installing the software on your system, indicated by the **%prep**, **%build**, and **%install rpm** macros. You can skip any of these stages, say, if the software is already installed. You can also leave any of them out of the **spec** file or comment them out with a preceding #. The **spec** file is capable of taking a compressed archive, unpacking it, compiling the source code files, and then installing the program on your system. Then the installed files can be used to create the RPM package.

The **%prep** macro begins the prep segment of the **spec** file. The prep segment's task is to generate the software's source code. This usually means unpacking archives, but it may also have to update the software with patches. The tasks themselves can be performed by shell scripts you write. Special macros can also automatically perform these tasks. The **%setup** macro can decompress and unpack an archive in the **SOURCES** directory, placing the source code files in the **BUILD** directory. The **%patch** macro applies any patches.

The **%build** segment contains the instructions for compiling the software. Usually, this is a simple **make** command, depending on the complexity of your program. The **%install** segment contains the instructions for installing the program. You can use simple shell commands to copy the files or, as in the **bookspec** example that follows, the **install** command that installs files on systems. This could also be the **make install** command, if your Makefile has the commands to install your program.

```
%build
make RPM_OPT_FLAGS="$RPM_OPT_FLAGS"

%install
install -s -m 755 -o 0 -g 0 bookrec /usr/bin/bookrec
install -m 644 -o 0 -g 0 bookrec.1 /usr/man/man1
```

The **%files** segment contains the list of files you want placed in the rpm package. Following the **%files** macro, you list the different files, including their full pathnames. The macro **%config** can be used to list configuration files. Any files listed here are placed in the **/etc** directory. The **%doc** macro is used for documentation, such as README files. These are placed in the **/usr/doc** directory under a subdirectory consisting of the software's name, version, and release number. In the **bookspec** example shown here, the **README** file is placed in the **/usr/doc/bookrec-1.0-2** directory.

bookspec

```
Summary: bookrec program to manage book records
Name: bookrec
Version: 1.0
Release: 2
Copyright: GPL
Group: Applications/Database
Source: /root/rpmc/bookrec-1.0.tar.gz
%description
This program manages book records by title, providing
price information

%prep
%setup

%build
make RPM_OPT_FLAGS="$RPM_OPT_FLAGS"

%install
install -s -m 755 -o 0 -g 0 bookrec /usr/bin/bookrec
install -m 644 -o 0 -g 0 bookrec.1 /usr/man/man1

%files
```

```
%doc README

/usr/bin/bookrec
/usr/man/man1/bookrec.1
```

RPM Build Operation

To create an rpm software package, you use the **rpm build** options (listed in Table 32-3) with the **rpm** command, followed by the name of a **spec** file. The **-bl** option checks to see if all the files used for the software are present. The **-bb** option builds only the binary package, whereas **-ba** builds both binary and source packages. They expect to find the compressed archive for the software in the build tree's **SOURCES** directory. The **-ba** and **-bb** options execute every stage specified in the rpm spec script, starting from the prep stage, to unpacking an archive, and then compiling the program, followed by installation on the system, and then creation of the package. The completed rpm package for executable binaries is placed in a subdirectory of the build tree's **RPMS** directory. This subdirectory has a name representing the current platform. For a PC, this is **i386**, and the package is placed in the **RPMS/i386** subdirectory. The source-code package is placed directly in the **SRPMS** directory.

The following program generates both a binary and a software package, placing them in the build tree's **RPMS/i386** and **SRPMS** directories. The name of the spec file in this example is **bookspec**.

```
rpm -ba bookspec
```

An executable binary package has a name consisting of the software name, the version number, the release number, the platform name (**i386**), and the term **rpm**. The name, version, and release are separated by hyphens, whereas the release, platform name, and the **rpm** term are separated by periods. The name of the binary package generated by the previous example, using the **bookspec** spec script, generates the following name:

```
bookrec-1.0-2.i386.rpm
```

The source code package has the same name, but with the term **src** in place of the platform name:

```
bookrec-1.0-2.src.rpm
```

Option	Description
-ba	Create both the executable binary and source-code packages. Perform all stages in the spec file: prep, build, install, and create the packages
-bb	Create only the executable binary package. Perform all stages in the spec file: prep, build, install, and create the package
-bp	Run only the prep stage from the spec file (**%prep**)
-bl	Do a "list check." The **%files** section from the spec file is macro-expanded, and checks are made to ensure the files exist
-bc	Do both the prep and build stages, unpacking and compiling the software (**%prep** and **%build**)
-bi	Do the prep, build, and install stages, unpacking, compiling, and installing the software (**%prep**, **%build**, and **%install**)
--short-circuit	Skip to specified stage, not executing any previous stages. Only valid with **-bc** and **-bi**
--clean	Remove the build tree after the packages are made
--test	Do not execute any build stages. Used to test spec files
--recompile *source_package_file*	RPM installs the source-code package and performs a prep, compile, and install
--rebuild *source_package_file*	RPM first installs the named source package and does a prep, compile, and install, and then rebuilds a new binary package
--showrc	List the configuration variables for the **/etc/rpmrc** file

Table 32-3.   *The RPM Build Options*

APPLICATIONS

Chapter 33

Office Applications

A variety of office suites are now available for Linux. These include professional-level word processors, presentation managers, drawing tools, and spreadsheets. The freely available versions are described in this chapter. Currently, you can download personal (noncommercial) versions for both WordPerfect and StarOffice from the Internet for free. KOffice is an entirely free office suite planned for release with KDE 2.0. The Gnome Workshop Project is integrating Gnome applications into a productivity suite that will be freely available. You can also purchase commercial office suites, such as Applixware, from Red Hat and Corel Office. *Applixware* includes a word processor, spreadsheet, presentation graphics tool, drawing tool, an e-mail client, and an object-oriented application builder.

Accessibility to Microsoft Office

One of the primary concerns for new Linux users is what kind of access they would have to their Microsoft Office files, particularly Word files. The Linux operating system and many applications for it are designed to provide seamless access to MS Office files. The Intel version of Linux can directly mount and access any Windows partition and its files. The major Linux Office Suites including WordPerfect, KOffice, and particularly StarOffice, all read and manage any Microsoft Office files. In addition, these Office Suites are fast approaching the same level of support for office tasks as found in Microsoft Office.

If you want to use any Windows application on Linux, one important alternative is the VMware virtual platform technology. With Vmware, you can run any Windows application directly on your Linux system. For more information check the VMware Web site at **www.vmware.com.**

WordPerfect

The personal version of Corel's WordPerfect word processor is now available for Linux and is free (it is included with OpenLinux). The personal version is a fully functional word processor. However, it does not currently support TrueType fonts and it does not allow you to import other objects, such as images. You can download WordPerfect from the Corel Web site at **linux.corel.com**. WordPerfect is more than just a word processor. You can use it to create drawings, spreadsheets, and charts, as well as to edit and publish Web pages.

When you first start WordPerfect, a small window is displayed with the WordPerfect logo and four menus: Program, Preferences, Window, and Help. From the Program menu, you can select WordPerfect. In the Preferences menu, you can open a window with icons for configuring your printer, selecting fonts, choosing colors, and selecting conversion filters. The Window menu moves you to different open windows.

WordPerfect provides many of the standard word processing features, including cut-and-paste operations, font and paragraph styles, and document formatting. The extensive features for WordPerfect are indicated by its set of toolbars. WordPerfect includes such editing features as Grammar-As-You-Go, which checks and highlights suspicious phrases and offers suggestions. With Spell-As-You-Go, words are identified that might be misspelled as you type them. Corel Versions keeps track of document revisions for workgroup collaboration.

WordPerfect includes a chart and drawing tool for creating figures. You can perform drawing operations such as sizing and rotating images, as well as contouring text over image shapes. The drawing tool supports features such as gradients, patterns, and groupings. You can create a variety of different charts, including 3-D, area, and line charts. WordPerfect supports a number of spreadsheet functions with which you can create tables with spreadsheet cells. You can use such data to generate charts.

You can also use WordPerfect as a Web page editor and publisher, adding or changing HTML components. Use WordPerfect to create your HTML document with hyperlinks and bookmarks, and then place them on your Web site. Any text beginning with an Internet protocol, such as **www**, **ftp**, and **http**, is automatically set up as a hyperlink. You can also save Web pages as WordPerfect documents for easy editing.

WordPerfect supports an extensive number of file formats, including Microsoft Word 97 files. With WordPerfect, you can effectively edit your Word files. WordPerfect also has its own file manager. You can use the file manager to locate and open files, but it also performs other operations. You can create directories and modify file permissions, as well as move and copy files.

KOffice

KOffice is an integrated office suite for the *KDE (K Desktop Environment)* consisting of several office applications, including a word processor, a spreadsheet, and graphic applications. All applications are written for the KOM/OP component model, which allows components from any one application to be used in another. This means you can embed a spreadsheet from KSpread or a drawing from KIllustrator in a KWord document. You can obtain more information about KOffice from the KOffice Web site at **koffice.kde.org**. The first release of KOffice is scheduled as part of KDE version 2.0.

Currently, KOffice includes KSpread, KPresenter, KDiagram, KImage, KIllustrator, KFormula, Kword, Katabase, KImageShop, and KoHTML (see Table 33-1). KSpread is a spreadsheet, KPresenter is a presentation application, KIllustrator is a vector drawing program, KWord is a Publisher-like word processor, KDiagram charts and diagrams, KFormula is a formula editor, and KImage is a simple image viewer, and KoHTML is an HTML viewer.

Embedded components support real-time updates. For example, if you use KDiagram to generate a chart in a KWord document using data in a KSpread

Application	Description
KSpread	Spreadsheet
KPresenter	Presentation program
KIllustrator	Vector drawing program
KWord	Word processor (desktop publisher)
KFormula	Mathematical formula editor
KChart/KDiagram	Tool for drawing charts and diagrams
KImage	A simple image viewer
Katabase	A database not unlike Paradox and Access
KoHTML	An HTML viewer
KImageShop	An image manipulation program

Table 33-1. *KOffice Applications*

spreadsheet and then change the selected data in the spreadsheet, the KDiagram automatically updates the chart in the KWord document. In effect, you are creating a compound document, one made up of several applications. This capability is implemented by the KDE object model known as *K Object Model/OpenParts* (*KOM/OP*). KOM/OP is based on CORBA 2.2, the industry standard for communication between distributed objects. KOM/OP is not dependent on the K Desktop and can be used by any application designed for it on any interface, including Gnome. A Gnome application can be written to use KOM/OP and operate entirely on the Gnome GUI. This feature makes KOffice a possible candidate for a Linux and UNIX standard.

With *KOffice,* you create one kind of document rather than separate ones for different applications. The different applications become views of this document, adding their components to it. KWord sets up the publishing and word processing components, KIllustrator adds drawing components, while KSpread adds spreadsheet components. You use the appropriate application to view the different components in the single document. This means you can have separate windows open at the same time for different components of the document.

KSpread is the spreadsheet application, which incorporates the basic operations found in most spreadsheets, with formulas similar to those used in Excel. You can extend KSpread capabilities with Python scripts. It supports features such as embedded buttons for customized functions, automatic completion for cell contents, and formatting options, such as backgrounds, borders, and font styles. To generate a diagram using selected cells, select the Insert Diagram entry from the KSpread menu. This starts up KDiagram, which you then use to create the diagram—which is then embedded in the spreadsheet. You can also embed pictures or formulas using KImage, KIllustrator, or KFormula.

With *KDiagram,* you can create different kinds of charts, such as bar graphs, pie charts, and line graphs. To generate a chart, you can use data in KSpread or you can use KDiagram tables to enter your data.

With *KPresenter,* you can create presentations consisting of text and graphics modeled using different fonts, orientations, and attributes such as colors. You can add such elements as speech bubbles, arrows, and clip art, as well as embed any KOffice component. KPresenter supports standard editing operations such as shading, rotating, and coloring objects, as well as cut-and-paste and undo/redo capabilities. You can generate templates from a KPresenter document, in effect, enabling you to use a document's configuration to create other documents. With KPresenter, you can also create special effects such as simple animation.

KIllustrator is a vector-based graphics program, much like Adobe Illustrator and Corel Draw. It supports the standard graphic operations such as rotating, scaling, and aligning objects. KIllustrator also includes text formatting capabilities such as alignment to irregular boundaries. You can create complex illustrations using layers, using a layer manager to control the layers. KIllustrator also supports a number of import and export filters for image files of different types like .jpeg, .gif, and .eps.

KWord can best be described as a desktop publisher, with many of the features found in publishing applications like Microsoft Publisher and FrameMaker. Although it is also a fully functional word processor, KWord is not page-based like Word or WordPerfect. Instead, text is set up in frames that are placed on the page like objects Frames, like objects in a drawing program, can be moved, resized, and even reoriented. You can organize frames into a frame set, having text flow from one to the other. Formatting can be applied to a frame set, changing features in all the frames belonging to it at once. The default frame set up for you when you first create a document is the same size as the page. This gives you the effect of a page-based word processor, enabling you to work as if you were using a standard word processor. You can, of course, change the size of your frame and add new ones, if you want.

You can also insert images, illustrations, tables, and other KOffice components such as diagrams and spreadsheets. You can set up a frame to contain an image and place it on top of a text frame, configuring the text frame to flow its text around the image.

KWord uses templates to set up a document. You have two different sets of templates from which to choose: one for *desktop publishing* (*DTP*) and the other for standard word processing (Wordprocessing). The desktop publishing templates enables you to move frames freely, whereas in the word processing templates, the frames are fixed to the size of the page.

KWord supports the standard word processing features for formatting paragraphs, text, and document elements, such as headers and footers, as well as lists and multiple columns. You can also define your own paragraph layouts, specifying features such as indentation, fonts, borders, and alignment. Layouts are the same as styles used in other word processors. Tables are implemented as frames, where each cell is its own frame.

KFormula is a formula editor used to generate mathematical formulas. Although KFormula does not have the power of TeX, you can use it to create fairly complex formulas. It supports standard components like roots, integral, and fractions, as well as fonts for Greek symbols.

Currently, *KImage* is used only to display images. Later, it will be enhanced with image editing capabilities. For now, you can use it to display images embedded in different KOffice applications. *KoHTML* is another applet used to display Web pages. It is useful for displaying Web pages embedded in KOffice applications.

KImageShop, which is currently under development, is an image editor much like PhotoShop. *Katabase* is a database application designed to work with KOffice applications.

Gnome Workshop Project

Office applications such as the Gnumeric spreadsheet have been developed independently for Gnome. Currently, the Gnome Workshop Project is attempting to integrate the various office applications into a productivity suite. Although most are still under development, some have stable working versions you can download and install. You can find out more from the Gnome Workshop Project Web site at **www.gnome.org/gw.html**. Here, you can download current versions and view screen shots. A current listing is shown in Table 33-2. All implement the CORBA model for embedding components, ensuring drag-and-drop capability throughout the Gnome interface.

The *Gnumeric* is the Gnome spreadsheet, a professional-level program meant to replace commercial spreadsheets. Like Gnome, Gnumeric is freely available under the GNU Public License. Gnumeric is included with the Gnome release and you will find it installed with Gnome on the Red Hat and SuSE distributions. You can download current versions from **www.gnome.org/gnumeric**. Gnumeric supports standard GUI spreadsheet features, including autofilling and cell formatting, and it provides an extensive number of formats. It supports drag-and-drop operations, enabling you to select and then move or copy cells to another location. Gnumeric also supports plug-ins, making it possible to extend and customize its capabilities easily.

StarOffice

StarOffice is a fully integrated and Microsoft Office-compatible suite of office applications developed and supported by Sun Microsystems. It includes Web-enabled word processing, spreadsheet, presentation, e-mail, news, chart, and graphic applications. Versions of StarOffice exist for Linux, Windows, Mac, Solaris, and OS/2. With StarOffice, you can access Microsoft Office (including 2000) files and data to create spreadsheets, presentations, and word processing documents. You can save

Application	Description
Achtung	Presentation manager
GWP	Word processor
GO	Word processor
AbiWord	Cross-platform word processor
Gnumeric	Spreadsheet
Guppi	Statistical tool for plotting data
Genius	Scientific calculator
Dia	Diagram and flowchart editor
Electric Eyes	Image viewer
Gnome Help Browser	Enhanced for Web browsing
GYVE	Vector drawing package
GIMP	GNU image manipulation program
gnome-db	Database architecture for Gnome
GNOME Personal Information Manager	Calendar/organizer and an address book

Table 33-2. *Gnome Workshop Project*

StarOffice documents in Microsoft formats or as HTML files that you can post on Web sites.

StarOffice is free for all noncommercial, private users, as well as students. You can download a free copy of StarOffice from the Sun Web site at **www.sun.com/ products/staroffice**. The package is about 65 megabytes. The Web site also contains information such as online manuals and FAQs.

StarOffice describes itself as implementing a task-oriented approach to office projects. You can complete an entire project using a variety of different tools in just one place, StarOffice. In addition, StarOffice applications are fully Internet-aware, enabling you to connect directly to Web sites and access information from your word processor, spreadsheet, or presenter.

When you start up StarOffice, you are presented with the StarOffice Desktop window. From here, you can create documents and access other StarOffice applications. The left pane in this window is the Explorer. This is a tree menu that lists the different resources you can use, such as an address book, a gallery of clip art, and FTP server URLs. The main window of the StarOffice Desktop shows icons for applications you can use, your StarOffice documents, and other tools.

To use StarOffice, you create projects. In a particular project, you can place resources such as images, Internet links, e-mail messages, or office documents, such as spreadsheets and word processing documents. To create a new document, click the New button in the bottom status bar and select the application you want to use from the pop-up menu. You can create spreadsheets, word processing documents, presentation files, mail messages, charts, images, mathematical formulas, and even Web pages (see Table 33-3). You can also create frame sets for use in Web page frames. Initially, windows are attached (docked) to the Desktop window. You can unattach them from the Desktop window to their own floating windows by double-clicking the gray area between them.

StarOffice has its own mail and news clients. With StarMail, you can define mail accounts and access your e-mail, as well as compose and send messages. With StarDiscussion, you can access newsgroups, saving articles and posting your own. You can set up icons and entries for mail accounts and newsgroups on your Desktop and Explorer window.

The StarWriter word processor supports standard word processing features, such as cut-and-paste, spell-checker, and text formatting, as well as paragraph styles. You can also insert objects in your text, such as images, diagrams, or text frames. Text can be configured to flow around them. A text frame can be further edited to create banner-like text, coloring, blending, and shaping text. The Navigator enables you to move through the document by page or by object, such as from one image to another.

You can open and save documents in the MS Office, WordPerfect, Lotus 1-2-3, and AmiPro formats. This means you can effectively edit MS Word documents with StarOffice. StarWriter also functions as a Web browser—capable of displaying HTML pages—and supports Java, JavaScript, Navigator, and Explorer plug-ins. At the same time, you can edit a Web page, turning StarWriter into a Web page editor.

You can embed objects within documents, such as using StarChart to create a bar chart using data in the spreadsheet. With StarMath, you can create formulas that you can then embed in a text document.

With the presentation manager (StarImpress), you can create images, such as circles, rectangles, and connecting elements like arrows, as well as vector-based illustrations for presentations. StarImpress supports advanced features like morphing objects, grouping objects, and defining gradients. You can also create animation effects and use layers to generate complex images. Any components from other StarOffice applications can be embedded in a presentation document. You can also import Microsoft PowerPoint files and save presentation files as HTML files. An AutoPilot Wizard for StarImpress walks you through the steps for creating a presentation.

StarDraw is a sophisticated drawing tool that includes 3-D modeling tools. You can create simple or complex images, including animation text aligned on curves. You can use StarDraw to create buttons and icons for your Web page.

StarSchedule provides scheduling and task management that can be used to coordinate efforts by a group of users. You can use it to track events and to-do lists, connecting automatically to the address book. StarSchedule includes a reminder system to display pop-up alerts and to send e-mail reminders. The StarSchedule server operates independently from StarOffice to provide scheduling services to any client on your network. StarBase is a relational database, somewhat like MS Access, which supports drag-and-drop operations for importing data to your StarOffice applications.

Application	Description
StarDesktop	Main desktop window for StarOffice applications
StarWriter	Word processor
StarImpress	Presentation manager
StarDraw	Drawing tool
StarChart	Chart and graph creator
StarMail	E-mail client
StarDiscussion	Newsgroup client
StarMath	Mathematical formulas
StarImage	Image editor
StarCalc	Spreadsheet
StarSchedule	Schedule manager
StarBase	Relational database

Table 33-3.   *StarOffice Applications*

Chapter 34

Database Management Systems, Graphic Tools, and Multimedia

861

Avariety of database management systems are now available for Linux. These include high-powered, commercial-level database management systems, such as Oracle, IBM, and Sybase. Most of the database management systems available for Linux are designed to support large relational databases. For small personal databases, you can use the desktop database management systems being developed for KDE and Gnome. In addition, some software is available for databases accessed with the xBase database programming language. These are smaller databases using formats originally developed for dBase on the PC. Various database management systems available to run under Linux are listed in Table 34-1.

You can also use a wide range of graphic tools, ranging from simple image viewers like kimage to sophisticated image manipulation programs like the GIMP. You also have newer graphic tools for Gnome and KDE desktops, as well as the older X Window System, from which to choose. Graphics tools available for use under Linux are listed in Table 34-2.

Database Management Systems

Database software can be generally organized into three categories: SQL, xBase, and desktop databases. *SQL-based databases* are professional-level relational databases, whose files are managed by a central database server program. Applications that use the database do not access the files directly. Instead, they send requests to the database server, which then performs the actual access. *SQL* is the query language used on these industrial-strength databases.

The *xBase language* is an enhanced version of the dBase programming language used to access database files whose formats were originally developed for dBase on the PC. With xBase, database management systems can directly access the database files. xBase is used mainly for smaller personal databases, with database files often located on a user's own system.

Desktop databases are being developed for both Gnome and KDE. Currently, these are personal databases, designed for individual users. Katabase is meant to be used with a user's KOffice applications, and Gaby, for a user's personal records. Both, however, are designed with a plug-in structure that can easily extend their capabilities.

SQL Databases (RDMS)

SQL databases are *relational database management systems* (*RDMS*) designed for extensive database management tasks. Many of the major SQL databases now have Linux versions, including Oracle, Informix, Sybase, and IBM (but, of course, not Microsoft). These are commercial and professional database management systems of the highest order. Linux has proved itself capable of supporting complex and demanding database management tasks. In addition, many free SQL databases are available for Linux that offer much the same functionality. Most commercial database also provide a free personal version, as with Oracle, Adabas D, and MySQL.

PostgreSQL

PostgreSQL is based on the POSTGRES database management system, though it uses SQL as its query language. POSTGRES is a next-generation research prototype developed at the University of California, Berkeley. Linux versions of PostgreSQL are included in Red Hat, Debian, and Slackware distributions. Updates can be obtained from respective distribution update sites, such as **ftp.redhat.com.** You can also download current versions from the PostgreSQL Web site at **www.postgresql.org**. Development is being managed by a team of developers over the Internet.

Oracle

Oracle offers a fully functional version of its Oracle8 database management system for Linux, as well as the Oracle Application Server. You can download trial versions effective for 30 days from the Oracle Web site at **www.oracle.com**. Oracle8 is a professional database designed for large databases. Expect to use a gigabyte of memory just to install it. The Oracle Application Server provides support for real-time and commerce applications on the Web. As Linux is a fully functional version of UNIX, Oracle is particularly effective on it. Oracle was originally designed to operate on UNIX, and Linux is a far better platform for it than other PC operating systems.

Oracle offers extensive documentation for its Linux version that you can download from its Documentation page, to which you can link from the Support pages on its Web site. The documentation available includes an installation guide, administrator's reference, and release notes, as well as the generic documentation. You can find specific information on installing and configuring Oracle for Linux in the Oracle Database HOW-TO, available at **www.linux.org**.

Informix

Informix offers an entire line of database products for Linux, including its Dynamic Server, Informix SE, Informix 4GL, and C-ISAM. Informix Dynamic Server features Dynamic Scalable Architecture, making it capable of effectively using any hardware setup. Informix SE (special edition) is a user-friendly and reliable database server that requires little database administration, while it provides fast and consistent access supporting SQL. Informix 4GL includes database tools, such as a debugger and compiler. C-ISAM is a library of C functions for indexed sequential access methods. Informix database systems provide flexible indexing, data consistency, integrity constraints, and security. Informix only provides commercial products. No free versions exist, though the company currently provides special promotions for Linux products. You can find out more about Informix at **www.informix.com/linux**.

Informix strongly supports Linux development of its Informix line. It provides developer support through its Informix Developer Network (**www.informix.com/idn**). Informix has a close working relationship with Red Hat and plans to provide joint technical support for their products.

APPLICATIONS

Sybase

Sybase offers a line of database products ported to Linux free. You can download them through the Sybase Web site at **www.sybase.com** or from its FTP site at **ftp.sybase.com/linux**. The free products include the Adaptive Server Enterprise server, the Open Client/C library (unsupported), and SQL Anywhere Studio (evaluation version). You can currently download the Adaptive Server Enterprise server from the Web page **www.sybase.com:80/products/databaseservers/linux/**, or from the Sybase FTP site at **ftp.sybase.com/linux**. The Sybase Enterprise database features data integration that coordinates all information resources on a network. SQL Anywhere is a database system designed for smaller databases, though with the same level of complexity found in larger databases.

DB2

IBM provides a Linux version of its DB2 Universal Database software. You can download it free from the IBM DB2 Web page for Linux, **www.software.ibm.com/ data/db2/linux/**. DB2 Universal Database for Linux includes Internet functionality along with support for Java and Perl. With the Web Control Center, administrators can maintain databases from a Web browser. DB2 features scalability to expand the database easily, support for Binary Large Objects, and cost-based optimization for fast access. DB2 is still very much a mainframe database, though IBM is currently working on refining its UNIX/Linux version.

Ingres II

Ingress II is an industrial-strength relational database provided by Computer Associates. You can download a free copy of Ingress II as part of the Computer Associates Open Beta program for Linux. You can find a link for the download at the Computer Associates Web site at **www.cai.com/products/ingres.htm** or at **www.ingres.com**. The Beta version include the complete Ingress II database engine, with features like variable page size, support for Binary Large Objects, interfaces for C, compatibility with IngPerl (database access with the Perl scripting language), and Internet publishing capabilities. A complete set of online documentation is also included.

Adabas D

Adabas D is an intermediate relational database, not quite as powerful or as large as Oracle, which is meant for use on smaller networks of personal databases. It still provides the flexibility and power found in all relational databases. Adabas D provides a free personal version for Linux . For commercial uses, you have to purchase a copy. You can find online documentation, including manuals and FAQs, at the Caldera Web site at **www.calderasystems.com**. You can also check the Adabas D Web site at **www.softwareag.com**.

MySQL

MySQL is a true multiuser, multithreaded SQL database server, develop by TcX. MySQL is free for personal and noncommercial use. You can download a copy from its Web site at **www.mysql.com**. The site also includes detailed documentation including manuals and FAQs. RPM packages are available for Red Hat and OpenLinux at the Red Hat contrib site at **contrib.redhat.com**.

MySQL is structured on a client/server model with a server daemon (`mysqld`) filling requests from client programs. MySQL is designed for speed, reliability, and ease of use. It is meant to be a fast database management system for large databases and, at the same time, reliable with intensive use.

GNU SQL

GNU SQL is the GNU relational database developed by a group at the Institute for System Programming of the Russian Academy of Sciences and supported by the GNU organization. It is a portable multiuser database management system with a client/server structure that supports SQL. The server processes requests and performs basic administrative operations, such as unloading parts of the database used infrequently. The clients can reside on any computer of a local network. GNU-SQL uses a dialect of SQL based on the SQL-89 standard and designed for use on a UNIX-like environment. You can download the database software from the GNU FTP site at **ftp.gnu.org**. For more information, contact the GNU-SQL Web site at **www.ispras.ru/~kml/gss**.

xBase Databases

Databases accessed with *xBase* are smaller in scale, designed for small networks or for personal use. Many are originally PC database programs, such as dBaseIII, Clipper, FoxPro, and Quicksilver. Currently, only Flagship provides an interface for accessing xBase database files, although the Harmony project is currently developing a Clipper clone that may run on Linux systems.

Flagship is a compiler with which you can create interfaces for querying xBase database files. The interfaces support menus and dialog boxes, and have function calls that execute certain database queries. Flagship can compile dBaseIII+ code and up. It is compatible with dBase and Clipper, and can access most xBase file formats, such as **.dbf**, **.dbt**, **.fmt**, and **.frm**. One of Flagship's key features is that its interfaces can be attached to a Web page, enabling users to update databases. Flagship is commercial software, though you can download a free personal version from its Web site at **www.fship.com/free.html**.

Desktop Database

Both Gnome and KDE also have database management applications that take advantage of their respective desktops. KDE's Katabase is part of KOffice and is fully integrated with its other applications. Gnome's Gaby takes advantage of the interface to display and search user databases.

Katabase (KOffice)

Katabase is a database management system that is part of the K Desktop's KOffice suite of programs. It is a desktop database, somewhat like Microsoft Access and Paradox; however, it makes full use of its integration with other Koffice programs by means of KOM/OpenParts. As part of KOffice, any part of Katabase can be embedded into another Koffice application, and Koffice components can be embedded into Katabase. You can find out more about Katabase at **koffice.kde.org**.

The main structure of Katabase is a plug-in framework that operates as a base manager. The database is composed of different parts serviced by a KOM application that plugs into the base manager. *Kdataparse* is where the methods plug in to access different data types. The interface looks the same to the user no matter what method is being used. At Kdataparse, you enter a SQL query. Kforms displays forms, Kreports generates reports, Ktable displays tables, and Kscripts runs scripts. Katabase's modular design allows the addition of other components, expanding its capabilities.

Gaby

Gaby is a small personal database manager using GTK+ and Gnome. It provides access to user databases, such as those for addresses, books, even photos. Gaby's plug-in design makes it easily extensible. You can find out more about Gaby at **gaby.netpedia.net**. Its interface has the same browser-like tools found in most Gnome applications. You can download the current version of Gaby from the Gnome software map at **www.gnome.org**.

Graphic Tools

Gnome, KDE, and the X Window System support an impressive number of graphic tools, including image viewers, window grabbers, image editors, and paint tools. On the KDE and Gnome desktops, these tools can be found under either a Graphics submenu or the Utilities menu.

KDE Graphic Tools

The *kview program* is a simple image viewer for GIF and JPEG image files. The *ksnapshot program* is a simple screen grabber for KDE, which currently supports only a few image formats. The *kfourier program* is an image-processing tool that uses the Fourier transform to apply several filters to an image at once. The *kshow program* is a simple image viewer. The *kuickShow program* is an easy-to-use, comfortable image browser and viewer, based on imlib. The *kpaint program* is a simple paint program with brushes, shapes, and color effects.

System	Site
Oracle	Oracle database **www.oracle.com**
Sybase	Sybase database **www.sybase.com**
DB2	IBM database **www.software.ibm.com/data/db2/linux**
Informix	Informix database **www.informix.com/linux**
Ingress II	Computer Associates database **www.cai.com/products/ingres.htm**
Adabas D	Adabas D database **www.softwareag.com**
MySQL	MySQL database **www.mysql.com**
GNU SQL	The GNU SQL database **www.ispras.ru/~kml/gss**
PostgreSQL	The PostgreSQL database **www.postgresql.org**
Flagship	Interface for xBase database files **www.fship.com/free.html**
Katabase	KOffice desktop database **koffice.kde.org**
Gaby	Gnome desktop personal database **gaby.netpedia.net**.

Table 34-1. *Database Management Systems for Linux*

Gnome Graphic Tools

ImageShaker is a digital image-processing tool that includes an extensive set of graphic filters, such as alpha blending and median. It uses a stream-like approach that allows batch processing.

Electric Eyes is a simple image viewer. Right-click its window to display a pop-up menu with options. You can load images, and also move back and forth through previously viewed ones. You can even make an image your background.

GQview is a simple image viewer supporting features like click file viewing, thumbnail preview, zoom, drag-and-drop, and external editor support, as well as slideshow and full-screen options. Multiple files can be selected for moving, copying, deleting, renaming, or dragging. See **gqview.netpedia.net** for more information.

The *GIMP* is the *GNU Image Manipulation Program*, a sophisticated image application, much like Adobe Photoshop. You can use GIMP for such tasks as photo retouching, image composition, and image authoring. It supports features like layers, channels, blends, and gradients. GIMP makes particular use of the GTK+ widget set. You can find out more about the GIMP from its Web site at **www.gimp.org**. You can also download the newest versions from here. GIMP is freely distributed under the GNU public license.

X Graphic

The *xv program* is a screen capture and image-editing program. After displaying the main screen, right-click it to display its control screen. Use the Grab button to scan a window or a section you select with a drag operation using your middle mouse button. Once you have scanned a window or screen section, you can crop it with a drag operation with your left mouse key and then use crop to reduce to that selected section. With xv, you can also convert an image file from one format to another. Just load the image and then save it as another file using a different image format.

The *xpaint program* is a painting program, much like MacPaint. You can load paint pictures or photographs, and then create shapes, add text, and add colors. You can use brush tools with various sizes and colors. The xfig program is a drawing program, and xmorph enables you to morph images, changing their shapes.

Multimedia

There are an extensive number of applications available for both Video and Sound, including sound editors, mp3 players, and video players. Linux sound applications include Mixers, digital audio tools, CD audio writers, mp3 players, and network audio support. The Linux Midi and Sound Pages currently at **www.xdt.com/ar/linux-snd** hold links to Web and FTP sites for many of these applications. Many sound applications are currently under development for Gnome including sound editors, mp3 players, and audio players. Check the software map at **www.gnome.org** for current releases. For KDE there are a variety of applications including a media player (kmedia), mixer (kmix), mp3 player (KJukeBox), and CD player (kscd). Check **www.kde.org** for recent additions.

Several projects are underway to provide TV, Video, and DVD support for Linux. The site **linuxtv.org** provides detailed links to DVD, Digital TV (DVD), and Analogue TV Linux projects. The XFree86 version 4.0 with the Xv extensions will include support for video in a window for selected platforms. Several projects have already developed applications. The Video 4 Linux project has created the Video4Linux software package that allows you to play Mpeg1 video sources on Linux. Video4Linux is included with Linux distributions, including Red Hat. Currently under development is Video for Linux Two (V4L2). This is a separate project that has established a set of APIs and standards for handling video devices on Linux, providing a common API for video and tuning sources, teletext, and other TV-related VBI data. It includes a suite of related driver specifications for different types of video devices and video-related data.

KDE	Description
kview	Simple image viewer for GIF and JPEG image files
ksnapshot	Screen grabber
kfourier	Image processing tool that uses the Fourier transform
kuickShow	Image browser and viewer
kshow	Simple image viewer
kpaint	Paint program
Gnome	
Gqview	Image viewer
ImageShaker	Digital image processing
GIMP	GNU Image Manipulation Program
Electric Eyes	Image viewer
X Window System	
xv	Screen grabber and image conversion
xpaint	Paint program
xfig	Drawing program
xmorph	Morphs images
xfractals	Generates fractal images

Table 34-2.   *Graphic Tools for Linux*

It is intended as a replacement for Video for Linux. Several applications currently support it, including XawTV, Gnomevision, and kTuner.

For KDE, several video applications are currently under development including a video player (action), a TV tuner (kwintv and kTuner), and an Mpeg1 video player (ZZplayer). Currently under development for Gnome are TV tuners (Gnomevision and gnome-tv), a video player (Gnome-Video), and a video editor (trinity).

For DVD, the Linux Video and DVD Project (LiViD) at **www.linuxvideo.org** supports the development of Mpeg2 (DVD) software. LiViD DVD and multimedia players are currently under development. LSDVD (**www.csh.rit.edu/lsdvd/**) is currently developing a DVD player that will eventually include fully compliant DVD software decoding. You can obtain information about recent efforts to develop Linux DVD at **www.opendvd.org.**

The LinuxDVD Project at **linuxdvd.corepower.com** is hosting links and information for the different efforts to develop DVD support on Linux. From here you can access the different DVD and video projects easily.

The Complete Reference

Linux

Chapter 35

Editors

Linux distributions include many text editors. These range from simple text editors for simple notes to editors with more complex features such as spell-checker, buffers, or pattern matching. All generate character text files and can be used to edit any Linux text files. Text editors are often used to change or add entries in Linux configuration files found in the **/etc** directory or a user's initialization or application dot files located in a **home** directory. You can use any text editor to work on source code files for any of the programming languages or shell program scripts.

Traditionally, most Linux distributions include the cursor-based editors Vim or Emacs. *Vim* is an enhanced version of the Vi text editor used on the UNIX system. These editors use simple, cursor-based operations to give you a full-screen format. You can start these editors from the shell command line without any kind of X-Window system support. In this mode, their cursor-based operations do not have the ease-of-use normally found in window-based editors. There are no menus, scroll bars, or mouse-click features. However, the K Desktop and Gnome do support powerful GUI text editors with all these features. These editors operate much more like those found on Mac and Windows systems. They have full mouse support, scroll bars, and menus. You may find them much easier to use than the Vi and Emacs editors. These editors operate from their respective desktops, requiring you first have either KDE or Gnome installed, though the editors can run on either desktop. Vi and Emacs, on the other hand, have powerful editing features that have been refined over the years. Emacs, in particular, is extensible to a full-development environment for programming new applications. Newer versions of Emacs, such as GNU Emacs and XEmacs, provide X-Window system support with mouse, menu, and window operations. They can run on any window manager or desktop. In addition, the gvim version of Vim editor also provides basic window operations. Table 35-1 lists several GUI based editors for Linux.

K Desktop Editors: KEdit, KWrite, Kjots, and KWord

All the K Desktop editors provide full mouse support, implementing standard GUI operations, such as cut-and-paste to move text, and click-and-drag to select text. The KEdit program is the default editor for the K Desktop (see Figure 35-1). It is a simple text editor meant for editing simple text files like configuration files. A toolbar of buttons at the top of the KEdit window enables you to execute common editing commands easily, using just a mouse click. With KEdit, you can also mail files you are editing over a network. The entry for KEdit in the K menu is listed simply as Text Editor. You can start up KEdit by entering the **kedit** command in a terminal window. The KOffice Office Suite also includes a word processor called *KWord,* which is a high-powered word processor you can also use as a simple editor.

A more advanced editor is *KWrite,* with features like spell-checker. Formatting options can be set in the options menu and implemented using CTRL-J. Most commands

The K Desktop	Description
KEdit	Text editor, default for K Desktop
KWrite	Text and program editor
KJots	Notebook editor
KWord	Desktop publisher, part of KOffice
Gnome	
gEdit	Text editor
gXedit	Text and HTML editor
gnotepad+	Notebook editor
X-Windows	
XEmacs	X-Window system version of Emacs editor
GNU Emacs	Emacs editor with X-Window system support
gvim	Vim version with X-Window system support
WordPerfect	Word processor that can edit text files

Table 35-1. *Desktop Editors*

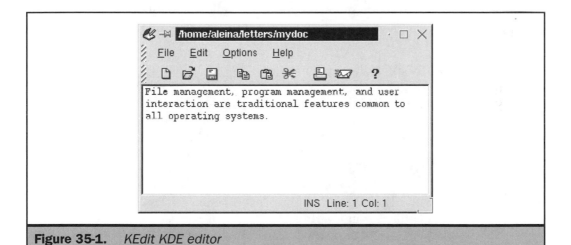

Figure 35-1. *KEdit KDE editor*

can be selected using menus. A toolbar of icons for common operations is displayed across the top of the kwrite window. A click on the right mouse button displays a pop-up menu with entries for Cut, Copy, and Paste, as well as Open and Save. At the bottom of the KWrite menu is a message box that displays the current operation or any error messages. The entry for KWrite in the K menu is Advanced Editor. You can also start up KWrite by entering the `kwrite` command in a terminal window.

KWrite is designed to be a program editor for editing source code files. Although KWrite does not have all the features of Emacs or Vi, it can handle most major tasks. The Highlight entry in the Options menu enables you to set syntax highlighting for different programming languages, such as C, Perl, Java, and HTML. In addition, KWrite also has the capability to access and edit files on an FTP or Web site.

The editor *KJots* is designed to enable you to jot down notes in a notebook. It organizes notes you write into notebooks, called simply *books*. You can select the one you want to view or add to from the Books menu. To start KJots, select its entry in the Utilities menu or enter the `kjots` command in a terminal window.

Gnome Editors: gEdit, gXedit, gnotepad+

All the Gnome editors provide full mouse support, implementing standard GUI operations, such as cut-and-paste to move text, and click-and-drag to select text. *gEdit* is a basic text editor for the Gnome desktop (see Figure 35-2). You can use gEdit to perform most text editing tasks, such as modifying configuration files. It features a plug-in menu that provides added functionality, and it includes plug-ins for spell-checking, project management, encryption, and e-mail.

A more powerful editor, *gXedit,* includes standard features such as spell-checking, formatting, autosave, and encryption. Menus contain all the gXedit commands, and a toolbar of icons for commonly used commands is displayed across the top of the gXedit window. The gXedit editor supports a full range of file operations, enabling you to merge, sort, or compare files. You can easily insert the date and the contents of your signature file. You can also use gXedit to compose Man pages, inserting the Man tags for the header, synopsis, description, and options. In addition, gXedit can also compose and edit Web pages. You can easily insert HTTP elements, such as links, image references, or headings, and gXedit can then access Netscape to preview the page. You configure gXedit using the Settings window, which has panels for display, network, macro, and command settings. Settings are saved in the user's **home** directory in the file **.gxedit**.

The gXedit editor is network-aware. You can compose files and then send them as e-mail messages, edit news articles obtained from your news server directly, and access and edit files located on FTP or Web sites. The network setting first must be entered in the network panel in the Setting's window. In addition, gXedit also has a mirror function that works somewhat like the talk utility. You can have gXedit operate as a server, letting other users connect to your program and view everything you type in your gXedit window. You could also connect to someone else running gXedit to view what he is displaying.

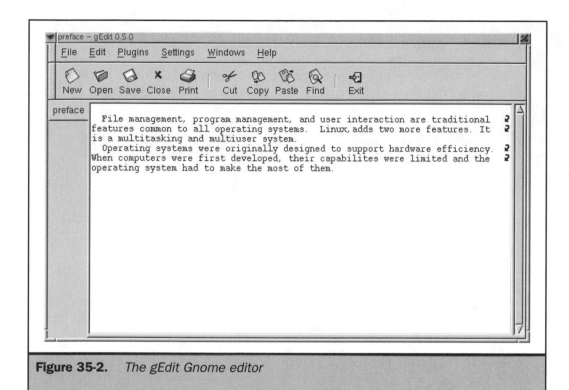

Figure 35-2.   *The gEdit Gnome editor*

The editor, *gnotepad+*, is a simple editor for making small text files. gnotepad+ does, however, have a toolbar for Web page composition containing several of the more common HTML elements. You can insert links, headings, and lists, as well as other basic Web page components.

The Vi Editor: vim and gvim

The *Vim editor* included with most Linux distributions is an enhanced version of the Vi editor. It includes all the commands and features of the Vi editor. *Vi*, which stands for *visual*, remains one of the most widely used editors in Linux. Keyboard-based editors like Vim and Emacs use a keyboard for two different operations: to specify editing commands and to receive character input. As editing commands, certain keys perform deletions, some execute changes, and others perform cursor movement. As character input, keys represent characters that can be entered into the file being edited. Usually, these two different functions are divided among different keys on the keyboard. Alphabetic keys are reserved for character input, while function keys and control keys specify editing commands, such as deleting text or moving the cursor. Such editors can rely on the existence of an extended keyboard that includes function and control keys. Editors in UNIX, however, were designed to assume a minimal keyboard with alphabetic characters, some control characters, as well as the ESC and ENTER keys. Instead of dividing the command and input functions among different keys, the Vi editor has two separate modes of operation for the keyboard: command mode and input mode. In *command* mode, all the keys on the keyboard become editing commands; in the *input* mode, the keys on the keyboard become input characters. Some of the editing commands, such as **a** or **i**, enter the input mode. On pressing the **i** key, you leave the command mode and enter the input mode. Each key now represents a character to be input to the text. Pressing ESC automatically returns you to the command mode, and the keys once again become editor commands. As you edit text, you are constantly moving from the command mode to the input mode and back again. With Vim, you can use the CTRL-O command to jump quickly to the command mode and enter a command, and then automatically return to the input mode. Table 35-2 lists this basic set of Vi commands you need to get started in Vi.

Key	Cursor Movement
h	Moves the cursor left one character
l	Moves the cursor right one character
k	Moves the cursor up one line
j	Moves the cursor down one line
w	Moves the cursor forward one word
W	Moves the cursor forward one space-delimited word
b	Moves the cursor back one word
B	Moves the cursor back one space-delimited word
e	Moves the cursor to the end of the next word
E	Moves the cursor to the end of the next space-delimited word
0	Moves the cursor to the beginning of the line
$	Moves the cursor to the end of the line
ENTER	Moves the cursor to beginning of next line
–	Moves the cursor to beginning of previous line

Table 35-2.   *Vi Editor Commands*

Key	Cursor Movement
(	Moves the cursor to beginning of sentence
)	Moves the cursor to the end of sentence; successive command moves to beginning of next sentence
{	Moves the cursor to beginning of paragraph
}	Moves the cursor to end of paragraph
CTRL-F	Moves forward by a screen of text; the next screen of text is displayed
CTRL-B	Moves backward by a screen of text; the previous screen of text is displayed
CTRL-D	Moves forward by one-half screen of text
CTRL-U	Moves backward by one-half screen of text
G	Moves the cursor to last line in the text
*num*G	Moves the cursor to specific line number: **45G** places the cursor on line 45
H	Moves the cursor to line displayed onscreen
M	Moves the cursor to middle line displayed onscreen
L	Moves the cursor to bottom line displayed onscreen
' '	Moves the cursor to its previous location in the text
m*mark*	Places a mark on a line of text; the mark can be any alphabetic character
'*mark*	Moves the cursor to the line with the mark
Input	All input commands place the user in input; the user leaves input with ESC
a	Enters input after the cursor
A	Enters input at the end of a line
I	Enters input before the cursor
I	Enters input at the beginning of a line
o	Enters input below the line the cursor is on; inserts a new empty line below the one the cursor is currently on

Table 35-2. *Vi Editor Commands* (continued)

Key	Cursor Movement
O	Enters input above the line the cursor is on; inserts a new empty line above the one the cursor is currently on
Text Selection (vim)	**Cursor Movement**
v	Visual mode; move the cursor to expand selected text by character. Once selected, press key to execute action: c change, d delete, y copy, : line-editing command, J join lines, U uppercase, u lowercase
V	Visual mode; move cursor to expand selected text by line
o	Expand selected text backward
Delete	**Effect**
x	Deletes the character the cursor is on
X	Deletes the character before the character the cursor is on
Dw	Deletes the word the cursor is on
Dd	Deletes the line the cursor is on
D	Deletes the rest of the line the cursor is on
d0	Deletes text from the cursor to beginning of line
d*c*	Deletes specified component, *c*
J	Joins the line below the cursor to the end of the current line; in effect, deleting the new line character of the line the cursor is on
Change	Except for the replace command, **r**, all change commands place the user into input after deleting text
s	Deletes the character the cursor is on and places the user into the input mode
C	Deletes the rest of the line the cursor is on and places the user into input mode
cw	Deletes the word the cursor is on and places the user into the input mode

Table 35-2. *Vi Editor Commands* (continued)

Key	Cursor Movement
c0	Changes text from cursor to beginning of line
r	Replaces the character the cursor is on; after pressing **r**, the user enters the replacement character; the change is made without entering input; the user remains in the Vi command mode
R	First places into the input mode, and then overwrites character by character; appears as an overwrite mode on the screen, but actually is in input mode
c*c*	Changes the specified component, *c*
Move	Moves text by first deleting it, moving the cursor to desired place of insertion, and then pressing the **p** command. (When text is deleted, it is automatically held in a special buffer.)
p	Inserts deleted or copied text after the character or line the cursor is on
P	Inserts deleted or copied text before the character or line the cursor is on
dw p	Deletes a word, and then moves it to the place you indicate with the cursor (press **p** to insert the word *after* the word the cursor is on)
d*c* p	Deletes specified component, *c*, then moves it to the place you indicate with the cursor (press **p** to insert the word *after* the word the cursor is on)
yy or Y	Copy the line the cursor is on
y*c*	Copies component specified, *c*
Component References	**Description**
w	Word the cursor is on
b	To beginning of a word
W	Space-delimited word
B	Beginning of a space-delimited word

Table 35-2.   *Vi Editor Commands* (continued)

Key	Cursor Movement
)	Sentence
}	Paragraph
G	Rest of the file
m	The *m* is a mark
L	To bottom of the screen
yH	To top of the screen
Search	The two search commands open up a line at the bottom of the screen and enable the user to enter a pattern to be searched for; press ENTER after typing in the pattern
/*pattern*	Searches forward in the text for a pattern
?*pattern*	Searches backward in the text for a pattern
n	Repeats the previous search, whether it was forward or backward
N	Repeats the previous search in opposite direction
/	Repeats the previous search in forward direction
?	Repeats the previous search in backward direction
Buffers	There are 9 numbered buffers and 26 named buffers; named buffers are named with each lowercase letter in the alphabet, *a-z*. Use the double quote to reference a specific buffer
"*buf-letter*	Named buffer—references a specific named buffer, **a**, **b**, and so forth
"*num*	Numbered buffer—references a numbered buffer with a number 1-9
Help (vim)	**Effect**
:help *command*	Starts help utility; you can specify a command
F1	Same as :help

Table 35-2. *Vi Editor Commands* (continued)

Key	Cursor Movement
Line-Editing Commands	**Effect**
w	Saves file
r *filename*	Inserts file text
q	Quits editor, **q!** quits without saving
d	Deletes a line or set of lines
m*Num*	Moves a line or set of lines by deleting them and then inserting them after line *Num*
co*Num*	Copies a line or set of lines by copying them, and then inserting the copied text after line *Num*
Line Reference	**Description**
Num	A number references that line number
Num, Num	Two numbers separated by a comma references a set of lines
Num–Num	Two numbers separated by a dash references a range of lines
–Num	The minus sign (-) preceding a number offsets to a line before the current line
+Num	The plus sign (+) preceding a number offsets to a line after the current line
$	The dollar sign symbol ($) references the last line in the file
/*Pattern***/**	A line can be located and referenced by a pattern; the slash searches forward
?*Pattern***?**	A line can be located and referenced by a pattern; the question mark (?) searches backward
g/*Pattern***/**	A set of lines can be located and referenced by a repeated pattern reference; all lines with a pattern in it are referenced

Table 35-2. *Vi Editor Commands* (continued)

APPLICATIONS

Key	Cursor Movement
Special Character	**Effect**
.	Matches on any one possible character in a pattern
*	Matches on repeated characters in a pattern
[]	Matches on classes of characters, a set of characters, in the pattern
^	References the beginning of a line
$	References the end of a line
/<	References the start of a word
>/	References the end of a word
Substitution Command	**Description**
s/pattern/ replacement/	Locates pattern on a line and substitutes pattern with replacement pattern
*s/pattern/ replacement/***g**	Substitutes all instances of a pattern on a line with the replacement pattern
Num-Num **s**/*pattern/ replacement/*	Performs substitutions on the range of lines specified
1, $ **s**/*pattern/ replacement/***g**	Substitutes all instances of a pattern in the file with the replacement pattern

Table 35-2.   *Vi Editor Commands* (continued)

Although the Vi command mode handles most editing operations, it cannot perform some, such as file saving and global substitutions. For such operations, you need to execute line-editing commands. You enter the line editing mode using the Vi colon command, **:**. The colon is a special command that enables you to perform a one-line editing operation. Upon pressing the colon, a line opens up at the bottom of the screen with the cursor placed at the beginning of the line. You are now in the line editing mode. In this mode, you enter an editing command on a line, press ENTER, and the command is executed. Entry into this mode is only temporary. Upon pressing ENTER, you are automatically returned to the Vi command mode, and the cursor returns to its previous position on the screen.

Although you can create, save, close, and quit files with the Vi editor, the commands for each are not all that similar. Saving and quitting a file involves the use of special line-editing commands, whereas closing a file is a Vi editing command. Creation of a file is usually specified on the same shell command line that invokes the Vi editor. To edit a file, type **vi** or **vim** and the name of a file on the shell command line. If a file by that name does not exist, the system creates it. In effect, giving the name of a file that does not yet exist instructs the Vi editor to create that file. The following command invokes the Vi editor, working on the file **booklist**. If **booklist** does not yet exist, the Vi editor creates it.

```
$ vim booklist
```

After executing the **vim** command, you enter Vi's command mode. Each key becomes a Vi editing command, and the screen becomes a window onto the text file. Text is displayed screen by screen. The first screen of text is displayed, and the cursor is positioned in the upper-left corner. With a newly created file, there is no text to display. This fact is indicated by a column of tildes at the left-hand side of the screen. The tildes represent the part of a screen that is not part of the file.

Remember, when you first enter the Vi editor, you are in the command mode. To enter text, you need to enter the input mode. In the command mode, the **a** key is the editor command for appending text. Pressing this key places you in the input mode. Now, the keyboard operates like a typewriter and you can input text to the file. If you press ENTER, you merely start a new line of text. With Vim, you can use the arrow keys to move from one part of the entered text to another and work on different parts of the text. After entering text, you can leave the input mode and return to the command mode by pressing ESC. Once finished with the editing session, you exit Vi by typing two capital Z's, **ZZ**. Hold down the SHIFT key and press **Z** twice. This sequence first saves the file and then exits the Vi editor, returning you to the Linux shell. To save a file while editing, you use the line editing command **w**, which writes a file to the disk. **w** is equivalent to the Save command found in other word processors. You first press the colon key to access the line editing mode, and then type in a **w** and press ENTER.

You can use the **:q** command to quit an editing session. Unlike the **ZZ** command, the **:q** command does not perform any save operation before it quits. In this respect, it has one major constraint. If any modifications have been made to your file since the last save operation, then the **:q** command will fail and you will not leave the editor. However, you can override this restriction by placing a **!** qualifier after the **:q** command. The command **:q!** will quit the Vi editor without saving any modifications made to the file in that session since the last save.

To obtain online help, enter the **:help** command. This is a line-editing command. Press the colon, enter the word **help** on the line that opens at the bottom of the screen, and then press ENTER. You can add the name of a specific command after the word **help**. The F1 key also brings up online help.

APPLICATIONS

gvim

As an alternative to using Vim in a command-line interface, you can use *gvim*, which provides X-Windows-based menus for basic file, editing, and window operations. To use gvim, enter the **gvim** command at an X-Windows terminal prompt or select it from a Window manager menu. The standard Vi interface is displayed, but with several menu buttons displayed across the top. All the standard Vi commands work just as they are described here. However, you can use your mouse to select items on these menus. You can open and close a file, or open several files using split windows or different windows. The editing menu enables you to cut, copy, and paste text as well as undo or redo operations. In the editing mode, you can select text with your mouse with a click-and-drag operation, use the Editing menu to cut or copy, and then paste the selected text. Text entry, however, is still performed using the **a**, **i**, or **o** commands to enter the input mode.

Options in Vi: set and .exrc

Vi has a set of options with which to configure your editor. You set an option with the **set** line-editing command. You can set options within Vi using the Vi line editing mode. The **set** command followed by the option name sets the option on. If the characters "no" are attached to the beginning of the option name, then the option is set off. For example, the command **set number** sets the number option, which numbers your lines; whereas the command **set nonumber** turns off the number option. The command **set** by itself provides a list of all options the user has set. If an option is already set, the command **set** followed by that option's name displays the value of the option. The command **set all** displays the settings of all the options.

Vi options can be used to control search operation, text display, and text input. If you set the **ignorecase** option, then searches ignore uppercase or lowercase characters in making matches. A search for **/There** retrieves both "there" and "There." You can abbreviate the **ignorecase** option with **ic**. The commands **set ignorecase** and **set ic** turn the option on, whereas **set noignorecase** and **set noic** turn it off. The **wrapscan** option allows a search to wrap around the file. While in the input mode, you can automatically start a new line at a specified margin (**wrapmargin**), you can automatically indent a new line (**autoindent**), you can check for an opening parenthesis when entering a closing parenthesis, and you can determine the number of spaces you can backtab when in input.

You may want to set certain options for every file you edit. Instead of setting these options manually for each file each time you edit them, you can place these options in your **EXINIT** shell variable or in editor initialization files, and have them automatically set for you. To use the **EXINIT** variable to set your options automatically, you need to assign the **EXINIT** variable a quoted **set** command specifying what options you want set. Whenever you invoke Vi, the **set** command stored in **EXINIT** is automatically executed. In the next example, the user assigns to the **EXINIT** variable the quoted **set** command to set both the **nu** option for numbering lines and the **ic** option for ignoring case in searches:

```
$ EXINIT='set nu ic'
```

Although you can assign the **set** command to the **EXINIT** variable in your shell, you would normally assign it in your login or shell initialization files. Then, whenever you log in, the **EXINIT** variable is automatically assigned its **set** command. In the next example, the quoted **set** command is assigned to **EXINIT** in the user's **.bash_profile** initialization file. Options set in this way are set for every file you edit. You may need some options for only a selected set of files. For example, you may want to number lines in only your C source code files and word wrap your lines only in your document files. You can tailor your options for a selected set of files by using an editor initialization file called **.exrc**. The **.exrc** file contains commands to configure your editor. When Vi is invoked, the shell first searches for an **.exrc** file in the current working directory. If one is there, the shell runs it, executing the commands. These usually are **set** commands, setting the options for the editor. If no **.exrc** file is in your working directory, the shell searches your **home** directory for an **.exrc** file. You can have a separate **.exrc** file in as many directories as you want. This enables you to customize the editor according to the files you have in a given directory.

The Emacs Editor

Emacs can best be described as a working environment featuring an editor, a mailer, a newsreader, and a Lisp interpreter. The editor is tailored for program development, enabling you to format source code according to the programming language you use. Many versions of Emacs are currently available for use on UNIX and Linux systems. The versions usually included with Linux distributions are either GNU Emacs or XEmacs. The current version for GNU Emacs is 20.*x* and is X-Windows system capable, enabling GUI features such as menus, scrollbars, and mouse-based editing operations. See Chapter 11 for a discussion of the GNU Emacs mailer, and Chapter 12 for one on its newsreader. Check the update FTP sites for your distribution for new versions as they come out, and also check the GNU Web site at **www.gnu.org,** and the Emacs Web site at **www.emacs.org**. You can find more information about XEmacs at its Web site, **www.xemacs.org**. Currently, GNU Emacs is distributed with Red Hat systems, and XEmacs is distributed with OpenLinux.

Emacs derives much of its power and flexibility from its capability to manipulate buffers. Emacs can be described as a buffer-oriented editor. Whenever you edit a file in any editor, the file is copied into a work buffer, and editing operations are made on the work buffer. In many editors, only one work buffer exists, enabling you to open only one file. Emacs can manage many work buffers at once, enabling you to edit several files at the same time. You can edit buffers that hold deleted or copied text. You can even create buffers of your own, fill them with text, and later save them to a file. Emacs extends the concept of buffers to cover any task. When you compose mail, you open a mail buffer; when you read news, you open a news buffer. Switching from one task to another is simply a matter of switching to another buffer.

The Emacs editor operates much like a standard word processor. The keys on your keyboard are input characters. Commands are implemented with special keys, such as control (CTRL) keys and alternate (ALT) keys. There is no special input mode, as is in Vi or Ed. You type in your text and, if you need to execute an editing command, such as moving the cursor or saving text, you use a CTRL key. Such an organization makes the Emacs editor easy to use. However, Emacs is anything but simple—it is a sophisticated and flexible editor with several hundred commands. Emacs also has special features, such as multiple windows. You can display two windows for text at the same time. You can also open and work on more than one file at a time, and display each on the screen in its own window. You invoke the Emacs editor with the command **emacs**. You can enter the name of the file you want to edit or, if the file does not exist, it is created. In the next example, the user prepares to edit the file **mydata** with Emacs:

$ emacs mydata

Emacs is a full-screen editor that supports menus even when used on the command line. In the case of a newly created file, the screen is empty except for the bottom two lines. The cursor is positioned in the upper-left corner. The bottom line is called the *Echo area*, and it functions as a kind of Emacs command line. The *Echo area* is also used to display Emacs messages. The line above it is called the *mode line* and is used to display status information about the text being edited. The mode line is highlighted in reverse video. The GNU version of Emacs also displays a list of menus at the top of the screen. If you are working from the shell, you can access the menu entries by pressing the F10 key. If you are working on a desktop, you can use your mouse (see Figure 35-3).

To enter text, simply start typing—you are always in the input mode. Editing commands, such as movement commands, are implemented with CTRL keys. For

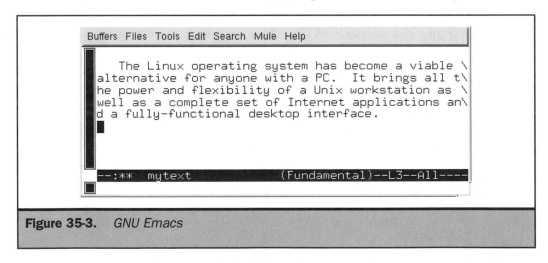

Figure 35-3. *GNU Emacs*

example, to move the cursor right, use CTRL-F, and to move the cursor left, use CTRL-B. To move up one line, use CTRL-P, and to move down one line, use CTRL-N. You can save your text at any time with the CTRL-X-CTRL-S command sequence. Many Emacs commands are made up of CTRL key combinations. The command sequence to quit the editor is CTRL-X-CTRL-C. When you finish editing the file, first save the file with CTRL-X-CTRL-S before quitting the editor with CTRL-X-CTRL-C.

Emacs provides several help utilities, such as an online manual and a tutorial. You access the help utilities through a CTRL-H sequence. CTRL-H followed by another CTRL-H lists the many possible options. An option of special note is the tutorial. CTRL-H-T places you into an online tutorial that provides you with special lessons on Emacs. Table 35-3 lists the Emacs help commands.

Cursor Movement	Effect
CTRL-B	Moves left one character (backward to the previous character)
CTRL-F	Moves right one character (forward to the next character)
CTRL-N	Moves down one line (the next line)
CTRL-P	Moves up one line (the previous line)
CTRL-V	Moves forward one screen
CTRL-Z	Moves backward one screen
CTRL-L	Moves to the center of screen
ALT-F	Moves forward one word
ALT-B	Moves backward one word
ALT-]	Moves to the next paragraph
ALT-[	Moves back to the previous paragraph
CTRL-A	Moves to the beginning of a line
CTRL-E	Moves to the end of a line
ALT-<	Moves to the beginning of buffer, usually beginning of file
ALT->	Moves to the end of buffer, usually end of file
ALT-*num*	Repeats the following command *num* number of times
ALT-X	Moves to the Echo area to enter a command

Table 35-3.   *Emacs Commands*

Deletion	Effect
DEL	Deletes the character before the cursor
CTRL-D	Deletes the character after the cursor
Kills and Yanks	**Effect**
CTRL-K	Removes the remainder of a line (kills the rest of the line)
CTRL-K-CTRL-K	Removes the remainder of a line and the new line character at the end
ALT-D	Removes the word after the cursor
ALT-DEL	Removes the word before the cursor
ALT-K	Removes the remainder of a sentence
CTRL-W	Removes a region (deletes a block)
CTRL-Y	Inserts (yanks) the contents of a kill buffer into the text
CTRL-X-U	Undoes the previous command
Search and Replace	**Effect**
CTRL-S	Searches for a pattern forward in the text
CTRL-R	Searches for a pattern backward in the text (reverse)
ALT-CTRL-S	Searches for a regular expression forward in the text
ALT-CTRL-R	Searches for a regular expression backward in the text
`replace string`	Performs a global substitution
`replace regexp`	Performs a global substitution using regular expression
`query-replace-regexp`	Searches for a regular expression in query and replace operation
ALT-% *pattern* ENTER *replacement* ENTER	Queries and replaces a pattern: **Key** SPACEBAR Replaces and moves to next instance DEL Does not replace and moves to next instance ESC Quits search-replace operation . Replaces and exits ! Replaces all remaining instances ^ Moves back to previous replacement

Table 35-3.   *Emacs Commands* (continued)

Region	Effect
CTRL-@ or CTRL-SPACEBAR	Marks a region (block)
CTRL-X-CTRL-X	Exchanges cursor (point) and marks
ALT-H	Marks a paragraph as a region
CTRL-X-CTRL-P	Marks a page as a region
CTRL-X-H	Marks the entire text in buffer as a region

Text Format	Effect
auto-fill-mode	Sets fill mode option
ALT-*num* CTRL-X-F	Sets position of right margin
ALT-Q	Justifies a paragraph
ALT-Q	Justifies a region

Window Command	Effect
CTRL-X-2	Splits to a new window vertically
CTRL-X-5	Splits to a new window horizontally
CTRL-X-O	Selects other window
CTRL-X-P	Selects previous window
ALT-CTRL-V	Scrolls the other window
CTRL-X-0	Closes current window
CTRL-X-1	Closes all but the current window
CTRL-X-^	Extends the current window vertically
CTRL-X-}	Extends the current window horizontally

File Buffer Command	Effect
CTRL-X-CTRL-F	Opens and reads a file into a buffer
CTRL-X-CTRL-S	Saves the contents of a buffer to a file
CTRL-X-CTRL-C	Quits the editor

Table 35-3.   *Emacs Commands* (continued)

File Buffer Command	Effect
CTRL-X-CTRL-V	Closes the current file and opens a new one (visiting a new file)
CTRL-X-I	Inserts contents of a file to a buffer
CTRL-X-CTRL-Q	Opens a file as read-only; you cannot change it
CTRL-X-D	Enters the dired buffer that has a listing of your current directories; moves to different file and directory names; displays other directories; selects and opens files
Buffer Command	**Effect**
CTRL-X-B	Changes to another buffer; you are prompted for the name of the buffer to change to (to create a new buffer, enter a new name)
CTRL-X-K	Deletes (kills) a buffer
CTRL-X-CTRL-B	Displays a list of all buffers
ALT-X `buffer-menu`	Selects different buffers from a list of buffers
Help Command	**Effect**
CTRL-H-CTRL-H	Lists possible help options
CTRL-H-I	Accesses the Emacs manual
CTRL-H-T	Runs the Emacs tutorial
CTRL-H-B	Displays keys and the commands they represent

Table 35-3. *Emacs Commands* (continued)

GNU Emacs X-Windows Support

You can run GNU Emacs either from an X-Windows window manager or from the shell command line. Many window managers or desktops may already have an entry in their main menu. If not, you can open a terminal window and enter the command **emacs**. When run from a terminal window, Emacs operate with X-Windows support, enabling mouse-based editing and menu selection. You can also run Emacs from a standard shell command line, without X-Windows. In this case, mouse-based operations are not enabled. However, the Emacs menu headings are still displayed at the top of the screen. You can access a menu by pressing F10. The screen will split, with the lower section listing menus and keys you press to access them. Once you select a menu, the items for that menu are listed with keys to press to select one. For example, to open a file you press F10, the **f** to list the file menu items, and then the **o** to select the open item.

The GNU Emacs editor now supports a X-Windows graphical user interface. To enable X-Windows support, start Emacs within an X-Windows environment, such as a KDE, Gnome, or fvwm desktop. The basic GUI editing operations are supported: Selection of text with click-and-drag mouse operations; cut, copy, and paste; and a scroll bar for moving through text. The Mode line and Echo areas are displayed at the bottom of the window, where you can enter keyboard commands. The scroll bar is located on the left side. To move the scroll bar down, click it with the left mouse button. To move the scroll bar up, click it with the right mouse button.

From the menus at the top of the window, you can execute most file, edit, and buffer operations. The Buffers menu lists your active buffers. You can use it to switch to another buffer, in effect, switching to other files you are editing or to other tasks, such as composing mail messages. The File menu manages buffers, windows, and frames. The Edit menu handles edit operations like cut, copy, and paste, as well as search and replace. The Search menu lists search operations, such as searching with regular expressions. An Options menu enables you to set options for editing and printing. From the Tools menu, you can access mail and the newsreader. The Help menu lists several help documents, including FAQs and Web pages. The menus are helpful for more complicated Emacs operations, such as opening multiple frames or windows on a text, as well as managing buffers and file buffers. When you execute an operation through a menu item, its equivalent keyboard command appears in the Echo area. Figure 35-3 shows the Emacs window.

XEmacs

XEmacs is the complete Emacs editor with a graphical user interface and Internet applications. The Internet applications, which you can easily access from the main XEmacs button bar, include a Web Browser, a mail utility, and a newsreader. If an entry exists for XEmacs in the Desktop menu, you can use that to start it. Otherwise, you can open a terminal window and enter the **xmacs** command at the prompt. The main XEmacs window is displayed with a button bar across the top for basic editing operations and for Internet applications. XEmacs supports the basic GUI editing operations: Selection of text is done with click-and-drag mouse operations: cut, copy, and paste; and a scroll bar for moving through text. At the bottom of the XEmacs window, the Mode line and Echo areas are displayed as on the standard Emacs editor. You can enter keyboard commands in the Echo area, just as you would in the Emacs editor. From the XEmacs menus at the top of the window, you can execute most file, edit, and buffer operations. The File menu manages buffers, windows, and frames. The Edit menu handles edit operations like cut, copy, and paste, as well as search and replace. An Options menu enables you to set options for editing and printing. From the Apps menu, you can access other applications, like mail, the newsreader, and the Web browser. The Buffers menu lists your active buffers. The Help menu lists several help documents including FAQs and Web pages. The XEmacs menus are helpful for more complicated Emacs operations, such as opening multiple frames or windows on a text, as well as managing buffers and file buffers. When you execute an operation through a menu item, its equivalent keyboard command appears in the Echo area.

Meta-Keys, Line Commands, and Modes

The Emacs editor operates much like any normal word processor. Only one mode, the input mode, exists. If you hit any character key, you are entering data into the file. All character keys are input characters, not commands. A *character key* can be thought of as any key you type in directly, as opposed to CTRL keys or ALT keys. Character keys are any keys you could type in at a typewriter. Commands are assigned to CTRL keys, as well as meta-keys. In this version of Emacs, a *meta-key* may be either an ALT key sequence or an escape (ESC) key sequence. On other systems, they may be one or the other. ALT key sequences operate like CTRL keys. While you hold down the ALT key, you press another key, and then let up on both. The ESC key sequence is slightly different. First, you press ESC and let up on it. Then you press another key. CTRL keys and meta-keys constitute only part of the many commands available in Emacs. All commands can be entered using command words typed in the Echo area. The meta-key commands ALT-X or ESC-X place you in the Echo. Once in the Echo area, you execute a command by typing in the command and any of its arguments, and by pressing ENTER. Table 35-3 lists the Emacs editing commands.

The mode line displays status information about the text being edited. The mode line is made up of several components, with the following form:

```
-ST-Emacs: BufferName  (major minor)------Place--
```

The first field, ST, indicates whether the file has been saved since the last change to the text. If the field displays two asterisks, **, the text has been changed, but not yet saved. If the field displays two dashes, - -, the text has not been changed since the last save. If the field displays two percent signs, %%, the file is read-only and cannot be modified.

The NAME field is the name of the buffer. In the case of files, this is the name of the file. The PLACE field indicates how far you are positioned in the file. For example, if the PLACE field is 40 percent, the text being displayed is 40 percent of the way through the file. In the next example, the mode line indicates the file has not been saved since the last change, the name of the buffer is **mytext**, and the cursor is positioned at the top of the file.

```
-**-Emacs: mytext        (text fill)----   --Top--
```

The MAJOR/MINOR field indicates the major and minor modes for editing the file. Emacs recognizes several major modes, the most common of which is the text mode. Different types of files require special editing configurations. A C program file, for example, may need special indentation features. For this reason, a special editing mode exists for C programs. Emacs recognizes other standard modes, such as nroff and Lisp. Emacs determines the mode by examining the extension used in the filename. A **.c** extension indicates a C program file. In that case, Emacs uses the C mode. If there is no extension, Emacs uses the text mode. If, for some reason, Emacs cannot determine the mode for the file, it uses the fundamental mode, which offers no special features. Emacs has three minor modes: fill, overwrite, and abbrev. The *fill mode* is usually the default and automatically wraps long lines in the file. The *overwrite mode* enables you to overwrite text, and the *abbrev mode* enables you to use abbreviations when entering text.

Index

M

O

P

Z

red**hat**®

www.redhat.com

About the CD

The Linux distribution CD-ROM, Red Hat Linux 6.2, Publisher's Edition, is included in the book. Standard installation also installs and configures the Apache Web server and an FTP server, automatically making your Linux system a Web and FTP site. You can find the latest information about Red Hat at **www.redhat.com**.

The CD includes both the Gnome and the K Desktop Environment (KDE) graphical user interfaces (GUIs), along with an extensive number of Gnome and KDE applications. Red Hat 6.2 installs both Gnome and KDE, as well as a comprehensive set of Linux software applications including the GNU software packages (graphics, communications, publishing, editing, programming, games), development tools, and Internet servers (ftp, Web, mail, news, and DNS). Red Hat 6.2 also installs a complete set of Internet clients such as mail, news, FTP, and Web browsers, including Netscape Communicator. There are clients for both the Gnome and KDE desktops, as well as for shell and window manger interfaces.

The CD and the Red Hat Web site (**www.redhat.com**) include extensive documentation including HOW-TO documents, tutorials in Web-page format, and online manuals. Three very helpful Red Hat guides are the *Red Hat Installation Guide*, the *Red Hat Getting Started Guide*, and the *Official Red Hat Linux Reference Guide*. All are in Web-page format and can be viewed with any Web browser on any system. The *Red Hat Installation Guide* is located on the Red Hat CD in the **doc/install-guide** directory and can be read directly from the CD. The *Red Hat Installation Guide* provides a detailed walk-through of the installation procedure with the help of graphics and helpful suggestions. It is best to check it before you install Red Hat. The *Red Hat Getting Started Guide* provides an overview of basic Red Hat operations, such as working with Gnome and basic configuration. The *Official Red Hat Linux Reference Guide* covers administration and configuration tasks in detail, and can be located on the CD with this pathname:

```
\doc\install-guide\index.htm
```

For added functionality, you can download free personal editions of the StarOffice office suite from **www.sun.com**, KOffice from **koffice.kde.org**, and WordPerfect from **linux.corel.com**. Also, the Java Development Kit is available for free at **www.blackdown.org**. Databases are available from their respective Web sites, such as Oracle from **www.oracle.com**. Numerous applications in the easy-to-install RPM package format are available for download from **contrib.redhat.com** and **updates.redhat.com**. You can both download and install these applications using either the Gnome or KDE file managers. Several popular Internet sites where you can easily obtain Linux applications are listed here:

Linux Applications	Internet Site
Java Development Kit	www.blackdown.org
Window manger and desktop themes	www.themes.org
Gnome applications	www.gnome.org
KDE applications	www.kde.org
Netscape Communicator and Navigator	Any distribution site such as ftp.redhat.com or ftp.calderasystem.com
StarOffice	www.sun.com
Tk/Tcl Applications	www.scriptics.com
Perl Applications	www.perl.com
Applications for Red Hat	contrib.redhat.com
Linux Applications	www.linuxapps.com and www.xnet.com/~blatura/linapps.shtml
WordPerfect	linux.corel.com
Linux World	www.linuxworld.com
Linux Journal	www.linuxjournal.com
Online Linux	www.linux.org
Linux Documentation Project	metalab.unc.edu/LDP/
Linux Application in RPM packages	www.rpmfind.net
New Linux Applications	www.freshmeat.net

The Red Hat Linux distribution installs a professional-level and very stable Linux system with KDE and Gnome GUI interfaces, providing you with all the advantages of a UNIX workstation on your PC, combined with the same ease of use and versatility found on GUI systems like Windows and Mac OS. An extensive set of Internet servers is also included, which are automatically installed along with flexible and easy-to-use system configuration tools like Linuxconf.

This book includes a copy of the Publisher's Edition of Red Hat Linux from Red Hat Software, Inc., which you may use in accordance with the GNU General Public License. The Official Red Hat Linux, which you may purchase from Red Hat Software, includes the complete Official Red Hat Linux distribution, Red Hat Software's documentation, and 90 days of free e-mail technical support regarding installation of Official Red Hat Linux. You also may purchase technical support from Red Hat Software on issues other than installation. You may purchase Official Red Hat Linux and technical support from Red Hat Software through the company's Web site (**www.redhat.com**) or its toll-free number: 1 (888) REDHAT1.

Due to space considerations on the Red Hat 6.2 CD-ROM, some rarely used files such as TeX, some foreign-language Xfree86 fonts, a DOS emulator, and some Alpha and Sparc source code files are not included. Check **README.publishers-edition** file on the CD-ROM for all listings. Should you happen to want any of these files, they can be downloaded from **ftp.redhat.com**.